INTRASITE SPATIAL ANALYSIS IN ARCHAEOLOGY

INTRASITE
SPATIAL ANALYSIS
IN ARCHAEOLOGY

EDITED BY HAROLD J. HIETALA

Associate Professor of Anthropology and Associate Professor of Statistics, Southern Methodist University, Dallas

with editorial contributions by

PAUL A. LARSON, Jr

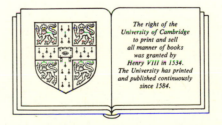

The right of the
University of Cambridge
to print and sell
all manner of books
was granted by
Henry VIII in 1534.
The University has printed
and published continuously
since 1584.

CAMBRIDGE UNIVERSITY PRESS

CAMBRIDGE

LONDON   NEW YORK   NEW ROCHELLE

MELBOURNE   SYDNEY

Published by the Press Syndicate of the University of Cambridge
The Pitt Building, Trumpington Street, Cambridge CB2 1RP
32 East 57th Street, New York, NY 10022, USA
296 Beaconsfield Parade, Middle Park, Melbourne 3206, Australia

© Cambridge University Press 1984

First published 1984

Printed in Great Britain at the University Press, Cambridge

Library of Congress catalogue card number: 84-5900

British Library Cataloguing in Publication Data
Intrasite spatial analysis in archaeology.——
(New directions in archaeology)
1. Archaeology——Methodology
I. Hietala, Harold J. II. Series
930.1′01′8   CC75

ISBN 0 521 25071 4

To my wife
Barbara Joyce Bernhardt

CONTENTS

CONTRIBUTORS

Jeffrey H. Altschul, Statistical Research, PO Box 31865, Tucson, Arizona.

Kenneth J. Berry, Department of Sociology, Colorado State University.

Richard Ciolek-Torrello, Department of Archaeology, Museum of North Arizona, Flagstaff.

George Cowgill, Department of Anthropology, Brandeis University.

C. Reid Ferring, Institute of Applied Sciences, North Texas State University.

Roland Fletcher, Department of Anthropology, University of Sydney.

Brian Hayden, Department of Archaeology, Simon Fraser University.

Harold J. Hietala, Departments of Anthropology and of Statistics, Southern Methodist University, Dallas.

Francoise Hivernel, Department of Archaeology, University of Cambridge.

Ian Hodder, Department of Archaeology, University of Cambridge.

Glynn Ll. Isaac, Department of Anthropology, Peabody Museum, Harvard University.

Ian Johnson, Department of Anthropology and Sociology, University of Queensland.

Ellen M. Kroll, Department of Anthropology, University of Wisconsin.

Kenneth Kvamme, Department of Anthropology, University of California, Santa Barbara.

Paul W. Mielke, Department of Statistics, Colorado State University.

Frederick C. Munday, Infotec Development Incorporated, Earth Sciences Division, Department of Archaeology, Sonora, California.

Rebecca S. Sload, The Wyatt Company, Wellesley Hills, Massachusetts.

Brian Spurling, Archaeological Resource Management Section, Heritage Conservation Division, Saskatchewan Culture and Recreation, Regina.

Robert Whallon, Museum of Anthropology, University of Michigan.

PREFACE

Intrasite spatial analysis has existed informally since archaeologists first started making observations about the internal structure of historic and prehistoric sites. Nevertheless, Leroi-Gourhan's work at the Magdalenian open-air site of Pincevent spawned considerable formal interest in the topic. Although European archaeologists were in the forefront of these investigations, American archaeologists were soon to follow. In the early and middle 1970s, we tried to use techniques and methods borrowed from ecological studies. Unfortunately, plant communities develop in more restricted ways than do social communities. In consequence, we found that the borrowed ecological methods did not work very well.

By 1980, we had recognized the multidimensional complexities of intrasite spatial analysis and were aware that analytical methods had to be tailored to the archaeological sites under investigation. It should have been obvious from the outset that different approaches were needed for different problems and different sites. Clearly, the problems and quality/quantity of data of an open-air palaeolithic site are different from those of an urban metropolis; the former type of site also has fewer 'knowns'.

This volume covers spatial analysis approaches and methods for sites ranging from those of early man in Africa to a major Mesoamerican metropolis. In addition, two sites occupied during this century are considered. The contents of this volume are briefly discussed in the first chapter while an admittedly personal overview of future directions is given in the last chapter.

Each chapter in the volume was extensively reviewed by combinations of the various contributors, as well as others, and thus the volume is as much theirs as it is mine. I would like especially to thank Bonnie Hole, Frank Hole, and Fred Wendorf who served as outside reviewers for some of the contributions. A special note of gratitude must be extended to Paul Larson who convinced me to persue the concept of this volume, but who, unfortunately, left archaeology, in 1980, after finishing his dissertation. His editorial contributions during the early stages of this volume were of exceptional importance and it is sad that he departed from archaeology to become a professional geologist.

I also wish to thank the staff at Cambridge University Press and Mrs Sandi Irvine for their unflagging help in seeing the progress of the volume through to completion. Finally, I would like to thank my wife, Barbara J. Bernhardt, who gave me unquestioned support even when she was sure this project would never end.

Dallas H. J. H.
April 1984

Chapter 1

**Intrasite spatial analysis:
a brief overview**
Harold J. Hietala

This volume explores the topic of intrasite spatial analysis by utilizing the talents of scholars from the international community. The individual contributions cover a broad spectrum of theoretical and methodological perspectives with data applications ranging from early hominid sites to a Mesoamerican urban center, and including ethnographic studies devoted to determining the intricate relationships between ethnographic and archaeological data. Since intrasite spatial analyses involved with theory, method and data are so different between early man and urban center studies, it is unrealistic to assert the existence of unique methodological approaches which characterize general archaeological problems in a unified fashion. In addition, investigating a given geographical region at a specific time period will require different approaches for different archaeological questions. Since this volume on intrasite spatial analysis in archaeology involves sites ranging from those of early man to the complex ones of modern man, with geographical locations in the New and Old Worlds, it seems appropriate to outline some of the objectives of the volume before considering specific approaches.

General background

At the formative stage in the development of this book, the main thrust was to promote an international scientific dialogue on intrasite spatial analysis in archaeology. Scholars across the international community were initially approached with guidelines emphasizing the notion that theory, *a priori* principles, assumptions, methods, data, applications and interpretations were to be integrated. Specifically, theoretical approaches were expected to explicate potential archaeological applications with suggested methodological and analytical tools. For example, theoretical spatial patterns derived from ethnographic studies were expected to have explicit quantitative characteristics which could be directly related to archaeological material culture. On the other hand, methodological approaches were expected to consider the effects of multiple-activity areas, multiple or repeated occupations and multiple-component configurations. The sensitivity and robustness of particular methods are of interest here since, even in the purest case, local and global notions of variability might affect results and, therefore, interpretations. Whether these minimal goals were met is left to the judgement of the reader.

On the other hand, the breadth and depth of resulting approaches are impressive, since the contributions, taken as a whole, emphasize the areas of theory, method, applications, and ethnographic analogy in such a way that all four approaches bridge paleolithic and complex civilization studies with intervening cases. A consideration of time depth (Table 1) shows that the intrasite efforts range from early man to complex civilization studies in the Old World, and from hunter–gatherer to complex civilization studies in the New

Table 1. *Site parameters by chapter*

Chapter	Approximate dates	Site types	Geographical locations
2	> 1 500 000 B.P.	Early man	Kenya, Tanzania
3	80 000 B.P.	Middle Paleolithic	Israel
4	45 000 B.P.	Middle Paleolithic/Upper Paleolithic transition	Israel
5	27 000 B.P.	Upper Paleolithic	Israel
6	14 000 B.P.	Upper Magdalenian	France
7	2 000 B.P.	Neolithic	Kenya
8	1 400 A.D.	Plains Village	Oklahoma, USA
9	1 300 A.D.	Pueblo	Arizona, USA
10	600 A.D.	Urban Metropolis	Central Mexico
11	1 250 A.D.	Medieval Fortress	Turkey
12	1 910 A.D.	Historical	Australia
13	1 970 A.D.	Modern	Alaska, USA

World. It should be noted (Table 1) that the chapters are ordered strictly by approximate time depth for their dated site applications, with the only exceptions (Chapters 8–11) occurring between the beginnings of the Christian era and the discovery of the New World by Christopher Columbus. The order of chapters in these instances accommodates two principles. First, Chapters 8–10 are all North American sites and progress from a hunter–gatherer site (Delaware Canyon) to an organized community site (Grasshopper Pueblo) and then to an urban metropolis site (Teotihuacán). Secondly, Chapter 11 continues the strict ordering for all other sites and, as a medieval fortress site application, is conveniently placed adjacent to the chapter on Teotihuacán applications. The applications in Chapters 2–13, nevertheless, have much in common.

Organizing principles

The broad swath of general archaeological perceptions seems to be oriented toward integrating theory, methods, and data so that particular archaeological questions of interest can be adequately explored. Many questions of interest can be organized under the categories of post-depositional movement, artifact conjoins, multiple occupations, index variability, statistical approaches, ethnographic studies and complex sites. These categories are discussed sequentially.

Post-depositional movement

It is of crucial interest in non-stratified sites that vertical movement, as a possible mechanism of artifact location, be negated before attempting spatial analyses by artificial level. Hivernel and Hodder (Chapter 7) investigate this problem at the site of Ngenyn in Kenya.

Artifact conjoins

The refitting of artifacts can be very useful when investigating vertical movement of artifacts (Kroll and Isaac, Chapter 2). Other applications have been involved with interpreting intrasite structure (Cahen *et al.*, 1979; Hietala, 1983) and in interpreting technological change (Volkman, 1983).

Multiple occupations

Of major interest in any site is whether or not the excavated portion represents a single occupation or is a result of repeated occupations. This problem is considered by Ferring (Chapter 8).

Index variability

Often, two or more sites are compared and contrasted through one or more indices. Intersite differences for a particular index are meaningful only if intrasite variability, for the index, is significantly smaller than intersite variability. This topic is explored by Munday (Chapter 3) but has also been studied by Jones (1984). Fletcher (Chapter 11) also uses indices (spatial messages) for identifying the presence or absence of dimensional order. He applies his approach to the site of Taşkun Kale in Turkey.

Statistical approaches

Several methods are advocated which tend, in different ways, to minimize the nature of global assumptions. Hietala (Chapter 4) considers local and global applications based on multivariate categorical data methods. Berry, Mielke and Kvamme (Chapter 5) offer a non-parametric test statistic for investigating global association. Johnson (Chapter 6) offers an extension of shared area methods based on comparing local and global densities and Whallon (Chapter 13) considers a local approach which he calls 'unconstrained cluster analysis'.

Ethnographic studies

A theoretical consideration of ethnographic analogy applications to early man studies is given by Kroll and Isaac (Chapter 2). Ciolek-Torrello (Chapter 9) contrasts an ethnographic model of room function to a model statistically derived from the archaeological remains at Grasshopper Pueblo. In addition, Spurling and Hayden (Chapter 12) consider the relationship between global tests of association and global interpretations of behaviour using ethnographic data, while Whallon (Chapter 13) compares his derived spatial patterns from the Mask site to known behavioral patterns.

Complex sites

Practical and theoretical considerations toward complex site variational studies are given by Ciolek-Torrello (Chapter 9) and Cowgill, Altschul and Sload (Chapter 10). The latter give serious thought to local and global considerations in the fundamentally difficult question of *barrio* definitions, in space, at Teotihuacán.

The above summary does not intend, in any way, to delimit the general questions posed by each author. For example, Kroll and Isaac (Chapter 2) consider definitions for spatial patterns representing hominid behavior and activities; Munday (Chapter 3) considers local and global space; Hietala (Chapter 4) gives an application for multivariate index variation (when the data are categorical); Berry, Mielke and Kvamme (Chapter 5) consider their method relative to size, shape and density parameters; Johnson (Chapter 6) considers the problems of depositional areas versus activity areas; Hivernel and Hodder (Chapter 7) contrast the use of nearest-neighbor and associational statistics; Ferring (Chapter 8) successfully uses SYMAP descriptions for archaeological interpretation; Ciolek-Torrello (Chapter 9) contrasts the use of numerous multivariate techniques; Cowgill, Altschul and Sload (Chapter 10) consider the problem of repeated occupations; Fletcher (Chapter 11) is certainly involved with a complex site in conjunction with a novel approach; Spurling and Hayden (Chapter 12) seriously consider the interrelationships between activity areas and depositional areas; and, finally, Whallon (Chapter 13) realistically discusses the background to his new approach *vis-à-vis* those he has previously documented. Although many authors (including myself) have taken or currently take Whallon (1973, 1974) to task for his early publications on spatial analysis, he, and he alone, gives the best discussion regarding their weaknesses. That he was above the criticism and developed a better system is to his credit as a scholar.

The above comments illustrate some of the variability in approaches taken by scholars concerned with intrasite variability. Although it is certainly true that the problems and approaches are not always statistical, it is nevertheless true that statistical problems have been centrally involved in intrasite spatial analysis. To this extent, a short discussion of statistical approaches seems to be appropriate.

Statistical approaches

There has been, in the past, an unwelcome tendency for scholars associated with spatial analyses in archaeology to seek out analytical methods and techniques which work well in other disciplines and attempt to apply them in archaeology. Negative aspects of these methods are given heavy emphasis in many publications (see e.g. other chapters of this volume) and will not be commented upon here. Instead, I prefer to present some general statistical considerations.

Spatial analysis is a logical extension of ordinary aspatial analysis in any applied science which has a spatial component of variability. Useful analytical methods are potentially unlimited since the single scientific requirement is an appropriate integration of the spatial provenience variables into the overall analytical scheme. After all, if one or more spatial variables are appended to a list of aspatial variables, the basic statistical problems have not been theoretically expanded, outside of dimensional expansion through the addition of more variables. The spatial aspect of variability is treated with particular respect, however, since many questions are posed in relation to it.

Of importance in archaeological applications is whether or not the assumptions of the statistical analyses are met by the archaeological data. The notion of local versus global variability is discussed by Hietala (Chapter 4), Johnson (Chapter 6) and Whallon (Chapter 13). It is certainly of importance that archaeological assumptions are met and tested by statistical algorithms. These considerations are discussed by other authors in the volume.

A possible broad conclusion is that we need to go much further. I think, however, that we are on the right track. Statistical techniques, such as autocorrelation studies and spatial series analysis, not discussed here, are deferred to the last chapter of the volume.

Summary

This volume emphasizes many concepts and many approaches applied to studies ranging from those on early man in the Old World through those on an urban metropolis in the New World. Readers interested in spatial analysis should read the entire volume, since many questions of archaeological interest are similarly posed in different regions of the globe at different periods of hominid evolution.

References

Cahen, D., Keeley, L. H. and Van Noten, F. L. (1979). Stone tools, tool kits and human behavior in prehistory. *Current Anthropology* 20: 661–83.

Hietala, H. J. (1983). Intralevel and interlevel spatial analyses at Boker Tachtit, *Prehistory and Paleoenvironments in the Central Negev, Israel*, Vol. III, *The Avdat/Aqev Area*, Part 3, ed. A. E. Marks, pp. 217–81. Department of Anthropology, Southern Methodist University: Dallas, Texas.

Jones, M. (1984). The use of technological indices: a case study for the Levantine Mousterian. In *Statistical Analysis of Archaeological Data Structures,* ed. C. Carr. Academic Press: New York. (In press.)

Volkman, P. (1983). Boker Tachtit: core reconstructions. In *Prehistory and Paleoenvironments in the Central Negev, Israel,* Vol. III, *The Avdat/Aqev Area,* Part 3, ed. A. E. Marks, pp. 127–90. Department of Anthropology, Southern Methodist University: Dallas, Texas.

Whallon, R. (1973). Spatial analysis of occupation floors. I. Application of dimensional analysis of variance. *American Antiquity* 38: 266–78.

Whallon, R. (1974). Spatial analysis of occupation floors. II. Application of nearest neighbour analysis. *American Antiquity* 39: 16–34.

Chapter 2

**Configurations of artifacts
and bones at early
Pleistocene sites in
East Africa**
Ellen M. Kroll and Glynn Ll. Isaac

Archaeologists can trace a trail of apparent refuse concentrations from the present back to a time around 2 million years ago. The younger segments of the trail include substantial ruined structures, food remains, and artifacts made from stones, ceramics, metals, leather, wood and other materials. Until the industrial revolution, accumulations of ruins and rubbish were most commonly formed at and around 'settlements', where humans lived. But before 12 000 years ago, at most sites, structures were absent or insubstantial, and the principal classes of trash consisted of stone artifacts, and broken bones that seem to have been food refuse. Material remains localized at relatively recent settlements are generally attributed to familiar kinds of human activity, but the significance of very old accumulations of stones and bones is more problematic. Because apes and monkeys, the closest living evolutionary relatives of humans, do not create long-lasting concentrations of litter in their daily lives, the following questions arise: (1) when in the course of evolutionary differentiation and cultural development did the human tendency to create durable litter first develop, and (2) what were the economic, cultural and social circumstances associated with the first concentrations? This essay explores the contribution which archaeological spatial analysis may make toward answering those evolutionary questions.

Archaeological reconstructions of 2 to 1 million year old hominid behavior frequently rely on evidence preserved in the sedimentary deposits at Olduvai Gorge, Tanzania, and Koobi Fora, Kenya (see Fig. 1).[1] Well-preserved and firmly dated material remains exist at both places because of geological circumstances created by the development of the Eastern Rift Valley. Isaac (1976a), Hay (1976), and Bishop (1978) summarize the palaeo-geographic settings and sedimentary contexts. The archaeological evidence consists of a widespread, diffuse scatter of recently eroded artifacts and broken bones, with localized concentrations observable in some places. The anomalously high density concentrations, normally designated as sites, identify target areas for excavation. Excavations typically yield assemblages of technologically simple stone artifacts alone or with broken bones.[2] Clark (1970), Leakey (1971), and Isaac and Harris (1978) provide basic information on the archaeology of the early sites.

The existence of concentrations of stone artifacts and broken bones was used by Isaac (e.g. 1976b, 1978a) and Leakey (1971) to infer aspects of the socio-economic organization of early hominids, and specifically to support the hypothesis that, by $1\frac{1}{2}$ to 2 million years ago, some hominids lived in social groups involved in the kinds of behavior that distinguish modern humans from contemporary non-human primates. The interpretation by Isaac, that some of the concentrations represent fossil 'home bases' or 'camps' to which food was transported for collective consumption, is illustrative. Many of the interpretations came from the nature of the

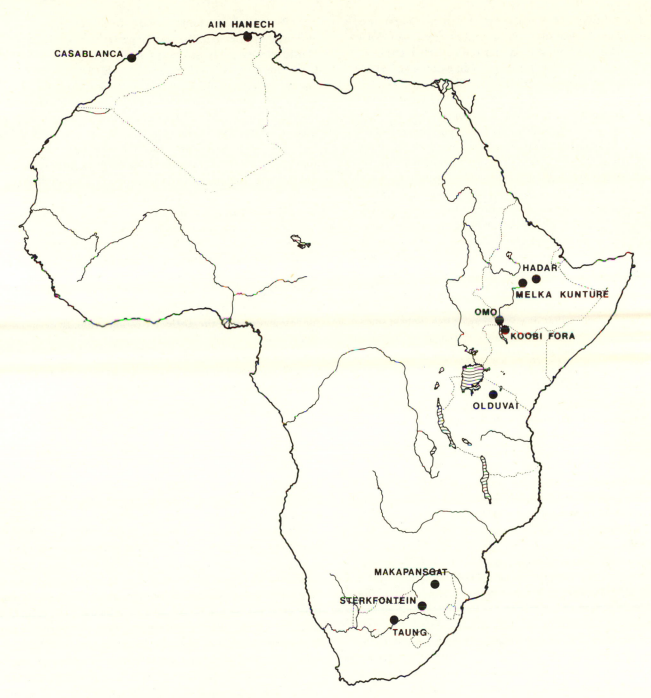

Fig. 1. Map showing the locations of various Plio-Pleistocene archaeological sites in east Africa.

artifact-and-bone assemblages and their concentration co-occurrences, rather than specifically from the internal spatial arrangements of the concentrations. The artifact assemblages documented technical skills and indicated some tool-related activities. Assemblages of broken bones, interpreted as hominid food refuse, provided dietary and subsistence information. Some sites showed distinctive intrasite distributions (e.g. the stone circle at DK, the high density cluster of flakes, flake fragments and bone fragments at FLK *Zinjanthropus*) suggestive of hominid 'activity' or 'occupation' areas. Various

publications provide general discussions of archaeological interpretations of the Plio-Pleistocene evidence (Isaac 1969, 1976*b*, 1978*a*, 1978*b*, 1980, 1981*a*, 1981*b*; Leakey 1971, chapter 10; Harris 1978, chapter 5; Bunn *et al.* 1980; Binford 1981; Isaac and Crader 1981; Bunn 1982*a*). Some of the fundamental issues discussed here have been addressed elsewhere by Isaac, but this essay represents our first attempt to discuss the potential contribution of intrasite spatial analysis toward answering evolutionary questions.

Since the late 1960s there have been many publications

aimed specifically at the analysis of spatial configurations within archaeological sites. Those studies vary in approach from visual inspection of point pattern or scale maps (e.g. Leroi-Gourhan and Brézillon 1972; Van Noten *et al.* 1980) to quantitative measurements of coordinate matrices or densities per 1 m × 1 m square (Dacey 1973; Whallon 1973, 1974; Freeman 1978; Hietala and Stevens 1977). For the palaeolithic, previous studies generally share the identification of palaeo-activity areas as a goal. For well-preserved late Pleistocene and younger sites which include a variety of material remains, especially those with structures and hearths, the search for activity areas does not usually require justification, although determinations of contemporaneity, secondary refuse dumps, and meaningful functional associations may be difficult. At older sites, however, where the material remains are less varied and structures and hearths are not commonly preserved, problems related to mode of accumulation, temporal and functional associations, and disturbance are more acute. Those problems, in combination with the possibility that human behavior has evolved since the early sites were formed, create a particular challenge for spatial analysis of the early sites.

In the mid-1970s as part of the work of the Koobi Fora Research Project, one of us (EMK) embarked on a study of the spatial configurations of artifacts and bones within selected Plio-Pleistocene archaeological sites, specifically involving detailed descriptions and analyses of a series of sites from Koobi Fora and Olduvai Gorge (Kroll 1984). Previously published studies of the intrasite spatial patterns at one or more sites at Olduvai Gorge include those by Larson (1975), Ohel (1977), Davis (1976, 1978), and Hietala and Larson (1979). Isaac *et al.* (1976) and Harris (1978) discuss aspects of the spatial patterns excavated before 1977 at Koobi Fora.

The purpose of this essay is to elucidate the questions and problems that arise for archaeologists seeking to interpret the arrangements of objects at very early sites. Some of the problems are held in common with the investigation of sites of all ages, but others are special and particular to the early period. For example, consideration of the geological mechanisms by which sites were formed is of particular importance when, as is the case for most early sites, the archaeological materials are stratified in fluviatile or lake margin deposits (Isaac, 1967, 1977; Binford 1977, 1981). Therefore, before we present our data, methods of intrasite analysis and preliminary observations, we will examine basic assumptions about early hominid use of space and scrutinize ideas about how very ancient concentrations of artifact and bone refuse may have formed. The data used include published spatial configurations recorded in excavations at Olduvai Gorge (Leakey 1971) and at Koobi Fora (Isaac *et al.* 1976; Harris 1978), and additional information available to us through our own involvement in the current research at Koobi Fora. We have drawn on data and methods being developed by the Koobi Fora Research team (see Acknowledgements).

We propose that one method for exploring the antiquity of some familiar human patterns in the Plio-Pleistocene data may be the systematic comparison of distributions progressing from recent to old. The archaeological record may well show subtle changes through time which may mark the development of the human tendency to create litter in an organized space. If we subtract features such as hearths and hut remains from the plans of the younger sites, the comparison of the distribution of the residual stone and bone remains may provide a useful basis for assessing whether the patterns at early sites are similar or contrastive.

Hominid land use patterns

Fossils contemporaneous with the very early archaeological evidence show that hominids with brains relatively smaller than those of modern humans made the artifacts and perhaps the concentrations of material refuse (Pilbeam 1972; Walker and Leakey 1978). The fact that there are no living counterparts of Plio-Pleistocene proto-humans creates both the fascination and the difficulty of behaviorally oriented archaeological studies. We must consider whether archaeologists can accurately reconstruct aspects of the lives and behaviors of early hominids that are not simply untested extrapolations from familiar modern patterns.

Ethnographic studies show that the use of space by all recent human societies is very different from that of extant monkeys and apes (Isaac 1981*a*). Some non-human primate land use patterns include sleeping recurrently in the same spatially focused social groups without daily radiative departures and returns by individuals. Other non-human primate patterns include wide-ranging individual trajectories with periodic social groupings, but without recurrently occupied spatial foci. None includes the continual or even intermittent transport of food and materials to particular places. In contrast, modern human societies are characterized by groups who recurrently sleep and eat in proximity to one another, although the actual location of sleeping and eating may shift. During each day, some members of the groups commonly go to different places, but then return to the current sleeping place. Notably, food is transported to the collective place, as are materials for making equipment and other items of material culture. It is the cumulative effect of that pattern of movement, transport, and ultimate littering that tends to create the camp and settlement sites that are so prominent in the relatively recent archaeological record.

In summary, there are several behavior patterns that are quasi-universal among recent humans which tend to have fairly marked effects on their use of space and hence on the configuration of their refuse. Those include the tendency of modern humans (1) to carry food to special places, (2) to feed at those places, (3) to sleep at those places, and (4) repeatedly to make and repair equipment at those same places. The locations are the 'home bases', 'camps', or 'settlements' that are familiar to us all. Because that land use pattern is not held in common with other primates, it follows that, at some stage in the evolutionary divergence of human ancestors from their non-human primate relatives, the human pattern of social–spatial organization began to differentiate.

Although we cannot assume that whole behavioral systems of recent humans have a great antiquity, we can explore the evolution of some specific behaviors. Given the four potentially independent behavior sets outlined above, we can draw a matrix of some possible combinations. The combinations comprise six alternative hypotheses for investigation:

Behaviors	Alternative hypotheses					
	1	2	3	4	5	6
Repeated manufacture of tools at a locale	+	+	+	+	+	+
Feeding at the locale	−	+	+	−	+	+
Carrying food to the locale	−	−	+	−	−	+
Sleeping on the ground at the locale	−	−	−	+	+	+

+ = behavior present, − = behaviour absent.

Combination number 6 is the modern human condition.

In setting out the matrix we have eliminated some combinations: archaeologists studying the sites tend to document repeated tool manufacture, so we have not listed those combinations which lack tool manufacture, even though such locales may well have existed in the total early hominid behavior repertoire. We have also discounted the possibility that food was carried in but not consumed. 'On the ground' is used in opposition to 'in the trees', i.e. the common non-human primate sleeping place which may well have been retained until late phases of evolution. For recent humans the activity of sleeping on the ground at a locale is often marked by a sheltering structure and by the existence of a cleared area of ground surface. In the dry tropics the structures made by hunter–gatherers are commonly very flimsy, but they usually exist and serve to demarcate segments of intrasite space.

Another quasi-universal factor in the organization of the activity areas of recent humans is *controlled* fire. For hominids during the past several hundred thousand years, many aspects of life have been organized around hearths. That spatial focus is deeply embedded in attitudes and in symbolic systems. Indeed the word 'focus', which is derived from the Latin word for 'fireplace', 'hearth', or 'the center of the home', involves that metaphor. Ethnographic records show that, in many recent hunter–gatherer home base sites, a series of hearths was in simultaneous use. These hearths are commonly juxtaposed to shelters and reflect the segmentation of the occupying group into a series of 'modules' or 'house-

holds'. Numbers of well-preserved late Quaternary archaeological sites appear to provide convincing evidence of the same kind of patterning (e.g. the Russian sites summarized by Klein 1969; Pincevent by Leroi-Gourhan and Brézillon 1972; Borj Mellala by Tixier 1976). Earlier possible examples include the Mousterian site of Molodova (Klein 1973) and the Acheulian site of Terra Amata (de Lumley 1969).

From those comparative ethnographic and middle to late Pleistocene observations, several questions confront archaeologists concerned with the investigation of intrasite configurations in a sequence of earlier sites:

1. When did the controlled use of fire become a regular part of hominid behavior, and at what stage do we find evidence of intrasite segmentation associated with repeating hearth and/or structural modules, perhaps indicative of social units?

2. Are objects discarded at sites that seem to antedate the controlled use of fire arranged differently from objects discarded at sites formed thereafter?

Other large-scale questions relate to the patterns of movement and amount of time involved in the formation of early Pleistocene sites. Some recent tropical hunter–gatherers were restlessly nomadic, rarely basing themselves for more than a few weeks at any one spot, although their overall round of movement covered a limited area. Other tropical hunter–gatherers appear to have remained at one camp for many months or longer, when some critical resource such as a waterhole, fishing ground, or collecting area was in use. Non-human primate patterns of moving, feeding, and sleeping are similarly varied. Likewise, the movement patterns of social carnivores, and their use or not of 'dens' and 'lairs' for breeding and communal feeding, are highly varied both within and between species.

Early hominid patterns were also probably flexible and varied. Yet, it would clearly be of interest for archaeologists to be able to assess hominid time and mobility patterns from their use of a localized space, as imprinted at a sample of early refuse configurations. Therefore, other important questions for spatial analysis are:

1. Can we distinguish between patterns generated by very brief activity episodes and patterns formed during sustained occupation over many days, weeks, or months?

2. Can we distinguish between sites formed by one uninterrupted occupation episode and sites formed by several partially or wholly superimposed episodes?

These are some fairly far-reaching questions arising from comparative archaeological, ethnographic and primatological studies concerning hominid land use patterns. They challenge spatial analysts to find patterns that will help to test the alternative hypotheses associated with the questions. Although part of our research is aimed in the direction of such hypothesis testing, enquiry can not begin there. Rather, we must first deal with site formation processes, the 'middle range theory' of Binford (1981).

Site formation processes

On the basis of material composition and density, Isaac and Harris (1978) identified three different types of concentrations among the early archaeological sites at Koobi Fora: (1) artifacts with little or no bone (type A), (2) artifacts with bones from a single large carcass (type B), and (3) artifacts with bones from many different carcasses (type C).[3] Leakey (1971) identified analogous types at Olduvai Gorge.

The major possible mechanisms known to us which may have been involved in forming the three types of concentrations are represented in Table 1. Clearly, each mechanism alone could produce a concentration. Of six such possibilities, four would be entirely natural (S1, B1, B2, B3) and two hominid-induced (S2, B4). Likewise, a concentration could result from various combinations of the mechanisms.

The concentrations which would have the highest anthropological interest are those in which there is a co-occurrence of stone artifacts and bones related principally to hominid activity (S2 and B4). For the FLK *Zinjanthropus* site at Olduvai and the KBS site at Koobi Fora, among others,

Table 1. *Possible modes of site formation. An archaeological concentration may result from a single mode or various combinations. Concentrations of stone artifacts and bones (S2 and B4) would have the highest anthropological interest. Recently discovered concentrations of bones with cut-marks (B2 or B4) at Koobi Fora present new research possibilities*

Stones	Bones
S1. Artifacts were washed in and deposited as a concentration by flowing water.	B1. Parts of dead carcasses or bare bones were washed in and deposited as a concentration by flowing water.
	B2. One or more animals died or were killed at the locality leading to the formation of a concentrated patch of bones.
	B3. Animals (e.g. hyenas, wild dogs, leopards, porcupines, etc.) transported parts of dead carcasses and/or numerous bones to the locale and deposited them there.
S2. Hominids transported artifacts and/or unmodified stones to the locale, with or without subsequent flaking of the stones on the spot.	B4. Hominids transported bones and/or whole or parts of dead carcasses to the locality and discarded the bones there.

After Isaac and Crader 1981.

the co-occurrence of artifacts and bones has been tacitly attributed to hominid activity. That attribution led to the further interpretation that those sites represent fossil 'camp' or 'occupation' sites (Leakey 1971) formed from the early manifestation of the home base pattern of behavioral organization (Isaac 1969, 1978b). There is now a growing realization, discussed below, of the importance of treating the 'home base' interpretation as one of several alternative hypotheses to be tested.

Various kinds of evidence suggest how the early concentrations of stone artifacts and bones formed. Characteristics of the encasing sediments, and the abrasion, size sorting, and orientations of the archaeological objects themselves, may all help to indicate whether water currents were the principal agent of transport and deposition at the sites in question (i.e. mechanisms S1 and B1) (Isaac 1967; Behrensmeyer 1975a, 1975b; Harris 1978; Shackley 1978; Kroll 1981; Schick 1984).

The presence of bones at a site because of the death of one or more animals at that locale (B2) is particularly difficult to distinguish from their presence because of transport by hominids (B4). Where a large part of a single very large animal (e.g. elephant or hippopotamus) is found, common sense tends to indicate mechanism B2 rather than B3 or B4. The occurrence of remains of numerous different kinds of animals at a place which shows no signs of having been a natural trap tends to imply mechanism B3 or B4. Mechanism B3, carnivore accumulation, may be distinguished from mechanism B4 by the representation of body parts in the bone assemblage and the prevalence of specific damage patterns which carnivores inflict on bones (Klein 1975; Brain 1976; Behrensmeyer and Hill 1980; Binford 1981; Bunn 1982b). Ultimately, the best indicators that early hominids were intensely involved in handling bones, presumably in relation to getting meat and marrow as food, come from damage patterns of a kind specifically resulting from human action. Cut-marks and fractures from hammers have been found on bones from both Koobi Fora and Olduvai Gorge (Bunn 1981) and from Olduvai Gorge (Potts and Shipman 1981).

To avoid seeking anthropological meaning in spatial configurations that were primarily created by non-hominid agencies, we advocate that the sites selected for study should be restricted to those that meet most of the following criteria: (1) the sites should be located outside of water courses, (2) the archaeological remains should be encased in silt matrices which are indicative of low-energy deposition of sediments, (3) the bones, if present, should show cut-marks and/or signs of hammer fracture, and (4) the archaeological remains should be restricted to a single horizon.

Table 2 lists the Koobi Fora and Olduvai sites that we view as candidates for spatial analysis. Sites known to fulfill all of the above four criteria include the FxJj 20 site complex, FxJj 50, FxJj 64, FLK *Zinjanthropus,* and FLK N Levels 1/2. Sites which fulfill some of the criteria have been

Table 2. *Palaeo-geographic contexts of Plio-Pleistocene archaeological sites from Koobi Fora (Lower and Upper Members) and Olduvai Gorge (Bed I and Lower and Middle Bed II). Asterisks identify the most promising candidates for spatial analysis*

Region	Lake margin/floodplain	Alluvial and river bank floodplain	Partially silted river channel
Koobi Fora		FxJj 10	FwJj 1
		FxJj 17	FxJj 1
		*FxJj 20 Main	FxJj 3
		*FxJj 20 East	
		FxJj 20 AB	
		*FxJj 50	
		*FxJj 64	
Olduvai Gorge	DK	MNK Skull	
	*FLK *Zinjanthropus*		
	FLK NN Level 3		
	*FLK N Level 1/2		
	FLK N Levels 3–6		
	HWK E 1		

included for comparative analysis. Because all of the very early sites yet reported have been buried and preserved by sediments deposited by moving water, albeit gently moving water, the question must always be asked, how much has the moving water affected the arrangement of objects? That question is being explored by several members of the Koobi Fora Research Project (Isaac 1981*b*), and, as we will show, spatial analysis of conjoined, oriented, or size-sorted artifacts and bones can help to provide an answer.

The early sites as analytic entities

Figure 2 illustrates the patterning uncovered by excavations at a series of Plio-Pleistocene sites. Each diagram presents the plan of an excavation area, and each point marks the position of a specimen plotted *in situ*. At present, the diagrams omit quantities of small specimens collected by the screening of sediments recovered from gridded excavation areas (i.e. 1 m × 1 m squares) in systematic spits. The excavation areas range in size from approximately 300 (FLK *Zinjanthropus*) to 30 (FxJj 3) square meters (see Table 3). At all of the sites the erosion slope (see dashed lines in Fig. 2), which allowed the archaeologist to detect the existence of a concentration, also destroyed part of the concentration. Figure 3, which illustrates the spatial relationship between the surface stones and bones exposed on the erosion slope and the specimens recovered *in situ* by excavation at FxJj 64, typifies the situation of discovery of most Plio-Pleistocene sites. At most of the sites, the excavation margins do not reach the edges of the concentration of material which the excavation was designed to investigate. Exceptions may be FxJj 3 (also called HAS), FxJj 20E, FxJj 50, FxJj 64, and FLK *Zinjanthropus*, where the excavations appear to sample a relatively large part of a concentration. Even at those excavations, one or more trench margins transect high densities of material remains. We must thus determine how to reconstruct the various overall configurations of the sites from the excavated samples.

Varied approaches and methods of analysis are required for studying the different sizes of excavated samples. For us, the investigation of overall configuration covers questions about the following: (1) the overall size of a concentration; (2) the number, spacing, shape, and density of clusters, scatters, and gaps within a concentration; and (3) the possible differences in composition between clusters and scatters. The study of small samples may also explore internal clustering, but without gaining as much information as can be extracted from the large samples about the total size and range represented at the particular site. The detection of regularities in the positive or negative spatial association of classes of objects should be possible for both scales of samples.

Figure 4 provides a series of sections through six excavation areas at Koobi Fora. Each diagram represents the vertical distribution of specimens relative to one of the horizontal axes (i.e. north–south or east–west). In few recorded sites do the pieces lie on a simple, flat surface; rather, they commonly form a zone of variable thickness. Leakey (1971) noted the variable thicknesses of individual archaeological zones at several sites at Olduvai Gorge. Although she did not record the elevations for each excavated piece, she classified the sites into (1) those concentrations on a palaeo-land surface with material remains dispersed through only about 10 cm of sediment (e.g. FLK *Zinjanthropus*, FLK NN Level 3), and (2) those with material remains dispersed through a considerable thickness of clay or fine-grained tuff (e.g. FLK N Level 5).

Most archaeologists would treat a laterally extensive zone only a few centimeters thick as an indivisible archaeological horizon. Spatial analysis of its horizontal configuration (x, y axes) could proceed without undue concern over small differences in elevation (z axis). Where the vertical spread is

(a)

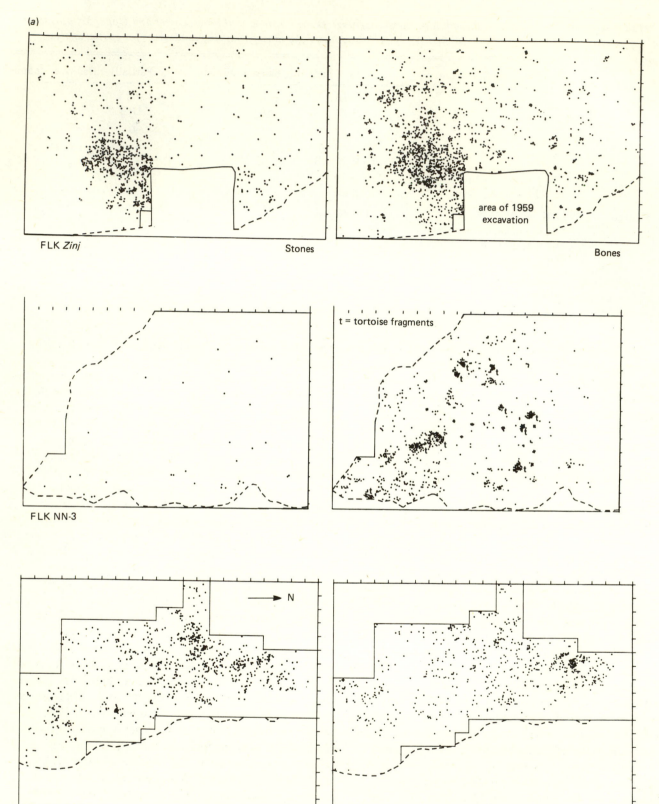

Fig. 2. Plans of the excavations at Koobi Fora and Olduvai Gorge show the positions of plotted stones (*left*) and bones (*right*) all at the same scale (1 scale mark = 1 m). In addition to the points shown, each site yielded smaller screened pieces which were not individually plotted. The dashed lines mark the edges of the erosion slope (except FLK N Level 5). The diagrams of FxJj 20 Main and FxJj 20 East do not include the trenches or remains excavated since 1977.

(b)

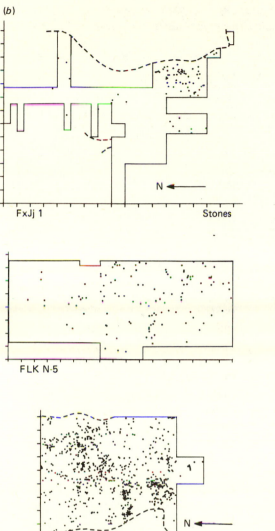

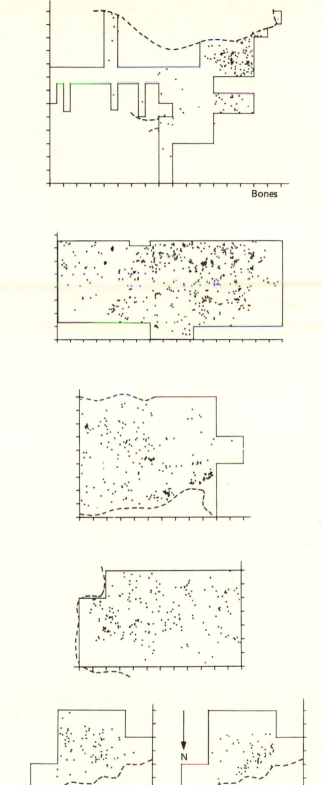

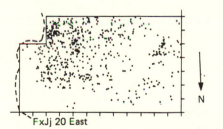

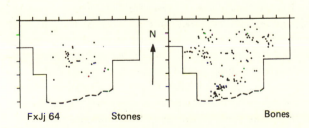

Fig. 2(b).

Table 3. *Approximate numbers of excavated stones and bones from excavations at Koobi Fora (Bunn 1982b, Bunn et al. 1980, Harris 1978, Isaac et al. 1976), and at Olduvai Gorge (Leakey 1971), and approximate areas of excavation. The site size data are highly tentative estimates*

Sites	Stone artifacts (n =)	Unmodified stones (n =)	Bones/ teeth (n =)	Approximate excavation area (m²)	Estimated site size		
					Geometric approximation	Radius (m)	Area (m²)
FxJj 1	139	5	688	55	Circle	7–8.5	150–230
FxJj 3	118	3	239	33	Circle	3–3.75	28–44
FxJj 10	332	2	3	13	Circle	2–3	12–28
FxJj 17	263	1	326	23	?Ellipse?	(6 × 2)	9
					?Circle?	(2 ⩾ 3)	12–⩾ 28
FxJj 20M	2497	19	4570	85	Circle	5	75–85
FxJj 20E	1205	25	3124	80	Circle	6	100–120
FxJj 20AB	3462	10	1634	12	?Circle?	2–⩾ 3	12–⩾ 28
FxJj 50	1405	76	2100	200	Circle or ellipse	12 (22 × 10)–(24 × 15)	450 173–282
FxJj 64	45	0	579	40	Circle	3–4	25–50
DK 1–3	1198	–	9984	231	Circle or ellipse	7 (24 × 15)	155 282
FLK *Zinj*	2470	96	3510	300	Circle	10–12	315–450
FLK NN-3	48	24	2158	230	Indeterminant – ?concentration?		
FLK N-6	123	7	614	35	Ellipse or circle	(9 × 6) 4.5	42 55–65
FLK N-5	151	29	2210	115	?Circle?	⩾ 6	⩾ 110
FLK N-4	67	17	929	80	?Circle?	⩾ 4	⩾ 50
FLK N-3	171	39	1254	110	?Circle?	⩾ 6	⩾ 110
FLK N-1/2	1205	210	3294	100	?Circle?	⩾ 8	⩾ 201
MNK-SK	689	67	378	40	Indeterminant		
HWK E-1	154	163	425	95	Indeterminant		

more extensive, however, consideration of the sediment substrate and the possible causes of dispersal becomes essential. Those causes include the following:

1. *Depositional dispersal* involving continual sedimentation with artifact and bone discard being spaced through time. Later increments would be deposited above earlier ones.
2. *Post-depositional dispersal* involving the initial deposition of archaeological materials on a single, but not necessarily flat, ground surface which would be covered later by sediment. During or subsequent to burial, the materials would become vertically dispersed away from the old ground surface by bioturbation (e.g. burrowing, root action, trampling by humans or animals), sediment shrinkage and swelling, and other processes.

Clearly, the processes of vertical dispersal could operate individually at a site or they could operate in combination, with additive effects on the magnitude of dispersion.

Our analytic work thus far strongly suggests that, where the East African Plio-Pleistocene open-air sites formed on loose sandy or silty substrates, post-depositional processes could have readily dispersed an archaeological zone through a thickness of at least 10 to 15 cm of sediment. Archaeological zones spread through more than 15 cm of sediment pose problems for the spatial analyst on how to demarcate a useful analytic entity. For the time being, exploration of the following approaches seems best to us: (1) allowing the network of conjoining stone and bone pieces to define segments of the vertically dispersed zone as horizontal units for spatial analysis, and (2) defining arbitrary vertical subdivisions and searching for coherent spatial patterns within them on an iterative, trial and error basis.

The sections in Fig. 5 present the networks of conjoining stones and bones at three Koobi Fora sites. At FxJj 50, the material remains in the southern part of the site form a zone only a few centimeters thick. The more northerly remains span some 50 cm of sediment, and at one place appear as two superimposed vertical zones of high density. The small number of conjoining pieces that link the two zones may be significant for interpreting whether the two zones represent two distinguishable phases of site use.

We suggest two alternative hypotheses for the formation of the observed configuration:

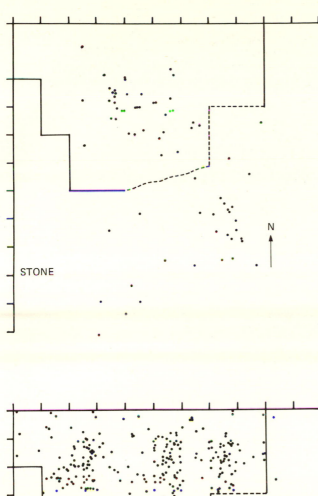

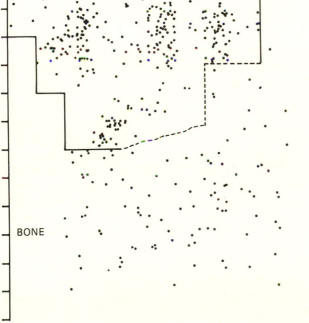

Fig. 3. Plans of the excavation area at Koobi Fora site FxJj 64 show the spatial relationship between surface stones and bones exposed on the erosion slope and those recovered *in situ.* Conjoins between surface and excavated stones confirm the association between at least some of the surface and excavated pieces. In addition to the pieces plotted *in situ,* the plans include pieces recovered by screening and subsequently assigned random positions within their 1 m × 1 m units of recovery for analytical purposes (1 scale mark = 1 m).

1. There were two distinguishable phases of site use that were separated by the accumulation of a few tens of centimeters of silt; the conjoining links could have been established by the re-use of artifacts by hominids during the second phase of site use or by downward or upward migration of pieces induced by bioturbation.

2. Stone artifacts and bones may have accumulated on an undulating land surface during a gap between sedimentation episodes; after burial, natural processes churned the sediments and dispersed the archaeological materials downward or upward, into two zones in some places.

Our excavation at FxJj 50 uncovered abundant evidence of extensive bioturbation in the form of calcium carbonate casts which appear to be fossilized subterranean termite burrows. The greatest vertical dispersal of archaeological materials occurs in precisely the area where evidence of termite disturbance is most abundant. This fits predictions of hypothesis 2 rather than those of hypothesis 1. We therefore have tentatively accepted this as our working hypothesis, and here we are treating the distribution of material at FxJj 50 as a single entity for analysis. In other more detailed studies, we will explore alternative analytic procedures.

In selecting our analytic entity, we must remember that many of the available spatial patterns are possibly the cumulative products of behavioral events that were spaced through time. Based on that premise, much of the available record is 'time averaged', and we must try various techniques for discovering the processes that have contributed to the aggregate configurations.

In summary, we present an analogy that illustrates the different scales of resolution and perception. Through a wide-angle lens, the array of stone artifacts and broken bones in an excavation area would probably appear as a concentrated patch in a regional configuration that included other high density patches, surrounded by vast areas which had very low densities of artifacts or which were entirely vacant. A view of the same excavation through a normal lens would reveal a mosaic of higher and lower densities of objects within the patch. A telephoto lens would show specific localized configurations of objects with individually distinguishable characteristics. Clearly, if spatial analysis of the early sites is to develop and contribute to our understanding of early proto-human ways of life, analysis at the different scales is an important step toward effectively integrated overall models.

Intrasite spatial configurations: patterns and processes

The tacit assumption has been made in many publications, that many of the early sites are living floors which record a refuse composition and spatial configuration imposed by a single, continuous occupation event. From that assumption follows a sense of legitimacy in discussing the layout of an archaeological concentration as if it were a coherent entity functioning as an organized campsite. That interpretation may ultimately be found to be true for some of the early sites, but we have come to realize that the underlying assumption

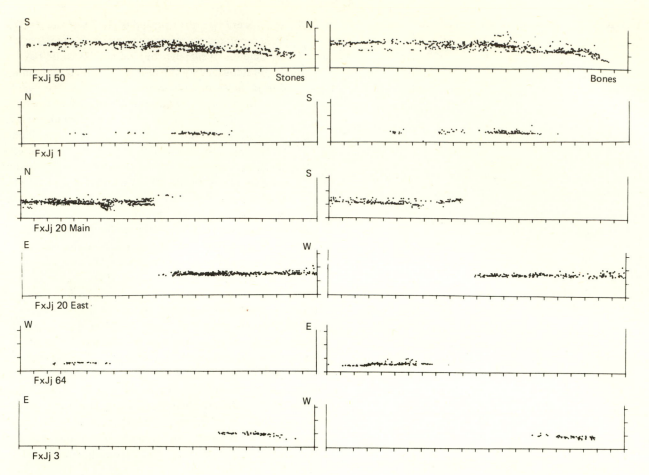

Fig. 4. Vertical profiles of the Koobi Fora sites with the elevations of plotted stones (*left*) and bones (*right*) all at the same scale (1 scale mark = 1 m). In addition to the points shown, each site yielded smaller screened pieces which were not individually plotted. The sections of FxJj 20 main and FxJj 20 east do not include remains recovered since 1977.

is dangerous. Alternatives must be considered. For example, perhaps a concentration did not form as a single, continuous occupation, but formed as separate, sequential events, each of which resulted in the deposition of a set of items which were either superimposed on, or juxtaposed to, the discarded items from previous use of the site. In other words, the early sites may have formed as *complex organized entities* in which the total configuration is now indicative of associated uses of space, or may have formed as *compound entities* in which the meaningful behavioral patterns can best be determined if the separate site uses can be resolved.

With either pattern of site formation, the behavioral processes that have intelligible material manifestation in a configuration of stone and bone objects found at a Plio-Pleistocene open-air locality include the following:

1. Stone knapping producing small patches of debitage.
2. Discard of stone-cutting implements dulled during the performance of a task.
3. Discard of implements or introduced stones (manuports) at the end of performing some task, or when the occupying individuals leave the site.
4. Discard of whole bones after meat has been removed from them.
5. Dropping of bone fragments and splinters broken in the process of meat and marrow removal.
6. Transport or re-use of stones or bones which had been discarded previously.

The foregoing are all site-forming behaviors performed by hominids. Each would have had its own frequency and spatial distribution in any given episode of site use (Ammerman and Feldman 1974). Items dropped essentially where they were used have been referred to as 'primary refuse' (Schiffer 1972, 1976). Items that the occupants deliberately removed or tossed from the area of use have been called 'secondary refuse'. The latter may be concentrated or dispersed, but would probably be peripheral to areas of activity. As mentioned above, scavengers, moving water, and the processes of bioturbation may also affect the distributions which archaeologists unearth.

Putting aside the potential effects of post-occupation disturbances, behavioral processes 1 to 6 can be used to construct some expectations of spatial patterns. Figure 6

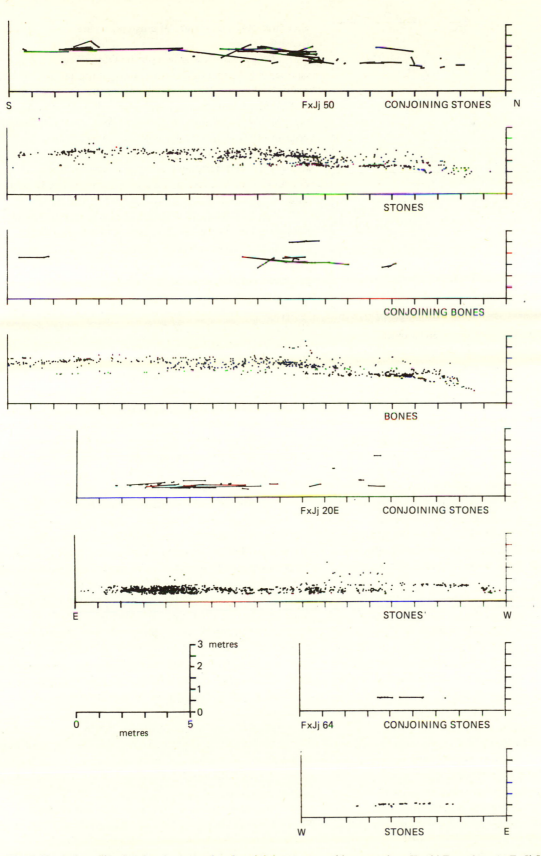

Fig. 5. Vertical profiles showing the networks of conjoining stones and bones at three Koobi Fora sites. At FxJj 50, the 40 cm separation between conjoining sets documents the value of conjoining for discerning vertically indivisible units. The sections of FxJj 20 east include stone and bone remains excavated since 1977.

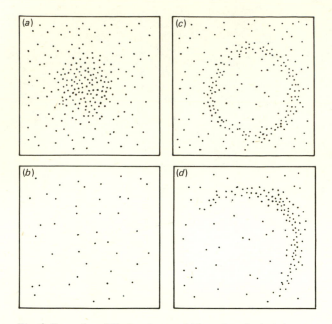

Fig. 6. Examples of ideal patterns within archaeological sites; (*a*) cluster and peripheral scatter, (*b*) unclustered scatter, (*c*) and (*d*) variations of the *O'Connell size differentiation pattern.*

shows some of the theoretical possibilities but there may well be others.

If an activity, for example stone knapping or bone breaking, were pursued with some intensity at a single spot, and if the refuse were *not* cleared away, then a central cluster with a periphery of diminishing densities might be expected (Fig. 6*a*). That configuration might also result from the occurrence of several refuse generating activities at one spot during an entire occupation. The persistent focusing of activities might well be induced by the existence of a particularly comfortable shade tree. We shall call that pattern of primary refuse a *cluster and peripheral scatter* or simply a *cluster pattern.*

If a refuse forming activity or series of activities occurs in an area, but the larger items of refuse were tossed or cleared out of that area, a pattern which is in some sense the converse of the *cluster pattern* may form. The densest accumulations of large items would be peripheral to the activity area instead of at its focus (Fig. 6*c, d*). The formation of that kind of secondary refuse pattern has been well documented by James O'Connell (personal communication) in modern encampments of Australian aborigines. Living areas were kept clear of larger refuse items, which accumulated as a crescentic midden around each living area. We shall term that kind of configuration an *O'Connell size differentiation pattern.*

If refuse forming activities were not spatially concentrated at any one time, or if they shifted about frequently, a quasi-random-dispersed scatter could form within the site (Fig. 6*b*). We shall term that an *unclustered scatter pattern* of primary refuse.

An excavation area may expose any one of the theoretical patterns or a combination of patterns. The latter suggests

that sites may be clusters of clusters, separated by gaps in density.

Two previous workers on the Olduvai spatial patterns each opted for one of the four configurational models without overt discussions of the overall conceptual framework. Ohel (1977) identified clusters, which he called elongate and circular concentrations, as places of food preparation and food consumption, respectively; whereas Davis (1978) identified sparsely littered central areas as communal activity areas and densely littered peripheral areas as places for butchery and consumption. At present, we are treating those and other interpretations as rival hypotheses to be tested.

Inspection of Fig. 2 shows the early sites as variable configurations of clusters and gaps. Comparison of the point pattern diagrams with the shaded density diagrams presented in Fig. 7 shows the repetitive occurrence of stone and bone clusters and scatters exposed by large (FxJj 50) and small (FxJj 64) excavation areas at Koobi Fora. At both sides, the overall distributions of stones and bones overlap, although the high density peaks do not coincide exactly. The excavations at FxJj 64 exposed a cluster of flakes and flake fragments, overlapping and contiguous with three clusters of bone fragments discernible by eye. The larger excavation at FxJj 50 exposed a southern, a central, and a northern cluster of stones, and a southern and a northern cluster of bones. The northern clusters clearly are clusters of clusters. Comparisons of those and other Plio-Pleistocene patterns with the theoretical patterns outlined above, will involve quantitative as well as visual analysis.

The sizes of early refuse concentrations

The range of variation in the sizes of the concentrations is of interest, particularly the anthropological meaning of any regularities which might emerge between site size and (1) the configuration and/or composition of refuse; (2) the environmental context; or (3) the predominant season of site use, if that can be determined. For example, if large and small sites have similar material compositions and configurations, we might relate the size differences to duration or intensity of activities, or to the number of hominids. But if large and small sites consistently differ in their material compositions and configurations, we might associate size differences with different processes of formation (e.g. different refuse producing activities).

All of those comparisons and correlations depend on our ability to determine site size, which is not as simple as might be supposed. Two obstacles must be overcome: (1) we must excavate on a scale sufficient to reach the edges of a refuse concentration at two or more widely spaced points, and (2) to do that we must know how to recognize the edges. There has been a tendency to treat a decrease in density towards a margin of an excavation as an indication of an edge. But once we recognize that many sites are clusters of clusters with gaps in between, more rigorous tests for the existence of edges become necessary. We need to determine the boundaries

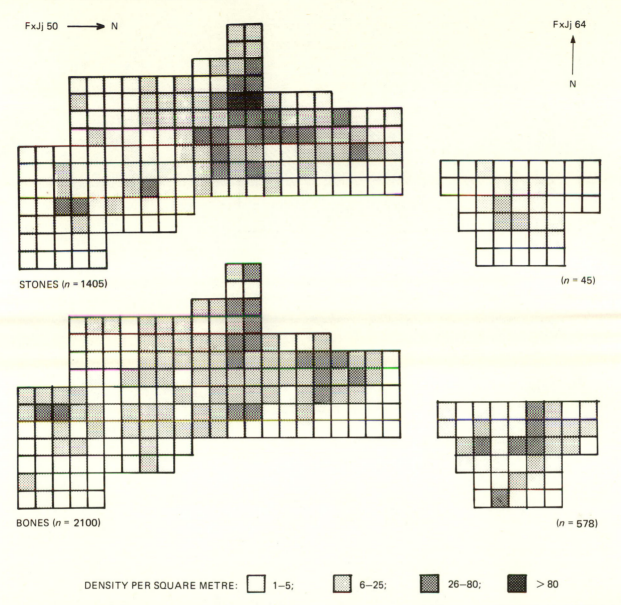

DENSITY PER SQUARE METRE: ☐ 1–5;   ▨ 6–25;   ▨ 26–80;   ■ > 80

Fig. 7. Shaded diagrams showing the stone and bone densities per meter square at FxJj 50 and FxJj 64. The densities include pieces plotted *in situ* and smaller pieces recovered by systematic screening. The overall distributions of stones and bones overlap, although the high density peaks do not exactly coincide.

between hominid refuse and background densities of material remains.

At Koobi Fora, the archaeologists have begun to employ field methods aimed at the excavation of sample trenches that transect apparent site margins. Figure 8 illustrates the conceptual problem and the approach thus far adopted for the determination of edges (see also Isaac and Harris 1980, for the scatter-between-the-patches study of background densities).

As already indicated, few excavations of early sites have been of sufficient extent for reliable determination of the size of the total Plio-Pleistocene refuse concentration. From the excavated samples, only tentative estimates of Plio-Pleistocene 'site' sizes can be offered. Table 3 presents the data, tentative though they are. Estimates of group size and other related

computations should probably not be attempted until we understand more about how the sites formed.

In the formative years of Plio-Pleistocene archaeological research a major aim was the recovery of large assemblages, especially of stone artifacts. Hence, areas producing a maximum density of material remains in a restricted space were sought for excavation. That approach clearly produced very biased statistics of site size and density, and deliberate steps will have to be taken to overcome the bias. Further, if one accepts the possibility that large, dense concentrations may result from superpositioning of separate, small-scale refuse generating events (i.e. 'compound entities'), then an attempt to excavate examples of isolated occurrences of refuse, resulting from segregated refuse generating events, becomes crucial.

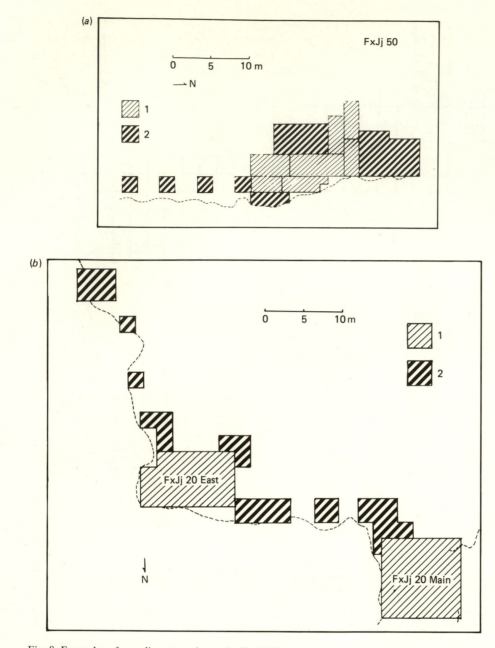

Fig. 8. Examples of sampling strategies at the Koobi Fora excavations (*a*) FxJj 50 and (*b*) FxJj 20 site complex. Shading 1 shows the trenches excavated to expose areas of maximum density; shading 2 shows trenches excavated to determine the edges of each concentration.

At Koobi Fora, we have identified a few such 'mini-sites'. Plans of one, FxJj 64, were referred to above (see Figs. 2, 3, and 7). The conjoining of 17% of the debitage at that site and the macroanalysis of raw material suggest that the stone artifact assemblage may have formed from on-the-spot knapping of a few basalt cobbles. The presence of cut-marks on one elephant-sized rib indicates that at least some of the bones were functionally related to hominid activities at the site (Henry Bunn personal communication). The analysis of similar 'mini-sites' should isolate sets of activities and their spatial manifestations, which may then be teased out of sites which formed as 'compound entities'.

Oldowan assemblages and methods of study

As emphasized at the outset of this essay, the corpus of material remains found at Oldowan sites is different from and less varied than that found at more recent sites. The Oldowan stone assemblages are technologically simple, with the elaboration of retouched types minimal relative to that found in younger assemblages (Vertes 1968; Isaac 1972). Oldowan assemblages generally include two broad categories: (1) cores, and (2) flakes and flake fragments. The cores may be viewed as tools themselves, and/or as the sources of sharp-edged flakes.

For the purposes of industrial taxonomy, Leakey (1971) divided the assemblages from Olduvai Gorge into 25

Table 4. *Simplified version of Mary Leakey's* (1971) *classification of Plio-Pleistocene stone artifact assemblages. Classes X, Y, and Z may be further subdivided functionally by edge angle, mass, and other specific attributes related to cutting, hacking, pounding, and other actions*

Mary Leakey's categories

Tools	proto-bifaces bifaces cleavers choppers polyhedrons discoids modified battered nodules and blocks heavy-duty scrapers *outils écailles*	Core tools	Class X relatively large lumps with one or more sharp edges
Debitage	core fragments	Waste cores	
Utilized	anvils		
Tools	subspheroids spheroids	Utilized cobbles and blocks	Class Y relatively large minimally flaked lumps
Utilized	hammerstones cobbles, nodules, and blocks		
Manuports	unmodified cobbles, nodules and blocks	Unmodified cobbles and blocks	
Tools	light-duty scrapers burins awls laterally trimmed flakes	Flake tools	Class Z relatively thin, sharp slivers
Utilized	heavy-duty flakes light-duty flakes		
Debitage	flakes resharpening flakes broken flakes, chips	Waste flakes	

typological entities. Laboratory study has shown that items assigned to a single type have very different functional potentials. Two specimens categorized as choppers, by their morphology, may differ in maximum dimension by as much as 100 millimeters or more, with even more marked differences in weight. Consequently, although the distributions of the morphological types deserve attention, for many purposes of spatial analysis we think that the 25 typological entities can be reduced to three categories of which the functional potentials are more-or-less known. Table 4 summarizes an alternative system for categorizing the stone artifacts.

In general, if cores were used only as a source of flakes and if the refuse from stone knapping (i.e. small flakes and flake fragments) were segregated from other refuse, we might expect significant numbers of cores to be found in association with flaking debris. Cores tossed away might be found surrounding clusters of flaking debris. However, if knapping areas were not segregated from other activity areas, then we might expect to find cores associated with a wider range of materials, but still predominantly near higher densities of flaking debris. But if the sharp edges or the butt ends of the cores were used for various purposes, we might expect a different distribution pattern. Interpretation of the alternative distribution patterns may become more feasible after further use–wear analysis of the artifacts (Keeley and Toth 1981). Ultimately, the value of pursuing the different spatial possibilities is relative to the amount of post-activity disturbance and removal of materials.

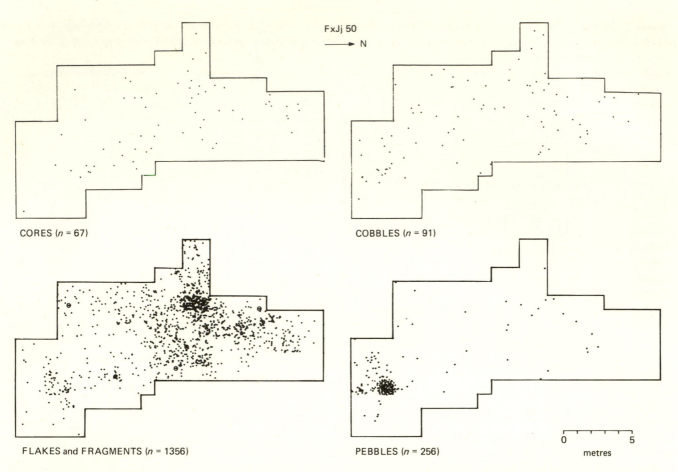

Fig. 9. Dissected plans of FxJj 50 showing the distributions of cores, flakes and flake fragments, cobbles, and pebbles. The plans include pieces plotted *in situ,* and pieces recovered by screening and subsequently assigned random positions within their 1 m X 1 m units of recovery.

The plans of FxJj 50 in Fig. 9 show the spatial distributions of the three simplified categories of stone artifacts presented in Table 4. The excavation at FxJj 50, as at most Oldowan sites, yielded a low density of cores compared to debitage. The clusters of debitage, flakes and flake fragments, are highly suggestive of stone knapping areas as discussed in the next section. The distributions of cores and cobbles each appear less clustered than the distribution of debitage, but the composite distribution of cores and cobbles covers the same overall area as the distribution of debitage. Although pebbles are present at most of the Koobi Fora floodplain sites, their distribution pattern at FxJj 50 is an anomalously high density cluster.

In undertaking the research on which this paper is based, we have been fortunate to work with both the original site plans and the collections from Olduvai Gorge and Koobi Fora (see Acknowledgements), whereas previous spatial analysts of the Olduvai sites (e.g. Ohel 1977; Davis 1978) used only published information from Leakey (1971). Our access to the collections and primary field records is enabling the gathering of a variety of data and the exploration of various analytic approaches as outlined below.

First, the artifact specimens have been examined and classified according to the standard Mary Leakey system and according to modified versions of her system (see Table 4). In addition, attribute data, which have been recorded for each item, enable the study of spatial distributions of categories that cross-cut the standard typological categories. We regard the following as particularly important classes of attribute data: (1) size (e.g. maximum dimensions and weight), (2) edge characteristics (e.g. suitability for cutting, chopping, or pounding), and (3) type of stone (e.g. raw material).

Secondly, searches are underway for artifacts that fit together (conjoin). Joins are sought among (1) spatially contiguous pieces, (2) complementary technological categories (e.g. left- and right-half split flakes), and (3) specimens of matching, distinct raw materials.

Thirdly, the stone objects themselves have been laid out on laboratory tables in scale replicas of their spatial configurations. Neighboring items may be examined as sets with possible technological or functional (activity) significance. At site FxJj 50 (Figs. 2 and 7), we laid out both the stones and the bones in their spatial configuration at full scale on the floor of the excavation. That provided valuable insight into how conspicuous and obtrusive various densities of refuse might have been to hominids occupying the surface on which the items were accumulating (see discussion section below).

Fourthly, selected bone assemblages from Koobi Fora and Olduvai Gorge have been studied by Bunn (1982*b*). He is working with Ellen Kroll on a joint spatial analysis of the bone data (e.g. distributions of taxonomic and skeletal categories, conjoining sets, and differently sized bone fragments).

Fifthly, Mary Leakey's published plans of the Olduvai floors have been digitized, and the digitized plan coordinates (*x, y* axes) are being merged with the catalogue and attribute data records. The Koobi Fora sites already have three-dimensional (*x, y, z* axes) coordinate data. With all those data as computer input, plots are being prepared for each site. Each category of data can be projected separately or in combination with other categories. Figure 9 provides an example of a series of dissected plots for FxJj 50. The dissected computer plots can be scanned with reference to other field and laboratory records and to plans showing the locations of conjoining pieces.

At this stage, specific questions should be asked. Does the eye perceive clusters and gaps? If so, are there differences in the composition of the refuse between the clusters and the gaps? Does the composition of the refuse differ between areas in the center of the site and areas at the margins? Can we recognize stone knapping areas and events? Do the various size and other categories show congruent density patterns, or do the peaks and troughs of densities differ for some size categories? Answers to those and other questions (or potential hypotheses) are being sought initially by inspection. Where a feature of interest emerges, quantitative assessment of the strength of the pattern and tests of significance will commonly be needed, but in our view elaborate quantitative methods should be employed after elementary methods have been used to explore and identify basic patterns.

For our analysis, we will formulate testable hypotheses in two ways: (1) deductive hypotheses derived from considerations of comparative human and animal behaviour studies (we have discussed this in our introduction), and (2) hypotheses inspired by the recognition of seemingly regular relationships in an existing archaeological data set. The second class of hypotheses might be thought of as 'inductive', but in our view such hypotheses can become useful and legitimate components of organized knowledge, *if* they are recast as deductive propositions, and if they are tested against fresh data sets which were not used in the initial formulation process.

Conjoining sets of stones and bones

Perhaps the most exciting new line of spatial evidence comes from the conjoining (refitting) of stone artifacts and broken bones. When it has been possible to invest the time, for sites with suitable materials, conjoining pieces have been found among the artifacts and bones. Conjoins have been recorded for the stone specimens from a series of Koobi

Fora sites by Henry Bunn, Ellen Kroll, Kathy Schick, and Nick Toth, and for several sites at Olduvai Gorge by Ellen Kroll. Conjoins have been recorded for the bones from both places by Henry Bunn. At least 10% of the flaked stones from sites FxJj 3, FxJj 50, and FxJj 64 conjoin. Other sites with conjoining sets include FxJj 10, FxJj 17, FxJj 20 Main, FxJJ 20 East, FxJj 20 AB and FxJj 63. Approximately 4% of the identifiable bones conjoin from FxJj 50 and from the FLK *Zinjanthropus* site (Henry Bunn personal communication). Bunn *et al.* (1980) provide a preliminary report of the conjoining at FxJj 50.

Successful conjoining of artifacts has been accomplished at a number of Pleistocene and younger sites, including Boker Tachtit (Hietala 1983), Bordj Mellala (Tixier 1976), Gonnersdorf (Bosinski 1979), Isoyama (Serizawa 1977), Meer (Cahen *et al.* 1979), Pincevent (Leroi-Gourhan and Brézillon 1972), Solvieux (Sackett and Gaussen 1976), and Terra Amata (de Lumley 1969; Villa 1978). At those and the Plio-Pleistocene sites, the distribution patterns of conjoining pieces have been a powerful tool in spatial analysis. First, at sites where archaeological materials are dispersed through an appreciable thickness of sediments, the vertical distribution of the network of conjoining pieces can help to assess post-depositional disturbances and analytic units. Secondly, at sites where conjoining pieces tend to cluster spatially, we gain confidence that there has been minimal post-depositional disturbance and that the spatial configuration can be used for behavioral inferences. The most obvious behavioral inference is that the overlapping conjoining sets of stone demarcate knapping areas. Thirdly, for each site, comparison of the composite plan with the plan showing the distribution of conjoining sets, makes possible the search for residual patterns perhaps indicative of other activities. Fourthly, the discovery of conjoining sets sometimes indicates the existence of objects which must have been present at the site at some stage, but have since been removed, at least from the area sampled. That helps to establish that the refuse found at an archaeological site is only the partial residue of a complex input–output system. Finally, when use–wear studies are further advanced, and those results are compared with patterns of conjoining, it should become feasible to explore the relationships between implement making and activity areas (e.g. Cahen *et al.* 1979).

Figure 10 shows the distribution of conjoining artifacts at three Koobi Fora sites. Using FxJj 50 as an example, there are two networks of conjoining stone sets. The southern has seven overlapping sets, involving 33% of the debitage in that area. For three sets, the cores are absent, presumably having been removed for use elsewhere as cores and/or as tools. In the northern cluster of 30 overlapping and contiguous stone sets, more material is crowded together. Comparison of Figs. 2 and 7 shows the high density of flakes and flake fragments, and broken bones, in that area. Nine sets of conjoining bones and several bones with cut-marks also occur in that area.

The identification of stone knapping areas from the

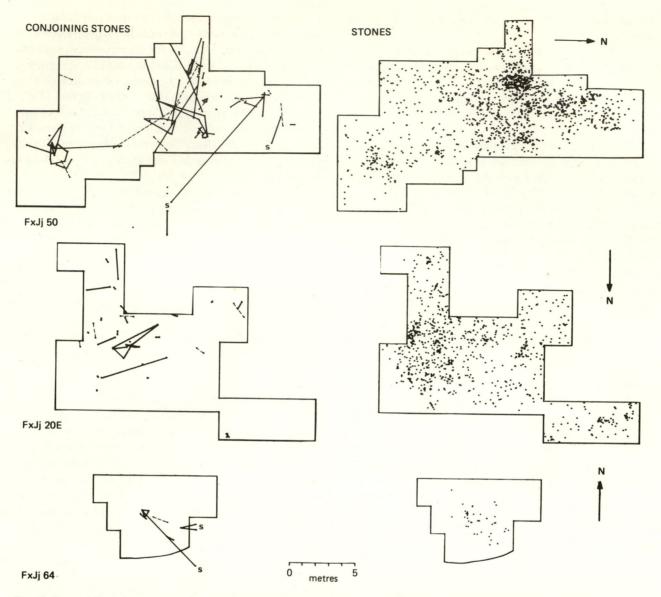

Fig. 10. Plans of three sites at Koobi Fora show the distributions of conjoining artifacts. The webs of conjoining lines may demarcate stone knapping activity areas. Solid lines indicate sets of conjoins which reconstruct a flaking sequence (e.g. between a core and flakes), whereas dashed lines indicate sets of conjoins which reconstruct a single flake (e.g. between a knapped flake and its distal end). The plans include pieces plotted *in situ*, and pieces recovered by screening and subsequently assigned random positions within their 1 m × 1 m units of recovery. S = surface.

clusters of conjoining pieces is especially significant for the early sites, which at times have been attributed to non-hominid processes of accumulation. The distribution patterns in Fig. 10 resemble the patterns interpreted as stone knapping areas at several younger sites (e.g. Pincevent, Meer). Nevertheless, there are two alternative hypotheses to test:

1. The clustered networks of conjoining artifacts demarcate minimally disturbed areas of stone knapping *in situ*.
2. The clustered networks of conjoining artifacts result from stone knapping elsewhere with the fortuitous re-location of pieces either by flowing water, hominid transport of refuse, scuffage by hominids or other animals, or other agents of transport.

Fluvial transport experiments to date (e.g. Isaac 1967; Harris 1978; Schick 1984) have emphasized the dispersal and rearrangement of concentrations of replicated artifacts. They provide size-sorting evidence that demonstrates the subtractive effects of fluvial processes. But until the additive effects of fluvial processes have been fully explored, aspects of hypothesis 2 cannot be adequately tested. The fortuitous accumulation of concentrations of conjoining sets by flowing water is one such proposition.

Meanwhile, there are several reasons for treating hypothesis 1 as the intuitive working hypothesis in accounting for the clusters of conjoining sets of artifacts at FxJj 50. First, the sedimentary context provides a significant clue about the

FxJj 50   LIMB AND RIB ORIENTATIONS

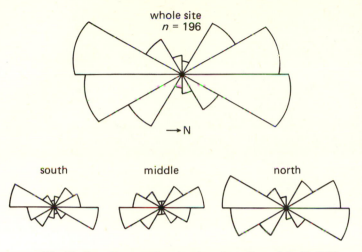

Fig. 11. Rose diagrams showing the orientations of the FxJj 50 rib and limb shafts which are at least twice as long as they are wide (Bunn 1982*b*). Elongate bones are among the most sensitive indicators of palaeocurrents.

environment of deposition. The silty-sand and sandy-silt floodplain deposits suggest that the material remains were buried by sediments deposited by gently flowing water. The water flow presumably removed some tiny pieces (Bunn *et al.* 1980), and oriented many rib and limb shafts (see Fig. 11). Yet, the overall size representation of artifacts and bones includes pieces of different transport potential, and a high percentage of small pieces of debitage. That representation suggests a lack of the kind of size-sorting indicative of fluvial transport and can be compared further with size frequency information from fluvial transport experiments (Isaac 1967; Harris 1978; Voorhies 1969; Schick 1984).

Figure 12 shows the spatial distributions of small, medium, and large stone artifacts at FxJj 50 and FLK *Zinjanthropus*. It is important to note that the top right and middle frames at FLK *Zinjanthropus* include many hundreds more unplotted tiny pieces recovered by the screening of sediments from the vicinity of the dense circular cluster. It is interesting that, at FxJj 50, the distribution of the smallest-size artifacts mimics the distribution of conjoining sets (compare Figs. 10 and 12). At both FxJj 50 and FLK *Zinjanthropus*, the high density spatial concentrations are composed of small-sized artifacts. That similarity argues against attributing the FxJj 50 spatial patterns solely to fluvial processes, because FxJj 50 and FLK *Zinjanthropus* show similar distributions, although the sites sample an alluvial floodplain context and a lake-margin context, respectively (see Table 2). Further support of the stone knapping interpretation as a viable working hypothesis comes from replicative experiments by Nick Toth and Kathy Schick to calibrate the sizes and shapes

of modern knapping debris scatters. In their experiments, the maximum extent of flaking scatter varied from approximately 1 to 3 m (Bunn *et al.* 1980), not unlike the areas defined by the archaeological sets. Whether or not the early hominids transported or cleared refuse is a subject of speculation and interest as discussed below.

Attention must also be given to understanding why certain sites yield a low number of conjoins. Lack of conjoining does not meet our expectations for undisturbed occupation debris, unless the lack of conjoining reflects (1) the skill or time of the conjoiner, (2) the limited sampling of a Plio-Pleistocene site, (3) deliberate removal by hominids of key pieces, or (4) the absence of stone knapping by hominids at the site. Kathy Schick, along with other members of the Koobi Fora Research Project, is conducting experiments to calibrate the effects of time and removal on conjoining. That should help us to interpret the significance of the near lack of conjoining pieces at various sites.

Another promising line of evidence comes from Henry Bunn's faunal analysis and involves the spatial distributions of modified and conjoined bones. Figure 13 shows that, at FxJj 50, the sets of conjoined bones are spatially concentrated in two areas. The fracture patterns on some of those bones suggest hominid breakage for the extraction of marrow.

In Fig. 14, the top right frame shows the point pattern distribution for all plotted bones at FLK *Zinjanthropus*. That pattern has received considerable attention in the archaeological literature with various interpretations of the composition and significance of the very high density circular concentration and the less dense, elongate concentration seen above it. Leakey (1971) noted the high density of small pieces of stone and bone in the circular concentration and the scatter of larger pieces of stone and bone in the other areas of the excavation. She reported Desmond Clark's suggestion that the gap between the circular and elongate concentrations of bones may represent the position of a windbreak over which hominids tossed bones which may first have been fractured in the area of the circular concentration and then discarded. Ohel (1977) speculated that the elongate concentration may represent an area where hominids butchered carcasses, whereas the circular concentration may represent an area where hominids consumed carcasses. He related the presence of small sharp pieces of debitage in the circular concentration to the cutting and slicing of meat. In contrast, Binford (1981) attributed the accumulation of bones at FLK *Zinjanthropus* to non-hominid carnivores, perhaps followed by scavenging hominids.

The coupling of data from Bunn's recent analysis of the FLK *Zinjanthropus* bones with digitized coordinate data provides significant evidence for the interpretation of the agents and processes of bone accumulation. In Fig. 14, the top left frame shows the localized distribution of the sets of conjoined bones. The web of lines connects the circular and elongate concentrations. Knowing that some of the bones have been modified by hominids and/or large carnivores (Bunn

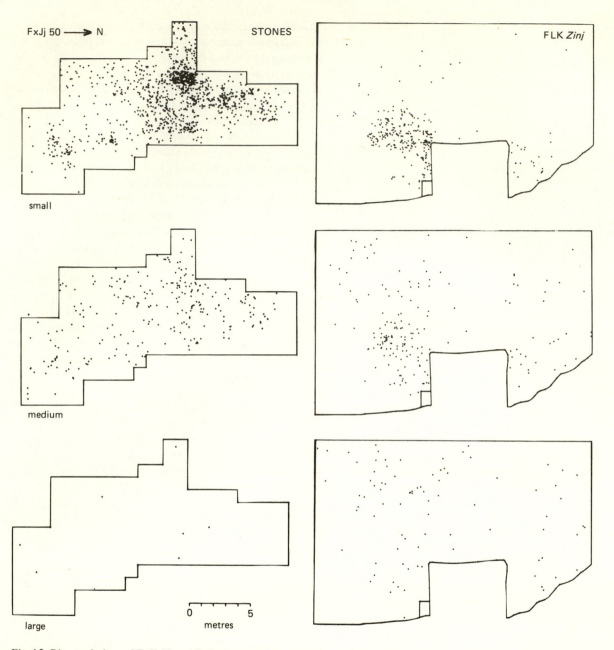

Fig. 12. Dissected plans of FxJj 50 and FLK *Zinjanthropus* showing the distributions of small (0–19 mm), medium (20–39 mm), and large (> 40 mm) pieces of flakes and flake fragments. The co-occurrences of the clusters of small pieces of debitage with the webs of conjoining artifacts at FxJj 50 further suggest that those were areas where hominids knapped stone. The plans include pieces plotted *in situ* and pieces recovered by screening and assigned random positions within their 1 m X 1 m units of recovery.

1981; Potts and Shipman 1981), we can ask, what agent or agents were responsible for the distinctive spatial patterns at FLK *Zinjanthropus*? What do we find when we compare the distribution patterns of carnivore modified, cut-marked, and unmodified (i.e. not gnawed, not cut) bones? Although we cannot assume that carnivores gnawed every bone they may have moved, or that hominids left cut-marks or diagnostic fractures on every bone they butchered, we can isolate the bones we know to have been modified by carnivores or hominids. That gives us the middle right frame, in which we can see that carnivores left their 'calling cards' across the whole excavation area.

In the lower right frame we can examine the remaining distribution of cut-marked and unmodified bones. It is quite interesting that the distributions of both the carnivore modified bones and the cut-marked and unmodified bones resemble the overall distribution of all bones (top right frame).

Bones from the same taxon as well as some individual bone specimens were modified by both carnivores and hominids. Which came first is an important and tantalizing question for unraveling the sequence of events that led to the accumulation of artifacts and bones at FLK *Zinjanthropus*. By intuition, it seems unlikely that hominids would have

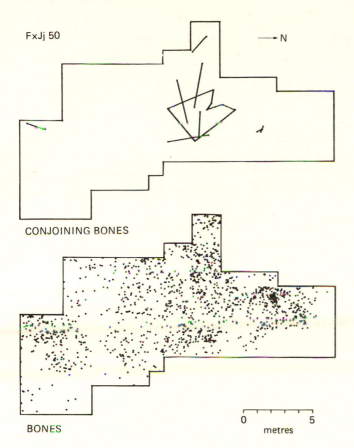

FxJj 50

→ N

CONJOINING BONES

BONES

0 ————— 5
metres

Fig. 13. Plan showing the distribution of conjoining bones at
FxJj 50 (Bunn 1982*b*). The network of conjoins may demarcate
areas where hominids broke open bones to extract marrow.

scavenged bones that had already been de-fleshed, gnawed,
and broken by non-hominid carnivores. Hence, if we assume
that hominids were the principal accumulators of the bones
because of the high incidence of cut-marks (Bunn 1981), then
we can examine the sequence of agents which created the
spatial distribution of bones. The right-hand frames of Fig. 14,
in sequence from top to bottom, show that the overall distribution pattern (top frame) consisting of the dense circular
concentration, the elongate concentration, and the lower
density scatter of other bones, persists through the apparent
carnivore filter (middle frame) and seems to have been the
pattern left from hominid involvement with the bones
(bottom frame). That persistence may begin to answer our
question about who arranged the bones. The working hypothesis that hominids formed the spatial pattern of bones is
consistent with the fact that the spatial pattern of stone artifacts, which would not have been a major attraction for carnivores, largely coincides with the bone pattern.

As shown by the left-hand frames of Fig. 14, the major
concentration of conjoining bones in one area of the
excavation also seems to have survived the activity of non-
hominid carnivores. Although the concentration of conjoining pieces will receive further attention during more detailed

analysis (Henry Bunn and Ellen Kroll unpublished), it is
difficult not to reach the preliminary conclusion that the
processing of animal carcasses by hominids was a fairly
localized activity. The conjoining sets which connect the
circular and elongate concentrations may ultimately document
the relationship between different parts of the site, and may
be useful in assessing the interpretations offered by Clark
(in Leakey 1971) and Ohel (1977). We should add that we
omitted the dissected plot showing those sets that conjoin
cut-marked with gnaw-marked bones. That plot has the
potential for tracing hominid and/or carnivore transport of
bones across the site.

Comparative observations

As already mentioned, one important way of determining distinctive patterns for early hominid use of space is
to compare the plans of the Plio-Pleistocene sites with those
of later prehistoric sites. That is easier said than done, as
many of the available plans of stone and bone refuse at
open-air pre-agricultural sites have not yet been published
in full detail. The sample that we are using for comparative
purposes is growing and at present includes the following:
Bordj Mellala (Tixier 1976), Gonnersdorf (Bosinski 1979),
Gwisho (Gabel 1965), Latamne (Clark 1967), Meer (Cahen
et al. 1979; Van Noten *et al.* 1978, 1980), Mwanganda
(Clark and Haynes 1970), Orangia (Sampson 1976), Pincevent (Leroi-Gourhan and Brézillon 1966, 1972), Solvieux
(Sackett and Gaussen 1976), Star Carr (J. G. D. Clark 1954),
Les Tartarets II (Brézillon 1971; Hesse 1971), Terra Amata
(de Lumley 1969; Villa 1978), Torralba (Freeman 1978),
various other French (e.g. de Lumley 1969; Leroi-Gourhan
et al. 1980), central European (e.g. Banesz 1976; Bosinski
1976), and Russian sites (e.g. Klein 1969, 1973), and sites
in the Sahara (e.g. Wendorf and Schild 1980) and in the
central Negev (e.g. Marks 1971). Our study of the corpus
of comparative material has not yet passed the stage of
scanning the plots for *potential* contrasts. We offer the
following preliminary observations:

1. There are basic similarities linking many of the stone age
   hunter–gatherer intrasite spatial patterns: (*a*) the refuse
   consists of a jumble of flaked stones interspersed with
   broken bones (although the peak densities of stone and
   bone do not necessarily coincide); (*b*) the sizes of
   individual concentrations seem to range from 8 to 20 m
   in diameter; (*c*) within the concentrations, there are
   commonly one or more zones of higher refuse density.
2. The maximum densities of refuse items per square meter
   hitherto observed in the very early sites seem to be lower
   than the values that are common in later sites.
3. The assemblages from the Plio-Pleistocene sites contain
   fewer distinct forms and varieties of retouched tools
   than do later assemblages; consequently, the early site
   plans are simpler to dissect, although as complex to
   interpret.
4. Hearths and fireplaces have not been identified with any

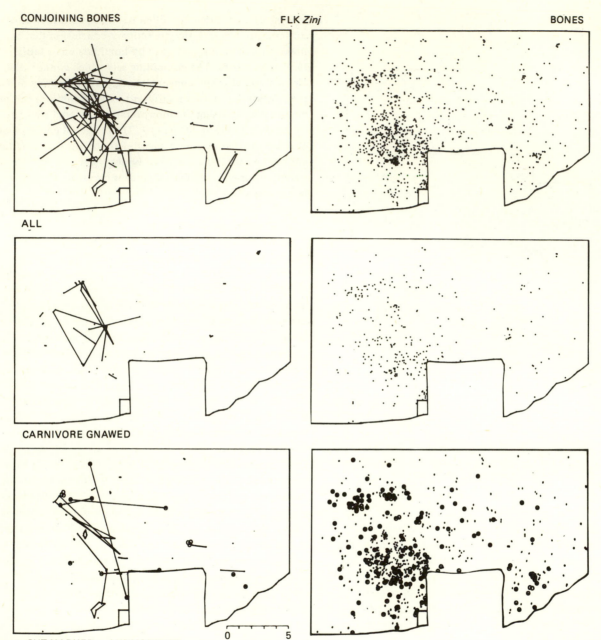

Fig. 14. Plans showing the distribution of modified and conjoined bones at FLK *Zinjanthropus* (bone data from Bunn 1982*b*). For a discussion of the patterns see pp. 23–5. (Unmodified = not gnawed, not cut.)

certainty from the Plio-Pleistocene sites, although discolored patches that may be traces of fire have been found at FxJj 20 East (Harris 1978). The absence of evidence for fire should not be taken at face value, because charcoal does not often survive the ground water conditions of Rift Valley sedimentary contexts.

5. Clearly defined modular divisions within the sites have not yet been observed in the Oldowan sites. These are in evidence through multiple hearths or multiple hut traces at later sites, for example, Bordj Mellala or Pincevent. But if the visible traces of the hearths themselves

were subtracted from many of the later period sites, it is not clear that the former existence of hearth and household modules would be detectable from the stone and bone refuse alone.

6. Refuse dumps are evident at some, but not all, of the later sites. While inspection has not revealed incontrovertible clear-cut secondary refuse accumulations in the Plio-Pleistocene sites, the possibility remains that either the scatter at the periphery of some sites or the dense internal clusters are in fact secondary refuse zones.

7. With the possible exception of the DK stone circle, traces of shelters or structures have not yet been detected at the early sites. While structures are evident at some late stone age sites, they are by no means universally present.

Our preliminary inspection suggests that the differences in archaeological expression of intrasite use of space between very early and later Pleistocene hominids are fairly subtle. That may reflect the early establishment of fundamentals of the human pattern of socio-economic organization which remained stable throughout pre-agricultural evolution, while elaboration and development occurred in other spheres of culture. On the other hand, similar refuse patterns could have been generated by markedly contrasting socio-economic patterns. The latter possibility emphasizes the importance of pursuing more rigorous comparisons of early and late sites and of generating alternative hypotheses with carefully worked-out test implications (Kroll 1984).

Discussion

Following our review of approaches and methods, it is fair to ask whether we can answer, however tentatively, any of the large-scale questions posed earlier in this essay. First and foremost, is spatial analysis helping us to understand how the early sites formed and what role those places played in the lives of early hominids? Intrasite distribution patterns seem to confirm that stone knapping and the processing of animal carcasses both occurred within the same confined area (e.g. FxJj 50, FLK *Zinjanthropus*). That combination of hominid actions is predicted by the home base and food-sharing model of early hominid socio-economic organization (Isaac 1978*a*, 1978*b*). We must immediately admit, however, that several other conceivable models of behavior could also account for spatial contiguity between stone-flaking and the breaking of bones. We now need to find appropriate test implications that will allow us to distinguish between the spatial patterns that would have been generated at a home base, and patterns that would have formed in other ways.

Secondly, how long did the hominids spend at the sites? Did they stay overnight, and if so, did they sleep on the ground or in trees? Comments rather than answers are all that can yet be offered in response to those questions. The number of artifacts at most of the early sites could have been made by one or two vigorous, competent stone-knappers in an hour or less. But the amount of stone imported to most sites would have required a dozen or more person-trips to and from the source of stones if some sort of container were used, and more trips if the stones were carried directly in the hands. Likewise, the variety and number of animals at the sites seem to imply a substantial accumulation period, although the unweathered condition of most bones suggests that they were not subjected to sub-aerial weathering processes for more than a year or so (Henry Bunn personal communication). Thus, the formation of many of the sites presumably does represent a fair number of return visits. Whether that implies a sustained stay during which the site was a base of operation, or whether it implies a series of brief visits spaced through time, we do not yet know.

At one stage we supposed that using spatial analysis to test for the *O'Connell size differentiation pattern* might help to distinguish sustained periods of site use from a succession of casual short-term visits. The secondary refuse processes observed in Australia would only be detectable where occupation had been sustained. Those processes may be indicative of a widespread phenomenon that was previously unreported. The *O'Connell size differentiation pattern* may yet be detected in some of the early sites. Based on preliminary inspectional analysis, the distribution at the FLK *Zinjanthropus* excavation area may be the earliest example of that pattern. The bulk of the refuse found at the early sites so far, however, is of a size that would not necessitate clearance. When we set up a full scale reconstruction of the refuse scatter at FxJj 50 (which in Fig. 2 appears to be a fairly densely littered site), we saw that the hominids who generated the litter probably would have been blissfully unaware of the garbage underfoot. Given a sandy substrate and a little leaf mold, they could have squatted, sat, or slept on the artifact-and-bone scatter without noticing it. One of the few researchers who has previously worked on the Olduvai plots and published his findings decided that the densest refuse areas were peripheral to the locations of activities (Davis 1978). In our view that remains plausible but requires more rigorous testing.

Thirdly, can activity areas be distinguished by visual inspection? The answer must be cautious. The locations of several of the primary refuse generating activities sometimes appear to be spatially distinct. Those activities are, of course, stone knapping and the breaking of bones, and their locations may be marked by clusters of conjoining pieces (see Figs. 10, 13 and 14). Ohel (1977) suggested that areas of butchery and meat preparation can be distinguished from areas of meat consumption by the quantity of flakes and bone splinters concentrated at the meat consumption areas. We find his hypothesis interesting, but as we have indicated, it requires further exploration as one of a set of explicitly stated alternative hypotheses. Whether wood whittling, hide preparation, the pounding of foods, or other activities were part of early hominid life remains to be determined. If they were, then we must determine whether the places where those activities occurred are archaeologically detectable.

Under equatorial conditions, the patchy distribution of comfortable shaded areas seems a critical factor in the localization of human activities and the resultant refuse (Yellen 1977). The majority of Plio-Pleistocene sites are very likely fossilized, shady picnic spots which were used recurrently, but the trees and bushes that were originally important are gone, leaving scant traces if any. We do have leaf impressions at FxJj 1 (also called KBS) and tree root casts at FxJj 50. Archaeological ingenuity is needed for the formulation of testable hypotheses about shade and its effect on the use of space and the distribution of refuse. The study of modern analogue environments and the determination of the properties of shaded areas will be necessary. Meanwhile, it seems that dense patches of refuse as have been recovered from FxJj 50 at Koobi Fora or FLK *Zinjanthropus* at Olduvai Gorge would all fit perfectly well into the shade areas afforded by trees growing in comparable situations in modern East Africa. In addition to providing shade, the trees may also have provided the hominids with a refuge from on-the-ground difficulties.

As has been shown, there are spaces within sites that remained clear of large items of refuse. They would have been suitable for sitting or lying down and sleeping. However, there is no repeating pattern that we would interpret as sleeping areas.[4]

In summary, the patterns of early hominid behavior may well have been profoundly different from those of any living system that we can observe. If we are to explore the record and detect its originality, we need to avoid adopting interpretations and hypotheses that project ethnographic or primate patterns into the remote past. That means that, in addition to using the kinds of rigorous quantitative techniques which have been developed by some archaeological spatial analysts over the past decade, we need to engage in restless thinking about processes and patterns, and to develop a hierarchy of testable hypotheses. This essay has dealt mainly with the process of groping towards such hypotheses. We have attempted to show that through spatial analysis of the Plio-Pleistocene stone artifact and bone configurations and comparisons with experimental and later Pleistocene patterns, we can, without wild extrapolations or giant leaps backward, begin to decipher some of the earliest evidence for the refuse-producing behaviors of hominids.

Our research group, like many others, has become increasingly conscious of the need to understand processes as a prerequisite to interpreting the excavated record. That is leading to a regular alternation between scrutiny of the archaeological record and experimentation and/or the study of analogous situations. In pursuing that kind of approach, we hope to make the interpretations of Plio-Pleistocene sites, including their spatial configurations, more realistic and more interesting.

Notes

1. Well-preserved sites have been discovered and investigated principally at Olduvai Gorge Beds I and II (Leakey 1971), at Koobi Fora (Isaac *et al.* 1976; Harris 1978; Isaac and Harris 1978), at Melka Kunturé (Chavaillon and Chavaillon 1971; Piperno and Bulgarelli-Piperno 1974–75), in the Shungura Formation at the Omo (Merrick *et al.* 1973; Chavaillon 1976; Merrick 1976), and most recently at the Hadar (Roche and Tiercelin 1977). At many of those sites, work is still in progress and/or full reports are in preparation for publication. Appropriate data are not available for early sites in South or North Africa.
2. The artifact assemblages older than 1½ million years have been assigned to the Oldowan Industry (Olduvai Beds I and Lower II),

the Developed Oldowan Industry (Olduvai Middle and Upper Bed II), the KBS Industry (Koobi Fora Formation Lower Member) and the Karari Industry (Koobi Fora Upper Member). All of those industries are components of the 'Oldowan Industrial Complex' (Harris 1978).
3. The discovery of GaJi 5 at Koobi Fora by Bunn (1981) shows another category of sites consisting exclusively of bones of many carcasses. Although no stone artifacts were recovered, the presence of cut-marks on some of the bones indicates their functional association with hominid activities.
4. The DK hut circle (Leakey 1971, Fig. 7) is a possible example of such an organized space.

Acknowledgements

Our study of intrasite spatial patterns is a part of the collaborative venture of the archaeological segment of the Koobi Fora Research Project. We have drawn data and ideas from our colleagues on the project, notably A. K. Behrensmeyer, H. Bunn, I. Findlater, J. W. K. Harris, A. B. Isaac, Z. Kaufulu, K. Schick, J. Sept, and N. Toth. We thank them and the other individuals who have participated in field seminars at Koobi Fora. We have also benefited from discussions with J. D. Clark, J. O'Connell, R. Potts, J. Portugali, J. Speth and others.

We make extensive use of data from excavations that have involved years of hard, skilled work by teams of excavators from the Kenya National Museum under the foremanship of Muteti Nume, Kitivi Kimeu, and Mukilya Mangoka. We have made use of the Koobi Fora field records and excavations plans of J. W. Barthelme, H. Bunn, J. W. K. Harris, and F. Marshall. We are especially grateful to J. W. K. Harris for his data from many of the Karari sites and his advice to Ellen Kroll. Likewise, Henry Bunn has generously given us access to his bone data, has helped with many aspects of the analysis, and has contributed ideas.

Mary Leakey generously gave us access to the specimens from her excavations at Olduvai Gorge, and to the catalogs and original field plans.

The Koobi Fora Research Project has its headquarters in the National Museums of Kenya, and its work has been made possible through the support of the Museum and the Kenya government. We thank Richard Leakey and his staff. Financial support has come largely from National Science Foundation grants to Glynn Isaac and National Geographic Society grants to Richard Leakey.

R. Blumenschine, H. Bunn, M. Kroll, J. Sept, and A. Vincent have helped with the completion of this paper. Barbara Isaac helped with the illustrations. M. Anderson provided invaluable guidance for computer compilations and plotting; the Plio-Pleistocene point pattern diagrams were drawn by a Tektronix plotter using a Data General MV/8000. Funds for computer time came from the Department of Anthropology, University of California, Berkeley, and we thank E. A. Hammel and W. H. Geoghegan for their continued support.

References

Ammerman, A. J. and Feldman, M. W. (1974). On the making of an assemblage of stone tools. *American Antiquity* 39(4): 610–16.

Banesz, L. (1976). Les structures d'habitat au Paléolithique superieur en Europe Centrale. *UISPP 9th Congress* 8: 8–53.

Behrensmeyer, A. K. (1975*a*). The taphonomy and paleo-ecology of Plio-Pleistocene vertebrate assemblages east of Lake Rudolf, Kenya. *Bulletin of the Museum of Comparative Zoology at Harvard University* 146(10): 473–578.

Behrensmeyer, A. K. (1975*b*). Taphonomy and paleoecology in the hominid fossil record. *Yearbook of Physical Anthropology* 19: 36–50.

Behrensmeyer, A. K. and Hill, A. P. (eds.) (1980). *Fossils in the Making: Vertebrate Taphonomy and Paleoecology.* University of Chicago Press: Chicago.

Binford, L. R. (1977). Olorgesailie deserves more than the usual book review. *Journal of Anthropological Research* 33(4): 493–502.

Binford, L. R. (1981). *Bones: Ancient Men and Modern Myths*. Academic Press: New York.

Bishop, W. W. (ed.) (1978). *Geological Background to Fossil Man*. Scottish Academic Press: Edinburgh.

Bosinski, G. (1976). Middle Paleolithic structural remains from western central Europe. *UISPP 9th Congress* 11: 64–77.

Bosinski, G. (1979). *Die Ausgrabungen in Gönnersdorf 1968–1976: Und die Siedlungsbefunde der Grabung 1968*. Franz Steiner: Wiesbeden.

Brain, C. K. (1976). Some principles in the interpretation of bone accumulations associated with man. In *Human Origins: Louis Leakey and the East African Evidence*, ed. G. L. Isaac and E. R. McCown, pp. 97–116. W. A. Benjamin: Menlo Park, California.

Brézillon, M. (1971). Les Tarterets II, site paléolithique de plein air à Corbeil-Essonne (Essonne) I. *Gallia Préhistoire* XIV(1): 3–40.

Bunn, H. T. (1981). Archaeological evidence for meat-eating by Plio-Pleistocene hominids from Koobi Fora and Olduvai Gorge. *Nature* 291: 574–7.

Bunn, H. T. (1982a). Animal bones and archaeological inference. (Book Review of *Bones: Ancient Men and Modern Myths*, by L. R. Binford.) *Science* 215: 494–5.

Bunn, H. T. (1982b). Meat-eating and human evolution: studies on the diet and subsistence patterns of Plio-Pleistocene hominids in East Africa. Ph.D. thesis, Department of Anthropology, University of California, Berkeley.

Bunn, H. T., Harris, J. W. K., Isaac, G., Kaufulu, Z., Kroll, E., Schick, K., Toth, N. and Behrensmeyer, A. K. (1980). FxJj50: An early Pleistocene site in northern Kenya. *World Archaeology* 12(2): 109–36.

Cahen, D., Keeley, L. H. and Van Noten, F. L. (1979). Stone tools, toolkits, and human behavior in prehistory. *Current Anthropology* 20(4): 661–83.

Chavaillon, J. (1976). Evidence for the technical practices of early Pleistocene hominids: Shungura Formation, Lower Omo Valley, Ethiopia. In *Earliest Man and Environments in the Lake Rudolf Basin: Stratigraphy, Paleoecology and Evolution*, ed. Y. Coppens, F. C. Howell, G. Ll. Isaac and R. E. F. Leakey, pp. 565–73. University of Chicago Press: Chicago.

Chavaillon, M. J. and Chavaillon, N. (1971). Présence eventuelle d'un abri Oldowayen dans le gisement de Melka-Kontouré (Ethiopie). *Comptes rendus des Séances de l'Académie des Sciences* 273: 623–5.

Clark, J. D. (1967). The middle Acheulian occupation site at Latamne, northern Syria. *Quaternaria* 9: 1–68.

Clark, J. D. (1970). *The Prehistory of Africa*. Thames & Hudson: London.

Clark, J. D. and Haynes, C. V. (1970). An elephant butchery site at Mwanganda's Village, Karonga, Malawi, and its relevance for Palaeolithic archaeology. *World Archaeology* 1(3): 390–411.

Clark, J. G. D. (1954). *Excavations at Star Carr: an Early Mesolithic Site at Seamer, near Scarborough, Yorkshire*. Cambridge University Press: Cambridge.

Dacey, M. F. (1973). Statistical tests of spatial association in the locations of tool types. *American Antiquity* 38(3): 320–8.

Davis, D. D. (1976). Spatial organization and subsistence technology of lower and middle Pleistocene hominid sites at Olduvai Gorge, Tanzania. Ph.D. thesis, Department of Anthropology, Yale University.

Davis, D. D. (1978). Lithic assemblage variability in relation to early hominid subsistence strategies of Olduvai Gorge. In *Lithics and Subsistence: The Analysis of Stone Tool Use in Prehistoric Economies*, Publications in Anthropology, No. 20, ed. D. D. Davis, pp. 35–86. Vanderbilt University Press: Nashville.

de Lumley, H. (1969). A paleolithic camp at Nice. Reprinted in *Old World Archaeology: Foundations of Civilization*, ed. C. C. Lamberg-Karlovsky, pp. 33–41. W. H. Freeman: San Francisco.

Freeman, L. G. (1978). The analysis of some occupation floor distributions from earlier and middle Paleolithic sites in Spain. In *Views of the Past*, ed. L. G. Freeman, pp. 57–116. Mouton: The Hague.

Gabel, C. (1965). *Stone Age Hunters of the Kafue: The Gwisho A. Site*. Boston University Press: Boston.

Harris, J. W. K. (1978). The Karari industry: its place in East African prehistory. Ph.D. thesis, Department of Anthropology, University of California, Berkeley.

Hay, R. L. (1976). *Geology of the Olduvai Gorge*. University of California Press: Berkeley.

Hesse, A. (1971). Les Tartarets II, site paléolithique de plein air à Corbeil-Essonnes (Essonne). II. Comparison par le calcul des distributions horizontales des vestiges lithiques. *Gallia Préhistoire* XIV(1): 41–6.

Hietala, H. J. (1983). Boker Tachtit: intralevel and interlevel spatial analysis. In *Prehistory and Paleoenvironments in the Central Negev, Israel*, vol. III, *The Avdat/Aqev Area*, Part 3, ed. A. E. Marks, pp. 217–81. Department of Anthropology, Southern Methodist University: Dallas, Texas.

Hietala, H. J. and Larson, P. A., Jr (1979). SYMAP analyses in archaeology: intrasite assumptions and a comparison with TREND analysis. *Norwegian Archaeological Review* 12(1): 57–64.

Hietala, H. J. and Stevens, D. E. (1977). Spatial analysis: multiple procedures in pattern recognition studies. *American Antiquity* 42(4): 539–59.

Hill, A. (1975). Taphonomy of contemporary and late Cenozoic East African vertebrates. Ph.D. thesis, Bedford College, London.

Isaac, G. Ll. (1967). Towards the interpretation of occupation debris: Some experiments and observations. *Kroeber Anthropological Society Papers* 37: 31–57.

Isaac, G. Ll. (1969). Studies of early culture in East Africa. *World Archaeology* 1: 1–28.

Isaac, G. Ll. (1972). Chronology and tempo of cultural change in the Pleistocene. In *Calibration of Hominoid Evolution*, ed. W. W. Bishop and J. Miller, pp. 381–430. Scottish Academic Press: Edinburgh.

Isaac, G. Ll. (1976a). East Africa as a source of fossil evidence for human evolution. In *Human Origins: Louis Leakey and the East African Evidence*, ed. G. Ll. Isaac and E. R. McCown, pp. 121–37. W. A. Benjamin: Menlo Park, California.

Isaac, G. Ll. (1976b). The activities of early African hominids: a review of archaeological evidence from the time span two and a half to one million years ago. In *Human Origins: Louis Leakey and the East African Evidence*, ed. G. Ll. Isaac and E. R. McCown, pp. 483–514. W. A. Benjamin: Menlo Park, California.

Isaac, G. Ll. (1977). *Olorgesailie: Archaeological Studies of a Middle Pleistocene Lake Basin*. University of Chicago Press: Chicago.

Isaac, G. Ll. (1978a). The food-sharing behavior of proto-human hominids. *Scientific American* 238: 90–108.

Isaac, G. Ll. (1978b). Food-sharing and human evolution: archaeological evidence from the Plio-Pleistocene of East Africa. *Journal of Anthropological Research* 34: 311–25.

Isaac, G. Ll. (1980). Casting the net wide: a review of archaeological evidence for early land use and ecological relations. In *Current Argument on Early Man*, ed. L.-K. Königsson, pp. 226–51. Royal Swedish Academy of Sciences and the Nobel Foundation, Karlskoga.

Isaac, G. Ll. (1981a). Stone Age visiting cards: approaches to the study of early hominid land use patterns. In *Patterns in the Past*, ed. I. Hodder, pp. 131–55. Cambridge University Press: Cambridge.

Isaac, G. Ll. (1981*b*). Emergence of human behaviour patterns: archaeological tests of alternative models of early hominid behavior: excavation and experiments. *Philosophical Transactions of the Royal Society of London, Ser. B* 292: 177–88.

Isaac, G. Ll. and Crader, D. (1981). To what extent were early hominids carnivorous? An archaeological perspective. In *Omnivorous Primates: Gathering and Hunting in Human Evolution,* ed. R. Harding and G. Teleki, pp. 37–103. Columbia University Press: New York.

Isaac, G. Ll. and Harris, J. W. K. (1978). Archaeology. In *Koobi Fora Research Project,* vol. 1: *The Fossil Hominids and an Introduction to their context, 1968–1974,* ed. M. G. Leakey and R. E. Leakey, pp. 64–85. Clarendon Press: Oxford.

Isaac, G. Ll. and Harris, J. W. K. (1980). A method for determining the characteristics of artifacts between sites in the Upper Member of the Koobi Fora Formation, East Lake Turkana. In *Proceedings of the VIII Pan African Congress on Prehistory, Nairobi,* ed. R. E. Leakey and B. A. Ogot, pp. 19–22. TILLMIAP: Nairobi.

Isaac, G. Ll., Harris, J. W. K. and Crader, D. (1976). Archaeological evidence from the Koobi Fora Formation. In *Earliest Man and Environments in the Lake Rudolf Basin: Stratigraphy, Paleoecology and Evolution,* ed. Y. Coppens, F. C. Howell, G. Ll. Isaac and R. E. F. Leakey, pp. 533–51. University of Chicago Press: Chicago.

Isaac, G. Ll., Marshall, F. and Behrensmeyer, A. K. (1984). FxJj 64. In *Koobi Fora Research Project,* vol. 3: *Archaeology,* ed. G. Ll. Isaac and J. W. K. Harris. Clarendon Press: Oxford. (In press.)

Keeley, L. and Toth, N. (1981). Microwear polishes on early stone tools from Koobi Fora. *Nature* 293: 464–5.

Klein, R. G. (1969). *Man and Culture in the Late Pleistocene: A Case Study.* Chandler Publishing Company: San Francisco.

Klein, R. G. (1973). *Ice-Age Hunters of the Ukraine.* University of Chicago Press: Chicago.

Klein, R. G. (1975). Paleoanthropological implications of the non-archaeological bone assemblage from Swartklip I, southwestern Cape Province, South Africa. *Quaternary Research* 5(2): 275–88.

Kroll, E. M. (1981). 'Spatial configurations at Plio-Pleistocene archaeological sites at Koobi Fora, Kenya, and Olduvai Gorge, Tanzania.' Paper presented at the 46th Annual Meeting of the Society for American Archaeology, San Diego, April 30–May 2.

Kroll, E. M. (1984). The anthropological meaning of spatial configurations at Plio-Pleistocene archaeological sites in East Africa. Ph.D. thesis, Department of Anthropology, University of California, Berkeley. (In preparation.)

Larson, P. (1975). Trend analysis in archaeology: a preliminary study of intrasite patterning. *Norwegian Archaeological Review* 8: 75–80.

Leakey, M. D. (1971). *Olduvai Gorge,* vol. 3: *Excavations in Beds I and II, 1960–1963.* Cambridge University Press: Cambridge.

Leroi-Gourhan, A. and Brézillon, M. (1966). L'habitation magdalénienne no. 1 de Pincevent près Montereau (Seine-et-Marne). *Gallia Préhistoire* XI: 263–385.

Leroi-Gourhan, A. and Brézillon, M. (1972). Fouilles de Pincevent: essai d'analyse ethnographique d'un habitat magdalénien (la section 36). *Gallia Préhistoire* supplement 7. Paris: CNRS.

Leroi-Gourhan, A., Audouz, F. and Karlin, C. (1980). Analyses du rapport à l'éspace. Processus de structuration de l'éspace: la structuration de l'éspace en Préhistoire. Thème C. Gestlon des Ressources Raves. Organisation de l'espace et population, pp. 143–151.

Leroi-Gourhan, A. and Brézillon, M. (1972). Fouilles de Pincevent: Essai d'analyse ethnographique d'un habitat magdalénien (la section 36). *Gallia Préhistoire,* supplement VII. Paris: CNRS.

Marks, A. E. (1971). Settlement patterns and intrasite variability in the central Negev, Israel. *American Anthropologist* 73: 1237–44.

Merrick, H. V. (1976). Recent archaeological research in the Plio-Pleistocene deposits of the Lower Omo Valley, Southwestern Ethiopia. In *Human Origins: Louis Leakey and the East African Evidence,* ed. G. Ll. Isaac and E. R. McCown, pp. 461–82. W. A. Benjamin: Menlo Park, California.

Merrick, H. W., de Heinzelin, J., Haesaerts, P. and Howell, F. C. (1973). Archaeological occurrences of early Pleistocene age from the Shungura Formation, Lower Omo Valley, Ethiopia. *Nature* 242: 572–5.

Ohel, M. J. (1977). Patterned concentrations on living floors at Olduvai, Beds I and II: experimental study. *Journal of Field Archaeology* 4: 423–33.

Pilbeam, D. R. (1972). *The Ascent of Man.* Macmillan: New York and London.

Piperno, M. and Bulgarelli-Piperno, G. M. (1974–5). First Approach to the ecological and cultural significance of the early Palaeolithic occupation site of Garba IV at Melka-Kunturé (Ethiopia). *Quaternaria* 18: 347–82.

Potts, R. and Shipman, P. (1981). Cutmarks made by stone tools on bones from Olduvai Gorge, Tanzania. *Nature* 291: 577–80.

Roche, H. and Tiercelin, J. J. (1977). Découverte d'une industrie lithique ancienne *in situ* dans la formation d'Hadar, Afar Centrale, Ethiopie. *Comptes rendus hebdomadaires des Séances de l'Académie des Sciences* Série D 289(19): 1871–4.

Sackett, J. and Gaussen, J. (1976). Upper Paleolithic habitation structures in the Sud-Ouest of France. *UISPP 9th Congress* 13: 55–83.

Sampson, G. (1976). The stone structures from Orangia, O.F.S. South Africa. *UISPP 9th Congress* 11: 7–34.

Schick, K. (1984). Towards the interpretation of early archaeological sites: Experiments in site formation processes. Ph.D. thesis, Department of Anthropology, University of California, Berkeley. (In preparation.)

Schiffer, M. (1972). Archaeological context and systemic context. *American Antiquity* 37: 156–65.

Schiffer, M. (1976). *Behavioral Archaeology.* Academic Press: New York.

Serizawa, C. (1977). *Isoyama. Records of Archaeological Material,* No. 1. Department of Archaeology, Faculty of Arts and Letters, Tohoku University: Sendai, Japan.

Shackley, M. L. (1978). The behavior of artefacts as sedimentary particles in a fluviatile environment. *Archaeometry* 20(1): 55–61.

Tixier, J. (1976). *Le Campement Préhistorique de Bordj Mellala, Ouargla, Algérie.* Editions du Cercle de Recherches et d'Etudes Préhistoriques 13: Paris.

Van Noten, F., Cahen, D. and Keeley, L. (1980). A paleolithic campsite in Belgium. *Scientific American* 242(4): 48–55.

Van Noten, F., Cahen, D., Keeley, L. H. and Moeyersons, J. (1978). *Les Chasseurs de Meer.* De Temple: Brugge.

Vertes, L. (1968). Rates of evolution in Palaeolithic technology. *Acta Archaeologica Academiae Scientiarium Hungaricae* 20. Fasc. 1–4.

Villa P. (1978). The stone artifact assemblage from Terra Amata: a contribution to the comparative study of Acheulian industries in southwestern Europe. Ph.D. thesis, Department of Anthropology, University of California, Berkeley.

Voorhies, M. R. (1969). Taphonomy and population dynamics of an Early Pliocene vertebrate Fauna, Knox County, Nebraska. *Contributions to Geology, Special Paper* No. 1. University of Wyoming: Laramie.

Walker, A. and Leakey, R. E. F. (1978). The hominids of East Turkana. *Scientific American* 239(2): 54–66.

Wendorf, F. and Schild, R. (eds.) (1980). *Prehistory of the Eastern Sahara*. Academic Press: New York.

Whallon, R. R. (1973). Spatial analysis of occupation floors. I. Application of dimensional analysis of variance. *American Antiquity* 38(3): 266–78.

Whallon, R. R. (1974). Spatial analysis of occupation floors. II. Nearest neighbor analysis. *American Antiquity* 39(1): 16–34.

Yellen, J. E. (1977). *Archaeological Approaches to the Present: Models for Reconstructing the Past*. Academic Press: New York.

Postscript

Our paper was drafted in 1979 and reworked in 1981. Since then, several of our colleagues have completed relevant Ph.D. dissertations and publications. The dissertations include Henry Bunn's (1982) comparative study of archaeological bone assemblages from Koobi Fora and Olduvai Gorge and various modern bone assemblages, Zefe Kaufulu's (1983) study of the microstratigraphic evidence for site formation at the Koobi Fora archaeological sites, Richard Potts' (1982) study of the stone artifact and bone assemblages from five of the Olduvai Gorge Bed I sites, and Nicholas Toth's (1982) experimental study of the manufacture and use of ancient stone artifacts from Koobi Fora. Several other dissertations are nearly complete with 1984 target dates of completion. Those include Ellen Kroll's comparative study of the horizontal and vertical spatial patterns at 20 archaeological excavations at Koobi Fora and three at Olduvai Gorge, Kathy Schick's experimental study of site formation processes and the effects of floods on refuse scatters, and Jeanne Sept's study of contemporary vegetation patterns in topographic situations analogous to the ancient archaeological sites at Koobi Fora. The volume of the Koobi Fora Research Monograph Series on the archaeological excavations at Koobi Fora from 1970–9, edited by Glynn Isaac, is in press.

Glynn Isaac (1984, in press) now advocates moving to a more neutral, less anthropocentric terminology for some behaviors hypothesized as having been involved in site formation. He has replaced 'home base' and 'food-sharing' labels with the zoological term, 'central place foraging'.

The spatial data reported and discussed remain consistent with the hypothesis that the sites were central places to which food (i.e. meat and marrow, at least) was carried and collectively consumed. We are currently exploring the spatial patterns with several alternative behavioral models in mind.

Chapter 3

Middle Paleolithic intrasite variability and its relationship to regional patterning
Frederick C. Munday

This chapter explores some ramifications of intrasite spatial patterning in lithic material for intersite comparison and interpretation. Data used comes from Central Negev Mousterian sites previously subjected to intersite, interlevel, and/or intralevel analysis (Munday 1976, 1977*a*, 1977*b*, 1979; Hietala and Stevens 1977; Marks and Friedel 1977).

Most intrasite spatial analyses are conducted so as to improve understanding of the human behavior that produced the observed archaeological patterning. Examples include analyses of paleolithic living floors (Hietala and Stevens 1977; Kroll and Isaac, Chapter 2); space confined by structures (Raper 1977; Hill 1968; Cowgill *et al.*, Chapter 10); and modern hunter–gatherer refuse distributions (Yellen 1977; Binford 1978; Whallon, Chapter 13). This chapter emphasizes the contribution that intrasite analysis can make to producing sounder interpretations of, and conclusions about, intersite or interlevel comparisons. Specifically, contrary to emphasizing intrasite behavioral patterning, I stress the contribution of intrasite analysis as a tool for testing implicit assumptions that underlie many contemporaneous intersite or interlevel comparisons.

The intrasite basis of intersite comparisons

Many scolars concerned with paleolithic research compare sites on the basis of their technological and typological indices; these are computed on the basis of relative-frequency occurrences of tools, debitage, or manufacturing procedures (cf. Bordes 1961; Skinner 1965; Jelinek 1975; Schick and Stekelis 1977). Clusters of Mousterian assemblages with similar indices have been interpreted as being culturally (Bordes and de Sonneville-Bordes 1970) or temporally different (Mellars 1969, 1970). A variation on this analytic theme is the text edited by Binford and Binford (1966), which proposed an activity basis for Mousterian assemblage variability. In these analyses the comparative measures were computed from total assemblages. It was implicitly assumed, therefore, that indices were behaviorally or culturally representative, i.e. the areas the artifacts came from were assumed to be homogeneous with respect to the measures used. Recognizing this assumption is important because it indicates that the researcher also implicitly assumes little intrasite variation in the behavior represented by the index or comparative measure used. I am as guilty as others in avoiding the testing of *at least* this assumption as it affects my interpretation of interlevel and intersite Mousterian variability.

The following is a theoretical example of the pertinence of intrasite analysis to intersite and interlevel comparisons. If flake dimensions were dependent on core reduction stage and tool production activities, intrasite variation in flake lengths, widths, and thicknesses may have varied across an occupation floor depending on the occurrence of core decortification, later reduction, or tool manufacturing activities in different site areas. Ideally, these areas should be partitioned for analytic purposes because single measures calculated for the occupation floor assemblage would blend data from different activities. This would render both behavioral interpretation and intersite analysis meaningless. Another example of an unreliable assemblage measure would be use of a single index to describe sidescraper occurrence for an occupation floor where there was significant numerical or density variation in this tool.

Intrasite analysis is therefore applicable to intersite studies which consider the locational or temporal dimensions of a series of assemblages. While the focus of intersite studies might philosophically vary from cultural identification to behavioral understanding, one should *at least* minimally investigate site-specific artifact and behavioral patterning before proceeding to inter-assemblage comparisons. When levels within a site are treated as different assemblages, one basic assumption to be tested is that of intralevel index homogeneity. High intralevel index variability, as with high intrasite variability, might invalidate its use in interlevel and in intersite comparisons. While implications of the assumption of index homogeneity are not always explicitly recognized, they almost certainly lie in the background of most researchers' thoughts. They can be formally investigated through the analysis of intrasite or intralevel patterning.

The preceding discussion considered indices or summary measures calculated for a single typological or technological element, e.g. a sidescraper index or average flake length. Such measures can be termed *simple* indices. An additional problem arises if one considers an index which is an aggregate of different typological or technological elements. Such measures can be termed *compound* indices. One example is Bordes' Upper Paleolithic Index; this is the sum percentage occurrence of several tool types (Bordes 1961). If one considers these tool types were associated by virtue of use in a specific activity, we might expect them to be spatially associated. In an activity sense, therefore, spatial covariance of the component parts of a compound index might be a prerequisite for its use in intersite or interlevel comparisons. Such covariance patterning may, however, be muddied by *at least* activity area overlap, curation, and dropping and ·passing rates (Ammerman and Feldman 1974). Other research interests might dictate other intrasite patterning requirements. All research interests might still require that spatial homogeneity of a compound index be confirmed before it can be considered to be a useful measure for comparing whole assemblages.

The Levallois Index, the sum percentage occurrence of Levallois flakes, blades, and points in a Mousterian assemblage (Bordes 1961), is one such compound index used by myself (Munday 1977a) and many others (cf. Skinner 1965; Marks and Crew 1972; Crew 1975; Jelinek 1975; Schick and Stekelis 1977) in intersite and/or interlevel comparisons. Because these lithic types are direct byproducts of core reduction, we might expect them to covary spatially by virtue of a common origin.

Therefore, a useful intersite or interlevel comparative measure might consist of those spatially related types. This notion is complicated by the possibility that Levallois flakes, blades, and points, and combinations thereof, may have been produced from slightly different core types. This might weaken any anticipated spatial covariation if, for example, points were produced from distinctive cores in areas adjacent to flake and blade production areas. Thus, while Levallois elements may have originated from core reduction activities, they might not spatially covary.

Even if the component parts of the Levallois index had a common origin, spatial covariation might not be expected if different debitage types were subsequently incorporated into different activities. For example, the consistent spatial association of points, but not flakes and blades, with a variety of retouched tools at the Mousterian site of Rosh Ein Mor (Hietala and Stevens 1977) suggests they may have functioned as tools even though themselves unretouched. Frequent intralevel segregation of flakes and blades and their more common segregation from points suggest a variety of behavioral contexts for these Levallois elements. Under these conditions, the inclusion of flakes, blades, and points in a single compound index might be inadvisable for either intrasite consideration or intersite comparison. These and other data (Munday 1977a, pp. 166–77) suggest that the Levallois Index as used in contemporaneous publications may be of dubious value in intersite and interlevel comparisons. These preliminary indications of violations of assumptions that underlay intersite comparisons need further examination before previous research conclusions can be accepted.

Research background

Previous research related to Mousterian studies in the Negev includes work by Price-Williams (1973, 1975) and Gilead (1980). More comprehensive analyses resulted from the Central Negev Archaeological Project in the Avdat/Aqev area (Marks 1976, 1977). Sites from this project that are discussed in this Chapter are illustrated in Fig. 1.

Work by Marks and Crew (1972), Crew (1976), and Munday (1976, 1977a, 1977b) on Mousterian occupations emphasized single-site analyses or intersite technological and typological comparisons. Broader discussions that emphasize regional and diachronic patterning are Marks and Freidel (1977) and Munday (1979). The only article to consider intralevel and interlevel typological patterning simultaneously is that by Hietala and Stevens (1977). For purposes of this chapter, intersite and interlevel technological comparisons by Munday (1976, 1977a, 1977b, 1979) and intralevel and interlevel typological comparisons by Hietala and Stevens (1977) merit review.

Intersite technological comparisons by Munday (1976, 1977a) indicated that Mousterian flint knappers were strongly motivated by a desire economically to use time, work, and flint resources; this was reflected in a greater reduction of cores, and the production of larger numbers of smaller and

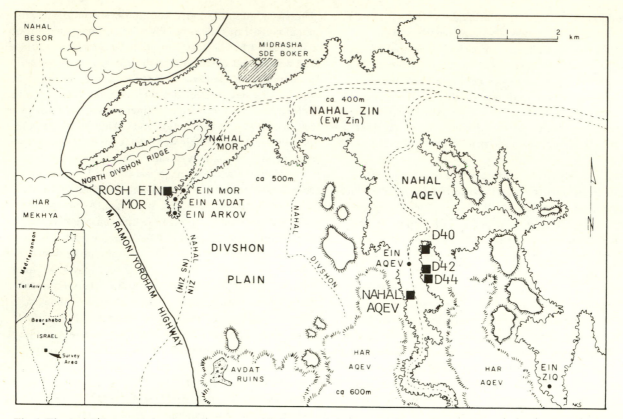

Fig. 1. The Avdat/Aqev area showing major topographic features, drainages, and sites discussed in the text. (Modified after Munday 1976.)

more highly prepared flakes with increased distance from raw material sources. In general, knappers partially overcame flint scarcity by increasing preparatory input into core reduction. Thus, labor substitution extended a core's flake-production life and reduced the number of trips to a raw material source. This economizing behavior was reflected in interassemblage variation for several measures. Average flake length, width, and thickness, and flake and core sizes were smaller in assemblages further from flint sources. Platform and dorsal scar flaking patterns were more complex, and the overall number of flakes per core were higher where flint was scarce (Munday 1977*a*, pp. 89–108). Other, traditional, comparisons included inter-site variation in the Levallois Index, a measure discussed earlier and one considered by Bordes (1961) to have had cultural significance. While site indices were low – the proportional occurrence of Levallois debitage was always less than 30% – variability was largely related to the amount of core reduction at different sites; the greater the reduction, the lower the Index (Munday 1977*a*, pp. 166–77). Because approaches to core reduction appeared to be directly related to raw material availability, this suggests an indirect relationship between the Levallois Index and site/resource relationships. Similar arguments have been proposed by Collins (1969), Binford (1972), and Fish (1978). Overall, these data suggest that intersite spatial variation in this technological index relates more to resource than cultural factors. Interlevel technological analyses likewise indicate that non-cultural factors influenced other aspects of assemblage variability.

Interlevel comparisons at Nahal Aqev (Munday 1977*b*, 1979) suggest that flake-production methods also changed over time. Flake shape, and platform and dorsal flaking patterns appear to have temporally covaried in non-linear fashion. A preliminary interpretation suggested this pattern was related to paleoenvironmental change and demographic shifts. In this sense, preparatory input into flake production changed because of shifts in area occupation mode. Given these technological patterns, it seems clear that various aspects of core reduction strategies were related not only to resource availability (intersite patterning) but also to temporal change (interlevel patterning). However, my efforts for both of these types of patterning were predicated on the assumption that intralevel variability was sufficiently small that average and overall measures were valid for intersite and interlevel comparisons. Other work on intralevel typological patterning suggests this assumption warrants testing.

The single intrasite typological analysis conducted to date (Hietala and Stevens 1977) indicates the presence of distinct typological patterning at the site of Rosh Ein Mor. Their work suggests a long-lived spatial association between burins, endscrapers, notches, Levallois points, and possibly perforators; this artifact group consistently aggregated in the same areas of the site in consecutive levels. Therefore typological indices varied depending on the area of the site examined. Relevant to my intersite analyses is the fact that Levallois points, flakes, and blades – the component parts of the Levallois Index – may not spatially associate at Rosh Ein

Mor. In addition, the recurring spatial patterning of behavior within the site would have produced typological index heterogeneity. Both considerations, soon to be addressed in greater detail, warn against interlevel or intersite comparisons based on overall assemblage indices. It should be noted, however, that Hietala and Stevens stressed the abundant typological data from Rosh Ein Mor. My analyses emphasized technological data because most Mousterian sites in the Central Negev had small typological samples. It cannot be assumed that intrasite typological heterogeneity implies the same for intrasite technological indices.

The preceding comments about previous Mousterian research in the Central Negev, and the pertinence of intrasite analysis to intersite comparisons, can be tested in preliminary fashion on technological data from several sites in the Avdat/Aqev area.

Data base

The 21 known Mousterian sites in the Avdat/Aqev area date to an early Levantine Mousterian technocomplex similar to that from Tabun, Bed 39 (Jelinek *et al.* 1973). Radiocarbon dates from Rosh Ein Mor (Fig. 1) indicate occupation prior to 50 000 years ago, while Nahal Aqev (Fig. 1) was probably temporally related to a nearby travertine (Goldberg 1976) that dates to about 80 000 ± 10 000 years ago (Schwartz *et al.* 1979). These dates, plus palynological data from Rosh Ein Mor, Nahal Aqev, and Tabun, suggest occupation during an early Würm stadial when the Negev was moister than today.

Only five of these sites seem suitable for intrasite analysis of some of the measures of interest. Rosh Ein Mor contains cultural material *in situ* through a single subsurface layer that averages about 75 cm thick (Crew 1976). Nahal Aqev contains three subsurface levels (Munday 1977b). Levels 1 and 2 each contain low densities of cultural material through about 20 cm of deposit. The lowest – level 3 – contains dense lithic debris through about 70 cm of deposit. Excellent artifact condition in all three levels, especially level 3, suggests little post-occupation disturbance. The remaining three sites, D40, D42, and D44 are surface occurrences that exhibit varying densities of lithic material (Munday 1976, 1977a). Minimal post-occupation surface deflation may have occurred at D42 and D44 and comparisons within and between lithic concentrations are probably meaningful. D40 lies on a flat–gently-sloping surface where minimal downslope movement may have occurred. Two distinct lithic clusters lie adjacent to each other; comparisons between clusters are probably more meaningful than comparison within clusters because of minimal intrasite artifact movement.

Data from Rosh Ein Mor and Nahal Aqev come from contiguous block and trench style excavations, respectively. Although 45 m² were excavated at Rosh Ein Mor, technological data beyond that reported by Crew (1976), Marks and Crew (1972), and Munday (1976, 1977a) are not yet available; there are forthcoming analyses (H. J. Hietala, personal communication). The site has been subjected to

intensive intralevel and interlevel typological analysis (Hietala and Stevens 1977). The technological sample reviewed here comes from a 1 m × 12 m area, 5 cm thick; this lies between 45 and 50 cm from the surface and reflects a sample from level 10. Within Nahal Aqev, data come from between 22 m² grids for level 1 to 5 m² for the bottom of level 3. Here, as in previous papers, level 3 is discussed in terms of seven 10 cm spits. Levels and spits delineated for Rosh Ein Mor and Nahal Aqev are not living floors *per se*; this clearly limits interpretive potential concerning intralevel technological patterning. In addition, some areas excavated at Nahal Aqev are extremely small. Therefore, it is impossible to relate reported samples to prehistoric activity areas. These data can, however, be used for preliminary estimates of the degree of intralevel technological variation.

For the surface sites, lithic material was systematically collected and analyzed from 136 m², 36 m², and 17 m² for D40, D42, and D44, respectively. In all cases, two areas from each site were collected; these amount to 32 m² and 104 m² from two distinct clusters within D40; 20 m² and 16 m² from two concentrations within D40 and 10 m² and 7 m² from two concentrations within D44. These are far from ideal conditions for conducting intrasite spatial analysis because areas collected are mostly small and some post-occupation artifact movement has undoubtedly occurred. Only at D40 were potentially complete activity areas collected.

Analytic approaches

For an index value to be useful in intersite or interlevel comparisons, it might be assumed that it displays little or no intralevel or intrasite variability. Thus, all areas within a given site or level should exhibit similar indices if a summary measure is to be used for intersite comparisons. Even where variability exists, it might still be possible to use an assemblage index if intrasite differences are 'smaller' than intersite differences.

Technological indices reviewed here are flake length, width, and thickness; three shape indices, flake length/width, length/thickness, and width/thickness; and the spatial covariation of Levallois flakes, blades, and points. These indices are of interest for my own work (Munday 1977a, 1977b, 1979) and that of others (Jelinek 1975, 1977; Schick and Stekelis 1977). 'Size' measures are reviewed because intersite flake dimensions were apparently dependent on site distances to resources such as flint. 'Shape' measures are reviewed because interlevel and intersite variation apparently related to technological change overtime. 'Levallois' debitage occurrence is reviewed because of the necessity to estimate intrasite and intralevel covariation patterns prior to constructing a compound index.

One approach that can be taken to test the notion of index homogeneity is to compare mean indices across grid units. For example, we can test to see if means of flake dimensions or shape indices come from the same population. Preliminary analysis indicated that samples of flakes from many grid units were small, particularly in D40, D42, and D44. In addition, sample variances differed by an order of magnitude of 2 to 5 even after data transformations to reduce those differences. Therefore, use of a parametric procedure seemed inadvisable. The non-parametric Kruskall–Wallis H-test (Friedman 1937, 1940) that compares three or more independent samples to see if they differ in average rank seems to be an appropriate comparative measure. This is because the procedure accomodates small samples and, if one wishes to make no assumptions about frequency distribution shapes, mean ranks can be compared (Harshbarger 1977). This selection was also more appealing for other reasons. For example, indices reviewed here are computed for attributes that are products of core reduction processes. Despite artisan intent, core reduction involves considerable production error. Therefore, because an absolute value for an observation on a flake may only approximately reflect the artisan's intent, it should not be interpreted literally. The use of ranked observations aids this because, by implying that one flake is only longer, broader or thicker than another, ranks play down absolute differences.

To test the spatial association of Levallois flakes, blades and points, Fisher's Exact and chi-square tests of association are used. Fisher's Exact test is used for comparisons of 30 or less grid units; the chi-square test is used elsewhere. Relatively high alpha levels will be considered because of the many small samples of grid units compared. A typical test compares the presence/absence of flakes versus blades over a series of grid units. Presence within a grid unit is defined as a frequency greater than the median value of a debitage type over the area analyzed. Absence is defined by occurrence less than or equal to that median value. The terms aggregation and segregation are used following definitions by Hietala and Stevens (1977). These relatively weak tests of spatial association are chosen because debitage sample sizes and the number of grid units compared are often small. In addition, the elongated, trench-style excavations only minimally permit investigation of aboriginal occupation areas.

Three types of comparisons will be made when testing the spatial homogeneity of simple size and shape indices or the spatial association of parts of the compound Levallois Index. These are analyses *within lithic concentrations* defined by fieldwork, *between concentrations* within individual sites, and *between all grid units* within a site or level; the last of these amounts to overall intrasite analysis.

Data analysis
Data analysis will proceed by investigating first patterning in simple indices and then patterning in parts of the compound Levallois Index.

Simple indices: flake dimensions and shape
Using the notation in Table 1, 19 of the 156 comparisons exhibit grid unit differences in various flake size and shape indices. If comparisons using grid units with less than five flakes are eliminated (i.e. those in D40A, and Nahal Aqev 1, 2 and 3b), 18 of 132 comparisons exhibit significant intrasite variability. Assuming errors are normally distributed, we might expect 15.6 and 13.2 cases of chance significant differences with alpha at 0.1 for these two groups of comparisons. Overall, the frequency of significant intrasite variations only marginally exceeds that expected by chance, suggesting that overall intrasite variation is small. However, closer inspection of Table 1 suggests the following weak patterns: (1) 11 of 18 significant differences occur for flake length and thickness indices; (2) size index differences outnumber shape index differences; (3) index differences within concentrations occur less frequently than those between concentrations, within sites, or within levels; (4) D40 exhibits a high proportion of all index intrasite differences. The weakness of these patterns must be stressed. The primary reason for mentioning them is that they afford preliminary insight into intrasite patterning and hence, with data from larger areas and under sounder testing conditions, they suggest future research orientations.

Intrasite variation in flake length and thickness
Significant length variation appears to predominate in Rosh Ein Mor and Nahal Aqev, both intensive occupation sites (Munday 1977a). Alternatively, significant thickness variation predominates in D40 and D42, both limited activity sites. The resultant cross-tabulation (Table 2) mildly suggests an association between intrasite variation in certain flake indices and site type using an alpha level of 0.2 as significant. This relatively high alpha level is appropriate in light of the small sample analyzed (Cowgill 1977). Because this association is weak, it cannot be interpreted definitively although some suggestions can be made about factors underlying variation.

An association between intrasite flake length variation and occupation sites may relate to a relationship between core reduction and tool manufacturing practices (Munday 1977a). This research indicated that artisans at intensive occupation sites tried to maintain production of long flakes even as cores became smaller with increased core reduction. Longer flakes were apparently required for tools and intrasite flake variation may be the byproduct of spatial variation in flake producing and tool manufacturing efforts. The precise relationship between these behaviors cannot be specified because of limited excavation and small tool sample sizes from Nahal Aqev. Ongoing research at Rosh Ein Mor (H. J. Hietala, personal communication) may clarify this patterning.

A second possible reason for flake length differences within occupation sites also relates to core reduction practices. At Nahal Aqev and Rosh Ein Mor, core size varied from the large ones brought to the site to small ones discarded when exhausted. This size range would have produced variation in the surface area of flake removal faces on cores and hence the potential for a wide range of flake sizes. Consequently, flake lengths may have varied spatially depending on the size of cores reduced at specific locations.

Table 1. *Kruskall–Wallis comparisons of mean ranks for index homogeneity tests*[a]

Site comparison	Number of grid units	Grid unit area (m²)	Unit sample sizes	Average unit sample sizes of complete flakes	Length	Width	Thickness	L/W	L/TH	W/TH
					Flake indices					
D40A	9	4	3 n's < 5	6.00						
D40A	6	4	all n's > 5	7.50						
D40B	10	8	all n's > 5	13.10			+		++	
D40A vs D40B	16	24 vs 30	all n's > 5	102.00	+	++			+++	++
D40 overall	2	mixed	all n's > 5	11.00		++			++	
D42A	10	2	all n's > 5	23.30			++			
D42B	8	2	all n's > 5	19.88						
D42A vs D42B	2	20 vs 16	all n's > 5	196.00						
D42 overall	18	2	all n's > 5	21.78			+			
D44A	3	2	all n's > 5	9.00						
D44B	5	2	all n's > 5	14.00						
D44A vs D44B	2	6 vs 10	all n's > 5	48.50						
D44 overall	8	2	all n's > 5	12.13						
Rosh Ein Mor, level 10	12	1	all n's > 5	20.67	++					
Nahal Aqev 1	22	1	5 n's < 5	16.59						
Nahal Aqev 1	17	1	all n's > 5	21.47						
Nahal Aqev 2	10	1	1 n < 5	17.30	+					
Nahal Aqev 2	9	1	all n's > 5	19.22	+					
Nahal Aqev 3a	14	1	all n's > 5	26.50	++					
3b	9	1	1 n < 5	31.33						
3b	8	1	all n's > 5	35.25						+
3c	6	1	all n's > 5	23.50			+			
3d	5	1	all n's > 5	34.60		++	++			
3e	5	1	all n's > 5	60.60						
3f	5	1	all n's > 5	18.40						+
3g	5	1	all n's > 5	28.20						
9 levels/spits within Nahal Aqev: interlevel comparisons				216.00	+++	+++	+++	+++	++	++
20 Avdat/Aqev area assemblages: intersite comparisons				183.00	+++	+++	+++	+++	+++	+++

[a] Notation is as follows. Significance between 0.10 and 0.05: +, between 0.05 and 0.01: ++, and less than 0.01: +++. These can be thought of as weak, intermediate, and strong grid unit differences respectively. Grid unit size varies to increase unit flake sample sizes. Repeated grid unit comparisons, i.e. D40A, and Nahal Aqev 1, 2, and 3b, eliminate grid units with less than five flakes. Collapsing 1 m × 1 m grid units to increase sample sizes eliminated 1 m² from D44A.

The association between intrasite flake thickness variation and limited activity sites may relate to the earlier core reduction stages that predominate at D40, D42, and D44 (Munday 1977a). Under such core reduction conditions, the contrast of thicker cortical flakes with thinner, intermediate reduction stage flakes may have produced grid unit differences. By inference, this suggests some degree of spatial segregation to different flake production activities, e.g. nodule testing, initial reduction, and the later production of desired flakes. Such a notion is weakened by the absence of intrasite flake thickness variation in one limited activity site (D44) and in one cluster in each of D40 and D42. However, five instances of significant flake thickness variation out of 12 possible comparisons for limited activity sites suggest the occurrence of real intrasite variation in this index in this site type.

Intrasite variation in flake 'size' versus 'shape'

Of the 19 instances of intrasite index variation, 13 are for 'size' indices – flake length, width, and thickness – while only 6 are for 'shape' indices (Table 1). The occurrence of only 6 examples of intrasite flake 'shape' variation is essentially equal to the 7.9 chance variations expected from 78 possible comparisons using an alpha level of 0.1; thus, no real

Table 2. *Relationship between site type and significant intrasite index variation*

	Frequency of significant intrasite variation (to at least the 0.10 level)	
	Flake length	Flake thickness
Limited occupation sites	1	5
Intensive occupation sites	3	2
Fisher's Exact probability (1-tailed): 0.196		

flake 'shape' variation appears to exist. This statement needs qualification because four of the six examples occur within D40 and most relate to between cluster differences. The overall lack of flake 'shape' variation probably results from 'shape' being controlled by the technical approach to core reduction. Providing a core reduction approach was uniformly adopted by artisans in a specific time period, little intrasite variation might be expected. A uniform approach to core reduction was undoubtedly promoted by extensive use of a unidirectional Levallois core reduction technique and the generally conservative behavior suggested for the Levantine Mousterian (Crew 1975). Intrasite differences can be attributed to deposition of flakes from different 'techno-logical' time periods or to random variation within a single time period. The relatively frequent occurrence of flake 'shape' variations within D40 may represent time differences given spatial separation of the clusters within the site.

The stronger occurrence of flake 'size' differences should be expected since these attributes were a function of *at least* core and raw material size. Possible reasons for intrasite flake size differences were discussed in the previous section.

Intrasite variation within concentrations vs other comparisons

When considering the type of comparison made, there is a weak and statistically non-significant tendency for less variation within concentrations (8.3% of all possible compari-sons) as opposed to between-concentration and within-site/ level comparisons (16% of all possible comparisons (Table 3)). This is somewhat emphasized when considering only flake length and thickness (Table 3), the indices most frequently characterized by significant intrasite variation. This patterning is interpretable.

If a concentration represents a single or minimal number of behavioral events, little within-concentration variation is expected because it should exhibit considerable technological homogeneity. This would be the result, given an individual's production skills or production by a group of individuals using a time-specific technological approach to core reduction. Such within-concentration homogeneity might be strongest if the lithic clusters resulted from a single or small numbers of occupations. Between-concentration contrasts should occur, given flake production by different individuals, groups of individuals, or for different activities. A contrast might be especially strong if concentrations were formed at different time periods and technological change occurred over time. Within-site/level contrasts might occur under those conditions described for between-concentration comparisons. However, weaker contrasts may occur because occupation overlap or difficulty in discerning refuse from single activities

Table 3. *The occurrence of significant variation within types of spatial comparisons conducted*[a]

	Within-cluster	Between-cluster	Within-site/level	Between-cluster + within-site/level
Flake length	0	1	3	4
Flake width	0	0	1	1
Flake thickness	2	1	4	5
Flake length/width	0	0	0	0
Flake length/thickness	1	1	1	2
Flake width/thickness	0	1	2	3
Total significant variations	3	4	11	15
Possible significant variations	36	18	78	96
Total relative to possible	8.3%	22.2%	14.1%	16.0%
Flake length and thickness only				
Total significant variations	2	2	7	9
Possible significant variations	12	6	26	32
Total relative to possible	16.7%	33.3%	26.9%	28.0%

[a] Possible contrasts include only those that meet minimum sample size requirements for all grid units.

may blur boundaries between separate debris depositions. Consequently, while significant within-site/level variation existed, it may be masked or even be undetectable because of practical considerations related to site formation processes. This point leads naturally into the discussion of D40 patterning.

Intrasite variation within D40

The occurrence of almost half (45%) of all significant index variations within D40 suggests that all previous comments about weak patterning need tempering. In fact, excluding D40, the remaining 126 possible comparisons (Table 1) should produce 12.6 chance significant variations with alpha at 0.1. This is essentially equal to the 11 instances of significant intrasite differences for non-D40 sites. This would suggest no overall intrasite variation existed for the indices reviewed. This comment needs qualification in the light of possible reasons for the strong patterning within D40.

Of the eight examples of index variation within D40, two are for between-clusters and two for intrasite comparisons. Both of the latter occur where there is between-cluster variation. Clearly, cluster differences underly intrasite patterning. This can be attributed to the spatial distinctiveness of the clusters and the low lithic density – less than two complete flakes per square meter – for each cluster; this is the lowest for all sites discussed. These characteristics may mean that limited activity took place at D40 relative to other sites discussed and that activities were spatially segregated. Both factors would have contributed to minimal blending of debris from recurrent activities and hence would facilitate detection of intrasite technological variation. If so, patterning within D40 has repercussions for other comparisons made. Because of higher lithic densities and the arbitrary nature of areas and spits analyzed for non-D40 sites, behavioral events are spatially less distinct than those at D40. Consequently, in all non-D40 comparisons, activity overlap through time may have blurred intrasite variation so that detection is currently difficult or impossible. In fact, observed variation may only marginally represent that which actually existed. If so, previous attention paid to weak intrasite patterns was warranted because they may actually represent lithic distributions formed from overlapping aboriginal behaviors and hence interdigitation of spatially and temporally distinct activity sets. Were it possible to discriminate between these, detection of stronger intrasite variability might be possible. Conjoining of flakes, tools, and cores (Cahen *et al.* 1979) is one methodological approach to dissection of activity structure and hence one way to reduce this problem.

Compound indices: the Levallois Index

Of the 57 associational tests between Levallois flakes, blades, and points, only 8 reveal spatial aggregation (Table 4); most of these are weak associations and no examples of segregation were detected. This compares with the 10.4 expected by chance with alpha at 0.2. Because of the small samples of debitage in grid units, repeats of these comparisons were based

on strict absence/presence of lithic classes. Only minor changes from that recorded in Table 4 were noted; these were trivial changes in associated probabilities, deletion of the flake/blade aggregation in D40A, and addition of a strong aggregation for flakes and points in 3d. These data, along with the random patterning to significant aggregations in Table 4, suggests no spatial reality to the Levallois Index as traditionally used. While it is tempting to argue that this results from the small size of the areas examined and the small debitage counts per grid unit, more rigorous associational tests at Rosh Ein Mor (Hietala and Stevens 1977) failed to confirm consistent aggregation for any pair of Levallois debitage classes. In fact, some evidence suggested segregation between Levallois points and flakes. It should be noted, however, that Levallois points strongly aggregate with Levallois flakes and blades in the collapsed spits from Nahal Aqev level 3 (Table 4). This appears to result from the cumulative effects of several instances of non-significant aggregation in spits with small grid and debitage samples. These patterns suggest that if one assumes consistency in patterning within Nahal Aqev level 3, larger excavations may yet confirm several aggregative pairs and hence patterning that contrasts with the lack of aggregation for these lithic classes over the collapsed data from all spits within Rosh Ein Mor (see Hietala and Stevens 1977, figure 12*b*).

It is reasonable to ask why Levallois flakes, blades, and points do not appear to aggregate in light of their common core reduction origin. In D40, D42, and D44 at sites on or near flint sources, the dominance of the Levallois core reduction technique is attested to by the strong presence of Levallois cores (Munday 1977*a*). There are usually more cores than associated forms of Levallois debitage which clearly indicates exportation of finished Levallois blanks from these sites (Crew 1976; Munday 1977*a*). Therefore, associational patterns present under production conditions were subsequently disturbed because of flake, blade, and/or point exportation; this makes detection of original patterning impossible. At occupation sites, the foci of Levallois core and debitage importation (Crew 1976; Munday 1977*a*), at least two factors operated to reduce association between Levallois debitage classes. Imported flakes, blades and points may have been differentially absorbed into activities and Levallois debitage produced on site from imported cores may have been subjected to intrasite movement depending on activity structure. The net result produced little evidence of aggregative patterning until data from Nahal Aqev level 3 spits were collapsed into a single analytic unit. Significantly, at Rosh Ein Mor, Levallois points strongly and consistently aggregate with a variety of retouched tools while blades and flakes, which sometimes aggregate, only occasionally associate with this same complex of retouched tools. Differential participation in activity structure at Rosh Ein Mor is suggested for different Levallois debitage classes.

Clearly, given development of a core reduction procedure oriented towards production of blanks preferred for stone tools, Levallois debitage was prone to major partici-

Table 4. *Tests of spatial association between Levallois flakes (FL), blades (BL), and points (PT)*[a]

Site	Number of grids	Grid size (m)	Average number of Levallois pieces per grid unit			Spatial comparison		
			FL	BL	PT	LF/LB	LF/LP	LB/LP
D40A	9	2 × 2	1.67	2.44	0.89		+	
D40B	25	2 × 2	2.24	1.44	0.32			
D40	34	2 × 2	2.09	1.41	0.47			+
D42A	20	1 × 1	0.35	0.40	0.10	+	++	
D42B	16	1 × 1	0.81	0.38	0.19			
D42	36	1 × 1	0.56	0.39	0.14			
D44A	6	1 × 1	1.67	0.17	0.33			
D44B	10	1 × 1	3.00	0.90	0.00			
D44	16	1 × 1	2.50	0.63	0.14			
Rosh Ein Mor	12	1 × 1	1.42	1.00	1.00			
Nahal Aqev 1	22	1 × 1	1.50	0.64	1.09	+++		+
Nahal Aqev 2	10	1 × 1	0.20	0.60	0.30			
Nahal Aqev 3a	14	1 × 1	0.57	0.64	0.57			+
3b	9	1 × 1	2.00	0.44	1.11		+	
3c	6	1 × 1	0.67	1.00	1.83			
3d	5	1 × 1	1.80	2.20	1.80			
3e	5	1 × 1	3.20	4.20	4.60			
3f	5	1 × 1	0.80	0.80	1.40			
3g	5	1 × 1	1.00	0.80	2.20			
Nahal Aqev 3	49	1 × 1	1.31	1.20	1.61		+++	+++

[a] Notation is as follows. Significance between 0.2 and 0.1, +; between 0.05 and 0.1, ++; and less than 0.05, +++.

pation in both intrasite and intersite passing and dropping patterns. Under these conditions, spatial association between classes would only be strongly detectable if flakes, blades, and points were incorporated together into tool-using activities or where remnants of core reduction activities remain intact or identifiable.

Implications of intrasite patterning for regional patterning

Overall, there are no compelling reasons to believe that intrasite variability invalidates the use of site indices in intersite or interlevel comparisons. The most notable exception within the comparisons conducted is the lack of utility of the Levallois Index because of scant evidence for spatial aggregation of Levallois flakes, blades, and points. Preliminary analysis of some indices does, however, suggest weak intrasite patterning that should be tested under more suitable conditions with larger areas and where aboriginal activity variation can be detected. These weak patterns and Levallois debitage patterning may have implications for regional studies in the Levantine Mousterian.

Some flake size indices may exhibit intrasite variability that is a function of site type. This potentially relates to core reduction practices that vary with site resource availability. Preliminary examination indicates that the weakness of intrasite variability relative to intersite patterning in the Avdat/Aqev area is not a function of small samples of flakes in grid units. This is indicated when equivalent-sized random samples are drawn from all sites and compared (Table 5). These comparisons exhibit strong and consistent interlevel and intersite differences even under very small sample size conditions. Therefore, because intrasite patterning is small relative to intersite variability and 'size' indices relate strongly to resource availability, the economizing behavior model described by Munday (1977a) is not invalidated.

Beyond the Avdat/Aqev area, these data are also significant. Intersite flake size indices may vary because of resource availability or potentially because of intrasite sampling differences. For sites that exhibit intrasite index homogeneity, intersite variation may be a function of access to raw material. Where intrasite index variation occurs, intersite variation may be a function not only of resource access but of intrasite sampling differences. Currently, controlling intrasite flake index variation is not important because comparisons primarily involve typological and technological indices developed by Bordes (1950, 1961). As model testing

Table 5. *Comparisons of random samples drawn from Nahal Aqev (interlevel) and all sites (intersite)*

	Average, n^a							
Index	10	10	15	15	20	20	21.4	21.4
Comparison of 20 sites								
L	++	+	+++	+++	+++	+++	+++	+++
W	+++	++	+++	++	+++	++	+++	+++
T	+++	++	+++	+++	+++	+++	+++	+++
L/W								
L/T	+++	+	+++	++	+++	+++	+++	+++
W/T	+		+++		+++		+++	+++

	Average, n^a							
Index	15	15	20	20	25	25	29.74	29.74
Comparison of 9 levels								
L	++		+++		++	++	++	
W				+				++
T	++		++		++		++	
L/W			+					
L/T			+					
W/T	+						+	

^{a} Sample sizes are equivalent to or less than average flake samples for grid units in interlevel and intersite comparisons in Table 1. Average flake sample size for *intersite* comparisons is 21.4. This is equivalent to the mean number of flakes per grid unit when considering all sites compared in Table 1. Average flake sample size for *interlevel* comparisons is 29.74. This is equivalent to the mean number of flakes per grid unit when considering levels 1, 2, and 3 in Nahal Aqev.

L = length; W = width; T = thickness.

situations develop which utilize other indices of behavioral significance, control of intrasite variability in 'size' indices and intersite resource availability may become increasingly important for adequate intersite and interlevel comparisons.

The paucity of significant variation in flake shape indices bodes well for interlevel and intersite comparisons aimed at identifying measures with temporal and adaptive significance in the Levantine Mousterian (Jelinek 1977; Munday 1979). The intralevel stability of shape indices is not a function of small sample sizes because interlevel and intersite comparison of random samples of equivalent size (Table 5) produce strong intersite differences for all save the flake length/width index; the length/thickness index is the most variable under a wide range of small sample size conditions. While few interlevel differences occur (Fig. 5), the flake length/width and width/thickness indices exhibit patterned interlevel *trends* in contrast to random patterning for the length/thickness index (Table 6). Clearly, the aspatial comparisons reported in Tables 1 and 5 underestimate the true nature of interlevel patterning. The use of these two indices as temporal markers may ultimately be validated given the intrasite stability reported here. Significantly, while they may exhibit complementary temporal trends within Nahal Aqev, the notion that they represent different aspects of temporal change in Middle Paleolithic technology might be entertained. Jelinek (1977) described steady, long-term temporal change in flake width/thickness indices at Tabun Cave. He suggested this pattern may have long term significance for the evolution of technological processes in the Levant. Munday (1979) suggested adaptive change contingent on environmental shifts as the basis for temporal variation in the flake length/width index. These models warrant further research and both may be acceptable if indices measure different aspects of temporal change in Middle Paleolithic technology.

Table 6. *Raw and two-point smoothed means for shape indices in levels and spits of Nahal Aqev*

Level/spit	Size index						
	Flake length/width		Flake length/thickness		Flake width/thickness		
	Raw	Smooth	Raw	Smooth	Raw	Smooth	n
1	1.40		6.61		5.12		371
		1.46		6.71		5.02	
2	1.52		6.80		4.91		173
		1.52		6.98		5.08	
3a	1.51		7.16		5.24		371
		1.52		6.92		5.05	
3b	1.52		6.67		4.85		282
		1.58		7.17		4.88	
3c	1.64		7.66		4.91		141
		1.63		7.22		4.75	
3d	1.62		6.78		4.59		173
		1.61		7.03		4.74	
3e	1.60		7.28		4.88		303
		1.56		7.09		4.90	
3f	1.51		6.90		4.91		92
		1.54		6.96		4.99	
3g	1.56		7.01		5.06		141

Table 7. *Comparisons of the relative frequency of intrasite, interlevel, and intersite significant variation under equivalent sample size conditions*

| | Comparison | | | | | | |
| | Intralevel comparisons (see Table 1) | | Interlevel comparisons (see Table 5) | | Intersite comparisons (see Table 5) | | |
Index	Significant differences/ total comparisons	%	Significant differences/ total comparisons	%	Significant differences/ total comparisons	%
Size indices	12/66	18	11/24	46	24/24	100
Shape indices	6/66	9	4/24	17	13/24	54
All indices	18/132	14	15/48	31	37/48	77

It is also significant that when considering size and shape indices, the relative frequency and strength of contrasts increases when moving from intralevel to interlevel and then to intersite comparisons (Table 7). This patterning is stronger and more emphasized for 'size' than 'shape' indices. It may be that the greater overall stability of 'shape' indices suggests they may have only responded to major factors such as long term technological change. Overall, these data indicate that a multitude of factors probably operated to produce intersite patterning while few operated on intralevel variation. I might suggest that in addition to factors related to behavioral partitioning and core reduction that affected intralevel patterning, temporal technological change probably affected interlevel variability and both temporal change and resource variability affect intersite variation. Therefore, when moving from intralevel to interlevel then intersite comparisons, increasingly complex arrangements of behavioral and resource factors produced increasingly stronger contrasts in comparisons. If so, appeals to cultural (Bordes and de Sonneville-Bordes 1970), temporal (Mellars 1970) and activity factors (Binford and Binford 1966) as bases for intersite variations underestimate the complexity of phenomena that lie behind archaeological variability.

Scant evidence suggesting a lack of spatial aggregation of Levallois points in sites discussed here and by Hietala and Stevens (1977) indicates that collapsing these lithic classes into a compound index is unwarranted on a site-by-site basis. This pessimistic conclusion actually has little effect on either inter-site Mousterian studies in the Avdat/Aqev area or on Levantine Mousterian studies in general. In the Avdat/Aqev area, lithic classes were analyzed separately as well as in a compound index because they were clearly differentially related to core reduction and intersite movement of artifacts. In the Levantine Mousterian, the index is most often used for classification purposes when combined with other indices (Perrot 1968; Skinner 1965). In addition, researchers treat the index cautiously because, given that it is calculated by relating Levallois debitage to all debitage and tools, intersite numerical values may reflect variation in excavation and lithic retention procedures. The index, however, remains a basic assemblage feature reported under increasingly standardized excavation and lithic retention conditions.

Lack of any spatial reality to the Levallois Index on a site-by-site basis does not preclude its use under other conditions. Given Levallois debitage was moved between sites, production rates of Levallois debitage cannot be estimated for individual sites. It may, however, be possible to estimate the degree to which the Levallois technique occurs in an area by combining the Levallois features of sites that were temporally and functionally related. Thus, sites with varying Levallois indices but which were temporally and behaviorally related might be combined for purposes of calculating an area's Levallois Index. Resultant indices can be compared between regional site complexes in order to evaluate the spatial and temporal occurrence on the Levallois technique. Significantly, this practice may combine sites with high and low indices. The traditional practice has been to separate such sites into different groups for classification purposes (Skinner 1965; Bordes 1968; Perrot 1968). Such practices ignore the differential participation of sites in a dynamic system where artisans moved items between sites during their regular use of a variety of locations. While these comments are aimed at use of the Levallois Index, they apply to other intersite comparisons; sites should be related by virtue of participation in a behavioral system and not by virtue of a look alike contest!

Conclusions

Because minimal intrasite index variation is minimal, previous models for the Mousterian of the Avdat/Aqev area ascribing intersite variability to resource availability and interlevel variability to adaptive change are not invalidated. Preliminary examination of intrasite patterning suggests potential effects of site type, core reduction practices, activity area overlap, and intersite movement of lithic material on intersite patterning. These weak patterns merit additional research under more robust testing conditions.

References
Ammerman, A. and Feldman, M. (1974). On the 'making' of an assemblage of Stone Tools. *American Antiquity* 39: 610–15.

Binford, L. R. (1972). Model building paradigms and the current state of paleolithic research. In *An Archaeological Perspective*, ed. L. R. Binford, pp. 252–94. Seminar Press: New York.

Binford, L. R. (1978). *Numamuit Ethnoarchaeology: A Case Study in Archaeological Formation Processes*. Academic Press: New York.

Binford, L. R. and Binford, S. R. (eds.) (1966). A preliminary analysis of functional variability in the Mousterian of Levallois facies. *American Anthropologist* 68 (2–2): 328–95.

Bordes, F. (1950). Principes d'une méthode d'étude des techniques de débitage et de la typologie du Paléolithique ancien et moyen. *L'Anthropologie* 54: 19–34.

Bordes, F. (1961). *Typologie du Paléolithique ancien et moyen*. Publications de l'Institute de Préhistoire de l'Université de Bordeaux, Mémoire 1.

Bordes, F. (1968). *The Old Stone Age*. McGraw-Hill: New York.

Bordes, F. and de Sonneville-Bordes, D. (1970). The significance of variability in paleolithic assemblages. *World Archaeology* 2(1): 61–73.

Cahen, D., Keeley, L. H. and van Noten, F. L. (1979). Stone tools, tool-kits, and human behavior in prehistory. *Current Anthropology* 20: 661–84.

Collins, D. (1969). Culture traditions and environment of early man. *Current Anthropology* 10: 267–96.

Cowgill, G. (1977). The trouble with significance tests and what we can do about it. *American Antiquity* 42: 350–68.

Crew, H. (1975). *An Examination of Variability of the Levallois Method: Its Implications for the Internal and External Relationships of the Levantine Mousterian*. University Microfilms: Ann Arbor, Michigan.

Crew, H. (1976). The Mousterian site of Rosh Ein Mor. In *Prehistory and Paleoenvironments in the Central Negev, Israel*, ed. A. E. Marks, pp. 75–112. Southern Methodist University Press: Dallas, Texas.

Fish, P. (1978) 'Beyond tools: Debitage analysis and cultural inference in the Middle Paleolithic.' Paper presented to the Annual Meeting of the Society for American Archaeology: Tucson, Arizona.

Friedman, M. (1937). The use of ranks to avoid the assumption of normality implied in the analysis of variance. *Journal of the American Statistical Association* 32: 607–11.

Friedman, M. (1940). A comparison of alternative tests of significance for the problem of *m* rankings. *Annals of Mathematical Statistics* 11: 86–92.

Gilead, I. (1980). A Middle Paleolithic open-air site near Tell Far'ah, Western Negev: preliminary report. *Israel Exploration Journal* 30(1–2): 52–66.

Goldberg, P. (1976). Upper Pleistocene geology of the Avdat/Aqev area. *Prehistory and Paleoenvironments in the Central Negev*, ed. A. E. Marks, pp. 25–56. Southern Methodist University Press: Dallas, Texas.

Harshbarger, T. H. (1977). *Introductory Statistics: A Decision Map*. Macmillan: New York.

Hietala, H. and Stevens, D. (1977). Spatial analysis: Multiple procedures in pattern recognition studies. *American Antiquity* 42(4): 539–59.

Hill, J. (1968). Broken K Pueblo: patterns of form and function. In *New Perspectives in Archaeology*, ed. S. R. Binford and L. R. Binford, pp. 103–42. Aldine: Chicago, Ill.

Jelinek, A. (1975) A preliminary report on some Lower and Middle Paleolithic industries from the Tabun Cave, Mount Carmel (Israel). In *Problems in Prehistory: North Africa and the Levant*, ed. F. Wendorf and A. E. Marks, pp. 297–316. Southern Methodist University Press: Dallas, Texas.

Jelinek, A. (1977). A preliminary study of flakes from the Tabun Cave, Mount Carmel. *Eretz-Israel, Archaeological, Historical and Geographic Studies*, vol. 13: *Moshe Stekelis Memorial Volume*, ed.

B. Arensburg and O. Bar-Yosef, pp. 27–96. The Israel Exploration Society: Jerusalem.

Jelinek, A., Farrand, W., Haas, G., Horowitz, A. and Goldberg, P. (1973). New excavations at the Tabun Cave, Mount Carmel, Israel, 1976–1972: a preliminary report. *Paleorient* 1(2): 151–83.

Marks, A. E. (ed.) (1976). *Prehistory and Paleoenvironments in the Central Negev, Israel*, vol. 1. *The Avdat/Aqev Area*, Part 1. Southern Methodist University Press: Dallas, Texas.

Marks, A. E. (ed.) (1977). *Prehistory and Paleoenvironments in the Central Negev, Israel*, vol. 2, *The Avdat/Aqev Area*, Part 2, *and the Har Harif*, Southern Methodist University Press: Dallas, Texas.

Marks, A. E. & Crew, H. (1972). A preliminary report on Rosh Ein Mor: an open-air Mousterian site in the Central Negev. *Current Anthropology* 13(5): 591–593.

Marks, A. E. and Freidel, D. (1977). Prehistoric settlement patterns in the Avdat/Aqev area. In *Prehistory and Paleoenvironments in the Central Negev, Israel*, vol. 2, ed. A. E. Marks, pp. 131–58. Southern Methodist University Press: Dallas, Texas.

Mellars, P. (1969). The chronology of Mousterian industries in the Perigord region of south-west France. *Proceedings of the Prehistoric Society* 6: 134–70.

Mellars, P. (1970). Some comments on the notion of 'functional variability' in stone tool assemblages. *World Archaeology* 2(1): 74–89.

Munday, F. C. (1976). Intersite variability in the Mousterian occupation of the Avdat/Aqev area. In *Prehistory and Paleoenvironments in the Central Negev, Israel*, vol. 1, ed. A. E. Marks, Southern Methodist University Press: Dallas, Texas.

Munday, F. C. (1977a). *The Mousterian in the Negev: A Description and Explication of Intersite Variability*. University Microfilms: Ann Arbor, Michigan.

Munday, F. C. (1977b). Nahal Aqev (D35): a stratified, open-air occupation in the Avdat/Aqev area. In *Prehistory and Paleoenvironments in the Central Negev, Israel*, vol. 2, ed. A. E. Marks, pp. 35–60. Southern Methodist University Press: Dallas, Texas.

Munday, F. C. (1979). Levantine Mousterian technological variability: a perspective from the Negev. *Paleorient* 5: 87–104.

Perrot, J. (1968). La prehistoire palestinienne. In *Supplément au Dictionnaire de la Bible* 8(43), pp. 286–446. Letouzey et Ané: Paris.

Price-Williams, D. (1973). Preliminary report of the environmental archaeological survey of Tell Fara, 1972. In *Archaeological Theory and Practice*, ed. D. Strong, pp. 193–216. Academic Press: London.

Price-Williams, D. (1975). The environmental background to prehistoric sites in the Fara region of the Western Negev. *Bulletin of the Institute of Archaeology of the London University* 12: 125–43.

Raper, R. A. (1977). The analysis of the urban structure of Pompeii: a sociological examination of land-use (semi-micro). In *Spatial Archaeology*, ed. D. Clarke, pp. 189–221. Academic Press: New York.

Schick, T. and Stekelis, M. (1977). Mousterian assemblages in Kebara Cave, Mount Carmel. In *Eretz-Israel, Archaeological, Historical and Geographic Studies*, vol. 13: *Moshe Stekelis Memorial Volume*, pp. 97–149. The Israel Exploration Society: Jerusalem.

Schwartz, H. P., Blackwell, B., Goldberg, P. and Marks, A. E. (1979). Uranium series dating of travertine from archaeological sites, Nahal Zin, Israel. *Nature* 277(5697): 558–560.

Skinner, A. (1965). *The Flake Industries of Southwest Asia*. University Microfilms: Ann Arbor, Michigan.

Whallon, J. (1979). 'Multilevel clustering.' Paper presented to the Annual Meeting of the Society for American Archaeology, Vancouver, British Columbia.

Yellen, J. (1977). *Archaeological Approaches to the Present: Models for Reconstructing the Past*, Academic Press: New York.

Chapter 4

**Variations on a categorical
data theme: local and global
considerations with
Near-Eastern paleolithic
applications**
Harold J. Hietala

General questions posed at an archaeological site include
those of context. On an intrasite level of inquiry, typical
questions involve the nature of the material deposition
processes (natural and cultural) giving rise to the archaeological
record. Pertinent questions in this regard are considered by
other authors in this volume (see e.g. Kroll and Isaac, Chapter
2; Hivernel and Hodder, Chapter 7; and Ferring, Chapter 8).
On the other hand, specific archaeological questions typically
revolve about space utilization and behavior associated with
the inhabitants of a site, insofar as it is recognizable in the
material record. These considerations, among others, lead us
toward attempts to understand quantitative spatial
patterning within archaeological sites; it does not need to be
mentioned that interpretations of assumed or *a posteriori*
spatial patterns have their own difficulties.

An *a priori* perception of what constitutes archaeological
spatial patterning, however, is confronted with its own
problems, not the least of which is whether a legitimate
pattern should be site wide (global) or representative of only a
portion of the site (local). It seems apparent that the holistic
viewpoint in archaeology has contributed to biases in intrasite
investigational perceptions in that cultural history has
traditionally emphasized global patterns at the expense of
local patterns. Behavioral archaeology has attempted, in a
broad sense, to counter this by searching for the anthropological correlates of behavior in the archaeological record. Just

as any living community is more than its holistic description,
an archaeological site is more than its material inventory
description. The material inventory undoubtedly has
variability of behavioral significance within and between
different areas of an excavated site. Spatial patterns may be
local or global but the search for such patterns has frequently
been heavily biased in one direction or the other, depending
on the viewpoint of the investigator. A global approach, for
example, might fail to recognize a local pattern if it is
sufficiently localized. On the other hand, a local approach
might fail to recognize a global pattern if local variability is in
excess of the variability between areas of the site. In any case,
the nature of spatial patterning should be tied to the notions
of local and global variation.

The purpose of this chapter is to illustrate the general
applicability of multivariate categorical data methods for the
study of intrasite spatial patterning in archaeology. The
general methods are broad enough to be able to consider local
and global variation simultaneously.

Local and global considerations
Spatial patterns are frequently represented, in
mathematical terms, by single variable distributions,
associations or relationships between pairs of distributions or
structural configurations in multivariate space. If certain
variables are expected, for example, to covary in an area

restricted to a single activity, then such covariation might not be expected to occur in other areas. In this sense, a local pattern might escape detection if the statistical procedure utilized all of the site-wide data, with equal weight given to each data point. On the other hand, a site-wide associational pattern might not be statistically detected if the procedure balanced different area effects against each other (e.g. local positive correlations balanced by other local negative correlations). Even as archaeological patterns may be local or global, so may the statistical algorithms used for their detection. It is important here to recognize that the application of any statistical procedure requires a tacit acceptance of certain *a priori* assumptions and, thus, has its own built-in strengths and weaknesses.

The search for patterns at a descriptive level *vis-à-vis* spatial mapping techniques, for example, suggests that local procedures are more congruent with archaeological data sets than are global procedures (Hietala and Larson, 1979, p. 58). Other arguments establishing a need for congruency between data and methods are given by Whallon (Chapter 13). In the investigation of associational patterns, Hietala and Stevens (1977) have discussed the relationships between several competing procedures. Whether or not such procedures should be globally or locally applied depends, in part, on the nature of the material record in space. It should be stressed, however, that local and global considerations are hardly unique to intra-site spatial analysis in archaeology and, in fact, are common in aspatial statistical analyses. For example, a reasonable investigator would not forcefully argue in favor of a linear regression application for the purposes of assessing the strength of relationship between two variables if the data suggested a quadratic fit. The data might suggest, for example, a positive linear relationship for low values of the independent variable, a negative linear relationship for high values of the independent variable, but a lack of linear relationship overall. The lack of a global linear relationship does not suggest the lack of any relationship. It merely suggests, in this case, that a linear association coefficient is not appropriate. In this presumed quadratic relationship, it would be reasonable to postulate different relationships in different domains (areas) of the independent variable. The domain space in this hypothetical example suggests the importance of space (conceptual or real) in statistical applications. This point is further illustrated in the following two examples, the first of which is an anthropological application while the second is archaeological.

The first example is an ethnographic study among the Lacandone Maya in the southern highlands of Mexico (Nations, 1978), where an imbalance in the sex ratio of male to female children was posited. It was expected that there would be more male than female children, because of the Lacandone tendency toward the practice of polygyny (Divalle and Harris, 1976). Investigations were carried out at three nearby Lacandone villages (Mensabok, Naja and Lacanja), where it was found that the overall proportion

(0.523) of male children surviving more than one year was well in accord with a 50/50 ratio of boys to girls. For monogamous and polygamous marital unions the proportions were 0.520 and 0.549, respectively. Thus, it would appear that an overall child sex ratio for the three Lacandone villages is consistent with a hypothetical sex ratio balance. This, however, is where location rears its ugly head. The proportions of male children in the villages of Mensabok, Naja and Lacanja were 0.647, 0.500 and 0.430, respectively. This variability, with significant sex ratio imbalances in the villages of Mensabok and Lacanja, was shown to be primarily related to post-marital residence patterns (Nations and Hietala, 1978). The Mensabok marital unions were dominated by a patrilocal residence pattern, with a sex ratio bias toward boys. In contrast, the dominant pattern at Lacanja was matrilocal, with a sex ratio bias toward girls. Interestingly, Naja was bilocal and had a balanced sex ratio. This example illustrates a situation in which the index of sex ratio was globally uninformative while the corresponding local indices provided much needed information. There is no reason to presume that archaeological indices, based on site-wide data, potentially would not suffer from similar problems.

The second example is afforded by Wendorf and Schild (1976; Schild and Wendorf, 1981), whose investigations at Bir Sahara (site BS-13, main level) in the western desert of Egypt revealed a horizontal distribution of Mousterian artifacts. Quantitative analyses were performed on the spatial locations of tools using a simplified Wroclaw dentrite (Florek *et al.*, 1951; Kostrubiec, 1971) which showed general clustering in the northern part of the site. When spreading the nearest-neighbor based dentrites (Góralski, 1974) over denticulates as one set and sidescrapers and points together as another, two distinct patterns emerged. One pattern indicated a clustering of sidescrapers and points in the southwestern area of the general cluster of tools while the other suggested a random distribution of denticulates there and elsewhere. Wendorf and Schild (1976, p. 25) remark:

> The importance of this observation becomes more obvious when one realizes that at this site, obviously undisturbed and quite possibly associated with a single occupation, one portion is more Denticulate oriented in the composition of tools, while the other, southwestern, is more Typical Mousterian in its character.

However one interprets this situation, it is obvious that a global description of the tools would have been pure folly without an adequate understanding of their local descriptions. This was rectified through a simultaneous consideration of local and global space.

The above two examples illustrate not only the need to consider local and global space simultaneously but also the need not to prejudge the size or shape of areas considered at the local level. It may be noted that the local areas used in the analysis in the first example were obvious and disjoint while those in the second were determined from the data and were overlapping. This observation is not without relevance since reasonable intrasite analyses may generally require the judicious exploitation of areas of different size and shape which overlap spatially. Congruent archaeological and statistical methods should allow for the determination of over-lapping spatial areas.

The problematic issues, however, are at the methodo-logical level. If we had a time machine, we might be able to trace the material inventory through production, use, main-tenance and discard phases, identify activity and depositional areas and then be able to determine which statistical algorithms would be best to answer which archaeological questions. In all likelihood, different statistical procedures would be optimal for different questions. Some of the procedures would probably be global while most would require varying degrees of local and global assumptions. The different procedures would probably require the determination of different areas for different questions and the areas would probably be unconstrained in size, shape, and overlapping characteristics. However, in reality we must rely on consider-able variability in our approaches and considerable expertise in our applications.

These thoughts are in complete accord with ethnographic evidence where, for example, Yellen (1977) and Binford (1978) argue that activities are not always spatially segregated, some tasks take place in a multiplicity of areas and many tasks occur in the same generalized area. Schiffer (1981, p. 905) summarizes their collective viewpoints as follows:

> Binford denies that such activity patterning leaves the archaeological record devoid of distributional informa-tion for inferring past activities and their placement . . . (while) . . . Yellen has never claimed that behavioral inferences are impossible as a consequence of complex activity patterning, only that analysis becomes more dif-ficult once the simplistic correlation between areas and activities is rejected . . . .

We would be philosophically bankrupt if we pursued the illusionary goal of finding a single approach to answer all of our intrasite archaeological questions. A combination of statistical algorithms seems to be required where the application of a particular method is not based on prejudice *a priori* but on the statistical assumptions common in the archaeological data to hand and relevant theory for the considered archaeological question(s).

Since a majority of the archaeological record is characterized by nominal data, it is surprising that correspond-ing spatial analyses have not been more involved with statistical methods for discrete data. It is even more surprising when it is realized that discrete methods generally make few assumptions, are multivariate in scope, and have widespread possibilities in applications.

Multivariate categorical data methods

In this section, some general thoughts are devoted to the use of discrete data techniques in archaeology. The log-linear model is defined and some important partitioning results, applicable to the simultaneous consideration of local and global variability, are presented. The section ends with some within-site archaeological considerations.

Introduction

Most archaeologists are familiar with two-way contingency tables and the applications of Pearson's chi-squared statistic for testing homogeneity (by row or column) or independence between the rows and columns of a con-tingency table. While some are familiar with McNemar's test or the logistic model (Cox, 1970), few are acquainted with the theories, methods and applications of multidimensional cross-classified categorical data developed over the past two decades. In this period, advances in statistical theory coupled with the easy availability of high-speed computers (and associated soft-ware) led to an abundance of texts on multivariate categorical data analysis (Lindsey, 1973; Haberman, 1974; Plackett, 1974; Bishop *et al.*, 1975) with an excellent introductory version for non-statisticians by Fienberg (1977). Although there does not exist a text on discrete methods in archaeology there have been numerous multivariate applications ranging from problems and statistical tests for symmetry and conditional independence hypotheses (Hietala and Close, 1979), typo-logical classifications (Reid, 1974), decision-making criteria (Clark, 1976), intrasite pattern recognition studies (Hietala and Stevens, 1977), intersite faunal comparisons (Butler *et al.*, 1977), to combined intrasite and intersite spatial analyses (Hietala and Larson, 1980; Hietala, 1983*b*). These applica-tions have been predominantly associated with the log-linear model even though other possibilities exist (see Chapter 10 of Bishop *et al.*, 1975). Advantages of the log-linear model rest in its logical simplicity (similar to analysis of variance models) and its ability exactly to partition variability into components which are asymptotically independent.

The log-linear model

The general log-linear model is discussed in detail in Bishop *et al.* (1975) with a 'readable' version in Fienberg (1977). For purposes of this discussion, a simple presentation of the model is given for a two-way contingency table. An elaborated version is then given for a three-way table and, finally, a heuristic version is given for higher-order tables. The general log-linear model is similar to a factorial analysis of variance model (Scheffé, 1959: p. 121), where the natural logarithms of the cell frequencies are characterized by a linear sum of parameters associated with a general effect, main effects for the individual variables, two-way interaction effects linked with pairwise combinations of the variables, and so forth.

For a two-way contingency table, the general model is

$$\log(n_{ij}) = \mu + \alpha_i + \beta_j + (\alpha\beta)_{ij} + \epsilon_{ij},$$

where n_{ij} is the frequency of the (i, j) cell, α_i is the effect of the i-th row, β_j is the effect of the j-th column, $(\alpha\beta)_{ij}$ is the interaction effect between the i-th row and the j-th column, and ϵ_{ij} is the error due to real data departures from the assumed model. A particular model is said to be 'saturated' when all possible effects are assumed *a priori* to be non-zero. The term 'saturated' has cognitive meaning, since in this case the error terms are zero. In other words, the saturated model gives a perfect fit between the data and the model. On the other hand, an unsaturated model admits *a priori* zero values for some of the effects. For example, a hypothesis of independence between the row and column variables requires that the joint probability of an observation occurring in the (i, j) cell equals the product of the unconditional (marginal) probability that an observation occurs in the i-th row and the unconditional probability that an observation occurs in the j-th column. Taking logarithms, the corresponding logarithm of the joint probability would be the simple sum of a row effect and a column effect. In consequence, the traditional hypothesis of independence between the rows and columns of a two-way contingency table can be stated as a formal hypothesis in terms of the parameters of the general log-linear model. Specifically, the traditional hypothesis of independence is formally equivalent to the hypothesis that all interaction effects are equal to zero. A hypothesis of row homogeneity, on the other hand, requires not only that the interaction effects are zero but, in addition, that the column main effects are also zero. Less well-known hypotheses are characterizable through constraints on the parameters of the log-linear model. One example is a hypothesis of symmetry for square tables where intuition dictates that the probability of an observation in the (i, j) cell equals the probability of an observation in the (j, i) cell. The formal null hypothesis associated with the log-linear model requires that $\alpha_i = \beta_i$ and that $(\alpha\beta)_{ij} = (\alpha\beta)_{ji}$ for all rows and columns. Additional hypotheses are characterized in Bishop *et al.* (1975). It is not sufficient, however, simply to characterize these hypotheses, since we must be able to subject the propositions to statistical tests.

Fortunately, hypotheses associated with the log-linear model may be statistically tested through the G^2 statistic (Fienberg, 1977, p. 36). Interestingly, this statistic is a function of the likelihood ratio statistic (Rao, 1965, p. 350), based on maximum likelihood estimates of the model parameters. If λ denotes the likelihood ratio statistic, then $G^2 = -2 \log \lambda$ and if, in addition, the alternative hypothesis is the simple negation of the null hypothesis (corresponding to the saturated model), then

$$G^2 = 2 \sum_i \sum_j n_{ij} \log (n_{ij}/m_{ij}),$$

where n_{ij} is the observed frequency of the (i, j) cell and m_{ij} is the expected frequency of the (i, j) cell based on estimating the cell probabilities by the principal of maximum likelihood. If the null hypothesis is correct (i.e. if the fitted model is correct) and the sample size is not small, then the statistic has an approximate chi-squared distribution with degrees of freedom equal to the number of independent constraints, under the null hypothesis, placed on the parameters of the model. The sample size is considered adequate if the expected frequencies are generally no smaller than five. Degree of freedom calculations are straightforward providing one notes,

as in analysis of variance models, that a contingency table with r rows and c columns has $(r - 1)$ independent main effect parameters for rows, $(c - 1)$ independent main effect parameters for columns, and $(r - 1)(c - 1)$ independent parameters for row by column interactions. Thus, the conventional hypothesis of independence has $(r - 1)(c - 1)$ degrees of freedom while the hypothesis of row homogeneity has $(c - 1) + (r - 1)(c - 1) = r(c - 1)$ degrees of freedom. Similarly, the hypothesis of symmetry has

$$(r - 1) + \frac{(r - 1)^2 - (r - 1)}{2} = \frac{r(r - 1)}{2}$$

degrees of freedom. The null hypothesis is rejected at the α level if the observed G^2 value is in excess of the corresponding critical value for the chi-squared distribution. The two-way model easily extends to the three-way model as follows.

A three-way contingency table is characterized by

$$\log (n_{ijk}) = \mu + \alpha_i + \beta_j + \gamma_k$$
$$+ (\alpha\beta)_{ij} + (\alpha\gamma)_{ik} + (\beta\gamma)_{jk}$$
$$+ (\alpha\beta\gamma)_{ijk} + \epsilon_{ijk}$$

where the global effect is denoted by μ, the main effects associated with the three classificatory variables are denoted by simple Greek letters with subscripts (α_i, β_j and γ_k), the two-way interaction effects are denoted by pairwise combinations of the main effect symbols [$(\alpha\beta)_{ij}$, $(\alpha\gamma)_{ik}$, $(\beta\gamma)_{jk}$], the three-way interaction effect is denoted by $(\alpha\beta\gamma)_{ijk}$ and, finally, the residual effect is given by ϵ_{ijk}. As in the two-way model, the saturated model includes all possible effects with consequent zero values for the residual terms. Applications are theoretically similar to those for the two-way model in that G^2 and associated degrees of freedom calculations are based on the same principles. There are, however, many more testable hypotheses. In addition to the hypotheses associated with the two-way marginal tables, there are hypotheses unique to the three-dimensional configuration. For example, a hypothesis of mutual independence between the three classificatory variables is now possible. Note that pairwise independence between the variables in the two-way marginal tables does not imply mutual independence. This hypothesis would require that all two-way and three-way interaction terms are zero for all rows, columns and layers. Another unconditional hypothesis of interest might be independence between the third variable (layer classification) and the other two variables (row and column classifications). The associated log-linear model would require that all interactions including a layer (γ) term are zero, i.e. $(\alpha\gamma)_{ik}$, $(\beta\gamma)_{jk}$ and $(\alpha\beta\gamma)_{ijk}$ are zero for all rows, columns and layers. This could be of special interest if one or more of the variables represented space or spatial factors. Conditional hypotheses are also of interest. Consider, for example, the hypothesis of conditional independence between any two variables given the other variable. This hypothesis states that the two variables are independent of each other in each of the individual two-way tables corresponding to the individual values of the other variable (perhaps spatial areas). It should be noted that conditional independence does not imply, nor is it implied by, unconditional (marginal) independence. These notions are conceptually akin to notions of partial and zero-order correlations (Fienberg, 1977, p. 45). The above only illustrate a few of numerous unsaturated models characterized by zero and non-zero parameter sets. In addition, there are hypotheses of total symmetry, marginal symmetry, and marginal homogeneity, as well as the conditional hypotheses associated with partitioning theorems and the differences between hypothetical states in hierarchies of nested models.

The number of possibilities becomes larger for four-way contingency tables where there are four main effect parameter sets, six two-way interaction parameter sets, four three-way interaction parameter sets, and one four-way interaction parameter set. The methods, however, do not change although we restrict ourselves to the class of hierarchical models for which the maximum likelihood estimates of the cell frequencies can always be found through the principle of iterative proportional fitting (Fienberg, 1977, p. 60). This is not a real restriction, since a four-way table has 113 different hierarchical models (Fienberg, 1977, p. 60) and includes all of the hypotheses of homogeneity and independence. One powerful feature of the general log-linear model is its ability to partition the test statistic, G^2, into components which are asymptotically independent. Often, this can be accomplished so that a global hypothesis partitions into a sum of other specific hypotheses.

Useful partitioning results

A full discussion of partitioning results for the log-linear model is beyond the scope of this chapter. The results offered here are based primarily on the Goodman partitioning calculus summarized by Bishop *et al.* (1975, p. 169–75). The partitioning results allow a comparison of two different log-linear models when one model is a special case of the other. In the two-way table, the hypothesis of row homogeneity is a special case of the hypothesis of independence between the two variables. In a three-way table, the hypothesis of mutual independence between all three variables is a special case of independence between the third variable and the other two variables. Without loss of generality, let model 2 be a special case of model 1 and let G_2^2 and G_1^2 denote their respective test statistics against the general alternative hypothesis. It can be shown (Fienberg, 1977, p. 49) that the conditional hypothesis for testing the validity of model 2, given the *a priori* validity of model 1, has a test statistic value of

$$G_{2/1}^2 = G_2^2 - G_1^2.$$

Furthermore this statistic is asymptotically chi-squared with degrees of freedom equal to the difference of the degrees of freedom between models 2 and 1. In addition $G_{2/1}^2$ is asymptotically independent of the test statistic for model 1. Stated more precisely, if model 2 is correct, then the test statistic for model 2 uniquely partitions into two asymptotically and

independently distributed components where one component is the test statistic for model 1, the other component is the conditional test statistic for model 2 given model 1, both statistics have chi-squared distributions and their degrees of freedom sum to the degrees of freedom for the model 2 test statistic. The above example illustrates the general nature of partitioning theorems where the focus of interest is on the relationship between models nested in a hierarchical format (Fienberg, 1977, p. 49).

This focus has apparently led to archaeological applications where conditional hypotheses have been represented in terms of model selection problems (Clark, 1976; Hietala and Stevens, 1977). Other applications where conditional hypotheses have represented locational differences have been supplied by Butler *et al.* (1977), Hietala and Stevens (1977), Hietala and Larson (1980) and Hietala (1983a, 1983b). Since these applications do not seem to have induced readers to internalize the methods, a reasonable explication of intrasite possibilities seems to be required.

Intrasite considerations

Because the determination of patterns has been conceptually aligned with notions of local and global variation, it seems reasonable to amplify the problems with an ecological example. Suppose two tree species are differentially adapted to altitudes above 1500 meters, one species favoring lower, and the other higher, regions. A global analysis of the pertinent data would suggest that the two species tend to segregate. On the other hand, the two species might locally aggregate at all altitudes with density variation based on soil type, water availability and drainage systems. In this case, a situation exists where global segregation occurs in the presence of local aggregation.

An archaeological example of local aggregation and global segregation could occur in Archaic sites in Texas if bifacial thinning flakes were abundant around firepits (because of maintenance activities) and primary flakes were generally found in areas distant from firepits (because of core reduction activities). The reverse situation of local segregation with global aggregation could occur in southwestern US Indian pithouse communities or in Old World upper paleolithic scatters. In the former case, one could have spatially distinct activities occurring inside the structural features (pithouses), yielding local segregation of certain artifact classes. A global analysis based on all within-structure and outside-structure information might yield a conclusion of global aggregation for the same artifact classes. In the latter case, a similar situation could occur if multiple or repeated occupations have occurred on the same landscape with a minor degree of overlapping concentrations.

The situation of local aggregation with global segregation is illustrated in the next section. Local segregation with global aggregation, on the other hand, is illustrated in Table 1 where variable *A* represents two artifact classes, variable *B* represents two areas and variable *C* represents two subareas within each

Table 1. *Hypothetical variable frequencies with a partition of the G^2 statistic*

		Area $B1$ Subareas		Area $B2$ Subareas		Areas	
		$C1$	$C2$	$C1$	$C2$	$B1$	$B2$
Artifact	$A1$	25	10	5	20	30	30
classes	$A2$	5	15	10	5	15	20
G^2 statistic		5.709		4.405		0.227	

Hypothesis	G^2	d.f.	Conclusion
$(A \oplus C \vert B1)$	5.709	1	Segregation
$(A \oplus C \vert B2)$	4.405	1	Segregation
$(A \oplus C \vert B)^a$	10.114	2	Segregation
$(A \oplus B)^b$	0.227	1	Aggregation
$[A \oplus (B, C)]^c$	10.341	3	Patterned

[a] A and C are conditionally independent given B.
[b] A and B are marginally independent.
[c] A is jointly independent of B and C together.
d.f. = degrees of freedom.

of the two areas. The G^2 statistic for testing the hypothesis that variable A is independent of variables B and C together can be partitioned into a G^2 statistic for testing the hypothesis that variables A and C are conditionally independent given variable B (the sum of the statistics for testing independence within areas) and a G^2 statistic for testing marginal independence of variables A and B (the statistic for testing independence between areas). The hypothetical artifact classes are clearly segregating within areas but aggregating between areas. Many possible applications ensue through appropriate variation in the definitions of the three variables. For example, in spatial analyses at Bir Tarfawi, an Aterian site in the western desert of Egypt, Hietala and Larson (1980, pp. 383–6) used partitioning results to study intersite variability of technological and tool class distributions as well as within-site and between-site variability in the same classes. Using distance information within one of the sites, a study of the spatial variability between cores, debitage, tools and fauna was performed. It should be noted that if one of the categorical variables is an ordered sequence of Euclidean distance categories, then one can test the hypothesis that an association between two artifact classes and their corresponding nearest neighbors is independent of distance. The test statistic is a generalization of certain statistics utilized by Hanson (1972) and Whallon (1974) and has, as one of its features, the ability to determine if nearest-neighbor patterns are uniform in local and global space.

Another study (Hietala and Stevens, 1977) used partitioning theorems for two purposes. The first was used to select models in the determination of global associational patterns. The second used partitioning theorems for the determination of within-level and between-level associational modes (defined in terms of spatial consistency through the levels) for particular artifact classes. In addition, associational consist-

ency, by level, between classes was tested to give an overall test of specific consistency of artifact classes through and within levels. This study has been criticized as global in nature. In the applications section, I will illustrate that a local approach determines areas which are variable in size, shape and overlapping characteristics.

A third study (Hietala, 1983a, 1983b) utilized areas defined through artifact conjoin distributions. These areas were tested for bidirectionality relationships between the conjoins by symmetry tests discussed earlier. In addition, variability within levels (between areas) and between levels was systematically studied for technological and tool class variables. In the applications section, one new approach is developed which, as it turns out, greatly simplifies the technological studies. The approach is based on the simple observation that if a partitioning theorem is used to separate technological variability (for specific variables observed on particular artifact classes) into within-level and between-level components, then (under the hypothesis of unpatterned total variability), the G^2/degrees of freedom statistic for between-level variability divided by the G^2/degrees of freedom for within-level variability will, asymptotically, be an F-statistic with numerator and denominator degrees of freedom given by the degrees of freedom for the statistics in the numerator and denominator of the ratio. This result is logically derived from the combination of three separate theorems. The first theorem (Bishop *et al.*, 1975, p. 254) asserts asymptotically independent chi-squared distributions for the components of G^2. The second theorem (Rao, 1965, p. 104; Bishop *et al.*, 1975, p. 472) affirms that the distribution of the ratio of two statistics converges, in law, to the distribution of the ratio of their limiting (asymptotic) statistics. The third, and most well known, states that the ratio of two independent chi-squared variables divided by their respective degrees of freedom is an

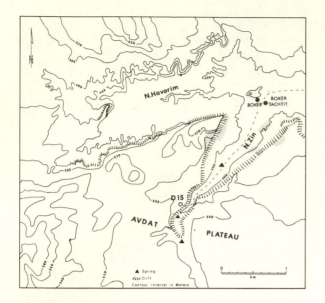

Fig. 1. Location of the sites Rosh Ein Mor (D15) and Boker Tachtit, in the Central Negev, Israel.

F-statistic (Scheffé, 1959, p. 414). This *F*-statistic can be used to determine if between-level variability is substantially larger than within-level variability. Needless to say, the same concept can be employed for studying within-area and between-area variability and, hence, can be used to study local and global patterning.

Applications

The two sites considered in these applications are Rosh Ein Mor (D15) and Boker Tachtit (Fig. 1), both located in the Central Negev of Israel. The former site is an Early Levantine Middle Paleolithic occurrence (Hietala and Stevens, 1977) while the latter is a stratified Middle to Upper Paleolithic transitional site (Marks, 1983). The Rosh Ein Mor site will be used to illustrate how the G^2 statistic can be used to determine areas of homogeneous content while the site of Boker Tachtit will be used to illustrate an application of the *F*-statistic for technological transition studies.

To determine areas of homogeneous content for artifact classes, one can utilize the G^2 statistic for testing independ-

Table 2. *Artifact class frequencies and relative frequencies for the 3 × 4 unit configuration at Rosh Ein Mor*

Sidescrapers				Denticulates				Sidescrapers to denticulates			
15	11	12	21	15	11	9	13	0.50	0.50	0.57	0.62
9	7	18	16	25	14	21	17	0.26	0.33	0.46	0.48
3	7	8	15	13	13	14	17	0.19	0.35	0.36	0.47
Levallois points				Levallois flakes				Points to flakes			
97	25	33	71	78	92	79	78	0.55	0.21	0.29	0.45
84	28	26	68	63	89	90	83	0.57	0.24	0.22	0.48
136	34	31	73	82	93	97	67	0.62	0.27	0.24	0.52

Table 3. *Areas defined by cluster analysis using the G^2 statistic for selected artifact pairs*

Sidescraper and denticulate comparisons

Units defining areas				Comparison	G^2	d.f	*p*-value
2	2	2	2	Within Area 1	2.011	4	> 0.700
1	1	2	2	Within Area 2	2.598	6	> 0.800
1	1	1	2	Between Areas	13.594	1	< 0.001

Levallois point and Levallois flake comparisons

Units defining areas				Comparison	G^2	d.f.	*p*-value
5	3	3	4	Within Area 3	2.710	5	> 0.700
5	3	3	4	Within Area 4	2.147	2	> 0.300
5	3	3	4	Within Area 5	1.497	2	> 0.500
				Between Areas	161.503	2	< 0.001

d.f. = degrees of freedom.

Table 4. *Blade frequencies for Boker Tachtit attributes by area for all levels*

Attributes	Level 1			Level 2					Level 3		Level 4		
	L	M	R	L	ML	MR	TL	TR	In	Out	L	R	T
Platforms													
Simple	21	46	12	24	87	80	126	38	13	16	156	110	57
Dihedral	8	11	4	8	32	26	79	10	3	12	36	33	17
Multiple	12	46	21	18	67	50	132	53	19	22	118	85	24
Cortical	3	3	1	0	5	6	6	5	3	2	10	6	4
Crushed	14	45	11	8	32	24	32	3	14	19	27	14	12
Tip shape													
Blunt	32	71	22	22	100	102	190	42	24	44	136	106	56
Pointed	19	55	14	17	73	58	108	45	22	18	147	114	46
Hinged	8	20	9	15	47	22	66	13	10	10	50	24	8
Profile													
Flat	10	38	2	10	23	33	37	25	17	22	90	64	39
Incurvate	19	41	19	9	54	53	109	25	7	12	101	47	40
Twisted	31	74	28	41	151	104	233	61	33	41	165	140	35
Cortex													
None	31	111	29	38	144	91	242	69	34	55	220	169	78
1–24%	19	30	12	15	52	73	67	28	19	13	83	53	17
25–49%	10	12	8	9	32	26	70	14	4	7	53	29	19
Bulbs													
Diffuse	22	48	21	23	61	93	90	28	20	26	88	54	48
Normal	22	55	20	34	99	69	185	69	29	38	206	143	54
Pronounced	14	46	7	3	65	17	92	13	7	10	55	46	5
Cross-section													
Triangle	22	68	21	27	90	90	130	33	29	25	146	95	39
Rt Triangle	5	9	2	4	12	10	31	6	4	5	14	9	11
Trapezoid	29	66	25	27	125	87	218	72	24	41	182	141	56
Shape													
Tri./Rect.	44	118	34	40	177	155	302	75	40	44	263	190	100
Ovoid	2	1	1	3	5	2	7	0	3	1	8	5	0
Canted	3	11	6	6	10	7	16	10	4	11	23	21	2
Expanding	11	23	7	6	31	23	48	20	10	18	52	32	10
Scar Patterns													
Unidir.	27	46	25	32	85	89	119	44	39	30	266	184	93
Bidir.	14	70	55	13	92	50	206	43	10	26	29	39	7
Bi-crossed	10	19	5	9	25	22	31	15	5	13	29	14	5
Change	2	3	0	1	4	3	0	1	1	2	4	2	0
Other	7	15	4	5	22	26	23	18	2	4	28	12	9
Sample size	60	153	49	60	228	190	379	111	57	75	356	251	114

Tri. = Triangle; Rect. = Rectangle; Rt = right-angled; L, denotes the left area of level 1; other characters denote other areas for other levels.

ence in two-dimensional tables with the first variable (A) representing two artifact classes and the second variable (B) representing grid unit cells. Using the G^2 statistic as a measure of similarity (it is also a test statistic) one can use a cluster analysis to determine grid unit areas of similar content for the variable pairs. If this is performed separately for all pairs of variables, areas will be defined which are not restricted in size or overlapping characteristics. Clearly, they are partially restricted in shape since it combines grid units. If the initial units are not defined as grid units, then this restriction would be eased. At Rosh Ein Mor, the data (Table 2) are utilized to compare the areas defined by Levallois points and Levallois

Table 5. *F-statistics for comparing within- and between-level technological variation for Boker Tachtit blades*

	Between-levels		Within-levels			
Variable	G^2	d.f.	G^2	d.f.	*F*-statistic	*p*-value
Scar patterns	290.85	12	109.36	36	7.98	0.000
Tip shape	29.69	6	34.00	18	2.62	0.007
Platform type	114.92	12	67.09	36	5.14	0.000
Profile	69.69	6	58.24	18	3.59	0.001
Bulb	37.56	6	108.75	18	1.04	0.444
Shape	18.69	9	41.78	27	1.34	0.263
Cross-section	6.67	6	32.38	18	0.62	0.712
Cortex	9.51	6	52.63	18	0.54	0.771

d.f. = degrees of freedom.

flakes, on the one hand, and denticulates and sidescrapers, on the other hand.

For the sidescraper–denticulate comparisons, the first units grouped together are those in the first row and first two columns. Since the (1,1) unit has 15 sidescrapers and denticulates each and the (1,2) unit has 11 sidescrapers and denticulates each, the G^2 statistic has a value of zero. At step number two, the (2,3) and (3,4) units are grouped together while in the next step, the (3,2) and (3,3) units are clustered. At the fourth step, the (2,3) unit is clustered with units clustered in the first step. This stepwise procedure is continued until the clustering algorithm yields a G^2 statistic larger than the critical value for rejecting the null hypothesis of independence between the variables and group units considered at this step. Any further clustering will yield G^2 values which are larger yet. In this case the (3 × 4) unit configuration defines two areas (Table 3) which are each homogeneous but are different from each other. The Levallois point–Levallois flake comparisons yield three areas. It is noted (Table 3) that the two sets of areas equal those defined by the earlier study (Hietala and Stevens, 1977, p. 555) and are clearly overlapping. In general applications, the clustering mechanism and the stopping rules may vary.

The data for the technological study at Boker Tachtit (Table 4) are used to calculate the G^2 statistics for within-level and between-level comparisons of the technological variables listed. Table 5 gives the *F*-statistics and associated *p*-values for all of the technological variables measured on blades. Here it is seen that only significant *F*-statistics are for scar patterns, tip shape, platform type and profile. Interestingly, this conclusion is identical with that obtained in the earlier study (Hietala, 1983*a*, 1983*b*), although the amount of effort required is marginal in comparison. The reader is urged to read the original papers for detailed conclusions regarding the patterns at Boker Tachtit and Rosh Ein Mor.

Acknowledgement
The data for the Rosh Ein Mor and Boker Tachtit applications were obtained through NSF grants GS-42680, BNS 76-81646 and BNS 79-04931.

References
Binford, L. R. (1978). Dimensional analysis of behavior and site structure: learning from an Eskimo hunting stand. *American Antiquity* 43: 330–61.
Bishop, Y. M. M., Fienberg, S. E. and Holland, P. W. (1975). *Discrete Multivariate Analysis: Theory and Practice*. MIT Press: Cambridge, Mass.
Butler, B. H., Tchernov, E., Hietala, H. J. and Davis, S. (1977). Faunal exploitation during the Late Epipaleolithic in the Har Harif. In *Prehistory and Paleoenvironments in the Central Negev, Israel*, Vol. II, *The Avdat/Aqev Area*, Part 2, *The Har Harif*, ed. A. E. Marks, pp. 327–45. Department of Anthropology, Southern Methodist University: Dallas, Texas.
Clark, G. A. (1976). More on contingency table analysis, decision making criteria and the use of log linear models. *American Antiquity* 41: 259–73.
Cox, D. R. (1970). *Analysis of Binary Data*. Methuen: London.
Divalle, W. T. and Harris, M. (1976). Population, warfare, and the male supremacist complex. *American Anthropologist* 78: 521–38.
Fienberg, S. E. (1977). *The Analysis of Cross-Classified Categorical Data*. MIT Press: Cambridge, Mass.
Florek, K. J., Lukaszewicz, J., Perkal, J., Steinhaus, H. and Zubrzycki, S. (1951). Sur la liaison et la division des points d'un ensemble fini. *Colloquia Mathematica* 2: 282–5.
Góralski, A. (1974). *Metody Opisu i Wnioskowania Statystycznego w Psychologii*. Warszawa.
Haberman, S. J. (1974). *The Analysis of Frequency Data*. University of Chicago Press: Chicago, Ill.
Hanson, N. R. (1972). *Patterns of Discovery*. Cambridge University Press: Cambridge.
Hietala, H. J. (1983*a*). Boker Tachtit: spatial distributions. In *Prehistory and Paleoenvironments in the Central Negev, Israel*, vol. III, *The Avdat/Aqev Area*, Part 3, ed. A. E. Marks, pp. 191–216. Department of Anthropology, Southern Methodist University; Dallas, Texas.
Hietala, H. J. (1983*b*). Boker Tachtit: intralevel and interlevel spatial analyses. In *Prehistory and Paleoenvironments in the Central Negev, Israel*, Vol. III, *The Avdat/Aqev Area*, Part, 3, ed. A. E. Marks, pp. 217–81. Department of Anthropology, Southern Methodist University: Dallas, Texas.
Hietala, H. J. and Close, A. E. (1979). Testing hypotheses of independence on symmetrical artifacts. *Journal of Archaeological Science* 6: 85–92.
Hietala, H. J. and Larson P. (1979). SYMAP analyses in archaeology: intrasite assumptions and a comparison with TREND analysis. *Norwegian Archaeological Review* 12: 57–64.

Hietala, H. J. and Larson, R. (1980). Intrasite and intersite spatial analyses at Bir Tarfawi. In *The Prehistory of the Eastern Sahara: Paleoenvironments and Human Exploitation,* ed. F. Wendorf and R. Schild, pp. 379–88. Academic Press, New York.

Hietala, H. J. and Stevens, D. E. (1977). Spatial analysis: multiple procedures in pattern recognition studies. *American Antiquity* 42: 539–59.

Kostrubiec, B. (1971). Analiza matematyezna zbioru osiedli wojewodztwa opolskiego, In *Struktury i Procesy Osadnicze*, ed. S. Golachowski. Pople–Wroclaw.

Lindsey, J. K. (1973). *Inferences from Sociological Survey Data: A Unified Approach.* Elsevier: New York.

Marks, A. E. (1983). The sites of Boker Tachtit and Boker: a brief introduction. In *Prehistory and Paleoenvironments in the Central Negev Israel,* Vol. III, *The Avdat/Aqev Area,* Part 3, ed. A. E. Marks, pp. 15–37. Department of Anthropology, Southern Methodist University: Dallas, Texas.

Nations, J. D. (1978). Population ecology of the Lacandon Maya. Ph.D. Thesis, Southern Methodist University: Dallas, Texas.

Nations, J. D. and Hietala, H. J. (1978). 'Sons, sex ratios, and selective neglect.' Paper presented at the 77th annual meeting of the American Anthropological Association: Los Angeles, Cal.

Plackett, R. L. (1974). *The Analysis of Categorical Data.* Griffin: London.

Rao, C. R. (1965). *Linear Statistical Inference and Its Applications.* John Wiley and Sons: New York.

Reid, D. (1974). Some comments on typologies in archaeology and an outline of a methodology. *American Antiquity* 39: 216–42.

Scheffé, H. (1959). *The Analysis of Variance.* John Wiley and Sons: New York.

Schiffer, M. B. (1981). Some issues in the philosophy of archaeology. *American Antiquity* 46: 899–908.

Schild, R. and Wendorf, F. (1981). *The Prehistory of an Egyptian Oasis.* Polska Akademia Nauk Instytut Historii Kultury Materialnej: Wroclaw.

Wendorf, F. and Schild, R. (1976). The Middle Paleolithic of North-eastern Africa: new data and concepts. *UISPP 9th Congress* 3: 8–34.

Whallon, R. (1974). Spatial analysis of occupation floors. II. Application of nearest neighbor analysis. *American Antiquity* 39: 16–34.

Yellen, J. E. (1977). *Archaeological Approaches to the Present: Models for Reconstructing the Past.* Academic Press: New York.

Chapter 5

**Efficient permutation
procedures for analysis
of artifact distributions**
Kenneth J. Berry, Paul W. Mielke
and Kenneth L. Kvamme

Because tool types and artifacts owe their spatial distributions within a site, at least in part, to the patterned behavior of prehistoric peoples, the spatial analysis of tool-type and/or artifact distributions within a site is potentially informative regarding the activities and organization of prehistoric societies. Early analyses of intrasite spatial patterns were primarily based on maps of artifact classes within a site and suffered from a lack of objective, rigorous, quantitative techniques, relying heavily on inspection and visual assessment (Whallon 1973, p. 266). Recognizing that the spatial distributions of artifact classes within a site are a meaningful type of archaeological data and, consequently, that the analysis of artifact distributions warrants more than visual inspection and impressionistic interpretation, more recent work (*vide,* Clarke 1968, 1977; Dacey 1973; Duda and Hart 1973; Whallon 1973, 1974; Rogers 1974; Hodder and Orton 1976; Schiffer 1976; Hietala and Stevens 1977; Hodder and Okell 1978) applies quantitative analytical techniques, usually of a statistical nature, to the analysis of spatial distributions of artifacts within a site.

Presented in this chapter are rigorous permutation tests designed to detect locational differences among artifact classes within a site. As permutation tests, they require neither distributional assumptions nor spurious data restrictions and allow either point-plot or count-per-grid data in one-, two-, or three-dimensional archaeological space, thus permitting simultaneous analysis of occupation floors and/or levels. Moreover, the tests tolerate odd-shaped and/or non-contiguous site structures and permit the inclusion of unclassified (or unclassifiable) artifacts.

The following sections present (1) the basic results together with (2) worked examples that illustrate a variety of site conditions, (3) location/dispersion estimation techniques which provide a description of each artifact class as well as possible differences among classes, (4) the special handling of very large data sets, (5) a discussion of the relationship of the permutation tests to several well-known classical inference techniques, and (6) an appendix containing complete mathematics for all sections of the chapter.

A permutation approach – MRPP
The multi-response permutation procedures (MRPP) presented in this chapter are analogous, in application, to one-way multivariate analysis of variance (MANOVA). However, the MRPP are based upon a principle entirely different from conventional MANOVA, where location measurements of individual artifacts are the primary units of analysis. The MRPP utilize the average between-artifact distance among artifacts within classes as their primary analysis unit.

Consider a hypothetical site location containing two types of artifacts, borers and scrapers, and imagine that these

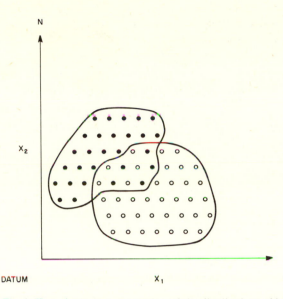

N

X_2

DATUM X_1

Fig. 1. Hypothetical representation of the distributions of borers (dots) and scrapers (circles) within a site space.

two artifact classes possess distinct but overlapping distributions on the site floor. Figure 1 graphically represents the distributions of the borers and scrapers within the site space: X_1 represents the east–west axis, X_2 represents the north–south axis, the borers are symbolized by dots and the scrapers by circles. It is clear from a visual inspection of Fig. 1 that there is partial separation between the borers and scrapers within the site, and that borers and scrapers tend to be located in different areas of the site. This separation and clustering may be characterized more rigorously and numerically by examining the distance, $\Delta_{I,J}$, between all possible pairs of points (i.e. all combinations taken two at a time) in Fig. 1, where

$$\Delta_{I,J} = [(X_{1I} - X_{1J})^2 + (X_{2I} - X_{2J})^2]^{\frac{1}{2}}, \qquad (1)$$

and where I and J represent two different artifact locations. [Note: extensions to higher dimensions and complete mathematical formulations of the entire set of multi-response permutation procedures is contained in the appendix to this chapter.]

The clustering of the artifacts into the two classes can now be considered numerically by forming two averages (ξ_B = borers and ξ_S = scrapers) of the $\Delta_{I,J}$ distances, one average over each artifact class. Let N represent the total number of artifacts, n_B the number of borers, and n_S the number of scrapers, then the average distance among borers,

$$\xi_B = \sum_{I<J} \Delta_{I,J} \binom{n_B}{2}, \qquad (2)$$

and the average distance among scrapers,

$$\xi_S = \sum_{I<J} \Delta_{I,J} \binom{n_S}{2}, \qquad (3)$$

where $\sum\limits_{I<J}$ is the sum over all I and J within the i-th artifact class (here i is either B or S) such that $1 \leqslant I < J \leqslant n_i$, and $\binom{n_i}{2}$ is the number of distinct pairs of artifact locations (i.e. distances between artifacts) that can be formed from the i-th artifact class. Now the average separation (clustering) of the N artifacts into the two artifact classes is the weighted mean (δ) of the two ξ_i values:

$$\delta = \frac{n_B}{N} \xi_B + \frac{n_S}{N} \xi_S. \qquad (4)$$

To recapitulate, $\Delta_{I,J}$ is the distance across the site location between any two (I-th and J-th) artifact locations; ξ_i is the average of the $\Delta_{I,J}$ distances among all $\Delta_{I,J}$ values in the i-th artifact class, and δ is the weighted within-class average of the distances between all possible pairs of artifact locations in the same artifact class, where the weight (n_i/N) is the proportional size contribution of the i-th artifact class.

It is important to recognize that the partition of the N artifacts plotted in Fig. 1 into dots and circles, i.e. borers and scrapers, is but one of many partition possibilities. This is to say that the N artifacts can be partitioned into two distinct artifact classes each having, respectively, a fixed number (n_B, n_S) of points in precisely $M = N!/(n_B!n_S!)$ ways. Each of the M possible partitions can be given a fixed probability ($1/M$) of occurrence under the null hypothesis, thereby generating a sample space, and δ can be calculated for each of these M partitions. The problem is to determine if the observed δ for a particular partition is unusual with respect to other possible partitions with the same size structure (n_B, n_S) that could have been made with these N artifacts.

If the observed partition is such that the two artifact classes are tightly clustered and tending toward complete separation, then the two ξ_i values will be relatively small (i.e. the average within-class distances will both be small) and, consequently, the weighted-mean of the ξ_i values (δ) will also be small, compared to other possible δ values. The observed δ value will then fall somewhere near the left tail of the discrete distribution of all possible δ values. The probability of such an extreme, or more extreme, δ value (i.e. the probability of the observed clustering or a tighter clustering of artifact classes) is the probability of the observed δ value plus the sum of the probabilities of all smaller δ values. If the probability value is small, then there is evidence of a location difference between the artifact classes within the site.

Approximate sampling distribution of δ

Because the calculation of the probability value of an observed δ requires that M values of δ be obtained and because the calculation of M possible values of δ is not computationally feasible in most applications (e.g. with $N = 60$ and $n_B = n_S = 30$, $M = 1.1826 \times 10^{17}$), an approximate test becomes necessary. To obtain the approximate probability value, consider the distribution of the standardized test statistic $T = (\delta - \mu_\delta)/\sigma_\delta$, where T is approximated by the Pearson type III distribution (Mielke *et al.* 1981*a*) and where, if δ_j signifies the j-th value among the M possible values of δ, the mean (μ_δ), the variance (σ_δ^2), and the skewness (γ_δ) are given by

$$\mu_\delta = \frac{1}{M} \sum_{j=1}^{M} \delta_j, \tag{5}$$

$$\sigma_\delta^2 = \frac{1}{M} \sum_{j=1}^{M} (\delta_j - \mu_\delta)^2, \tag{6}$$

and

$$\gamma_\delta = \frac{1}{M} \sum_{j=1}^{M} (\delta_j - \mu_\delta)^3 / \sigma_\delta^3. \tag{7}$$

Computational procedures to obtain μ_δ, σ_δ^2, and γ_δ for an observed set of data are described by Mielke (1979) and Mielke *et al.* (1976) and also in the appendix to this chapter. An alternative for determining the probability value is to employ tabulated quantile values of the Pearson type III distribution (Harter 1969). The only entries required for obtaining interpolated probability values with the Harter (1969) tables are the quantities T and γ_δ. An obvious drawback to interpolated probability values involves cases which exceed the limits of the finite table. For this reason, all probability values reported in subsequent examples are based on the approximate technique described above.

Incidentally, an interesting statistic closely related to the MRPP statistic was recently suggested by Hodder and Okell (1978), but because their statistic is a ratio statistic, attainment of its associated probability value unfortunately requires the use of Monte Carlo sampling procedures (also termed re-randomization).

Numerical illustration of the MRPP

To illustrate the calculation of the MRPP, consider an assemblage of seven ($N = 7$) scrapers classified into two types: endscrapers ($n_E = 3$) and carinated scrapers ($n_C = 4$). Two measurements of location (X_1 and X_2) have been taken on each scraper. Specifically, X_1 is the distance in meters east from the site datum and X_2 is the distance in meters north from the site datum. Therefore, each scraper possesses two scores (site coordinates) and can be located precisely in a two-dimensional space such as an occupation floor. Table 1 lists the site coordinates for the seven scrapers and Fig. 2 locates the seven scrapers on an occupation floor. Now, without prior classification knowledge, the three endscrapers might be any three of the seven scrapers (A, B, C; A, B, D; A, B, E; . . . ; E, F, G) and the four carinated scrapers might be any four of the seven scrapers (D, E, F, G; C, E, F, G; . . . ; A, B, C, D). Here there are $M = 7!/(3!4!) = 35$ possible allocation combinations of the seven scrapers to the two classes. Put another way, if there are three endscrapers and four carinated scrapers, then there are 35 possible ways to arrange the endscrapers and carinated scrapers among the seven locations mapped in Fig. 2,

Table 1. *Hypothetical site coordinates for seven scrapers*

Scraper	X_1 (m)	X_2 (m)
A	4	5
B	3	4
C	4	3
D	2	3
E	2	2
F	3	2
G	3	1

given that the mapped locations do not indicate the type of scraper found there. Column 2 of Table 3 lists the 35 possible allocation combinations.

Consider each of the $\binom{7}{2} = 21$ pairs of scraper locations (one pair at a time) and calculate the distance, $\Delta_{I,J}$, between pairs of scraper locations. Visualize these distances as straight lines (21 in all) drawn between all possible pairs of the seven locations mapped in Fig. 2 (see Fig. 3). Among the resulting 21 values of $\Delta_{I,J}$ (see Table 2), scraper locations close together (e.g. F and G) will have a small value of $\Delta_{I,J}$ (e.g. 1.0000) and scraper locations far apart (e.g. A and G) will have a large value of $\Delta_{I,J}$ (e.g. 4.1231), since $\Delta_{I,J}$ is merely the distance in meters between the locations of the I-th and J-th scrapers.

There will be $2M = 70$ values of ξ_i calculated for this problem: 35 for each of the two types of scrapers. The ξ_i values, averages of the $\Delta_{I,J}$ distances within each artifact type, are given in columns 3 and 4 of Table 3 for each of the 35 possible combinations. The test statistics of interest (δ's),

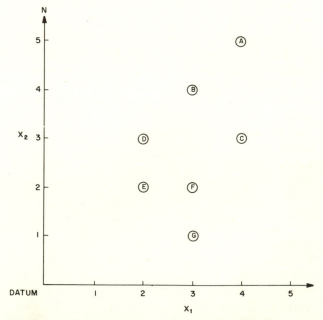

Fig. 2. Map of occupation floor with seven scrapers with coordinates as in Table 1.

Table 2. $\Delta_{I,J}$ distances for locations A through G from Table 1, Fig. 2, and Fig. 3

Pair number	Pair	Distance (Δ) (m)
1	A,B	1.4142
2	A,C	2.0000
3	A,D	2.8284
4	A,E	3.6056
5	A,F	3.1623
6	A,G	4.1231
7	B,C	1.4142
8	B,D	1.4142
9	B,E	2.2361
10	B,F	2.0000
11	B,G	3.0000
12	C,D	2.0000
13	C,E	2.2361
14	C,F	1.4142
15	C,G	2.2361
16	D,E	1.0000
17	D,F	1.4142
18	D,G	2.2361
19	E,F	1.0000
20	E,G	1.4142
21	F,G	1.0000

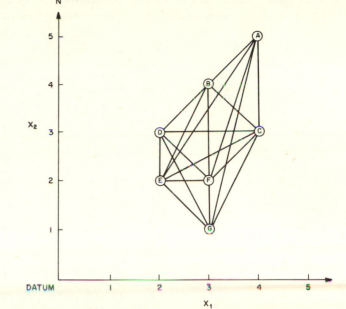

Fig. 3. $\Delta_{I,J}$ representations for locations A through G from Table 1 and Fig. 2.

weighted averages of the ξ_i values for each of the 35 combinations, are given in column 5 of Table 3. If the three endscrapers are first considered to be in locations A, B, and C (see Fig. 2), then the four carinated scrapers are, necessarily, in locations D, E, F, and G, and δ is the weighted within-class average of all $\Delta_{I,J}$'s associated with each scraper type where the weight of each scraper type is its proportion of all artifacts (i.e. 3/7 for endscrapers and 4/7 for carinated scrapers). The calculations for this combination follow. For endscrapers A, B, and C, $\Delta_{A,B} = 1.4142$, $\Delta_{A,C} = 2.0000$, $\Delta_{B,C} = 1.4142$, the sum of the $\Delta_{I,J}$ values = 4.8284, and $\xi_E = 4.8284/3 = 1.6095$. For carinated scrapers D, E, F, and G, $\Delta_{D,E} = 1.0000$, $\Delta_{D,F} = 1.4142$, $\Delta_{D,G} = 2.2361$, $\Delta_{E,F} = 1.0000$, $\Delta_{E,G} = 1.4142$, $\Delta_{F,G} = 1.0000$, the sum of the $\Delta_{I,J}$ values = 8.0645, and $\xi_C = 8.0645/6 = 1.3441$. Thus, $\delta = (3/7)(1.6095) + (4/7)(1.3441) = 1.4578$. Notice that the two clusterings (A, B, C; D, E, F, G) are quite tight (see Fig. 2) and the low δ value of 1.4578 represents this tight clustering.

Now assume that the three endscrapers are in locations A, B, and D and the four carinated scrapers are in locations C, E, F, and G. Then, for endscrapers A, B, and D, $\Delta_{A,B} = 1.4142$, $\Delta_{A,D} = 2.8284$, $\Delta_{B,D} = 1.4142$, the sum of the $\Delta_{I,J}$ values = 5.6568, and $\xi_E = 5.6568/3 = 1.8856$. For carinated scrapers C, E, F, and G, $\Delta_{C,E} = 2.2361$, $\Delta_{C,F} = 1.4142$, $\Delta_{C,G} = 2.2361$, $\Delta_{E,F} = 1.0000$, $\Delta_{E,G} = 1.4142$, $\Delta_{F,G} = 1.0000$, the sum of the $\Delta_{I,J}$ values = 9.3006, and $\xi_C =$

9.3006/6 = 1.5501. Thus, $\delta = (3/7)(1.8856) + (4/7)(1.5501) = 1.6939$.

Repeating these calculations $M = 35$ times (i.e. all possible three–four partitions) results in the sampling distribution of the 35 possible values of δ (each δ having endscrapers associated with a distinct combination of three locations and carinated scrapers associated with a distinct combination of four locations). If each of these M (35) possible combinations is given a fixed probability of occurrence of $1/M$ (1/35), i.e. the null hypothesis, and the associated values of δ are ordered from low to high (see Table 4), then the probability of a particular combination, or one more extreme, is the number of combinations having δ values equal to or less than the observed combination, divided by M. If the observed partition of scrapers is tightly clustered and tending toward separateness, with endscrapers lying in a portion of the occupation floor different from where the carinated scrapers are found, then the δ for this partition will be small relative to the other δ values and will fall near the top of the ordered list in Table 4 or near the left tail of the discrete distribution of all M possible δ values (see Fig. 4). For example, if endscrapers = A, B, and C and carinated scrapers = D, E, F, and G, then $\delta = 1.4578$. On the other hand, if endscrapers = A, C, and E and carinated scrapers = B, D, F, and G, then the clustering is less and the separateness is almost non-existent (see Fig. 2) and $\delta = 2.1740$, which is considerably larger than $\delta = 1.4578$.

To carry the example through to completeness, consider that the three endscrapers were found in locations C, F, and G and the carinated scrapers were found in locations A, B, D, and E (see Fig. 2). Then, for endscrapers C, F, and G, $\Delta_{C,F} =$

Table 3. ξ *and* δ *values for all combinations of endscrapers and carinated scrapers*

Case number	Three–four combination	Mean (ξ) of first group (m)	Mean (ξ) of second group (m)	Mean (δ) of combination (m)
1	A,B,C; D,E,F,G	1.6095	1.3441	1.4578
2	A,B,D; C,E,F,G	1.8856	1.5501	1.6939
3	A,B,E; C,D,F,G	2.4186	1.7168	2.0176
4	A,B,F; C,D,E,G	2.1922	1.8537	1.9988
5	A,B,G; C,D,E,F	2.8458	1.5107	2.0829
6	A,C,D; B,E,F,G	2.2761	1.7750	1.9898
7	A,C,E; B,D,F,G	2.6139	1.8441	2.1740
8	A,C,F; B,D,E,G	2.1922	1.8834	2.0157
9	A,C,G; B,D,E,F	2.7864	1.5107	2.0575
10	A,D,E; B,C,F,G	2.4780	1.8441	2.1158
11	A,D,F; B,C,E,G	2.4683	2.0894	2.2518
12	A,D,G; B,C,E,F	3.0625	1.7168	2.2935
13	A,E,F; B,C,D,G	2.5893	2.0501	2.2812
14	A,E,G; B,C,D,F	3.0476	1.6095	2.2258
15	A,F,G; B,C,D,E	2.7618	1.7168	2.1646
16	B,C,D; A,E,F,G	1.6095	2.3842	2.0522
17	B,C,E; A,D,F,G	1.9621	2.4607	2.2470
18	B,C,F; A,D,E,G	1.6095	2.5346	2.1381
19	B,C,G; A,D,E,F	2.2168	2.1684	2.1891
20	B,D,E; A,C,F,G	1.5501	2.3226	1.9915
21	B,D,F; A,C,E,G	1.6095	2.6025	2.1769
22	B,D,G; A,C,E,F	2.2168	2.2364	2.2280
23	B,E,F; A,C,D,G	1.7454	2.5706	2.2169
24	B,E,G; A,C,D,F	2.2168	2.1365	2.1709
25	B,F,G; A,C,D,E	2.0000	2.2783	2.1591
26	C,D,E; A,B,F,G	1.7454	2.4499	2.1480
27	C,D,F; A,B,E,G	1.6095	2.6322	2.1939
28	C,D,G; A,B,E,F	2.1574	2.2364	2.2025
29	C,E,F; A,B,D,G	1.5501	2.5027	2.0944
30	C,E,G; A,B,D,F	1.9621	2.0389	2.0060
31	C,F,G; A,B,D,E	1.5501	2.0831	1.8547
32	D,E,F; A,B,C,G	1.1381	2.3646	1.8389
33	D,E,G; A,B,C,F	1.5501	1.9008	1.7505
34	D,F,G; A,B,C,E	1.5501	2.1510	1.8935
35	E,F,G; A,B,C,D	1.1381	1.8452	1.5421

1.4142, $\Delta_{C,G} = 2.2361$, $\Delta_{F,G} = 1.0000$, the sum of the $\Delta_{I,J}$ values = 4.6503, and $\xi_E = 4.6503/3 = 1.5501$ (see Tables 2 and 3). For carinated scrapers A, B, D, and E, $\Delta_{A,B} = 1.4142$, $\Delta_{A,D} = 2.8284$, $\Delta_{A,E} = 3.6056$, $\Delta_{B,D} = 1.4142$, $\Delta_{B,E} = 2.2361$, $\Delta_{D,E} = 1.0000$, the sum of the $\Delta_{I,J}$ values = 12.4985, and $\xi_C = 12.4985/6 = 2.0831$ (see Tables 2 and 3). Thus, $\delta = (3/7)(1.5501) + (4/7)(2.0831) = 1.8547$ (see

Table 3). Turning to Table 4, the value of $\delta = 1.8547$ is the sixth value in the ordered list of 35 δ values; therefore, the probability of a clustering this close or closer is 6/35 = 0.1714. Figure 4 displays the ordered δ values from Table 4 graphically and the observed δ value of 1.8547 is the sixth value from the left.

It is clearly impractical to calculate a probability value

Fig. 4. Discrete frequency distribution of δ for three–four combinations of endscrapers and carinated scrapers.

Table 4. *Ordered values of δ for endscrapers and carinated scrapers*

Order	Combination	Mean (δ) (m)
1	A,B,C; D,E,F,G	1,4578
2	E,F,G; A,B,C,D	1.5421
3	A,B,D; C,E,F,G	1.6939
4	D,E,G; A,B,C,F	1.7505
5	D,E,F; A,B,C,G	1.8389
6	C,F,G; A,B,D,E	1.8547
7	D,F,G; A,B,C,E	1.8935
8	A,C,D; B,E,F,G	1.9898
9	B,D,E; A,C,F,G	1.9915
10	A,B,F; C,D,E,G	1.9988
11	C,E,G; A,B,D,F	2.0060
12	A,C,F; B,D,E,G	2.0157
13	A,B,E; C,D,F,G	2.0176
14	B,C,D; A,E,F,G	2.0522
15	A,C,G; B,D,E,F	2.0575
16	A,B,G; C,D,E,F	2.0829
17	C,E,F; A,B,D,G	2.0944
18	A,D,E; B,C,F,G	2.1158
19	B,C,F; A,D,E,G	2.1381
20	C,D,E; A,B,F,G	2.1480
21	B,F,G; A,C,D,E	2.1591
22	A,F,G; B,C,D,E	2.1646
23	B,E,G; A,C,D,F	2.1709
24	A,C,E; B,D,F,G	2.1740
25	B,D,F; A,C,E,G	2.1769
26	B,C,G; A,D,E,F	2.1891
27	C,D,F; A,B,E,G	2.1939
28	C,D,G; A,B,E,F	2.2025
29	B,E,F; A,C,D,G	2.2169
30	A,E,G; B,C,D,F	2.2258
31	B,D,G; A,C,E,F	2.2280
32	B,C,E; A,D,F,G	2.2470
33	A,D,F; B,C,E,G	2.2518
34	A,E,F; B,C,D,G	2.2812
35	A,D,G; B,C,E,F	2.2935

(p) in this manner whenever M is large, e.g. for $N = 20$ and $n_E = n_C = 10$ the number of values of $\Delta_{I,J}$, $\binom{20}{2}$, is 190 and the number of values of δ, M, is 184 756. Since the sampling distribution of all possible values of δ is very often highly skewed in a negative direction (see Fig. 4), a reasonable approximation to the discrete sampling distribution of δ is given by the continuous Pearson type III distribution. The area under the Pearson type III distribution between the observed value of T (i.e. the standardized value of δ) and $-\infty$ yields the required probability value (p). To determine this area, four values are necessary: the mean of the sampling distribution of δ (μ_δ), the variance of the sampling distribution

of δ (σ_δ^2), the skewness of the sampling distribution of δ (γ_δ), and the value of δ based on the observed distribution of artifacts (see equations (4), (5), (6), and (7)). Given these four values, an appropriate approximation of the sampling distribution of δ based on the Pearson type III distribution can be determined and the probability value (p) can be obtained by numerically integrating from $-\infty$ to the observed value of T (Mielke *et al.* 1981a).

For these data, $\delta = 1.8547$, $\mu_\delta = 2.0547$, $\sigma_\delta^2 = 0.0396$, and $\gamma_\delta = -1.3523$. Thus, $T = (\delta - \mu_\delta)/\sigma_\delta = -1.0048$ and integration (Simpson's rule) yields $p = 0.1454$ which compares favorably with the exact value (0.1714) given that only 35 points are available in the discrete distribution. If an appropriate correction for continuity is utilized or if M is large, the results are nearly identical. In the following analyses, the data are such that M is always extremely large and the approximate solution is used throughout. Complete computational techniques for obtaining μ_δ, σ_δ^2, and γ_δ for an observed set of data are described in the appendix to this chapter.

Differences in location are detected by the MRPP when the observed δ value is less than the expected δ value (μ_δ) and the associated probability value (p) is small. However, a small value of p may arise from essentially two types of location differences: separation and/or concentration. The ξ_i values provide the vehicle for interpreting the type of location difference encountered for a specific set of data. A location difference can be attributed to *separation* when p is small and all values of ξ_i are similar in magnitude and are less than μ_δ, i.e. all artifact classes are clustered to about the same degree and the difference is the result of the artifact-class clusters being separated in the site space (see Fig. 5a). In contrast, a location difference is attributed to differential *concentration* when p is small, the ξ_i values differ in magnitude, and one or more values of ξ_i are greater than μ_δ, i.e. the degree of clustering of the artifact classes is great relative to their separation in the site space (see Fig. 5b). In the event that the small p value results from a combination of separation and concentration, an examination of the plotted data will indicate the nature of the difference encountered (see Fig. 5c).

To illustrate the types of location differences, look again at Fig. 2. Consider first that the endscrapers are in locations A, B, and C and the carinated scrapers are in locations D, E, F, and G. In this case, $\xi_E = 1.6095$ and $\xi_C = 1.3441$ (see Table 3) are roughly equivalent in magnitude and are both less than $\mu_\delta = 2.0547$. The MRPP are detecting the differential locations (i.e. separation) of endscrapers and carinated scrapers which, as can be seen from Fig. 2, appear in different site spaces, possess about the same degree of concentration (1.6095 and 1.3441), and are similar to the representation in Fig. 5a. Consider now that the endscrapers are in locations A, E, and G and the carinated scrapers are in locations B, C, D, and F (see Fig. 2). In this case, $\xi_E = 3.0476$ and $\xi_C = 1.6095$ (see Table 3) are different in magnitude and, with $\mu_\delta = 2.0547$, one ξ_i value is less than μ_δ (1.6095) and the other is greater than μ_δ (3.0476). The MRPP are detecting the differential concentrations of endscrapers and carinated scrapers which, as can be seen from Fig. 2, are roughly in the same site location but possess differential concentrations (similar to the representation in Fig. 5*b*).

Now consider the extended example above where the endscrapers are in locations C, F, and G and the carinated scrapers are in locations A, B, D, and E (see Fig. 2). In this case, $\xi_E = 1.5501$ and $\xi_C = 2.0831$ (see Table 3) are different in magnitude and, with $\mu_\delta = 2.0547$, one ξ_i value is less than μ_δ (1.5501) and the other is greater than μ_δ (2.0831). The MRPP are detecting both the differential concentrations of endscrapers and carinated scrapers (see Fig. 2) as well as their separation within the site space (see Fig. 5*c*).

Thus, the values of ξ_i and of μ_δ provide the basis for interpreting the type of location difference observed and indicate whether the location difference is the result of separation, differential concentration, or a combination of the two. This type of analysis is treated in more detail in a later section.

Example MRPP analyses

Recent work at two Old World sites provides excellent data for illustrating applications of the MRPP to archaeological analysis. The first site is Sde Divshon, an Upper Palaeolithic site on the Divshon plain in the Central Negev, Israel (Marks 1971; Dacey 1973; Ferring 1976). This 800 m² site (see Fig. 6, site D27B) is an undisturbed surface scatter of lithic artifacts. Artifact locations in 225 m² of this site have been mapped, the locations of endscrapers, burins, and carinated scrapers for over 63 m² of the site have been published by Marks (1971) and Dacey (1973). These data are utilized here to illustrate the application of the MRPP (see also Berry *et al.* 1980). The second site is Rosh Ein Mor (see Fig. 6, site D15), an immensely rich Middle Palaeolithic site lying less than 2 km southwest of Sde Divshon. Rosh Ein Mor is an open-air Mousterian site in the western part of the Divshon plain (Marks 1971; Marks and Crew 1972; Crew 1976; Hietala and Stevens 1977). The extent of the site is estimated at 1200 m² of which 45 m² in the center portion were excavated: horizontal units of 1 m × 1 m were dug in 5 cm ground-contour levels.

Table 5. *Sde Divshon data analysis*

Artifact	n_i	ξ_i (m)
Endscrapers	118	3.9072
Carinated scrapers	27	3.8322
Burins	81	3.9121

Because of small artifact class frequencies in the 1 m × 1 m units, 12 1 m × 3 m units were judiciously constructed, eliminating 9 of the original units to preserve a rectangular format (Hietala and Stevens 1977). Another procedure collapsed the 45 1 m × 1 m units through levels. It is these data, reported by Hietala and Stevens (1977, p. 546), which are utilized here to illustrate the MRPP.

Example 1

The mapped portion of Sde Divshon (Marks 1971, pp. 1241–3; Dacey 1973, p. 322) contains a total of $N = 226$ artifacts belonging to three artifact classes: endscrapers, carinated scrapers, and burins. The 63 m² mapped area is of a living floor and each artifact has been placed within a 1 m × 1 m grid overlay (Dacey 1973, p. 322). Considering all three artifact classes simultaneously, the MRPP (see Table 5) yield $\mu_\delta = 4.0365$, $\gamma_\delta = -1.3729$, $T = -8.6641$, with $p = 7.9536 \times 10^{-6}$, i.e. the probability ($p$) of observing by chance alone a distribution of endscrapers, carinated scrapers, and burins this unusual or more unusual. The probability value indicates marked locational differences among the three artifact classes within the site. Since all three values of ξ_i (see Table 5) are roughly equal in magnitude and all are less than μ_δ (4.0365), this indicates that the location difference observed results principally from the spatial separation of the endscrapers, carinated scrapers, and burins within the excavated area.

It should be noted that these calculations yield numerical results which differ from those in Berry *et al.* (1980). The MRPP have undergone a series of refinements since their

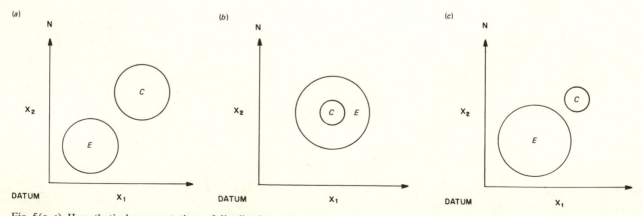

Fig. 5(*a–c*). Hypothetical representations of distributions of endscrapers (*E*) and carinated scrapers (*C*).

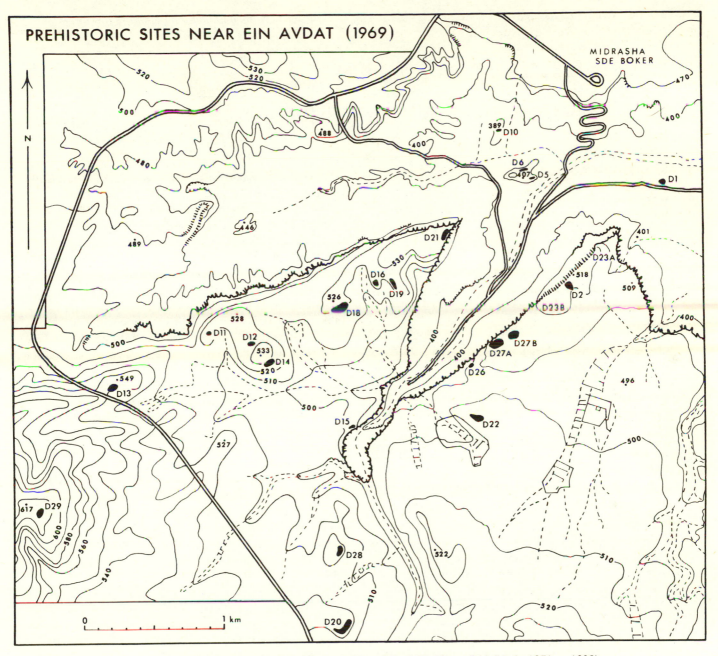

Fig. 6. Map of prehistoric sites with Sde Divshon designated as D27B and Rosh Ein Mor as D15 (Marks 1971, p. 1238).

inception, including a compensatory mechanism for unequal artifact class sizes which was not available for the earlier analysis. Although identical results are obtained when artifact class sizes are exactly equal, the current MRPP are far more efficient in discriminating locational differences when unequal artifact class sizes are encountered. It is this latter approach which is utilized for all analyses in this chapter.

Given that there are appreciable intrasite location differences among endscrapers, carinated scrapers, and burins, a pair-by-pair analysis might yield further information about the nature of this difference. A comparison of only endscrapers and carinated scrapers yields $\mu_\delta = 4.0068$, $\gamma_\delta = -1.8341$, $T = -6.7048$, with $p = 3.3403 \times 10^{-4}$, indicating

a marked intrasite location difference (separation) between endscrapers and carinated scrapers (note that the two ξ_i values from Table 5 are both less than μ_δ). A comparison of endscrapers and burins yields $\mu_\delta = 4.0043$, $\gamma_\delta = -2.0001$, $T = -7.5489$, with $p = 1.9095 \times 10^{-4}$, indicating a substantial intrasite location difference (separation) between endscrapers and burins. Similarly, a comparison of carinated scrapers and burins yields $\mu_\delta = 3.9633$, $\gamma_\delta = -2.0448$, $T = -3.0018$, with $p = 0.0186$, indicating an intrasite location difference (separation) between carinated scrapers and burins. Thus, the pair-by-pair analyses confirm that the three types of artifacts occupy distinctly different site locations within the excavated area.

Table 6. *Artifact classes and frequencies from Rosh Ein Mor*

Artifact	n
Endscrapers	170
Sidescrapers	141
Burins	228
Levallois flakes	971
Levallois blades	645
Levallois points	698
Notches	401
Denticulates	180
Borers	28
Bone	97

Table 7. *Rosh Ein Mor data analysis*

Artifact	n_i	ξ_i (m)
(Two-dimensional analysis)		
Burins	29	5.0643
Endscrapers	28	5.1474
Sidescrapers	32	4.2391
Denticulates	28	4.7312
(Three-dimensional analysis)		
Borers	28	20.0776
Bone	97	9.5998

Table 8. *Non-commensurate ξ_i values for borers and bone from Rosh Ein Mor*

Artifact	n_i	ξ_i (m)
Borers	28	6.2272
Bone	97	1.9463

Example 2

The Rosh Ein Mor site is an extremely rich site with tens of thousands of artifacts, thus requiring non-visual procedures for the detection of spatial patterns. Hietala and Stevens (1977, p. 546) report on a portion of the excavated area containing 3559 artifacts belonging to 10 artifact classes. The classes and their sizes are reported in Table 6. The three illustrations which follow draw upon selected portions of the data in various combinations.

The first illustration considers data on burins, endscrapers, sidescrapers, and denticulates drawn from level 4, the first undisturbed level. The $36 \, \text{m}^2$ non-contiguous site area is of an occupation floor and each artifact has been placed within a $1 \, \text{m} \times 3 \, \text{m}$ grid structure (Hietala and Stevens 1977, pp. 545–6). Considering all four artifact classes, the MRPP yield $\mu_\delta = 4.6979$, $\gamma_\delta = -1.4326$, $T = 0.5130$, with $p = 0.6346$. One of the four ξ_i values in Table 7 is less than μ_δ and three are greater. The obtained probability value indicates no locational differences (separation of concentration) among burins, endscrapers, sidescrapers, and denticulates in level 4. Incidentally, examination of the six possible pair-by-pair comparisons of the four artifact classes yields similar results,

with probability values ranging from $p = 0.2867$ (burins and denticulates) to $p = 0.7718$ (burins and sidescrapers).

The second illustration considers data drawn from borers and bone over all six reported levels (4 through 9), permitting a three-dimensional analysis: the two horizontal coordinates plus the level in which the artifact was discovered. The comparison of borers and bone yields $\mu_\delta = 13.2195$, $\gamma_\delta = -2.3218$, $T = -14.7170$, with $p = 5.5332 \times 10^{-7}$, indicating, since the ξ_i values straddle the value of μ_δ (see Table 7), a marked locational difference (concentration) between borers and bone in the excavated site area.

Now, an MRPP analysis of this type entails an additional consideration: the three axes (dimensions) must be approximately commensurate. Both the surface axes are reported in meters ($3 \, \text{m} \times 13 \, \text{m}$) while the six levels are 5 cm ground-contour levels, for a total reported excavation depth of 1 m. The vertical dimension was made commensurate in this analysis with the two surface (horizontal) axes. The reason that the measurements associated with the axes must be made commensurate is to insure proper weighting among the various dimensions. Failure properly to weight the dimensions may mean that the effect of one dimension may be obscured by another. To illustrate, re-analysis of the same data *without* the commensurate adjustment yields $\mu_\delta = 3.3918$, $\gamma_\delta = -1.9911$, $T = -26.9192$, with $p = 4.2756 \times 10^{-13}$ (ξ_i values are reported in Table 8). This p value, compared with the commensurate-adjusted p of 5.5332×10^{-7} reported above, indicates that the horizontal (surface) dimensions may be exerting a stronger influence on the magnitude of the probability value than the vertical dimension (levels). That is, since the commensurate-adjusted probability value is markedly different, the horizontal dimensions with their larger scales must be suppressing the relative contribution of the vertical scale.

A third illustration considers these points in more detail. Given that a substantial location difference (concentration) between borers and bone was found in the three-dimensional analysis, it follows that further analyses might clarify the nature of the difference. There are two modes of data-dredging that should be considered: first, whenever there are more than two artifact classes, various combinations of classes should be examined in order to determine which combinations are contributing to the difference; this procedure is analogous to a multiple-means test *a posteriori* following a conventional one-way analysis of variance, such as a Scheffé test, and was

Table 9. *Borers and bone from Rosh Ein Mor collapsed over levels*

Artifact	n_i	ξ_i (m)
Borers	28	5.3667
Bone	97	1.3251

Table 10. *Borers and bone from Rosh Ein Mor collapsed over horizontal (surface) dimensions*

Artifact	n_i	ξ_i (m)
Borers	28	2.0159
Bone	97	1.0009

utilized above in the pair-by-pair comparisons of burins, endscrapers, and carinated scrapers from Sde Divshon. Because only two classes of objects are considered here (borers and bone), this mode does not apply. Secondly, whenever there is more than a single dimension, various combinations of dimensions (or single dimensions) should be examined in order to isolate the meaningful dimension(s). In this analysis there are three dimensions: two on the surface (horizontal dimensions) and one consisting of levels (the vertical dimension). It might be that the vertical dimension is making the entire contribution to the locational difference and the horizontal dimensions are making none. That is, it is possible that successive encampments over time where borers and bone (or, borers or bone) were discarded is the key to their locational difference. For example, if only borers (no bone) were found in levels 4, 5, and 6 and only bone (no borers) was found in levels 7, 8, and 9 and, in addition, all the borers and bone from all levels had the same identical horizontal placements, then the vertical dimension would be making the entire contribution and the horizontal dimensions would be making none.

On the other hand, it might be that the horizontal dimensions are making the entire contribution to the locational difference and the vertical dimension is making none. For example, if the borers and bone had non-overlapping horizontal placements at each level, and each and every level had the same identical horizontal placements of borers and bone, then the horizontal dimensions would be making the entire contribution and the vertical dimension would be making none.

Finally, it might be that *both* the horizontal and vertical dimensions are contributing to the locational difference. Analyzing the horizontal and vertical dimensions separately will reveal the nature and extent of each contribution. Looking first at the two horizontal dimensions collapsed over the vertical levels, the analysis of borers and bone yields $\mu_\delta = 2.6522$, $\gamma_\delta = -2.1556$, $T = -22.1070$, with $p = 2.3498 \times 10^{-10}$, indicating a definitive locational difference (concentration) between borers and bone in the horizontal dimensions (ξ_i values are given in Table 9). Turning attention to the vertical dimension and ignoring the effects of the horizontal dimensions, the analysis of borers and bone yields $\mu_\delta = 1.3419$, $\gamma_\delta = -2.2827$, $T = -11.0885$, with $p = 1.2690 \times 10^{-5}$, indicating a marked locational difference (concentration) between borers and bone in the vertical dimension (ξ_i values are given in Table 10). Note here that *both* the

horizontal and vertical dimensions are contributing to the substantial difference in location (concentration) between borers and bone, the horizontal dimensions somewhat more than the vertical dimension. Note also that this result confirms the previously mentioned suspicions concerning the commensurate adjustment of the vertical levels, i.e. in the absence of a commensurate adjustment the contribution of the vertical scale measurements (5 cm) was being suppressed by the larger horizontal scale measurements (1 m) and the horizontal axes were exerting a stronger influence on the magnitude of the probability value ($p = 2.3498 \times 10^{-10}$) than the vertical axis ($p = 1.2690 \times 10^{-5}$). For comparison, the previously stated probability value for both the horizontal and vertical axes was $p = 5.5332 \times 10^{-7}$.

Location/dispersion estimation techniques

The inference techniques presented thus far constitute the principal statistical methods for analyzing intrasite spatial relations among artifact classes; that is, the MRPP provide a means for the assessment of similarities or differences between the distributions of two or more artifact classes in a one-, two-, or three-dimensional site space. Of additional importance is the investigation of why similarities and/or differences between artifact class distributions within a site have occurred. In particular, and as noted in previous sections, dissimilar artifactual distributions can be attributed to (1) differences in separation where artifact classes are spatially segregated within the site, (2) differences in concentration where the artifact classes are overlapping but the spatial dispersions of two or more classes are unequal, or (3) differences in both separation and concentration (see Fig. 5a–c).

As an aid to the analysis of such patterning, three location and dispersion (separation and concentration) estimators are defined which allow the representation of intrasite artifactual data in a descriptive manner: first, a measure of intrasite location for each artifact class; secondly, a measure of intrasite locational differences (separation) between all distinct pairs of artifact classes; and thirdly, intrasite dispersion (concentration) measures of artifacts about the measure of intrasite location for each artifact class.

The first estimator is the r-dimensional median, λ_i, of the i-th artifact class. In particular, λ_i of the i-th artifact class is that point in the r-dimensional site space ($r = 1, 2,$ or 3) around which the sum of all Δ_{I,λ_i} distances is minimized ($I = 1, \ldots, n_i$). For example, in a two-dimensional site space such as an occupation floor, Δ_{I,λ_i} for the i-th artifact class is defined as

$$\Delta_{I,\lambda_i} = [(X_{1I} - \lambda_{1i})^2 + (X_{2I} - \lambda_{2i})^2]^{\frac{1}{2}}, \qquad (8)$$

where λ_i is $(\lambda_{1i}, \lambda_{2i})$ and λ_{1i} and λ_{2i} are the two-dimensional coordinates of the median for the i-th artifact class. In practice, the estimation of the r-dimensional median of the i-th artifact class, λ_i, is obtained by an iterative procedure utilizing the r-dimensional mean as the initial estimate. The iterative procedure is continued until all coordinate differences between subsequent iterations are less, in absolute value, than some preselected minimum, say 10^{-8}. Detailed procedures for obtaining λ_i values are contained in the appendix to this chapter.

Secondly, in order to identify locational separation or, alternatively, proximities between the i-th and j-th artifact classes, the distance between all pairs of artifact-class medians may be calculated. For example, the distance between any two medians, λ_i and λ_j, in a two-dimensional space is given by

$$\Delta_{\lambda_i,\lambda_j} = [(\lambda_{1i} - \lambda_{1j})^2 + (\lambda_{2i} - \lambda_{2j})^2]^{\frac{1}{2}}, \qquad (9)$$

which is simply the distance across the occupation floor between the median of the i-th artifact class and the median of the j-th artifact class and has a structure identical to the definition of $\Delta_{I,J}$ given above in equation (1).

Thirdly, having determined λ_i for each artifact class as well as the intermedian distances between pairs of medians, $\Delta_{\lambda_i,\lambda_j}$, it is convenient also to have measures of the concentration of each artifact class about its median. Given λ_i, $\bar{\Delta}(\lambda_i)$ is a measure of the concentration of artifacts about λ_i in the i-th artifact class. In particular, $\bar{\Delta}(\lambda_i)$ is the average Δ_{I,λ_i} distance the artifacts lie from λ_i. It is important not to confuse $\bar{\Delta}(\lambda_i)$ and ξ_i. The latter is the mean of the $\Delta_{I,J}$ distances within an artifact class while the former is the mean within-class distance of every artifact from the median location, λ_i, of that class. In addition it is helpful to describe various quantiles: the q-th quantile for the i-th artifact class is simply that minimum distance, D_q, from λ_i such that at least $100q$ % of all artifact locations are contained within the r-dimensional hypersphere having the prescribed radius D_q. For example, in a two-dimensional space such as an occupation floor, $D_{0.25}$ is the length of the radius of a circle with λ_i at the center, such that 25% of artifact locations in the i-th artifact class are contained within the circle. Suggested values of q are 0.25, 0.50, 0.75, and 0.90; in addition, it is recommended that the distance between λ_i and the most distant artifact location (the maximum) be given to indicate the total range of values.

Consider Fig. 7 which is a hypothetical distribution of 20 artifacts on a 5 m × 5 m occupation floor. The point (*) in the center is λ_i (3, 3); $D_{0.25}$ is 0.50 m and is indicated by the innermost circle and encloses 25% (i.e. 5 of 20) of the artifact locations, which are represented by dots. $D_{0.50}$ is 0.75 m and is indicated by the second circle from the center and it encloses 50% (i.e. 10 of 20) of the artifact locations. The third circle (dashed line) is $\bar{\Delta}(\lambda_i)$ and indicates the average distance to

Table 11. *Dispersion/concentration measures for the data represented in Fig. 7*

Dispersion measure	Artifact location (m)
Average	1.000
$D_{0.25}$	0.500
$D_{0.50}$	0.750
$D_{0.75}$	1.250
$D_{0.90}$	2.000
Maximum	2.500

each of the 20 artifact locations from λ_i. Successive circles represent $D_{0.75}$, $D_{0.90}$, and the maximum distance. Table 11 summarizes the various distance measures for Fig. 7.

The three quantified distance measures (medians, intermedian distances, and quantiles) are useful and important adjuncts to the data-dredging procedures detailed in the previous section. They provide coefficients of the magnitude of locational differences between and within artifact classes. These three coefficients complement the ξ_i, μ_δ, and p values given by the MRPP and, together, permit a comprehensive analysis of artifact locations. Most importantly, the three coefficients permit the assessment of separation, concentration, or a combination of the two without constructing full plots. Three hypothetical examples based on the data in Table 1 and Fig. 2 follow.

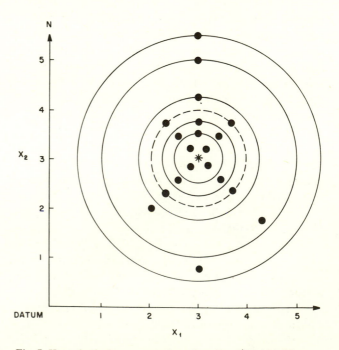

Fig. 7. Hypothetical representation of median (*) and 0.25, 0.50, 0.75, 0.90, and maximum quantiles about the median in a two-dimensional space.

Table 12. *Dispersion/concentration measures for endscrapers (A, B, C) and carinated scrapers (D, E, F, G) from Table 1, Fig. 2, and Fig. 8*

Dispersion measure	Artifact class	
	Endscrapers (m)	Carinated scrapers (m)
Average	0.9107	0.8090
$D_{0.25}$	0.4227	0.5000
$D_{0.50}$	1.1547	0.5000
$D_{0.75}$	1.1547	1.1180
$D_{0.90}$	1.1547	1.1180
Maximum	1.1547	1.1180

Table 13. *Dispersion/concentration measures for endscrapers (A, E, G) and carinated scrapers (B, C, D, F) from Table 1, Fig. 2, and Fig. 9*

Dispersion measure	Artifact class	
	Endscrapers (m)	Carinated scrapers (m)
Average	1.6553	1.0000
$D_{0.25}$	0.3799	1.0000
$D_{0.50}$	1.1854	1.0000
$D_{0.75}$	1.1854	1.0000
$D_{0.90}$	3.4005	1.0000
Maximum	3.4005	1.0000

First, consider that the endscrapers are in locations A, B, and C and the carinated scrapers are in locations D, E, F, and G (see Fig. 2). In this case, $\lambda_E = (3.4227, 4.0000)$, where the abscissa ($X_1$ axis) is given first, and $\lambda_C = (2.5000, 2.0000)$. The two medians ($\lambda_E$ and λ_C) are displayed graphically by asterisks in Fig. 8. The intermedian distance between endscrapers and carinated scrapers ($\Delta_{\lambda_E, \lambda_C}$), which is designated simply as Δ in the following discussion, is displayed by a dashed line drawn between the two medians and is $\Delta = [(3.4227 - 2.5000)^2 + (4.0000 - 2.0000)^2]^{\frac{1}{2}}$, which is equal to 2.2026 m. The dispersion/concentration quantiles are given in Table 12 and, for purposes of visual assessment, the average distances, $\bar{\Delta}(\lambda_E)$ and $\bar{\Delta}(\lambda_C)$, are drawn in Fig. 8 as circles about the median values; the radii of the circles are equal to the average distances in Table 12. It is clear from an

inspection of Fig. 8 that the median values are widely *separated*, that both groups possess similar *concentrations*, and that, on average, any difference is the result of location within the site space rather than differential concentration. This is the same conclusion reached utilizing the ξ_l and μ_δ values in the previous section.

For the second example, imagine that the endscrapers are in locations A, E, and G and the carinated scrapers are in locations B, C, D, and F (see Fig. 2). In this case, $\lambda_E = (2.3798, 2.0103)$ and $\lambda_C = (3.0000, 3.0000)$. The two medians are displayed graphically by asterisks in Fig. 9. The intermedian distance between endscrapers and carinated scrapers (Δ) is displayed by a dashed line and is equal to 1.1680 m. The dispersion/concentration quantiles are given in Table 13 and the average distances about the medians (from

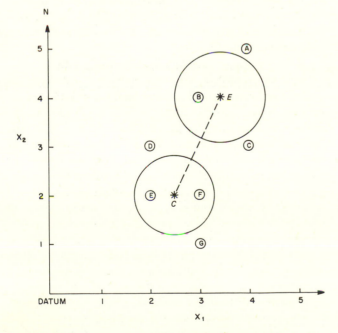

Fig. 8. Graphic representation of medians (*), intermedian distance, and average distances for endscrapers, *E* (A, B, C), and carinated scrapers, *C* (D, E, F, G), from Table 1 and Fig. 2.

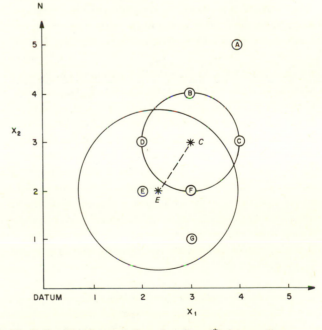

Fig. 9. Graphic representation of medians (*), intermedian distance, and average distances for endscrapers, *E* (A, E, G), and carinated scrapers, *C* (B, C, D, F), from Table 1 and Fig. 2.

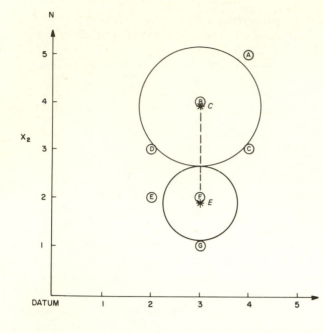

Fig. 10. Graphic representation of medians (*), intermedian distance, and average distances for endscrapers, E (C, F, G), and carinated scrapers, C (A, B, D, E), from Table 1 and Fig. 2.

Table 14. *Dispersion/concentration measures for endscrapers (C, F, G) and carinated scrapers (A, B, D, E) from Table 1, Fig. 2, and Fig. 10*

Dispersion measure	Artifact class	
	Endscrapers (m)	Carinated scrapers (m)
Average	0.8047	1.2661
$D_{0.25}$	0.0000	0.0028
$D_{0.50}$	0.9999	1.4115
$D_{0.75}$	0.9999	1.4169
$D_{0.90}$	1.4142	2.2332
Maximum	1.4142	2.2332

Table 13) are drawn as circles in Fig. 9. Inspection of Table 13 and Fig. 9 reveals that the median values are not widely *separated*, that the two artifact classes possess dissimilar *concentrations*, and that, on the average, any difference results from differential concentration rather than from spatial separation within the site space. Again, this is the same conclusion reached utilizing the ξ_i and μ_δ values in the previous section.

For the third example, imagine that the endscrapers are in locations C, F, and G and the carinated scrapers are in locations A, B, D, and E (see Fig. 2). In this case, $\lambda_E = (3.0000, 1.9999)$ and $\lambda_C = (2.9987, 3.9975)$. The two medians are displayed graphically by asterisks in Fig. 10. The intermedian distance between endscrapers and carinated scrapers (Δ) is displayed by a dashed line and is equal to 1.9975 m. The dispersion/concentration quantiles are given in Table 14 and the average distances about the medians (from Table 14) are drawn as circles in Fig. 10. Inspection of Table 14 and Fig. 10 reveals that the median values are widely *separated*, that the two artifact classes possess dissimilar *concentrations*, and that, on the average, any difference is caused by *both* separation and differential concentration. Again, this is the same conclusion reached by utilizing the ξ_i and μ_δ values and visual inspection of the site plot in the previous section.

Example location/dispersion analyses

The descriptive utility of the three location/dispersion estimators, λ_i, $\bar{\Delta}(\lambda_i)$, and $\Delta_{\lambda_i, \lambda_j}$, for intrasite spatial analysis are more fully illustrated below with three archaeological examples drawn from the Sde Divshon and Rosh Ein Mor data.

Example 1

Returning to the Sde Divshon data analyzed above, it was determined that there were marked locational differences among burins, endscrapers, and carinated scrapers within the site. Calculation of the medians, the interclass distances between paired medians, and the intraclass dispersion measures of artifact locations, permits a visual assessment of the intrasite locational differences among burins, endscrapers, and carinated scrapers.

Sde Divshon (Marks 1971), it will be recalled, is a two-dimensional 63 m² site of rectangular configuration (7 m × 9 m). The location/dispersion analysis reveals that endscrapers have a two-dimensional median $\lambda_E = (2.9445, 6.0533)$, carinated scrapers have a median $\lambda_C = (5.3147, 6.1236)$, and burins a median $\lambda_B = (4.0000, 4.9999)$. Clearly, the three artifact classes differ considerably in terms of median location (separation). Figure 11 illustrates the distributions of the three artifact classes within the site where the medians are represented by asterisks.

To confirm this separation, the interclass distances between paired medians are considered (see the dashed lines in Fig. 11). Between endscrapers and burins $\Delta = 1.4911$ m, between endscrapers and carinated scrapers $\Delta = 2.3712$ m, and between carinated scrapers and burins $\Delta = 1.7294$ (see Fig. 11). It should be noted at this point that the probability values of the MRPP do not depend on these intermedian distances, but rather utilize the distances between all possible pairs of artifact locations. This is important since it is erroneous to assume that larger $\Delta_{\lambda_i, \lambda_j}$ values will yield smaller probability values. Compare the following: between endscrapers and carinated scrapers $\Delta = 2.3712$ m and $p = 3.3403 \times 10^{-4}$, between endscrapers and burins $\Delta = 1.4911$ m and $p = 1.9095 \times 10^{-4}$, and between carinated scrapers and burins $\Delta = 1.7294$ m and $p = 0.0186$.

Turning attention to the concentration of artifact locations about their artifact-class medians, the six realized dispersion measures are presented in Table 15, with average distances plotted as circles in Fig. 11. Although the three artifact classes differ very little in their average dispersion, the

Table 15. *Dispersion/concentration measures of endscrapers, carinated scrapers, and burins from Sde Divshon*

| | Artifact class | | |
	Endscrapers (m)	Carinated scrapers (m)	Burins (m)
Dispersion measure			
Average	2.8251	2.7118	2.8343
$D_{0.25}$	1.9475	1.6899	2.2361
$D_{0.50}$	2.8279	2.4750	3.0000
$D_{0.75}$	3.6230	3.1626	3.6056
$D_{0.90}$	4.4956	4.4547	4.1231
Maximum	6.8251	6.1023	4.4721

Table 16. *Interclass distances between burins, endscrapers, sidescrapers, and denticulates from Rosh Ein Mor, level 4*

Artifact classes	Distance (m)
Burins and endscrapers	2.0493
Burins and sidescrapers	0.0000
Burins and denticulates	0.0106
Endscrapers and sidescrapers	2.0493
Endscrapers and denticulates	2.0388
Sidescrapers and denticulates	0.0016

quantiles in Table 15 reveal three interesting facts: first, most of the carinated scrapers are heavily concentrated about their median, relative to the endscrapers and burins, with a small percentage scattered some distance away, i.e. 25% of the carinated scrapers lie within 1.6899 m from λ_C, while 25% of the endscrapers and 25% of the burins lie 1.9475 m and 2.2361 m from λ_E and λ_B, respectively. Secondly, the burins have a light concentration in the close vicinity of their median, but have, overall, a tighter concentration of locations than the carinated scrapers and the endscrapers (indicated by their

maximum values: 4.4721 m versus 6.1023 m and 6.8251 m). Thirdly, the endscrapers occupy a middle position between the other two classes, having greater concentration in close to the median than the burins, but less than the carinated scrapers. A point worth emphasizing is that the quantiles in Table 15 obviously yield far more information regarding a dispersion/ concentration pattern than can be obtained with a single dispersion measure such as $\bar{\Delta}(\lambda_i)$.

Example 2

Two sets of artifactual data from the Rosh Ein Mor site were utilized in a previous section to illustrate the MRPP. Analysis of the first data set revealed that there were no locational differences of consequence between burins, endscrapers, sidescrapers, and denticulates. Attention is now focused on calculating the intraclass medians of these four artifact classes, the interclass distances between the intraclass medians, and the intraclass dispersion/concentration measures of artifact locations.

The four artifact classes are drawn only from level 4 of the Rosh Ein Mor excavation, thus a two-dimensional 39 m^2 site of rectangular configuration (3 m × 13 m) is considered, with a 3 m × 1 m unreported rectangle dividing the level into two equal (3 m × 6 m) sections (see Fig. 12). Burins have a median $\lambda_B = (3.0000, 5.9999)$, endscrapers have a median $\lambda_E = (3.0927, 8.0472)$, sidescrapers a median $\lambda_S = (3.0000, 6.0000)$, and denticulates a median $\lambda_D = (2.9999, 6.0106)$. It is clear that the median locations of burins, sidescrapers, and denticulates are essentially identical and that the median location of endscrapers differs by only about 2 m from the other three artifact classes (see Fig. 12).

The interclass distances between paired medians confirm the analysis above of the individual medians. As indicated in Table 16, the class of endscrapers is the only artifact class which differs substantially in any manner from the other three artifact classes. The dispersion/concentration measures for the four artifact classes are presented in Table 17. Sidescrapers and denticulates have very similar distributions over level 4, while endscrapers have both the highest average distance and the lowest 0.90 quantile. This suggests that the overall distribution

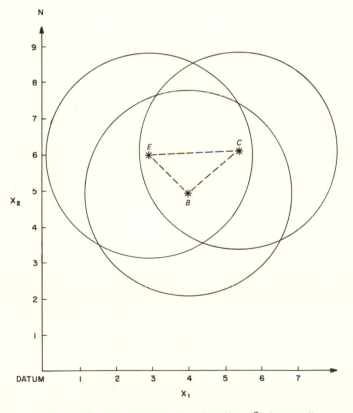

Fig. 11. Graphic representation of medians (*), intermedian distances, and average distances for endscrapers (*E*), carinated scrapers (*C*), and burins (*B*) from Sde Divshon.

Table 17. *Dispersion/concentration measures for burins, endscrapers, sidescrapers, and denticulates from Rosh Ein Mor, level* 4

Dispersion measure	Artifact class			
	Burins (m)	Endscrapers (m)	Sidescrapers (m)	Denticulates (m)
Average	3.8765	4.0310	3.1921	2.9981
$D_{0.25}$	2.9999	2.2377	0.9999	1.0000
$D_{0.50}$	3.1623	5.0352	3.1623	3.0106
$D_{0.75}$	4.1231	5.1281	3.9999	4.1129
$D_{0.90}$	7.0710	5.1642	7.0711	6.9894
Maximum	7.0710	5.1642	7.0711	7.0606

of endscrapers is more tightly concentrated than the other three classes, but that they are sparsely distributed near their middle area. Burins possess a distribution similar in size to the sidescrapers and the denticulates except that they also have a sparsely distributed middle area like the endscrapers.

Example 3

The MRPP analysis of borers and bone from Rosh Ein Mor indicated a marked locational difference (concentration) between these archaeological classes. In this case a three-dimensional site is considered, identical to that described in the last illustration, but now with the addition of six 5 cm vertical levels (4 through 9). Borers have a three-dimensional median location of $\lambda_B = (2.9942, 11.2293, 6.8805)$, with the vertical dimension listed last; while bone has a three-dimensional median location of $\lambda_O = (3.1627, 12.9539, 8.3712)$. It is immediately apparent that the differences in median location between borers and bone occur, first, in the vertical dimension, where the distance is 1.6 levels (the median value for borers lying between levels 6 and 7 (6.8805) and the median value for bone lying between levels 8 and 9 (8.3712)) and, secondly, along one axis of the horizontal dimensions (X_2), where the distance is 1.7 m. The interclass distance, Δ, between the two median locations is 2.2858 m,

reflecting a combination of both the horizontal and vertical distances.

The dispersion measures for the borers and the bone are presented in Table 18. Disregarding the maximum distance, the bone is much more concentrated than the borers; this is clear from a comparison of the average distance estimators and/or any quantile. For example, on average the bones lie only 1.3732 m from their median, while borers lie 4.7713 m from their median, i.e. 3.47 times as much dispersion for borers compared with bone. Furthermore, 25% of all the bones lie less than a meter away (0.9171 m) from their median, while 25% of all the borers lie more than two meters away (2.2186 m). To taken an extreme case, 75% of all the bones lie within 1.3226 m of their median, while 75% of all borers lie within 8.2899 m of their median. Clearly, it is this overwhelming disparity in concentration which is contributing to the MRPP finding of a locational difference (concentration) between borers and bone. Note, the intermedian distance is only 2.2858 m which is considerably less than the difference between the two averages ($4.7713 - 1.3732 = 3.3981$ m) meaning that the average sphere with radius = 4.7713 m drawn about the median value of borers will completely envelop the average sphere with radius = 1.3732 m drawn about the median value of bone. Put another way, on average, bones lie within the

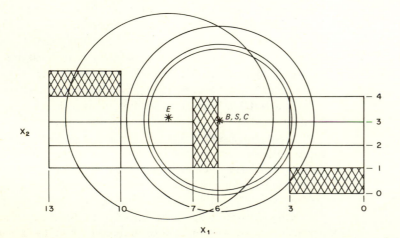

Fig. 12. Graphical representation of medians (*) and average distances for burins (*B*), endscrapers (*E*), sidescrapers (*S*), and denticulates (*D*) from Rosh Ein Mor, level 4.

Table 18. *Dispersion/concentration measures for borers and bone from Rosh Ein Mor (levels 4–9)*

Dispersion measure	Artifact class	
	Borers (m)	Bone (m)
Average	4.7713	1.3732
$D_{0.25}$	2.2186	0.9171
$D_{0.50}$	2.9393	1.0481
$D_{0.75}$	8.2899	1.3226
$D_{0.90}$	8.4414	2.6413
Maximum	8.7767	9.9959

Table 19. *Comparison of the MRPP with and without re-randomization*

Statistic	MRPP without re-randomization	MRPP with re-randomization
μ_δ	4.0365	4.0365
ξ_E	3.9072	3.9072
ξ_C	3.8322	3.8322
ξ_B	3.9121	3.9121
σ_δ^2	2.4842×10^{-4}	2.4842×10^{-4}
γ_δ	-1.3729	-1.3864
T	-8.6641	-8.6641
p	7.9536×10^{-6}	8.4397×10^{-6}

sphere occupied by borers – any real difference is clearly the result of differential concentration.

Analysis of large assemblages

It is often important to perform intrasite spatial analyses on very large assemblages. Whenever analyses involve large numbers of artifacts (e.g. $N > 300$), a computational problem arises in the calculation of the skewness term γ_δ. In general, the MRPP buy freedom from distributional assumptions with increased computational effort. Specifically, the problem is that the numerical calculation of γ_δ requires in excess of $\binom{N}{3}$ conceptual steps and quickly becomes prohibitive in computational cost and time as N becomes large. If F represents the number of conceptual steps, then when $N = 41$, $F > 10\,000$; when $N = 86$, $F > 100\,000$; when $N = 183$, $F > 1\,000\,000$; and when $N = 393$, $F > 10\,000\,000$. However, the problem is solvable and an efficacious solution is discussed in this section such that very large assemblages (up to roughly $N = 10\,000$) can be efficiently analyzed.

Unlike γ_δ, the exact values of the mean, μ_δ, and the variance, σ_δ^2, can be obtained from very large complete assemblages without great cost because they require only a fixed multiple of $\binom{N}{2}$ conceptual steps. As a consequence, the calculation for very large assemblages is accomplished in two steps. First, the exact values of μ_δ and σ_δ^2 are obtained from the entire assemblage of artifacts. Secondly, γ_δ is estimated from one or more samples randomly drawn from the entire assemblage (i.e. re-randomization).

To accomplish the first step, a limited set of calculations is performed on the complete assemblage, yielding μ_δ and σ_δ^2 for the entire set of artifacts; computational formulas for μ_δ and σ_δ^2 remain as defined above in equations (5) and (6). The second step is more involved, requiring both sampling and additional computations which are essential in obtaining an efficient unbiased estimator of γ_δ ($\bar{\gamma}$). To obtain $\bar{\gamma}$ for the complete assemblage, one or more independent random samples are drawn without replacement from the entire assemblage (artifact classes are ignored) and the estimates of γ_δ are calculated for each random sample in a manner

analogous to the previous computation for the exact result in equation (7). The individual estimators for each random sample are both unbiased and extremely efficient estimators of γ_δ because of well-known optimal properties of U-statistics (Hoeffding 1948; Nandi and Sen 1963). If $\hat{\gamma}_j$ is the j-th of n estimates of γ_δ, then $\bar{\gamma}$ is defined by

$$\bar{\gamma} = n^{-1} \sum_{j=1}^{n} \hat{\gamma}_j. \tag{10}$$

A convenient measure of the precision of $\bar{\gamma}$, when n is at least 2, is the estimated standard error of $\bar{\gamma}$ given by

$$\hat{\sigma}_{\bar{\gamma}} = \left[(n^2 - n)^{-1} \sum_{i=1}^{n} (\hat{\gamma}_i - \bar{\gamma})^2 \right]^{\frac{1}{2}}. \tag{11}$$

Complete procedures for obtaining $\bar{\gamma}$ are given in the appendix to this chapter.

On the basis of empirical work with this large-assemblage re-randomization procedure, it is recommended that each replication be about size 50. Large samples, while yielding greater precision, increase computation time at an enormous rate. In addition, replicates which are somewhat smaller than size 50 appear to have poor precision. Moreover, the number of replicates of size 50 is recommended to be between 10 and 25; this approach will yield satisfactory results for most applications.

Example large assemblage analysis

To illustrate the application of the MRPP with large assemblages, the Sde Divshon data is re-analyzed. While this data set is clearly not a 'large assemblage' with $N = 226$, it does provide an opportunity to illustrate the large-assemblage re-randomization procedure by comparing it with the previously described MRPP applied to the same data set.

It will be recalled that the mapped portion of Sde Divshon discussed previously contained a total of $N = 226$ artifacts belonging to three artifact classes: endscrapers, carinated scrapers, and burins. Table 19 lists the relevant data from both sets of calculations. Note that the μ_δ, ξ_i, σ_δ^2, and T values are identical, as they should be. With 10 subsamples of size 50 each, drawn without replacement from the original 226 artifacts, the estimated value of γ_δ ($\bar{\gamma}$) is $= -1.3864$, with an estimated standard error ($\hat{\sigma}_{\bar{\gamma}}$) of 0.0683. Note that the large-assemblage re-randomization skewness value of -1.3864 compares favorably with the MRPP skewness value of -1.3729 and that the estimated standard error value, 0.0683, is very small. The re-randomization probability value of $p = 8.4397 \times 10^{-6}$ is essentially the same as the original MRPP probability value of $p = 7.9536 \times 10^{-6}$.

MRPP and classical inference techniques

Although based upon apparently different principles, the MRPP nevertheless possess interesting relationships with several well-known classical inference techniques. This section briefly describes the nature of the relationships between the MRPP and several of the better-known parametric and non-parametric tests.

In order to relate the MRPP to existing inference techniques (in the present notational context), it is first necessary to introduce a more general version of the distance measure $\Delta_{I,J}$. When previously defined in an earlier section, $\Delta_{I,J}$ was presented in a two-dimensional format as

$$\Delta_{I,J} = [(X_{1I} - X_{1J})^2 + (X_{2I} - X_{2J})^2]^{\frac{1}{2}}, \qquad (12)$$

which is simply the ordinary Euclidean distance in any two-dimensional space. Rewritten, in a two-dimensional space, with a summation,

$$\Delta_{I,J} = \left[\sum_{k=1}^{2} (X_{kI} - X_{kJ})^2 \right]^{\frac{1}{2}}, \qquad (13)$$

and in an r-dimensional space,

$$\Delta_{I,J} = \left[\sum_{k=1}^{r} (X_{kI} - X_{kJ})^2 \right]^{\frac{1}{2}}. \qquad (14)$$

If it is desired to vary the measure of distance, then a still more general version of $\Delta_{I,J}$ may be defined. Specifically, let

$$\Delta_{I,J} = \left[\sum_{k=1}^{r} (X_{kI} - X_{kJ})^2 \right]^{v/2}, \qquad (15)$$

where $v > 0$. This generalization obviously includes the previously defined $\Delta_{I,J}$ when $v = 1$. Also, the $\Delta_{I,J}$ corresponding to $v = 2$ involves the traditional least-squares type statistics which are associated with some of the most commonly applied test statistics at this time.

The MRPP yield very efficient inference techniques in their ability to discriminate between locational differences in artifact classes. The efficient discrimination characteristics of the MRPP are consistent with the fact that special cases of the MRPP are coincident with well-known parametric and non-parametric techniques which provide optimum efficiency under prescribed conditions. For example, suppose that N artifacts are exhaustively divided between two or more classes, that $r = 1$, and that $v = 2$ (i.e. a squared Euclidean distance, $\Delta_{I,J}$, is utilized over a single dimension such as meters north

of a site datum). Then the resulting univariate version of the MRPP corresponds to the permutational analog of the presently popular two-sample t test (with two classes) and one-way ANOVA (with two or more classes) class of tests. It should be emphasized that this version of the MRPP remains appropriate when assumptions (such as normality) essential to inferences based on common tables for the t and ANOVA tests are not met, i.e. if the assumptions are violated, then inferences based on the MRPP remain valid whereas inferences based on routinely used tables for the t and ANOVA tests are not valid. As a consequence, this version of the MRPP maintains all of the advantages, without the disadvantages of the classical t and ANOVA tests, except, of course, an increased computational effort. Furthermore, the choice of $v = 1$ (which has been employed in all the foregoing analyses) has no parametric counterparts; however, by its inherent construction, it also is an efficient inference technique and, in addition, possesses the intuitive appeal of being based on Euclidean distances and thereby operating within the framework of a metric space. The well-known statistical techniques based on $v = 2$ (t and ANOVA) are, of course, *not* within the framework of a metric space and involve a complicated non-metric space in which the triangle inequality is not satisfied. The next paragraph indicates some of the advantages of $v = 1$ over $v = 2$ in the context of *non-parametric* inferences.

If N artifacts are exhaustively partitioned among two or more classes and, as above, $v = 2$ and $r = 1$, and the univariate artifact measurements are replaced by ranks (i.e. a squared Euclidean distance, $\Delta_{I,J}$, is utilized over a single dimension such as number of levels below the site surface), then the resultant univariate non-parametric version of the MRPP is equivalent to the two-sample Mann Whitney–Wilcoxon (with two classes) and Kruskal–Wallis (with two or more classes) tests. In contrast, if N artifacts are exhaustively partitioned among two or more classes, $r = 1$, the univariate artifact measurements are replaced by ranks, but $v = 1$, then the resultant univariate non-parametric version of the MRPP is substantially superior to the version with $v = 2$ for detecting location shifts associated with either a double-exponential or a U-shaped distribution (Mielke *et al.* 1981*b*). Even when logistic and normal distributions are considered, the version of the MRPP with $v = 2$ yields only a slight improvement over the version with $v = 1$. A point worth mentioning is that none of the known types of non-parametric tests coincides with the present univariate non-parametric versions of the MRPP indexed by $v > 0$, with the obvious exception of $v = 2$.

Summary

The methodology of spatial analysis is in need of new and suitable statistical techniques possessing assumptions which can be met and enjoying properties which adhere to the nature of the archaeological data base. The multi-response permutation procedures (MRPP) introduced here provide such an approach. The MRPP offer a comprehensive means for detecting differences in the spatial distributions of artifact classes within a site. Location and dispersion estimates provide needed insight into the nature of the difference (i.e. separation, concentration, or a combination thereof). Moreover, the MRPP eliminate several problems current in intrasite spatial analysis. Namely, (1) the MRPP require no distributional assumptions such as normality and homogeneity of variance, (2) the MRPP utilize all locational information in the data, (3) the MRPP permit analyses of count-per-grid or point-plot data in one-, two-, or three-dimensional archaeological space, (4) the MRPP tolerate any grid shape and/or site shape, including non-contiguous site structures, and (5) the MRPP define their own site area based on the proveniences of the artifact classes under consideration, eliminating a common problem in other statistical approaches caused by zero-count grids and/or areas with an absence of artifacts of a particular class.

In a problem-oriented approach, the MRPP can be employed to test specific hypotheses concerning differences in the spatial distributions of artifact classes specified *a priori*. As a data-dredging technique, entire site assemblages can be analyzed and, when differences are found, comparisons of selected combinations of artifact classes may be analyzed to determine those making a substantial contribution to the observed difference. Similar analyses of each spatial dimension, or combinations of dimensions, can isolate those dimensions contributing to the difference.

Although the impetus which stimulated the development of the MRPP was simply the need to be able to make inferences which do not require the invocation of distributional assumptions which may be totally unfounded, it is abundantly apparent that the MRPP are general inference techniques and, consequently, possess a broad spectrum of potential applications. Although, as noted above, special cases of the MRPP are equivalent to several commonly employed statistical techniques (e.g. Mann Whitney–Wilcoxon, Kruskal–Wallis, two-sample *t*, and one-way ANOVA tests), the extent of potential applications of the MRPP to intrasite spatial analysis in particular, and to archaeology in general, is virtually unlimited.

APPENDIX

Let $\Omega = \{\omega_1, \ldots, \omega_N\}$ designate a finite assemblage of N artifacts (a finite population) from within a site; let $x'_I = [x_{1I}, \ldots, x_{rI}]$ denote the transposed column vector, x_I, of r commensurate coordinate measurements for artifact ω_I ($I = 1, \ldots, N$); let $S_1, \ldots, S_{g+1}$ represent an exhaustive partitioning of the N artifacts comprising Ω into g well-defined disjoint artifact classes plus an additional disjoint subset, S_{g+1}, consisting of unclassified artifacts (S_{g+1} may be a null subset); let n_i ($i = 1, \ldots, g$) be the number of artifacts in the i-th artifact class; and let

$$n_{g+1} = N - \sum_{i=1}^{g} n_i$$

be the number of artifacts which are unclassified and therefore not assigned to any of the g artifact classes. Also, let $\Delta_{I,J}$ be a distance measure between ω_I and ω_J. The form of $\Delta_{I,J}$ is presently limited to

$$\Delta_{I,J} = \left[\sum_{k=1}^{r} (x_{kI} - x_{kJ})^2 \right]^{v/2},$$

where $v > 0$ and x_{kI} is the k-th coordinate measurement of artifact ω_I. If $v = 1$, then $\Delta_{I,J}$ is the Euclidean distance between artifacts ω_I and ω_J. Then the test statistic of interest is defined as

$$\delta = \sum_{i=1}^{g} C_i \xi_i,$$

where

$$\xi_i = \binom{n_i}{2}^{-1} \sum_{I < J} \Delta_{I,J} I_{S_i}(\omega_I) I_{S_i}(\omega_J)$$

is the average of the distance measures between artifacts of the i-th class ($i = 1, \ldots, g$), $\sum_{I<J}$ is the sum over all I and J such that $1 \leqslant I < J \leqslant N$; $I_{S_i}(\omega_I)$ is an indicator function and is unity if ω_I belongs to artifact class S_i and is zero otherwise for $I = 1, \ldots, N$; $n_i \geqslant 2$ is the number of (classified) artifacts in artifact class S_i ($i = 1, \ldots, g$); $C_i = n_i/K$ is the proportional size contribution of S_i; $K = \sum_{i=1}^{g} n_i$; and $n_{g+1} = N - K$ is the number of remaining (unclassified) artifacts in artifact class S_{g+1}. Thus defined, δ is the weighted within-class average of the Euclidean distances between all possible pairs of artifacts in the same artifact class. Weights other than $C_i = n_i/K$ have been considered (O'Reilly and Mielke 1980; Mielke *et al.* 1981*a*). The only restriction placed on the weights is that $\sum_{i=1}^{g} C_i = 1$ and $C_i > 0$ for $i = 1, \ldots, g$.

Utilizing δ, consider H_0: the artifact classes *a priori* $S_1, \ldots, S_g$ correspond to a random distribution of the artifacts $\{\omega_1, \ldots, \omega_N\}$ to the classified artifact classes with a given size structure $(n_1, \ldots, n_g)$ versus H_1: the artifact classes correspond to a non-random distribution of the N artifacts to the g artifact classes. The one-sided lower-tail probability value (p) corresponding to a realized value of δ,

$$p = P[\delta \leqslant \text{realized value of } \delta \,|\, H_0],$$

provides a measure of the effectiveness of the classification *a priori* of artifacts. Procedures for obtaining values of p for real data are given in the subsequent discussion.

The permutation distribution of δ under H_0 implies that each of the

$$M = N! \Big/ \left(\prod_{i=1}^{g+1} n_i! \right)$$

possible allocation combinations of the N artifacts to the $g+1$ classes will occur with equal probability. With the permutation distribution of δ under H_0 assumed, let μ_δ, σ_δ^2, and γ_δ represent the mean, variance, and skewness of δ, respectively.

If δ_j signifies the j-th value among the M possible values of δ, then

$$\mu_\delta = \frac{1}{M} \sum_{j=1}^{M} \delta_j,$$

$$\sigma_\delta^2 = \frac{1}{M} \sum_{j=1}^{M} (\delta_j - \mu_\delta)^2,$$

and

$$\gamma_\delta = (E[\delta^3] - 3\mu_\delta \sigma_\delta^2 - \mu_\delta^3)/\sigma_\delta^3,$$

where

$$E[\delta^3] = \frac{1}{M} \sum_{j=1}^{M} \delta_j^3.$$

The computing formulas for μ_δ, σ_δ^2, and γ_δ (Mielke 1979) are given by

$$\mu_\delta = D(1),$$

$$\sigma_\delta^2 = 2\{(g + L_1)K^{-2} - [N(N-1)]^{-1}\}[D(2) - 2D(2') + D(2'')] + 4(K^{-1} - N^{-1}) \times [D(2') - D(2'')],$$

and

$$\gamma_\delta = \kappa_3(\delta)/\sigma_\delta^3,$$

where $\kappa_3(\delta)$, the third cumulant of δ, is given by

$$\kappa_3(\delta) = E[\delta^3] - 3\mu_\delta \sigma_\delta^2 - \mu_\delta^3$$

and

$$
\begin{aligned}
E[\delta^3] = K^{-3}\{ & 4(L_1 + L_2)D(3) + 8(g - L_2)[3D(3') \\
& + D(3^*)] + 8(K - 3g - L_1 + 2L_2)[3D(3^{**}) \\
& + D(3^{***})] + 6[(K-2)(g + L_1) \\
& - 2(g - L_2)]D(3'') + 12[(K-6)(K - g - L_1) \\
& + 6(g - L_2)]D(3''') + [K^3 - 6K(2K - g - L_1) \\
& + 8(5K - 7g - 4L_1 + 3L_2)]D(3'''')\},
\end{aligned}
$$

with

$$L_1 = \sum_{i=1}^{g} (n_i - 1)^{-1}$$

and

$$L_2 = \sum_{i=1}^{g} (n_i - 1)^{-2}.$$

The symmetric function model parameters (Mielke $et\ al.$ 1976) which appear in the above expressions for μ_δ, σ_δ^2, and $E[\delta^3]$ are given by

$$D(1) = \frac{1}{N^{(2)}} \sum_{J_1,J_2} \Delta_{J_1,J_2},$$

$$D(2) = \frac{1}{N^{(2)}} \sum_{J_1,J_2} \Delta_{J_1,J_2}^2,$$

$$D(3) = \frac{1}{N^{(2)}} \sum_{J_1,J_2} \Delta_{J_1,J_2}^3,$$

$$D(2') = \frac{1}{N^{(3)}} \sum_{J_1,J_2,J_3} \Delta_{J_1,J_2} \Delta_{J_1,J_3},$$

$$D(2'') = \frac{1}{N^{(4)}} \sum_{J_1,J_2,J_3,J_4} \Delta_{J_1,J_2} \Delta_{J_3,J_4},$$

$$D(3') = \frac{1}{N^{(3)}} \sum_{J_1,J_2,J_3} \Delta_{J_1,J_2}^2 \Delta_{J_1,J_3},$$

$$D(3'') = \frac{1}{N^{(4)}} \sum_{J_1,J_2,J_3,J_4} \Delta_{J_1,J_2}^2 \Delta_{J_3,J_4},$$

$$D(3''') = \frac{1}{N^{(5)}} \sum_{J_1,J_2,J_3,J_4,J_5} \Delta_{J_1,J_2} \Delta_{J_1,J_3} \Delta_{J_4,J_5},$$

$$D(3'''') = \frac{1}{N^{(6)}} \sum_{J_1,J_2,J_3,J_4,J_5,J_6} \Delta_{J_1,J_2} \Delta_{J_3,J_4} \Delta_{J_5,J_6},$$

$$D(3^*) = \frac{1}{N^{(3)}} \sum_{J_1,J_2,J_3} \Delta_{J_1,J_2} \Delta_{J_1,J_3} \Delta_{J_2,J_3},$$

$$D(3^{**}) = \frac{1}{N^{(4)}} \sum_{J_1,J_2,J_3,J_4} \Delta_{J_1,J_2} \Delta_{J_1,J_3} \Delta_{J_2,J_4},$$

and

$$D(3^{***}) = \frac{1}{N^{(4)}} \sum_{J_1,J_2,J_3,J_4} \Delta_{J_1,J_2} \Delta_{J_1,J_3} \Delta_{J_1,J_4},$$

where J_1, J_2, J_3, J_4, J_5, and J_6 denote distinct integers from 1 through N and $N^{(k)} = N!/(N-k)!$. Efficient computational techniques for obtaining the above symmetric function model parameters (which are finite population U-statistics) for a realized set of data are described in the appendix of Mielke $et\ al.$ (1976). Incidentally, asymptotic distributional properties of δ (i.e. as $N \to \infty$) are described elsewhere (Mielke 1979; O'Reilly and Mielke 1980).

Because the calculation of p, based on obtaining all M possible values of δ, is not computationally feasible even with relatively small artifact classes, an approximation of the underlying permutation distribution of δ is requisite. To obtain the approximate value of p, consider the distribution of the standardized test statistic given by

$$T = (\delta - \mu_\delta)/\sigma_\delta,$$

where T is approximately distributed as the Pearson type III distribution. In particular, the Pearson type III distribution compensates for the fact that the underlying permutation distribution of δ is often very skewed in the negative direction (i.e. $\gamma_\delta < 0$). The probability value (p) for a realized value of δ (say δ_0) is given by

$$p = P[\delta \leqslant \delta_0] \doteq \int_{-\infty}^{T_0} f(y)\,dy,$$

where

$$
f(y) = \frac{(-2/\gamma_\delta)^{4/\gamma_\delta^2}}{\Gamma(4/\gamma_\delta^2)} [-(2 + y\gamma_\delta)/\gamma_\delta]^{(4-\gamma_\delta^2)/\gamma_\delta^2} \\
\times e^{-2(2+y\gamma_\delta)/\gamma_\delta^2},
$$

$-\infty < y < -2/\gamma_\delta$, and $T_0 = (\delta_0 - \mu_\delta)/\sigma_\delta$. The value of p based on the Pearson type III distribution is evaluated with Simpson's rule over the interval $(T_0 - C, T_0)$ where $C > 0$ and is given by

$$p \doteq \frac{C}{6H}\left[f(T_0 - C) + f(T_0) + 4\sum_{j=1}^{H} f\left(T_0 - C\right.\right.$$

$$\left.\left. + \frac{(2j-1)C}{2H}\right) + 2\sum_{j=1}^{H-1} f\left(T_0 - C + \frac{jC}{H}\right)\right],$$

where H is an integer ≥ 2. In this chapter all calculations are based on $C = 9$ and $H = 250$.

An alternative procedure for determining p is to employ tabulated quantile values of the Pearson type III distribution (Harter 1969). The only entries required for obtaining interpolated values of p with these tables are the quantities T and γ_δ. An obvious drawback to interpolated values of p involves cases which exceed the limits of a finite table. For this reason, all p values reported in this chapter are based on the previously described technique which utilizes the Pearson type III distribution and Simpson's rule.

Whenever analyses involve large numbers of artifacts (e.g. $N > 300$), a computational problem arises in the calculation of the skewness term γ_δ. Specifically, the problem is that the numerical calculation of γ_δ requires in excess of $\binom{N}{3}$ conceptual steps and quickly becomes prohibitive in computational cost and time as N becomes large. Unlike γ_δ, the exact values of the mean, μ_δ, and the variance, σ_δ^2, can be obtained for very large complete assemblages without great cost because they require only a fixed multiple of $\binom{N}{2}$ conceptual steps. As a consequence, the calculations for large assemblages are accomplished in two parts. First, the exact values of μ_δ and σ_δ^2 are obtained from the entire assemblage of artifacts. Secondly, γ_δ is estimated from one or more samples randomly drawn from the complete assemblage (i.e. re-randomization).

To accomplish the first part, a limited set of calculations are performed on the entire assemblage, yielding μ_δ and σ_δ^2 for the complete set of artifacts. The computational formulas for μ_δ and σ_δ^2 have been previously defined in equations (5) and (6). However, the second part is more involved, requiring both sampling and additional computations which are essential in obtaining an efficient unbiased estimator of

$$\kappa_3(\delta) = E[\delta^3] - 3\mu_\delta\sigma_\delta^2 - \mu_\delta^3,$$

which is a linear combination of the finite population U-statistics, i.e. $D(3), \ldots, D(3'''')$. The previously stated expression for $E[\delta^3]$ is also a linear combination of these finite population U-statistics. The two remaining terms, $\mu_\delta\sigma_\delta^2$ and μ_δ^3, expressed as linear combinations of the finite population U-statistics are given by

$$\mu_\delta\sigma_\delta^2 = \frac{a_1}{[N^{(2)}]^2}[2N^{(2)}D(3) + 4N^{(3)}D(3') + N^{(4)}D(3'')]$$

$$- \frac{2a_1 - a_2}{N^{(2)}N^{(3)}}[4N^{(3)}D(3') + 2N^{(3)}D(3*)$$

$$+ 4N^{(4)}D(3**) + 2N^{(4)}D(3***) + N^{(5)}D(3''')]$$

$$+ \frac{a_1 - a_2}{N^{(2)}N^{(4)}}[4N^{(4)}D(3'') + 8N^{(4)}D(3**)$$

$$+ 8N^{(5)}D(3''') + N^{(6)}D(3'''')]$$

and

$$\mu_\delta^3 = \frac{1}{[N^{(2)}]^3}\{4N^{(2)}D(3) + 8N^{(3)}[3D(3') + D(3*)]$$

$$+ 8N^{(4)}[3D(3**) + D(3***)] + 6N^{(4)}D(3'')$$

$$+ 12N^{(5)}D(3''') + N^{(6)}D(3'''')\},$$

where $a_1 = 2\{(g + L_1)K^{-2} - [N(N-1)]^{-1}\}$, $a_2 = 4(K^{-1} - N^{-1})$, $K = \sum_{i=1}^{g} n_i$, $L_1 = \sum_{i=1}^{g}(n_i - 1)^{-1}$, and $N^{(k)} = N!/(N-k)!$.

Let $\hat{\kappa}_{3,j}(\delta)$ be the j-th of n estimates (say $n = 10$) of $\kappa_3(\delta)$ where the finite population U-statistics are estimated by corresponding sample U-statistics based on a without-replacement simple random sample of a specified size (say 50). If $\hat{\gamma}_j = [\hat{\kappa}_{3,j}(\delta)]/\sigma_\delta^3$ for $j = 1, \ldots, n$, then the unbiased estimator of γ_δ is given by

$$\bar{\gamma} = n^{-1}\sum_{j=1}^{n} \hat{\gamma}_j.$$

Providing $n \geq 2$, an estimated standard error of $\bar{\gamma}$ is given by

$$\hat{\sigma}_{\bar{\gamma}} = \left[(n^2 - n)^{-1}\sum_{j=1}^{n}(\hat{\gamma}_j - \bar{\gamma})^2\right]^{\frac{1}{2}}.$$

In particular, $\bar{\gamma}$ is an extremely efficient estimator of γ_δ because of well-known properties of U-statistics (Hoeffding 1948; Nandi and Sen 1963).

Although the inference techniques presented thus far constitute the principal statistical method for analyzing intrasite spatial relations among artifact classes, it is nevertheless important also to have a related method for presenting these relations in a more descriptive manner. As an aid to representing intrasite artifactual data in a descriptive fashion, three intuitively defined location and dispersion estimators are considered: (1) a measure of intrasite location for each artifact class, (2) intrasite dispersion measures of artifacts within an artifact class, and (3) a measure of intrasite locational differences between all distinct pairs of artifact classes. These three quantified distance measures are useful and important adjuncts to the previously described inference procedures. They provide measures of locational differences between and within artifact classes. These measures complement the probability value given by the MRPP and jointly provide a comprehensive analysis of artifact locations.

The first estimator is the r-dimensional median, λ_i, of the i-th artifact class: $\lambda_i' = [\lambda_1, \ldots, \lambda_r]$, where λ_{k_i} is the coordinate of the k_i-th dimension, $k_i = 1, \ldots, r$ and $i = 1, \ldots, g$. (The appended subscript i in terms such as k_i is intended simply to associate various observations and parameters with the i-th artifact class.) In particular, λ_i is that point in the r-dimensional archaeological space which minimizes the average distance, $\bar{\Delta}$, of all n_i artifact locations in the i-th artifact class from λ_i; that is,

$$\bar{\Delta}(\lambda_i) = n_i^{-1} \sum_{j=1}^{n_i} \left[\sum_{k_i=1}^{r} (X_{kij} - \lambda_{k_i})^2 \right]^{\frac{1}{2}}, \quad i = 1, \ldots, g.$$

The estimation of the r-dimensional median of the i-th artifact class is obtained by an iterative procedure. The m-th iterative estimate of λ_i is denoted by $\lambda'_{i(m)} = [\lambda_{1(m)}, \ldots, \lambda_{r(m)}]$ where the k_i-th coordinate of the m-th iteration is given by

$$\lambda_{k_i(m)} = \frac{\sum_{j=1}^{n_i} X_{kij} \left[\sum_{h_i=1}^{r} (X_{h_i j} - \lambda_{h_i(m-1)})^2 \right]^{-(1/2)}}{\sum_{j=1}^{n_i} \left[\sum_{h_i=1}^{r} (X_{h_i j} - \lambda_{h_i(m-1)})^2 \right]^{-(1/2)}},$$

$$k_i = 1, \ldots, r.$$

A convenient initial estimate of λ_i is the r-dimensional mean; namely, $\lambda'_{i(0)} = [\bar{X}_1, \ldots, \bar{X}_r]$ with

$$\bar{X}_{k_i} = \frac{1}{n_i} \sum_{j=1}^{n_i} X_{kij}, \quad k_i = 1, \ldots, r.$$

The iterative procedure is continued until all coordinate differences between subsequent iterations are less, in absolute value, than some preselected minimum (say 10^{-8}).

For the purpose of identifying locational proximities between the i-th and j-th artifact classes, the Euclidean distance is calculated between all pairs of artifact-class medians, e.g. the distance between any two medians, say λ_i and λ_j, is given by

$$\Delta_{\lambda_i, \lambda_j} = \left[\sum_{k_i = k_j = 1}^{r} (\lambda_{k_i} - \lambda_{k_j})^2 \right]^{\frac{1}{2}}.$$

Having determined λ_i ($i = 1, \ldots, g$), the average Euclidean distance to each of the artifact locations from λ_i, $\bar{\Delta}(\lambda_i)$, is a measure of dispersion of the i-th artifact class. In addition, the q_i-th quantile distance is defined as that minimum distance, D_{q_i}, from λ_i such that at least $100q$ % of all artifact locations are contained within the r-dimensional hypersphere having the prescribed radius D_{q_i}. Suggested values of q_i are 0.25, 0.50, 0.75, and 0.90; in addition, it is recommended that the distance between λ_i and the most distant artifact location be given to indicate the total range of values.

Acknowledgements

This work has been supported by the Office of Atmospheric Resources Management, Bureau of Reclamation, United States Department of the Interior, Contract No. 8-07-83-V0009.

References

Berry, K. J., Kvamme, K. L. and Mielke, P. W. (1980). A permutation technique for the spatial analysis of the distribution of artifacts into classes. *American Antiquity* 45: 55–9.

Clarke, D. L. (1968). *Analytical Archaeology*. Methuen: London.

Clarke, D. L. (1977). *Spatial Archaeology*. Academic Press: New York.

Crew, H. L. (1976). The Mousterian site of Rosh Ein Mor. In *Prehistory and Paleoenvironments in the Central Negev, Israel*, ed. A. E. Marks, vol. I: *The Avdat/Agev Area*, pp. 75–112. Southern Methodist University Press: Dallas, Texas.

Dacey, M. F. (1973). Statistical tests of spatial association in the locations of tool types. *American Antiquity* 38: 320–8.

Duda, R. O. and Hart, P. E. (1973). *Pattern Classification and Scene Analysis*. Wiley: New York.

Ferring, C. R. (1976). Sde Divshon: an Upper Paleolithic site. In *Prehistory and Paleoenvironments in the Central Negev, Israel*, vol. I: *The Avdat/Agev Area*, ed. A. E. Marks, pp. 199–226. Southern Methodist University Press: Dallas, Texas.

Harter, H. L. (1969). A new table of percentage points of the Pearson type III distribution. *Technometrics* 11: 177–87.

Hietala, H. J. and Stevens, D. E. (1977). Spatial analysis: multiple procedures in pattern recognition studies. *American Antiquity* 42: 539–59.

Hodder, I. R. and Okell, E. (1978). An index for assessing the association between distributions of points in archaeology. In *Simulation Studies in Archaeology*, ed. I. R. Hodder, pp. 97–107. Cambridge University Press: Cambridge.

Hodder, I. R. and Orton, C. R. (1976). *Spatial Analysis in Archaeology*. Cambridge University Press: Cambridge.

Hoeffding, W. (1948). A class of statistics with asymptotically normal distribution. *Annals of Mathematical Statistics* 19: 293–325.

Marks, A. E. (1971). Settlement patterns and intrasite variability in the Central Negev, Israel. *American Anthropologist* 73: 1237–44.

Marks, A. E. and Crew, H. L. (1972). Rosh Ein Mor: an open-air Mousterian site in the Central Negev, Israel. *Current Anthropology* 13: 591–3.

Mielke, P. W. (1978). Clarification and appropriate inferences for Mantel and Valand's nonparametric multivariate technique. *Biometrics* 34: 277–82.

Mielke, P. W. (1979). On asymptotic non-normality of null distributions of MRPP statistics. *Communications in Statistics: Theory and Methods* A8: 1541–50.

Mielke, P. W., Berry, K. J. and Brier, G. W. (1981a). Application of multi-response permutation procedures for examining seasonal changes in monthly mean sea-level pressure patterns. *Monthly Weather Review* 109: 120–6.

Mielke, P. W., Berry, K. J., Brockwell, P. J. and Williams, J. S. (1981b). A class of nonparametric tests based on multi-response permutation procedures. *Biometrika* 68: 720–4.

Mielke, P. W., Berry, K. J. and Johnson, E. S. (1976). Multi-response permutation procedures for *a priori* classifications. *Communications in Statistics: Theory and Methods* A5: 1409–24.

Nandi, H. K. and Sen, P. K. (1963). On the Properties of U-statistics when the observations are not independent: part II, unbiased estimation of the parameters of a finite population. *Calcutta Statistical Association Bulletin* 12: 124–48.

O'Reilly, F. J. and Mielke, P. W. (1980). Asymptotic normality of MRPP statistics from invariance principles of U-statistics. *Communications in Statistics: Theory and Methods* A9: 629–37.

Rogers, A. (1974). *Statistical Analysis of Spatial Dispersion*. Pion: London.

Schiffer, M. B. (1976). *Behavioral Archeology*. Academic Press: New York.

Whallon, R. (1973). Spatial analysis of occupation floors. I. Application of dimensional analysis of variance. *American Antiquity* 38: 266–77.

Whallon, R. (1974). Spatial analysis of occupation floors. II. The application of nearest neighbor analysis. *American Antiquity* 39: 16–34.

Chapter 6

**Cell frequency recording and
analysis of artifact
distributions**
Ian Johnson

This paper discusses the use of small, high-resolution collection units for the recording and analysis of artifact distributions. It is argued that this form of data collection can often replace two-dimensional coordinate recording without appreciable loss of information. However, conventional quadrat analysis methods are generally unable to exploit the information content of high-resolution collection units. Methods of handling such data are therefore proposed and illustrated by application to the Upper Magdalenian site of Pincevent near Paris.

The work described here was stimulated by an attempt at quantitative spatial analysis of artifact distributions at the site of Les Tarterets in northern France (Hesse 1971) and by time spent on open-area excavations in France and Germany. Hesse's analysis was an experimental application of the quadrat frequency correlation method also discussed by Whallon (1973b) and applied by him to the site of Guila Naquitz, Oaxaca Valley, Mexico. Hesse found that the correlation of quadrat frequencies for Les Tarterets gave inconsistent results, quite at variance with one another and with his subjective assessment of the obvious patterning present. He suggested that these inconsistencies arose from the inclusion of part-empty quadrats and he tested a correction factor which gave only marginal improvements. Other contributing factors are probably the highly skewed distribution of quadrat frequencies and the effect of imposing an arbitrary grid of quadrats on the artifact concentrations present. The implications for Whallon's detailed activity interpretation of Guila Naquitz are obvious, and other objections to his procedures have been raised by Riley (1974) and Hietala and Stevens (1977).

My first experiments with spatial analysis were based on data extracted from the published site plans for Les Tarterets (Brézillon 1971), a total of some 1100 artifacts divided into four categories (blocks of unretouched stone, stone tools, blades and cores) and distributed over an area of $140 \, \text{m}^2$. My initial approach was based on coordinate data, as it was apparent, not only from the few archaeological applications of quadrat methods but from the much longer established studies in statistical ecology, that the problems associated with the use of quadrats were far from being resolved. I soon realised, however, that archaeological data were not going to lend themselves conveniently to a coordinate-type analysis, owing to the problems of collection of the smaller and (generally) more numerous types of artifact, notably small debitage. This led me to question the logic of applying highly disparate levels of recording precision within a single site; typically, coordinate data to the nearest centimetre for an impure sample of the larger finds, and collection by metre squares for the remainder. I reasoned that, by reducing the size of the cells used in the initial collection of the data, one could increase their resolution to a point at which there was no substantial difference in archaeologically interpretable information content as compared with coordinate data. The time saved in not recording coordinate data of dubious validity (owing to the impurity of the sample) can be fed into increasing the resolution of the cells used, thus increasing the overall information content of the data (note that it may still be relevant to employ mapping of occupation floors and/or recording of coordinate data for the larger finds whose collection *in situ* can be guaranteed by virtue of their size).

Cell frequencies as a source of information

If we employ the proposed strategy of increasing the resolution of the collection units (cells) used, and largely dispensing with coordinate data, we are likely to run into methodological problems associated with low cell frequencies. These problems are symptoms of the transfer of spatial information from the cell frequencies themselves to the spatial relationships between cells. Taking the extreme case, for coordinate data (for which the cells are, in theory, infinitely small) the cell frequencies are all either 0 or 1 (unless objects are co-incident) and the only information contained in the cell frequencies is the total number of objects. In this case *all* the spatial information is contained in the spatial relationships between the cells (coordinate locations).

I would contend that most, if not all quadrat analysis methods at present in use fail to exploit *either* the information locked up in the spatial relationships between collection units (cells) *or* the full information available from the cell frequencies themselves (cf. Hietala and Stevens 1977, p. 539). The commonest methods, such as quadrat frequency correlation analysis (Hesse 1971; Whallon 1973*b*) and various sorts of chi-squared analysis (Dacey 1974; Wintermann 1975), treat each quadrat as an isolated sampling unit and therefore fail to exploit specifically the spatial relationships between the quadrats. The grouping of the original collection units into larger quadrats, while making limited use of the spatial-relationship component, destroys the resolution of the data collected. Contiguity ratio analysis (Dacey 1968, 1974), in reducing interval data to presence/absence level, does not fully exploit the frequency data, though more effective use is made of the spatial relationships between collection units. As a result, these methods, and particularly the commoner ones, not only fail to do justice to the information content of excavation-square type data but will be unable to handle data from smaller, higher-resolution collection units.

The purpose of this paper, therefore, is to suggest ways in which we can extract information effectively from cell frequency data by exploiting both the frequencies themselves and the spatial relationships between the collection units employed. My approach involves the assumption of some degree of (positive) spatial autocorrelation (Cliff *et al.* 1975, p. 145) of cell frequencies, allowing the use of various methods of approximation, interpolation and smoothing in the calculation of association coefficients and the generation of artifact distribution density surfaces and simulated point

distributions. A wide range of techniques current in the geographical literature can be employed, and my discussion is intended as a proposal of directions rather than as an exhaustive review.

The first section of this paper will be devoted to general discussion of different conceptual approaches to spatial analysis. Consideration will be given to the sorts of archaeological situation required for different approaches, together with more detailed discussion of terminology, data collection strategies and the manipulation of cell frequency data.

The main methodological section of the paper presents a method of quantitative spatial analysis which can be applied either to coordinate data or to cell frequency data. This method has been termed Local Density Analysis and has been fully described by Johnson (1976). Apart from exploiting the information content of both the cell frequencies and the spatial relationships between collection units, Local Density Analysis has the advantage of mathematical simplicity. This encourages users to understand how the method works and gets us away from the black box syndrome. Being devised specifically with archaeological use in mind, the method was conceived in terms of the sorts of patterning likely to interest archaeologists, viz. clustering of artifacts and the association between artifact categories, rather than those of interest to disciplines such as geography or botany. Consequently I have concentrated on developing Local Density Analysis as a robust descriptive method rather than as a statistical test or model-fitting method.

The methodology developed will be illustrated by a test application to one of the occupation units at the Upper Magdalenian site of Pincevent, near Paris (Leroi-Gourhan and Brézillon 1966, 1972). The sample, totalling 3400 artifacts, is classified into 24 categories and distributed over an area 10 m × 11 m. Whilst the area covered and the choice of artifact categories place this application in the realm of a methodological test, the sample analysed and the results obtained compare favourably with other published applications and have yielded archaeologically useful information. It is later hoped to extend the data to include the full range of excavated material and an area covering several occupation units.

Field of application

My discussion is directed towards sites lacking internal physical boundaries which might otherwise serve *a priori* as delimiters of potential activity loci. This is the case for the majority of hunter–gatherer sites, where physical barriers such as walls or windbreaks have decayed or never existed. Though my discussion will be in terms of hunter–gatherer sites, the methodology proposed can be applied to any sites lacking formalised permanent structures.

Central to my reasoning is the concept of an assemblage as an unstratified archaeological site or a minimal subdivision of a stratified archaeological sequence. Assemblages store archaeological information in two ways: by differences between assemblages and by internal patterning (including artifact variability and spatial distribution). The former is often referred to as intersite variability (more correctly inter-assemblage variability) and potentially bears information on diachronic variations, exploitation patterns, activities and artifact function. The latter is generally referred to as intra-site variability (or intra-assemblage variability) and is poten-tially suited to questions of spatial organisation or patterning of prehistoric occupations, activities performed and functional interpretations of artifact categories. The results of intra-assemblage analysis may serve as additional variables in an interassemblage analysis.

In this paper I am concerned with one aspect of intra-assemblage patterning, the spatial distribution of 'discrete' artifacts (i.e. artifacts which can be counted as individuals) which can reasonably be treated as points on a site-plan. Whilst this aspect is one of the most informative and readily quanti-fied components of spatial patterning, it is not the only one. Other components include the orientations of the long axes of discrete artifacts and, more importantly, the patterning of artifacts which are not discrete objects and/or are of significant size in relation to the site. Examples of the latter are scatters of ochre or comminuted charcoal, scooped-out hollows, piles of plant material or complex features such as constructed hearths.

Spatial analysis (more correctly, areal analysis) of point distributions is a topic which has received considerable atten-tion in the fields of geography and plant ecology (e.g. Greig-Smith 1952, 1961; Clark and Evans 1954; Kershaw 1957, 1961; Berry and Marble 1968; Cole and King 1968, p. 163 *et seq.*; Pielou 1969). Over the past few years methods developed in these fields have been borrowed by archaeologists (e.g. Whallon 1973*a*, 1973*b*, 1974; Hodder and Orton 1976) not only for intra-assemblage spatial analysis but also for intersite spatial analysis (i.e. patterning of sites or find-spots on the landscape). However, although similar methods may be applic-able, the underlying models are quite different. Geographers commonly wish to compare the fit between an observed distri-bution and a model derived from a theoretical perspective. They are frequently concerned with the *spacing* of points. Plant ecologists also work in terms of models of spacing. Archaeologists, on the other hand, do not often have expecta-tions concerning the patterning they are likely to find, other than vague general notions of clustering and of differential distributions of different artifact categories. They are therefore more concerned with *exploratory* analyses intended to detect correlations of artifact types and zones of concen-tration. Central to much archaeological reasoning in the field of spatial analysis is the concept of a *feature*, a unique palimpsest or patterning of archaeological material or modifi-cation of the occupied surface. This concept does not appear often in the geographical or ecological literature, where greater emphasis is placed on repetition of patterning than on unique occurrences.

Approaches to spatial patterning

Features embody the patterning of an assemblage and are frequently given interpretative terminology, e.g. knapping pile, post-hole, sleeping hollow. More generally, however, features are simply observations of apparent patterning, and may or may not be of archaeological significance. Leroi-Gourhan (Leroi-Gourhan and Brézillon 1972, p. 325), makes a distinction between *obvious* features (features identified during excavation) and latent features (features identified during analysis). I prefer to make a different distinction, between *descriptive* terminology used to refer to any aspect of patterning detected, without any implication that it is the product of human activities, and *interpretative* terminology which seeks to apply a particular interpretation to the pattern-ing observed. Interpretative terminology is often applied during excavation to unambiguous features such as hearths, whilst less characteristic features such as areas of artifact con-centration and impoverishment may never be attributed specific interpretative terminology, although contributing to the overall interpretation of the site.

Owing to their complex characteristics and particular-istic nature, the features we isolate may not themselves be amenable to quantitative analysis, and in hunter–gatherer sites will often be treated subjectively at the interpretative stage of an inductive research design. This approach, which I shall call the 'feature' approach, clearly presupposes the distinction of a unique occupation of a site, or of repetitive occupations with replication of patterning. Unfortunately there is no easy way of verifying that these conditions have been met, least of all statistical testing of the distributions (see later). Our only recourse is to intuition, based on assessment of the thinness of the occupation horizon, clarity of the features distinguished and general 'coherence' of the patterning observed.

In the context of the 'feature' approach, quantitative analysis can serve as a means of detecting and describing features (in a non-statistical sense) or of defining them (in a statistical sense). Its role is primarily to reduce to some degree the subjective content of visual assessments of artifact distri-butions (see Hodder and Orton 1976, p. 4 *et seq.*, figs. 1.2–1.5, for a succinct demonstration of how easily the eye can be deceived). The key to this approach is therefore *simplification*. One way of achieving this is by the reduction of a number of point-maps or cell-frequency maps of artifact categories to a single matrix of association coefficients or a multivariate solu-tion in two or three dimensions. A second way is to reduce the data to contoured artifact density plots, ideally based on groupings of artifact categories established by the first method; in this way the patterning of an assemblage can be summarised in a limited number of 'factor' density maps whose patterning is more easily grasped than that of the source maps (see for example Figs. 7*a*, *b* and 8*a*, *b*).

The 'feature' approach is primarily concerned with the spatial organisation of archaeological sites, and is therefore relevant to questions of changes in spatial organisation through time or across the landscape. The 'feature' approach is also relevant to questions of tool function and activity 'signatures', but this is more fully embodied in a second approach, formally proposed by Whallon (1973*a*, pp. 115-18) as the 'functional' approach:

> Binford . . . has drawn one major implication from his proposed explanation of the variability among middle palaeolithic assemblages. . . . We would like to consider another. . . that artifacts, classified into separate tool types, should be differentially distributed on prehistoric occupation floors as a result of their differential utilization in the various separate activities carried out by human groups at each location used or inhabited. . . . We would [expect] that groups of tool types will be mutually correlated in terms of their pattern of distribution, particularly in the larger and richer sites. These groups should represent functionally associated tools, or 'tool kits', which were used in the same activity or activities.

Whallon's argument presents an optimistic vista of 'tool-kits' and functional information. To decide whether this view is justified, we must examine some of Whallon's explicit and implicit assumptions:

1. 'Tools' were differentially utilised in different activities.
2. 'Tools' used in an activity were discarded together and subsequently displaced together.
3. The products of different activities were to some degree spatially segregated.
4. The correlation of tool types belonging to an activity will be stronger in the larger and richer sites.

Though Whallon uses the term 'tools', it is clear from his subsequent discussion (1973*b*) that his assumptions have been applied more generally to the full range of artifact types. It may indeed be reasonable to assume that waste products of activities, such as bone fragments or debitage, are generated in proportion to the time and intensity of performance of an activity, and find their way directly into the archaeological record at or near their point of production. These artifacts can be considered as 'expedient' and relating uniquely to a particular activity. In contrast, intentionally fashioned tools may be used in a number of activities and may be carried from site to site. Such artifacts are termed 'curated' (Binford 1972, 1977), and there is no guarantee that they will find their way into the archaeological record in a similar proportion to the 'expedient' products of individual activities with which they are associated (Ammerman and Feldman 1974). In some cases discard of curated tools may be strongly correlated with *maintenance* of the tool (e.g. replacement of an adze flake) rather than *use* of the tool. We might expect a use-related distribution of curated tools only if discard were directly related to breakage or other functional inadequacy and occurred immediately. Even in this case, breakage may be related primarily to the nature of the task rather than to the frequency with which it is performed.

Direct studies of the factors affecting discard of curated tools are rare, and the factors may well vary considerably from case to case. In many cases, discard of the elements of composite tools may well be related to tool maintenance rather than to tool use. However White and Modjeska (1978, p. 283) argue that the spatial pattern of the loss of highly curated blades among the Duna of Papua New Guinea is related more closely to environmental conditions (humidity and vegetation cover) than to the spatial patterning of where they were used or maintained.

Even if discard of a particular tool category does occur at the point of use, it will only be possible to detect a correlation between this category and other products of the activity(ies) in which it is involved if the sample size is large enough. To generate a sufficient sample size for curated tools, a longer period of occupation and/or greater intensity of site usage will be required than will be the case for expedient tools or waste products (cf. Yellen 1977, p. 82). This, in turn, implies a greater chance of blurring of patterning through superimposition of activities, clearing of debris and recycling of artifacts. On balance, therefore, we are more likely to obtain information on the existence of spatial distribution of activities from waste products or expediently used tools than from tools which have been curated and used in a number of activities.

The assumption that the products of different activities are spatially segregated and that the products of a single activity are displaced together have been questioned in a number of ethnographic and archaeological studies. From his studies of the !Kung Bushmen, Yellen (1977, p. 85 *et seq.*) argues that it is the social context of activities rather than their nature which is the prime determinant of their spatial location in the sites studied. He sees Bushmen camps as divided into nuclear family units, each with a hut, a hearth in front of this structure and a surrounding area in which a wide range of domestic activities are carried out. The space enclosed between these units is seen as a communal area in which activities such as dancing and sharing of game occur. A few activity-specific areas occur around the perimeter of the camp in response to space requirements or messiness of particular activities. On the basis of these observations, Yellen questions the assumption of spatial segregation of activities which underlies most attempts at quantitative spatial analysis.

Binford's discussion (1978) of a Nuniamut Eskimo hunting stand presents a contrary view of the factors affecting intrasite patterning. This view more closely parallels Whallon's model and involves the spatial patterning of activities according to functional (in the broadest sense) requirements rather than social context. Though Binford implies that many of the differences between his conclusions and those of Yellen arise from differences in approach we must bear in mind that Yellen's sites are 'base' camps associated with a day-to-day foraging economy and occupied by family units, whilst Binford's site is a special-purpose site in a storage economy, occupied by a limited cross-section of the society. Binford's study does not invalidate Yellen's conclusions but serves to point out the danger of cross-cultural ethnographic analogy (cf. Binford 1978, p. 358).

Ethnoarchaeological observations on contemporaneous Aboriginal camp sites in Central Australia and in Arnhem Land have shown that even for short-term occupations, site maintenance activities are the prime determinant of spatial patterning (J. F. O'Connell personal communication; B. Meehan and R. M. Jones personal communications). Site maintenance is strongly size-biased, so that only tiny waste products remained where the activities were carried out. The bulk of the products of all activities ended up in common waste dumps around the perimeters of the sites.

A similar situation is evident in the patterning of the open-air occupations at Pincevent, excavated by Leroi-Gourhan and Brézillon (1966, 1972). At Pincevent, lithic waste and bones occur in well-marked dumps, in some cases shared between adjacent hearth units, whilst the area surrounding each main constructed hearth is characterised by a carpet of tiny chips and small bone fragments. The distribution of shattered hearth-stone fragments also supports the site-maintenance interpretation of this patterning (see later).

One conclusion that we can draw from these examples, notably the Australian Aboriginal and !Kung studies, is that the patterning of occupation sites in which a full range of subsistence and maintenance activities have occurred may well be strongly influenced by site maintenance and/or social organisation and may not satisfy the assumptions of segregation set out by Whallon. The latter are more likely to be satisfied by more specialised types of site. Clearly we must examine the contrasting hypotheses when attempting to interpret site layout, and show that one or the other is untenable, rather than immediately interpret any patterning detected in terms of the hypothesis which appeals to us most.

Whallon's fourth assumption raises the problem of defining what we mean by a 'site'. In the Australian examples mentioned above, 'sites' extend over large areas, several hundred metres in diameter. The individual occupation units with one or more hearths, a windbreak, domestic, sleeping and dump zones are specific groupings of people within the site (family unit, young men's camp etc.). Each of these units corresponds fairly closely in size and range of features to the individual hearth units at Pincevent or to ethnographic and archaeological accounts of rockshelter occupations (e.g. Hale and Tindale 1934; Leroi-Gourhan 1961, 1976; de Lumley *et al.* 1969; Parkington and Poggenpoel 1971).

Although the individual occupation units in the ethnographic sites mentioned do not contain detailed activity information, the sites as a whole are likely to be more informative because specialised activities which are messy, communal or which require a great deal of space occur in the gaps between occupation units. These areas are generally less subject to site maintenance activities than the more intensively used space within the individual occupation units. The same sort of specialised activity loci between hearth units are apparent at Pincevent (Leroi-Gourhan and Brézillon 1972, p. 230). Unfortunately few excavations cover sufficient area, and in the case of rockshelters we are often dealing with islands of deposits preserved without surrounding terrain. Thus the 'site' in common archaeological usage is more readily equated with occupation units in the ethnographic situation.

What sort of sites lend themselves to spatial analysis? Ideally we should excavate large areas of open-air sites so as to include specialised activity areas as well as occupation units. In this way, our data will be amenable to both a 'feature' approach and a 'functional' approach. Excavation of single occupation units on open-air sites or of the interior of small-to-medium sized rockshelters is unlikely to yield detailed activity information owing to site maintenance activities and the omission of specialised activity areas potentially located outside the unit or shelter. Obviously very large rockshelters may contain a full range of activity areas, but excavation of a sufficient area is likely to pose even greater problems than for a limited-duration open-air site.

Occupation floors and significance tests

It has been noted that the 'feature' approach to spatial analysis necessitates the distinction of an 'occupation floor', in the sense that the assemblage analysed must represent use of the site in a spatially consistent fashion. This implies replication of the spatial organisation of the occupation if the assemblage represents several visits to the site. On the other hand the 'functional' approach might be able to extract information from a limited number of superimposed occupations provided there is replication of the activities performed (but not necessarily of spatial organisation – cf. Hietala and Stevens' (1977, p. 544) definition of 'consistent generic pattern').

Several authors (e.g. Whallon 1973*b*, p. 266; Dacey 1974, pp. 321, 328) have suggested that the first stage of spatial analysis should be to test the distributions of individual artifact categories for conformity to randomness. It is implied that, if all artifact categories are found to be randomly distributed, there is no point in carrying out further analysis. This approach can be criticised on several counts. In the present context 'randomness' means that we were unable to reject the null hypothesis that the distribution in question might have been generated by a random process (with given probability). This does not mean that it *was* generated by a random process, and in archaeological situations we can state fairly confidently that this is not in fact the case (cf. Dacey 1968, p. 172). Thus 'random' in this case really means unpatterned, on a continuum from clustered through unpatterned to regularly spaced (underdispersed to over-dispersed). This fact has been widely recognised in the geographic literature:

Indeed, the concept of randomness with respect to

settlement patterns might well be disregarded, except for the fact that the value of $R = 1$ is a convenient and useful origin from which to measure the tendencies toward aggregation or uniform spacing of settlements (King 1968, p. 166).

> ... in the real world it is perhaps more meaningful to view a given pattern as a deviation from one or other of these extremes [clustering and regularity] .... In reality, forces controlling the location of points are unlikely to operate at random

(Pinder and Witherick 1972).

A 'random' result obtained with a particular statistic will reflect not so much the lack of patterning of the distribution but the power (in a statistical sense) of the statistic used. If the test applied is powerful, the null hypothesis will probably be rejected even if the patterning is far too weak to be of archaeological importance (cf. Wright 1974). If the test applied is weak (as is the case with most quadrat methods), quite significant archaeological patterning may fail to invalidate the null hypothesis (a type II error). Dacey (1974) has illustrated the problem of interpreting the contradictory results generated by repeated applications of a test based on quadrats of different shape and size. In addition 'random' distributions are not necessarily *independent*, so that if the assumptions set out for the 'functional' approach are satisfied we could obtain a set of 'random' but dependent distributions.

Since statistical tests of randomness merely tell us something about the strength of patterning present, such tests are of no help in elucidating whether we are dealing with individual occupations or a replication of patterning. Nor can they tell us whether the patterning detected is archaeologically significant or the result of post-depositional disturbance. Our only guides to these questions are observations made at the time of excavation and the coherence of the results of our analyses. Probably the best test of archaeological significance is repeatability between assemblages, of the activity groupings or spatial layout detected. For the moment, however, there are few areas where we can compare such information for a number of assemblages. We are therefore obliged to fall back on internal coherence (i.e. can the patterning be explained (in the multivariate statistical sense) with a small number of factors, and are these factors readily interpretable in a sensible fashion (e.g. clear size effect, clear separation of lithic material and organic refuse)), and on basic observations such as pellicularity of an occupation horizon, clearly defined features and lack of evidence of post-depositional disturbance.

An added problem with statistical testing of distributions for randomness is the question of site area. The fact that a site has been distinguished in the first place implies that the distributions of at least some of the artifact categories are patterned. If we include areas of scattered finds surrounding the main concentration of an open-air site, most artifact categories will appear clustered. It may be possible to turn the question around and define the area of the site in such a way that the distribution of a particular set of artifact categories

conforms to randomness. Such an approach clearly renders meaningless the testing of individual categories. Alternatively, the boundary of the site can be delineated subjectively on a site plan and the enclosed area is measured. In some cases the area will be delimited by the limits of the excavation, whereas in others a decision will have to be made as to where the distributions become too diffuse to be considered significant. The only cases in which testing for randomness might have *some* meaning are partial excavations not extending out to the edges of a site or physically restricted occupations such as rockshelter sites.

Data for spatial analysis

Data for intra-assemblage spatial analysis are collected either as coordinate data for individual artifacts (generally to the nearest centimetre) or as frequency data for a number of artifact categories in areal subdivisions of the site. I refer to the latter as *cell frequency* data because the arbitrary areal divisions of the site are often squares with between 20 cm and 2 m side on a regular lattice, and are thus closely analogous to the cells of a bivariate frequency distribution. These two methods of recording spatial data are frequently applied side by side because it is generally impossible to record coordinate data for all the artifacts excavated, either by virtue of their numerical importance or because a proportion are missed during excavation and are recovered in the sieves, or both. This heterogeneity of much spatial data in archaeology is a stumbling block rarely, if ever, encountered in geographical or botanical work. Consequently archaeologists have borrowed methods from these disciplines without the methodology needed for the special conditions of archaeological data.

If each artifact category was recorded *either* purely as coordinate data *or* purely as cell frequency data, we could carry out two separate analyses, one for the coordinate data and a second for the cell frequency data with the coordinate data reduced to cell frequencies. In practice, however, the recording method used for any *particular* artifact is dependent on a hodgepodge of factors including size and shape of the object, colour and texture contrast with the deposits, the texture and humidity of the deposits and the competence and mood of the person excavating. Several of these factors may be spatially correlated.

The commonest approach to analysing coordinate data is to assume that the artifacts recorded with individual coordinates are a random (or total) sample of any categories involved. Whilst this may be a reasonable assumption for some categories, it is unlikely to be the case for categories containing small specimens such as microliths, burin spalls or isolated teeth. If such an assumption is made *it must be explicitly stated and justified*. This can best be done by showing that a negligible proportion of artifacts belonging to categories used in the coordinate analysis have been recorded by the cell frequency method.

It will often be necessary to eliminate some categories of smaller artifact from the coordinate analysis, with a consequent jettisoning of information that one has been at pains to collect. Such jettison is the mark of a poorly designed recording system for which the parameters controlling recording methods have not been explicitly formulated. In addition, if this results in only a small proportion of the material being analysed by coordinate methods, then it is doubtful whether the coordinate analysis will add much information to the results obtained from the cell frequency analysis.

Coordinate data are generally recorded as a response to the poor pattern resolution of the excavated squares (cells). The problem is best solved, not by recording coordinate data for an impure sample of the larger finds, but by decreasing the size of cells used. The increased resolution of the cell frequency data applied to the *full* range of excavated material has a higher and more easily exploited information content than a mixed recording system with lower resolution cells. If the resolution of the cells is increased to a point where they resolve at the level of post-depositional 'noise' or of uninterpretable archaeological detail, no extra information is available from coordinate data. In practice we are probably talking in terms of the reduction of 1 m × 1 m or 2 m × 2 m square excavation units to 20 cm × 20 cm or 25 cm × 25 cm cells for a clear occupation floor and perhaps 50 cm × 50 cm cells for an extensive and thick or poorly patterned archaeological horizon. Examples of this sort of recording are Leroi-Gourhan and Brézillon's (1966; 1972) use of 20 cm × 20 cm cells for collecting small debitage and bone fragments at Pincevent (large finds are individually mapped and numbered) and Ranson's (1981) use of 25 cm × 25 cm cells as the sole recording system on his excavation of a midden structure at Sundown Point, Tasmania.

Density mapping of cell frequency data

If the cells used to record an artifact distribution are small enough to resolve patterning in the form of concentrations of artifacts, artifact frequencies in adjacent cells will be related. In general, high values will occur with high values and low with low. This is known as (positive) spatial autocorrelation (Cliff *et al.* 1975, p. 145) and we must exploit it if we are to make the best use of cell frequency data. We can do this by using a number of techniques to smooth the cell frequencies so as to reduce the 'noise' introduced by dividing up the distribution into cells. In so doing we assume that the cell frequencies are finite samples of a continuous artifact density distribution, which can be represented as a surface whose 'height' above the XY plane at any point indicates the artifact distribution density at that point. This surface can be used in several ways, for example:

1. For visual presentation of the distribution of an artifact category (or of a group or factor of categories) the density surface can be presented as an isopleth (contour) map.
2. The density surface can be treated as a probability surface for the simulation of the original point distribution.

The latter approach may be required simply for visual presentation of the data as a point-map, but may also be used as a basis for further analysis. This may be necessary where coordinate data have been recorded for the majority of artifacts in a site and it is required to generate coordinate data for the remainder so that all artifact categories can be treated in a single (coordinate) analysis. However, great care must be taken in assessing the results of this sort of manipulation, as it is easy to make inappropriate assumptions, e.g. that the sieve finds have a similar distribution to the finds *in situ*.

The simplest way of exploiting the autocorrelation of cell frequencies is by the use of a moving-average, i.e. the cell frequencies are averaged over several cells (with equal or unequal weightings) and the resulting value is attributed to the central cell (Cole and King 1968, p. 201 *et seq.*). This technique serves to stabilise the cell frequencies against chance variation resulting from low numbers. The number of neighbouring cells and the weightings used will depend on the degree of autocorrelation and magnitudes of the cell frequencies (Robinson *et al.* 1978, p. 163 *et seq.*). The application of Local Density Analysis to cell frequency data (see later) is effectively based on the use of an unweighted moving-average.

Figure 1 illustrates the application of a moving-average to interval data in one dimension (a one-dimensional example is used for clarity of presentation, but is closely analogous to the two-dimensional situation). Diagram 1*a* shows the original point distribution, which is reduced to a histogram of interval frequencies in diagram 1*b*. These are stabilised by application of equally weighted moving-averages over three intervals (diagram 1*c*) and five intervals (diagram 1*d*). Both these histograms provide a clearer picture of the two concentrations of points in the original distribution than does the histogram of interval frequencies in diagram 1*b*. The moving-average histograms (including the original interval data) are smoothed (by eye) in diagram 1*e*, which can be compared with a plot of distance to nearest-neighbour (diagram 1*f*). The smoothed moving-average curves are a much clearer representation of the distribution of the points than either the original interval data or the unsmoothed moving-average histograms.

A bivariate analogue of the univariate histogram is illustrated in Fig. 2(*a–d*). In this case the histogram can be drawn as an isometric view, but such histograms are both tedious to draw and generally not very informative because of hidden detail. An alternative is to represent the histogram by shading on a plan, as I have done for the data from Pincevent (Fig. 7*c*). Such a plan, however, only gives a general idea of the location of concentrations and little idea of their shape or extent.

If we smooth the bivariate histogram using a moving-average technique and interpolate between the resulting values (treating the value for each cell as a point determination of artifact distribution density at the centre of the cell), we end up with a surface such as that shown in Fig. 2*c*. This distribution density surface is even more difficult to draw in isometric

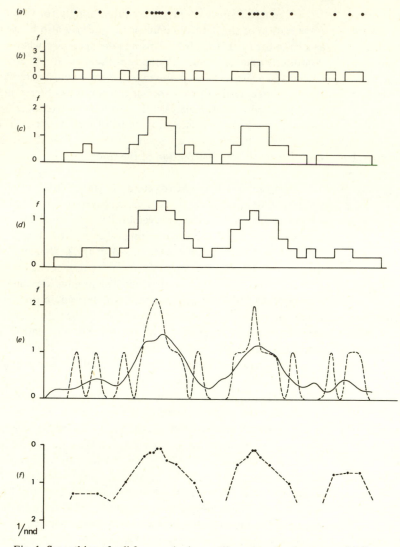

Fig. 1. Smoothing of cell frequencies in one dimension. f = frequency. (*a*) Source distribution. (*b*) Cell frequencies (interval data). (*c*) Moving-average over three intervals. (*d*) Moving-average over five intervals. (*e*) Cell frequencies (dashed) and five-interval moving-average (continuous) smoothed by eye. (*f*) Reciprocal of nearest neighbor distance (nnd).

perspective than the frequency histogram, though it can be done by computer (e.g. Zubrow and Harbaugh 1978, figs. 9–18). However, it can be more easily and more usefully represented as isopleths (contours) of density on a plan of the site (Fig. 2*d*, see also the plans for Pincevent, Figs. 7*b* and 8*b*). The visual information provided by these plans is far greater than that available from the plan of cells shaded according to cell frequency, giving information on shape and size of concentrations as well as on their spatial location.

The density-contour plans produced by this method provide a more easily assessed representation of the source distributions than do the original point-distribution plans, and are thus less open to differential interpretation by several observers (but see comments below). Furthermore they allow the representation of two types of distribution which cannot be represented as simple point-plans. First, distributions where the concentration of objects is too great for individual objects

to be reproduced on a plan at the scale desired, or for which objects cannot be distinguished because of overlap. These situations are commonly encountered when dealing with piles of chipping waste. Secondly, cases in which point-maps showing individual objects are meaningless; for instance, the distribution of factors or components derived from a multivariate analysis of the associations between artifact categories. Density mapping is therefore a useful complement to both quantitative analysis and visual assessment of artifact distributions when we are dealing with isolated or replicated occupation floors.

Choice of parameters

The plan generated by the smoothing and contouring process is dependent on the parameters of the method. In practice, this variation is likely to be at the level of coherence of the isopleths rather than of the overall structure. For

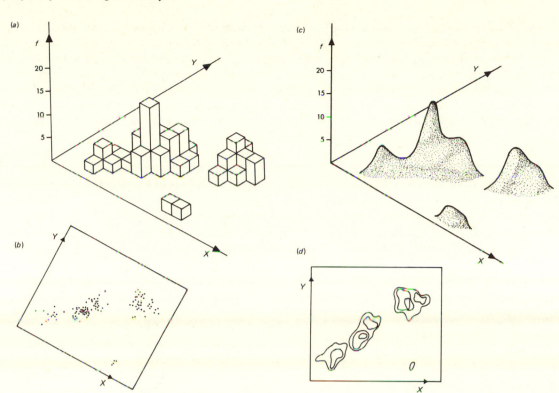

Fig. 2. Smoothing of cell frequencies in two dimensions. (*a*) Isometric three-dimensional graph of cell frequencies. (*b*) Source distribution. (*c*) Isometric view of smoothed density surface. (*d*) Contour plan of smoothed density surface. (*c*) and (*d*) drawn by hand, not mathematically derived from (*b*).

optimum resolution of patterning, the cell size and the number of cells used for the moving-average should be as small as possible. However, too few cells for the moving-average (or excessive weighting of a few cells) will cause the main lines of patterning to be lost in a wealth of uninterpretable detail at the same order of scale as the original cells.

I have not investigated the effect of interpolation algorithm and isopleth intervals. For Pincevent, I was dealing with closely and regularly spaced density determinations and strong patterning so that I doubt whether different algorithms would give different results at an archaeologically significant level. I would tentatively generalise this statement to say that the sorts of patterning in which we are interested for a 'feature' approach to spatial data are above the level of method-dependent variation, given the regular spacing of control points implied by the smoothing technique used. The choice of isopleth intervals is covered in some detail in the geographical literature (see Robinson *et al.* 1978, pp. 168–79, for discussion and references). In archaeological situations it may be relevant to choose isopleth intervals in terms of some statistical notion of clustering such as that advanced by Wintermann (1975, p. 28 *et seq.*) or by Whallon (1974, p. 23). Most workers, however, would probably be satisfied with a choice based on examination of the frequency distribution of the control point density determinations; this was the technique I used for the Pincevent analysis reported below.

Local Density Analysis

Local Density Analysis is a means of calculating a matrix of association coefficients between the distributions of a number of artifact categories. The elements of the diagonal of the matrix are a measure of clustering of individual artifact categories. The matrix can serve both as a directly interpretable summary of the relationships between the distributions of different artifact categories and of their degree of clustering (aggregation), and as input to a multivariate analysis designed to extract groups or factors of artifact categories showing related distributions. These groups or factors may in turn be interpreted directly or used as the basis for artifact-group distribution density plans. Local Density Analysis is therefore relevant to both a 'feature' and a 'functional' approach to the analysis of spatial patterning.

Local Density Analysis was originally conceived as a method of analysing coordinate data, the stimulus being provided by the obvious problems inherent in the quadrat frequency correlation method used by Hesse (1971) and Whallon (1973*b*). At a later stage it was realised that the method lent itself to an approximation which would allow the use of the basic algorithm with cell frequency data. Initially, however, I will present the method in terms of coordinate data. A full discussion is contained in Johnson (1976; see also Graham 1979).

Let us define the *local* density of one category (*j*)

in the vicinity of an object of another category (i) as being the number of j objects per unit area within a circular sampling unit, radius r, centred on the object of category i. We can write the *local* density of category j for the k-th object of category i, as $(M_{ij})_k/\pi r^2$ where $(M_{ij})_k$ = number of objects of category j within radius r of the k-th object of category i. M_{ij} is known as the *neighbour count* for *centres* of category i and *neighbours* of category j.

The *global* density of category j is defined as the total number of objects of this category (N_j), divided by the total area of the site, A. [I have commented above on the problems associated with the estimation of site area. For Local Density Analysis the area appears as a common factor in all the terms of the association matrix and can be eliminated later in the analysis.]

The index of association of category j with category i is termed $C_{ij(r)}$ (for sampling units of radius r), and is defined as:

$$C_{ij(r)} = \sum_{k=1}^{N_i} \frac{(M_{ij})_k/N_i\pi r^2}{N_j/A}$$

$$= \frac{\text{Mean Local Density of category } j \text{ in the vicinity of objects of category } i}{\text{Global density of category } j}.$$

Note that $C_{ii(r)}$ is a measure of clustering or aggregation of the objects of category i, and that $C_{ij(r)} = C_{ji(r)}$ for total samples of finite distributions.

If the two categories i and j are not associated within the area A, at the scale represented by the sampling unit radius chosen (see discussion later), the density of category j objects near objects of category i (the *local* density of category j) should be (on average) the same as the mean density of category j over the whole site (the *global* density), and the expected value of the association index will therefore be unity.

If the two categories i and j are positively associated within the area A, the density of category j objects in the vicinity of category i objects will tend to be higher than the mean density over the whole site (i.e. *local* density greater than *global* density) and the association index should be greater than unity. Conversely a dissociation or mutual exclusion should be reflected by indices less than unity. The limiting values are 0 for dissociation (no objects of one category within a distance r from objects of the other) and $A/\pi r^2$ for association (the maximum distance between any two objects belonging to the two categories is less than or equal to r). It should be noted that the index is strongly asymmetrical about unity, so that a log transformation may be used to give a more symmetrical index with zero indicating lack of association. However, it is less easy to assess the meaning of the transformed indices in terms of the source patterning represented.

Elimination of the site area

Since the area of the site appears as a constant factor in all the association indices calculated for a particular situation, it can be eliminated by any operation that takes account only of the ratio of (or, after log transformation, difference between) the terms in the association matrix. One solution is the calculation of a correlation coefficient between pairs of rows (or columns) of the association index matrix. This generates a matrix of correlation coefficients which can be used directly as input to a Principal Components Analysis or similar.

However, although the area of the site can be eliminated in this way, it is often useful to obtain the intermediate results, notably the indices of clustering of the individual categories. The area of the site may be estimated subjectively from the site plan, and in most cases this will prove satisfactory. As an alternative, the area of the site can be calculated from the matrix of association indices in such a way as to give this matrix a particular configuration, e.g. a mean value of unity for the elements of the diagonal. A third approach is the use of some other statistic to arrive at an area for the site, e.g. Whallon's use of a version of Nearest-Neighbour Analysis to define the limits of a cluster (Whallon 1974, p. 23).

Unless there are few categories, the correlation matrix is more stable than the association index matrix, as the correlation coefficients are based on the relationships between a pair of categories and all other categories. This smooths out chance variations which may occur in a single association index if the neighbour count is small. In addition the correlation coefficients are easier to assess, owing to their familiarity and ± 1.0 limits. However, further work is required to assess the ways in which different types of association are reflected in the correlation coefficient matrix and the effects of inserting or removing extra artifact categories with particular configurations (e.g. evenly spaced, highly clustered).

Choice of the neighbourhood distance

The neighbourhood distance is defined as the radius, r, of the circular sampling units used for the analysis. As the neighbourhood distance is increased, the analysis becomes progressively less sensitive to the smaller scales of patterning. This is simply a resolution effect rather than the sort of scale sensitivity exhibited by quadrat methods and noted as an undesirable characteristic by Hodder and Okell (1978, p. 97). The best results will generally be obtained with the smallest possible value of r. However, the reduction of the neighbourhood distance is limited by the reduction of the neighbour counts on which the association indices are based (i.e. the total number of objects of one category within the neighbourhood distance of objects of another category). As this becomes smaller, chance fluctuations become more important, resulting in increased 'noise' in the association indices matrix. Unstable indices (r too small) can be detected by the lack of strong positive or negative values in the correlation matrix and inconsistencies in the association and correlation matrices. Inconsistencies typically take the form of two categories, mutually associated, showing widely divergent associations with other categories. The use of a multivariate analysis to choose the

Table 1. *Cell cluster size and equivalent radius for cell frequency based Local Density Analysis*

D^a (m)	Number of cells included	r^a	Equivalent radius (cm) for $20\,\text{cm} \times 20\,\text{cm}$ cells
1.0	1	0.56	11.5
1.4	5	1.26	25
2.0	9	1.69	34
2.2	13	2.03	41
2.8	21	2.59	52
3.0	25	2.82	57
3.2	29	3.04	61
3.6	37	3.43	69
4.0	45	3.78	76
4.1	49	3.95	79

^{a}Measured in units of one cell edge length.

Values for D are approximate change-over point between different neighbourhood areas.

optimum neighbourhood distance is illustrated below in my analysis of the Pincevent data. Elsewhere (Johnson 1976, pp. 79–83) I have given a more detailed discussion of the effects of changes in the neighbourhood distance on the resolution of patterning, whilst Graham (1979) illustrates graphs of clustering and association indices against neighbourhood distance for distributions of graves and artifacts in an Iron Age cemetery.

Application to cell frequency data

Having presented Local Density Analysis as a coordinate method, a simple approximation allows the application of the method to cell frequency data. If we approximate the circular sampling units used for a coordinate-based analysis by a cluster of cells of the same area, we can write:

$$C_{ij(r)} = \sum_{k=1}^{N_c} \frac{(M_j)_k \cdot (L_i)_k / N_i \pi r^2}{N_j/A},$$

where r is termed the 'equivalent radius' or 'equivalent neighbourhood distance' of the analysis. It is the radius of a circle of the same area as the cluster of cells used (including the k-th cell). I have chosen to define the cluster as being those cells whose centres lie within a given distance, D, of the centre of the k-th cell (note that it will be constant over most of the area analysed, but may be reduced for peripheral cells). Table 1 shows the relationship between D and r. Note that r is not a continuous variable but takes a series of discrete values.

$(m_j)_k$ = Number of objects of category j in all cells whose centres lie at less than D from the centre of the k-th cell. N_c = Total number of cells. $(L_i)_k$ = Number of objects of category i in the k-th cell.

Note that if i and j are the same (i.e. calculation of C_{ii}) the term $(M_i)_k$ must be replaced by $[(M_i)_k - 1]$ to allow for objects 'counting' themselves as neighbours.

Analysis of isolated sampling units

I have noted earlier that most quadrat analysis methods take no specific account of the spatial relationships between the sampling units used. This may be a positive advantage if the original collection units are not necessarily contiguous, as in the case of a random or structured sampling procedure or of collection units situated in separate excavations. When applying Local Density Analysis under these circumstances the individual collection units are treated as complete sampling units for the determination of the *local* densities, without reference to adjacent units. This method can accommodate collection units of regular or irregular shape and size, through the following modification to the formula:

$$C_{ij(r)} = \sum_{k=1}^{N_c} \frac{[(L_j)_k \cdot (L_i)_k / S_k]/N_i}{N_j/A},$$

where S_k is the area of the k-th collection unit.

Provided the area of empty zones is not included in the value of A (and for the correlation matrix and multivariate analysis, even if it is) the results of a Local Density Analysis based on isolated collection units are unaffected by empty or part empty units. This is an important difference compared with correlation analysis, where 'dummy' quadrats can have a profound effect on the results (cf. Hesse 1971, p. 42; Whallon 1973b, p. 274).

Test application to Les Tarterets II

Table 2 shows the results of Local Density Analysis applied to four artifact categories at the site of Les Tarterets II, an Upper Magdalenian open-air site approximately 30 km south of Paris. This is the site on which Hesse (1971) carried out his correlation analyses. The table serves to illustrate the close agreement between the results of a coordinate-based Local Density Analysis and one based on 1 m × 1 m quadrats treated as isolated sampling units. This is not to imply that such a close agreement is to be expected in cases where patterning is less marked. The results of the coordinate based Local Density Analysis correspond closely with subjective assessment of the clustering and similarities of the distributions (Hesse 1971, Johnson 1976, p. 115). A correlation analysis of the same data, also using 1 m × 1 m quadrats, is tabulated for comparison.

Local density analysis of Pincevent section 36, V105

The site of Pincevent (Leroi-Gourhan and Brézillon 1966, 1972) is situated approximately 60 km southeast of Paris in the valley of the Seine. The deposits extend over several hectares and contain scattered Upper Magdalenian camp sites at various levels within a sequence of some 2.5 m of flood loams. The individual camp sites consist typically of one major constructed hearth surrounded by fine debitage and ochre staining on one side, and a spread of bones, fractured hearth stones and debitage on the other (Leroi-Gourhan and Brézillon 1972, pp. 240–50; 1966, p. 322 *et seq.*). Around the perimeter of this area there are generally one

Table 2. *Spatial analysis results for Les Tarterets II*

	Blocks	Tools	Cores	Blades	
Blocks	8.7				*Local Density Analysis*[a]
Tools	0.6	4.7			(coordinate data)
Cores	1.7	2.5	2.3		
Blades	1.1	1.2	1.2	1.4	
	Blocks	Tools	Cores	Blades	
Blocks	6.7				*Local Density Analysis*[b]
Tools	0.6	4.1			(1 m × 1 m quadrat data)
Cores	1.7	2.2	2.4		
Blades	1.2	0.9	1.1	1.5	
	Blocks	Tools	Cores	Blades	
Blocks	1.0				*Quadrat frequency correlation Analysis*
Tools	−0.06	1.0			(1 m × 1 m quadrat data)
Cores	0.16	0.28	1.0		
Blades	0.12	0.01	0.11	1.0	
	Blocks	Tools	Cores	Blades	
Number of artifacts	464	78	44	532	

[a] Area of site taken as $130\,m^2$, neighbourhood distance for coordinate Local Density Analysis = 56 cm.
[b] The 1 m × 1 m quadrats are treated as isolated sampling units. Equivalent neighbourhood distance = 56 cm.

or two smaller hearths, ash dumps and piles of debitage and a thin scatter of cumbersome items such as reindeer antlers.

The extraordinary preservation of features at Pincevent, attested by the presence of undisturbed piles of ash and charcoal, is attributed to prompt burial by low energy overbank flood deposits. Faunal material is also well preserved and is almost exclusively reindeer.

Leroi-Gourhan and Brézillon (1972, p. 246 *et seq.*) tentatively interpret the basic unit of occupation with its constructed hearth and associated artifact scatter, as representing some form of tent, perhaps a simple conical structure of skins on converging poles, with the main hearth situated at the opening. The dichotomy between the artifactual material on either side of the hearth is seen as the difference between a living space within the tent, characterised by small material and ochre stains, and an artifact disposal zone outside the tent, characterised by a fuller range of artifact sizes. The peripheral zone of scattered artifacts, hearths, ash piles and other small features is interpreted as a zone of specialised activities. Despite the excellent preservation and the minutely detailed décapage excavation, no post-holes have been found and there is no evidence for an arc of retaining stones. However, an experimental tent made without post-holes and with the cover weighted by sand alone has held up on the site for several years.

Although the hypothesis of a tent is based on the excavators' extensive study and familiarity with the Pincevent occupation units, we cannot afford to overlook an alternative hypothesis. The evident polarisation of the artifact distribu-tions could arise, not from a covered structure, but from wind direction and the placement of windbreaks such as those observed in the ethnographic studies mentioned above. In particular, the linear spread of ochre, faunal and lithic remains apparent for the V105 unit (Figs. 3, 7a and 8a) is suggestive of some form of windbreak running from northwest to southeast and situated 2 or 3 m southwest of the hearth. Movement between the windbreak and the hearth could account for the two diffuse ochre trails which spread in opposite directions from the dense patch near the hearth, whilst these trails cut across the walls of the hypothetical tent model.

In some cases two or more of the major hearths occur in fairly close proximity and at the same stratigraphic level. This is the case for the hearths in squares V105, L115 and T112[1] (Fig. 3) which were reported together in a single publication (Leroi-Gourhan and Brézillon 1972). There is some interchange between these units, such as borrowing of hearth stones. The pattern of borrowing (*ibid.* pp. 85–6, fig. 53) suggests that L115 may have been posterior to the other two hearths (the L115 hearth incorporates some of the larger fragments of hearth stones whose outer fragments are found around and within the V105 and T112 hearths and in a common dumping zone in QRS 107–8 which contains conjoins of pieces found around these two hearths). The spread of material around V105 appears to avoid the area surrounding hearth T112 (see Figs. 7b and 8b).

The initial choice of Pincevent as a test case for the application of Local Density Analysis was made for three main reasons:

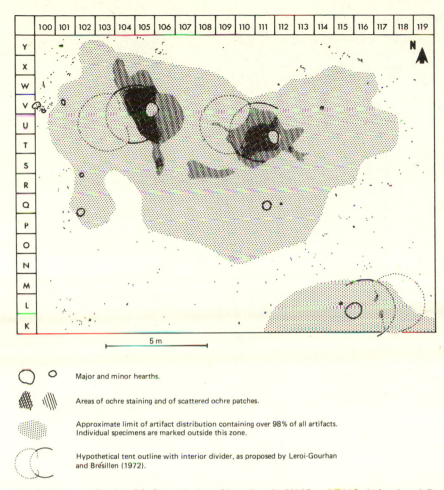

Major and minor hearths.

Areas of ochre staining and of scattered ochre patches.

Approximate limit of artifact distribution containing over 98% of all artifacts. Individual specimens are marked outside this zone.

Hypothetical tent outline with interior divider, as proposed by Leroi-Gourhan and Brésillen (1972).

Fig. 3. Pincevent Section 36. General plan of hearth units V105 and T112. (After Leroi-Gourhan and Brézillon 1972, figs. 52, 54, 60, 76.)

1. The ideal state of preservation of what are apparently single short-term occupations with clearly visible features provides a 'minimum noise' situation eminently suitable for an experimental application of the method.

2. The publications on Pincevent are probably the most comprehensive distribution studies available at the present time. This allows a direct assessment of the results of Local Density Analysis in terms of a careful and detailed qualitative study.

3. The exceptionally well-organised recording system greatly facilitated the collection of the basic data. The data were extracted from 1:20 scale working plans for each artifact type.

The V105 hearth and its associated features were chosen for analysis as being one of the three occupation units treated in the most recent and most detailed report on Pincevent (Leroi-Gourhan and Brézillon 1972). The analysis was restricted to the V105 unit as the area and artifact sample were sufficient for a satisfactory test application of Local Density Analysis. The area analysed was arbitrarily chosen to include most of the material believed to be associated with the V105 hearth on the basis of contiguity of distribution and the distribution of conjoins. It extends from O to Y and 100 to 109

(see Fig. 3). Parts of this area contain very few remains, so that the subjectively drawn limit of the distribution shown on Fig. 3 contains 98.5% of the total sample of objects.

A total of 3426 artifacts was recorded for this analysis, comprising most of the identifiable bones, formalised tools and hearth stone fragments. The material was divided into 24 artifact categories (Table 3), 14 of which were different skeletal parts of reindeer and 6 of which were formalised lithic types, including burin spalls and cores. Hearth stone fragments were divided into those larger and those smaller than 7 cm in maximum dimension (this arbitrary division was based on a subjectively assessed break in the distribution between 'large' and 'small' hearth stone fragments). The two remaining categories were skeletal remains of hare (the next commonest animal after reindeer) and pieces of an imported brown flint which is interpreted (Leroi-Gourhan and Brézillon 1972, p. 94) as representing the initial toolkit of the occupants of the site. Since the analysis was intended merely as a test of Local Density Analysis within the context of a minor research degree, I abandoned the recording of debitage and unidentifiable bone fragments which numbered several tens of thousands of specimens.

Final analysis of the Pincevent data was based on cell

Table 3. *Pincevent Section 36: V105. Abbreviations and sample size for artifact categories*

			Sample Size
	Reindeer skeletal remains		
1	ANTL	Antlers and fragments	17
2	MAXI	Maxilliaries	36
3	MAND	Mandibles	105
4	TOOTH	Isolated teeth	79
5	RIB	Ribs	210
6	SCAP	Scapulae and pelvises	64
7	HUME	Humeri	45
8	FEMR	Femurs and rotules	78
9	TIB	Tibias	92
10	ULRAD	Ulnas and radii	94
11	METT	Metatarsals	77
12	METC	Metacarpals	71
13	METP	Metapodials (METT + METC + Unident')	180
14	PHAL	Phalanges, residual phalanges and sesamoids	249
15	HARE	Hare bones	60
16	>7 CM	Hearth stone fragments exceeding 7 cm length	154
17	<7 CM	Hearth stone fragments less than 7 cm long	634
	Worked stone artifacts		
18	CORE	Cores	103
19	BURI	Burins	97
20	SPALL	Burin spalls	293
21	BBL	Backed bladelets	505
22	AWL	Awls and micro-awls	47
23	ENDS	Endscrapers and truncated blades	75
24	BRFLT	Artifacts in brown flint	61

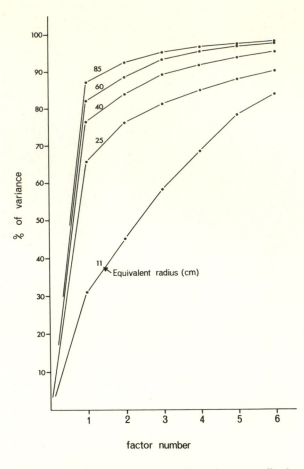

Fig. 4. Pincevent 36: V105. Cumulative variance contributions of Correspondence Analysis factors.

frequencies in 2750 20 cm × 20 cm cells, using an equivalent radius of 40 cm. The neighbour area consists of the centre cell and its 12 nearest neighbours. The choice of the optimum radius was based in the present instance on the results of analysis at equivalent radii of 11, 25, 40, 60 and 85 cm. Figure 4 shows the cumulative variance contribution of the first six factors of a Correspondence Analysis (Benzecri 1973) based on the matrix of association indices calculated for each of these scales. The first factor accounts for over 75% of the total variance in the association index matrix for $r = 40$, 60 and 85 cm, over 65% for $r = 25$ cm, but only 31% for $r = 11$ cm. For $r = 11$ cm the second and subsequent factors are all of considerable importance, whereas for the larger scales they are not. This pattern indicates the introduction of a lot of 'noise' into the association matrix at $r = 11$ cm, because of insufficient neighbour counts. This effect appears to be getting under way at $r = 25$ cm, so that this graph alone points to $r = 40$ cm as being the optimum neighbourhood distance.

In Table 4 I have calculated correlation coefficients between the columns of the factor matrices for $r = 11$, 25, 40 60 and 85 cm in such a way that the first column (representing the first factor) for each matrix is compared with the first column in each of the other matrices, the second column with the other second columns etc. The correlation coefficients illustrate the similarity between the factors extracted for different equivalent neighbourhood distances. The first factor is effectively identical for all the neighbourhood distances used. For the second and third factors there is little correlation between the $r = 11$ cm results and those for larger scales, whilst the latter, from $r = 25$ cm to $r = 85$ cm, show a high degree of correlation. The coherence of the results from $r = 25$ cm upwards, but not for $r = 11$ cm, again points to the introduction of noise into the association index matrix for the smallest scale, resulting from the low neighbour counts (see also Graham 1979, p. 16). For the fourth and fifth factors (not included on Table 4), there is little correlation between either the $r = 11$ cm or $r = 25$ cm results and those for larger scales, but the $r = 40$ cm, $r = 60$ cm and $r = 85$ cm maintain a stable pattern.

These results indicate that for the first three components of a multivariate analysis of the Local Density Analysis results,

Table 4. *Pincevent Section 36: V105. Correlation comparison of the results of Correspondence Analysis for different scales of Local Density Analysis*

Equivalent radius (cm)

	11	25	40	60	85
11	1.0				
25	0.99	1.0			
40	0.97	0.99_5	1.0		
60	0.96	0.99_0	0.99_7	1.0	
85	0.95	0.98	0.99_9	0.99	1.0
	11	25	40	60	85

First factor

Equivalent radius (cm)

	11	25	40	60	85	11	25	40	60	85
11	1.0									
25	−0.05	1.0								
40	0.04	0.97	1.0							
60	0.04	0.59	0.63	1.0						
85	−0.01	0.58	0.62	0.99	1.0					
11	0.10	0.27	0.28	−0.02	−0.08	1.0				
25	0.07	0.01	0.05	0.77	0.74	0.07	1.0			
40	0.05	−0.03	0.00	0.76	0.75	−0.13	0.98	1.0		
60	−0.11	−0.68	−0.72	0.00	0.01	−0.16	0.57	0.63	1.0	
80	−0.26	−0.54	−0.60	0.03	0.02	−0.17	0.53	0.56	0.92	1.0
	11	25	40	60	85	11	25	40	60	85

Second factor   *Third factor*

all equivalent neighbourhood distances from 25 cm to 85 cm give essentially the same solutions. The $r = 25$ cm results do, however, show an increasing 'noise' effect, which might be expected to show up in unreliable results for very sparse categories, so an equivalent neighbourhood distance of 40 cm was selected for the final analysis.

Results

Tables 5 and 6 show the association and correlation matrices produced by Local Density Analysis of the Pincevent data using the chosen equivalent radius of 40 cm. Initial inspection of these matrices indicates that there is a clear dichotomy between the 14 reindeer bone categories and the six categories of lithic material. This pattern is best seen in the correlation matrix, both because the correlation coefficients are less prone to 'noise' and because they are easier to appreciate. An intermediate group consists of cores, which show an association with the faunal remains rather than the other lithic remains as one might have expected, hare bones which are associated slightly more closely with the lithic group than with the other faunal remains, and the two size classes of hearth stone fragments. The larger hearth stones (over 7 cm length) are associated with the lithic group, and the smaller hearth stones with the faunal group. The same relationships are apparent in the Correspondence Analysis factor matrix, presented diagrammatically in Fig. 5. A similar plot, shown in Fig. 6, was obtained using SPSS factor analysis (principal factors with iteration, singular correlation matrix, maximum off-diagonal element used as initial estimate of communality, factors 1 and 2 account for 56% and 28% of variance, Varimax rotation).

The dichotomy between faunal and lithic remains is of no surprise if one examines the plans for these artifacts (Figs. 7a, b and 8a, b), which show them as clearly segregated into separate, although overlapping areas (e.g. faunal remains in U106–7, lithic remains centred on the V105 hearth). On perçoit très bien l'apport des déchets par amas successifs tantôt dominées par le silex, tantôt par les déchets culinaires (Leroi-Gourhan and Brézillon 1972, p. 244, figs. 162 and 175). This segregation appears very clearly on the distribution density plans for reindeer bones and lithic artifacts (compare the three main concentrations in Fig. 8a with those in Fig. 7a). The interest of the results lies in the less obvious details. The first and most important of these is the association of cores and the larger hearth stone fragments with the faunal remains group, contrasting with the association between the smaller hearth stone fragments and the lithic remains group. Examination of the plans suggests that the larger hearth stone frag-

90

Table 5. *Local Density Analysis, Pincevent Section 36: V105. Association indices*

Category	ANTL	MAXI	MAND	TOOTH	RIB	SCAP	HUME	FEMR	TIB	ULRAD	METT	METC	METP	PHAL	HARE	>7CM	<7CM	CORE	BURI	SPALL	BBL	AWL	ENDS	BRFLT
ANTL	1.06																							
MAXI	2.10	3.40																						
MAND	2.65	2.76	4.29																					
TOOTH	2.45	3.06	3.59	3.85																				
RIB	2.60	2.56	3.30	3.12	3.58																			
SCAP	2.63	2.30	2.56	3.58	2.90	2.63																		
HUME	1.69	1.67	3.00	2.53	2.56	2.43	1.73																	
FEMR	3.45	2.90	3.85	3.09	3.09	2.83	2.69	3.72																
TIB	1.29	2.20	2.36	2.16	2.37	2.26	2.76	2.25	3.00															
ULRAD	1.87	1.90	2.95	2.89	2.49	2.45	2.80	2.63	2.55	2.62														
METT	2.37	3.07	2.97	3.58	3.16	2.39	1.79	3.36	2.17	2.79	3.10													
METC	1.86	1.76	3.20	3.07	2.75	2.40	2.65	2.93	2.42	2.85	2.69	2.73												
METP	2.20	2.43	3.12	3.29	2.95	2.35	2.32	3.10	2.30	2.82	3.76	3.50	2.93											
PHAL	3.35	2.82	3.58	3.30	3.30	3.29	3.25	3.53	2.60	3.16	2.86	3.40	3.10	3.95										
HARE	2.66	2.25	3.10	2.93	2.97	2.27	2.17	2.99	2.27	2.79	2.96	2.36	2.83	3.09	3.63									
>7CM	2.62	2.06	3.75	3.10	3.63	2.73	2.42	3.59	2.07	3.02	2.90	3.27	3.13	3.49	3.17	5.12								
<7CM	1.93	1.50	2.29	2.09	2.15	1.49	1.69	2.37	1.54	2.06	2.42	1.94	2.25	2.06	2.56	1.93	4.78							
CORE	0.99	1.27	2.37	1.77	1.99	1.60	2.07	2.49	2.40	2.90	2.02	2.02	2.17	2.67	2.46	2.86	1.89	3.26						
BURI	2.52	1.39	1.94	2.35	3.02	2.75	1.80	2.17	1.82	1.72	2.33	2.19	2.29	2.59	3.09	2.55	1.72	2.19	3.93					
SPALL	2.02	1.14	2.16	1.76	2.62	1.47	1.33	1.86	1.50	1.56	1.90	1.80	1.92	2.25	3.19	2.36	1.79	2.73	4.02	5.99				
BBL	1.54	1.13	2.23	2.04	2.83	1.56	1.22	1.87	1.16	1.50	1.69	1.36	1.64	2.10	3.22	2.42	1.57	2.43	4.33	6.29	7.29			
AWL	2.50	1.52	2.29	2.16	3.45	2.09	1.56	2.19	1.09	1.20	2.70	1.66	2.25	2.32	3.05	2.70	1.30	2.77	4.45	5.52	5.79	5.69		
ENDS	1.90	1.53	2.09	2.15	2.12	1.76	1.73	2.10	1.37	1.84	2.32	1.69	1.99	1.93	2.35	1.52	1.46	2.70	2.35	2.97	2.85	3.25	2.12	
BRFLT	2.49	1.89	2.90	2.55	3.55	2.42	1.87	2.32	1.43	1.70	1.80	1.80	1.96	2.83	3.09	2.76	1.69	2.50	3.55	4.66	5.15	5.53	3.09	5.08
	ANTL	MAXI	MAND	TOOTH	RIB	SCAP	HUME	FEMR	TIB	ULRAD	METT	METC	METP	PHAL	HARE	>7CM	<7CM	CORE	BURI	SPALL	BBL	AWL	ENDS	BRFLT

Reindeer bones — *Lithic industry*

Table 6. *Local Density Analysis, Pincevent Section 36: V105. Correlation matrix*

Category	ANTL	MAXI	MAND	TOOTH	RIB	SCAP	HUME	FEMR	TIB	ULRAD	METT	METC	METP	PHAL	HARE	>7 CM	<7 CM	CORE	BURI	SPALL	BBL	AWL	ENDS	BRFLT
ANTL	1.00																							
MAXI	0.50	1.00																						
MAND	0.56	0.67	1.00																					
TOOTH	0.59	0.83	0.73	1.00																				
RIB	0.72	0.33	0.56	0.64	1.00																			
SCAP	0.56	0.68	0.66	0.77	0.60	1.00																		
HUME	0.42	0.52	0.71	0.62	0.27	0.64	1.00																	
FEMR	0.47	0.75	0.87	0.78	0.43	0.67	0.62	1.00																
TIB	0.10	0.46	0.43	0.46	−0.05	0.42	0.73	0.43	1.00															
ULRAD	0.21	0.49	0.71	0.62	0.09	0.49	0.76	0.70	0.82	1.00														
METT	0.57	0.77	0.65	0.78	0.44	0.60	0.51	0.68	0.30	0.46	1.00													
METC	0.48	0.55	0.80	0.75	0.40	0.68	0.81	0.74	0.69	0.85	0.67	1.00												
METP	0.48	0.67	0.75	0.81	0.42	0.62	0.65	0.77	0.54	0.75	0.77	0.81	1.00											
PHAL	0.45	0.62	0.85	0.75	0.48	0.81	0.75	0.86	0.60	0.73	0.52	0.79	0.69	1.00										
HARE	0.51	0.01	0.28	0.12	0.63	0.14	0.01	0.15	−0.29	−0.06	0.24	0.13	0.17	0.11	1.00									
>7 CM	0.51	0.33	0.79	0.56	0.69	0.56	0.57	0.71	0.31	0.59	0.50	0.71	0.65	0.74	0.48	1.00								
<7 CM	0.08	−0.33	−0.22	−0.33	−0.13	−0.47	−0.34	−0.26	−0.52	−0.33	−0.05	−0.27	−0.17	−0.51	0.27	−0.24	1.00							
CORE	0.12	0.05	0.43	0.13	−0.02	0.09	0.61	0.31	0.66	0.73	0.15	0.58	0.40	0.39	0.15	0.53	−0.12	1.00						
BURI	0.19	−0.43	−0.33	−0.34	0.43	−0.18	−0.43	−0.47	−0.68	−0.66	−0.29	−0.44	−0.40	−0.39	0.61	−0.04	0.27	−0.41	1.00					
SPALL	0.03	−0.60	−0.44	−0.54	0.22	−0.45	−0.59	−0.61	−0.75	−0.74	−0.43	−0.58	−0.54	−0.58	0.57	−0.18	0.41	−0.35	0.92	1.00				
BBL	0.07	−0.55	−0.40	−0.49	0.27	−0.40	−0.56	−0.60	−0.72	−0.72	−0.41	−0.55	−0.53	−0.55	0.58	−0.15	0.37	−0.34	0.92	0.99	1.00			
AWL	0.16	−0.47	−0.38	−0.41	0.38	−0.31	−0.59	−0.51	−0.79	−0.75	−0.32	−0.54	−0.48	−0.51	0.58	−0.13	0.40	−0.47	0.94	0.96	0.96	1.00		
ENDS	0.22	−0.36	−0.29	−0.31	0.30	−0.32	−0.53	−0.44	−0.75	−0.67	−0.18	−0.46	−0.35	−0.49	0.56	−0.22	0.65	−0.43	0.80	0.85	0.84	0.89	1.00	
BRFLT	0.22	−0.41	−0.27	−0.35	0.45	−0.23	−0.48	−0.45	−0.75	−0.71	−0.29	−0.50	−0.46	−0.41	0.59	−0.06	0.34	−0.43	0.92	0.94	0.75	0.97	0.87	1.00
	Reindeer bones																		*Lithic industry*					

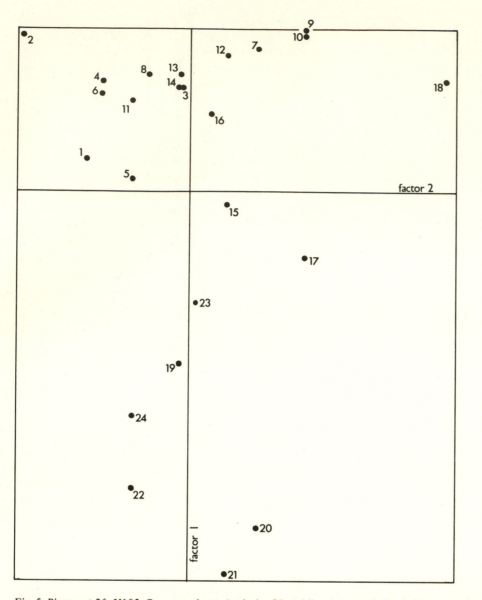

Fig. 5. Pincevent 36: V105. Correspondence Analysis of Local Density association indices; factor matrix plot. (See Table 3 for list of artifact categories.) Equivalent neighbourhood distance = 40 cm, factors 1 and 2 account for 76% and 7% of variance.

ments, the cores and the bulk of the faunal remains occur in common disposal areas east of the main hearth (squares U106, U107 and S107), whereas the smaller hearth stone fragments and the lithic remains occur in and around the main hearth (squares V105, U105 and U106) and in a different suite of disposal areas (squares X102 and R107). The hypothesis offered to explain these observations is that food remains and bulky items were disposed of immediately onto a 'midden' away from the main hearth, whereas the smaller hearth stone fragments and the lithic artifacts concentrated in and around the main hearth and were the subject of periodic removal to subsidiary dumps, notably those around X102 and R107.

Observations paralleling this situation have been made in the ethnographic context by J. F. O'Connell (personal communication) on recent Aljawara camp sites in Central

Australia. In this case, a windbreak protects a series of hearths, bordering a large semicircular area in which most domestic activities are carried out. This area contains mostly small artifacts, larger ones being immediately rejected, or periodically swept, onto an arc of middens on the perimeter opposite the windbreak. Artifacts are further spread by the activities of dogs and children.

The suggestion of size-influenced rejection patterning at Pincevent is further supported by the observation that the two most clustered and most highly associated artifact categories are backed bladelets and burin spalls, which appear to be clustered around the west of the hearth and in the two main concentrations of lithic remains (Leroi-Gourhan and Brézillon 1972, figs. 70 and 71). Subjective assessment of the distribution of very small debitage (based on field records, see also *ibid*. fig.

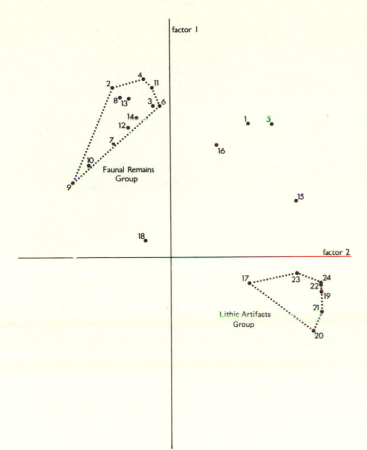

Fig. 6. Pincevent 36: V105. Factor Analysis of Local Density association indices; factor matrix plot. (See Table 3 for list of artifact categories.) Equivalent neighbourhood distance = 40 cm, factors 1 and 2 account for 56 % and 28 % of variance.

59) suggests that this is even more clustered. Other lithic types are progressively less associated with burin spalls and backed bladelets and show lesser degrees of clustering as their mean size increases. Whilst these observations may imply activity determinants, the survival of very highly clustered distributions of small artifacts and the progressive decrease in clustering with artifact size suggest a size filtering effect which may be the result of site maintenance activities.

The present analysis shows one very strong factor (over 75 % of variance) which is interpreted as representing differential disposal patterns for bulky artifacts and faunal material on the one hand, and for smaller lithic material on the other. The second and third factors of the multivariate analysis also maintain a stable configuration through a wide range of analysis scales. These factors appear to translate the peculiarities of the distributions of particular artifact categories, notably the separation of cores and maxillaries from the faunal remains group in opposite directions on factor 2, and of the smaller class of hearth stone fragments from all other artifact categories on factor 3. Certainly there is no sign of neat 'toolkit' factors, but this is hardly to be expected in such a clear-cut case of patterning by site maintenance activities.

Conclusion

In this chapter I have set out to do two things. Firstly, to structure a discussion of different conceptual approaches to spatial data and of different ways of recording such data. Secondly, to propose a particular methodology for the analysis of spatial data collected as cell frequencies, and to illustrate this methodology with an application to data from Pincevent.

I have argued that cell-frequency recording of artifacts need not be considered as a poor cousin of coordinate data to be reserved for sieve finds and other artifacts too small or too numerous to be bothered with. Used intelligently, cell frequency recording provides a method of rapidly and accurately recording spatial information at a uniform level of precision. This is contrasted with the weaknesses inherent in conventional recording strategies involving a combination of coordinate and cell frequency data. These weaknesses not only result in inefficient use of excavation resources, but in many cases give rise to data whose impurities it is tempting to ignore. The underlying problem is simply that the resolution of conventional grid-squares is insufficient to exploit the full information potential of the majority of excavated sites. Increased resolution of collection units (i.e. smaller units), together with more limited and explicitly controlled use of coordinates or mapping for larger finds, is seen as the solution to these problems.

In the middle part of the chapter, I have considered ways of exploiting the information content of cell frequency data. I have argued that many conventional quadrat methods fail to exploit the data efficiently, and I have proposed the Local Density Analysis technique as a means of calculating a matrix of association coefficients between categories. Emphasis was placed on description and visual presentation because these were considered to be of paramount importance in archaeological situations. The main advantages of Local Density Analysis were seen as its mathematical simplicity and robustness.

The application of Local Density Analysis and the other techniques discussed to archaeological data was demonstrated on data from Pincevent. Despite the methodological test nature of the analysis, it proved possible to suggest hypotheses which were not immediately apparent from subjective assessment of the distributions. The prime determinant of artifact distribution patterning at Pincevent appears to be site maintenance, occurring either as immediate disposal of material or as periodic clearing. The present analysis suggests that we are unlikely to obtain detailed activity information from the spatial patterning of the Pincevent occupation units, which appear to correspond more closely with a social-context model of spatial patterning as proposed by Yellen (1977) than with an activity-specific model such as those discussed by Whallon (1973b) or Binford (1978). This is a conclusion which might, however, be modified by the inclusion of the small unprepared hearths scattered between the larger, more complex and very much richer prepared hearths and associated features.

This discussion is obviously no more than a tentative

(a)

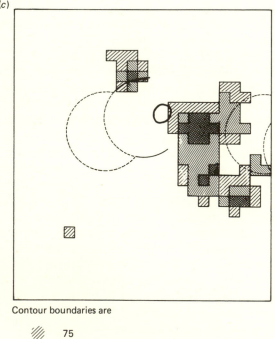

(b)

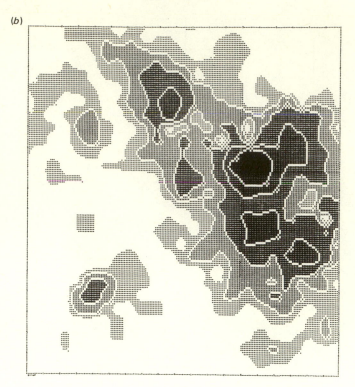

(c)

Contour boundaries are

/// 75

     110

     155

finds per square metre

Fig. 7. (*a*) Pincevent 36: V105. Distribution of faunal remains. (After Leroi-Gourhan and Brézillon 1972, fig. 76.) (*b*) Pincevent 36: V105. Computer generated density map of faunal remains (categories 1–14). Unweighted five-cell moving average, control point spacing 40 cm, interpolation and contouring by SYMAP. Contour boundaries are 3.7, 21.3, 55, 126, 218 finds per square metre, darkest shading is highest density. (*c*) Pincevent 36: V105. Unsmoothed (proximal) density map of faunal remains (categories 1–14). Unweighted five-cell moving average calculated at 40 cm intervals.

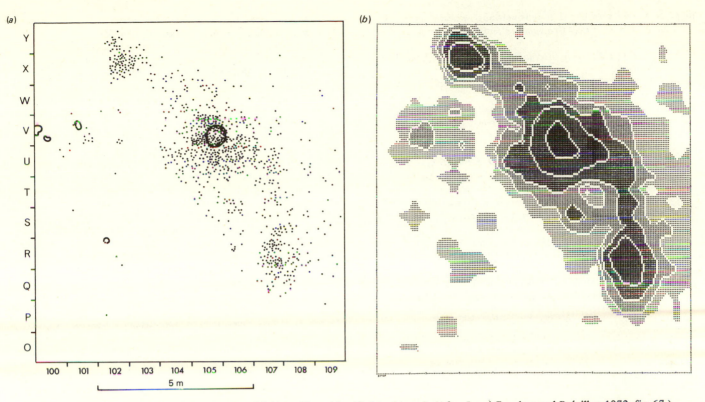

Fig. 8. (*a*) Pincevent 36: V105. Distribution of lithic artifacts (classified tool types). (After Leroi-Gourhan and Brézillon 1972, fig. 67.)
(*b*) Pincevent 36: V105. Computer generated density map of lithic artifacts (categories 19–24). Unweighted five-cell moving average, control point spacing 40 cm, interpolation and contouring by SYMAP. Darkest shading is highest density.

step towards the use of intrasite spatial data and specifically towards the efficient use of cell frequency data. I hope that in some degree it may serve as a basis for further developments. However, I believe that the methodology proposed is already workable, and I hope that I have shown this through the analysis of the Pincevent data.

I am in no sense a statistician and I have deliberately ignored statistical assessment of the Local Density method, although I think I have a fairly clear idea of how the association indices behave when faced with different types of patterning. Whilst statistical and simulation studies should undoubtedly be a prerequisite to the widespread adoption of a particular spatial analysis technique, the analysis of spatial distributions is not a simple problem for which there is a 'right' technique. Different situations and different underlying assumptions will require different methods, often used together in a single study (cf. Hietala and Stevens 1977). I feel that we have now reached a stage in intrasite spatial analysis where the first priority should be to complete and publish substantial numbers of non-trivial analyses, preferably applying and comparing several different methods on the same data. Only then will we be in a position to assess the strengths and weaknesses of different techniques and to choose appropriate methods for a given situation. With a wide range of techniques now available for quantitative spatial analysis, it is probably in the development of our underlying concepts and

assumptions that we can expect to see the greatest progress over the next few years. The influence of ethnoarchaeological work will doubtless be of crucial importance in this respect.

Acknowledgements

This chapter is based mainly on work carried out at the Institut du Quaternaire, Bordeaux University, in 1975. Professor F. Bordes and J-Ph. Rigaud encouraged the undertaking of the project and generously provided the necessary facilities and advice. Professor A. Leroi-Gourhan and his team not only made freely available the results of their excavations at Pincevent but also the facilities of their field station for the collection of the data and the writing of parts of this chapter. Many ideas have arisen through discussion with Paul Callow, whose criticisms and suggestions I gratefully acknowledge. A number of people read and criticised drafts of this paper, of whom I should like to thank particularly Jim Rhoads for his constructive demolition of my first draft and Peter White for succinctly targetting its weaknesses. I am indebted to Ouma Sananikone and Maureen Johnson for typing drafts of this paper.

Note
1. Each major hearth and its associated features is referred to by the metre square in which it was first encountered.

References
Ammerman, A. J. and Feldman, M. W. (1974). On the making of an assemblage of stone tools. *American Antiquity* 39: 610–16.
Benzecri, J. P. (1973). *L'analyse des Données*, vol. 2, *L'analyse des Correspondances*. Dunod: Paris.

Berry, B. J. L. and Marble, D. F. (eds.) (1968). *Spatial Analysis: A Reader in Statistical Geography*. Prentice Hall: Englewood Cliffs, New Jersey.

Binford, L. R. (1972). *An Archaeological Perspective*. Seminar Press: New York.

Binford, L. R. (1977). *For Theory Building in Archaeology*. Academic Press: New York.

Binford, L. R. (1978). Dimensional analysis of behavior and site structure: learning from an Eskimo hunting stand. *American Antiquity* 43: 330–61.

Brézillon, M. (1971). Les Tarterets II, site paléolithique de plein air à Corbeil-Essonnes (Essonne) I. *Gallia Préhistoire* XIV, 3–40.

Clark, J. P. and Evans, F. C. (1954). Distance to nearest neighbour as a measure of spatial relationship. *Population Ecology* 35: 445–53.

Cliff, A. D., Haggett, P., Ord, J. K., Bassett, K., Davies, R. B. (1975). *Elements of Spatial Structure: A Quantitative Approach*. Cambridge University Press: Cambridge.

Cole, J. P. and King, C. A. M. (1968). *Quantitative Geography: Techniques and Theories in Geography*. Glasgow University Press, Glasgow.

Dacey, M. F. (1968). Modified Poisson provability law for point pattern more regular than random. In *Spatial Analysis: A Reader in Statistical Geography*, ed. B. J. L. Berry and D. F. Marble, pp. 172–9. Prentice Hall: Englewood Cliffs, New Jersey.

Dacey, M. F. (1974). Statistical tests of spatial association in the location of tool types. *American Antiquity* 38: 320–8.

de Lumley, H. *et al.* (1969). Une cabane Acheuléenne dans la grotte du Lazaret (Nice). *Memoires de la Société Préhistorique Française*, 7.

Graham, I. (1979). Spatial analysis and distance methods in the study of archaeological distributions. *Journal of Archaeological Science* 6: 1–25.

Greig-Smith, P. (1952). The use of random and contiguous quadrats in the study of the structure of plant communities. *Annals of Botany, London* 16: 293–316.

Greig-Smith, P. (1961). Data on pattern within plant communities. I. The analysis of pattern. *Journal of Ecology* 49: 695–702.

Hale, H. M. and Tindale, N. B. (1934). Aborigines of the Princess Charlotte Bay, North Queensland. *Records of the South Australia Museum* 5: 117–72.

Hesse, A. (1971). Les Tarterets II, site paléolithique de plein air à Corbeil-Essonnes (Essonne). II Comparaison par le calcul des distributions horizontales des vestiges lithiques. *Gallia Préhistoire* XIV: 41–6.

Hietala, H. J. and Stevens, D. E. (1977). Spatial analysis: multiple procedures in pattern recognition studies. *American Antiquity* 42: 539–59.

Hodder, I. and Okell, E. (1978). An index for assessing the association between distribution points in archaeology. In *Simulation Studies in Archaeology*, ed. I. Hodder, pp. 97–108. Cambridge University Press: Cambridge.

Hodder, I. and Orton, C. (1976). *Spatial Analysis in Archaeology*. New Studies in Archaeology I. Cambridge University Press: Cambridge.

Johnson, I. (1976). Contribution méthodologique à l'étude de la répartition des vestiges dans des niveaux archéologiques. DES Thesis, Université de Bordeaux I.

Kershaw, K. A. (1957). The use of cover and frequency in the detection of pattern in plant communities. *Ecology* 38: 291–9.

Kershaw, K. A. (1961). Association and covariance analysis of plant communities. *Journal of Ecology* 49: 643–54.

King, L. J. (1968). A quantitative expression of the pattern of urban settlement in selected areas of the United States. In *Spatial Analysis: A Reader in Statistical Geography*, ed. B. J. L. Berry and D. F. Marble. Prentice Hall: Englewood Cliffs, New Jersey.

Leroi-Gourhan, A. (1961). Les fouilles d'Arcy-sur-Cure. *Gallia Prehistoire* IV: 3-16.

Leroi-Gourhan, A. (1976). Les Structures d'habitat au Paléolithique supérieur. *La Préhistoire Française*, I: 656–63.

Leroi-Gourhan, A. and Brézillon, M. (1966). L'habitat magdalénien no. 1 de Pincevent près de Montereau (Seine-et-Marne). *Gallia Préhistoire* IX, Fasc. 2: 263–385.

Leroi-Gourhan, A. and Brézillon, M. (1972). Fouilles de Pincevent. Essai d'analyse ethnographique d'un habitat magdalénien (la section 36). *Gallia Préhistoire*, suppl. VII. CNRS: Paris.

Parkington, J. and Poggenpoel, C. (1971). Excavations at De Hangen, 1968 *South African Archaeological Bulletin* 26: 3–36.

Pielou, E. (1969). *An Introduction to Mathematical Ecology*. John Wiley: New York.

Pinder, D. A. and Witherick, M. E. (1972). The principles, practice and pitfalls of nearest-neighbour analysis. *Geography* 57, 77–88.

Ranson, D. (1981). Open areas excavations in Australia. A plea for bigger holes. In *Holier Than Thou*, Proceedings of the 1978 Kioloa Conference on Australian Prehistory, ed. I. Johnson, pp. 77–90. Department of Prehistory, Australian National University: Canberra.

Riley, T. J. (1974). Constraints on dimensions of variance. *American Antiquity* 39: 489–90.

Robinson, A., Sale, R. and Morrison, J. (1978). *Elements of Cartography*. John Wiley: New York.

Whallon, R. E. Jr (1973*a*) Spatial analysis of palaeolithic occupation areas. The present problem and the 'functional argument'. In *The Explanation of Culture Change*, New York. Academic Press: ed. C. Renfrew, pp. 115–29.

Whallon, R. E. Jr (1973*b*). Spatial analysis of occupation floors. I. Application of dimensional analysis of variance. *American Antiquity* 38: 266–77.

Whallon, R. E. Jr (1974). Spatial analysis of occupation floors. II. Nearest neighbor analysis. *American Antiquity* 39: 16–34.

White, J. P. and Modjeska, N. (1978). Acquirers, users, finders, losers: The use axe blades make of the Duna. *Trade and Exchange in Oceania and Australia,* ed. J. Specht and J. P. White, pp. 276–87. Sydney University Press: Sydney, New South Wales.

Wintermann, R. (1975). Problems in the horizontal analysis of archaeological remains from Upper Palaeolithic sites. Master's Thesis: University of California, Los Angeles, Cal.

Wright, R. V. S. (ed.) (1974). *Stone Tools as Cultural Markers: Change, Evolution and Complexity*. Australian Institute of Aboriginal Studies: Canberra.

Yellen, J. E. (1977). *Archaeological Approaches to the Present*. Academic Press: New York.

Zubrow, E. B. W. and Harbaugh, J. W. (1978). Archaeological prospecting: Kriging and simulation. In *Simulation Studies in Archaeology,* ed. I. Hodder, pp. 109–22. Cambridge University Press: Cambridge.

Chapter 7

Analysis of artifact distribution at Ngenyn (Kenya): depositional and postdepositional effects
F. Hivernel and I. Hodder

Analysis of artifact distributions can be carried out at many different analytical levels. If an archaeological deposit is not too thick and the density of artifacts not too great, patterning of the artifacts may sometimes be noticed during the excavation process or else noticed on the final maps. But more often the density of Old World archaeological material is too high for patterning to be noticed during excavation, and the resulting maps are frequently too crowded to be easily read. Consequently one has to turn to statistical methods in order objectively to assess whether non-random patterns are present and in order to describe them.

On the other hand, in the interpretation of archaeological spatial patterns, initial consideration should be of the deposition and later disturbance of the artifacts. Without this prior 'filtering', assessment of prehistoric behaviour and activities on sites is potentially dangerous. Realisation of the importance of *depositional factors* in the interpretation of site formation and artifact distributions, while implicit in many earlier studies, has only recently been emphasised. The concepts have now been defined (Schiffer 1976) and a series of hypotheses developed (e.g. Yellen 1977). It is obvious that depositional processes are often very difficult to trace, save in very exceptional circumstances such as at Pincevent (Leroi-Gourhan and Brézillon 1972), where the full story of a tool could be traced from its manufacture, use, resharpening and transformation to its abandonment. But testable hypotheses can be developed which may at least encourage the archaeologist to consider his data from a different perspective. One example of such a hypothesis concerns the effects of curation on site assemblages (Hayden 1976; Binford 1978). A rather different depositional hypothesis will be examined in this chapter. Schiffer (1976), Yellen (1977) and R. Gould (personal communication) have suggested that a multipurpose, 'home base' occupation may result in a continual resorting and movement of artifacts (as a result of kicking and trampling etc.), so that the association between activities and artifacts resulting from those activities is disturbed. On a shorter term or special activity site there would be lower probabilities of movement and disturbance of artifacts. Many artifacts will remain at the location of the original activities which produced them.

Yet interpretation in terms of depositional processes must also take *postdepositional factors* into account. There is a definitional difficulty in deciding whether a process such as kicking of bones or artifacts by man is depositional or postdepositional. Presumably an intentional kick might be considered depositional and an unintentional kick postdepositional! In view of such difficulties, 'postdepositional' will be used in this article to refer to non-human agencies. Several different non-human processes may act on an archaeological site once it has been abandoned. They may preferentially affect the faunal remains (Isaac 1971; Kroll and Isaac, Chapter 2), as in the case of scavengers dispersing or destroying bones.

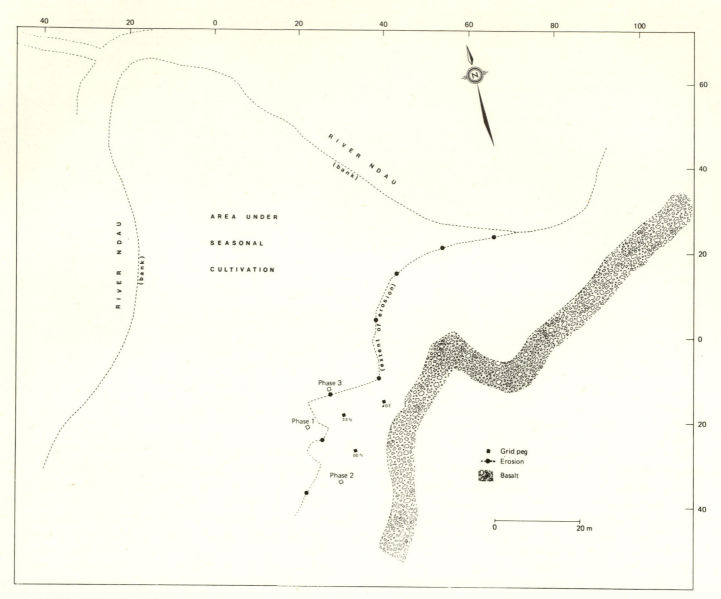

Fig. 1. Site location, Ngenyn, Kenya.

Erosion and weathering (wind, rain, sun, termites etc.) can occur before the site is buried. Gifford (1978) has shown how, in a part of Kenya (the Turkana area) adjacent to that studied here, trampling by animals can re-sort bone material into different sizes at different depths below the ground surface. Disturbance may also result during the burial of a site. For example, the flow of water and silt may rearrange artifact distributions into new configurations. Such postdepositional effects are likely to be highly specific to each locality – to each site or even part of a site. It is essential, therefore, that they be discussed in terms of the local environment and palaeoenvironment. In the following section, then, the site of Ngenyn (Fig. 1) is described and the particular natural processes relevant to the build up of layers on the site are discussed.

The Ngenyn site and the local postdepositional effects

The aim of this chapter is to show how an explicit consideration of depositional and postdepositional factors can aid the analysis and interpretation of spatial information. The particular site used as an example is Ngenyn, situated in the Kapthurin River Basin, west of Lake Baringo, north central Kenya. The excavation of the 3 m Holocene terrace of the River Ndau in the Tugen Hills revealed three different periods of occupation separated by sterile sediment (Hivernel 1978). Phase 3 provided a ^{14}C date of 1970 ± 150 b.p. Cattle and ovicaprids were found, and the pottery was decorated. The deposit of this phase has a thickness of 44 cm and was very close to, and sometimes even eroding out at, the surface. Spatial analysis was carried out over a 3 m × 3 m area of the deposit. Phase 2 was dated to 2020 ± 130 b.p. Cattle and goats were present and the pottery was undecorated. It was dug over 2 m × 4 m and encountered 1.20 m below ground level. The layer had a thickness of 32 cm. Phase 1 is still undated, but was stratigraphically earlier than the other two phases.

No cattle were recovered, but ovicaprids were present. The pottery was mainly undecorated. It was excavated over 2 m × 7 m and the layer was first encountered 2 m below present ground level. The layer had a thickness of 25 cm.

During the excavation of these phases, the deposits were divided into arbitrary vertical divisions (spits) of approximately 2 cm thickness. Each artifact was given a two-dimensional spatial coordinate (measured in the field to 0.50 cm), but depth was only recorded by placing the items in spits. The purpose of the spits was to assess the degree of mixing and variation in assemblage through the depth of one period of occupation.

Artifacts which could be rejoined often occurred in the same or adjacent spits in each occupation phase (Hivernel 1978), which suggests some degree of secondary movement. Similarly, no distinct narrow horizons of artifacts could be identified within the phases. This evidence of slight disturbance of the archaeological layers must be considered in relation to the specific postdepositional factors at work at Ngenyn. Fortunately, detailed sedimentological and geological studies have been carried out in the Tugen Hills by Tallon (1976) and his findings are used in the following discussion of the natural build up, movement and erosion of the layers.

The occupation areas at Ngenyn were covered by silt deposited by the flooding river. The site was situated at the periphery of the floodplain, backing onto a ridge, and the disturbance caused by silt deposition would not have been great. It is rare that sites are buried entirely after one year, and several rainy seasons or episodes may go by before the sites are completely covered. Sometimes several severe rains can speed up the process. For example, in northern Kenya (Gifford and Behrensmeyer 1977) in an environment similar to that at Ngenyn, about 30 cm of sediment accumulated on a site during four or five rains between 1973 and 1974.

In addition, erosion may occur in conjunction with deposition. Among the processes isolated by Tallon which can have a bearing on the explanation of the archaeological record at Ngenyn, the most important are raindrop erosion and surface wash. Raindrop erosion is significant in sparsely vegetated areas. Stones or pebbles lying on a ground surface protect the soil underneath them, but the raindrops still affect the uncovered areas adjacent to the stones. This often results in stones being left standing on pedestals of earth a few centimetres high. This process can affect the stratigraphy of an archaeological floor by artificially lowering the small elements, while the large ones stand high. Tallon notes (1976, p. 241) that perched pebbles are common in the Tugen Hills. Such factors would have been especially significant if there had been a more humid environment in the past. In semi-arid areas, this form of erosion is an important factor in soil creep.

Another form of erosion which still acts in the Ngenyn area today is surface wash. This is a process combining elements of sheet flood, raindrop erosion and soil creep, and it is active in all areas of semi-arid open bushland. During heavy rains, the upper 5–10 cm of the ground surface become waterlogged. If the gradient of the ground is small the still water as well as the surface water travels down the slight gradient as sheet wash. Any angular fragments of rocks which have rolled down the slope of an adjacent area of positive relief are slowly moved down the gradient by the surface wash. Smaller particle sizes transported by surface wash travel as slurry in the upper layers of the ground surface and in suspension in water travelling over the surface. In the Kapthurin, the slurry can shift pebbles whose long axis measures up to 15 cm (Tallon 1976). The steeper the gradient, the greater is the transportation capacity of surface wash. After the rain has stopped, the material in suspension is redeposited as the water dries up. Partly because of this and partly because the larger rock fragments are transported in and not on slurry, pebbles initially lying on top of the ground are usually submerged in a sea of silt. The depth of the sheet flood varies between 10 cm and 25 cm. Discrete irregularities or hollows on a primary depositional surface tend to be infilled and smoothed out by surface wash (Tallon 1976, p. 242).

Most of the stone artifacts from phase 3 (which is very close to the surface) exhibit concretions of calcium carbonate indicating some prolonged water action. No such concretions were noticed in Phase 2, but they occur again in Phase 1. Surface wash is certainly a process still affecting Phase 3 today and could account for the fact that next-to-no artifacts could be rejoined or matched together. Phases 1 and 2 are more deeply buried and may in the past have been less affected by this surface wash (see also below).

The various postdepositional factors described above provide the essential background for any analysis and interpretation of spatial distributions of artifacts at Ngenyn. They have some immediate effects on the way the data are organised. The spits by means of which the site was excavated and the material coded can be given very little significance in view of the postdepositional distortions. In particular, when the sample of artifacts from each spit is very small, it would seem to be of little value to examine the spatial patterning of that spit separately. Accordingly, during the analysis which follows, all the spits from one phase or adjacent spits within a phase have frequently been 'collapsed' and considered together. But, in addition, variation in spatial patterning at different depths within one deposit is also examined for those phases with larger sample sizes and thicker deposits (Phases 2 and 3), in order to obtain some indication of variability within the overall collapsed distributions. But the arbitrary nature of these spits must always be borne in mind. Figures 2 to 12 are illustrative only of particular spits and groups of spits since it would have been impossible in the context of this book to provide maps of all the material (for a full acount see Hivernel 1978).

The postdepositional effects will be considered in all the stages of analysis and interpretation that follow. The aim of these analyses is to determine whether, after the postdepositional effects have been 'filtered' out, hypotheses concerning depositional processes and on-site behaviour can be identified. In particular, attempts will be made to suggest whether specific phases are the result of 'home base' or short term occupation. In view of these aims it is now necessary to consider which techniques of analysis are most appropriate.

Quantitative methods of spatial analysis

The first concern is to examine whether artifacts of different types and at different depths are more or less clustered in their spatial distribution. Evidence of variation in spatial clustering according to friability of different artifact categories and their ease of transport by natural processes will allow the differential effects of such disturbance as water flow across the site to be assessed. Variation of spatial patterning with depth may occur because of the surface wash described above. It is necessary then to use techniques of point pattern analysis which are most sensitive to degrees of clustering and randomness.

Since the artifacts had been given grid coordinates in the field, it seemed sensible to use this detailed information rather than to agglomerate artifacts into quadrats. Quadrat methods of point pattern analysis have been shown (Hodder and Orton 1976, pp. 36–8) to be heavily dependent on the size of quadrat used. Any method based on frequency occurrence of artifacts in grid units results in a loss of spatial information. Thus, in this analysis, the Clark and Evans (1954) distance measure was used which takes as its data the grid coordinates of artifacts (Hodder and Orton 1976, pp. 38–43). The R coefficient measures a first-order difference between the observed distribution distances and those expected from a random distribution. An observed random distribution has a theoretical R value of 1.0, a clustered distribution has an R value less than 1.0 and a uniform (regular) distribution a value greater than 1.0. Levels of significance can also be calculated. However, these significance levels are seriously disturbed if distributions are studied without a surrounding boundary or 'buffer' zone. Hodder and Orton (1976, p. 42), Donnelly (1978) and Pinder *et al.* (1979) discuss some of these edge effects. As noted above, however, the aim of this study is to examine the *relative* patterning of different kinds of artifacts rather than to determine the statistical significance of the patterning of individual kinds of artifacts. There is little value, then, in decreasing the already small area of the distributions by incorporating a buffer zone around the edge or by incorporating edge effect adjustments.

After having identified the degree of clustering in artifact distributions at different depths in the deposits, the next concern is to examine whether the patterning of one artifact type is related to the patterning of another, for example by having clusters in similar areas. Such evidence is again important for assessing the degree of postdepositional effects. For example, it might be found that artifacts of similar friability and ease of movement had similar distributions. But association analysis is also important for examining ideas concerning depositional processes. For example, are the artifact types relatively well re-sorted and randomly intermingled (as in a 'home base' occupation), or are they clustered in separate localities (as in a short or special activity occupation)? A further possibility in a long

Table 1. *Artifact classes*

Artifact class	Variable number	Map symbol
Bones	1	+
Basalt	2	|
Pottery	3	v
Fresh obsidian	4	$
Silicified obsidian	5	*
Burned clay	6	▣
Charcoal	7	☉
Ostrich egg shell	8	△
Pebbles	9	◇
Hard compacted clay	10	×
Altered obsidian	11	1
Holes	12	2
Seeds	13	3
Wood	14	4
Features	15	5
Mother of pearl	16	6
Concretions	17	7

term, high density occupation would be distinct clusters of many artifact categories associated together in refuse 'dumps'.

The second type of analysis thus examined the spatial relationship between the distributions of all pairs of artifact categories. Hodder and Okell (1978) have introduced a new statistical coefficient for this purpose which they have demonstrated to be more sensitive to many types of spatial patterning than a range of existing measures. As with the nearest-neighbour statistic, the A coefficient uses distance measures rather than quadrat counts and so retains greater spatial information. Because the coefficient uses all the distances between the locations of both the artifact types being compared, it uses more detailed information and is more able to detect segregation and association than several other distance measures (for example, those described by Hodder and Orton (1976)). The A coefficient varies from 0, indicating complete segregation, to 1.0 indicating random intermingling, to greater than 1.0, indicating positive association in separate clusters. Significance levels for this measure have been empirically derived by Hodder and Okell (1978), and in contrast to the first type of analysis, edge effects do not prevent the use of these significance levels. Accordingly, results significant at $p = 0.05$ are indicated in the tables for the A coefficient. As already mentioned, significance levels for the R value would have little validity in the context of the Ngenyn data and they are not quoted in the tables.

Spatial analysis at Ngenyn

The nature of the artifact distributions (see Table 1) can now be examined for each phase using nearest-neighbour analysis and the A coefficient, in order to identify differences

Table 2. *Nearest-neighbour analysis (R) values for Phase 3*

Variables	(R)	Horizons															
		1	2	3	4	5	6	7	8	9	10	11	12–14	15	16–17	18–20	21–22
1	0.82	0.86	0.93	0.91	0.91	0.94	0.91	0.97	0.92	0.83	0.75	0.84	0.76	0.59	0.84	0.61	0.58
2	1.00	0.95	0.87	1.01	1.01	1.16	1.00	1.01	0.95	1.11	0.96	1.08	1.13	1.11	1.08	0.82	0.85
3	0.97	0.97	0.89	0.89	1.06	0.81	0.85	0.86	0.79	1.06	1.24	0.92	1.38	0.97	1.62	–	0.28
4	1.05	1.01	1.02	1.06	0.81	1.29	0.91	1.21	1.12	0.98	0.88	0.90	0.88	1.47	1.36	–	0.90
5	1.10	0.88	0.99	0.98	1.23	1.07	1.07	0.98	1.16	0.98	1.61	1.19	0.85	–	1.54	1.08	0.95
6	0.84	0.98	0.82	0.81	0.83	1.03	0.70	0.71	0.81	0.89	0.73	1.09	0.70	0.78	0.77	0.98	0.96
7	0.90	1.00	0.93	0.88	1.02	0.77	0.78	0.42	2.03	0.36	0.73	0.95	0.88	–	1.02	–	–
8	1.49	1.48	2.21	1.81	1.14	0.85	–	–	–	–	–	–	–	–	–	–	–
9	1.16	0.41	0.98	1.02	–	1.61	1.02	–	1.35	0.51	2.52	1.08	–	–	0.37	–	–
11	0.90	1.00	0.98	1.82	1.19	1.28	1.04	0.95	0.55	0.27	1.09	0.89	0.70	–	0.38	0.43	0.55
13	0.42	–	–	–	–	–	–	–	–	–	–	–	0.34	–	–	–	–
14	0.52	–	–	–	–	0.97	–	–	0.08	–	–	–	–	–	–	–	–
15	0.04	–	–	–	0.03	–	0.03	–	–	–	–	–	–	–	–	–	0.08

For list of variables see Table 1.

Each horizon or 'spit' is approximately 2 cm thick.

Missing values and variables occur where less than four artifacts occur.

Table 3. *Association (A) values for Phase 3*

Variables	1	2	3	4	5	6	7	8	9	11	13	15
1		0.96	*0.90*	0.95	0.94	0.92	*0.79*	0.95	0.97	*0.77*	*0.72**	*0.03**
2			*0.90*	0.96	0.95	0.91	*0.75*	1.13	0.96	*0.72*	*0.73**	*0.04**
3				0.93	*0.90*	0.85	*0.82*	1.13	0.93	*0.74*	*0.52**	*0.03**
4					0.98	0.95	*0.84*	1.11	0.97	*0.83*	*0.59**	*0.03**
5						0.92	*0.83*	1.05	0.94	*0.83*	*0.75*	*0.03**
6							*0.69**	0.86	0.88	*0.61*	*0.72**	*0.04**
7								1.08	*0.82*	*0.82*	*0.41**	*0.01**
8									1.07	*0.98*		*0.01**
9										1.02		*0.02**
11											*0.22**	*0.02**
13												*0.04**

* = significant at $p = 0.05$.

A values less than or equal to 0.90 are in italics.

For list of variables (see Table 1).

in patterning according to artifact type and according to depth within the deposits.

Phase 3. Nearest-neighbour analysis (Table 2)

When the vertically collapsed deposit of Phase 3 is considered as a whole, the nearest-neighbour R values can be grouped into two categories, one being slightly more clustered than the other. The first, more clustered, group (R less than 1.0) contains mainly easily friable material, except the petrographically 'altered' obsidian. Apart from ostrich egg shells, the contents of the second, less clustered, group consist largely of less friable stone objects.

Group 1		Group 2	
R	Artifact type	*R*	Artifact type
0.97	Pottery	1.49	Ostrich egg shell
0.90	Charcoal	1.16	Pebbles
0.90	Altered obsidian	1.10	Silicified obsidian
0.84	Burned clay	1.05	Fresh obsidian
0.82	Bone	1.00	Basalt
0.52	Wood		
0.42	Seeds		

The overall difference between the friability of the artifacts in the two groups could be the result of the original pattern of disposal of the two kinds of artifact. However, a more economical hypothesis would be that the difference arises because of postdepositional factors. Treading, earth movement and other localised disturbances could have led to the breaking up and small-scale concentration of the more friable and lighter material, in contrast to the heavier stone artifacts.

It is evident from Table 2 that Phase 3 (the largest and most productive excavation) shows greater artifact clustering with greater depth. This is especially clear in the bones which show a steady increase in clustering with depth. It was noted that soil creep affects the first 15 cm of the ground surface in the Ngenyn area. One interpretation is that the original clustered patterns (as seen at the bottom of the excavated deposit) have been gradually disturbed and lost in the upper portion. But other factors may also have been involved.

By comparing Figs. 2 and 3, it is clear that the overall number of bones in the upper portion of the deposit is considerably higher than at the bottom, and the same applies to all categories of artifact. The two figures may suggest that the overall 'random' pattern in the upper part of Phase 3 (Fig. 2) results from the superposition of a number of occupations like that in the lower part of the deposit (Fig. 3).

Any clustering in the bone distributions occurs at a very small scale (Fig. 3), and this localised scale of clustering is also seen for other sorts of artifacts (see Figs. 4–6) – the seed distributions in particular (see symbol '3' in Fig. 5). Figure 7 shows the lack of this small-scale localised clustering in the basalt distribution as an example of the Group 2 category.

One kind of artifact which does not support the division into Group 1 friable and Group 2 less friable in the lists above is ostrich egg shell. These shell fragments are light and friable and might be expected to have shown more clustering. Perhaps the solution is that the egg shell fragments were already broken into very small pieces before deposition so that further fragmentation and localised disposal was less possible. This explanation is supported by the fact that the shell pieces are small beads or beads in the process of being manufactured.

Phase 3. Association analysis (Table 3)

The analysis results show that most of the artifact categories are fairly randomly intermingled. However, the patterning of some of them consistently diverges from that

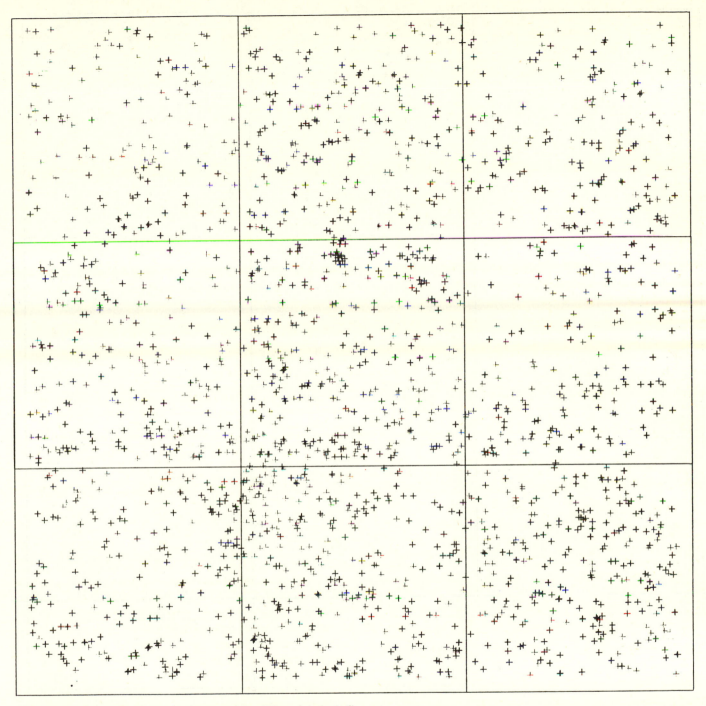

Fig. 2. Distribution of bones (+) in the upper spits of Phase 3 (spits 1–6).

of others (italic in Table 3). Low values of the *A* index of association (less than 0.90) are found for pottery, charcoal, the altered obsidian category, seeds, and the highly clustered 'features' (mainly holes of unknown significance). All these kinds of artifact occur in the more clustered Group 1 noted above. However, there is no evidence in the analysis results that the clusters of one sort of artifact are especially associated with the clusters of any other. The patterning of the different kinds of artifact is not organised in the same way.

The spatial patterning in Phase 3 thus fails to provide any evidence of the organisation of rubbish into distinct zones within the excavated area. There are no large clusters in which numerous artifact types are associated. Inspection of Figs. 3–5 shows that the clustering which has been observed in the nearest-neighbour analyses is very small scale (the clusters are only 10–30 cm across) hardly suggesting refuse dumps or activity areas. As already suggested, the fact that the degree of clustering is related to the friability of the material may indicate that the small scale clustering results from disturbance such as treading and kicking or by natural

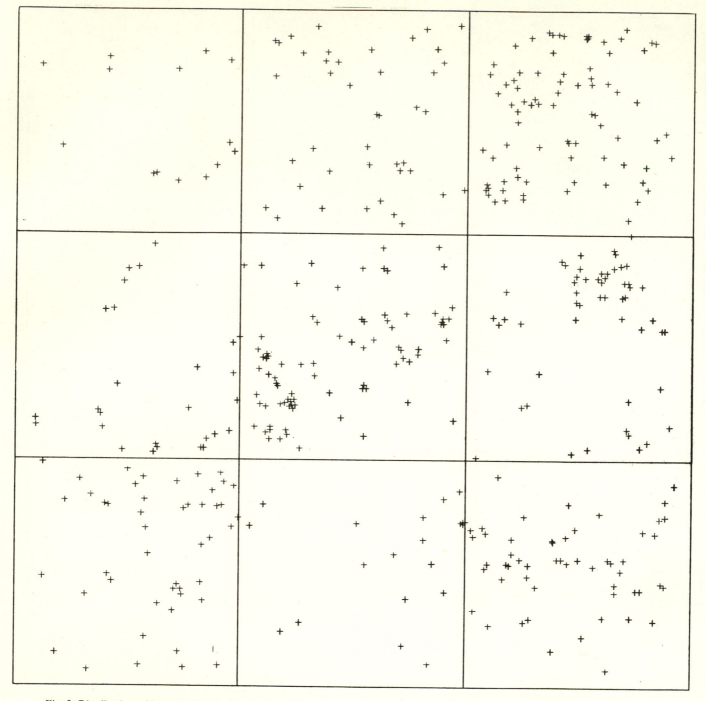

Fig. 3. Distribution of bones (+) in the lower spits of Phase 3 (spits 14–22).

processes. The less clustered, more random patterning in the upper portion of the deposit may be because of a greater and more blurred palimpsest of the small scale clusters found lower down, or the disturbance by soil creep.

Phase 2. Nearest-neighbour analysis (Table 4)

The spatial patterning of the artifacts in Phase 2 shows some differences from that in Phase 3. If the deposit is considered as a whole, without subdivision into spits, the R values for the artifact categories for which there is adequate infor-

mation can be classified less easily into the two groups noted in Phase 3. The more friable material (burned clay, bones, pottery and charcoal) has R values of 0.83, 0.63, 0.56 and 0.54, respectively. The stones (silicified obsidian, fresh obsidian, basalt) have values of 1.23, 0.93 and 0.73. Thus, although there remains some evidence for a more clustered, friable group and a less clustered, less friable group, there is some overlap in R values and the distinctions are generally less clear. Also in contrast to Phase 3, the nature of this clustering is rather different. The overall map of all artifacts

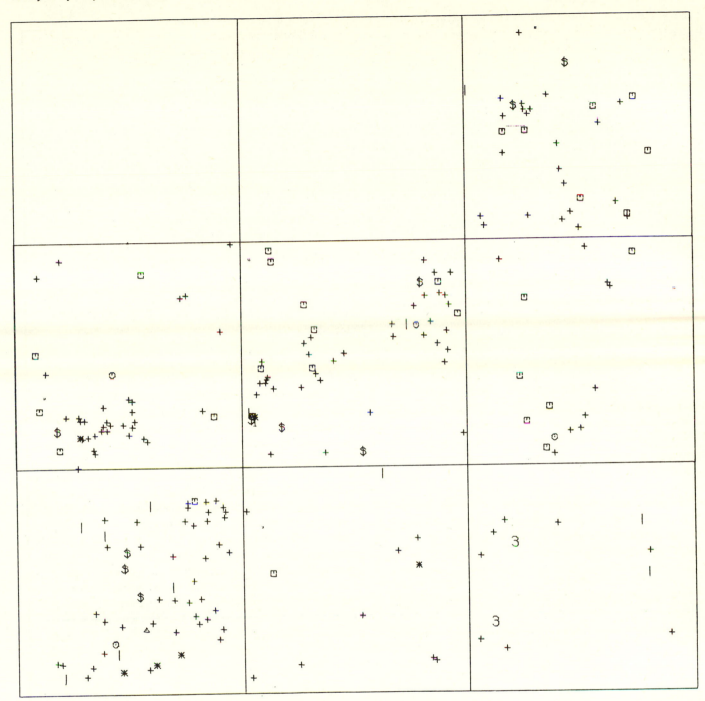

Fig. 4. Distribution of all artifact types in Phase 3 (spit 14). For symbols see Table 1.

at all depths (Fig. 8) and the total distribution of basalt artifacts (Fig. 9) show one clear major cluster. The evidence from the rejoining of flakes and cores showed that the cluster represented a knapping area (Hivernel 1978). The cluster is much larger and more distinct than any found in Phase 3. A cluster of similar dimensions is perhaps visible in the centre of the plan in Fig. 10 (obsidian artifacts), and comparison with Fig. 9 shows that the obsidian and basalt clusters occur at different locations. A large cluster is also visible in the distribution of 'burned clay' (Fig. 11), and once again this cluster

does not occur in the same place as the basalt and obsidian clusters.

In general, then, the nature of the clustering visible in Phase 2 is rather different from that in Phase 3, with clusters being 1–2 m across as opposed to 10–30 cm across. However, the latter smaller scale of clustering is seen in the Phase 2 bone distributions and perhaps in the pottery as well.

As in Phase 3, there is clear evidence (Table 4) that artifacts are more clustered in the lower portion of the deposit. Such evidence, in addition to the small scale of some of the

Table 4. *Nearest-neighbour analysis (R) values for Phase 2*

Variables	(R)	Horizon subdivisions				
		1	2–5	6–8	9–11	12–16
1	0.63	0.70	0.73	0.62	0.61	0.48
2	0.73	0.75	0.82	0.70	0.72	0.67
3	0.56	0.76	0.67	0.34	0.50	–
4	0.93	–	1.32	1.09	0.95	0.37
5	1.23	2.16	1.07	0.58	1.13	–
6	0.83	1.14	0.69	0.66	1.11	0.56
7	0.54	0.73	0.54	–	0.37	–
8	0.78	–	–	–	–	0.78

For list of variables see Table 1.
Each horizon or 'spit' is approximately 2 cm thick.
Missing values occur where less than four artifacts occur.

Table 5. *Association (A) values for Phase 2*

Variables	1	2	3	4	5	6	7
1		0.86	0.82	0.96	0.95	0.88	0.76
2			*0.74**	0.96	1.04	0.88	0.89
3				*0.75**	*0.68**	*0.69**	*0.61**
4					1.03	0.94	0.76
5						0.82	0.80

Significant at $p = 0.05$.
Low (A) values are in italics.

clustering and the division between friable and less friable material, indicates some disturbance of the type argued for Phase 3. However, the degree of such disturbance would appear to be less in Phase 2.

Phase. 2. Association analysis (Table 5)

A values indicating significant spatial segregation for artifacts are common only in the case of pottery. As in Phase 3, the localised patterning of this type of artifact is different

Table 6. *Nearest-neighbour (R) value for Phase 1*

Variables	R
1	0.71
2	0.75
3	0.81
4	0.91
5	0.73
9	1.06
12	0.53
17	0.54

For list of variables see Table 1.

from that of other categories. There are again no large scale clusters of associated artifacts which would suggest refuse dumps.

Phase 1. Nearest-neighbour analysis (Table 6) and association analysis (Table 7)

In this sample from a thinner deposit, the distinction between the degree of clustering of Group 1 and Group 2, less friable and friable artifacts, cannot be identified. In this respect the nearest-neighbour analysis results are more similar to those from Phase 2 than from Phase 3. This impression is strengthened when the nature of the clustering in Phase 1 is considered. As in Phase 2, one major cluster occurs (Fig. 12) and the small concentrations of Phase 3 cannot be distinguished. Basalt artifacts ($R = 0.75$) show a clear cluster in one area of the Phase 1 excavation where there is also a slight concentration of bones ($R = 0.71$). The concretions appear to form a similar cluster (it was noticed during the excavation that a number of these calcium carbonate concretions had formed around small fragments of bones). No table is provided of variation in R values with depth in the Phase 1 deposit. The deposit is already thin and the small

Table 7. *Association (A) values for Phase 1*

Variables	1	2	3	4	5	9	12	17
1		0.85	0.95	1.00	0.05*	0.69	0.79	0.45*
2			0.77	0.88	0.04*	0.95	0.49*	0.72*
3				0.90	0.05*	0.64	0.82	0.43*
4					0.05*	0.66	0.77	0.47*
5						0.04*	0.03*	0.03*
9							0.32*	1.14
12								0.20*

For list of variables see Table 1.
* = significant at $p = 0.05$.

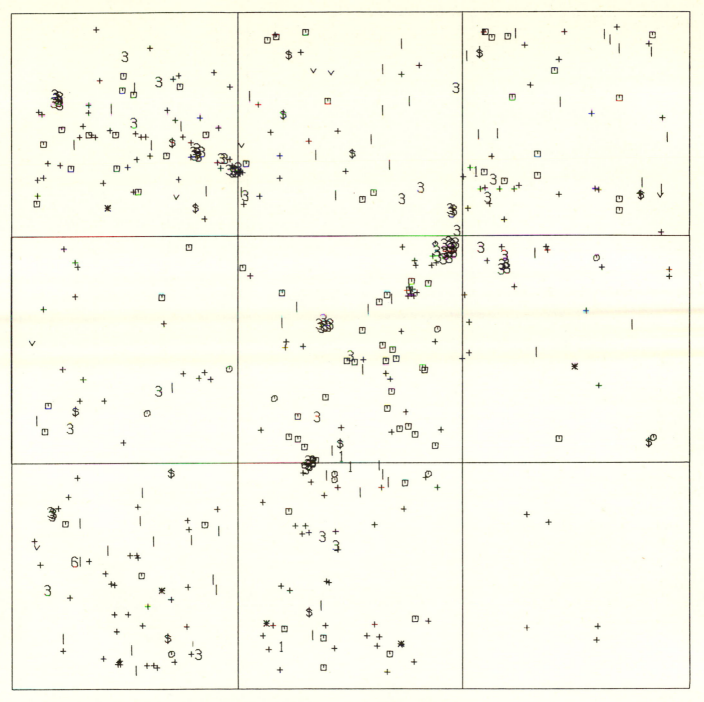

Fig. 5. Distribution of all artifact types in Phase 3 (spits 15–18). For symbols see Table 1.

sample size would have resulted in very low numbers of artifacts in each spit. Regarding the association analysis, it should be noted that the low *A* values for silicified obsidian (Table 7) are based on a very small sample (5).

Interpretation and conclusion

The spatial patterning in Phase 3 has a nature different from that of patterning in Phases 1 and 2. Apart from the higher density of artifacts and greater thickness of deposit in Phase 3, the scale of artifact clustering is much more localised than in Phases 1 and 2. In addition, the clearer difference in the patterning of the more easily friable material in Phase 3 argues for some disturbance of the material, for example by treading, kicking and by natural forces. It was suggested in the discussion of depositional processes in the introduction to this chapter that a multi-purpose, 'home base' occupation might be expected to result in a continual re-sorting and movement of the artifacts, so that the association between activities and artifacts resulting from those activities is disturbed. The wide range of artifact categories present, the density and thick-

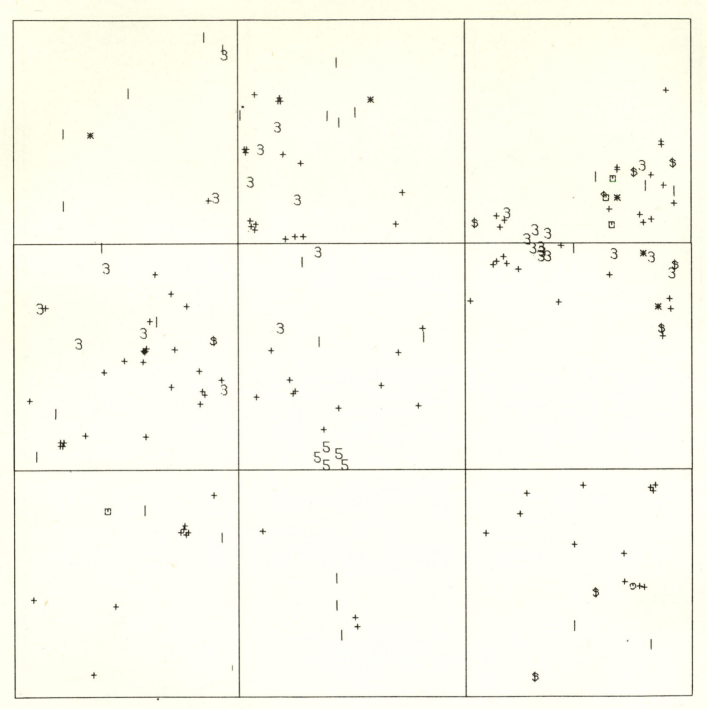

Fig. 6. Distribution of all artifact types in Phase 3 (spits 21–22). For symbols see Table 1.

ness of the deposit, and in particular the 'disorganised' nature of the patterning of the localised clusters of artifacts and their associations, all suggest that occupation in Phase 3 was relatively substantial. It is impossible to predict from the spatial patterning whether such occupation occurred in one or over several periods of use. But it has also been suggested that Phase 3 underwent considerable secondary disturbance from natural processes. The upper part of the deposit, in particular, was probably affected by surface wash, and the differences in the patterning of friable and less friable material could have resulted from natural sorting as much as from human agency of the kicking and scuffling kind. It is obviously difficult in this context to separate natural from human disturbance and corroboration for the 'home base' interpretation must be sought in other aspects of the evidence from the site (see below).

The patterning in the thinner and less dense deposits in Phases 1 and 2 suggests interpretations different from Phase 3. On a short term or special activity site there would be less likelihood of secondary movement and disturbance

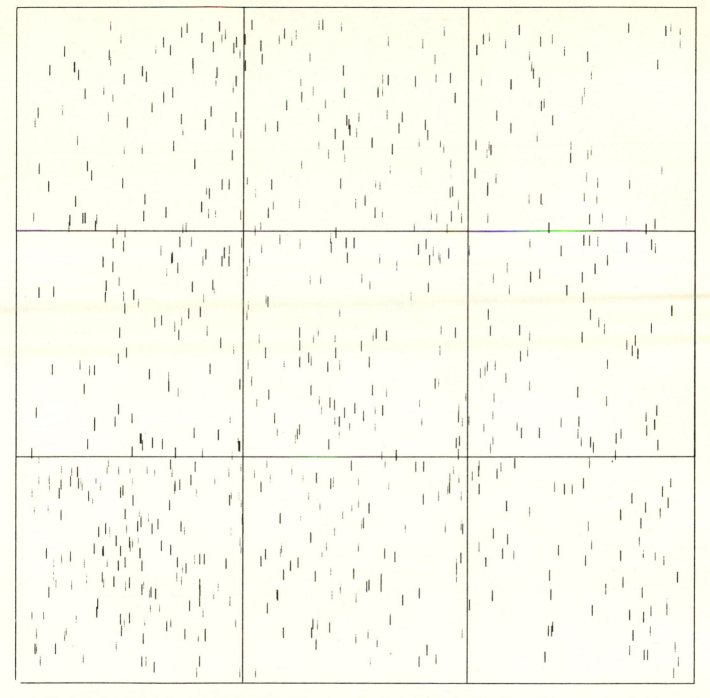

Fig. 7. Basalt artifact (ı) distribution in Phase 3.

of artifacts. Many will remain at the locations of the original activities which produced them. The cluster of basalt artifacts in Phase 2 (Fig. 8) can be interpreted as a knapping area (Hivernel 1978) and there are associated smashed bones. Similar large scale clusters occur for other artifact types in Phase 2 as well as in Phase 1.

There is little evidence of secondary disturbance of these clusters except by soil creep in the upper portion of the deposits. Lack of secondary dispersal compared to Phase 3 is also suggested by the less clear distinctions between the

patterning of friable and less friable artifacts in Phases 1 and 2. Unlike those in Phases 1 and 2, artifacts in Phase 3 had been well sorted after deposition into distinct categories based on weight and friability. In general, therefore, Phases 1 and 2 may represent shorter term occupations than Phase 3, less disturbed during use and probably exposed to other erosion processes for a shorter period of time.

Much caution should be exercised in considering the above interpretations. Similar spatial patterns can be produced by entirely different processes so that many of the assump-

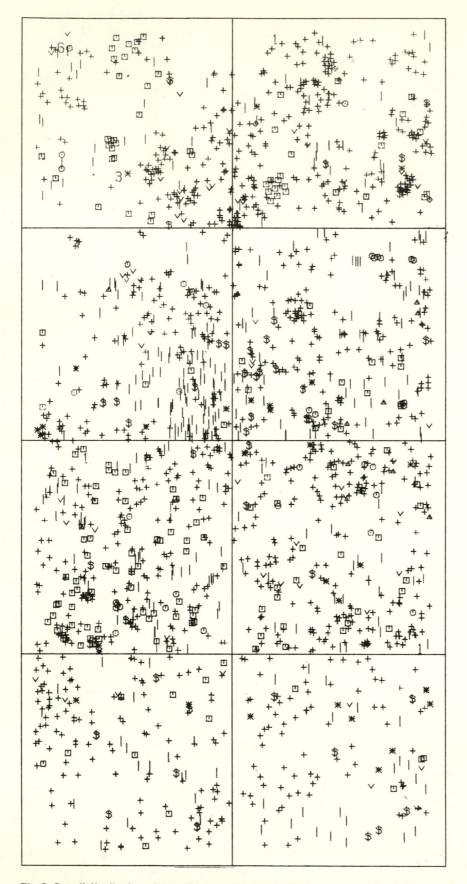

Fig. 8. Overall distribution of all artifacts at all depths in Phase 3. For symbols see Table 1.

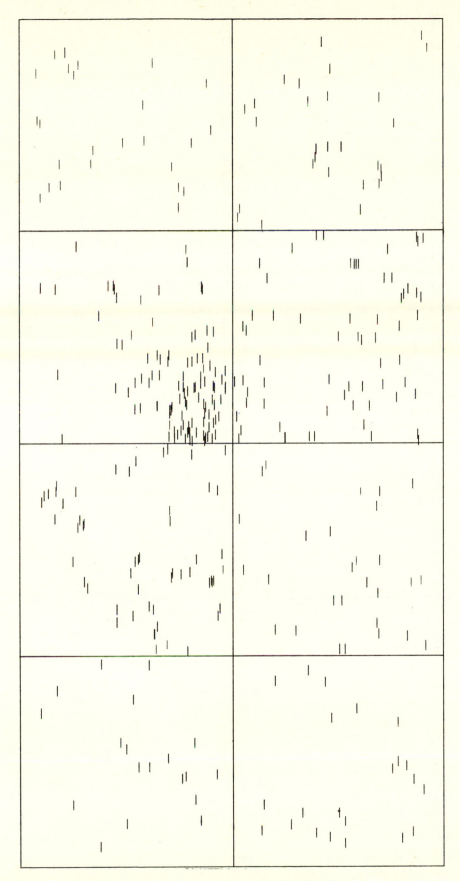

Fig. 9. Total distribution of basalt artifact (I) at all depths in Phase 2.

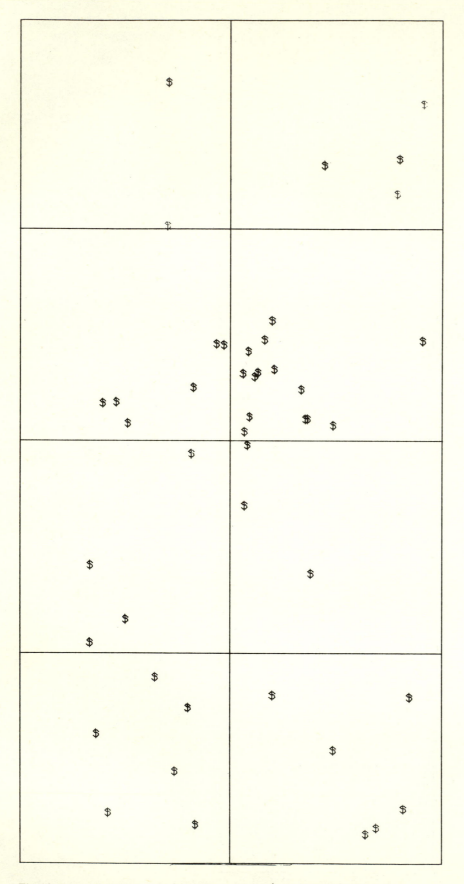

Fig. 10. Total distribution of fresh obsidian artifacts (**$**) at all depths in Phase 2.

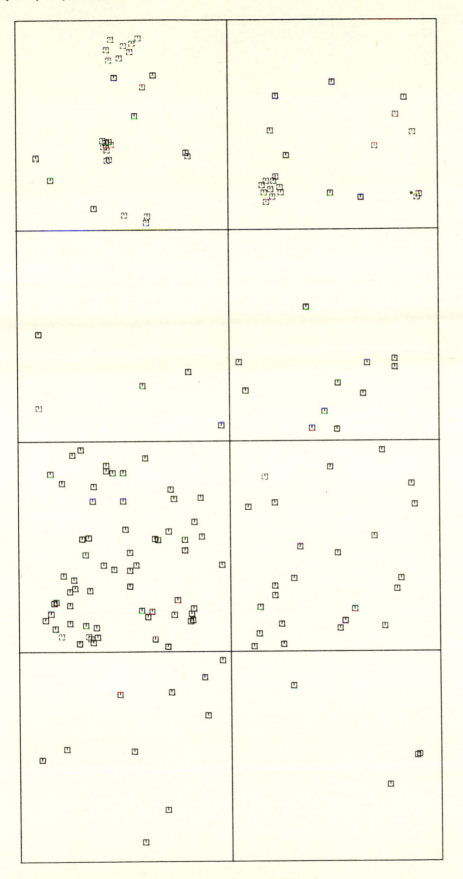

Fig. 11. Distribution of burned clay (▫) at all depths in Phase 2.

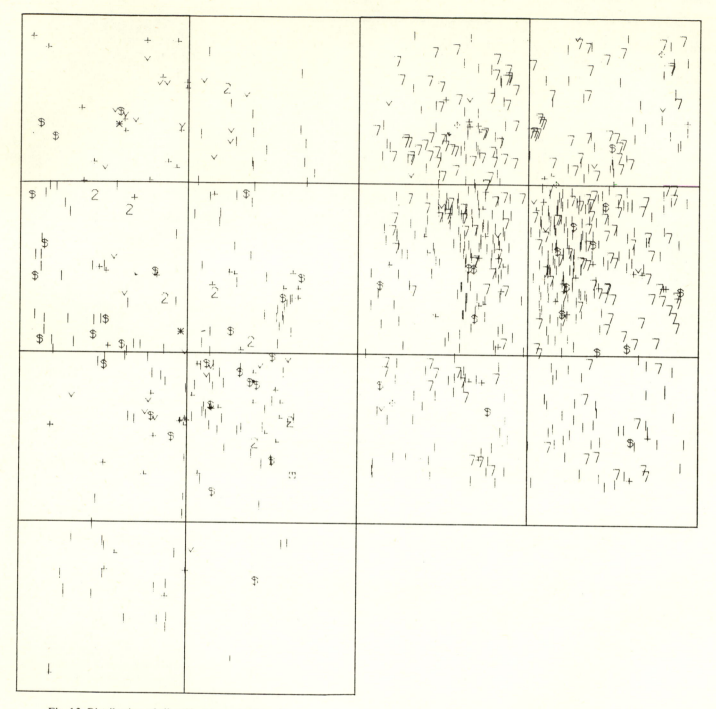

Fig. 12. Distribution of all artifact types in Phase 1.

tions used here may be incorrect. The differences in the artifact patterning between Phase 3 and Phases 1 and 2 could be largely the result of natural processes of erosion and earth movement. In addition, only small portions of the Ngenyn site were excavated so that the interpretations supplied above may not apply to the site as a whole in any one phase.

The results of the spatial analysis can, however, be compared with analyses of other aspects of the evidence from the site. The suggestions made above may gain more weight or be found inadequate when examined within the framework of the total evidence. The distinction between the 'home base' nature of Phase 3 and the short term or special activity nature of the other two phases is supported by the ratios of cores to tools in the different deposits. Phase 3 contains a high ratio of tools to cores while Phases 1 and 2 provide evidence of knapping floors with relatively more cores and flakes as opposed to tools. Phase 3 also had a wider range of wild fauna and a fuller range of the types of rodent fauna frequently associated with habitation and grain storage facilities. The plant remains in Phase 3 allowed the possibility of year-round occupation. The

Phase 3 deposit is thicker and has a greater density of artifacts of a wider range of functional classes. Taken on their own these various aspects of the evidence from the site and the spatial analysis results could be given little significance. But when considered in conjunction, the total evidence from the site suggests (Hivernel 1978) that Phase 3 may represent part of a 'home base' while Phase 2 represents an activity area and Phase 1 a short term occupation by a small, mainly hunter–gatherer group.

Criticisms of spatial analyses of occupation floors have concentrated on the assumption that the artifact patterning reflects past activities and behaviour (Schiffer 1976). The failure of these early analyses to consider depositional and postdepositional processes may have impeded the adoption and development of spatial analytical techniques in archaeology. We hope to have shown in this chapter that spatial analysis of occupation floors can be carried out within a framework which specifically concentrates on depositional and postdepositional effects, and that in this way the nature of a site and the past behaviour associated with it can be reconstructed more adequately.

Acknowledgements
The field research at Ngenyn carried out by F. Hivernel was supported by the Swan Fund (Oxford), The Gordon Childe Fund (Institute of Archaeology, London) and the Central Research Fund (London University).

References
Binford, L. (1978). *Nunamiut Ethnoarchaeology*. Academic Press: New York.

Clark, P. J. and Evans, F. C. (1954). Distance to nearest neighbour as a measure of spatial relationships in populations. *Ecology* 35: 445–53.

Donnelly, K. P. (1978). Simulations to determine the variance and edge effects of total nearest neighbour distance. In *Simulation Studies in Archaeology*, ed. I. Hodder, pp. 91–5. Cambridge University Press: Cambridge.

Gifford, D. (1978). Ethnoarchaeological observations of natural processes affecting cultural materials. In *Explorations in Ethnoarchaeology*, ed. R. Gould, pp. 77–101. University of New Mexico Press: Albuquerque, New Mexico.

Gifford, D. P. and Behrensmeyer, A. K. (1977). Observed formation and burial of a recent human occupation site in Kenya. *Quaternary Research* 8: 245–66.

Hayden, B. D. (1976). Curation: old and new. In *Primitive Art and Technology*, ed. J. S. Raymond, B. Loveseth, C. Arnold and G. Reardon, pp. 47–59. University of Calgary Archaeological Association: Calgary.

Hivernel, F. (1978). An ethnoarchaeological study of environmental use in the Kenya Highlands. Ph.D. thesis, University of London.

Hodder, I. and Okell, E. (1978). A new method of assessing the association between distributions of points in archaeology. In *Simulation Studies in Archaeology*, ed. I. Hodder, pp. 97–108. Cambridge University Press: Cambridge.

Hodder, I. and Orton, C. (1976). *Spatial Analysis in Archaeology*. Cambridge University Press: Cambridge.

Isaac, G. (1971). The diet of early man: aspects of archaeological evidence from Lower and Middle Pleistocene sites in Africa. *World Archaeology* 2: 278–99.

Leroi-Gourhan, A. and Brézillon, M. (1972). Fouilles de Pincevent: Essai d'analyse ethnographique d'un habitat magdalénien (la section 36). *Gallia Préhistoire,* supplément VII. CNRS: Paris.

Pinder, D., Shimada, I. and Gregory, D. (1979). The nearest-neighbour statistic: archaeological applications and new developments. *American Antiquity* 44: 430–45.

Schiffer, M. B. (1976). *Behavioral Archaeology*. Academic Press: New York.

Tallon, P. W. J. (1976). The stratigraphy, palaeoenvironments and geomorphology of the Pleistocene Kapthurin Formation, Kenya. Ph.D. thesis, University of London.

Yellen, J. (1977). *Archaeological Approaches to the Present. Models for Reconstructing the Past*. Academic Press: New York.

Chapter 8

**Intrasite spatial patterning:
its role in settlement–
subsistence systems analysis**
C. Reid Ferring

The tendency for humans to have patterned their behavior spatially in the past is evident; thus archaeological sites are traditionally recognized as fundamental spatial–cultural dimensions of analysis. Articles such as the ones in this volume increasingly demonstrate that behavior was also spatially patterned within sites. However, the simple observation that behavior was spatially 'patterned' within a site is too general to be of importance for prehistoric research. Quite obviously prehistorians are interested in which behaviors were spatially patterned and how that patterning may be exploited to better understand processes of adaptation and change.

Here, I will consider the potential significance of intrasite spatial patterning for the study of past settlement–subsistence systems. My concerns are more methodological than theoretical, yet I will intentionally avoid quantitative techniques of pattern detection. Rather I will focus on intrasite spatial patterning as an important, even critical, facet of broader research strategies dealing with the study of adaptation and change. The first part of the paper is concerned with archaeological correlates of spatially patterned behavior and their importance in the study of settlement–subsistence systems. In the second part of the paper an example of intrasite spatial patterning from a late prehistoric site in Oklahoma (USA) will be presented to illustrate some of the correlates and their implications.

Here, intrasite spatial patterning is regarded as the differential spatial distributions of things within a minimally dated horizon of an archaeological site. The context may be a buried living surface, an arbitrarily determined stratigraphic level, or a surface scatter. The things include artifacts (objects of human manufacture), ecofacts (bones, shells, plant macrofossils, and other subsistence debris) and features (hearths, pits, etc.). Sites with architectural features are not considered explicitly in these discussions, as my emphasis is on the study of hunter–gatherer populations which I will assume to have been predominantly non-sedentary.

Kinds of intrasite patterning

Two kinds of intrasite spatial patterning are considered here: spatial clustering (density patterning) and compositional patterning. Spatial clustering includes the areal extent as well as the absolute and relative spatial density of things on or within the minimally dated horizon. This criterion is usually employed to define the perimeter of the site itself. Within the site perimeter different kinds and different scales of clustering may be recognized. The scale of clustering may be measured by polymodal distributions of either cluster areas or their relative internal densities. Multiple clusters of similar dimensions, large clusters composed of smaller subclusters and other patterns have been recognized.

Compositional patterning is the density-free differential spatial distribution of selected categories of artifacts or ecofacts within the minimally dated horizon. This may be investigated independently from spatial clustering, for example by examining the spatial co-association of two tool classes without regard for their clustering tendencies. Compositional patterning may also be investigated together with spatial clustering. Once spatial clusters have been defined, their compositional patterning may be established simply by treating the individual clusters as comparative units, or subassemblages. Simultaneous evaluation of both kinds of patterning may be achieved by examining the mutual spatial clustering of preselected classes of data.

In behavioral terms both spatial clustering and compositional patterning are potentially significant, for together they may be used to infer not only the nature of past activities, but also the intensity or frequency with which they were carried out, and the possible interrelationships between different activities and their settlement system context.

Behavior and intrasite patterning studies: archaeological perspectives

Intrasite patterning studies must contend with the nature and spatial arrangement of both individual and group patterns of behavior. Variability in behavior patterns at these two levels are assumed to represent cultural choices, and therefore are useful for the analysis of adaptive strategies, mechanisms of change, etc. The archaeological perspective taken here simply defines behavioral constructs in terms which have empirical archaeological correlates and which are amenable to comparative archaeological analysis.

For purposes of intrasite spatial analysis the fundamental behavioral construct proposed here is the *activity*, defined as a specific task resulting in the deposition of diagnostic clustered archaeological remains. An example from flint knapping is decortification – recognized by flakes with dorsal cortex, abandoned cores or bifaces, etc.

The *group* is considered here to have been an aggregate of persons who carried out multiple activities in proximity, especially relative to others during the same occupational episode. If two or more groups occupied a site simultaneously, leaving spatially discrete remains of their activities, they are defined here as *subgroups*.

Since the activity is the building block for the other two constructs, it is important to emphasize that archaeological 'activities' are viewed as working hypotheses, generated out of archaeological or replicative experience and continually evaluated in archaeological contexts. Likewise, groups and subgroups are to be used as constructs dealing with the socio-economic contexts of multiple activities. These are approached in terms of multiple behaviors, but not in terms of numbers of persons involved. *A priori*, they contain no implied connotations with respect to the sex or kin affinities of the persons.

The settlement unit is the aggregate of persons, consisting of a group or subgroups, which carried out activities at a site during an occupational episode. Settlement units are viewed as socioeconomic components of a culture, subject to

transhumance as well as seasonal and/or periodic aggregation at a site or sites in the population territory. The archaeological correlate of the settlement unit is the occupation unit. This will be discussed later, within the context of settlement–subsistence system analysis.

Activities and groups/subgroups: archaeological correlates

The focus of intrasite spatial patterning studies should initially be on activities, and subsequently on group/subgroup structure; both of these must exhibit compositional and density patterning.

The proposed spatial correlate to the activity is the *activity area*, defined as an archaeologically consistent, spatially clustered, association of artifacts and/or ecofacts in a minimally dated archaeological horizon. Examples include decortification/preforming of cores or bifaces, initial butchering of large animals, etc.

It cannot be assumed that all activities resulted in the deposition of clustered debris; this does not render them unimportant, but clearly poses difficulties for the spatial analyst. Such 'dispersed activities' can be addressed after definition of the clustered activity areas via continued compositional patterning analysis.

The spatial correlate for the group is the *group cluster* while that for the subgroup is the *subgroup cluster*, both of which consist of multiple clustered activity areas, or single density-compositional clusters which are obviously multifunctional in character. The latter may reflect intense space utilization and overlapping activity areas. Although exceptions may certainly be envisioned, I suggest that activity areas are generally smaller than group/subgroup clusters by an order of magnitude.

Phased behaviors can be effectively used in activity area and cluster analysis. Study of the density-compositional patterning within a cluster can focus on activity areas related to phased behaviors, for instance lithic processing. Separate areas of initial core reduction, tool manufacture, tool maintenance and tool discard represent ideal phased activities. Butchering analysis may be addressed in a similar fashion. While some branching of an activity sequence may be evident, such as multiple areas of tool maintenance, this general situation would argue strongly for temporal affinity of the activity loci within the cluster. Spatially then, these loci help to define temporal contexts for the other debris in the cluster which may be less amenable to phase analysis. The importance of phased activity analysis for occupation unit definition will be indicated shortly.

Activity areas and group/subgroup clusters are viewed here as basic elements of intrasite spatial analysis. While the behavioral perspective developed earlier is necessary for their definition, full analysis and interpretation of these units requires consideration of the nature of intrasite variability as it relates to settlement–subsistence systems. How does spatial patterning within a site relate to the socioeconomic structure

Table 1. *Systems dimensions and archaeological correlates*

Analytical[a] Dimension	Behavioral Correlates	Empirical correlates	
		Intersite	Intrasite
Population	None	Number of sites	Artifact, ecofact densities; site size
(Functional) Differentiation	Demography; scheduling, geographic arrangement of procurement/processing activities	Functional (tool and ecofact assemblages) differences/similarities among sites; seasonality indicators	Activity segregation within occupation unit; spatial distributions of tools, debris, faunal, floral remains, feature associations
(Ethnic) Integration	Degree of shared behavioral traits between units	Stylistic similarities between assemblages (e.g. ceramic decorations, microlith shapes, lithic reduction style, etc.)	Intrasite spatial patterning and associations of stylistic data
Energy	Subsistence productivity	System productivity (caloric, nutritional); faunal, floral remains from all sites in system. Estimates of procurement costs (distance to resource, density of resource, etc.)	Occupation unit productivity

[a]Dimensions follow discussion of Plog (1977); behavioral and empirical correlates presented here as archaeological ramifications of Plog's dimensions.

of the settlement unit? Does the presence of multiple group/ subgroup clusters signify repeated (group) occupations or simultaneous (subgroup) manifestations? How do patterns of settlement unit composition and functional variability within one site relate to variability in other sites of the system?

Questions such as these clearly indicate the necessity of settlement–subsistence perspectives for intrasite spatial pattern detection and interpretation; moreover they imply that significant contributions to settlement–subsistence studies may be made by integrated intrasite–intersite analysis. Thus it is suggested that intrasite research strategies be formally linked to the study of multisite settlement–subsistence systems.

Intrasite spatial patterning and settlement–subsistence systems

The preceding discussions have defined behavioral constructs (activities and groups/subgroups) and their archaeological correlates (activity areas and group/subgroup clusters). These are essentially building blocks for spatial analysis; at the same time they are provisional in character in that continued research may well require modifications in their definitions. But to exploit these constructs and correlates in archaeological research, the systemic *context* of the activities and group/subgroup clusters must be established. This context is the settlement–subsistence system.

Dimensions of settlement–subsistence systems have both behavioral and empirical correlates (Table 1). The empirical (archaeological) correlates of the dimensions illustrate the key role which intrasite studies share in systems analysis. At the same time, the intrasite empirical correlates help structure spatial patterning studies *per se*, by providing explicit *goals* for those analyses.

The fundamental character of intrasite patterning is explicitly viewed as the result of activities conducted at a site. These activities were structured by the socioeconomic/ethnic composition of the settlement unit, by the relationship of the procurement/processing tasks to the whole subsistence system, the periodicity/intensity of occupations, and so on. This structure is clear (Table 1) especially for the arena of non-sedentary systems, for which seasonal/periodic changes in settlement unit composition, demographic arrangement, and economic activity are integral aspects of the system (Flannery 1968).

System analysis: behavior, time and intrasite spatial patterning

Settlement–subsistence system analysis must proceed from its basic components, within sites, to the intersite level. This sequence treats occupation units (composed of activities within a group or subgroup structure) as temporal–functional–social units of the system. Clearly these may be expected to have been dynamic with seasonal or periodic changes; nonetheless settlement–subsistence system analysis must begin with definition of the occupation unit. I contend that it is not possible to define occupation units without reference to their inherent behavioral, temporal and spatial dimensions. These three dimensions are extremely important aspects of archaeological data – how they are interrelated is illustrated by consideration of systems analysis.

Occupation units

Occupation units are the archaeological correlates of settlement units, that is they consist of debris generated at a site by a settlement unit during the course of a single occupational episode. If each occupational episode was sealed nicely between sterile layers of sediment, then the temporal dimension of occupation units could be dealt with during field excavations. This is rarely the case; we can make the assumption that all the debris on a 'living floor' was deposited during the same occupational episode only in special circumstances. So the temporal dimension of occupation units must be addressed vigorously.

Within minimally defined archaeological horizons (levels), time must be measured in behavioral–spatial terms, since by definition the temporal relationships of the data cannot be further treated by stratigraphic radiometric or other means. Thus the temporal relationships of artifacts on a buried surface must be examined via behavioral–spatial analysis in order better to define the occupational episode or episodes, to determine whether the settlement unit structure consisted of a single group or multiple subgroups, and so on.

Behavioral time relationships have already been suggested by reference to phased activities. Thus if a logical behavioral relationship can be established between two activity areas (e.g. areas of initial core reduction and final tool shaping), then these areas may be tentatively posed as part of the same occupation unit. This approach clearly recognizes the utility of linking behavior and time in spatial analysis, not to mention the key role which spatial analysis plays in the definition of occupation units for subsequent systems analysis.

Occupation units are therefore expected to include multi-activity group or subgroup clusters, and at least some temporal affinities should be utilized in occupation unit definition. Without evidence of phased behavioral linkage between clusters, intercluster functional/stylistic analysis can be used tentatively to define the occupation units.

Functional and stylistic data from clusters are used to evaluate the nature of functional and ethnic affiliations within and between occupation units. How these dimensions are approached for both single and multiple cluster data bases will be discussed next, considering the problem of single versus multiple occupational episodes.

Single clusters: simple occupation units

A single cluster (of activity areas) within a level is regarded as a straightforward example of a group cluster and a single occupation unit. It connotes a single occupation by a single functionally diverse group.

A single cluster occupation unit can be approached directly with respect to the system dimensions (Table 1). Functional differentiation is assumed to be represented by activity area variation, with task sharing among individuals (not groups) implied. Since single cluster occupation units are assumed to represent simple settlement unit structures, ethnic integration studies may be prohibited by the absence of repeated activity areas (containing suitable tools or ceramics) for comparison. Net subsistence productivity from the single occupational episode may therefore be estimated by the economic debris composition of the cluster.

Analysis of single cluster occupation units serves as an important research tool at the intersite level of study. Simply structured sites are important guides when later dealing with more complex (multiple cluster) spatial patterns. An example of a single cluster occupation unit from Delaware Canyon is described in the last part of this chapter.

Multiple clusters: single or repeated occupations?

As previously mentioned, the presence of multiple clusters in a horizon may reflect single or repeated occupations; this complicates occupation unit definition. For single occupations, each cluster would represent a subgroup cluster; for repeated occupations, each group cluster could represent a single occupation unit. For ease of discussion, repeated subgroup occupations will not be considered here – yet this complex situation could well be reflected in the archaeological record.

Cluster comparisons should begin with an extension of the compositional patterning study. Logical associations between clusters with respect to phased activities would be strong evidence that the cluster areas were occupied contemporaneously. Sharing of an area of initial core preparation or carcass dismemberment would be strong evidence for such relationships. An unusual demonstration of tool sharing between clusters was provided by core reconstruction at Boker Tachtit in the Central Negev (Hietala 1983, p. 20).

Cluster comparisons may be further enhanced by reference to the dimensions of functional differentiation and ethnic integration. Simultaneous occupation of a site by subgroups implies close ethnic affiliations, which can be addressed via analysis of stylistic attributes within artifact classes. At the same time, sharing of certain tasks, either at the procurement or processing level is expected for subgroup occupation patterns. These should be reflected as higher levels of functional differentiation, measured via tool class comparisons, ecofact remains, etc. Functional differentiation among socioeconomic subunits at a single site may be expected to increase as the number of subunits increases. Thus for a larger settlement unit greater task differentiation is expected as a mechanism to reduce competition and maximise efficiency of task scheduling (Plog 1977). Conversely, if a site was seasonally reoccupied by a single group, repetition of activity sets within multiple clusters is expected, especially since similar resource availabilities are likely contexts for separate occupations.

The combined temporal (e.g. phased activities), functional and stylistic approach to the analysis of multiple cluster data bases is espoused here as a means to structure spatial analyses and formally to recognize the importance of those dimensions for spatial patterning studies. Occupation unit definition and analysis, an explicit goal of intrasite patterning studies, must formally include functional and stylistic analysis in order to address the system dimensions of functional differentiation and ethnic integration.

Without attempts to define the temporal relationships among clusters, as a key aspect of occupation unit recognition, the character of occupation periodicity is ignored. For settlement–subsistence system analysis it is fundamentally important to address periodicity of site use. The implications of multiple clusters in a horizon would be totally different if they represented repeated occupations at one site and a complex multiple subgroup occupational episode at another. Here I have tried to emphasize that patterns of site use can be better understood by intrasite spatial patterning studies, especially if these studies formally recognize functional, ethnic and temporal dimensions of settlement–subsistence systems. In this analytical context intrasite spatial patterning studies are not viewed as isolated behavioral studies, but integral aspects of comprehensive archaeological investigations.

Turning now from general considerations to a specific example, spatial data from a site at Delaware Canyon will be briefly presented and discussed with reference to some of the preceding issues. The exceptional degree of intrasite spatial patterning at this site offers the opportunity to illustrate and emphasize some of the issues just discussed.

Spatial data from Delaware Canyon

At Delaware Canyon Oklahoma[1] (Ferring 1982*a*), excavations were carried out at several specific localities along the canyon, each of which is part of a late Holocene stratigraphic succession of occupations ranging from *ca* 2500 years B.P. to the latest prehistoric period (*ca* 350 years B.P.). Detailed field and laboratory studies by several scientists treated the geology, soils, invertebrate and vertebrate faunas, plant macrofossils and archaeological materials. A scenario of well preserved archaeological and paleoecological data fostered implementation of the research strategy focusing on changing adaptive strategies vis a vis changing local economic resource availabilities during the late Holocene (Ferring 1982*b*, 1982*c*). Spatial analyses were an integral part of the research strategy.

Delaware Canyon is located along a spring-fed northerly flowing tributary of the Washita River in southwestern Oklahoma (Fig. 1). Recent erosion has exposed approximately 10 m of late Holocene sediments rich in artifacts, charcoal and paleontological materials.

Two major periods of occupation are recorded. The first is dated to *ca* A.D. 0–1000, and consists of stratified Plains

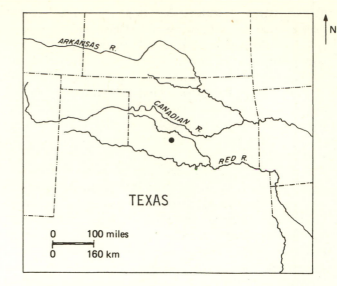

Fig. 1. Location map of Delaware Canyon, Oklahoma. Dot indicates location of Delaware Canyon, just south of Washita River (unlabelled).

Woodland materials in a 1 m thick paleosol. Subsequent Plains Village occupations are most common in a thinner buried paleosol dated to *ca* A.D. 1250–1650. Molluscan and soils analyses (Fullington and Fullington 1982; Pheasant 1982) indicate that the Plains Woodland period was the moistest in late Holocene times, with drier conditions prevailing during Plains Village occupations.

Locus CD 258 A is situated at the southern end of the canyon (Fig. 2). It consists of a thin Plains Village archaeological deposit *in situ* within the buried Delaware Creek paleosol. A total of 52 m^2 of the buried deposits were systematically excavated.

The archaeological deposits at the site occur within the paleosol, which has been eroded and subsequently covered by approximately 45 cm of colluvium. Recent slumping has truncated the horizontal extent of the deposit on the north, west and east sides of the site, while the deposits appear to thin and disappear to the south. Additional cultural materials in the same stratigraphic position are exposed in the east wall of the canyon, indicating that the materials excavated are only part of a larger occupation area. Unfortunately, none of these other areas could be tested.

Since earlier test excavations had defined the stratigraphic position of the archaeological materials, main excavations were directed at the exposure of horizontal distributions. After removal of overburden to just above the paleosol, 0.25 m^2 units were excavated in 10 cm levels, with all matrix being water screened through 2 mm mesh. Stratigraphic studies showed all the cultural materials occurred on a single paleo-surface which dipped slightly to the southeast following the approximately basin shaped configuration of the canyon at this point. Hearths, large faunal elements and artifact concentrations permitted accurate definition of this living surface.

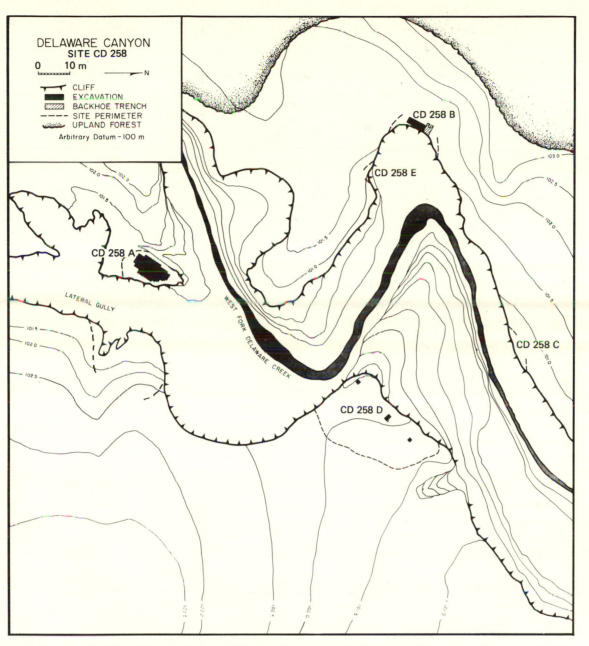

Fig. 2. Map of site CD 258, Delaware Canyon, Oklahoma. This is the southern portion of the canyon. Note locus CD 258 A, on eroded remnant. Greater original extent of this locus is indicated by materials *in situ* exposed in sediments along eastern edge of gully.

Although many specific artifactual or faunal elements were mapped in primary positions during excavations, all horizontal proveniences for the present report are by excavation unit (0.5 m × 0.5 m) only. Plots of tools were prepared by hand, while counts for other categories were used to generate the PSYMAP presented here.

Three distinct hearths were located in the northern area of excavation (Fig. 3). Another hearth may have been present in the southeast part of the site, where considerable charcoal and burned bone were found, but no hearth outline was detected. A total of just over 12 000 faunal elements were recovered, 918 of which were identifiable to species. These faunal remains exhibit marked differential spatial patterns.

Two distinct concentrations of deer define the two main areas of the site (Fig. 3): the northern (Area 1) and the southern (Area 2). It is significant that these bones appear to come from one individual, while a single immature element suggests that possibly two are represented (Butler and Yates 1982). Element distributions, however, support the single individual interpretation. The northern concentration is situated clearly among the hearths, while the southern one is perhaps peripheral to a hearth. Bison bones from a single individual are scattered within the southern area (Fig. 4). Rabbit bones are similarly concentrated in Area 2, but just west of the deer and bison (Fig. 5). Turtle remains are highly concentrated near the hearths in Area 1, but close inspection

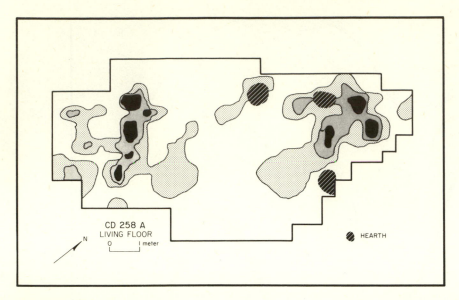

Fig. 3. PSYMAP of deer bone distributions at CD 258 A. 0.5 m × 0.5 m cells are used for this and subsequent PSYMAPs. In this and subsequent PSYMAP illustrations, shaded patterns have been used to indicate the density contours produced by the PSYMAP program. A contour interval of 20% was selected. The darkest pattern thus corresponds to the densest concentrations of the particular artifact or faunal element. The lowest density interval is not shaded.

reveals that they are predominantly south of the deer concentration there (Fig. 6). The distribution of burned bone fragments is clearly associated with the northern hearths, and the suspected hearth in the eastern part of Area 2 (Fig. 7).

A total of 3760 lithic artifacts were recovered. The distribution of debitage is strikingly separated into the two areas of the site (Fig. 8). The major concentration is in the southern part of the site where two or possibly three small subconcentrations are present. The other concentration is equally dense, but is smaller and situated just north of the hearths.

Technological analysis of these concentrations (Areas 1 and 2) revealed striking differences between these debitage

samples. The southern sample has a higher frequency of biface thinning flakes (39%) compared with the northern one (22%). Size analysis of these two samples indicate that there are no significant differences *within* the southern concentration but that a highly significant difference between flake and biface thinning flake sizes occurs in the sample from Area 1. The debitage from the southern concentration is also significantly smaller than that of the northern one. Raw materials are also different between the two areas. Alibates flint (from Texas) constitutes 24.5% of the material in the northern area but only 8.4% in the southern one. Kay County flint (from northern Oklahoma) is 3.3% and 12.6% in the respective areas.

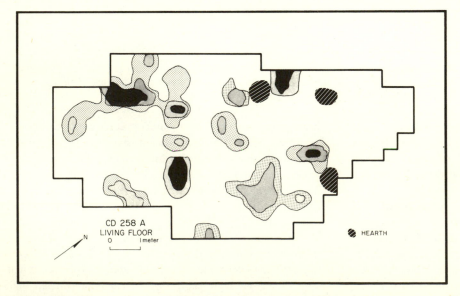

Fig. 4. PSYMAP of bison bone distributions at CD 258 A. These remains appear to be of a single individual.

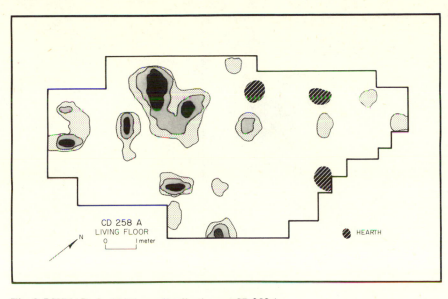

Fig. 5. PSYMAP of rabbit bone distributions at CD 258 A.

These patterns strongly suggest technological differences separate the two areas of the site.

Tool distributions offer considerable insight into the nature of these technological differences (Fig. 9). All but one of the biface preforms occur in the southern area. Without doubt this is an area of projectile point manufacture. More than one knapper or episode of manufacture is suggested by the subconcentrations yet no differences among the blanks from these areas are apparent.

The absence of a concentration of blanks, in addition to the technological differences indicated, show that biface manufacture was probably not associated with the northern concentration. The only tools there are a drill, two projectile points and one preform fragment. The best interpretation of this debitage concentration is that it represents an area of intense tool maintenance. The technological patterns suggest

that unifacial and possibly some bifacial tools were being maintained. The homogeneity of the debitage from the southern area seems to reflect the dominance of small biface production, although some maintenance spalls are probably represented as well, since this concentration includes several scrapers, retouched pieces and a knife. Virtually every pottery sherd occurs in the northern area; three vessels are represented in this sample.

This exceptionally well-defined evidence of activity segregation demands consideration of the possible occupation patterns at the site. The relative time of occupation is of paramount importance. No stratigraphic separation of these two clusters exists, and the materials must be treated as if they are on the same surface. This does not, *a priori*, indicate that the concentrations are necessarily synchronic; they could be separated by months or even years. Butler and Yates (1982)

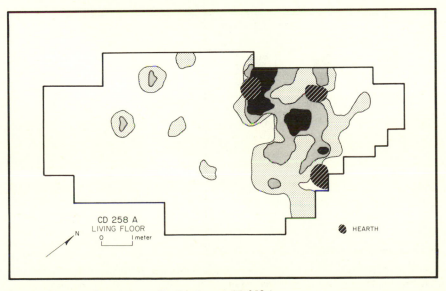

Fig. 6. PSYMAP of turtle bone distributions at CD 258 A.

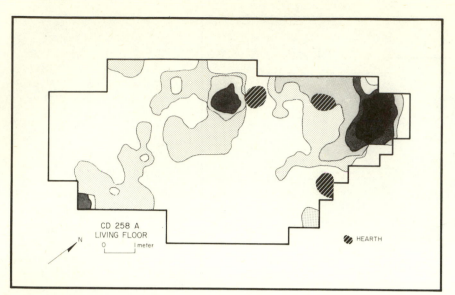

Fig. 7. PSYMAP of burned bone distributions at CD 258 A.

considered the seasonal implications of the fauna and have indicated that the turtle elements are suggestive of a non-winter occupation while the other elements are not seasonally diagnostic.

Discussion

The large samples of artifacts and faunal elements at site CD 258 A clearly exhibit a remarkable degree of spatial patterning. Distinct segregation of both artifactual and faunal classes is evident, while overall, two general concentrations may be defined, each consisting of faunal and artifactual elements. This patterning serves as a convenient means to consider some of the issues raised in the first part of the chapter.

Several distinct 'activity areas' can be defined. Two and possibly three areas of projectile point manufacture are present in the southern portion of the excavation area. Limited projectile point manufacture may have taken place in the northern part of the site, yet the evidence for this is much less clear than in the southern part. The main area of tool discard is also in the southern part of the site, and largely overlaps with the point manufacture areas. In the same portion of the site, however, distinct butchering areas are evident, and the scrapers and retouched pieces are probably related to butchering activities. Some of the debitage in the southern part of the site most probably relates to unifacial tool maintenance, yet the technological segregation of these pieces from the point manufacturing debris could not be made.

A more distinct area of tool maintenance debris occurs

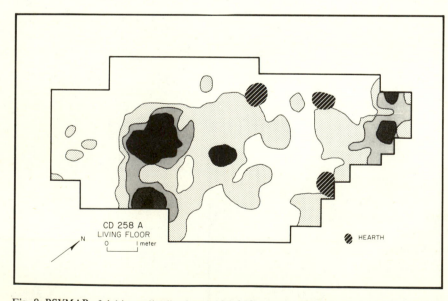

Fig. 8. PSYMAP of debitage distributions at CD 258 A. Note discussion in text of technological differences between concentrations in northern and southern portions of excavation area. Compare southern subconcentrations with distribution of bifacial preforms (for projectile points) in Fig. 9.

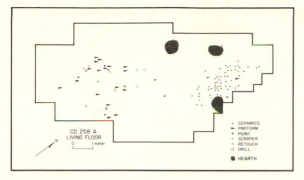

Fig. 9. Tool and ceramic distributions at CD 258 A. Note concentration of ceramics near hearths and areas of projectile point manufacture in southern portion of excavation area. All artifact locations plotted by hand within 0.5 m × 0.5 m excavation units.

in the northern part of the site; debitage attributes suggest marked functional differences from the southern areas. Faunal processing areas include the previously mentioned butchering areas in the southern portion of the site as well as cooking areas marked by concentrations of burned bone peripheral to the three hearths and near a possible unexcavated hearth. Differential processing of small game, illustrated here by the turtle and rabbit distributions, can also be viewed as constituting activity areas. With the exception of the partial bison carcass, each of these activity areas is well defined and limited to several square meters in area.

Turning to the issue of clustering, the apparent division of the site into northern and southern clusters should be considered in terms of the rather confined limits of the excavations. Without peripheral clearing, the visual impression of cluster definition may be quite misleading. When the evidence is considered from a compositional perspective, I would argue that the entire excavation area is best viewed as a group cluster, albeit not fully exposed and possibly near other unexposed clusters.

Stylistic comparisons of the activity areas are not possible owing to the remarkable functional segregation of the debris. The largely non-repetitive functional composition of the activity areas is suggestive of high functional differentiation and therefore probable occupational integration of the various activities. Shared or repeated activities are possibly indicated for projectile point manufacture and cooking only; neither of these situations argues strongly for a necessary case of repeated occupations.

I would suggest that these data from CD 258 A point strongly towards a case of a single functionally diverse occupation, marked by a single group cluster consisting of multiple, discrete 'activity areas'. It is important to consider that this small excavation ($52 \, \text{m}^2$) is only part of the largely eroded site, which probably had an extent of several hundred square meters. Full interpretation of this cluster, with respect to other possible clusters is not possible at present.

In terms of settlement–subsistence systems studies, the necessity of multiple cluster analysis at this site is clear.

Repetitive clusters, with little evidence of cluster integration would argue for repeated site occupations by small groups exploiting a diverse set of resources. At the same time it could be possible to demonstrate intercluster functional differentiation suggestive of subgroup occupations. The demographic and subsistence system implications of these alternates are obviously important to regional intersite analyses.

Summary and conclusions

Intrasite spatial analyses have been considered here as an integral, necessary component of settlement–subsistence system studies. Behavioral considerations provide for the definition of activities and group/subgroup settlement units, as well as their archaeological (empirical) correlates – activity areas and group/subgroup clusters. Occupation units are defined as the empirical correlate of an occupational episode by a settlement unit. Occupation unit definition is approached via phased activity analysis and functional/stylistic cluster comparison. These analytical efforts structure intrasite spatial patterning studies in an explicitly problem oriented manner, and relate those studies to broader investigations of multi-site or multi-level data bases.

Data from Delaware Canyon provide an example of spatially defined activity areas, clusters, and occupation units. The relationship of these to settlement unit composition and the periodicity of site utilization requires more extensive excavations, while the necessity of intrasite spatial patterning studies for settlement–subsistence pattern analysis is shown to be essential.

Note
1 This research was supported by Interagency Archaeological Services, National Park Service, Denver, and the Faculty Research Committee, North Texas State University.

References
Butler, B. and Yates, B. C. (1982). Animal exploitation in the Delaware Canyon area. In *The Late Holocene Prehistory of Delaware Canyon, Oklahoma* ed. C. R. Ferring, p. 117–56. Contributions in Archaeology, No. 1. North Texas State University: Denton, Texas.

Ferring, C. R. (ed.) (1982*a*). *The Late Holocene Prehistory of Delaware Canyon, Oklahoma*. Contributions in Archaeology, No. 1. North Texas State University: Denton, Texas.

Ferring, C. R. (1982*b*). Archaeology of the Delaware Canyon sites. In *The Late Holocene Prehistory of Delaware Canyon, Oklahoma*, ed. C. R. Ferring, pp. 195–250. Contributions in Archaeology, No. 1. North Texas State University: Denton, Texas.

Ferring, C. R. (1982*c*). Subsistence strategies and diachronic variability in the Late Holocene occupations of Delaware Canyon. In *The Late Holocene Prehistory of Delaware Canyon, Oklahoma*, ed. C. R. Ferring, pp. 251–69. Contributions in Archaeology, No. 1. North Texas State University: Denton, Texas.

Flannery, K. V. (1968). Archaeological systems theory and early Mesoamerica. In *Anthropological Archaeology in the Americas*, pp. 67–87. The Anthropological Society of Washington: Washington D.C.

Fullington, R. and Fullington, K. (1982). Molluscan Faunas from Delaware Canyon. In *The Late Holocene Prehistory of Delaware Canyon, Oklahoma*, ed. C. R. Ferring, pp. 95–116. Contributions in Archaeology, No. 1. North Texas State University: Denton.

Hietala, H. J. (1983). Boker Tachtit: intralevel and interlevel spatial analyses. In *Prehistory and Paleoenvironments in the Central Negev, Israel,* vol. III, *The Avdat/Aqev Area,* Part 3, ed. A. E. Marks, pp. 217–81. Department of Anthropology, Southern Methodist University: Dallas, Texas.

Pheasant, D. R. (1982). Soils analyses from Delaware Canyon. In *The Late Holocene Prehistory of Delaware Canyon, Oklahoma,* ed. C. R. Ferring, pp. 64–93. Contributions in Archaeology, No. 1. North Texas State University: Denton, Texas.

Plog, F. (1977). Explaining Change. In *Explanation of Prehistoric Change*, ed. J. N. Hill, pp. 17–57. University of New Mexico Press: Albuquerque, New Mexico.

Chapter 9

An alternative model of room function from Grasshopper Pueblo, Arizona
Richard Ciolek-Torrello

Since the beginning of organized archaeological research in the North American Southwest, there has been an enduring interest in the function of pueblo rooms and the activities that took place in them. This interest results in great part from the early recognition that these architectural structures were basic spatial units of households and other domestic and community groups that made up pueblo socities. It was rapidly discovered that a knowledge of room function provides important information about the organization of pueblo societies and their varying forms in time and space (cf. Fewkes 1909, 1919; Prudden 1914, 1918; Rohn 1965).

Most earlier studies of pueblo room function, however, have been limited in their analytical capability by dependence on a specific ethnographic model for interpreting room function. This model emphasizes the architectural characteristics of rooms as determinants of function. This chapter discusses the limitations of the method and presents an alternative approach that focuses on the activities that take place in rooms and the implements and materials used in those activities as definers of room function. This alternative approach is developed in the examination of room function at Grasshopper, a large fourteenth-century pueblo in the mountains of east-central Arizona.

An approach that focuses on activities enhances the archaeologists' ability to discover unique functional patterns relative to the approach that emphasizes architectural charac-

teristics. The discovery of unique patterns benefits the objective of studying the temporal and spatial variability of function and organization. But the relationship between activities and artifacts – the remains that represent activities in an archaeological context – is complex. Thus the examination of prehistoric activities requires more complex solutions than employed in earlier architectural studies.

Several multivariate analytic techniques are used here to accommodate the complex relationship between activities and their remains and to examine the wide range of variability exhibited by Grasshopper rooms. A knowledge of many activities that occur in these rooms is gained by analyzing artifacts found on floors using three R-mode analytic techniques that include factor analysis, principal components analysis, and multi-dimensional scaling. The results of these analyses are used to modify the data set which is then re-analyzed using a Q-mode technique. The room clusters produced by this last procedure are interpreted in terms of a room function typology.

The ethnographic model
Despite the antiquity of interest in room function, investigation proceeds even to this day from a very narrow perspective based on analogy with the pueblos described by ethnographers at the turn of the century. These early descriptions have been developed into what can be termed the

'ethnographic model' whose actual origins can be traced to the architectural studies of the Mindeleff brothers (Mindeleff 1891) among the historic and prehistoric pueblos of the Hopi and Zuni areas.

The ethnographic model identifies three functional room types: habitation, storage, and ceremonial. Habitation and storage rooms are distinguished on the basis of architectural characteristics such as room size and openings and the presence of non-portable facilities such as hearths and mealing bins. The ceremonial room is identified by a host of unique architectural features, the most prominent of which are a masonry bench with subfloor vent, hearth, and deflector. These rooms, known as kivas, are also usually subterranean. When rooms at an archaeological site under investigation exhibit characteristics that parallel those of historic pueblos, the model is applied to explain the function of the prehistoric rooms (cf. Wasley 1952).

This approach has been most clearly articulated by Hill (1968, 1970*a*, 1970*b*) in a pioneering but flawed study of rooms at Broken K Pueblo and applied with little modification to similar archaeological situations at small nearby pueblos (Hanson and Schiffer 1975; DeGarmo 1976). These applications provide a systematic elaboration of the ethnographic approach involving the use of hypothetico-deductive methods that test the relationship between architectural characteristics, in particular room size, non-portable facilities, and other room contents. Hill (1970*b*, p. 13) maintains that it is essential to demonstrate parallels rather than merely to propose them when inferring room function. Although, significantly, Hill employs artifacts for the first time in the analysis, it is important to remember that examination begins with a narrow set of room types.

Hill identifies three major room types at Broken K Pueblo on the basis of architectural variation. One type consists of small rooms averaging 5 m² in area and generally lacking facilities or other distinctive architectural characteristics. A second type is made up of larger rooms averaging 9.7 m² in area and usually containing mealing bins, firepits, and ventilators. Hill also found large subterranean rooms with the unique architectural features – bench, firepit, ventilator, and wall niches – usually associated with kivas. Surface ceremonial rooms were also found. The determination of function for all three types was based on direct analogy with the ethnographic model.

Notably, Hill took the ethnographic approach one step further. He attempted to verify these postulated functions by examining room contents such as artifacts and pollen in terms of activities that were predicted to occur in particular functional types. He was able to demonstrate an association between the postulated function and expected remains from activities.

This success is attributed in great part to strong architectural similarities between Broken K Pueblo and the historic pueblos. The results are questionable, however, because of two major problems in the analysis. First, the contents of all room floors (including 10 cm above the floor) were combined and compared with the combined contents of other types using chi-squared tests. No examination of the contents of individual rooms was included. Thus the internal variation within each of the functional types is unknown. It is highly likely that only a few rooms contributed to the significant differences encountered. Since storage rooms were distinguished primarily on a negative basis in terms of a paucity of artifacts, the same results could be achieved if all but a few habitation rooms contained few artifacts. Thus there may exist a greater variation within a particular type than between types. Secondly, and equally serious, many of the contents of rooms used in the analysis, e.g. pottery sherds, were most probably secondarily deposited as refuse from other activity areas rather than used on the floors on which they were found (cf. Schiffer 1972, 1973; Reid 1973). As a result, the artifacts found in a room may not represent the activities that occurred there.

Recently, Jorgenson (1975) has applied more mathematically sophisticated techniques in examining the ethnographic model of room function at the similar and nearby Table Rock Pueblo. Jorgenson avoids at least one of Hill's errors by using a factor analysis to examine the variation exhibited by individual rooms. For the first time a much greater emphasis is placed on artifacts as indicators of activities since both room floor contents and architectural characteristics are used as attributes. This sacrifices the independence of these two types of data, however, in future tests of the resultant typology.

Although several factors were derived that were interpreted as representing traditional pueblo activities, the factor analysis failed to distinguish the expected functional room types (Jorgenson 1975, p. 159). An 'implication analysis' was also carried out with similar results. This interesting outcome, in contrast to Hill's findings, suggests a significant difference in domestic organization from the historic pueblos upon which the ethnographic model is based.

This conclusion is untenable, however, since there are major deficiencies in Jorgenson's analysis. Again like Hill, Jorgenson failed adequately to consider whether floor contents actually represented remains of activities taking place in rooms or secondary deposition from other areas. She does argue for the relative contemporaneity of room use within a span of 20 to 40 years on the basis of the original excavators' analysis of pottery types. Even in the Southwest, however, ceramic types are not so well defined for such exact temporal distinctions. Clearly more precise controls are necessary to assume that the contents of room floors are comparable.

Jorgenson also fails adequately to screen the data before analysis and to report the original data frequencies, both of which are essential to evaluating the results. This is especially important in this case since all variables were reduced to presence/absence attributes. This involves a significant weighting of data that makes rare and common items equally important. Without the original frequencies, evaluation of the effects of this major alteration of the data is impossible.

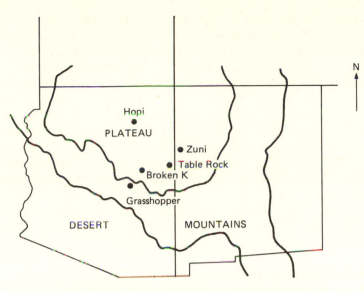

Fig. 1. Arizona and New Mexico, with locations of sites mentioned in text.

Finally, Jorgenson's expectation that the analyses she used could distinguish room types is mysterious. The analyses examined combinations of artifacts which at best – that is if unstated assumptions were valid – represented individual activities. It is unknown whether there was any direct attempt to identify groups of rooms with similar activities or combinations of activities which would indicate different functional types. Thus the analysis actually fell short of identifying what would have been previously undescribed types. It is doubtful, however, whether such types would have represented behaviorally significant types or merely statistical creations because of the inadequacies of the analysis.

To these shortcomings of earlier functional analyses can be added a major weakness in the use of the ethnographic model. The approach has been applied only to small pueblos in a very restricted area of the Southwest and is probably not generally applicable to other regions and temporal periods. The approach requires strong architectural parallels between historic pueblo rooms, on the one hand, and prehistoric pueblo rooms on the other hand. If architectural parallels are weak or non-existent, the approach is not useful.

It is possible, for example, that much of the apparent success of Hill and others is because of similar environmental circumstances. The historic Hopi and Zuni pueblos, Broken K Pueblo, and other prehistoric pueblos all occur on the semiarid Colorado Plateau (Fig. 1). Here, room size has been demonstrated to be the most significant criterion of function owing to the presence of a bimodal distribution in size at several prehistoric pueblos. The significantly smaller size of storage rooms can be attributed to the paucity of timber suitable for construction in the region. Since storage rooms are not regularly inhabited, their function could be met by several small spaces. Such constraints would not be expected to operate in the better-watered forested regions of the Southwest.

Architectural parallels cannot also be expected because of the changes that have occurred during prehistoric times and since. For example, between the time of the arrival of the Spanish and the study of pueblos by ethnographers, pueblo peoples have been considerably acculturated (Wilcox 1981). This is contrary to the often stated belief that pueblo culture has a history of retaining traits once they are introduced (Woodbury 1954). Although pueblo culture is noted for its conservatism, the fact should not go unrecognized that considerable changes have affected all aspects of pueblo life from subsistence to religion.

Recent architectural studies of historic pueblos reveal that tremendous reconstruction involving alteration of community spatial organization has taken place since prehistoric times (Adams 1978; Ahlstrom, Dean, and Robinson 1978; Ferguson and Mills 1978). We cannot assume that such changes have not also included significant alterations of domestic activity space and organization. In this light the extent of functional continuity between Broken K Pueblo and historic Hopi pueblos observed by Hill becomes quite doubtful, especially since the former is a relatively small single-storey pueblo in contrast to the much larger multistorey Hopi pueblos. Most interesting is the fact that Jorgenson failed to find an association between room size and artifact clusters at Table Rock Pueblo, which unlike other prehistoric examples happens to be a multistorey pueblo.

Thus the ethnographic model as articulated by Hill may not actually reflect architectural variability of the large historic pueblos. In fact, the derivation of the model is based on highly selective and non-representative data. No systematic study of the relationship between architectural patterns and room function exists at present for any historic pueblo, let alone a representative sample of pueblos. Thus the model provides only a very vague and general picture of the use of rooms in historic pueblos. It in no way accommodates the considerable variation observed between the Hopi and Zuni areas, for example. Yet such variation, related to different environmental and sociocultural contexts, is crucial to inferences about household and community organization and their change through time. Dependence on this model obscures this crucial information and even in the most ideal circumstances ultimately leads only to a sterile and rather uninteresting treatment of room function.

An alternative approach

Hill has pointed to a method for generating models of room function that is not dependent upon architectural information. This method focuses on the spatial loci of activity remains to infer room function (Hill 1970*b*, pp. 28–32). The approach proposes quantitatively to examine 'clusters' of remains, and then search for patterning in the spatial distributions of these clusters. The advantage of this method is that a broad range of variability in both architectural and artifactural data is considered before functional types are defined and tested. In this manner our opportunities to detect changes in the organization of activities are increased.

The problem for the archaeologist is one of identifying recurrent patterns in the spatial distribution of archaeological remains on room floors. These remains include the tools, facilities, debris, and raw materials used by individuals and groups in the performance of their tasks. Patterns are often identified by classifying these remains into functional types and grouping them on the basis of their spatial associations. It is then possible at times to interpret such groupings as functionally associated tools or 'toolkits' which were used in the same activity or related set of activities (Whallon 1973).

Within the last decade or two there has been a large number of such functional analyses that have experimented with various quantitative and associational statistical techniques. Many of these analyses which have dealt with relatively large and homogeneous occupation surfaces have focused on identifying statistically significant spatial units or parameters (Whallon 1973). This form of spatial analysis is not essential here, since pueblo communities are divided up into numerous small and distinct spatial units. Functional analyses of pueblos, however, would benefit from the identification of smaller spatial units within rooms. Such identification requires the use of techniques that can deal with the constraints placed upon the location of activities within rooms by the presence of walls, openings, and other architectural features. Clearly pueblo rooms are quite different from open-air sites or even cave surfaces.

Although frequently used in 'paleolithic' cultural contexts, quantitative and associational statistical techniques are equally applicable to the study of the more complex organization of later communities (see Chapters 10, 11 and 13, by Cowgill *et al.*, Fletcher, and Whallon). A major difference is that in many of the later communities significant spatial units are already defined.

The archaeological context of Grasshopper

Grasshopper is an example of what has been called 'Late Mogollon' or 'Prehistoric Western Pueblo' culture and is located in the forested mountain zone of Arizona (Longacre 1975) (Fig. 2). It consists of over 500 one- and two-storey rooms divided into 12 compact room blocks and 21 smaller groups (Fig. 3). The main part of the site contains three large room blocks located on either side of an old intermittent stream. These room blocks also delimit two large plazas

Fig. 2. Early photograph of Grasshopper ruins, showing rubble mounds of main pueblo before excavation. (Photographer: Byron Cummings, Arizona State Museum, University of Arizona.)

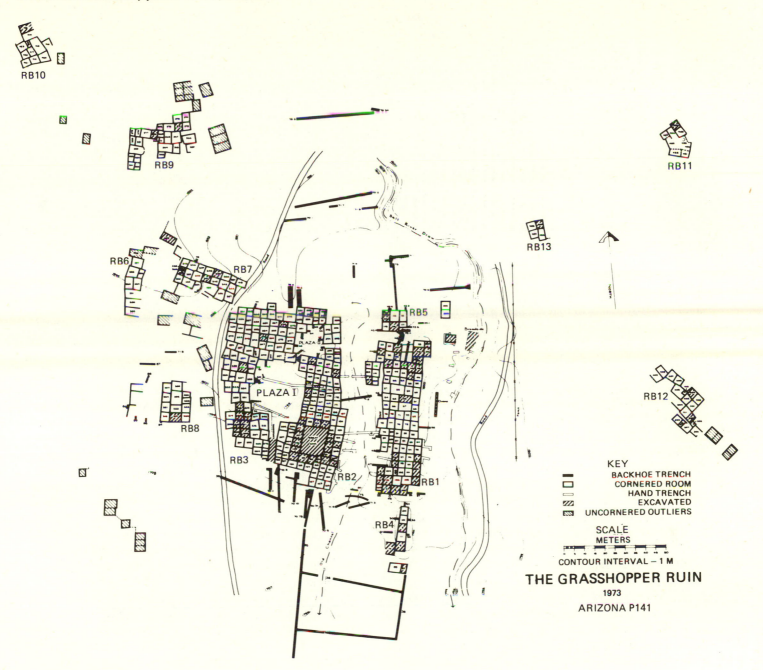

KEY

▬	BACKHOE TRENCH
▢	CORNERED ROOM
▭	HAND TRENCH
▨	EXCAVATED
▦	UNCORNERED OUTLIERS

SCALE
METERS

CONTOUR INTERVAL — 1 M

THE GRASSHOPPER RUIN
1973
ARIZONA P141

Fig. 3. The Grasshopper ruin.

and a Great Kiva — a very large surface ceremonial room. Surrounding these structures are the smaller room blocks which are scattered over an area of about 12 hectares in the valley bottom and encircling low hills.

Grasshopper is placed on a relatively firm chronological foundation by a relative sequence of room construction (Reid 1973; Longacre 1975) tied to absolute dates from tree ring analysis. From this information it has been surmised that initial construction at the site took place at the beginning of the fourteenth century (Ciolek-Torrello 1978) with the majority of the site completed by A.D. 1330 (Reid 1973). The community continued a slower expansion at least until the middle of the century. There is little evidence of growth after this time and the site was probably abandoned by the end of the century (Reid 1973; Longacre 1975). Recent investigations suggest that many of the smaller outlying room blocks were constructed during the middle or later phases of occupation (J. J. Reid, personal communication). Such rooms are not well dated but are architecturally different, being composed of insubstantial walls and roofs.

At the outset of this study it was apparent that the functional model employed by Hill at Broken K Pueblo was not applicable to Grasshopper. Of central importance is the fact that room size variability at Grasshopper does not corres-

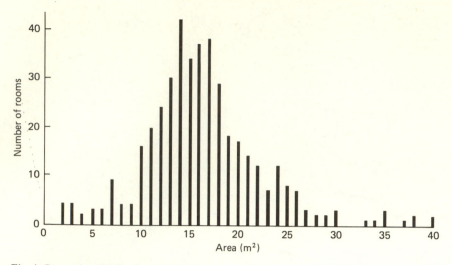

Fig. 4. Room size distribution.

pond in its patterning to that required by the model (Hill 1968, pp. 114–15). Rooms at Grasshopper are, on the average, almost twice the size (16.3 m² for all rooms) of those at Broken K Pueblo (cf. Hill 1968, p. 108) and their variability is much closer to a normal distribution with a single mode (14.9 m² for all rooms) (Fig. 4). The relatively large and uniform size of Grasshopper rooms is not unexpected, since large trees are available in the area for roof construction. Thus it is readily apparent that activity patterning at Grasshopper may be quite different from Broken K Pueblo and that room size may not be a significant indicator of room function.

The considerable remodeling at Grasshopper also weakens the expected relationship between room size and function. Many rooms, especially in the older parts of the main pueblo, have several superimposed floors. The earlier floors have been stripped of their contents and non-portable facilities removed, partially dismantled, or merely covered over. In some cases, rooms have been subdivided into several smaller rooms or new non-portable facilities have been added.

In addition, Sullivan (1974) found in a study of a small sample of rooms at Grasshopper that architectural characteristics such as room size and roofing material did not correspond with habitation and storage functions. He attributed this to remodeling, in particular, large rooms being converted to storage and other functions. This argument was based on an innovative approach for identifying original room function. Sullivan demonstrated that smaller than average sized rooms were often roofed with juniper which like other cedars is relatively immune to insect infestation. This characteristic would be very beneficial in a room where large quantities of grain are stored. Large rooms, in contrast, are usually roofed with pine, fir, or other woods whose characteristic of providing longer straighter beams is more important. Sullivan, however, failed to find a consistent association between rooms roofed with juniper and storage facilities on floors. Thus the remains on floors apparently reflected a change from the room's original function.

Finally, the presence of many two-storey structures makes the relationship between the upper and lower floors an equally, if not more, important influence on room function than the size of the lower floor. In multistorey structures of historic pueblos, for example, the upper floors are usually habitation areas while the lower floors are storage areas of the same household (Adams 1978). Thus the function of the lower floor is apparently determined by its complementary relationship with the upper floor rather than its size, since both floors are of equal size. Thus the situation at Grasshopper is clearly more complex than that of the small single-storey pueblos where Hill's ethnographic model has been previously applied.

Although architectural studies of room function do not appear to be productive, other aspects of the archaeological context of Grasshopper – in particular, the spatial, quantitative, and associational attributes of the remains preserved on floors – are especially amenable to the investigation of activities and room function. Unlike Broken K and many other pueblos, Grasshopper possesses large quantities of artifactual remains in their apparent location of use on room floors. For example, it is very common to find manos and metates in direct association with mealing bins, sooted bowls resting in hearths, large clusters of intact storage vessels, and numerous small domestic tools and raw materials resting on room floors. At the same time such room floors are usually covered only by the rubble of roofs and fallen walls and lack the deep deposits of refuse characteristic of many other sites. Thus it is possible to identify which activities took place on many room floors from the actual remains of those activities alone without reference to architectural information.

At first glance the situation at Grasshopper appears almost ideal for such analyses. The abundance and variety of remains left on most room floors suggest that many, if not most, classes of non-perishable items used in pueblo activities are represented in these rooms. This unusual situation may be the product of the rapid abandonment of the pueblo which corresponded with the abandonment of the larger surrounding region. The abandonment of Grasshopper, however, is poorly understood at present and several widely different views of its causes and effects are held (Reid 1973, 1978).

The archaeological context at Grasshopper is far more complex than this initial impression of abundance suggests. Even in the best of circumstances, archaeological samples are incomplete representations of systemic context materials because of the operation of formation processes and inadequate recovery procedures (Cowgill 1970; Schiffer 1972; Reid 1973; Collins 1975; Reid *et al.* 1975). Refuse disposal and remodeling activities are recognized as processes that have an important effect on the remains of activities at Grasshopper.

During its approximately 100 year occupation, a large community like Grasshopper would have accumulated sizable quantities of refuse and undergone extensive remodeling. This large accumulation of refuse requires a relatively complex disposal system, since all refuse could not be simply tossed across a room or out the door. The differential disposal of some refuse supports this supposition. Refuse at Grasshopper is primarily deposited in a few early-abandoned rooms, plazas, and especially in outdoor areas away from the main habitation areas (Whittlesey 1976). Different types of refuse are also deposited in different types of locations. The refuse from food processing activities such as animal bones, among the most noxious of refuse, is rarely deposited on occupied room floors while some rooms contain large quantities of manufacturing debris on their occupied floors.

It is apparent from this example of refuse disposal behavior that activities are represented on floors by disproportionate quantities and varieties of remains. Some activities are represented by a large number and variety of remains while others are represented by few or possibly none, even though they may have involved equal numbers of materials in the systematic context of the ongoing behavioral system. The quantity of remains of a particular activity found on a floor is not only related to the quantity of materials used or produced by that activity but also to the extent to which such materials are preserved or discarded in secondary refuse. The products of an important and very common activity such as cooking, for example, are either consumed, removed to middens, or lost to the processes of deterioration. In addition, few ceremonial paraphernalia, which play an important role in daily pueblo life, remain on room floors and were most likely curated at abandonment. Some of these paraphernalia, however, were preserved in burials which are not a part of the present analysis.

Another complicating factor, remodeling, is, as previously discussed, indicated by alteration of architectural features and facilities and the resurfacing of floors. Grasshopper grew through a relatively complex series of events (Reid 1973, 1978; Longacre 1975) which were apparently associated with several remodeling stages (Ciolek-Torrello 1978). In the process of renovating or remodeling rooms, the

previously occupied floors were apparently subjected to intense curating and scavenging. These floors contain few portable items, often broken or worn out, and occasionally partially demolished mealing bins, hearths, or other facilities. Some abandoned rooms were not reused and became filled with large quantities of secondarily deposited refuse most easily recognized by the unusually large numbers of sherds and lithic debris. Both kinds of abandoned floors are clearly not comparable to those that continued in use to the end of the occupation of Grasshopper. Schiffer (1976) has shown, however, that it is possible to identify activities from secondary refuse in some circumstances. This will not be attempted in the present analysis.

Natural formation processes also present problems. Erosion is not a significant factor in rooms although plazas and other outdoor areas are more seriously affected (Whittlesey 1976). Preservation, however, is relatively poor in rooms. Plant remains, cloth, hides, or wooden implements are rarely found. Burning of structures in some pueblos has resulted in the preservation of such materials on room floors. Virtually no rooms at Grasshopper, however, show evidence of being burned.

Another serious problem is presented by the collapse of structures after abandonment. Roofs and second-storey floors[1] were often intensively used for domestic activities. In several cases, groups of storage vessels, mealing bins, and hearths were found disturbed but intact resting on the collapsed remains of a roof or second-storey floor. Usually when these roofs collapsed, however, their associated materials became mixed with rubble and were often misinterpreted by excavators as secondary refuse. This was a particular problem when the first-storey floor of a room was abandoned and filled with refuse while the second-storey or roof continued in use for domestic activities. Even where this problem did not exist, recovery of materials from collapsed surfaces was poor relative to first-storey floors. Thus roofs and second-storey floors are also not comparable to first-storey floors even though all may have been subjected to similar cultural formation processes.

Thus despite this initial impression of completeness, the artifactual remains present on Grasshopper room floors do not directly represent 'toolkits.' Rather, several formation processes have operated systematically to distort the relationship between activities in the systemic context – the ongoing prehistoric behavioral system (Reid 1973; Schiffer 1973, 1976) – and their material remains in the archaeological context of the room floor as it exists when investigated by the archaeologist. The disproportionate preservation of some remains on room floors created by formation processes rather than the original activities can lead to meaningless results and major interpretive problems in a quantitative analysis.

It can, for example, contribute to the problem of 'abundance'. This is a general statistical problem resulting from the greater representation of some items relative to others. Those that are more abundant tend to exhibit greater variability and have a more significant influence in quantitative analyses than less abundant remains whose variability tends to be masked. Although this problem can be accentuated by formation processes, some items are in origin more abundant than others. For example, in food grinding activities several manos are usually used in conjunction with a single metate. Thus any methodology designed to investigate activities and room function must take into account the unequal representation of different remains. This is something that neither Hill (1968, 1970*a*, 1970*b*) nor Jorgenson (1975) adequately considered.

Methodology

The focus of this investigation is on the artifactual remains of activities found in large quantities on room floors. Because of remodeling and other factors, such remains are far better indications of room function than room size and other architectural features. It has been argued, however, that functional examination of artifactual remains presents the problem of controlling formation processes such as refuse disposal and differential preservation.

Much of this problem can be avoided by a careful selection of a set of rooms that are relatively contemporaneous and were subjected to the same general natural and cultural formation processes. Within this set of rooms additional control is provided by selecting and weighting the different types of remains using R-mode (variable clustering) analytic techniques. The results of this procedure are then employed in a Q-mode (object clustering) technique to derive a room function typology.

This approach has several advantages. The R-mode analyses are used to produce a highly selected, correlated, and weighted set of attributes that can be interpreted as the remains of a small number of important activities. In this way the typology is designed to compare rooms in terms of a set of equivalent, probably meaningful, attributes rather than the odd assortment of items that for a variety of reasons are found on a room floor. This approach examines, at least initially, a wider range of variability than considered in previous studies. At the same time the problems of abundance and formation processes are reduced if not controlled. Thus the analysis is directed towards producing a typology that eliminates extraneous processes and that can easily be interpreted in terms of meaningful behaviors such as activities.

R-mode analyses

R-mode analyses are useful as a preliminary stage for several reasons. Most object clustering methods measure correlations between variables on which the original measurements were made, for example, the frequency or relative frequency of artifact classes (Doran and Hodson 1975, p. 183). As a result, each variable is treated as equivalent in importance. Many of these variables are irrelevant, interdependent, or complex. A classification produced by the use of such variables could provide an accurate representation of the archaeological context remains but the systemic

context picture – in which the remains were used – would be a distorted one difficult to interpret in behavioral terms such as activities or function. The incomplete nature of archaeological remains and the disproportionate representation of different activities would result in still greater distortions. These problems can be alleviated through the selection and weighting of variables prior to classification. R-mode analytic techniques are a useful means of identifying and weighting the irrelevant, interdependent, and complex variables present in any analysis (Christenson and Read 1977).

Factor analysis is an R-mode technique that is specifically designed to partition out the major linear dimensions of variation that exist in a body of data and to approximate them with a smaller number of hypothetical variables called factors (Cattell 1965). Ideally, the disproportionate representation of different artifact types can be equalized by weighting and ranking variables which reduces the problem of abundance and provides some measure of control over the affects of formation processes. The interdependence of variables resulting from an activity that produces unusually abundant remains preserved on floors should be accounted for by the formation of a factor with which these variables are highly correlated. Irrelevant variables representing items not associated with any other type of item should have low correlations with all factors or form factors of their own (Christenson and Read 1977). Multifunctional tools represented by complex variables should associate with more than one factor (Christenson and Read 1977) or again form their own factor (Schiffer 1975).

Also under ideal circumstances the characteristics of factor analysis make it possible to distinguish overlapping spatial distributions of different tool assemblages sharing the same activity space (Vierra and Taylor 1977). In this respect it may be possible to identify different activities that take place in the same room.

Factor analysis can make possible the identification of meaningful relationships between variables. These relationships are indicative of activities assuming one is using a grossly functional classification of items (Binford and Binford 1966; Redman 1973; Schiffer 1975) and that the items are found in their location of use. Following the selection and weighting of variables, contents of rooms can then be compared or classified on the basis of a small number of dimensions of variation interpreted as the remains of activities rather than the odd assortment of artifacts that are usually preserved on floors. Thus classifications produced from the results of factor analyses can be more directly interpreted in behavioral terms.

In reality, however, factor analysis requires an extremely rigorous set of assumptions – unjustifiable in many archaeological analyses – in order to achieve these ends (Cowgill 1968; Lingoes 1970). The use of the techniques can have unforseen consequences.

Although R-mode analytic techniques in general can reduce the affect of abundance by replacing overly represented types with a smaller number of dimensions of variation, factor analysis can actually aggravate the problem. Variables with the highest variance have the greatest influence on the formation of factors. Since artifact types having the greatest frequencies usually also have the highest variance, such items will form the most factors.

A common solution to this particular problem is to use relative frequencies or percentages of artifact classes instead of raw counts (Cowgill 1968). This was attempted in an early foray into the Grasshopper room floor data but did not produce interpretable results. This poor result can be attributed in part to the fact that conversion to percentages requires an absolute or numerical scale of measurement or at least very high frequencies for all artifact classes. Because of such previously described problems as differential preservation and recovery of items, it is believed that artifact counts from room floors are best represented by ordinal or ranked scales. Reducing these counts to presence/absence values, an alternative solution commonly used in this situation, would have resulted in a considerable loss of information and resulted in problems similar to those encountered by Jorgenson (1975). Thus the problem of abundance cannot be so easily avoided in this analysis.

Another difficulty created by factor analysis is the focus on only a particular type of variation – common variance. Although the focus on common variance is an important means of eliminating irrelevant variables, the rejection of 'specific variance' in favor of 'common variance' in factor analysis has been a source of criticism (Doran and Hodson 1975, p. 205; Christenson and Read 1977, p. 167).

Specific variance may be very important in the present consideration. It is quite likely that a very important activity may be represented by very few artifact types because of poor preservation, refuse disposal, or other processes. The variables reflecting such activities could have a high variance but one that is not shared in common with other variables, i.e. a high specific variance. Since such a variable does not associate with other variables, its variance cannot be accounted for by the variance of other variables, i.e. a low common variance, and it will not attain an important position in the analysis results.

Thus factor analysis should be used with extreme caution. The results should be carefully examined to determine if a few relatively trivial variables have, because of their abundance, an undue influence on factor formation while what are believed to be important variables are ignored. This evaluation is facilitated by the use of two other R-mode techniques that utilize different assumptions and procedures as well as the results of the original data screening.

Room floor assemblages

The cases analyzed in this study are the assemblages of artifacts and facilities associated with room floors. A total of 100 rooms had been excavated at Grasshopper at the inception of the analysis. In order to eliminate the effects of some natural and cultural formation processes described

earlier, second-storey rooms and the lower floors in a superimposed sequence of floors are not included in the analysis. Remaining are 83 first-storey rooms representing about 20% of the total number of such rooms (Ciolek-Torrello 1978). Although these rooms were not selected for excavation according to a single consistent sampling strategy, they do accurately reflect the observed spatial and temporal variability of the community as well as size variability of all rooms (Ciolek-Torrello 1978).

A measure of room abandonment derived from an earlier formulation by Reid (1973, 1978) was used to provide additional relative temporal control over the excavated rooms and to determine which rooms were used primarily for refuse disposal (Ciolek-Torrello 1978). This measure examines the density of sherds in room-fill as an indicator of secondary refuse disposal activity (Reid 1973, 1978). The distribution of sherd densities was plotted and a cutoff determined at over 200 sherds m^{-2} (Ciolek-Torrello 1978). Rooms containing more than this number are classified as early-abandoned – prior to the pueblo's abandonment – and subsequently used primarily for refuse disposal. Rooms containing lower sherd densities are classified as late-abandoned rooms – abandoned near the end of pueblo occupation, which would have prevented the accumulation of much refuse. These rooms were probably used for ongoing domestic activities although it is possible that a room could be abandoned and not used as a midden, albeit an unlikely situation in a typical pueblo community.

This measure indicates that 68 of the 83 excavated ground floor rooms constitute a relatively contemporaneous class (Dean 1970) of late-abandoned floors. It should be recognized that not all these rooms are believed to have been occupied and abandoned at the same time. Rather, the remains of these floors represent a roughly contemporaneous occupation that occured within a maximum span of 20 to 40 years – most likely less – that probably followed the greatest expansion of the community.

Late-abandoned rooms usually contain much larger quantities of items in their presumed location of use, for example, whole vessels, than do early-abandoned rooms. This not only supports the proposition of ongoing domestic use but also indicates that most rooms with low frequencies – early-abandoned rooms – have been eliminated from the analysis. One late-abandoned room (No. 21) also had to be eliminated from the analysis. Although this large multistorey room contains large numbers of artifacts in their presumed location of use including numerous whole vessels, the unusually complex stratigraphy of the room made impossible the determination of which items were associated with each floor.

Thus 67 late-abandoned first-storey rooms remain to constitute the sample for functional analysis. The assemblages associated with these floors are analytically comparable since they are the product of generally similar formation processes and recovery procedures.

Artifact types

The variables employed in this analysis are general types or classes of artifacts found on floors. These include tools, non-portable facilities, ornaments, debris, and raw materials. These items were initially divided into 58 classes on the basis of reasonable functional interpretation generally employed by Southwestern archaeologists (see Kidder 1932; Woodbury 1954). The emphasis of these definitions is placed primarily on intuitive appraisals of formal and associational characteristics of artifacts rather than specific analyses of artifact functions, although some specific functional analyses have been performed. As a result, there probably exist some errors in the classification of individual artifacts or the functional interpretation of some types. But the multifunctional nature of most puebloan tools and the general level at which activities are examined here reduce the significance of such errors.

Lithic debitage and bone debris are not included among these 58 types, since they were not available at the time of the analysis. Perishable materials, including pollen and plant remains, are also not included. It should also be noted that non-portable facilities such as mealing bins and hearths are treated similarly to portable artifacts although the former are usually considered to be architectural characteristics. The present use of facilities is justified because these items are directly utilized in the performance of domestic activities, unlike room size for example. This close relationship of facilities with activities is reflected in their common removal or destruction when rooms are renovated and remodeled.

An initial review of the 58 classes of items on the 67 late-abandoned floors included an examination of the frequency distribution of each class of item, bivariate correlation, and in the case of facilities, contingency table analysis (Ciolek-Torrello 1978). As a result, the original 58 classes were reduced to 30 aggregated classes by a process of eliminating and combining types with extremely low frequencies. Similar classes of items were combined, especially when they were closely associated, while unique items occurring in very low frequencies were eliminated. A final list of the aggregated classes of artifacts and facilities and their mean frequencies is given in Table 1.

Analytic procedures

The data matrix used in this analysis consists of frequencies of 30 classes of items found on each of 67 late-abandoned ground floor rooms. The CDC 6400 and CYBER 175 computers at the University of Arizona were used in all computer assisted analyses. The analytic procedures used include three R-mode techniques – factor analysis, principal components analysis, and multidimensional scaling – to examine relationships between the variables and reduce them to a smaller set of weighted variables that will facilitate functional typology. The results of the factor analysis are then used in a Q-mode procedure to classify rooms into functional types.

Table 1. *Frequencies of classes of artifacts and facilities on late-abandoned floors (N = 67)*

Class	Sum	Mean	SD
1. Mealing bin	30	0.45	0.65
2. Cooking hearth	35	0.52	0.56
3. Other hearth	21	0.31	0.63
4. Storage box	18	0.27	0.70
5. Jar	380	5.67	6.92
6. Olla	85	1.27	2.18
7. Bowl	156	2.33	3.45
8. Plate	55	0.82	1.22
9. Slab	203	3.03	4.52
10. Cobble	141	2.10	2.94
11. Metate	106	1.58	1.66
12. Miscellaneous groundstone	46	0.69	0.98
13. Mano	357	5.33	5.42
14. Mano fragment	148	2.21	2.62
15. Handstone	193	2.88	3.83
16. Pebble	229	3.42	4.50
17. Hammerstone	198	2.96	3.36
18. Core	132	1.97	3.98
19. Chipped stone tool	248	3.70	6.11
20. Projectile point	156	2.33	3.06
21. Perforator	167	2.49	3.06
22. Arrowtool	63	0.94	1.52
23. Non-worked bone	141	2.10	4.72
24. Worked bone fragment	50	0.75	1.42
25. Pigment and clay	253	3.78	7.89
26. Stone axe	98	1.46	2.43
27. Boulder	14	0.21	0.56
28. Ornament	137	2.04	3.42
29. Mineral	53	0.79	1.72
30. Ceremonial object	46	0.69	1.63

SD = standard deviation.

Factor analysis

This R-mode procedure employs component programs of the BCTRY system (Tryon and Bailey 1970). These programs are combined in a standard factor analytic procedure using Pearson's r, the replacement of the main diagonal of the correlation matrix with communalities, and an oblique rotation of derived factors. It should be recognized immediately that this procedure makes the most demanding assumptions concerning the structure of the data, eliminates specific variance, and tends to magnify abundance while reducing the importance of non-abundant attributes.

The Empirical Key Cluster procedure (EKC) of the BCTRY system reduces the 30 variables to 5 factors. Each of these represents an underlying dimension of variation and can be described on the basis of the correlations (loadings) of the variables (Table 2). BCTRY identifies variables which are highly correlated with only one factor as definers of that

Table 2. *Loadings of variables on factors derived from BCTRY Empirical Key Cluster analysis*

Variable	Factor				
	1	2	3	4	5
Mealing bin	−0.086	0.005	0.818[a]	−0.230	−0.297
Cooking hearth	−0.161	−0.232	0.432[a]	−0.261	−0.204
Other hearth	0.004	0.090	−0.305	−0.062	0.074
Storage box	−0.140	−0.176	0.178	−0.071	−0.145
Jar	0.425	0.883[a]	0.163	0.281	0.252
Olla	0.151	0.699[a]	−0.012	0.180	0.138
Bowl	0.355	0.694[a]	0.251	0.184	0.328
Plate	0.345	0.471[b]	0.289	0.210	0.258
Slab	0.599[b]	0.558	0.102	0.133	0.542
Cobble	0.490[b]	0.439	0.412	0.124	0.100
Metate	0.343	0.167	0.759[a]	0.004	0.038
Groundstone	0.465[b]	0.300	0.409	0.128	0.092
Mano	0.565	0.522	0.586[a]	0.256	0.294
Mano fragment	0.520[a]	0.285	0.196	0.343	0.470
Handstone	0.425[b]	0.423	0.270	0.131	0.423
Pebble	0.693[a]	0.353	0.062	0.559	0.296
Hammerstone	0.783[a]	0.147	0.318	0.447	0.514
Core	0.595[b]	0.018	0.016	0.562	0.519
Chipped stone tool	0.829[a]	0.358	0.063	0.510	0.440
Projectile point	0.546	0.188	−0.012	0.568[b]	0.540
Perforator	0.743[a]	0.266	0.262	0.591	0.602
Arrowtool	0.750[a]	0.429	0.424	0.359	0.175
Non-worked bone	0.203	0.237	−0.081	0.129	0.601[a]
Worked bone fragment	0.521	0.182	−0.005	0.492	0.729[a]
Pigment and clay	0.871[a]	0.285	−0.004	0.758	0.323
Stone axe	0.477	0.621[b]	0.413	0.395	0.197
Boulder	0.176	−0.104	0.287	0.006	0.124
Ornament	0.683	0.154	−0.065	0.900[a]	0.548
Mineral	0.467	0.320	−0.084	0.773[a]	0.232
Ceremonial object	0.376[b]	−0.045	0.275	0.271	0.199
Cumulative proportion of converged communality	0.5066	0.6709	0.8369	0.9181	1.0057
Cumulative proportion of mean square of raw correlation matrix	0.7835	0.8479	0.9238	0.9368	0.9476

[a] Variables indicated by BCTRY as definers of factors.
[b] Other variables included in factor by BCTRY.

factor. Other variables which have lower correlations or correlations with several factors are also included in a factor.

These factors can also be interpreted by referring to the functional interpretations of the items that constitute each variable. It can be argued that this is a return to the use of ethnographic analogy that was criticized earlier. The use of analogy here is quite different, however, in that it refers to a broad body of functional data derived from numerous historic and prehistoric cases rather than a single ethnographic case. Furthermore, analogy is used here to interpret categories observed in the data rather than establish categories *a priori*.

Interpretation of factors

Factor 1 produced by EKC apparently represents the remains of generalized manufacturing activities that include the production of ceramics, stone tools, ritual objects, and ornaments. This is suggested by the high loadings (definers and other variables) of small tools such as mano fragments, handstones, pebbles (used as polishing tools and light hammerstones), hammerstones, retouched chipped stone tools (knives, scrapers, drills, etc.), perforators (bone awls, needles, and punches), and arrow tools. Also included are raw materials such as pigments (including clays) and cores.

Factor 2 is most easily interpreted as the remains of the storage of food and non-perishable items. Although no large quantities of food have been preserved in any Grasshopper rooms, pueblo food storage usually occurs in jars and ollas like those with high loadings on this factor. The limited pollen and flotation analysis that has occurred at Grasshopper supports this conclusion. Many jars, however, were also found to contain small tools and raw materials. Bowls and plates are generally believed to have been used primarily in food preparation and serving rather than storage activities. Thus their correlation with this factor is not readily interpretable. Similarly the high loading of axes is unexpected unless one considers that these items were stored with food and other objects when not in use.

Factor 3 apparently represents the remains of food preparation and cooking activities. This factor includes mealing bins and their commonly associated manos and metates. These are primarily used in preparing grains. Meat preparation and butchering are apparently not represented on room floors and most probably took place at kill sites and outdoor activity areas. Also included in this factor are cooking hearths which are small rectangular stone-lined firepits. These facilities occur almost exclusively in domestic rooms in contrast to other types of hearths that occur primarily in outdoor areas or ceremonial rooms.

The remaining two factors are more difficult to interpret, since they include primarily miscellaneous small objects such as projectile points, ornaments, and worked bone (fragments) with little apparent meaningful association. They can be most readily interpreted, however, as the remains of relatively minor manufacturing activities. The presence of non-worked bone (blanks) and worked bone fragments in Factor 5 suggest a bone tool manufacturing activity. No tools are included in this factor although numerous small tools have moderately high loadings on both Factor 5 and Factor 1. The fourth factor may also represent manufacturing since the minerals that define this factor are primarily raw materials such as turquoise used to manufacture ornaments.

Discussion of factor analysis

The results of the EKC analysis are unsatisfactory in their present form. As many as three factors (Factors 1, 4, and 5) appear to be measuring manufacturing activities while all other activities are measured by only two factors. This is clearly an example of the problem of abundance since many of the variables that define these three factors have among the highest average frequencies (see Table 1). EKC is obviously placing great weight on the variance exhibited by the large quantities of small tools, raw material and debris discarded on room floors although manufacturing activities are not the most important activities that are known to occur on both historic and prehistoric pueblo room floors.

In addition, the lack of concern with specific variance and non-abundant items is reflected in the fact that many variables are not included in any factor even though the

initial preview of data indicated that they were strongly associated with other items (usually not manufacturing) or exhibited interesting negative correlations.

The unsatisfactory results can also be attributed in part to the measurement scale assumed by factor analysis. It has been argued that the assumption of numerical scale data can not be supported in the analysis of frequency counts from an archaeological context. The distribution of artifact frequencies reflect relative differences between rooms rather than absolute ones because of measurement error and the differential effects of formation processes. Thus procedures employing numerical scales tend only to magnify the already inordinate variance of many small objects, while a ranked scale would reduce that variance. The use of numerical scales, therefore, can actually defeat the original purpose of using R-mode procedures.

As stated earlier, the usual solutions to this problem involving conversion of counts to relative frequencies did not work with this data. Other solutions, however, are possible. These include the use of R-mode techniques that have less demanding assumptions than factor analysis.

Principal components analysis

This procedure employs an SPSS Principal Factoring program without iteration (PA1) (Nie *et al.* 1975). The Spearman's correlation coefficient for ordinal scale measurements is used in place of the standard Pearson's *r*. This together with the fact that PA1 does not deal only with common variance should alleviate some of the problems encountered in the EKC factor analysis.

A Varimax rotation which maximizes the differences between variables was selected because of pragmatic reasons. This rotation produces the most easily interpreted final solution while other rotations attempted produce similar but generally more complex solutions.

The PA1 program reduces the 30 variables to 8 principal components that represent a dimension of variation somewhat similar to a factor. Each component has an eigenvalue greater than 1.00 and together they account for almost 73% of the variance. The value of 1.00 is the arbitrary default value of the program and is actually more sensitive than is necessary, since a large break in the distribution of eigenvalues occurs between the third and fourth component. The loadings of variables on each component are given in Table 3 and can be used to interpret the components in a manner similar to that carried out for the factors.

Interpretation and discussion of components

Although PA1 does not indicate defining variables, it is obvious from an inspection of variable loadings that the first three components are quite similar to the first three factors derived by EKC. Overall, however, the loadings of each variable are lower than in the EKC analysis. This indicates that in the Spearman's correlation matrix the variances of individual variables has been reduced which accords better with the rank differences in the original data.

Table 3. *Loadings of variables on principal components derived from SPSS PA1 analysis using a Spearman's correlation matrix*

Variable	Principal component							
	1	2	3	4	5	6	7	8
Mealing bin	−0.132	0.227	0.513	−0.418	0.179	0.032	−0.274	0.442
Cooking hearth	−0.211	−0.228	0.726	−0.214	0.061	0.079	−0.098	0.190
Other hearth	0.009	0.030	−0.176	0.865	0.025	−0.085	0.024	0.098
Storage box	−0.084	−0.110	0.073	0.113	−0.147	−0.003	0.007	0.850
Jar	−0.035	0.864	0.042	−0.089	0.170	0.116	0.029	−0.087
Olla	0.021	0.844	−0.106	0.182	0.193	−0.055	0.057	0.019
Bowl	0.139	0.738	0.162	0.009	−0.075	−0.125	0.099	−0.084
Plate	0.180	0.540	0.217	−0.186	−0.026	0.482	0.288	−0.096
Slab	0.092	0.269	0.162	0.191	0.397	−0.171	0.474	−0.027
Cobble	0.119	0.207	0.196	−0.144	0.706	0.266	0.222	−0.084
Metate	0.097	0.262	0.585	−0.209	0.497	0.186	−0.035	0.201
Miscellaneous groundstone	0.121	0.207	0.620	−0.062	0.098	−0.038	0.355	−0.247
Mano	0.371	0.536	0.265	−0.155	0.319	0.219	0.118	0.326
Mano fragment	0.285	0.079	0.042	0.047	0.754	0.047	0.270	−0.081
Handstone	0.317	0.310	0.442	0.394	0.066	0.401	0.099	−0.008
Pebble	0.595	0.192	0.139	0.124	0.216	0.244	0.256	−0.334
Hammerstone	0.455	0.059	0.179	0.117	0.625	0.118	0.245	−0.116
Core	0.452	0.184	0.064	−0.078	0.316	0.115	0.538	−0.240
Chipped stone tool	0.499	0.013	0.152	0.150	0.354	0.252	0.533	−0.109
Projectile point	0.356	0.079	−0.196	−0.060	0.092	0.106	0.721	0.083
Perforator	0.641	0.156	0.346	0.052	0.232	0.007	0.388	−0.056
Arrowtool	0.406	0.247	0.528	0.059	0.158	0.315	0.096	0.028
Non-worked bone	0.120	0.113	0.040	0.111	0.155	0.049	0.744	−0.068
Worked bone fragment	0.542	−0.051	0.090	0.151	0.082	0.052	0.501	−0.094
Pigment and clay	0.772	0.074	0.008	0.150	0.270	0.075	0.289	0.007
Stone axe	0.398	0.510	0.503	0.141	0.168	0.014	0.033	0.002
Boulder	0.033	−0.090	0.079	−0.058	0.211	0.880	0.036	0.021
Ornament	0.766	0.111	−0.065	0.040	0.017	0.049	0.262	0.009
Mineral	0.745	0.033	−0.046	−0.343	0.133	−0.085	−0.003	−0.026
Ceremonial object	0.403	−0.034	0.124	−0.310	0.212	0.016	0.604	0.213
Eigenvalue	9.96	3.44	2.33	1.41	1.35	1.22	1.07	1.02
Percentage of variance	33.2	11.5	7.8	4.7	4.5	4.1	3.6	3.4

Principal component 1 contains the many small tools and raw materials associated with manufacturing. Of interest here is the fact that worked bone, ornaments, and minerals also have high loadings on this component. This component is actually a composite of Factors 1, 4, and possibly 5 derived by EKC and thus the latter three factors are not independent but in fact correlated. This is not unexpected, since the oblique rotation used in factor analysis, unlike the orthogonal rotations of principal components analysis, can produce correlated factors. This is another way in which factor analysis may place unjustifiable weight on several variables or dimensions of variation.

Again the second principal component apparently represents the storage of food and non-perishable items. The high loadings of manos, however, contrasts with the factor analysis and is unexpected in this context. It can be explained by the fact that manos are among the most common tools and are used in many activities. Many manos are used in manufacturing in the process of grinding pigments and clays and as vessel supports in cooking and storage in addition to their best-known function as food grinding implements. This multi-functional character of manos is reflected by the moderate-to-high loadings on several components (and factors derived in the EKC analysis). Thus manos are poor diagnostics of any particular activity and should not be used as a definer of any single factor or component unless the class of manos is broken down into specific functional types on the basis of formal attributes, wear patterns (including traces of pigment), or fine-scale spatial associations.

The third principal component includes the remains of

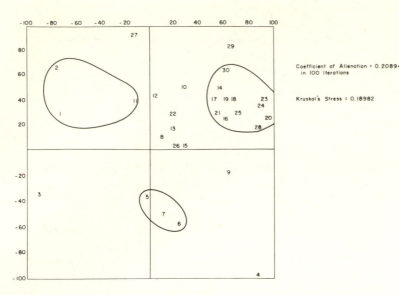

Fig. 5. Plot of variables from Guttman–Lingoes SSA-1 analysis. Clusters indicate association of variables in two-dimensional space. Encircled clusters correspond to Factors 1, 2, and 3 from BCTRY analysis. See Table 1 for variable identification.

food preparation and cooking activities. Mealing bins, cooking hearths, metates, and miscellaneous grinding stones are all highly correlated with this component. The high loadings of arrowtools and axes are unaccounted for. Manos have an unexpectedly low loading although this can be accounted for by the above discussion and is partially compensated for by handstones which have their highest loading on this component. The latter tools are small grinding stones that are even more multifunctional than manos, often being used for pounding as well as a variety of grinding activities.

The fourth principal component has only a single variable with a high loading – other hearths. The negative loadings of mealing bins and cooking hearths indicate that this component has little to do with normal food processing. It is possible that these other hearths were used in ritual activities (Stevenson 1904, p. 293) or merely room heating. Normally this component would be considered insignificant, since it measures specific variance and other hearths would be regarded as an irrelevant variable. The strong negative correlation with food preparation facilities and the association with kivas, however, indicates that this component may actually represent an important activity from which most other remains have either been curated or not preserved.

The remaining principal components 5–8 are difficult to interpret and may not be significant. Of these, the seventh and eighth appear to be the most interesting. The seventh apparently represents the use of stone and bone tools in manufacturing or processing activities. Little more can be said without specific analyses of the tools that make up this assemblage. The eighth component represents minor storage activities apparently associated with food processing. The correlation of storage boxes and mealing bins is unexpected. Storage boxes, if correctly interpreted, should correlate with storage facilities as suggested by ethnographic sources (Hill 1970*a*, p. 52). Later analysis, however, shows that these

facilities actually exhibit a complex associational pattern that is not well reflected in the principal components analysis.

In summary, it is obvious that the principal components analysis with its simpler assumptions has reduced the affects of abundance relative to the more stringent factor analysis. For example, manufacturing activities are accounted for primarily by a single uncorrelated component and several low frequency variables have formed factors of their own. It is equally clear, however, that the problem has not been completely eliminated since the first component is still dominated by high frequency variables. The final R-mode technique may go even further in reducing this problem.

Multidimensional scaling

The Spearman's matrix derived in the SPSS procedure was next input to a Guttman–Lingoes Small Space Analysis (SSA-1). Unlike factor analysis, this technique better preserves the rank order distances (Cowgill 1968, 1970) that are inherent in the ordinal scale of measurement of the input data. Neither PA1 nor EKC preserve rank orders when measuring the correlations between variables and components or factors even when the original data are in the form of a rank ordered matrix. Thus the SSA-1 procedure is a necessary check of the reliability of the other R-mode techniques.

The results of the SSA-1 procedure can only be presented graphically. Variable clusters identified by SSA-1 are displayed in two dimensions (no major differences in the overall relationships were noted in a three-dimensional display). These results tend to support the variable clusters – components and factors – defined by PA1 and EKC although it is apparent that the rank order distances between some associated variables are greater than the other procedures indicated.

Three distinct variable clusters can be identified in the SSA-1 results (Fig. 5). These correspond with variables correlated with the first three principal components derived by PA1 and the first three factors derived by EKC. A fourth intermediate cluster consists of multifunctional items which are correlated with more than one component or factor in the other analyses. SSA-1 also identifies three other variables as outliers to all of these clusters. These outliers coincide with the variables having high loadings on principal components 4, 6, and 8.

This technique theoretically should be least affected by the problem of abundance since it better preserves the rank order distances in measuring correlation between variables as well as between variables and the underlying dimensions of variation represented by variable clusters. Like the principal components analysis, however, it supports the derivation of the first three factors in the EKC analysis. Thus these appear to represent stable and significant variable clusters rather than mere statistical artifacts.

Modifying the factor analysis

Thus apart from several unsatisfactory aspects, the major elements of the BCTRY factor analysis are supported by the other R-mode analytic techniques. The objections raised concerning the factor analysis can be eliminated, at least in part, through several modifications of the results of the EKC analysis. The Preset Key Cluster (PKC) program of the BCTRY system (Tryon and Bailey 1970) is used for this purpose. This procedure eliminates the fifth factor which is apparently a redundant variable correlated with Factors 1 and 4. In addition, manos which are actually highly correlated with at least three factors is removed as a definer of Factor 3. The end product is a set of four factors that are more similar in composition to the first three components derived by PA1 and supported by SSA-1. The major difference is that principal component 1 is represented by two correlated factors – Factors 1 and 4.

Composite scores

Up to this point the original 30 variables consisting of artifact counts have been reduced to a set of empirically significant and independent (except for Factors 1 and 4) factors. Each factor describes relationships between variables that reflect patterning in spatial association of items. Variables are also weighted by their correlation or loading on the factor. Irrelevant variables (really a misnomer) which do not exhibit patterning shared by other variables are eliminated by low loadings on the factors. The effect of abundance which tends to be magnified by factor analysis is recognized and reduced somewhat by comparison with other R-mode techniques that better preserve rank-order distances.

More important, because the items were found in their presumed location of use and on a relatively uniform set of floors, these factors reflect what can be interpreted as the remains of at least three basic domestic activities – manufacturing, storage, and food processing. These are not the only activities that are believed to have taken place on Grasshopper

room floors. For example, ceremonial activities as well as others are not represented by any factor. The factors do represent the bulk of material preserved (and probably used) on most late-abandoned floors. In order to address other activities, means other than those described here must be used.

As a result of this work, room floor variability can now be re-examined and a typology derived using a small set of apparently meaningful dimensions of variation rather than the original assortment of items whose distribution is the result of a variety of processes in addition to function. This is achieved by deriving a new data matrix based on the selection and weighting of variables accomplished by the factor analysis. This new data matrix is then analyzed in the Q-mode.

A major advantage of the BCTRY system of programs is that it makes possible an easy interaction between R-mode and Q-mode analyses. In fact, the BCTRY system clusters variables as a standard preliminary step to object clustering (Tryon and Bailey 1970).

The Facs procedure (Tryon and Bailey 1970, p. 310) is used to produce a new composite variable that estimates each of the four derived factors. Composite variables are synthetic variables used to redescribe the original data based on the proportionate R-mode frequencies of the original measurements. The option employed here is to produce composite cluster scores which include only defining variables in deriving the composite variable (Tryon and Bailey 1970, p. 175). Cluster scores contrast with composite factor scores where all variables are included in defining each composite variable and each original variable shows the graded weight proportional to its correlation with the corresponding factor.

Composite cluster scores are calculated for each of the four factors and 67 late-abandoned rooms using the equally weighted defining variables. For example, each defining variable of Factor 1 in the modified PKC analysis is given a weight of 1.00 on composite variable 1 while all non-definers are given a weight of 0.00. All the scores are also standardized with a mean of 50 and a standard deviation of 10 so that all four composite variables have an equal variance and weight in the typology (Tryon and Bailey 1970, p. 140).

The calculation of cluster scores rather than factor scores facilitates the interpretation of the typology (Tryon and Bailey 1970, p. 175). At the same time equalizing the weights of each defining variable and each composite variable is an important means of reducing the effect of abundance since the most abundant items tend to correlate with the first factor which accounts for the largest amount of variance. Without such weighting this factor would have the greatest influence on the typology. Now, however, each dimension of variation – interpreted as an activity – is equally represented in the new data matrix. Each of the important defining variables is also treated equally in estimating each dimension. It should not be forgotten that manufacturing activities are still represented by two composite variables even though other R-mode analyses (PA1 and SSA-1) indicated that their

Table 4. *Mean composite cluster score of each object cluster (type) derived by BCTRY Condensation method*

	Mean composite score			
Type	Factor 1	Factor 2	Factor 3	Factor 4
1	45.51	43.96	42.62	47.33
	(4.92)	(2.32)	(4.68)	(4.64)
2	45.97	46.46	58.69	47.39
	(4.18)	(3.55)	(4.30)	(3.85)
3	48.56	57.67	43.57	46.15
	(5.70)	(4.50)	(4.34)	(1.82)
4	55.77	54.98	66.32	47.59
	(4.79)	(6.24)	(4.21)	(4.21)
5	70.37	41.76	42.98	77.34
	(0.82)	(0.00)	(0.90)	(12.10)
6	72.00	70.05	53.33	78.64
	(6.21)	(4.94)	(5.26)	(8.83)

Standard deviations in parentheses.

Table 5. *Composite cluster scores for reassigned rooms and previously unassigned rooms*

Room	Factor 1	Factor 2	Factor 3	Factor 4
438	49.53	45.21	39.11	57.01
231	57.15	45.79	49.25	52.18
108	53.04	44.05	51.79	56.98
145	58.58	43.48	46.70	60.28
19	41.32	51.61	41.66	44.18
15	41.59	41.76	54.30	44.18
22	56.11	44.05	56.93	57.01
44	55.98	90.70	41.66	47.40
13	43.48	81.00	39.11	77.78
43	93.34	67.70	49.29	50.62
21	Not included in R-mode or Q-mode analyses			

defining variables could be easily represented by a single dimension.

Q-mode analysis

The matrix of composite cluster scores are then input to a BCTRY Condensation program (Tryon and Bailey 1970, pp. 331–2). This is an iterative hierarchical object clustering procedure that uses composite scores in place of original variable measurements. It works by representing all the object (room floors) in a four-dimensional space defined by the scores on the four composite variables (Tryon and Bailey 1970, pp. 312–13). This space is divided into sectors by sectioning each dimension by the scores on that dimension. Sectors that have more objects falling within their boundaries define the first approximation of types. A mean score on each dimension is calculated for each of these trial types. Each object is then assigned to the trial type with which it has the smallest Euclidean distance. The means are then recalculated and the process reiterated until no type changes membership.

Six object clusters are defined by BCTRY in this manner. Each is inferred to represent a functionally distinct room type in terms of manufacturing, storage, or food processing. Type 4 rooms, for example, have the highest mean score for the composite variable that corresponds with Factor 3 representing food processing activities. Type 4 rooms also have moderate scores for the factors representing manufacturing and storage (Table 4). Type 2 rooms in contrast have a similar mean score for Factor 3 but much lower scores for the other factors. Thus it can be inferred that rooms of types 2 and 4 are the primary areas for food processing while Type 4 rooms are also used for manufacturing and storage.

This classification, however, is not satisfactory for several reasons. Although only three rooms (13, 43, and 44) could not be classified into a type, these rooms all exhibit unusually high scores on Factor 2 and either of Factors 1 or 4 and very low scores on Factor 3 (Table 5). These rooms also have very large numbers of almost all types of items including non-definers. In contrast almost a third of the rooms which have low scores on all factors (and generally contain few items) are placed in a single type. Thus the analysis is still being affected by the problem of abundance despite the derivation of other interesting types.

It is possible to ameliorate this situation by re-classifying several rooms on the basis of their composite scores and the values of the original variables. The latter are especially important at this stage, since several important variables, in addition to the trivial or irrelevant ones, have been excluded from the object cluster analysis. However, the number of clusters derived by BCTRY, and their basic composition, are retained intact. In fact, the differences between types are enhanced if one considers the changed type means (Table 6).

In the revised classification (Table 6) four rooms (108, 145, 231, and 438) were originally assigned by BCTRY to Type 1 but have been here reassigned to Type 5. Although these rooms have generally low scores on all four factors, they are highest on Factors 1 and 4 (Table 5), a situation most similar to Type 5 rooms as indicated by the original mean composite score for each type (Table 4). In addition, most of these rooms have very high scores on Factor 5 which was not used in the Q-mode analysis, a situation similar to most Type 5 rooms. A similar rationale is used to assign the three previously unassigned rooms to Type 6 which has the highest mean score for Factors 1, 2, and 4 and a very low score for Factor 3. The reason that these three rooms were not originally included in any type is that they exhibit extraordinarily high scores on Factor 2 and either Factor 1 or Factor 4. This is clearly an affect of abundance that may have been magnified in the typology despite all attempts to the contrary. Thus these reassignments can be seen as a final attempt to reduce the affects of abundance. A summary of the final classification of rooms and revised mean composite scores for each type is

Table 6. *Final classification of rooms[a] and revised mean composite cluster scores for each type*

Room					
Type 1	Type 2	Type 3	Type 4	Type 5	Type 6
26	211	434	11	279	246
18	100	215	216	187	39
352	114	35	116	269	13[b]
12	7	210	3	438(1)	43[b]
2	143	376	371	231(1)	44[b]
42	349	9	205	108(1)	21[c]
197	8	183	319	145(1)	
274	4	198	359	22(2)	
338	24	45			
360	398	19(1)			
206	27				
40	6				
195	218				
341	5				
121					
153					
425					
33					
404					
280					
37					
15(2)					
$N=$ 22	14	10	8	8	6 = 68

Factor	Revised mean composite cluster scores					
1	43.87	45.56	47.84	55.77	60.70	67.36
	(2.91)	(3.33)	(5.83)	(4.79)	(7.94)	(17.29)
2	43.39	46.97	57.07	54.98	43.48	75.90
	(1.83)	(3.48)	(4.64)	(6.24)	(1.49)	(9.27)
3	42.12	59.54	43.25	66.32	47.00	50.12
	(4.43)	(3.80)	(4.22)	(4.21)	(4.97)	(7.10)
4	45.64	46.93	45.95	47.59	64.43	66.62
	(2.32)	(3.07)	(1.82)	(4.21)	(12.61)	(15.46)

[a] When room assignment changed, assignment by BCTRY indicated in parentheses.

[b] Previously unassigned rooms.

[c] Not included in any R-mode or Q-mode analyses, given mean frequency of Type 6 rooms for original variables in remaining analyses.

given in Table 6. It should be noted that R21 which was not included in any of the analyses because of the inability to assign precise frequencies for each artifact type is also classified in Type 6. This assignment is based on an overall similarity of this room to the others in the type rather than a quantitative analysis.

Room function

The function of each of these revised types is described on the basis of their revised mean composite scores for each of the four factors used in the Q-mode procedure (Table 6). A return to the original artifact frequency data provides additional information about the classification and also takes into account important variables that were not used in the Q-mode analysis.

Figure 6 presents relative frequencies for the most significant variables in the form of multiple bar graphs for each room type. The defining variables for all five factors derived by the EKC analysis (Table 2) are included. Relative frequencies for other variables included by EKC in Factors 2

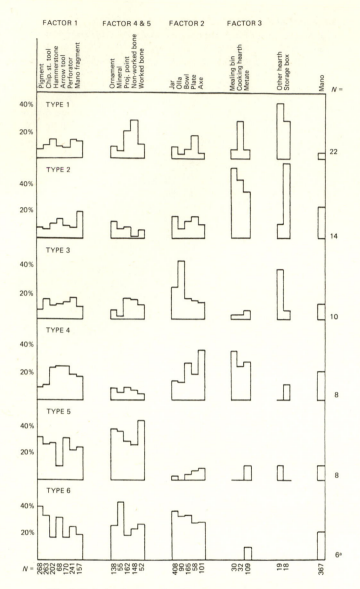

Fig. 6. Relative frequencies, by room type, of variables associated with five factors, other hearths, storage boxes, and manos. Chip. St. = chipped stone; Proj. = projectile. [a]Total includes R21 which is given mean frequencies of Type 6 rooms for each variable.

and 4 are also presented. These variables are grouped by factor cluster except in the case of manos which are presented separately, since this variable associates strongly with several factors. Finally, relative frequencies for storage boxes and other hearths are also included. The latter were not involved in the Q-mode analysis but reflect important specific variation as indicated by their placement on principal components 8 and 4, respectively, by the PA1 analysis.

The following functions are ascribed to the room types on the basis of this and distributional information:

    Type 1 – Limited Activity Rooms
    Type 2 – Habitation Rooms
    Type 3 – Domestic Storage Rooms
    Type 4 – Multifunctional Habitation Rooms

    Type 5 – Manufacturing Rooms
    Type 6 – Storage/Manufacturing Rooms

Limited Activity Rooms

These rooms have among the lowest mean scores for all factors indicating either limited use or use in activities that are not measured by the four factors. Inspection of the bar graphs, however, suggest considerable variation in this type. Over 40% of the other hearths with suspected ceremonial function are found in rooms of this type. Most of the rooms with these hearths also contain a storage box (Fig. 7). This type also contains the highest percentage of non-worked bone, including animal skulls and bird skeletons which a recent study suggests are used in a ceremonial or ritual context (Olsen 1980). Finally, three of the four rooms at Grasshopper that have masonry benches typical of kivas are contained in this type. The fourth kiva-like room was abandoned early and subsequently resurfaced and divided into two rooms (114 and 195). This is not to suggest that all Type 1 rooms are ceremonial rooms. Rather only about a third were apparently used for this function. BCTRY, however, could not distinguish these as a separate type.

Many of the remaining Type 1 rooms were used for limited food processing activities, probably as areas supplementary to habitation rooms. These rooms contain only a partial assemblage of the tools usually associated with this activity – a mealing bin, cooking hearth, or several grinding stones, but not all three. This supplementary function is clearly illustrated by the aforementioned R114 and R195. The latter is one of the smallest rooms (5.6 m^2) in the pueblo and contains only a mealing bin and a few associated tools (Fig. 8). It is adjacent to the larger R114 (Type 2) with more complete food processing activities. The mealing bin in the smaller room was probably used to supplement the two mealing bins found in the larger room. Independent use of the smaller room or use with some other room is not indicated, since both rooms lie in the corner of a small roomblock (RB5).

The function of a few other rooms in this type cannot be ascertained from the available data since they contain few associated artifacts or facilities. It is possible that they were used to a small degree as manufacturing areas or even that some are abandoned rooms that have not yet been used for refuse disposal.

Habitation Rooms

The factor scores for these rooms are generally similar to those of Type 1 rooms with the exception of the interpretation of Factor 3 as representing food processing activities. Rooms of this type invariably contain at least one and sometimes two mealing bins and cooking hearths along with several metates and grinding stones. Although they have low scores on the storage factor, they contain over 50% of the storage boxes. This partially accounts for the low correlation of this variable with other storage variables. The remaining storage

Fig. 7. Ceremonial hearth (other hearth) and storage box in R197, a Limited Activity room. Two small pits (lower left) and the top of a cooking hearth on an earlier floor (upper right) also shown. The few portable artifacts associated with these features were removed prior to the taking of this photograph. (Photographer: R. G. Vivian, Arizona State Museum, University of Arizona.)

boxes are associated with other hearths in other types of rooms. Type 2 rooms conform most closely with what has been described as the pueblo habitation room (Hill 1968, 1970*a*, 1970*b*).

Domestic Storage Rooms

These rooms appear to conform most closely to the typical pueblo storage areas associated with the above kind of habitation room. Unlike the other rooms with extensive storage facilities (Type 6 rooms), these are usually found adjacent to habitation rooms at Grasshopper (Fig. 9). The high scores on the storage factor alone suggest that they are used almost exclusively for storage. Such rooms usually contain large numbers of storage vessels, particularly jars and ollas in addition to a metate, some manos, and a few other domestic implements. A few of these rooms also serve an apparent secondary ceremonial function as suggested by the high percentage of other hearths (Fig. 10).

Multifunctional Habitation Rooms

A second type of habitation room (Fig. 11) is distinguished by moderate scores on manufacturing and storage activities in addition to high scores for food processing. These rooms contain higher frequencies of manufacturing materials and storage vessels than the other type of habitation room. A high frequency of bowls appears to lie behind the high scores on the storage factor although jars are also common. The abundance of bowls is as expected from our understanding of pueblo ethnography (Hill 1970*a*). The relative paucity of ollas, however, conflicts with expectations for habitation rooms (Mindeleff 1891, pp. 109–10).

Multifunctional habitation rooms also contain high frequencies of manos as one would expect in a food processing area. The earlier R-mode analysis, however, indicated a relatively low correlation between manos and food processing. How might this seeming contradiction be explained? The frequencies of manos in these rooms are only exceeded by

Fig. 8. Room 195: a small Limited Activity room with a mealing bin containing a metate and associated mano (center) and crushed storage jar (lower left). (Photographer: R. G. Vivian, Arizona State Museum, University of Arizona.)

those in Type 6 rooms which have the highest frequencies of storage vessels. Thus manos are apparently occurring in large numbers in two different types of contexts. The strong association of manos in these habitation rooms is being masked by the presence of relatively large numbers of storage vessels as well.

Manufacturing Rooms

High scores on Factors 1 and 4 suggest that these rooms are devoted almost exclusively to manufacturing activities. It is not clear, however, whether these rooms are the actual loci of manufacturing activities or merely areas for the storage and discard of manufacturing materials. Although manufacturing activities are recognized as a common part of puebloan domestic structure, specialized manufacturing rooms have not been previously described. At Grasshopper, however, there are rooms that contain few or none of the facilities that are common in other types of rooms. Instead, they contain large

quantities of pigments, clays, cores, worked bone, and small tools.

The question of whether manufacturing actually takes place in these rooms is unresolved at present. Most lack hearths of any kind or other sources of light. Thus it is difficult to imagine people carrying out various precision manufacturing activities in such locations. Furthermore, tools and debris often occur in thick deposits (10–20 cm deep) suggesting refuse disposal. Such rooms, however, lack the large numbers of sherds that are diagnostic of refuse disposal. It is possible that some of these rooms served as areas for storing and possibly discarding manufacturing materials only.

Storage/Manufacturing Rooms

These rooms are the fewest in number but contain among the highest frequencies of most classes of artifacts, especially storage vessels and manufacturing materials. In fact the six rooms in this type contain 30–40% of all the vessels and 40% or more of the pigments and minerals found on late-abandoned floors. It is clear in the case of these rooms that the manufacturing materials are being stored rather than used. A look at the floor plan of one of these rooms reveals that the entire room is filled with storage vessels leaving virtually no space for much work (Fig. 12). Despite the tremendous numbers of artifacts on these floors, there is an almost complete absence of all types of facilities such as mealing bins or hearths. Like Type 5 rooms, such rooms do not appear to have been described in any previous reports of either historic or prehistoric pueblos.

Discussion of functional types

The types derived by the multivariate analyses can be presented in the form of a model describing the range of functional variability found in rooms at Grasshopper. The model, however, is hypothetical at present. It is also incomplete, since roofs, second-storey floors and early floors, for example, are not included. It also focuses on an important but limited set of activities and excludes others. Despite such problems, its behavioral significance is suggested by several independent lines of evidence.

For example, there appears to be a partial correspondence between room function and certain architectural characteristics regardless of the considerable remodeling that has taken place in many rooms. Limited Activity rooms have the smallest mean size (12.4 m²) and include all rooms under 7 m² in area (Table 7). As indicated earlier, this type also contains all rooms having kiva features, in particular a masonry bench with ventilator shaft. When originally constructed, these benches were all associated with a round hearth (other hearth) (Fig. 7).

Most storage rooms (Type 3) are smaller than Habitation

Table 7. *Average floor area in m² by room type, including early-abandoned rooms*

Room type	Mean area
1	12.35
2	17.66
3	15.37
4	18.32
5	17.88
6	18.36
Early-abandoned	15.61
All rooms	15.79

rooms (Types 2 and 4) although they are still two to three times as large as their functional counterparts at Broken K Pueblo (Hill 1970*a*). Storage/Manufacturing rooms (Type 6), however, have the largest mean area of all types. The remaining Type 5 – manufacturing rooms – also tend to be quite large. The relatively large size of Type 5 and Type 6 rooms may result in part from the fact that they most often occur as the first floors of multistorey structures in which the upper floors apparently served as food processing areas as indicated by the presence of mealing bins, hearths, and several metates (Ciolek-Torrello 1978). More important, however, many of the Type 5 and Type 6 rooms occur in the oldest parts of the pueblo in the core construction units of the three large roomblocks (Longacre 1975). These rooms may have originally functioned as habitation areas as suggested by the common occurrence of cooking hearths on earlier resurfaced floors.

In contrast, the relatively small mean size of the 15

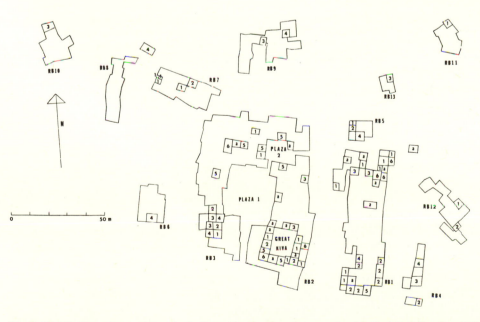

Fig. 9. Distribution of room types, including early-abandoned rooms. 1 = Limited Activity. 2 = Habitation. 3 = Domestic Storage. 4 = Multifunctional habitation. 5 = Manufacturing. 6 = Storage/Manufacturing. a = Abandoned, RB = roomblock.

Fig. 10. R210: a Domestic Storage room, containing about 12 large storage vessels and a ceremonial hearth (other hearth). The depression in the center is a test trench. (Photographer: Susan Luebberman, Arizona State Museum, University of Arizona.)

early-abandoned rooms (Table 7) – not examined here – suggests that they originally functioned as storage rooms. This provides further evidence that remodeling has indeed confused the original relationship between room size and function. Apparently large rooms tend to be remodeled while smaller rooms are abandoned. It must be recognized, however, that the difference in size between types is so slight, and the range in size within each type is so great, that predicting room function from a knowledge of size is an extremely tenuous procedure at Grasshopper. Prediction would be difficult even if we were able to control for remodeling because of the large number of other factors that impinge upon room function at this site.

The functional model presented here has also proved useful in the identification of organizational patterns within the community of Grasshopper. Different room types, for example, are not randomly distributed throughout the pueblo but usually occur within particular types of locations (Fig. 9).

Storage/Manufacturing rooms occur exclusively in the older parts of the community in and around the core construction units of the three large roomblocks and the Great Kiva. Domestic Storage rooms, in contrast, are located more commonly in peripheral areas that include the smaller outlying roomblocks and the peripheries of the three large roomblocks. Manufacturing rooms are primarily restricted to the older parts and the vicinity of the Great Kiva.

Again a contrasting situation is presented by both types of Habitation rooms which occur most often in the peripheral areas of the community. There are few indications of food processing activities characteristic of Habitation rooms in the older central parts of the pueblo, even when the upper floors of the multistorey structures are examined (Ciolek-Torrello 1978). Given this situation it is not surprising that virtually all early-abandoned rooms occur in the older central locations of the pueblo.

Finally the model also appears to be useful in the study

Fig. 11. R216: a Multifunctional Habitation room, containing a mealing area (upper right), storage area with 12 crushed vessels (left), cooking area (center), and numerous scattered small tools and debris. (Photographer: Susan Luebberman, Arizona State Museum, University of Arizona.)

of changing domestic organization. Recent analyses by the author suggest several intriguing patterns that can only be briefly mentioned here. The two types of Habitation rooms are probably associated with different-sized households which in turn have been interpreted as reflecting different stages in the developmental cycle of domestic groups at Grasshopper (see Ciolek-Torrello and Reid 1974). In the 1974 study, cooking hearth size was found to vary independently of room size and was postulated to be an indicator of household size (Fig. 13). Following the derivation of the room function typology, it was discovered that Type 2 Habitation rooms have significantly larger hearths than Type 4 Habitation rooms. Since the latter also contain storage and manufacturing facilities in addition to complete food processing facilities, it is inferred that Multifunctional Habitation rooms (Type 4) are the residence units of small single-room households. The other Habitation rooms (Type 2) have larger cooking hearths and virtually no storage and manufacturing facilities. They

are inferred to be the focal point of larger multiroomed households whose storage and manufacturing activities probably take place in adjoining rooms.

In addition, the Storage/Manufacturing rooms are associated with what appear to be a few very large households occupying multistorey structures in the older part of the pueblo. Domestic Storage rooms, in contrast, occur more commonly in the newer more peripheral areas of the community where they may be associated with smaller households. This discussion is not meant as a test of the room function typology: the results of these recent studies, however, are encouraging in regard to the validity of the typology.

Conclusion

A model of room function has been derived by focusing attention on the quantitative analysis of remains of activities on room floors. The derivation of this model has depended to a great extent on the use of multivariate analytic tech-

Fig. 12. R39: a Storage/Manufacturing room, containing 35 jars, ollas, and bowls and numerous small tools, ornaments and raw materials. (Photographer: R. G. Vivian, Arizona State Museum, University of Arizona.)

niques. These account for the multifunctional characteristics of many tools and can be used to accommodate the effects of formation processes by the selection and weighting of variables. Such techniques, however, have several important limitations. Overlapping distributions of artifact clusters cannot always be clearly distinguished, as in the case of manos. Although these tools probably associate equally with both storage and food processing activities, the different R-mode analytic techniques tend to emphasize their association with one or the other activity.

In addition, these multivariate techniques which measure linear associations are not able to accommodate significant variables with strong bimodal distributions, as in the case of other hearths and, to a lesser degree, storage boxes. Half the number of these hearths occurs in Ceremonial rooms while the remainder occur in Domestic Storage rooms. Storage boxes associate with both types of hearth but are rarely found alone. The low communalities of these two variables are clearly not

the product of the measurement of irrelevant variation. In contrast, boulders – another variable with low common variation – are apparently irrelevant since these objects are randomly distributed among all room types.

Measurement scale presents another problem. As the measurement scale assumed by the different multivariate techniques approaches an interval scale, apparently insignificant differences in measurements of the data are increasingly emphasized and more variable clusters defined. Multidimensional scaling, for example, made the fewest distinctions among manufacturing activities (one cluster) while the BCTRY factor analysis (EKC) made the most (three factors).

Such problems are not insurmountable. Many have been resolved in subsequent analyses by eliminating the use of the factor analyses and using the results of the principal components analysis with the rank-order correlation coefficient to derive composite cluster scores. Classical factor analysis with its rigid set of assumptions proved unsuitable

Fig. 13. Cooking hearth in R319, a habitation room, containing a soot covered bowl of a type often used in cooking. (Photographer: Margaret Thompson, Arizona State Museum, University of Arizona.)

for the analysis of frequency data from an archaeological context such as Grasshopper and probably most other Southwestern sites. The technique has a greater tendency than the other R-mode procedures to identify patterns or associations that are statistical artifacts resulting from common problems such as measurement error or abundance. More recent analysis of Grasshopper room floors has employed a simple clustering procedure that better accommodates rank orders between objects. The result has been a simpler and more parsimonious procedure but essentially the same typology.

Despite the analytic problems encountered in the quantitative analyses, the model of room function derived here describes a much wider range of variation in room function than was previously suspected from studies at other pueblos although types corresponding to the basic habitation, storage, and ceremonial rooms are recognized at Grasshopper. Two different types of habitation rooms and storage rooms, how-

ever, arc distinguished in addition to manufacturing rooms which have not been previously recognized as a distinct type.

These functional distinctions would not have been possible using the ethnographic model which focuses on architectural variability. Differences in size of most Grasshopper rooms are slight and any correspondence between room size and function has been complicated by considerable remodeling activity, the presence of multistorey structures and probably still other factors. The different types of habitation rooms, for example, are similar in size, presence of facilities and many of their contents, with the exception of manufacturing materials and storage vessels. Although these last two are only secondary aspects of the primary function of these rooms as food processing areas, this distinction is significant in the identification of different types of households.

Thus the functional model derived from a study of the

remains of activities has made possible not only the discovery of new types but also the identification of organizational patterns that would not have been recognized by focusing on architectural variability alone. The model derived here frees the investigator from the restrictions imposed by the use of the ethnographic model at other pueblos. The objections raised here are not against the use of ethnographic information, which has in fact proved very useful in past studies as well as the present one. Rather the objection is to the specific ethnographic model which has been used as a substitute for quantitative examination of a broad range of archaeological context data without adequate consideration regarding its appropriateness for such data. A better ethnographic model can be derived from an empirical examination of the historic pueblos – which was not carried out in the past. This is possible given recent studies in the Hopi (Adams 1978) and Zuni (Ferguson and Mills 1978) pueblos. Archaeological and ethnographic data can then be used in conjunction to enhance further the opportunity for identifying organizational changes rather than merely searching for parallels that can be identified in the archaeological record. For it is the evolutionary goals that inspired the early Southwestern archaeologists to study room function in the first place.

Acknowledgements

Materials analyzed in this paper were collected as part of 12 years of research by the University of Arizona Archaeological Field School at Grasshopper sponsored by the Department of Anthropology and the Arizona State Museum with the financial support of the National Science Foundation (GE-7781; GZ-22, 397, 745, 1493, 1924; GS-2566, 33436; SOC72-05334; BNS 74-23724-A01) and with the cooperation and encouragement of the White Mountain Apache Tribal Council. I also wish to express my appreciation to Donald Graybill, J. Jefferson Reid, and Michael B. Schiffer who encouraged this work and commented upon earlier drafts, to William A. Longacre, then Director of the Field School, who allowed me access to the data, and again to J. J. Reid who first introduced me to the data and who contributed significantly to all aspects of the work described here. Alas, blame for the content of this work falls upon no one but myself.

Note

1. First storey and second storey as used in this chapter correspond to ground floor and first floor in British terminology.

References

Adams, E. C. (1978). The architectural analogue to Hopi social organization and room use. Paper presented at the 77th Annual Meeting of the American Anthropological Association, Los Angeles.

Ahlstrom, R. V. N., Dean, J. S. and Robinson, W. J. (1978). Tree ring studies of Walpi Pueblo. Paper presented at the 77th Annual Meeting of the American Anthropological Association, Los Angeles.

Binford, L. R. and Binford, S. R. (1966). A preliminary analysis of functional variability in the Mousterian of Levallois Facies. In *Recent Studies in Paleoanthropology, American Anthropologist,* vol. 62, ed. J. D. Clarke and F. C. Howell, pp. 238–95.

Cattell, R. B. (1965). Factor analysis: an introduction to essentials. *Biometrics* 21: 190–215, 405–35.

Christenson, A. L. and Read, D. W. (1977). Numerical taxonomy, R-mode factor analysis, and archaeological classification. *American Antiquity* 42: 163–79.

Ciolek-Torrello, R. S. (1978). A statistical analysis of activity organization at Grasshopper Pueblo, Arizona. Ph.D. thesis, University of Arizona, Tucson.

Ciolek-Torrello, R. S. and Reid, J. J. (1974). Change in household size at Grasshopper. *The Kiva* 40: 39–47.

Collins, M. B. (1975). Sources of bias in processual data: an appraisal. In *Sampling in Archaeology,* ed. J. W. Mueller, pp. 26–32. University of Arizona Press: Tucson, Arizona.

Cowgill, G. L. (1968). Archaeological applications of factor, cluster and proximity analysis. *American Antiquity* 33: 367–75.

Cowgill, G. L. (1970). Some sampling and reliability problems in archaeology. In *Archeologie et Calculateurs,* ed. J. C. Gardin, pp. 161–75. Editions du Centre National de la Recherche Scientifique: Paris.

Dean, J. S. (1970). Aspects of Tsegi phase social organization: a trial reconstruction. In *Reconstructing Prehistoric Pueblo Societies,* ed. W. A. Longacre, pp. 140–74. University of New Mexico Press, Albuquerque, New Mexico.

DeGarmo, G. D. (1976). Identification of prehistoric intrasettlement exchange. In *Exchange Systems in Prehistory,* ed. T. K. Earle and J. E. Ericson, pp. 153–70. Academic Press: New York.

Doran, J. E. and Hodson, F. R. (1975). *Mathematics and Computers in Archaeology,* Harvard University Press: Cambridge, Mass.

Ferguson, T. J. and Mills, B. J. (1978). The built environment of Zuni Pueblo: the bounding, use and classification of architectural space. Paper presented at the 77th Annual Meeting of the American Anthropological Association, Los Angeles.

Fewkes, J. W. (1909). *Antiquities of the Mesa Verde National Park, Spruce-Tree House. Bureau of American Ethnology, Bulletin* 41, Washington.

Fewkes, J. W. (1919). *Prehistoric Villages, Castles, and Towers of Southwestern Colorado, Bureau of American Ethnology, Bulletin* 70, Washington.

Hanson, J. A. and Schiffer, M. B. (1975). The joint site – a preliminary report. In *Chapters in the Prehistory of Eastern Arizona, IV, Fieldiana Anthropology,* vol. 65, pp. 47–91.

Hill, J. N. (1968). Broken K Pueblo: patterns of form and function. In *New Perspectives in Archaeology,* ed. S. R. Binford and L. R. Binford, pp. 103–42. Aldine: Chicago, Ill.

Hill, J. N. (1970a). *Broken K Pueblo: prehistoric social organization in the American Southwest. Anthropological Papers of the University of Arizona* 18. University of Arizona Press: Tucson, Arizona.

Hill, J. N. (1970b). Prehistoric social organization in the American Southwest: theory and method. In *Reconstructing Prehistoric Pueblo Societies,* ed. W. A. Longacre, pp. 11–58. University of New Mexico Press: Albuquerque, New Mexico.

Jorgenson, J. (1975). A room use analysis of Table Rock Pueblo, Arizona. *Journal of Anthropological Research* 31: 149–61.

Kidder, A. V. (1932). *The Artifacts of Pecos.* Yale University Press: New Haven, Conn.

Lingoes, J. C. (1970). A general nonparametric model for representing objects and attributes in a joint metric space. In *Archeologie et Calculateurs,* ed. J. C. Gardin, pp. 277–97. Editions Du Centre National de la Recherche Scientifique: Paris.

Longacre, W. A. (1975). Population dynamics at the Grasshopper Pueblo, Arizona. In *Population Studies in Archaeology and Biological Anthropology: a Symposium, Memoirs of the Society for American Archaeology,* vol. 40, ed. A. Swedlund, pp. 71–6.

Mindeleff, V. (1891). A study of pueblo architecture: Tusayan and Cibola. *Bureau of American Ethnology Annual Report* 8, Washington, pp. 13–228.

Nie, N. H., Hull, C. H., Jenkins, J. K., Steinbrenner, K. and Bent, D. H. (1975). *Statistical Package for the Social Sciences.* McGraw-Hill: New York.

Olsen, J. W. (1980). A zooarchaeological analysis of vertebrate faunal remains from the Grasshopper Pueblo, Arizona. Ph.D. thesis, University of California, Berkeley, Cal.

Prudden, T. M. (1914). The circular kivas of small ruins in the San Juan watershed. *American Anthropologist* 16: 33–58.

Prudden, T. M. (1918). A further study of prehistoric small house ruins in the San Juan watershed. *Memoirs of the American Anthropological Association* 5: 3–50.

Redman, C. L. (1973). Multistage fieldwork and analytical techniques. *American Antiquity* 28: 61–79.

Reid, J. J. (1973). Growth and response to stress at Grasshopper Pueblo, Arizona. Ph.D. thesis, University of Arizona, Tucson, Arizona.

Reid, J. J. (1978). Response to stress at Grasshopper Pueblo, Arizona. In *Discovering Past Behavior: Experiments in the Archaeology of the American Southwest,* ed. P. Grebinger, pp. 195–213. Gordon & Breach, London.

Reid, J. J., Schiffer, M. B. and Neff, J. M. (1975). Archaeological considerations of intrasite sampling. In *Sampling in Archaeology,* ed. J. W. Mueller, pp. 209–24. University of Arizona Press, Tucson, Arizona.

Rohn, A. H. (1965). Postulation of socio-economic groups from archaeological evidence. *Memoirs of the Society for American Archaeology* 19, 65–9.

Schiffer, M. B. (1972). Archaeological context and systemic context. *American Antiquity* 37: 156–65.

Schiffer, M. B. (1973). Cultural formation processes of the archaeological record: applications at the Joint Site, east-central Arizona. Ph.D. thesis, University of Arizona, Tucson, Arizona.

Schiffer, M. B. (1975). Factors and toolkits: evaluating multivariate analyses in archaeology. *Plains Anthropologist* 20: 61–7.

Schiffer, M. B. (1976). *Behavioral Archaeology.* Academic Press: New York.

Stevenson, M. C. (1904). *The Zuni Indians: their Mythology, Esoteric Fraternities, and Ceremonies. Twenty-Third Annual Report of the Bureau of American Ethnology,* Washington.

Sullivan, A. P. (1974). Problems in the estimation of original room function: a tentative solution from the Grasshopper Ruin. *The Kiva* 40: 93–100.

Tryon, R. C. and Bailey, D. E. (1970). *Cluster Analysis.* McGraw-Hill: New York.

Vierra, R. K. and Taylor, R. L. (1977). Dummy data distributions and quantitative methods: an example applied to overlapping spatial distributions. In *For Theory Building in Archaeology,* ed. L. R. Binford, pp. 317–24. Academic Press: New York.

Wasley, W. W. (1952). The late pueblo occupation at Point of Pines, east-central Arizona. M.A. thesis, University of Arizona, Tucson, Arizona.

Whallon, R. (1973). Spatial analysis of occupation floors. I. Application of dimensional analysis of variance. *American Antiquity* 38: 266–78.

Whittlesey, S. M. (1976). Prehistoric pueblo plazas: interpretations of community organization. Paper presented at the 41st Annual Meeting of the Society for American Archaeology, St Louis.

Wilcox, D. R. (1981). Changing perspectives on the protohistoric pueblos, A.D. 1450–1700. In *The Protohistoric Period in the North American Southwest, A.D. 1450–1700, Arizona State University Anthropological Research Paper* 24, Tempe, ed. D. R. Wilcox and W. B. Masse, pp. 378–409.

Woodbury, R. B. (1954). *Prehistoric Stone Implements of Northeastern Arizona, Reports of the Awatovi Expedition*: 6 *Papers of the Peabody Museum of American Archaeology and Ethnology* 34, Cambridge, Mass.

Chapter 10

**Spatial analysis of
Teotihuacán: a Mesoamerican
metropolis**
George L. Cowgill,
Jeffrey H. Altschul and
Rebecca S. Sload

Teotihuacán is a very large prehistoric city in the central highlands of Mexico. It grew explosively in the last centuries B.C., flourished as the largest and most influential city in Meso-america during the early centuries A.D., and was in ruins before the end of the eighth century. At its height it covered over 20 km^2 and its population was probably well in excess of 100 000. It is a key site for understanding the culture history of Mesoamerica, and it is also a key instance of early large scale urbanism. Major recent sources on Teotihuacán and its cultural and environmental context in the Basin of Mexico include publications by Millon (1973, 1974, 1976, 1981), Sanders *et al.* (1979), and Wolf (1976).

The work we will discuss here is one outgrowth of the Teotihuacán Mapping Project, initiated in 1962 by René Millon, of the University of Rochester.[1] This project involved preparation of a very detailed 1:2000 topographic map covering the entire city and its surroundings. This topographic map was then used as the basis for a comprehensive foot survey (Millon 1973). Many of the survey results have been published in a volume consisting of 147 field data map sheets, each with a transparent overlay showing archaeological interpretations (Millon *et al.* 1973). This volume also includes separate map sheets showing archaeological interpretations of the central part of the city at 1:2000 and the entire city at 1:10 000, and the entire topographic map at 1:10 000. Versions of the archaeological interpretations map at 1:40 000

or a little smaller have also been published in a number of places, including Millon (1970*a*, 1973, 1974, 1976, 1981) and Sanders *et al.* (1979, pp. 112–13). We reproduce it here as Fig. 1. In Fig. 2 there is a broad outline of the chronology we are using, with estimated approximate dates. The local manifestation of the phase termed Coyotlatelco in Fig. 2 is called Xometla. Rapid growth of Teotihuacán occurred in the Patlachique and Tzacualli phases and its collapse at the end of Metepec. In pre-Patlachique and post-Metepec times there were significant occupations within our survey area, but they do not pertain to Teotihuacán as a major Mesoamerican center, and we will not discuss these earlier and later occupations in this paper. Our primary focus will be on spatial aspects of Teotihuacán during the approximately three-century period spanned by the Xolalpan and Metepec phases.

In the course of the survey directed by Millon, over 2000 substantial multi-family masonry apartment compounds were identified, as well as nearly 3000 other structural and spatial units. These others include pyramids; platforms; free-standing walls; areas probably occupied by insubstantial structures; plazas, avenues, streets, and passageways; caves; possible reservoirs; possible marketplaces; and other features. Approximately a million fragments of ceramics, obsidian, and other materials were systematically collected from the surfaces of these 5000 or so units. This combination of scale and intensity of coverage remains unprecedented in archaeology.

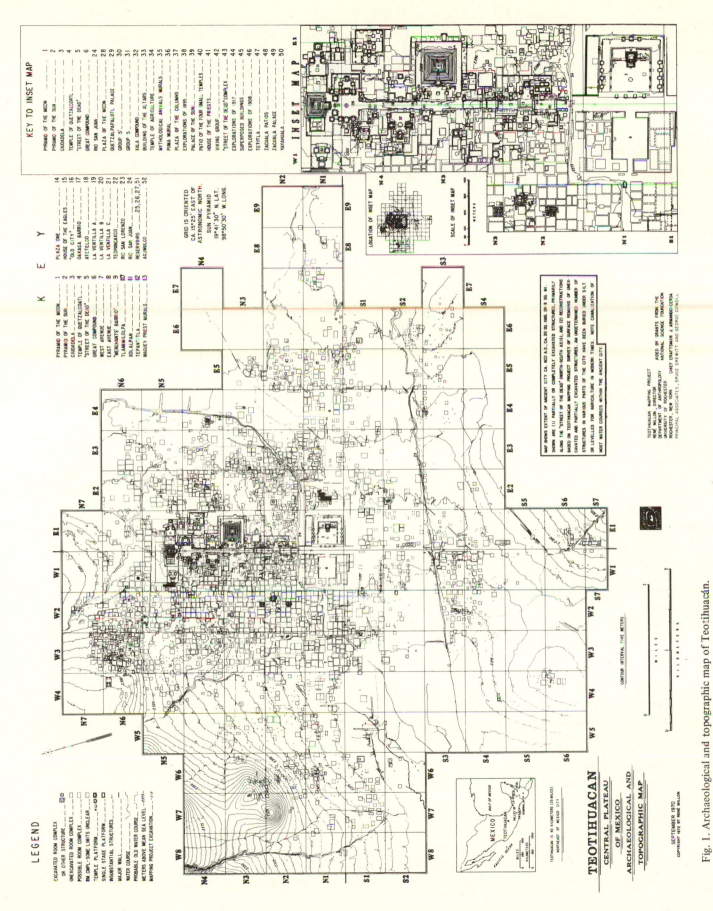

Fig. 1. Archaeological and topographic map of Teotihuacán.

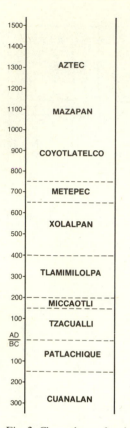

Fig. 2. Chronology of major ceramic phases at Teotihuacán. The term 'Coyotlatelco' is used here because of its broad applicability in the Basin of Mexico. The corresponding phase in the Teotihuacán Valley is called Xometla.

A second unprecedented aspect of the Mapping Project work is that all the collected materials have been saved, in an orderly and accessible fashion, in an archaeological research facility at Teotihuacán. The value of preserving such collections is still largely unappreciated by other archaeologists, and at present it is highly uncertain whether funding can be found to maintain these collections for the kinds of long term intensive reference and study for which they are uniquely suited. A large scale re-study of the ceramic components of these collections is underway, in order to recover considerably more data than were captured in the initial field analyses of ceramics, but even this study is no substitute for preserving the collections themselves. It is under the general supervision of Evelyn Rattray, while Paula Krotser has especially concentrated on identification of ceramic workshops.[2] Much of what we can already say about workshops in this paper would not have been possible if our collections had not been saved and available for re-study through 1981.

In addition to the map itself, many other aspects of the Mapping Project data have been studied by a number of workers and reported in a long series of articles and doctoral dissertations (see Millon 1981 for citations). Final reports are in preparation or are being revised for publication by the University of Texas Press. One such study, which has been our particular concern, involves development and analysis of a computerized data file. This file presently incorporates data from each of 5047 spatial units within the city. In Mapping Project terminology, most of these units are called 'sites'. We will follow this practice, although, in terms of 'intrasite' spatial analysis, the entire city of Teotihuacán is the 'site' and the 5047 spatial units are the elements by means of which we can study internal structure of the city. These minimal spatial units that we call sites correspond in most cases to single architecturally distinct structures or culturally meaningful spaces either between structures or otherwise bounding them, such as plazas or streets. In a few cases, field conditions made it impossible to be quite certain of a simple one-to-one correspondence between our units and ancient structures or other features.

We will discuss aspects of both *identification* and *interpretation* of spatial patterning in Teotihuacán archaeological materials, based largely (though by no means entirely) on data in our computer files. The distinction between identification and interpretation is important and is one of our major themes throughout this chapter. We would note particularly that identification of patterning is, in itself, a non-trivial series of operations, closely intertwined with interpretation of patterns, but nevertheless distinct.

We also want to call attention, early on, to two ways in which the nature of the object of our study, Teotihuacán, leads to approaches and results which differ from most of the other contributions to this volume. First, because Teotihuacán housed a complex urban society, many of the questions it is natural to ask differ considerably from those one asks of data on small village settlements or the camps of non-sedentary societies. Secondly, the spatial scale is very different. The entire city covers over 2000 hectares, that is, over 20 km². The mean area of our 5047 surface provenience units is about 3600 m², and over 80% of them are in the range from 500 to 8000 m² (0.05 to 0.8 hectares). Thus, our minimal spatial units are comparable in area to whole sites in many other intrasite studies. Some of our sites may correspond to single households, but many of them are apartment compounds, and others are localities where more than one insubstantial structure may have existed. Excavations of apartment compounds, both prior and subsequent to the beginning of the Mapping Project (e.g. Linné 1934, 1942; Armillas 1944, 1950; Séjourné 1959, 1966a, 1966b; Acosta 1964), have provided strong architectural evidence that each compound was occupied by several households of differing status (Millon 1976, p. 221; 1981, pp. 208–9). Millon (1970a, pp. 1079–80; and 1973, pp. 44–5) estimates that larger apartment compounds, on the order of 60 m × 60m, probably housed 60 to 100 persons. Intensive study of material from small provenience units on the surfaces of single compounds indicates that there is a great deal of internal spatial structure, not easily attributable to chance, in the distribution of materials within single unexcavated compounds (Altschul 1981). However, so far this kind of intensive surface study has been carried out for only a few sites, while detailed quantitative data on excavated material are not yet available for any sizable fraction of an apartment compound (or any other major structure) anywhere in Teotihuacán. What this means is that, at present, in most cases collections do not exist that would make it possible to study internal structure within single apartment compounds or other kinds of sites. Except in a few cases (Altschul 1981), we cannot address problems of variations among households within a single compound, much less activity areas or other spatial variations within single households. Most of our data on individual apartment compounds undoubtedly reflect several households – though probably groups of households which were closely linked and which may often have been corporate units. Rather than asking questions about spatial structure of activities within households, we have tended to ask questions about the spatial structure of neighborhoods (*barrios* or larger districts); about spatial patterning of types of sites, crafts and other spatial activities, and categories of persons within the city; and to seek evidence about spatial aspects of political administration, economic organization, and religion within the city. Cowgill (1974, 1977, 1979*a*) has also dealt with overall demographic trends.

One technical advantage of the spatial scale of our data is that problems of redeposition of surface materials and the relation between surface evidence and subsurface phenomena are considerably less acute than they are in studies that seek interpretable patterning within much smaller spatial units (Cowgill 1974, pp. 366–70).

Problems in connecting data and theory

Bringing computer techniques to bear so extensively on such a large and varied body of archaeological data has been unprecedented. A consequence is that there are no good exemplars, in the Kuhnian sense (Kuhn 1970) to guide our work. It has not been clear what we might accomplish, or how best to go about it. In contrast, archaeologists have good exemplars of work directed toward traditional concerns, such as time–space systematics.

We hope that, by applying techniques made possible by computers to data of the quantity and quality collected by the Mapping Project, we can draw conclusions about Teotihuacán society and culture that go far beyond what could be said a few years ago (except as plausible speculation or mere conjecture) and that are solidly based on good evidence and sound reasoning.

In fact, reflection on our own work to date, as well as everything else done by others in the name of 'new' or '*avant-garde*' archaeology, leads us to emphasize how serious the problems are that remain in connecting data with theory. Briefly, we have learned an enormous amount about the 'behavior' of archaeological materials at Teotihuacán. It would not have been possible to have learned so much if the fieldwork had been less intensive and systematic or if the material collected had not all been saved and remained accessible, and it would not have been feasible without the aid of computers. However, the archaeological variables themselves only

indirectly reflect the variables of real interest to us. There are some large technical tasks involved in summarizing and expressing the structure of the archaeological data. But these tasks seem manageable. Far more formidable are difficulties concerning the validity and relevance of the archaeological data as indicators of the social and cultural phenomena which are the proper subjects of theory.[3]

In addition to what we have learned about archaeological materials at Teotihuacán, in the past few years we have considerably sharpened our questions about the city by formulating more detailed models of various possible ways in which specific aspects of Teotihuacán society and culture may have been organized. But there remains a wide gulf between these two accomplishments. Many of the most interesting sociocultural hypotheses about Teotihuacán cannot be connected to present archaeological knowledge by really solid arguments. Faced with this situation, there is a temptation to substitute plausible or persuasive reasoning for hard reasoning.

Perhaps, on the whole, it may not be a bad thing that archaeologists have so often yielded to this temptation. The dialectic cycle of bold new hypothesis, followed by devastating criticisms – of which the new archaeology has furnished so many examples – has probably led to some real advances in our discipline. However, we would feel more sure of this if cases came to mind where the 'thesis' and 'antithesis' stages of the cycle had in fact been followed by some widely accepted new synthesis.

At any rate, we are uncomfortably aware that many of our favorite conjectures cannot yet be connected to our data by tightly reasoned arguments. The fact is that our models of Teotihuacán society are rarely unambiguous in their implications about what we should observe archaeologically, while what we do observe is often consistent with more than one model or hypothesis.

The conclusion we draw from these reflections is that it is well to make a clear distinction between discussions of hypotheses about Teotihuacán and other activities which are fundamentally descriptive. By the latter we mean identifying and summarizing structure in the archaeological data which cannot reasonably be explained as accidental or resulting from post-Teotihuacán phenomena, and which therefore must *somehow* reflect *something* about the Teotihuacanos themselves. Even if complex statistical procedures are used, including many forms of statistical inference, the approach is still 'data analytic' and the outcome is essentially descriptive. Our point is that it is respectable and indeed highly useful to operate on this level, even though the implications about Teotihuacán society furnished by our results may remain vague. A sizeable proportion of this chapter describes some of our techniques and results on this descriptive level.

These activities contrast with discussions of hypotheses about Teotihuacán (or interrelated sets of hypotheses), usually suggested by sociocultural theory, and both inductive and deductive arguments attempting to make connections between these hypotheses and our data. We feel it is most productive to operate in both 'deductive' and 'inductive' modes. That is, when, on the descriptive level, any sort of patterning in the archaeological data comes to our attention, it is proper and very useful to ask 'What are the data trying to tell us?' It is also useful to formulate hypotheses about Teotihuacán and to try to deduce archaeologically testable implications of these hypotheses. It is particularly useful to seek contrasting testable implications of competing alternative hypotheses. This may enable us to determine that the data are strongly against a number of rival alternatives. Although this does not *prove* that surviving hypotheses, not strongly opposed by the data, are correct, it does provide a rational basis for taking them more seriously than before.

Please notice that we are not simply saying that both inductive and deductive approaches are all right, and each person can follow his or her own tastes. We are saying that it is *wrong* to disdain inductive, empiricist methods, and it is also *wrong* to try to shy away from explicit theory. What is right is to make the most of both approaches, in conjunction with one another.

However, as we have already said, it is still rarely possible for us to connect our data and our hypotheses by arguments which we can accept as watertight. We will discuss hypotheses about Teotihuacán, point out how our archaeological evidence might *plausibly* be connected with these hypotheses, but also point out ambiguities which remain. By doing so, we hope to get credit for some imagination, but we also hope to set a good example for other archaeologists, and to stimulate improvements in at least three kinds of things: in hypotheses, in archaeological data, and in arguments connecting data with hypotheses.

The Nature of our data

Only a tiny fraction of Teotihuacán has yet been excavated. Of that fraction, recovery, recording, and preservation of data have rarely approached modern standards. Nearly all the information in our computer file is derived from surface evidence from structures unexcavated by archaeologists (although sometimes there were exposures because of erosion, looting, road cuts or other modern activities). Building debris is often visible on the surface, as are ceramics, obsidian, and other artifacts, in densities ranging from one every few square meters, up to hundreds in a single square meter. The most common building debris is the fine volcanic scoria (*cascajo*) from decayed concrete wall and floor facings. Stone rubble from wall cores and floor fills is often abundant. Many sites which appear to have been substantial structures exhibit small surface traces of *in situ* concrete-faced masonry walls and/or floors (cf. Millon 1973, Figures 50–56). Outer boundaries of substantial structures are usually fairly clear, because of mounding and/or concentrations of surface materials. However, standing architecture in unexcavated structures is usually exposed in small scattered patches, if at all, and individual room plans or other interior features can rarely be made out in sufficient detail to map. The archaeological map (Fig. 1) shows only outer boundaries of unexcavated structures. The very numerous apartment compounds shown as featureless rectangles would, if excavated, reveal scores of rooms, as well as inner courts, patios, passageways, platforms, and other features, similar to such excavated compounds as Tetitla, Zacuala 'Palace', and Yayahuala (Fig. 1, inset, numbers 47, 49, and 50).

Information on 291 variables for each site has been coded for the computer file. Variables include the date of the survey; personnel; impact of a variety of post-occupational phenomena, including erosion, silting, modern vegetation and land use, looting, controlled excavations, contemporaneous buildings, roads, and other alterations; visible surface evidence of ancient architecture, loose building materials and those *in situ*; field impressions about both architectural and functional nature of the site; counts of many categories of ceramics, lithics, and other artifacts collected from the surface; and persons responsible for the initial ceramic analysis.

Strengths and weaknesses of these data should be clearly understood. In a few places modern occupation had obliterated archaeological evidence. However, in most places the impact of modern activities was moderate or at least not catastrophic at the time of the survey. At present, parts of Teotihuacán are rapidly being built over by the growing contemporary population, and for many sites the only archaeological information we can ever expect is what was gathered in the Mapping Project survey.

Most visible architecture pertains to the Xolalpan and Metepec phases, although there are notable exceptions, such as the immense Pyramids of the Moon and Sun, the Ciudadela (including the 'Temple of Quetzalcoatl'), and the 'Great Compound' platforms (Fig. 1, inset, numbers 1, 2, 3, 4, and 6) all of which are earlier. However, surface ceramics on most sites include at least a few sherds from most of the periods shown in Fig. 2, from Tzacualli onwards. It appears that masking of surface ceramic evidence of earlier occupations by later occupations is not a serious problem (this topic is discussed in greater detail in Cowgill 1974).

'Total' collections were made from very few sites. In most cases, highly trained field workers covered the entire site, walking only a few meters apart, and collected all the rims, bases, handles, decorated and other special sherds (such as Thin Orange Ware), figurines, and non-ceramic artifacts that could be seen on a single pass. Intensive collection of all visible sherds, including plain body sherds, was out of the question. In a few cases where all sherds with dimensions over 3 or 4 cm were collected, the quantities obtained were approximately 10 to 100 times those obtained by 'standard' techniques. This suggests that truly intensive surface collecting from the entire city would have yielded something like 10 million to 100 million sherds. In retrospect, we wish that intensive collections had been made at more sites. However, really intensive collecting from all sites within the city was clearly not feasible. A conceivable strategy would have been to design some sort of spatial sample for the entire city, make 'total' collections from spatial units in the sample, and ignore all the rest. We feel very strongly that, unless the sampling fraction had been very large (which again would have made 'total' collecting unfeasible), any such sampling design would have missed a great deal of important spatial structure and variation.[4] For the future, we suggest that the best strategy for large sites would be some sort of mixture of controlled collection of diagnostics from *all* spatial units, plus 'total' collections from a limited sample of units.

We believe that variations in quantities of material collected per hectare resulting from variations in Mapping Project collecting practices, are mostly small relative to variations in actual densities of surface remains. There are a few exceptions we have identified and for which we have controlled. Variations in *ratios* of one type of artifact to another should be even less, although ratios may be somewhat affected in the relatively few sites where ceramics were very scarce or highly eroded.

Surface evidence is usually sufficient to indicate the existence and approximate dimensions of apartment compounds, but little about their internal structure. We can only assume that the rather diverse plans of the few which have been excavated are fairly representative of the whole range of variation (see Millon 1974, Figures 6 and 7; or 1976, Figures 13 and 14; for a juxtaposition of available plans of Teotihuacán residential structures at a uniform scale). Some 2300 apartment compounds appear to have been occupied in the Xolalpan phase, and most continued to be occupied into the Metepec phase. About 80 substantial residential structures which seem too small to have included multiple apartments are termed 'room groups'. There are about 250 relatively high mounds which are clearly remains of pyramids. There is little question that temples once stood on top of all these pyramids. About 300 other mounds are lower but stand out among the still lower ruins of apartment compounds. We are less sure whether all once supported temples, or whether many may have served other functions. We use the more non-committal term 'platform' for these lower mounds, which are quite diverse in size and shape. There are nearly 400 open spaces between structures, which we call 'plazas'. In addition, there are over 800 spatial units with substantial cover of ceramics and other artifacts, but negligible architectural debris. These sites are designated 'insubstantial structures'. There is no reason to assume that they comprise a homogeneous category. Some may have been dwellings made of adobes or other perishable materials, some may have been special-purpose structures or open areas used by residents of nearby sites, and a few may be merely scatters of debris from neighboring sites. It is significant that, even if all these sites were dwellings, they could have housed only a very small fraction of Teotihuacán's population, most of which must have lived in apartment compounds. An important logical implication is that, unless Teotihuacán had far fewer people of low status than of intermediate status, much of the low status population must have lived in architecturally substantial structures. As will be seen, several other lines of evidence support this conclusion.

Besides these categories, a few sites belong to well-defined special categories such as portions of streets or other access-ways (68), sections of free-standing walls (41), possible marketplaces (14), possible cemeteries (12), and caves (7). A residue of about 55 sites were difficult to assign to any well-defined architectural category, although they yielded enough ceramics of the Xolalpan and/or Metepec phases to suggest occupation during at least part of that timespan. Finally, 717 of the 5047 sites in our file do not appear to have been occupied or used during Xolalpan or Metepec times.

Computer-aided mapping of Teotihuacán data

Maps are a kind of graphic display of spatial data which, although familiar and often readily grasped, can be very powerful ways of summarizing and communicating information. Moreover, not all maps are simple. One can plot the spatial distribution of variables derived by complex computations from the raw data.

Most of our mapping work at present has a primarily descriptive emphasis. Some variables have been selected for mapping because we believe they have a fairly direct bearing on some of the hypotheses about Teotihuacán to be discussed in the next section. However, the majority have been chosen because they have intrinsic value as part of the *description* or *report* of our fieldwork. It should be of lasting value to put on record all the places where we found a high density of Xolalpan phase ceramics, for example, or all the places where the proportion of a given category (e.g. censers) is unusually high or unusually low, relative to other categories.

In the 1960s one of us (Cowgill) experimented with the SYMAP system but quickly concluded that it has a number of features which were not very useful to us and were formidably costly, in view of the number of maps we needed to produce (Cowgill 1967). Subsequently, with the assistance of Seth Reichlin and later Michael Ester, a program was developed that aggregated site data into arbitrary 250 m × 250 m units (each 6.25 hectares), and produced a printed output with each aggregated data value located in its correct spatial position relative to other data values (see Cowgill 1974, Figure 1, for an example of such a map). The choice of 6.25 hectare units was, we must emphasize, an expedient judged to be necessary in order to be able to summarize spatial data for the entire city at a scale of 1:40 000, which would permit publication of the resulting maps on single pages of reasonable size. In fact, site-by-site maps of small 25 or 50 hectare segments of the city (see e.g. Cowgill 1967) show that there is a good deal of spatial variation that is smoothed out and not represented by the 6.25 hectare aggregation units. This variation within units is not always small relative to the variation between units. Indeed, we now know that there is significant spatial variation in the distribution of artifacts on the surface even within individual sites (Altschul 1981). Nevertheless, maps based on 6.25 hectare units are a good compromise for displaying overall *regional* spatial trends in our data, rather than information about each specific site. For the multivariate statistical analyses to be described later, we have used individual sites, rather than aggregation units (except that, in some cases, a very few contiguous sites with small collections and similar architectural interpretations have been pooled).

A relatively simple program was acquired by Michael Ester (at the time a Brandeis graduate student and project research assistant) and adapted so as to use the output of the aggregation program to produce contour maps by a CalComp plotter. The resulting maps are highly useful for research, but not suitable for publication. For publication, we wanted to have the contours placed on the archaeological base map, and to have them labelled in spots which do not obscure important data on that map. After experimenting with either the plotter maps or the archaeological map as overlays over the other, we have concluded that the best method is to have a skilled archaeological illustrator (S. Whitney Powell) trace the plotter contours on to a slightly simplified version of the archaeological map. Figure 3, showing amounts collected per hectare of 'regular' Thin Orange Ware, is an example of such a map. In this and in all other maps of counts, we have adopted a standard set of levels: 400, 200, 100, 50, 25, 12, 6, and 3 per hectare. This follows a logarithmic scale; each level is half the preceding one. We find that this choice of levels works well both for displaying rather abundant categories, such as regular Thin Orange, and for much scarcer categories which rarely had overall densities greater than 6 per hectare in any aggregation unit. Remember that the quantities of material collected are only a small fraction of what might have been collected, if sites had been crossed and recrossed and even small body sherds collected. Thus, Fig. 3 shows that there was a small area in square N7W3[5] where the density of regular Thin Orange sherds *actually collected* was over 200 per hectare; about 67 times the density of 3 per hectare represented by the lowest contour line. Small amounts of regular Thin Orange were also collected from many additional sites outside the 3 per hectare line. Other categories also were often collected in densities of less than 3 per hectare. We did not want to omit this information entirely, but in regions where average collected amounts are as low as 3 per hectare, contour lines suggest a uniformity which has little relation to sparse patterns of actual discoveries. Our solution to this dilemma is to use small single digits to indicate specific sites, outside the 3 per hectare contour line, where examples of the mapped category were found. Digits indicate finds of one up to nine objects, while stars indicate sites where 10 or more examples were found. For many categories, finds of fewer than three or four sherds were not mapped, in order to avoid forests of '1's, '2's and '3's.

Thus, in Fig. 3, one can observe that in square N4E6, although the overall density of regular Thin Orange was less than 3 per hectare, there were two individual sites from which four and five sherds were collected. Stars, indicating 10 or more regular Thin Orange sherds from single sites in regions with densities less than 3 per hectare, appear in S4W4, S4W3, and S4E5.

Our choice of the 3 per hectare contour as the dividing point between generalized contours and site-by-site indications of actual counts is another compromise. Site-by-site counts in areas with densities higher than 3 per hectare result in an excessive quantity of numbers, often too closely spaced to be legible. However, even the 3 per hectare contour is a simplification and generalization of data which may be considerably more patchy in actual patterns of occurrence than is suggested by the contour lines. We have tried to remind the reader of this by using broken lines for the lowest mapped density contours.

We hope that other symbols and conventions used in our density contour maps are quite clear. One source of ambiguity is 'basins'; regions where water would collect if the contours represented actual topography. We have indicated basins by putting small tick marks on the 'downhill' sides of the contours surrounding them. Basins can occur at any density level. Thus, Fig. 3 shows basins which run below 50 per hectare (but not as low as 25 per hectare) in N3W2/N4W2 and N5W2. Basins lower than 3 per hectare occur in N2E4, S3E3, and elsewhere.

We have chosen regular Thin Orange Ware for an example of our density maps, because it is a very well-defined and abundant ceramic category at Teotihuacán that figures importantly in the statistical analyses to be discussed later. 'Regular' Thin Orange Ware is so-called because it contrasts with 'coarse' Thin Orange, a category that is more coarsely finished, with much larger temper inclusions and markedly different shapes. Coarse Thin Orange is not abundant at Teotihuacán. Regular Thin Orange is about 19% of all ceramics collected pertaining to the timespan from the Miccaotli through the Metepec phases, while coarse Thin Orange is only about 2% of this total. Since Thin Orange is easily recognized and was considered 'special' by field teams, there was a tendency to collect many smallish body sherds as well as rims and 'feature' sherds, so the actual overall proportion of regular Thin Orange vessels to other ceramics in use at any one time may have been considerably less than 19%. However, such estimates are further complicated by questions about the relative average longevity of different categories of ceramic vessels, as well as tendencies for different categories to break up into varying numbers and sizes of sherds. These are topics about which, for Teotihuacán, we still know very little. For present purposes, the relevant point is simply that, although the specific figure of 19% is not very meaningful, regular Thin Orange was not uncommon at Teotihuacán. Furthermore, as Fig. 3 demonstrates, it is quite widely distributed.

In spite of this, there is very good evidence that regular Thin Orange was not locally made. It has long been recognized that the fabric is not from any known local source (e.g. Sotomayor and Castillo 1963), and this is borne out by neutron activation analyses (Abascal 1974; Rattray 1976, 1980; Sayre and Harbottle 1979, pp. 25–31). Furthermore, Krotser and Rattray (1980 and personal communications) have not found any good evidence for regular Thin Orange

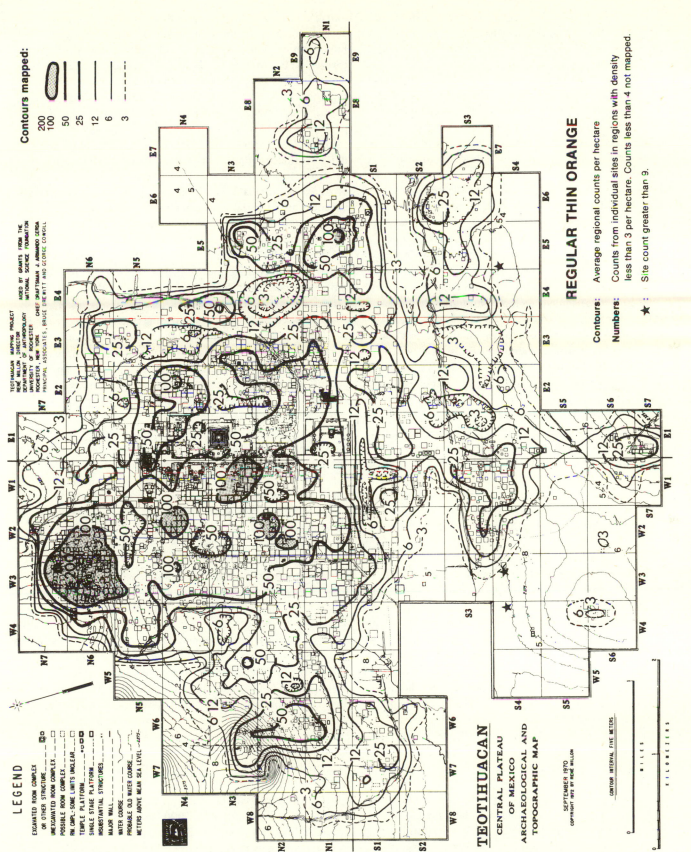

Fig. 3. Spatial distribution of regular Thin Orange Ware, derived from averages in 6.25 hectare regions.

production at Teotihuacán. A source somewhere in the state of Puebla has long been suspected, although, as far as we know, no incontrovertible evidence of manufacture there has yet come to light.

Regular Thin Orange occurs in a wide variety of shapes, including cylinder tripods and carved, incised, and modelled vessels that may perhaps be indicative of high social status. However, the great majority of regular Thin Orange vessels are well made but rather simple hemispherical bowls with ring bases. Some have incised and/or punctuate decoration (Séjourné 1966a, pp. 148, 149, 152; Linné 1934, Figs. 43–45, p. 70; 1942, Fig. 299, p. 161), but most of these bowls are plain. They look like serving bowls, but a few have quite noticeable wear on the bottom interior, very strongly suggesting that at least some were also used for grinding something, perhaps in food preparation (this is a point noted by Matthew Wallrath and Paula Krotser, as well as Cowgill). Since transport must have added to the cost of regular Thin Orange, we would expect that such vessels might be less common in the households of the very poor. Nevertheless, the simplicity, abundance, and wide spatial distribution of the hemispherical bowls within the city show that they cannot possibly have been a strong marker of high status. They must have been quite common in many households of intermediate status. Perhaps they played a role in some rituals, but it seems likely to us that much of their use was in non-ritualized contexts.

Unfortunately, it is not easy to date these hemispherical bowls, which form the bulk of the 'regular Thin Orange' category in our present computer file. Tiny amounts of regular Thin Orange occur as early as the Patlachique phase (Blucher 1971), but it is believed that the ware did not become abundant until late Tlamimilolpa times, after which it persisted in quantity throughout the Xolalpan and Metepec phases.

We have also generated a number of maps that show the areas where the *ratio* or proportion of one category, relative to some more inclusive set of categories, is exceptionally high or exceptionally low. It is worth pointing out that such maps are a special case of mapping residuals from a trend surface, where the trend surface is simply the horizontal plane representing a city-wide average ratio. We could, of course, carry this procedure further by computing higher-order trend surfaces and mapping residuals from them. However, we have not been very impressed by most other examples of archaeological trend surface mapping. Without a clear theoretical rationale, we doubt if such an exercise would give us additional insights. In contrast, our maps showing regions with above and below average proportions of a category have an obvious descriptive meaning, and we find them quite useful.

In order to produce contour maps of ratios, we begin by aggregating data from individual sites into the same 6.25 hectare units that we use for the density maps previously discussed. In nearly all ratio maps, the numerator category is a subset of the denominator categories, which means that resulting ratio values necessarily lie in the range from zero to

unity, and the absolute value of the numerator is less than or at most equal to the value of the denominator. In a few cases, numerator categories are not a subset of denominator categories; but even in these cases the average abundance of denominator categories is always so much greater than those in the numerator that aggregation units with numerators even slightly greater than denominators are extremely rare, if present at all. This has the important consequence that there is a pretty clear upper limit to ratios; for practical purposes, units with ratios appreciably greater than unity are non-existent. It also offers a simple way to deal with the problem of statistical unreliability of small samples. We are publishing contours only for those aggregation units with denominator counts greater than 50. Units with denominators less than 50 will have still smaller numerators, and we are not publishing the contours for such units – they are the areas outside the heavy black bordering lines of Figs. 4, 5, and 6. Since not all ratio maps base their denominator counts on the same categories, different maps have different boundaries. The choice of a count of 50 as the dividing line between 'reliable' and 'unreliable' is, of course, arbitrary. It leans toward trust in the data. In regions of low absolute sherd density, especially around the margins of the city, *isolated* aggregation units with exceptional ratios should be interpreted with caution. However, the chances are small that two or more contiguous units will accidentally show a similar extreme ratio.

To produce ratio maps, we experimented with computing the mean and standard deviation of the values of the ratio exhibited by each 6.25 hectare aggregation unit, and plotting contours which were multiples of one standard deviation above or below the mean. However, not surprisingly, the observed frequency distributions for most ratios are quite different from normal (i.e. Gaussian). Usually there are a sizable proportion of spatial units with low to moderate values of the ratio, but the number of units exhibiting a rather high ratio is far greater than would be expected if the distribution were normal: i.e. most distributions are skewed to the right, with a heavy upper tail. For such distributions, standard deviations are not especially good measures of dispersion, and it may not be even approximately true that about $\frac{1}{3}$ of all cases are more than one standard deviation above or below the mean or that only about 1/20th are more than two standard deviations from the mean. Percentile information seems more useful and more interpretable for these non-normal distributions. After some experimentation with other levels, we have chosen to map contours corresponding to the 10th, 25th, 75th, and 90th percentiles. Using these levels is rather common practice (Mosteller and Tukey 1977), and we feel they work well for us.

An example should make our methods more clear. In general we multiply ratios by 1000, so as to get rid of decimal points and convert from numbers ranging from zero to unity, to integers ranging from zero to 1000 (that is, to parts per thousand). In the case of regular Thin Orange, we computed, for each 6.25 hectare aggregation unit, the ratio of regular

Thin Orange relative to total Miccaotli–Metepec phase ceramics (of which regular Thin Orange is a subset).[6] We then ranked the aggregation units, from the one with the highest ratio to the one with the lowest. We discovered that 10% of the units had a ratio of regular Thin Orange greater than or equal to 282 per 1000 (i.e. 28.2%), while 90% of the units had a ratio lower than this. Similarly, 25% of the units had a regular Thin Orange ratio of at least 230 per 1000, 75% of the units had a ratio of at least 134 per 1000, and only 10% of the units had a ratio lower than 80 per 1000. This is the basis for four of the five contour levels used in Fig. 4.

For many categories, merely indicating the areas where ratios are at or above the 90th percentile did not seem enough. Within this upper 10% of spatial units, there are often a few that have ratio values far higher than any that would be expected to occur if the distribution of ratio values were approximately normal. These are the units that overload the extreme upper end of the distribution tail. In order to standardize the definition of such ratios, which we call 'superhigh', we reasoned as follows. For a set of scores whose frequency distribution is approximately normal, the 75th percentile will be about 0.675 standard deviations above the mean, and the 25th percentile will be about 0.675 standard deviations below the mean. The distance from the score at the 25th percentile to the score at the 75th percentile is called the interquartile range, and, for a normal distribution, will be 2×0.675, or 1.350 standard deviations. In a normal distribution, which is symmetrical, the mean will be at the center of the interquartile range, and a score whose distance above the mean is twice the interquartile range will be 2×1.350, or 2.70 standard deviations, above the mean. As can be seen from any table of areas under the normal curve (e.g. Blalock 1979, p. 602, Table C), the expected proportion of scores more than 2.70 standard deviations above the mean will be 0.0035, or about 1/286.

For most of our ratio maps, the number of spatial units with acceptably large denominators (at least 50 sherds) is around 300 to 400. This means that, if the frequency distribution of values of a given ratio were *in fact* normal, we should expect to observe slightly more than one unit per map with a ratio score more than twice the interquartile range above the mean ratio score. For example, 410 spatial units were used in Fig. 4. Since 0.0035×410 is 1.435, the expected number of units with a ratio of regular Thin Orange more than 2.70 standard deviations above the mean ratio would be 1.435 units, if we could assume that the distribution was normal.

At this point we might have continued by computing the exact mean of each distribution. However, it seemed more appropriate to use the median, since the median is closer to where the mean would have been if it were not for the 'heavy' upper tail in most distributions. Since most of the asymmetry in our distributions is in the tails, the midpoints of the interquartile ranges are good simple approximations to the medians, and we have used these midpoints in our next step. If X_{25} is the score corresponding to the 25th percentile, and X_{75} is the score corresponding to the 75th percentile, then the median of the distribution is approximated by $(X_{25} + X_{75})/2$. Recall that a 'superhigh' score is one that is greater than the mean by at least twice the interquartile range; that is, by at least $2(X_{75} - X_{25})$. If we let X_s stand for the superhigh threshold, then

$$X_s = [(X_{25} + X_{75})/2] + [2(X_{75} - X_{25})]$$
$$= (5X_{75} - 3X_{25})/2.$$

The same reasoning leads to a formula for computing X_1, a score below which scores can be regarded as 'superlow':

$$X_1 = [(X_{25} + X_{75})/2] - [2(X_{75} - X_{25})]$$
$$= (5X_{25} - 3X_{75})/2.$$

However, as would be expected, since the distributions almost always have a straggling upper tail but a truncated lower tail, computed superlow values are usually negative and not exhibited by any spatial units.

This whole method, more difficult to explain than to use, is a simple way of identifying those units with observed ratios higher than would be expected to occur more often than about once per map, if the distributions were in fact approximately normal. It is one reasonable way, among many which might have been chosen, to identify the places where scores are not merely in the top 10% (which, necessarily, will always be true of *some* 10% of all spatial units), but are in fact far out in the skewed upper tails of the distributions.

To use regular Thin Orange again as an example, the value of X_{25} is 134, and the value of X_{75} is 230. Substituting in our equation, we get

$$X_s = (5 \times 230 - 3 \times 134)/2 = 374.$$

The level for the superhigh contour actually used in Fig. 4 is 375. The values of 134 and 230 for X_{25} and X_{75} are rounded from more exact values used to obtain the value of 375 for X_s.[7] Superhigh areas in our contour ratio maps are emphasized by diagonal hatching. In Fig. 4, there are about eight spatial units with superhigh proportions of regular Thin Orange to total Miccaotli–Metepec phase ceramics, in contrast to the expectation of 1.435 units for a normal distribution. In Fig. 6, where the expected number is again about unity, the observed number of spatial units with superhigh ratios is upwards of 20.

After this discussion, we can turn to some interpretations of Fig. 4. Since regular Thin Orange occurs to some extent throughout the Miccaotli–Metepec timespan, the best choice for a denominator here is the total of all ceramics assigned to this timespan, including Thin Orange itself. Inspection of Fig. 3 shows that regular Thin Orange was collected in greatest abundance in the southeastern part of square N7W3, and it is relatively abundant in a broad area of the northern and central parts of the city, especially in and near square N6W3, and in squares N4W2, N3W1, and N2W2. Other areas of quite high abundance are in N1E5 and N4E2. However, most of these regions, especially in the southern part of N7W3 and all of N6W3, are areas where Miccaotli–Metepec phase

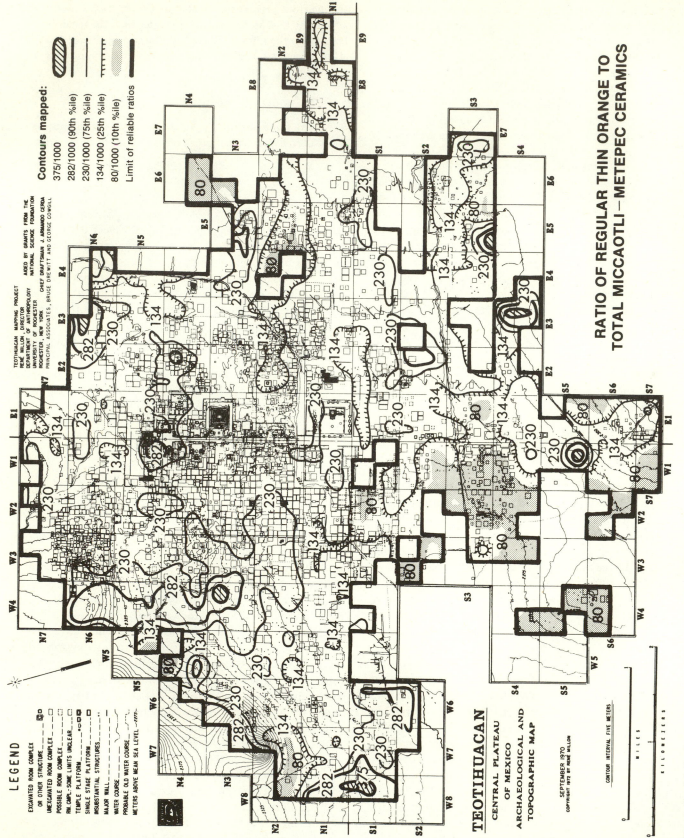

Fig. 4. Spatial distribution of ratios of regular Thin Orange to total Miccaotli–Metepec phase ceramics, derived from averages in 6.25 hectare regions.

ceramics in general were extremely abundant. Ceramics of this timespan were also extremely abundant in S3W1 and S3W2, where the abundance of regular Thin Orange is only moderately high. If we turn to Fig. 4, we see that the regions with high *proportions* of regular Thin Orange are strikingly different from the regions with high *densities* of the ware. Of the regions with high densities (over 100 sherds collected per hectare), only the northeast part of N4E2 is also above the 90th percentile of proportions. Most of N2W2 is above the 75th percentile, but only small parts of N6W3, N4W2, and N1E5 have proportions this high. All of N7W3 and N3W1 have unremarkable proportions, lower than the 75th percentile but higher than the 25th. The most striking region of high regular Thin Orange proportions is in a north–south strip near the western margin of the city, running from N6W4 to N3W4 and spreading from there, especially south-eastward. Most other regions of high regular Thin Orange proportions are near the margins of the city, with an almost continuous distribution in the northwest and southwest, and sporadic high spots elsewhere. Some of the peripheral high spots may reflect accidentally high ratios in regions with low total ceramic numbers, but the whole broad region on the north-western margin of the city cannot be dismissed as accidental, both because of the number of contiguous spatial units involved and because at least its eastward parts extend into regions of quite high ceramic density, where ratios are highly reliable. The statistical work to be described later indicates that some individual *sites* in the central parts of the city have very high proportions of regular Thin Orange, but the only extensive central region with a really high proportion is the strip beginning southwest of the Pyramid of the Moon; running east through the complex of temple groups, room complexes, plazas, and walls known as the Xala Compound (Fig. 1, inset, no. 32, also Millon 1973, p. 36 and Figure 42*a*, *b*) and extending to the cluster of apartment compounds which includes Tepantitla (Fig. 1, no. 12). The proportion is also somewhat above average on parts of the Great Compound and along the northern edge of the Ciudadela or the enclosure just north of it. The generally moderate proportions of regular Thin Orange near the 'Street of the Dead'[8] (Fig. 1, no. 5) are the more remarkable because, as Fig. 3 shows, density of the ware is fairly high in most of that area.

The proportion of regular Thin Orange is extremely low in much of the south and east, including the Tlajinga District (in and around squares S3W1 and S3W2) an important region of craft activity where there was large scale specialized production of San Martín Orange Ware and other ceramics. Proportions are relatively low along much of the eastern edge of the city, as well as in regions running inward as far as N2E2 and a region south and southeast of the Ciudadela. Isolated high proportions in S5W1, S4E3, and S3E5 are based on rather small sherd totals and are of doubtful cultural significance.

Summarizing Fig. 4, proportions of regular Thin Orange tend to be high in the northern and western regions of the city, especially toward the edges. Proportions tend to be low in the southern and eastern regions. Proportions are above average in a strip running from the Pyramid of the Moon to the neighborhood of Tepantitla, and on parts of the Great Compound and just north of the Ciudadela, but in most central parts of the city proportions are neither very high nor very low.

It is, thus, fairly easy to *describe* the spatial distribution of regular Thin Orange as a proportion of total Miccaotli–Metepec phase ceramics. How is one to interpret it? Since there are many reasons to believe that the ware was not made at Teotihuacán, we can rule out manufacture as a reason for any of the places with high densities or high ratios shown on Figs. 3 and 4. Some of the concentrations may represent places where imported Thin Orange vessels were warehoused. Except for such warehousing, the maps must reflect spatial patterns of Thin Orange consumption. It is somewhat surprising that regions near the center of the city do not show higher proportions of regular Thin Orange. Teotihuacán does not show a simple gradient from high social status in the center to lowest status on the outskirts, and there is evidence for marked differences in status between nearby residences (Millon 1976, p. 220). Nevertheless, there is a *tendency* for the proportion of residences judged to have been of high status to be higher in neighborhoods nearer to the center of the city, and lower towards the edges. Figure 4 certainly does not suggest that regular Thin Orange was the exclusive prerogative of high status households, or even that it was particularly uncommon outside high status or ritual contexts. This fact, while it deserves emphasis, is not very surprising, since we already knew in a general way that regular Thin Orange was quite abundant and was widely distributed spatially. What is very surprising, and indeed quite puzzling, about Fig. 4 is the extent to which very high proportions of regular Thin Orange are far out on the extreme western edges of the city. Some of these are areas where all ceramics were relatively scarce and/or eroded. It is possible that, in such situations, e.g. in the western parts of squares N6W4, N5W4 and N4W4, and in N3W4, there may have been a tendency to collect even small and eroded Thin Orange sherds, including body sherds, while eroded examples of other wares may have seemed undiagnostic and been rejected. However, this possibility would not explain the high proportions of regular Thin Orange in regions such as N3W3 and N2W2. At this stage in our work we remain puzzled. The ceramic reanalyses now underway, under the direction of Evelyn Rattray, are tabulating different forms of regular Thin Orange separately from one another, and this will provide more data with which to work. Paula Krotser (personal communication) has also been inspecting the hemispherical bowls for evidences of use and reuse. Site-by-site mapping of the spatial distribution of regular Thin Orange forms may also be enlightening. The statistical studies to be discusssed below add information that complements that in Figs. 3 and 4, although so far, as with so much else in our work, they had led to more focused questions rather than to satisfying answers.

San Martín Orange Ware is exceptionally different from regular Thin Orange Ware in all respects except that it is a ceramic and, doubtless confusingly to the uninitiated, contains the word 'orange' in its name. It is a 'no nonsense' utility ware, unslipped and undecorated; but sturdy, well made, and not unpleasing. By far the commonest shape is a large open 'crater' form, generally with roughened bottom and undoubtedly used for cooking. The only other common form is an amphora, whose shape suggests use for storage and perhaps transport (Séjourné 1966a, Plate 7, facing p. 48). Both of these shapes are very utilitarian, but it is reasonable to suppose that high status households, as well as others, would be well supplied with utilitarian vessels. We would expect, however, that, the higher the status of a household, the higher the proportion of other wares *in addition to* San Martín Orange. It does not seem likely that San Martín Orange would figure in any ritual contexts; except that food prepared in San Martín vessels might subsequently be consumed or offered in rituals. There is very extensive evidence that San Martín Orange was made at Teotihuacán, especially in specialized workshops in the Tlajinga District (in S3W1, S2W2, and the northern parts of S4W1 and S4W2), although some may have been manufactured elsewhere, for example, at sites in and near N6W3 (Evelyn Rattray and Paula Krotser, personal communications).

The spatial distribution of densities of San Martín Orange does not differ strikingly from that for regular Thin Orange (or, indeed, from many other ceramic categories), except that the highest densities of all, over 200 per hectare, were collected in the Tlajinga District, where numerous misfired sherds and potters' tools give evidence of manufacture. Densities of over 100 per hectare were also collected in and around N6W3, N3W1, N1W2, and N2E2. We have not included the density map for San Martín Orange here. However, the spatial distribution of *proportions*, shown in Fig. 5, differs strikingly from the density map, and it also differs greatly from Fig. 4, the map of proportions for regular Thin Orange. Note that in Fig. 5 the denominator is only total phased Xolalpan and Metepec ceramics. This denominator includes San Martín Orange itself, but excludes ceramics assigned to the Miccaotli and Tlamimilolpa phases (as well as Thin Orange, which cannot be phased), since Evelyn Rattray's stratigraphic studies indicate that San Martín Orange was only made during the Xolalpan and Metepec phases. However, little if any of the difference in general pattern between Figs. 4 and 5 can be attributed to different denominators.

Not surprisingly, the highest proportions (as well as densities) of San Martín Orange occur in the Tlajinga District, especially in S3W2. This is easily explained as a consequence of its specialized manufacture in that district. Other regions with unusually high proportions of San Martín Orange are mostly toward the center of the city; near, but not on, the 'Street of the Dead'. The proportion is very high in a zone running from N4W1 to N2W2, about 400 to 600 m west of the 'Street of the Dead'. It is also high in the northern parts of the Great Compound and just north of the Ciudadela, and in and

around N2E2 (also a region of high absolute density), in N2E5, and in S2E6. Other high spots in N2W7, N6E4, and S3E2 are based on rather small numbers of sherds and are of uncertain significance. Proportions in and around N6W3 are only somewhat above average, in spite of the quite high densities in that region.

Below average proportions of San Martín Orange occur mostly toward the edges of the city, especially in the north, though also to some extent in the south. In the north, low proportions extend as far south as the Pyramid of the Moon, and proportions are also below average at the Xala Compound and around the Pyramid of the Sun.

Comparing Figs. 4 and 5, we can see that there is little correlation (either positive or negative) between high proportions of regular Thin Orange and San Martín Orange. Both occur in above average proportions in a region along the northern parts of the Great Compound and just north of the Ciudadela. However, regular Thin Orange is also found in unusually high proportions near the Moon Pyramid, while San Martín proportions are below average in this area. Elsewhere along the northern 'Street of the Dead', proportions of regular Thin Orange are fairly average (at least when individual sites are aggregated into our 6.25 hectare spatial units), while proportions of San Martín Orange are average or below average. Outside of Tlajinga, most regions with unusually high proportions of San Martín Orange are less than 1.5 km from the northern half of the 'Street of the Dead', though usually not directly on the street. In contrast, a large region with high proportions of regular Thin Orange is markedly further west from the 'Street of the Dead'; except around N2W2 it overlaps little with the region of high San Martín Orange proportions. We find it very surprising that, aside from manufacture, the regions where the highest proportions of San Martín Orange seem to have been consumed are more central than are many of the regions with the highest proportions of regular Thin Orange. San Martín Orange is by no means rare anywhere. It comprises over 9.6% of total Xolalpan plus Metepec sherds in 90% of our spatial aggregation units and is over 17% of the total in 75% of the units. Nevertheless, Fig. 5, as well as some of our statistical investigations, suggests that it was used in highest proportions in households of intermediate status, and in lower proportions in low status sites as well as temples and high status residences. In higher status residences, this is probably because of the variety of ceramics in use in addition to San Martín Orange. In temples, presumably few if any of the activities called for San Martín Orange. Its relative unpopularity in low status sites is more surprising. It may be that a higher proportion of other rather plain wares, including burnished ollas, were in use on such sites, although this needs further confirmation from the reanalyses now in progress. Paula Krotser finds evidence that ollas were manufactured at a number of sites, but no evidence of concentrated or specialized workshops, and she suspects ollas may have been made in many districts by part-time potters, largely for local consumption (Paula Krotser, personal communication). We are

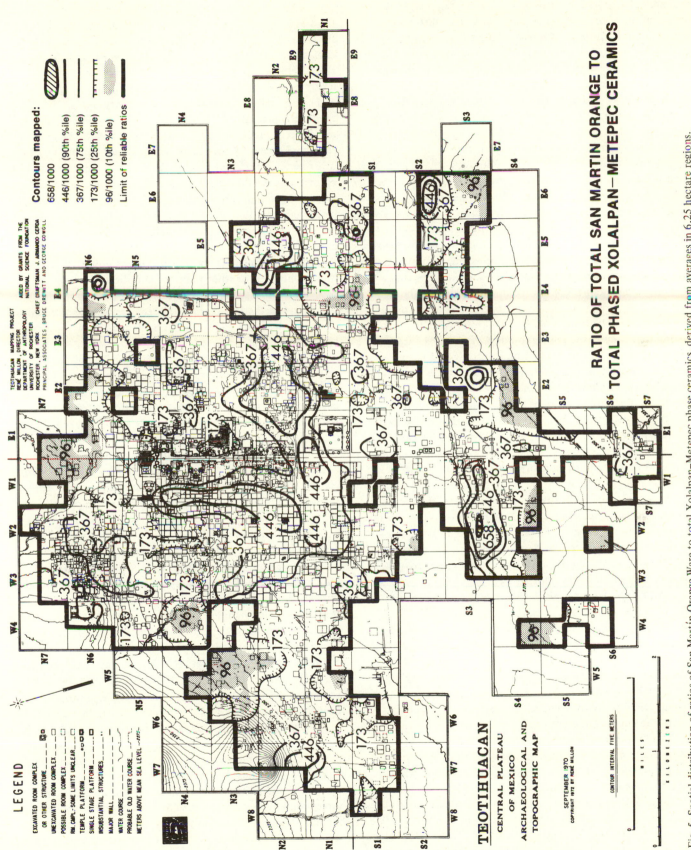

RATIO OF TOTAL SAN MARTIN ORANGE TO TOTAL PHASED XOLALPAN–METEPEC CERAMICS

Contours mapped:

658/1000
446/1000 (90th %ile)
367/1000 (75th %ile)
173/1000 (25th %ile)
96/1000 (10th %ile)
Limit of reliable ratios

LEGEND

EXCAVATED ROOM COMPLEX
OR OTHER STRUCTURE
UNEXCAVATED ROOM COMPLEX
POSSIBLE ROOM COMPLEX
RM. CMPL.—SOME LIMITS UNCLEAR
TEMPLE PLATFORM
SINGLE STAGE PLATFORM
INSUBSTANTIAL STRUCTURES
MAJOR WALL
WATER COURSE
PROBABLE OLD WATER COURSE
METERS ABOVE MEAN SEA LEVEL

TEOTIHUACAN MAPPING PROJECT
RENÉ MILLON, DIRECTOR
DEPARTMENT OF ANTHROPOLOGY
UNIVERSITY OF ROCHESTER
ROCHESTER, NEW YORK

AIDED BY GRANTS FROM THE
NATIONAL SCIENCE FOUNDATION
CHIEF DRAFTSMAN J. ARMANDO GERDA
PRINCIPAL ASSOCIATES, BRUCE DREWITT AND GEORGE COWGILL

TEOTIHUACAN
CENTRAL PLATEAU
OF MEXICO
ARCHAEOLOGICAL AND
TOPOGRAPHIC MAP

SEPTEMBER 1970
COPYRIGHT 1972 BY RENÉ MILLON

CONTOUR INTERVAL FIVE METERS

MILES
KILOMETERS

Fig. 5. Spatial distribution of ratios of San Martín Orange Ware to total Xolalpan–Metepec phase ceramics, derived from averages in 6.25 hectare regions.

probably glimpsing the outlines of major differences in the organization of production and distribution of different ceramic wares within Teotihuacán, with consequent differences in costs and in availability to various categories of persons using the vessels. It is also possible that significant differences in diet and/or size of households, related to social status, might lead to different food preparation techniques, in turn reflected in differing proportions of San Martín Orange, relative to other utility wares. There are a wide range of potential hypotheses here, waiting to be explored.

Of the many maps we have produced, a fourth example must suffice. Figure 6 shows proportions of 'handled covers' relative to total phased Xolalpan and Metepec ceramics (the same denominator as used in Fig. 5). Handled covers are a very distinctive and rather puzzling form within Rattray's (1981) Fine Matte Ware. They are evidently locally made, are usually well smoothed but not polished or burnished, are rarely if ever slipped, and are usually totally undecorated, except that a fair proportion have faint, shallow, stamped designs on the bottom. They are plates or shallow bowls, resting on three loop supports. The supports are often quite worn, in ways suggesting that they have seen a good deal of use on a hard flat surface. Some vessels appear burnt, as if they had been used to cook or at least heat food. Turned over, the plates become lids, which might have been secured by cords passed through the loops. Illustrated examples include Linné (1934, p. 81, Fig. 101; 1942, p. 129, Fig. 221) and Séjourné (1966a, p. 53, Fig. 31, and Plate 15, facing p. 218). Most Teotihuacán ceramic forms – jars, bowls, craters, plates, censers, *comales*, etc. – have counterparts in many other cultures. Their probable uses, in a general way, are not enigmatic, although there may be much to learn about the specifics. Handled covers, however, are, so far as we know, without close counterparts in other cultures,[9] and so far we have only been able to speculate about their role in Teotihuacán and the reasons for their unusual form. Spatial analysis, if it does not provide answers, at least provides relevant evidence.

By far the largest region with exceptionally high proportions of handled covers is along the 'Street of the Dead', especially the eastern side, including the Pyramid of the Sun and the Ciudadela. Other regions with high proportions are in and around N3W3 and in N6E2. Proportions are somewhat above average in the region of craft production in N6W3 and N6W2, and only slightly above average in a small part of the Tlajinga District. Below-average proportions occur mainly toward the edges of the city.

So far our best guess about the use of handled covers – and it is only a guess – is that they may possibly have been used by people consuming food some distance from where it had been prepared. We visualize the possibility of a sort of 'Teotihuacán lunchbucket'; some kind of container, not necessarily ceramic, into which the food was put, with the handled cover tied on to keep it relatively warm and fresh. At meal time, the handled cover could be removed and used as a serving plate, and it might also be put over a fire to reheat the food.

The spatial pattern of places with unusually high proportions of handled covers suggests a strong association with high status residences and/or temples, although by no means an exclusive association; handled covers comprise at least 1.2% of the Xolalpan–Metepec total in 75% of our spatial aggregation units. It is doubtful that they were used primarily in rituals,[10] and highly unlikely that they were status symbols. Perhaps they were most often used by very large households, or state institutions, preparing large quantities of food to be consumed elsewhere, either by their own personnel, or conceivably by other persons performing labor services.[11] If this hypothesis is correct, one would expect some handled covers to be found in scattered places where meals were consumed, but the really large concentrations should be in places where food was prepared and distributed in containers covered by handled covers.

Some handled cover concentrations doubtless reflect their manufacture rather than consumption. However we have no evidence that many were produced in close proximity to the 'Street of the Dead'. Paula Krotser (personal communication) has identified a few sites in N6W3 and N6W2 where they appear to have been made.

Handled covers occur in Teotihuacán burials, as do a very wide variety of other ceramic categories. However, relatively few Teotihuacán ceramic categories seem to have been intended primarily as grave furniture, and the substantial wear on many handled covers strongly suggests extensive use other than as grave furniture. Séjourné (1966a, p. 53 and Plate 15) illustrates two of these handled covers atop outcurving burnished bowls, and she asserts that this is a common association. Testing this hypothesis with our surface data will require results from the ceramic restudy now in progress in order to compare the spatial distribution of handled covers with that of Xolalpan and Metepec outcurving bowls. Insofar as 'nubbin' supports (mostly belonging to Miccaotli and Tlamimilolpa outcurving bowls) may be good indicators for outcurving bowls of all phases, our initial impression is that our evidence is against the association postulated by Séjourné. It is possible that handled covers are somewhat associated with *comales* and/or the Matte Ware ceramic stoves referred to as 'three-prong burners'. However, if either or both of these associations exists, it is much less strong than one might suppose. Certainly, neither burners nor *comales* show anything like the concentration of places with exceptionally high proportions near the 'Street of the Dead' exhibited by handled covers.

Our discussion of Figs. 3 through 6 is intended mainly to give examples of our computer-aided mapping of spatial patterns, together with the kinds of thought to which the maps give rise. These maps find their own justification as modes for describing some of our survey results. Richer interpretations depend on considering these few maps in conjunction with maps for many other categories, considering site-by-site distributions as well as regional patterns, and multivariate statistical investigations. Where possible, relevant data from excavations must also be brought to bear. In later sections

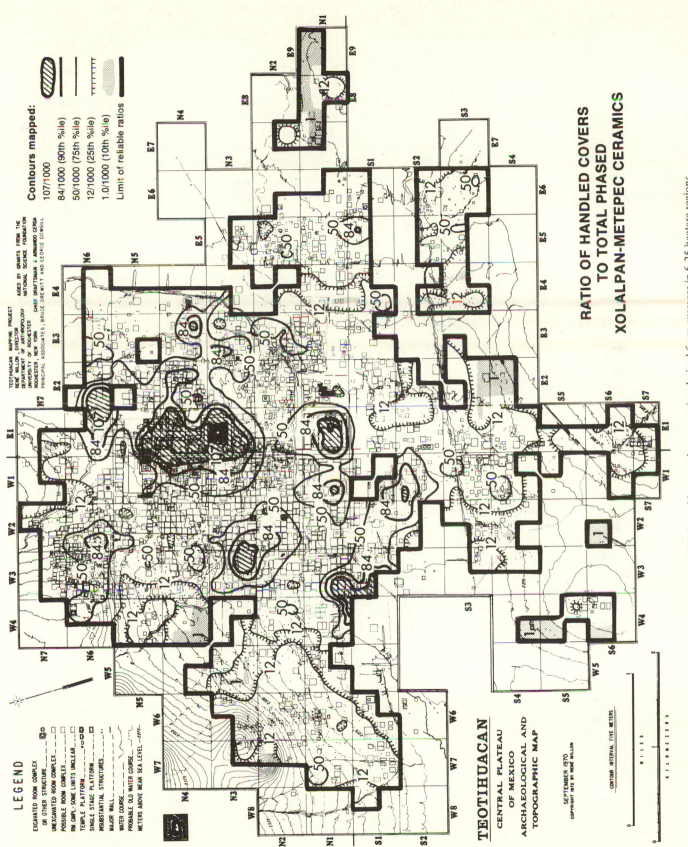

Fig. 6. Spatial distribution of ratios of handled covers to total Xolalpan–Metepec phase ceramics, derived from averages in 6.25 hectare regions.

we will return to regular Thin Orange, San Martín Orange, and handled covers, in the light of multivariate analyses.

For the volume now in preparation, approximately a hundred density and ratio maps of the types illustrated by Figs. 3 through 6 have been completed and others are in progress. The plotter maps have been done by Sload, in consultation with Cowgill, and the final maps by Powell, assisted by Elizabeth Wahle. Additional examples of earlier versions of some of these maps are given in Cowgill (1974). For rare categories (such as jade or polychrome 'stuccoed' sherds), where average collected densities are always less than 3 per hectare, the maps do not show contours, but consist entirely of counts from individual sites, and often even single occurrences are indicated. There are other categories of data, such as observations of specific architectural features or materials, functional interpretations of sites, etc., which are appropriately represented by presence/absence or nominal variables in contrast to counts of items of a given category collected, which are interval variables. For such nominal variables, our maps simply indicate the sites which belong to a given category or where a given feature was observed (e.g. all sites where painted plaster was seen).

Additional descriptive approaches

We have, of course, accumulated standard descriptive summary statistics for each of the 291 variables currently in our computer file. For large subsets of the variables measured on interval or ratio scales we have also computed matrices of correlation coefficients or other measures of association between all pairs of variables. Such matrices, if not guided by good theory, can be rather uninformative or positively misleading (cf. Keyfitz 1977, Chapter 12). Nevertheless, they provide a valuable kind of background information which aids in the design and interpretation of more theory-oriented investigations. One result of interest is that the spatial distribution patterns of categories assigned to a given phase tend generally to show higher correlations with one another than with spatial distributions of categories assigned to other phases. That is, most Xolalpan categories show greater similarity in spatial patterning to most other Xolalpan categories than to most categories of the Tlamimilolpa or other phases. Since most sites yielded substantial amounts of surface material from a number of different phases, it is noteworthy that multivariate statistical analysis can go so far toward disentangling this surface mixture. Nevertheless, we must emphasize that the Teotihuacán ceramic chronology has been developed quite independently of our computer studies, first by Bennyhoff (1967) and subsequently by Rattray (1973, 1981). Their work is based primarily on data from stratigraphic excavations and continues a line of earlier chronological analyses, notably those of Linné (1934, 1942, 1956), Vaillant (1938), Armillas (1944, 1950), Tolstoy (1958) and Müller (1978). Because of this chronology, we have felt free of the need to try to infer chronology from statistical analyses of surface materials. It is possible that such analyses, by themselves, might be able to go some way toward deriving a chronology. However, we have used our analyses, instead, to provide corroboration, from surface spatial patterns rather than stratigraphic excavations, of the chronology developed by James Bennyhoff and subsequently considerably refined by Evelyn Rattray.

Another simple descriptive activity involves listing the individual sites from which the highest quantities of a given artifact category were collected. The rationale is quite simple: maps such as Fig. 3 identify general regions where a category was found in highest densities, but we would also like to list the specific sites which yielded highest quantities, as a guide for future investigations.

Similarly, we would like to identify sites where the highest proportions of a given category were found, relative to something else, but here the matter is not so simple. Miriam Chernoff, a Brandeis graduate student, has worked on this task. For many sites, the count of the category (or set of categories) which forms the denominator will be a rather small absolute number, and thus subject to considerable sampling error. For example, suppose we want to identify the individual sites with the highest proportions of San Martín Orange, relative to total Xolalpan–Metepec ceramics. We might find one site where the proportion, in actual counts, is 5 out of 10, or 50%; while in another site the proportion might be 20 out of 100, or 20%. The proportion actually observed is higher in the first site. However, each collection must be considered to be a sample from the statistical population of all ceramics present on the surface of the given site, and the observed sample proportion in each site only provides an estimate of the true proportion of all ceramics on that site. Because of the lower numbers, a sample of 5/10 provides a much less reliable estimate, with a much larger standard error, than does a sample of 20/100. Given that typical proportions of San Martín Orange are between 17% and 37% (cf. Fig. 5), it is not at all obvious that the first site really has a higher proportion of San Martín Orange in its *population* of ceramics than the second site does, in spite of the fact that the first site has a higher proportion in its *sample*. If we simply ignore sample size, most of the extremely high or low ratios will come from sites with small collections, and these ratios will be quite unreliable estimates of the actual proportions in the populations of ceramics on each site.

Incidentally, readers should not confuse the populations of artifacts on each site with the population (what some would call the *universe*) of 5047 sites in our file. The sites are a set of 5047 distinct populations of artifacts, each of which is sampled by the material actually collected. Needless to say, in all cases we are using the term 'population' in its well-established statistical sense, rather than with its very different demographic meaning.

On the other hand, if we ignore all sites where the denominator is too small to enable the site sample to provide a highly reliable estimate of the true proportion of all ceramics on that site, then, for many variables, an excessive number of sites are eliminated. This rather arbitrary approach could be used with our ratio maps because sites were aggregated into 6.25 hectare blocks, and not too many of the resulting aggregates had excessively low denominators. For individual sites, something better is highly desirable, which will not totally discard information from sites with small collections, but will give more weight to information from sites with larger collections which provide more reliable estimates. At present we believe that a very promising approach is through a type of 'empirical Bayes' technique (Efron and Morris 1973, 1975, 1977; Carter and Rolph 1974; Efron 1975). This is the technique currently being applied by Miriam Chernoff.

Approaches where theory is primary

On a very high level of abstraction, many of the questions we are asking of Teotihuacán relate to two broad and rather ill-defined themes: *centralization* and *differentiation*. Many other researchers share interest in these topics, including Sanders *et al.* (1979, p. 4). However, both the specific questions we have asked and the techniques we use differ considerably from theirs. Most fundamentally, we begin with different assumptions. We do not accept their materialist paradigm. There is not the slightest question that Teotihuacán cannot be understood unless material, environmental, and technological factors are all taken into account. But we find their conceptualization of cultural phenomena oversimplified, and this sets limits on the kinds of hypotheses that can be entertained, limits that cannot be transcended by multivariate statistics (or any other technique) so long as one stays within a strongly materialist paradigm.

For better or worse, we are not prepared to state a crisply formulated and comprehensive paradigm of our own. Perhaps, for the present, we should not be too afraid of vague guiding ideas, as long as we are led to ask specific questions which lead to hypotheses which have archaeologically testable implications (cf. Mosteller and Tukey 1977, especially pp. 17–21, on the value of vague concepts in data analysis; and Adams 1966, p. 4, on 'untidy' problems).

On a somewhat less abstract level, here are some of the broad questions that concern us: How tightly was political authority centralized by the Teotihuacán state? To what extent were there groups or categories of people within the city who enjoyed a degree of autonomy? If there were such groups, how did they articulate with the central authority? As to differentiation, how much differentiation was there, and what were the axes along which significant differences were defined? There is abundant evidence for certain craft specialities, such as obsidian working (Spence 1967, 1979, 1981; Spence *et al.* 1979), ceramic manufacture (Krotser and Rattray 1980 and personal communications; Krotser 1979) and lapidary, bone, shell, and other workshops. At least for obsidian and ceramics, there is good evidence for further specialization in specific types of artifacts or wares. Spatial distributions of activities, such as these, that leave tangible evidence can be plotted. There is also clear evidence for an

ethnic neighborhood or *barrio* of Oaxaca-related people (Fig. 1, no. 17, N1W6), and much other evidence strongly suggestive of distinctive neighborhoods. There can be no doubt that there were many occupational specialities that leave less obvious evidence than do obsidian working or ceramic manufacture, and also that there was a wide variety of social statuses and sociopolitical roles. But evidence about these other kinds of differentiation is more elusive. How differentiated were 'political' offices, and what were the bases for their differentiation? Was there such a thing as high 'civil' office conceived by the Teotihuacanos as distinct from priestly office? To what extent were there special offices associated with the roles of war leaders? How much differentiation, if any, was there between priestly, military, and civil hierarchies? Undoubtedly there was a general correlation between great wealth and high office, but was it at all possible for merchants, large landholders, or others to hold great wealth apart from high office, or for persons who did not control great wealth to attain high office? Since we know essentially nothing about land tenure and very little about the organization of exchange, we cannot even be positive that categories such as 'merchant' or 'large landholder' had meaning in Teotihuacán culture.

For all of the above questions, there is every reason to suppose that the situation may have changed over time, and it would be good to discover and try to understand the trajectories of such change.

This is not the place to try systematically to relate the themes of centralization and differentiation to any comprehensive theory of early states. However, the questions we have listed are obviously relevant to such theory, and many of them have been current for some time. Some general relations can be sketched. There is an interplay between centralization and decentralization in all complex societies. Although individual cases differ significantly, the central authority often strives to acquire, and then to keep, relatively tight control over the entire system, while subordinates often struggle for greater autonomy. Frequently one observes a see-saw between these opposing tendencies (e.g. Cowgill 1979b; Yoffee 1979). In addition to the uniqueness of specific historical events and persons, factors which make for variations on the general theme include differences in environment and in technology of production, transportation, communication, and warfare. It is also useful to recognize that statecraft is itself a series of inventions, and the degrees of centralization and differentiation of large scale societies may well be influenced by the techniques of statecraft available and in use, as well as by numerous other factors.

This general model may well have applied to Teotihuacán, but we have almost no idea of the specific version, or of how it changed over time. There are several lines of evidence that suggest that centralization may have been extremely strong, at least early in the city's history. Throughout the entire city there is a remarkably close adherence to an orientation 15.5° east of true north for north–south features, and 16.5° south of true east for east–west features (Fig. 1; see also Millon 1973, pp. 37–8). Most of the clear evidence for these orientations dates to the Tlamimilolpa phase or later, but at least one (15.5°) was followed by the Pyramid of the Sun and the 'Street of the Dead' as early as the Tzacualli phase. Widely shared religious beliefs may have encouraged conformity to these orientations, but they still argue for strong centralization. Elsewhere in the Basin of Mexico, probably at or near the beginning of the Tzacualli phase, the number and size of settlements declined very rapidly, at the same time that Teotihuacán was growing very rapidly to become a 'primate city' (Blanton 1976; Sanders *et al.* 1979; Millon 1981). That is, Teotihuacán became very much larger than any other settlement in the Basin. The pattern differs drastically from the empirical generalization that the second-largest settlement is often about 1/2 the size of the largest, the next largest is about 1/3 the size of the first, and the *N*th is about 1/*N* the size of the first (Zipf's law), which fairly well describes many more developed settlement systems. The overwhelming size of Teotihuacán, relative to other Basin of Mexico settlements, is a further argument for a high degree of centralization. It is useful to think of a 'metropolitan' area (as suggested by Bernal 1966) in which local power was completely overshadowed by power from one or more sources within the city. This metropolitan area probably extended somewhat beyond the Basin of Mexico, possibly 50 to 100 km in various directions from the city.

The situation further away is less clear to us. Probably most Mesoamericanists are of the opinion that Teotihuacán, although very influential throughout Mesoamerica, subjugated some areas without much involvement in local administration, and acted in others as a powerful ally or dangerous rival of local potentates. However, it is not likely that investigations within the city itself will fully clarify these questions. Whether Teotihuacán's control of distant provinces was tighter than has been thought is a question that almost surely will require work addressed to this issue in the provinces themselves.

Within the city, signs of centrally imposed uniformity seem to stop at the outer walls of apartment compounds. Certainly, similar building techniques and materials were widely used, and features such as *talud-tablero* platforms recur repeatedly. Otherwise, what is most striking about the internal plans of excavated apartment compounds is not their uniformity, but their variety (Millon 1974, Figures 6 and 7; 1976, Figures 13 and 14; 1981, Figures 7–4 and 7–5). This is at least a hint that the apartment compound as a whole may have been the smallest unit dealt with directly by the central authority (Millon 1976, pp. 225–6).

While these lines of thought all suggest rather strong central authority, at least at the apartment compound level and above, and at least within the city and a surrounding 'metropolitan' area, one might entertain a contrary supposition. Since none of Teotihuacán's Mesoamerican antecedents had been nearly so large, there would have been no fund of experience in administering such a large and complex society, and presumably techniques of statecraft, at least at the outset, were somewhat poorly developed. This might have

made tight centralization impossible. However, the implications of this line of thought are ambiguous. Conceivably, a rather rigid centralization may have been needed *because* Teotihuacán had not yet developed sufficiently sophisticated techniques of statecraft to permit greater flexibility or to permit a certain amount of decentralization, without relinquishing control altogether. Armchair reasoning does not get us very far on this question. We need to derive archaeologically testable implications of these contrasting models – and then test them. We also need to improve the models by thinking more about evidence from other societies, including those historically well documented.

As we mentioned earlier, some interplay between centralization and decentralization seems universal. Central authorities often attempt to gain as much power as possible and to fill lesser offices with persons under their control, while removing or weakening the power of hereditary nobles or others with independent claims to authority. A reasonable guess about Teotihuacán is that the early period of very rapid expansion of the city was a time when an individual or very small ruling group was able to gain very strong centralized control over all important officeholders, and that this control was gradually weakened in the later phases of the city's life. Certainly such weakening control is likely in the regions outside the 'metropolitan' area. But it is far less clear that this was the actual story within the city itself. It may have been just the opposite, with centralized control increasing over time, or there may have been two or more cycles of centralization/ decentralization, or events may have been far more complex than any of these simple models. Again, testable implications and relevant evidence are urgently needed.

Concerning differentiation, we have the impression that it is often assumed that as societies develop increasingly state-like institutions, there is a unidirectional trend to increasing differentiation. Offices not only increase in number, they become more specialized. Is this idea a 'fruitful simplification' which liberates us from the complexities of individual cases and allows theory-building to proceed, or is it a naive *over-*simplification which stultifies theory? We believe it is the latter. In any case, clear archaeological evidence for or against growing sociopolitical differentation at Teotihuacán is of obvious relevance for theory.

We also have the impression, although we have not documented it, that it is widely supposed that Teotihuacán was less differentiated than the Aztec state which flourished a millenium later – particularly that there was less distinction between priestly, military and civil offices, and that a distinctive merchant class was perhaps less well developed. How solid is the evidence on which these suppositions rest? We suspect that they derive from four lines of evidence or reasoning: (1) representations of military figures who clearly contrast with priests appear to be only late in the still very incomplete corpus of Teotihuacán art; (2) the Aztec state incorporated many more people than the Teotihuacán, so Aztec sociopolitical organization must have been more differentiated; (3) the Aztec capital was not a primate center, but was merely the largest in a well-developed regional hierarchy of settlements, which argues for a more 'evolved' society with more developed statecraft; and (4) a tacit but perhaps influential assumption that merely because Teotihuacán was earlier, its society should not be 'more developed' than that of the Aztecs in any way.

It may very well be true that Teotihuacán started out far less differentiated than the Aztec state, grew more differentiated over time, but never reached the degree of differentiation exhibited by the sixteenth-century Aztecs. However, we would very much like to have better evidence for, or against, these notions.

Many of our questions about Teotihuacán probably would not have occurred to us if other archaeologists, social scientists, and historians had not raised these or related issues. We might not have insisted that our proposed answers meet standards of adequate scientific reasoning if there had not been recent emphasis on this by Binford, Spaulding, and other archaeologists. And we probably would not have dared to believe that we might actually obtain scientifically defensible answers to these questions, from prehistoric archaeological data, if it had not been for the optimism generated by the 'new archaeology' and the promise of mathematical and computer techniques of data analysis.

However, as we pointed out earlier, there is still often a gap between the kinds of questions we have just posed and the kinds of evidence we currently have at our disposal. Nevertheless, our evidence deserves to be summarized simply because it is useful for anyone undertaking further research on Teotihuacán. In addition, much of it at least points to steps toward eventual resolution of the questions we have raised. In the remainder of this paper we will discuss some of our recent efforts to use existing data to address four specific topics bearing on Teotihuacán society.

Four questions about Teotihuacán

The four topics or broad sets of questions we will discuss are (1) establishing a scale (or scales) of socioeconomic status, (2) the interpretation of insubstantial structures, (3) the problem of *barrios*, and (4) the nature of pyramids and platforms far from the 'Street of the Dead'. These are conceptually distinct but analytically related, because results bearing on one usually have relevance for the others.

First, there is the problem of establishing a valid and reasonably sensitive scale of social status. Our field data from most sites lend themselves only to some broad judgments, such as whether sites were architecturally substantial apartment compounds; smaller room groups; pyramids; lower platforms; or streets, walls, plazas, or other features. For reasons that are not always entirely clear to us, but which surely include quality of building materials and proximity to the 'Street of the Dead', field workers noted that some unexcavated apartment compounds and room groups were probably of exceptionally high status. Sites without evidence of substantial architecture were assumed to be either special activity areas or

residences of low status people. This leads to a crude three-level scale. Sites without substantial architecture are coded as 'low' status. Apartment compounds and room groups are coded 'high' status if field records so interpreted them. Remaining apartment compounds and room groups are lumped into an 'intermediate' category. However, René and Clara Millon's study of excavated compounds had led them to believe that at least six status levels might usefully be identified. These include the topmost élite (represented by the two palaces in the Ciudadela), and a lower high status level comprising most of the priestly and administrative hierarchy (exemplified by apartment compounds on the platforms of the Great Compound, and elsewhere). Next, perhaps separated by a major gap from higher levels, Millon sees evidence for at least three intermediate status levels exemplified respectively by compounds such as Zacuala Palace, Teopancaxco, and Xolalpan – numbers 49, 22, and 11 of Fig. 1. Millon (1976, pp. 227–8; 1981) sees a sixth still lower level represented by apartment compounds such as Tlamimilolpa and La Ventilla B – numbers 10 and 20 of Fig. 1. Sites without substantial architecture are presumably at the bottom end of this scale, and we surmise that many may have been occupied by persons of still lower status.

A status scale derived from indicators based on ceramics and other artifacts would be highly useful if it could be applied to unexcavated sites. It would permit us to corroborate and refine the judgments based on visible architectural evidence. Minimally, we would like to confirm or modify those judgments; to identify hitherto unrecognized sites which are likely to have had high status occupants; perhaps to demote some 'high status' sites to a lower position; and to identify other apartment compounds which, although architecturally substantial, housed occupants of relatively low status. More ambitiously, we would like to be able reliably to identify a larger number of status levels from surface evidence. In doing so, we should allow for the possibility that more than one status-related dimension is required adequately to reflect social differentiation at Teotihuacán. If wealth was not perfectly correlated with high office, or if priestly offices were distinct from military or civil offices, then there may be no single one-dimensional scale that neatly ranges households from the wealthy and powerful at one end, to the poor and insignificant at the opposite end. For example, if indeed there was a category of wealthy merchants, their household furnishings might be quite different from those of an important priest or high-ranking bureaucrat.

Good indices of socioeconomic and/or political–religous status at Teotihuacán would enhance our ability to interpret individual sites. Sizes and numbers of sites assigned to each status category would enable us to estimate proportions of the population belonging to each category, which in turn would have implications about the nature of the society. Distribution maps for sites of each category, or for scores on some index reflecting status, would be very revealing about the spatial patterning of residential groups of differing status within the city. Such evidence, when combined with evidence about possible wards (*barrios*), would have strong relevance for models of the sociopolitical organization of the city. For example, did neighborhoods tend to be relatively homogeneous in status, or were there marked variations within single *barrios*?

The second of the four topics we will discuss is the problem of sites with evidence of occupation but no substantial architecture. Plausibly, many may have been loci of very low status residences. However, some may have included workshops, storage facilities, or loci for other activities carried out by persons living in other structures. Field evidence suggests that this category encompasses a wide range of variation.

The third topic concerns the possible existence of well-defined *barrios* within the city. Ethnographic and historic sources indicate that in non-industrialized cities in various parts of the world one or more levels of social units have often mediated between the central authorities and individual households. These units have sometimes been used by the state for administration and control, for the organization of crafts or local activities, and/or by religious, kin, or ethnic groups to create sections with corporate identity. In Mesoamerican cities, corporate *barrio* units served many of these functions in Tenochtitlan, the Aztec capital (Calnek 1976, p. 295), and Blanton (1978, pp. 37–9, pp. 66–93) has argued that *barrios* existed at Monte Albán, the Zapotec capital in Oaxaca.

At Teotihuacán there is good evidence that at least some parts of the city were organized at a level above the apartment compound. In a tight spatial cluster toward the western edge of the city (in square N1W6) surface survey and excavation revealed an area clearly occupied by Oaxaca-related people. Throughout the city, workshops specializing in specific crafts are often found clustered together. Commenting on these occurrences, Millon (1981) observes that some spatial clusters of apartment compounds are '. . . so sharply set off from their immediate surroundings that *barrio* boundaries seem self-evident'. For earlier discussions of *barrios*, see Millon (1973, p. 40; 1976, p. 225).

Furthermore, there is a high probability *a priori* that *barrios* existed in Teotihuacán, because they have been present in so many other non-industrialized cities (Altschul (1981) reviews some of this evidence). Nevertheless, many questions about Teotihuacán *barrios* remain. Many apartment compounds *do not* belong to spatial clusters of compounds that are clearly set off from other such clusters and there are many parts of the city where we feel that sharply demarcated small neighborhoods are not immediately apparent from surface evidence.

Millon (1981) has approached the problem of neighborhood differentiation through examination of excavated apartment compounds. He concludes that there were 'significant differences in the status of occupants of adjoining compounds clearly belonging to the same *barrio* (Zacuala Palace and Zacuala Patios) . . . , and still greater differences between adjoining *barrios* (the two Zacuala compounds and Yayahuala) . . .'

(cf. Fig. 1, inset, numbers 49 and 48 in N2W2 and number 50 in N3W2). Millon adds that 'This and other evidence from our data . . . point . . . to abrupt disjunctions in status between *barrios*, rather than to any simple gradient in status from highest in the city center to lowest on the periphery.'

René Millon (personal communication) has also prepared a tentative *barrio* map for the entire city. Some of the spatial clusters proposed by Millon seem very clear. One example is a block in the northeastern part of N4E2; the Tepantitla compound is on its southern edge (Fig. 1, number 12). Others, especially in the more solidly built up parts of the city, seem less clear to us.

One aspect of our computer work is simply the search for spatial patterning that might confirm the pervasiveness of well-defined and sharply bounded small neighborhoods throughout the city. If they can be identified, a further set of questions can be asked about their sizes and boundaries. Do the boundaries approximately coincide with those on Millon's tentative *barrio* map, and are their sizes and numbers close to those he postulates? Inspection of Millon's map shows he is thinking of something like 150 to 200 *barrios* for the entire city. Taking 125 000 as a 'medium' estimate for the Xolalpan phase population, this implies an average of around 650 to 850 per *barrio*. The size and number of structures in some of the smallest and largest proposed *barrios* on Millon's map suggests a range from as few as 200 to as many as 3000 persons in individual *barrios*. Blanton (1978, pp. 30, 67) estimates a maximum population somewhere between 15 000 and 32 500 for Monte Albán, divided into 15 districts. This works out to an average somewhere between 1000 and about 2200 per district. Sanders *et al.* (1979, p. 160) say that census data indicates that Aztec *barrios* (*calpultin*) varied between 500 and 1000 people. It would be desirable to compare these figures with data from other documented non-industrialized cities.

A further aspect of our work on *barrios* concerns their social organization. Were there, in fact, corporate groups which more or less corresponded to the inhabitants of specific neighborhoods, and did such corporate groups form important lower level units in the administrative hierarchy of the city? If so, there might be a distinctive 'headquarters' site in each *barrio*. Identification of such sites would considerably strengthen the case for corporateness of *barrios*, would provide information about the actual number and average population of *barrios*, and might shed light on how *barrio*-level offices and organizations articulated with higher sociopolitical levels. Failure to identify 'headquarters' sites, however, would not argue strongly against the reality of *barrios* or their corporate character. *Barrios* and perhaps headquarters might be present and yet not be detected by our data and methods.

There is also evidence for districts larger than the numerous *barrios* postulated by Millon. Regions of around 30 to 100 hectares often seem rather distinctive. Examples are the district in and around N6W3, and the Tlajinga District (S3W1, S3W2, S4W1, and S4W2). Although distinct *barrios* can often be recognized within these districts, most sites in each of these districts share certain features of architecture and artifactual composition that distinguish them, as a district, from the rest of the city. Furthermore, long free-standing walls such as those in squares N5W4, N4W4, N6W3, N5W2, N4W2, N5W1 and N5E1 presumably marked socially significant boundaries (these walls, barely visible in Fig. 1, are readily seen in Millon *et al.* 1973). In some cases these walls mark edges of spatial clusters of apartment compounds. Other walls, within a few hundred meters of the 'Street of the Dead', probably bounded ritually and politically important precincts. In general, the contours of our distribution maps do not seem closely related to these walls, although this matter would bear further investigation.

A fourth set of questions is posed by temple-pyramids, platforms, and other special structures. If all these special structures were concentrated near the 'Street of the Dead', as the majority are, we would see no problem in interpreting them as the loci of activities of the high office-holders of the Teotihuacán state, together with staffs and households composed of lower-ranking people in the service of these officers. But there are very impressive pyramid complexes as much as 3 km from the 'Street of the Dead', as well as many lesser pyramids and platforms. With respect to any one of these special structures or complexes, three contrasting hypotheses occur to us. First, the principal occupants may have held rather high offices in a centralized administrative hierarchy controlled by the highest authority of the state. That is, the principal occupants were closely regulated by higher authority, by whom they could be appointed, transferred, or dismissed. A second, contrasting, hypothesis is that the principal occupants held offices that were not closely regulated by the state because the offices were of purely neighborhood or district significance and were not important enough. For example, a special structure might be one of the 'barrio headquarters' postulated above. In this model, *barrio* headmen might be accountable to higher authorities for furnishing taxes and personnel for state services, and for preventing or controlling trouble among the people under them, but otherwise free to operate without much state intervention. Recruitment to such offices might be a local matter, legitimized from within the group, although probably subject to approval by higher authorities. Probably many Aztec *calpulli* heads would fit this model.

Our third hypothesis is that occupants of a given special structure held offices that were not closely regulated by the central authority because they had an independent power base that was too strong for the central authority to capture. For example, the priesthood of a major temple complex might have successfully resisted domination by the state or, having come under its power, might have succeeded, over time, in regaining considerable autonomy. Or a great family or lineage might have enjoyed considerable independent wealth and power without any strong religious basis for their independence.

To epitomize all three hypotheses, the first is that the principal occupants of a given special structure were subordinate officials in a tightly centralized hierarchy; the second is that they were relatively autonomous minor functionaries of purely local importance, too insignificant to be closely controlled by the state; and the third is that they were too powerful and influential to be closely controlled by the state.

Readers may sense a discrepancy between our earlier discussion of a 'metropolitan' area, where we doubted if there were any very autonomous secondary centers within 50 to 100 km of Teotihuacán, and our third hypothesis, given here, that postulates highly autonomous groups within the city itself. These views are not incompatible. There could well have been a concentration of heads of all major power blocs within the city, without tight control of all these blocs by an all-powerful central authority.

There is no reason why the same hypothesis should apply to all temple or platform complexes. Different alternatives are more plausible for different sites. There are about 30 to 40 identified relatively small, low single platforms or pyramids that are quite distant from the 'Street of the Dead'. Some of these might be centers of localized cults, perhaps sanctioned but not controlled by the state. These are also plausible candidates for 'barrio headquarters'. However, if that is what they are, they cannot be the only ones, for there are far too few of them and there are large regions of the city where no platforms or pyramids at all have been identified. It seems likely that if there really were *barrio* headquarters, many (if not all) were in apartment compounds that, before excavation, show no conspicuous surface architectural differences from others. Millon (1976, p. 25) is inclined to accept Séjourné and Salicrup's (1965) suggestion that the Yayahuala compound housed a *barrio* temple, and Millon adds that it may also have housed the leader of the *barrio*.

At the other extreme, there are some 10 to 20 large and impressive pyramid groups, distant from the 'Street of the Dead' but surely not merely *barrio* headquarters. The principal persons associated with them must have been very important, and the real choice is between hypotheses one and three – to what extent were they independent of the highest central authority? Most of these groups are 'three-temple' complexes, a structural category we will discuss more extensively below. Notable examples are in N6W4, N6W3 (two), N3W2, and on the border between N6W2 and N5W2.

We give a range of numbers for these minor and major temples and platforms because there are about 30 others (among those distant from the 'Street of the Dead') whose physical scale is intermediate. We do not see discontinuities which would make it easy to decide on sharp dividing lines between 'minor', 'intermediate', and 'major'. Altogether we can identify about 75 of these platforms, pyramids, and pyramid complexes not closely associated with the 'Street of the Dead'.

In the sections that follow we will summarize some of our work addressed to the four topics we have discussed in this section.

Questions one and two: toward a scale of socioeconomic status, and the problem of insubstantial structures

We sense that it may be 'obvious' to some persons who have no direct acquaintance with Teotihuacán data that there must be clear ceramic indicators of high status or ritual activities. In fact, probable indicators of high status such as vessels with stucco painting, fine plano-relief carving, or objects such as jade ornaments are too scarce in surface collections to be very useful. Moreover, it is clear, from excavations as well as surface data, that these 'luxury' goods are present (perhaps in low proportions) in widely scattered parts of the city and in residences definitely not of high status. Furthermore, many individuals, and perhaps whole households, within a high status apartment compound will not, themselves, have been of high status. Our best chances of identifying status from surface data may be by relating status to tendencies for *different proportions* of relatively common categories of ceramics and other artifacts to occur.

Candeleros and censers are the principal ceramic categories we believe were primarily used in rituals. But *candeleros* are small, often relatively crude, and '. . . are so abundant and widespread in the city as to suggest that they were used in individual ritual practices of some kind' (Millon 1973, p. 62). The large elaborate censers were also not used exclusively in temples. They have been found in apartment compounds, but rarely in burials. They were probably used in commemorative rituals, among other activities. It is not obvious that *any* categories were limited to primary use in temple rituals. Teotihuacán murals often show processions of celebrants holding containers, but we see no evidence that the containers were ceramic (cf. Miller 1973).

In view of the difficulties in trying to use presence or absence of specific categories as indicators of status, Smith (1975, 1976) experimented with applying discriminant analysis to questions of socioeconomic status during the Xolalpan–Metepec timespan. Subsequently these investigations have been carried much further by Sload (1982). Some of her work has been published in greater detail elsewhere (Gottscho [Sload] 1977) but much is reported here for the first time. This section has been written primarily by Sload.

In contrast to cluster analysis, which yields groups of cases or variables, discriminant analysis begins with predefined groups of cases. Each case is scored on a number of variables (here, counts or proportions of artifact categories), and weights for the variables are derived, so as to discriminate maximally between the groups. The analysis leads to discriminant functions, each of which is a linear function of the input variables and represents one dimension of the data. Each function provides a distance scale, orthogonal to all the others, and cases can be plotted as points in the N-dimensional space defined by the N discriminant functions. Groups of cases having the greatest similarity will be closest together, while the two groups having the least in common on any dimension will be at opposite ends of the corresponding scale.

The analysis also furnishes insight into relations between variables. Each discriminant function is uncorrelated with (orthogonal to) all the others, and the investigator can determine which input variables correlate most highly with a given function. These correlations are better measures of the relation of a given variable to a given dimension than are the weights of the variables on the discriminant functions. These weights can be misleading and hard to interpret, especially if some of the input variables are highly correlated with one another.

Each discriminant function is interpreted by (1) seeing how the groups of cases score on it, and (2) examining the correlation with each variable to determine how much (or how little) each variable contributes to differentiating the groups. Pearson correlation coefficients were used, since the discriminant analysis model is linear. The square of this coefficient (r^2) indicates the proportion of a given variable's variance captured by the function. The sign of the coefficient indicates the direction of the relationship (i.e. a positive sign means that a higher score on the variable corresponds to a higher score on the discriminant function, while a negative correlation means the reverse).

'Reclassification' is a very important phase of the discriminant procedure. The original cases are reassigned to groups, solely on the basis of their discriminant function scores. If a case is reassigned to its original input group, it is scored as a 'hit'. Whether the observed proportion of hits is satisfactorily high is essentially a pragmatic question: it depends on what one hopes for from the analysis. Too low a proportion of hits could be the result of various reasons: initial groups that are badly chosen or not really very different, variables that are not very relevant for distinguishing between the groups, or serious violations of some of the assumptions of the mathematical model. On the other hand, a high proportion of hits is very reassuring, at least if the number of cases is much larger than the number of variables, since, even if one is uneasy about how well the real data conform to the mathematical model, one must be 'doing something right' in order to to get a high proportion of hits. If there were not many more cases than variables, one might be 'capitalizing on chance', but this is improbable if there are several times as many cases as variables.

Besides the assumption that the groups can be well separated by linear functions of the original variables (i.e. that non-linear relationships are unimportant), there are two others: that the variables have a multivariate normal distribution and that they have equal variance–covariance matrices within each group. We have already seen that many of our input variables (counts or proportions of categories) have highly skewed, non-normal distributions when the data are aggregated into 6.25 hectare units, and this is also the case when the units are individual sites. Fortunately, in practice discriminant analysis is very robust, so that assumptions regarding variable distributions and variance–covariance matrices 'need not be strongly adhered to' (Klecka 1975, p. 435). Nevertheless, high proportions of reclassification 'hits' are what really reassure us about the technique.

In the first discriminant analysis to be discussed, a preliminary sample was obtained by taking all 280 sites in the computer file coded 'high status residence', plus a systematic random sample consisting of one half of the sites with insubstantial structures coded 'low status residence' (313 sites). These 593 sites were examined in order to obtain a subset of sites with relatively clear evidence of their architectural category. Factors that disqualified a site were the presence of heavy erosion, redeposited fill, modern construction, and other evidence of a great deal of site disturbance, or a total sherd count of less than 50.

Sites coded 'high status' were divided into apartment compounds and room groups. The apartment compounds included in this study are all larger than about 50 m on a side, while the room groups are only 10 to 15 m on a side. We assumed that the small size of the room groups could not have permitted as many kinds of activities as would be expected in an apartment compound. Only room groups located within 250 m of the 'Street of the Dead' were used in this analysis. We used 38 sites for our 'high status room group' category and 41 sites represented 'high status apartment compounds'.

Insubstantial structures comprised two more input groups. 'Close' insubstantial structures were those less than 25 m from an apartment compound. 'Distant' insubstantial structures were all more than 60 m from any apartment compound. All of these sites were from among our sample of sites coded 'low status residences'. There were 42 sites in the 'close' group and 43 in the 'distant' group. Insubstantial structures between 25 and 60 m from the nearest apartment compound were excluded in order to get two clearly differing groups. The distinction was made because sites in the 'close' group may have been the loci of outbuildings for apartment compounds, while 'distant' sites, mainly located on the city peripheries, were much more likely to have been the loci of dwellings.

A fifth input group consisted of 42 apartment compounds from among the 1860 coded 'intermediate status' on the basis of field judgments. These were all less than 25 m from one (or more) of the 'close' insubstantial structures described above. These apartment compounds were included because, if the 'close' insubstantial structures were outbuildings (or possibly only redeposited fill) pertaining to apartment compounds, then these would probably be the compounds to which they were related.

To recapitulate, these five input groups were (1) high status apartment compounds, (2) high status room groups, (3) 'close' insubstantial structures, (4) 'distant' insubstantial structures, and (5) intermediate status apartment compounds chosen for their proximity to sites of group 3. A table will perhaps make these relationships clearer. Besides the dimensions of status judgments and architecture indicated in Table 1, groups 1 and 2 were differentiated on the basis of size, and groups 3 and 4 on the basis of proximity to apartment compounds.

The empty cells in Table 1 call for comment. We doubt if any Teotihuacanos of intermediate or high status resided in insubstantial structures, although they may have used

Table 1. *Input categories for the first discriminant analysis, classified by architectural evidence and field judgments of status. Numbers of cases in each category are given in parentheses*

Field judgment of status	Type of Architecture	
	Substantial, masonry and concrete	Insubstantial
High	(1) High status apartment compounds (41) (2) High status room groups (38)	
Intermediate	(5) Intermediate status apartment compounds (42)	
Low		(3) 'Close' insubstantial structures (42) (4) 'Distant' insubstantial structures (43)

insubstantial structures for some activities. We do think that many people of fairly low status may have lived in substantial structures, but we do not know how to identify such structures from surface evidence alone. One of the features of the 'reclassification' phase of discriminant analysis is that it can throw sites into the empty cells of Table 1. Among other things, this offers a possibility of identifying a discriminant function (or functions) that, on the basis of surface ceramic and artifact proportions, is diagnostic of low status associated with architecturally substantial apartment compounds.

If a linear discriminant function derived from our input variables adequately captures social status, and if the field judgments of status were correct reasonably often, then we should have a scale on which group 1 and group 2 sites are generally high, group 4 sites are low, and group 5 sites are in between. Our hypotheses about group 3 ('close' insubstantial structures) are more complex and are summarized in Table 2.

In this analysis 14 interval variables were used to characterize the 5 input groups. They pertained to ceramic categories including San Martín Orange Ware, regular Thin Orange Ware, coarse Thin Orange Ware, censers, three-prong burners, 'common' *candeleros*, all other *candeleros*, handled covers, 'puppet' figurines, Granular Ware, 'plaster-smoothers', ollas, *comales*, and 'rawcount'. 'Rawcount' is essentially the sum of the count of the 13 other categories just listed. It is the only artifactual count used without transformation as a variable in this analysis.

Table 2. *Hypotheses about functions of 'close' insubstantial structures (input category 3) and corresponding implications about positions of points representing collections from them in indiscriminate space. Note that comments in the righthand column refer only to locations in the abstract space defined by the discriminant functions, rather than to positions in 'on the ground' physical space*

Hypotheses	Implications
(1) Low status residences physically close to apartment compounds	Relatively near the centroid for 'distant' insubstantial structures (input category 4)
(2) Places where occupants of nearby apartment compounds carried out special activities	Not close to centroids for either 'distant' insubstantial structures or apartment compounds
(3) Used by occupants of nearby apartment compounds but not consistently for special activities	Relatively near the centroids for apartment compounds (mainly input category 5; possibly also categories 1 or 2)
(4) Largely redeposited artifacts from nearby apartment compounds	Relatively near the centroids for apartment compounds (same implication as for hypothesis 3)

The other 13 variables were derived from counts of the 13 ceramic categories on each site by expressing them as percentages of 'rawcount' for that site. Only those censers, ollas, and *comales* phased to the Xolalpan–Metepec timespan were counted. Other categories are virtually limited to this period or at least a high proportion of their counts belong to it. San Martín Orange, regular Thin Orange, and handled covers were discussed in connection with Figs. 3–6. Coarse Thin Orange occurs in the form of amphoras perhaps used in storage and transport. Censers were used in rituals, but were certainly not restricted to temples or to high status environments. Burners (Séjourné 1966*a*, plate 8) were probably used as stoves for both cooking and room heating. *Candeleros* are small, usually twin-chambered, and probably were used in individual rituals (Séjourné 1966*a*, Figs. 17–20, pp. 39–42). Varieties other than 'common' tend to be better made and may possibly be associated with somewhat higher status, although 'common' *candeleros* date mainly to the Metepec phase and the difference may be largely chronological rather than social. 'Puppet' figurines have separate, movable limbs. They were included as the best available substitute for all Xolalpan–Metepec figurines, because we do not yet have counts of most figurines by phase. 'Puppet' figurines are not limited to the Xolalpan–Metepec timespan but a large proportion belong to it. They were presumably used in household ritual. Granual Ware

occurs mainly as large, not very carefully decorated, amphoras ('group 7' of Séjourné 1966*a*, pp. 172–173). It is fairly common but probably was imported. It is not easy to phase, but much is probably earlier than Xolalpan. 'Plaster-smoothers' are non-ceramic objects of porous volcanic rock (*tezontle*). Their use is enigmatic; they seem remarkably ill-suited for smoothing plaster.[12] A high proportion seem to date to Xolalpan–Metepec times. Ollas are large burnished jar-shaped vessels, and *comales* are flat cooking griddles.

The SPSS (Statistical Package for the Social Sciences) version 6.01 DISCRIMINANT subprogram was used on Brandeis' DEC-10 computer. The analysis produced three significant discriminant functions. According to a formula given by Tatsuoka (1970, p. 48), 62% of the total sample variance were attributable to differences between the groups. Of this, 24% were accounted for by the first discriminant function, 23% by the second, and 10% by the third.

Functions 1 and 2 were of approximately equal importance. Function 1 distinguished between high status apartment compounds (group 1) at the positive end and 'distant' insubstantial structures (group 4) at the negative end. Function 2 distinguished between intermediate status apartment compounds (group 5) at the positive end and high status room groups (group 2) at the negative end. Function 3 was about half as important as the first two, since it captured only half as much variance. It contrasted 'close' insubstantial structures (group 3) at the positive end with high status room groups (group 2) at the negative end.

Variables that correlated positively with function 1 and that are therefore associated with high status were 'rawcount', San Martín Orange, three-prong burners, common *candeleros*, other *candeleros*, and handled covers. We were unable to discern a common theme underlying these variables that could be used to interpret the function. San Martín Orange, at least, which consists almost entirely of cooking and storage vessels, supports the idea that domestic activities were important in high status apartment compounds.

Function 2 was positively associated with *comales*, ollas, Granular Ware, and puppet figurines. It can perhaps be interpreted as a domestic cooking and living function. 'Plaster-smoothers' were also positively associated with function 2. Intermediate status apartment compounds showed the closest association with these categories, followed at some distance but about equally closely by both groups of insubstantial structures. The location of high status room groups at the far negative end of function 2 also supports the interpretation of this function as reflecting cooking and other domestic activities, since high status room groups are the category of sites that, *a priori*, would be expected to have the least evidence for such activities.

In the reclassification stage of this discriminant analysis, 54% of the sites were reassigned to their original input group. Based on group switching behavior, 'distant' insubstantial structures seem most like 'close' insubstantial structures. About 51% of 'close' insubstantial structures were reassigned to different groups, about equally distributed among 'distant' insubstantial structures, intermediate status apartment compounds, and high status apartment compounds. Intermediate status apartment compounds that were switched most often went to the 'close' insubstantial structure group. As a whole, 'close' insubstantial structures tend to be discriminated from both 'distant' insubstantial structures and from intermediate status apartment compounds. Hypotheses one, and three or four are consistent with those 'close' insubstantial structures switched to one of the other groups, but enough were not switched to suggest strongly that hypothesis two is correct for a good many 'close' insubstantial structures; they really were loci of special activities of some sort.

There were two noteworthy results pertaining to the high status apartment compounds and room groups. Handled covers were associated with both these groups. Unexpectedly, 41% of the variance of handled cover proportions was explained by their association with high status room groups. Figure 6 shows the spatial distribution of handled covers as a proportion of total Xolalpan–Metepec ceramics rather than relative to the categories used in this discriminant analysis. However, a contour map of handled covers as a percentage of exactly the categories used in this analysis shows a very similar spatial pattern. Figure 6 is consistent with the discriminant analysis results in showing a very high proportion of handled covers in the Ciudadela and along much of the northern part of the 'Street of the Dead'. This is also, of course, a region where many high status residences are found. Subsequent analysis of many apartment compounds in N4E2 and N2W2 indicates that these districts may also have been inhabited by people of above average status, so perhaps the somewhat above average proportions of handled covers in those regions may also be status linked.

Figure 6 shows other areas where the proportion of handled covers is very high. We have explored the possibility that some of these are regions where handled covers were made. We examined site records for all ceramic workshops identified in these regions before 1979. Most of these workshops did not show unusual numbers of handled covers, but some showed very high concentrations. One such workshop is in S4W1 and four others are in N6W3 and N6W2. Paula Krotser (personal communication) finds that about 50% of the handled cover fragments collected from these last four sites are defective sherds. We believe that high proportions of handled covers are found in these sections of the city because they were being produced there.

Since 1979 Krotser has re-examined more collections in the Mapping Project's Teotihuacán research facility for further evidence about ceramic workshops. Evidence for manufacture of handled covers is one of the topics of her research, stimulated in part by these results from our distribution mapping and discriminant analysis work.

The high proportion of handled covers on sites in the Great Compound, which may have included the main Teotihuacán marketplace, might be explained by handled covers having been stored there for distribution in the market, or by their use in food preparation stands. However, Millon suggests that the apartment compounds on the platforms of the Great Compound may be in his 'second highest status' group, so this region of high handled cover proportions may also be status-related. Since the use of handled covers is unknown, the basis for their association with high status remains obscure, although, as we discussed earlier, one conjecture is that they may have been used in connection with food prepared in one place, to be reheated and consumed elsewhere. If so, then they might be especially abundant in kitchens where food was distributed to numerous workers or retainers.

The second interesting result concerning high status residences came from the reclassification stage of the discriminant analysis. Five cases that were actually parts of the apartment compounds known as the House of the Priests and the Palace of the Sun, both of which are large enough so that they should have been given prior assignment to group 1, were mistakenly input as members of group 2 (Fig. 1, inset, numbers 41 and 39, in N3E1). These cases were consistently *not* switched out of the high status room group category, in this or in other discriminant analyses. Conversely, the two palaces in the Ciudadela, on either side of the Temple of Quetzalcoatl, were consistently switched from group 1 (high status apartment compounds) to group 2 (high status room groups).

Since the apartment compounds in the Ciudadela, the House of the Priests, and the Palace of the Sun appear to be of very high status, on the basis of their locations and architecture (Armillas 1964, p. 307; Millon 1973, pp. 34–5, and 55), an obvious possibility is that we are confronting distinctions between status levels within high status. The 'high status room group' category may actually reflect extreme high status, rather than the contrast between sites with few activities and those with many activities we originally thought we might capture by this analysis. Alternatively, these results could be interpreted spatially as a distinction between structures directly associated with the 'Street of the Dead' (high status room groups) versus structures further from the street (over a third of the sites in the high status apartment compound input group are more than 500 m from this principal avenue). A combination of both these alternatives was also possible, or perhaps the correct interpretation had not yet been formulated.

In an attempt to gain more understanding of the 'high status' sites, two more discriminant analyses were executed (also by Sload), using a different research design. Two input groups represented high status room groups. The definition of such sites was made more explicit. The architectural definition was changed little if at all, but sites were no longer restricted to those within 250 meters of the 'Street of the Dead'. Neither the house of the Priests nor the Palace of the Sun, both of which are high status apartment compounds, were treated as 'room groups' in these analyses. As defined for these analyses, a high status room group is a group of rooms on a platform adjacent or very close to a temple. Sites in this category are smaller than apartment compounds and presumably would not have involved as wide a range of activities. One input group included only sites whose interpretation was 'secure' in the sense that either the site records indicated that the site conforms to the above definition, or the location and architectural interpretation of the site along the 'Street of the Dead' clearly indicates that the definition holds. This input group contained 26 sites hereafter referred to as 'secure' high status room groups.

Membership criteria for the other input group of high status room groups were that the phased Xolalpan–Metepec sherd count should be at least 40% of the Miccaotli–Metepec total, and in addition that the interpretation of the site as a high status room group should be at least probable, though not necessarily as secure as for the 'secure' input group. Sites in this second group are referred to as 'high status room group with Xolalpan–Metepec 40% or more'. There were 21 sites in this input group, of which 15 also belonged to the 'secure' high status room group input group.

The two approaches to selecting sites for the 'high status room group' input group represent attempts to control for site interpretation and for time. The 'secure' group contained only sites whose architectural interpretations are as unequivocal as possible, given the nature of our surface data. No consideration was given to the proportion of Miccaotli and Tlamimilolpa phase ceramics relative to Xolalpan and Metepec; emphasis was on certainty that the sites actually belonged to the assigned input group. The other input group represents an attempt to control for time. By insisting that at least a fair proportion of the ceramics date to Xolalpan–Metepec, emphasis was placed on obtaining an artifact set that should be relatively contemporaneous, including categories, such as regular Thin Orange, that are not limited to the Xolalpan–Metepec timespan.

The same two approaches were used for obtaining high status apartment compound input groups. A site was judged a 'secure' high status apartment compound if the site record indicated both its residential function and its probable high status. The size of this input group was 21. To qualify as a 'high status apartment compound with Xolalpan–Metepec 40% or more' we required that Xolalpan–Metepec counts be at least 40% of the Miccaotli–Metepec total, and in addition that the site coded be 'high status apartment compound' on the computer file. If a site met these criteria, the original site record was re-examined to verify the coding judgment. There were 26 sites in this input group, 10 of which were also in the 'secure' high status apartment compound input group.

The fifth input group consisted of 22 sites with insubstantial structures. At the time of the analysis we believed that all these sites had been obsidian workshops during Xolalpan–Metepec times. Subsequent re-evaluation of these and other sites by Michael Spence produced the opinion that only a few of these were likely to have been obsidian workshops (personal communication). So, while this input group did consist of insubstantial structures with generally above average amounts of obsidian, it was not homogeneous with respect to any other characteristic, and it is difficult to interpret the results of the discriminant analyses regarding it.

These two analyses were designed to examine both ends of the status spectrum, but attention was concentrated on high status. The 'secure architecture' discriminant analysis used the 'secure' high status room groups, the 'secure' high status apartment compounds, and the insubstantial structures. The 'Xol–Met GE 40' analysis used the high status room groups and high status apartment compounds with Xolalpan–Metepec 40% or more of Miccaotli–Metepec, and the same set of insubstantial structures as in the 'secure' analysis. Note that sites judged to be intermediate status residences did not figure in either analysis. Almost the same variables were used as in the previous discriminant analysis. However, the proportion of each category in each site was multiplied by 1000, to give a number ranging from zero to 1000. In order to avoid the logarithm of zero, which is minus infinity, the constant one was added to each score, to give numbers ranging from unity to 1001. The common logarithm of each score was then computed (ranging from zero to 3.0004), and used as the input variable. This kind of 'log' transformation often gives better results in multivariate analyses. Among other things it reduces effects of the heavy upper tails in distributions skewed to the right and leads to more nearly normal distributions. The SPSS version 7.01 DISCRIMINANT subprogram was used with a stepwise procedure maximizing Rao's V.

Each discriminant analysis produced two discriminant functions (the maximum possible with three input groups). The relative positions of the input groups on each function were identical in each analysis. In each, function 1 reflects differences between the two high status groups and function 2 contrasts both high status room groups and insubstantial structures with high status apartment compounds. In the 'secure architecture' analysis the relative importance of the first function was more than three times that of the second function. In the 'Xol–Met GE 40' analysis function 1 was only twice as important as function 2.

The markedly greater importance of the first function in the 'secure architecture' analysis indicates that greater differences exist between the 'secure' high status sites and the insubstantial structure sample, than between the high status sites with Xolalpan–Metepec over 40% and the insubstantial structures. This point was also made in the reclassification stages of the analyses; 86% (19 cases) of the insubstantial structures were correctly reassigned to the same group in the 'secure architecture' analysis, while the corresponding percentage was 64% (14 cases) in the other analysis. These results suggest that the sites assigned to high status input groups in the 'secure architecture' analysis are in fact more securely high status than are those 'high status' sites used only in the analysis with Xolalpan–Metepec greater than 40%.

One of the hypotheses suggested by our first discriminant analysis was that differences between high status room groups and high status apartment compounds might arise because of differences in location relative to the 'Street of the Dead'. This hypothesis was tested and disconfirmed by this subsequent pair of analyses. Results clearly indicated that sites located on the 'Street of the Dead' include members of both the high status room group and high status apartment compound categories. It should be emphasized that, in this analysis, no apartment compounds were inappropriately assigned to 'room group' input categories.

The characteristics of the high status input groups, in terms of tendencies for low or high proportions of various ceramic categories to occur on their surfaces, were the same in these two later analyses as in the first discriminant analysis. The residential nature of high status apartment compounds received further support. These sites were characterized by 'common' *candeleros*, other *candeleros*, three-prong burners, handled covers, censers, San Martín Orange, *comales*, and decorated sherds (an aggregate category composed of stuccoed, plano-relief, and stamped). High status room groups were consistently associated only with handled covers, and more ambiguously with regular Thin Orange. Comparison of means and standard deviations of actual counts for all the high status input groups used in these logarithmic analyses revealed that, overall, high status room groups seem to have significantly fewer 'other' *candeleros*, puppet figurines, burners, San Martín Orange, and *comales* than do high status apartment compounds.

In the light of all these results, we can offer some interpretations. In general, the distinction between high status room groups and high status apartment compounds seems valid. The apartment compounds, as predicted, show wider and more intense use of categories associated with domestic activities. The functions of high status room groups are still uncertain, but at least two possibilities are consistent with the artifact distributions found on these sites. René Millon hypothesizes that they were actual residences of priests (personal communication). Another possibility is that they were special purpose rooms used by temple priests for activities such as meditation and personal ritual, entertaining or meeting with visiting dignitaries, resting during ritual cycles, or eating.

Neither of these hypotheses takes account of the need for places to perform activities classified as political and/or administrative in our cultural tradition. Such activities must have been important at Teotihuacán. Where were they carried out, and by whom? If the Teotihuacanos made little or no distinction between priestly and other offices, then many of these 'civic' activities might have been carried out in 'high status room groups', by persons associated with religious cults. Even if there was substantial differentiation of priestly and other offices, at least some of these room groups may have been places where politico-administrative activities were carried out.

The consistently higher proportion of handled covers on high status room groups should perhaps be viewed as a

tendency for low proportions of other categories to occur on such sites. It may be that food was being prepared elsewhere and carried in containers covered by handled covers to the occupants of high status room groups, if Cowgill's conjecture about the use of these objects is correct. Sload suggests that the higher the status, the more removed a person was from domestic activities. Thus, domestic activities may have been entirely absent in large sections of such presumably super-élite apartment compounds as the Ciudadela palaces, the House of the Priests and the Palace of the Sun; a possibility consistent with their being placed among 'room groups' by the first discriminant analysis discussed above.

A fourth analysis (also by Sload) involved 163 sites, predominantly those with insubstantial structures and 'intermediate status apartment compounds', from different regions of the city. Hierarchical clustering was applied to this set of sites, using both the 'complete linkage' and the 'Nature's Groups' algorithms. These methods will be explained in the next section. For the present, the essential point is that they generate subsets or 'clusters' of sites which in some sense are relatively similar to one another. In contrast to discriminant analysis, neither the membership of the clusters nor the number of clusters is specified in advance.

The clustering behavior of 'close' insubstantial structures and adjacent apartment compounds was different in different districts of the city. In N1E5, S1E5, and S1E4 (a craft workshop area) most insubstantial structures joined the same cluster as adjacent apartment compounds, which suggests that occupants of both types of structures were engaged in rather similar activities. In N7W3, N6W3, N7W2, and N6W2 (another district with many workshops) insubstantial structures clustered with adjacent apartment compounds only about half the time. These two regions of the city tended to maintain their spatial integrity in the cluster analysis. That is, most sites in each region joined separate large clusters. This is in direct opposition to what occurred in N2W6 and N3W6, where about one-third of the insubstantial structures joined the same cluster as adjacent apartment compounds, but these pairs were scattered among three different clusters. This indicates that many 'close' insubstantial structures in this district are not like adjacent apartment compounds, and also that adjacent apartment compounds are not like one another. Another clearcut result from these cluster analyses was that the majority of 'distant' insubstantial structures (or at least those on the city's periphery) do not cluster with either 'close' insubstantial structures or apartment compounds.

A point not revealed by the first discriminant analysis discussed above but made clear by this analysis is that neither 'close' nor 'distant' insubstantial structures can be treated as undifferentiated categories. Peripherally located insubstantial structures are different from insubstantial structures located in heavily built-up areas of the city, and they are also different from one another. Insubstantial structures within the densely settled areas of the city are also different from one another, depending upon what region of the city they are in. Even within regions, insubstantial structures may not be similar to one another. Unfortunately, we still cannot say precisely what functions were performed by these structures. A few individual cases that are probably redeposited fill turned up in this analysis. We still feel that most of these sites were probably either residences or outbuildings, but we would no longer postulate a simple dichotomy in which all peripheral insubstantial structures were residences and all more centrally located ones were outbuildings. There were probably some of both everywhere, as well as some 'insubstantial structures' which were special purpose open-air sites such as firing floors for ceramics, at least one of which has been identified by Paula Krotser (personal communication).

Some of the results presented in this section emerged consistently in several analyses. Others at present are merely 'indications' that must be pursued in further analyses. In general, we have found discriminant analysis to be a kind of multivariate statistical technique that can very usefully be applied to archaeological data. It is suitable for many problems, as long as groups of cases can be defined beforehand on the basis of criteria that are relevant but distinct from the set of variables from which the discriminant functions are derived and as long as the assumptions of the mathematical models are reasonably approximated. A great deal of further work along the lines discussed in this section is described by Sload (1982).

Question three: the problem of *barrios*

Using the ceramic data in our computer file, we have attempted to verify independently the existence of *barrios* in certain areas where Millon has defined them tentatively. Initial computer work on this problem was done by Matthew Freedman (1976), but most subsequent work has been by Altschul, who is the primary author of this section (see also Altschul 1981).

Early computer work conceptualized *barrios* as relatively homogeneous units composed of members affiliated through kinship, craft specialties, ethnic identity, and/or religious ties. Evidence consistent with this notion has been found in several areas of the city. For example, in square N1W6 a group of apartment compounds were occupied by people with strong ties to Oaxaca, about 500 km southeast of Teotihuacán. On the eastern periphery of the city another spatial cluster of sites has been interpreted as a neighborhood where merchants may have lived (Millon 1973, p. 40). In many sections of the city, however, Millon suggests that differences in status among those living in adjoining *barrios* was only slightly greater than internal variation within individual *barrios*. A wide variety of kinds of neighborhood organizations may have existed, intermediate between relatively homogeneous *barrios* at one extreme, and, at the other extreme, highly differentiated areas of the city that may not have been organized as *barrios* at all. Each kind of organization may have been characterized by different sets of features shared by its members, as well as by different sets on which members might vary. While future

excavations may lead to a better understanding of the diversity and nature of Teotihuacán *barrios*, we felt that with surface data the most fruitful approach would be to focus on the homogeneous type of organization. Thus we expected to distinguish only a small number of barrios and to obtain problematic results in many parts of the city, not necessarily because *barrios* did not exist in these areas, but because they were organized along different lines.

In attempting to identify homogeneous *barrios* we began with the working hypothesis that if such a type of neighborhood organization existed, examples should be recognizable as spatially contiguous groups of apartment compounds whose members not only resembled one another closely, but were also dissimilar in one or more ways from apartment compounds in neighboring groups. All that is needed to identify homogeneous *barrios* is a method that will define groups of sites that are similar in terms of some chosen set of attributes on which data are available. The method we have used is a form of hierarchical clustering in which each site represents an individual case (Q-mode). Each site was characterized by counts of 25 ceramic categories. Some categories (including regular Thin Orange, coarse Thin Orange, handled covers, three-prong burners, 'common' *candeleros*, other *candeleros*, puppet figurines, *copas*, and miniatures) were treated individually. Those censer, olla, *comal*, San Martín Orange, and Granular Ware sherds phased to either Xolalpan or Metepec were combined, so as to derive aggregate counts for each category, pertaining to the overall Xolalpan–Metepec timespan. Scarce categories such as all incised and finely decorated sherds were aggregated, as were all sherds identified as foreign. In all, 16 composite categories were counted for each site. The entire set was chosen to represent a wide range of categories believed to characterize residences and craft workshops. In lumping Xolalpan and Metepec, we had to assume that if a site was occupied at all during this timespan, its character had not changed drastically during this interval. Given the degree of chronological control in the original ceramic classification, this assumption was necessary. The ceramic reanalyses now being completed should permit better time control in future work.

For each pair of sites in a given analysis, a coefficient of similarity was computed. We have found a number of advantages in transforming counts into percentages of the total sum of counts for all 16 categories (Cowgill 1968). This removes absolute sizes of collections as a factor affecting similarity coefficients, while the problems that such a transformation creates for R-mode analyses (variable versus variable) do not affect Q-mode analyses (site versus site). Using these percentages, the Brainerd–Robinson similarity coefficient[13] was computed for each pair of sites and the resulting matrix was used as input for AGCLUS, a hierarchical clustering program developed by Donald Olivier of the Harvard School of Public Health. This program links the most similar pair of sites into an initial cluster. Stepwise linkage then successively joins the most similar sites and/or clusters until all sites have been linked within one all-inclusive cluster. A number of good general books on these and other clustering procedures are now available, including that by Sneath and Sokal (1973). AGCLUS offers seven options for criteria by which to evaluate similarity of clusters. Results are printed out as a 'dendrogram'; a tree structure that shows the sites and/or clusters linked at each step and the similarity level at which linking takes place.

Three important limits to hierarchical clustering should be noted. First, it simply generates groups that grow increasingly heterogeneous as the number of cases in them increases, until all groups are merged in one supercluster. There is no step in the linking process at which the number of groups is, in any clear sense, the 'right' number. It is up to the investigator to select a level of similarity at which well-defined and interpretable clusters exist. This decision is largely a matter of judgment and depends more on one's theoretical concerns or the nature of the problem than on finding some 'natural' level of similarity.

Secondly, changes in either the number of cases or the set of variables can produce major changes in the resulting clusters. One way of testing the robustness of a dendrogram is, obviously, to experiment with changing cases and/or variables. Another way is by trying more than one clustering option on the same set of similarity coefficients. To gain assurance about cluster reliability, we have used three different linking algorithms for each data set. One option, 'average linkage', joins clusters according to the mean similarity between all members of one cluster and all members of the other cluster. The second option, 'complete linkage', joins clusters on the basis of the least similar pair of members. The third option, a variation on the algorithm known as 'Nature's Groups', is based on a distance function that minimizes the within-cluster sum of squares over all clusters at each step. If similar clusters form under different linkage rules, our confidence that the groups are meaningful is increased.

The third limitation of hierarchical clustering is that although the technique can identify groups of sites, based on a specific set of variables, it does not provide a way for determining which variables are most distinctive of any particular group of sites. One way to determine the distinguishing characteristics of the groups is to use them as the input groups for a discriminant analysis. This use of discriminant analysis is logically quite different from the way we used it in the search for indicators of social status. There, discriminant analysis was used to test prior judgments based on architectural and locational evidence, by observing the behavior of input groups in analyses based on variables derived from surface collected materials. Here, the input groups are defined (in the hierarchical clustering stage) by the same variables as are subsequently used to derive the discriminant functions. The discriminant analysis is not used to test or refine the groups, but simply to identify the variables that principally characterize each group.

Although hierarchical clustering programs are relatively inexpensive compared to other kinds of multivariate statistics, difficulties mount rapidly if one tries simultaneously to cluster more than several hundred sites, and even for a hundred or so the output becomes rather unwieldy. Rather than dealing with all Teotihuacán at once, our initial search for *barrios* concentrated on three areas. Two of these, N1W2/S1W2 and N1E5/N2E5 were chosen primarily because many of the site collections were exceptionally large and therefore furnished exceptionally reliable estimates of true proportions of artifacts in the sites. The third area was the 200 hectare (1 km × 2 km) rectangle from N4W3/N4W2 to N7W3/N7W2. Much of this area was intensively occupied throughout Teotihuacán's history, a condition we felt might have led to the development of old, entrenched *barrios*.

Figure 7 maps results of an average linkage cluster analysis of sites in N1W2/S1W2, using 160 as the similarity level for separating clusters (possible values of the Brainerd–Robinson coefficient range from 0 to 200). The decision to use 160 as the cutoff level was merely a practical solution. Below this point the major clusters begin collapsing into each other, while above it they start to fragment into a large number of one- or two-pair groups. Sites not marked in Fig. 7 were excluded from the analysis because of the small size of artifact collections (less than 20 total objects from the combined 16 categories). Sites that are starred were included in the analysis but were not similar to any other site or cluster at the 160 level. Sites marked by dots are still accepted as obsidian workshops by Spence, after his recent re-evaluation (personal communication, October 1981). The results shown here are fairly typical of other sections of the city and we will confine our discussion to them (see Altschul (1981) for an expanded discussion). Several contiguous clusters can be discerned, especially in the northwest (cluster 1) and southeast (cluster 2) corners of N1W2. Cluster 1 corresponds fairly well with a localized group of obsidian workshops. Two other obsidian workshops in N1W2 appear in other clusters.

The ceramic-based clustering behavior of these latter workshops was puzzling and led Altschul to re-examine much of this area. Unfortunately, it has undergone vast alterations since the original survey. Nevertheless, the obsidian workshops that could be checked exhibited substantial variation, both in types of artifacts made and in the intensity of obsidian working. Most workshops in the northwest corner of N1W2 had pervasive obsidian surface covers that spread over the entire site. In other sections, however, workshops either contained much sparser collections or had intense obsidian concentrations in only one section of the site. It is possible, then, that in this area of the city, workshops varied between full-time, specialized obsidian workers in a number of contiguous apartment compounds and part-time workers producing primarily for use within a compound, some of which, as in clusters 2 and 3, may have been spatially clustered in larger social units on the basis of other attributes. Spence (1979, 1981) discusses this contrast between 'regional' and 'local' obsidian workshops.

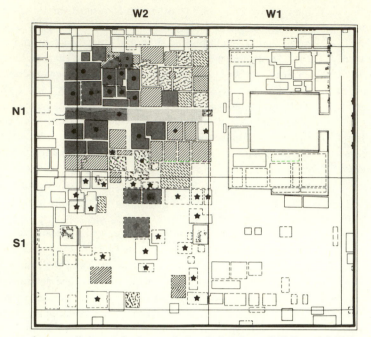

Average linkage cluster analysis of sites from N1W2 and S1W2.

N = 21 ■	Cluster 1	N = 4 ▨	Cluster 4
17 ▨	Cluster 2	3 ▨	Cluster 5
11 ▨	Cluster 3	4 ▨	Cluster 6

19 ★ Sites included in the analysis but which did not
         join clusters at the 160 level.

● Xolalpan—Metepec obsidian workshops.

Total = 79

Fig. 7. Spatial distribution of site groups derived from 'average linkage' hierarchical clustering in N1W2 and S1W2.

Although smaller spatially contiguous clusters exist in the northeast and southwest sections of N1W2, these clusters are much more difficult to interpret. There are at least four plausible hypotheses: (*a*) the clusters are artifacts of the statistical technique and small surface collections and do not reflect socially significant groupings, (*b*) *barrios* were non-existent in these areas, (*c*) *barrios* were much smaller, consisting of only three to five apartment compounds; or (*d*) *barrios* were organized along 'non-homogeneous' lines in which differences in status, occupation, and/or wealth existed between compounds within the same *barrio*. In this last case, it may be that the clustering technique is picking up similarities (e.g. in status or occupation) between members of different *barrios*.

At present we cannot reject or substantiate any of the four hypotheses advanced above. It must be remembered that there is nothing inherent in the statistical work we have carried out that 'naturally' leads to socially meaningful clusters. Thus

it is not always profitable, and can be misleading, to develop *ad hoc* links between each cluster and some social unit. We do not view the computer results as a final stage in archaeological research, but rather find that one of the most important and interesting aspects of our work is the spotting of unusual or hitherto unseen patterns in the surface material that should then be examined more closely in the field, if possible. At the same time, it should be pointed out that simultaneous existence of several different types of neighborhood organizations is widespread in non-industrialized cities (see Altschul 1981). It seems quite possible that there was more than one type of *barrio* organization at Teotihuacán. If so, René Millon's suggestion of a 'mosaic' aspect to the neighborhood structure of the city would be strengthened and made more complex.

Incidentally, city-wide summary maps such as Figs. 3–6 are probably of little use for identification of *barrios*, because the 6.25 hectare scale of site aggregation is too coarse. However, distribution maps for selected regions on a site-by-site basis are a potentially major complement to our statistical research on *barrios*.

Question four: pyramids and platforms not related to the 'Street of the Dead'

A combination of hierarchical clustering, discriminant analysis and other descriptive procedures has also been used to examine the relationship between neighborhood activities and the central authority of the city. This aspect of our work is also mainly by Altschul, who did much of the writing of this section. We have focused on pyramids and platforms, since these structures are believed to have been integrated into the city administration at all levels. Most of them are located on or in close relation to the 'Street of the Dead', forming a large district that we, in company with other students of Teotihuacán, assume was the scene of religous activities of major importance for the entire city and often, indeed, important far and wide in Mesoamerica. Higher levels, at least, of activities that we would categorize as political were undoubtedly also concentrated in structures related to the 'Street of the Dead'. In addition, a number of temples and temple complexes within this central district have been identified as centers of craft production (Millon 1966, 1970*b*, 1973; Spence 1967, 1981).

However, as we pointed out earlier, many pyramids and platforms are also found in other districts of the city. In this section we will use quotation marks and refer to all these pyramids and platforms as 'temples', although in the case of the lower platforms it is not clear that ritual activities were what made them special. It seems likely that these pyramids and platforms were associated with diverse activities. Some may have been established by the state to oversee craft production or to serve as administrative centers for certain sections of the city. Others may relate to ethnic groups, *barrios*, cults of distinctive deities, or craft associations whose religious practices may have differed substantially from the 'state' ceremonies performed along the 'Street of the Dead'. As noted earlier, some of these 'non-state' units may have been very powerful, with widespread influence, while others may have been of strictly local significance. In the work discussed here, we have concentrated less on evidence for power, and more on identification of non-central 'temple' sites whose ceramic proportions were similar to those characteristic of sites related to the 'Street of the Dead', in contrast to others with collections more similar to those from other sites in their immediate neighborhoods.

In one investigation, hierarchical clustering was performed on a sample of 102 sites, stretching from the northwestern periphery of the city (N7W3), through the 'Street of the Dead', and well into the east (N1E5). This sample, intended to be of manageable size for an initial investigation, is in no sense representative of the entire city, but consists of sites selected for their relevance to our specific questions. It includes 'temples', but also apartment compounds, generally 30 to 80 m distant from the 'temples'. The purpose of includ-

ing apartment compounds near 'temples' was to use sites representative of the neighborhoods in which 'temples' were found. At the same time, apartment compounds actually adjacent to 'temples' were avoided, partly to avoid collections that might be unduly affected by redeposited material washed down from 'temples', and partly because at least some of the residences adjacent to 'temples' may have been dwellings for priests or otherwise quite unrepresentative of their neighborhoods. Our notion was that if an outlying 'temple' was operated by the state it should cluster with sites along the 'Street of the Dead'. Alternatively, if an outlying 'temple' was associated with a *barrio* level of organization or a *barrio* cult, it should be quite distinct from 'temples' along the 'Street of the Dead', and *perhaps* more similar to neighboring apartment compounds.

The same 16 ceramic categories were used as in our work on *barrios*. They are listed in Table 3. Again, for each site, counts were converted to percentages (relative to these 16 categories) and we computed Brainerd–Robinson similarity coefficients for all the 5151 pairs of site collections in our sample of 102 sites.

AGCLUS was again used. With the average linkage option, we obtained eight major clusters at a similarity level of 145. Four of these clusters formed a well-defined supercluster, resembling one another at the 139 level but having an average similarity of only about 110 to the other clusters. Two clusters alone accounted for four-fifths of the sites in this supercluster. The first of these two clusters, with 17 sites, included most of the major temples of the city, including the three main pyramids (Sun, Moon, and Quetzalcoatl), as well as a few high status residences located near the temples. Nearly all the sites in this cluster belong to architectural complexes on or linked to the 'Street of the Dead', and none is outside the major north–south wall in N5W2 and N4W2.

The second major cluster of this supercluster included 22 sites. Most of the 'temples' in it were parts of three-temple complexes. More than 20 such complexes were already in existence in the city by the Tzacualli phase. Many are in the northern and western parts, while others, architecturally very similar, are along the 'Street of the Dead'. Those situated in outlying areas, such as in N5W2 and N6W3, are imposing, and their architecture contrasts sharply both with neighboring apartment compounds and with single 'temple' pyramids and platforms.

This supercluster, then, is composed mostly of impressive temple complexes, plus some high status residences, mostly near the 'Street of the Dead'. We feel rather confident that it can be related to the central authority, or at least to high ranking persons and activities. Only nine of the 'temples' in our entire sample of 102 sites did not join this 'high status' supercluster. All were relatively small single structures situated some distance from the 'Street of the Dead'. Six of these nine joined a rather large cluster that included 18 'intermediate status' apartment compounds. Sites in this cluster showed no clear spatial pattern, except that none was close to the 'Street of the Dead'.

186

Table 3. *Means and standard deviations of percentages of 16 ceramic categories in three groups of sites derived by hierarchical clustering. Group 1: Mainly pyramids and sites along the 'Street of the Dead'. Group 2: Portions of several large three-temple complexes, both close to and far from the 'Street of the Dead'. Group 7: apartment compounds and minor 'temples', not close to the 'Street of the Dead'*

Ceramic categories	Clusters		
	1 (N = 17) % ± %	2 (N = 22) % ± %	7 (N = 24) % ± %
Regular Thin Orange	82.6 ± 6.9	65.6 ± 4.4	46.9 ± 5.0
Coarse Thin Orange	2.5 ± 3.1	4.1 ± 4.7	3.1 ± 2.7
Comales	1.2 ± 3.1	0.5 ± 1.5	0.8 ± 2.3
Handled covers	2.7 ± 3.2	3.3 ± 3.8	2.2 ± 2.5
Incised and decorated	4.1 ± 4.8	3.4 ± 3.2	2.2 ± 2.6
Puppet figurines	0.4 ± 1.2	2.1 ± 3.1	2.3 ± 3.8
Foreign wares	0.3 ± 1.0	1.0 ± 2.1	1.4 ± 1.9
Censers	0.8 ± 2.1	1.1 ± 2.4	3.0 ± 4.3
Three-prong burners	0.5 ± 1.1	1.2 ± 1.4	1.9 ± 1.9
Granular Ware	0.4 ± 0.7	0.5 ± 1.1	0.6 ± 1.1
Miniatures	0.3 ± 0.8	0.3 ± 1.0	0.5 ± 0.9
Copas	0.2 ± 0.7	0.1 ± 0.4	1.0 ± 1.4
'Common' *candeleros*	0.7 ± 1.8	0.5 ± 1.0	4.9 ± 5.1
Other *candeleros*	0.1 ± 0.6	0.6 ± 1.1	3.0 ± 2.3
San Martín Orange	2.4 ± 4.1	14.0 ± 8.3	19.7 ± 5.3
Ollas	0.9 ± 1.8	1.5 ± 2.4	6.8 ± 3.2

These results suggest that we may be able to make distinctions, on the basis of surface collections alone, between 'temple' complexes occupied by persons of high status and/or where activities very similar to those along the 'Street of the Dead' were being carried out, and other 'temples' whose occupants and/or activities did not differ much from those in neighboring residences. Sites in the first category tend to be architecturally more imposing. The architectural evidence and that from ceramics are independent and mutually corroborative.

To ascertain which variables were most distinctive of each cluster, the clusters were used as input groups for a discriminant analysis. In addition to studying the behavior of the clusters in discriminant space we have found that a simple table of mean values and standard deviations of each variable for each group is a way to present results that is informative and relatively easy to interpret. Table 3 summarizes these data for the three clusters we have discussed above, which were the largest of the eight we obtained in this analysis. The other five, which included only two 'temple' sites, are less relevant for present purposes. The two variables that dominate the contrasts among these three clusters are proportions of regular Thin Orange and San Martín Orange, both of which we discussed earlier in connection with our density and ratio maps.

It is important to remember that the percentages in Table 3 are relative only to the 16 categories shown, and are not directly comparable to the percentages mapped in Figs.

3–6, which are based on *all* ceramics phased to Xolalpan–Metepec, or (for regular Thin Orange) to all Miccaotli–Metepec material. Percentages in Table 3 are much higher, for this reason. Also, the data in Table 3 are based on individual sites, while Figs. 3–6 are based on 6.25 hectare aggregates of sites.

From Table 3, we see that regular Thin Orange amounts to 80% or more (of the 16 categories) in most of the sites in cluster 1 (the cluster including the main pyramids), averages about 65% in the sites of cluster 2 (which includes many three-temple complexes, both on and far from the 'Street of the Dead'), but only about 47% in the sites of cluster 7 (which includes six minor 'temples' and 18 apartment compounds). In interpreting these figures, remember that we do not think that actual proportions of regular Thin Orange vessels in use on these sites at any specific moment were anywhere near this high. We do believe that the rank order of percentages of sherds in these collections correctly reflects the ranking of percentages of regular Thin Orange vessels actually in use relative to other ceramics.

San Martín Orange, in contrast, averages little more than 2% in cluster 1 sites, but averages around 14% in cluster 2 sites and about 20% in cluster 7 sites. Incidentally, comparison with Fig. 5 shows that few if any of these sites, even in cluster 7, have particularly high proportions of San Martín Orange, relative to all sites in the city.

None of the other 14 categories used in this study averages more than 7% in any of the clusters in Table 3, and most average much less. One's first thought is to question

Table 4. *Mean percentages of 14 ceramic categories in the same three groups of sites as in Table 3, restandardized to reduce effects of regular Thin Orange and San Martín Orange*

Ceramic categories	Clusters		
	1 (N = 17) (%)	2 (N = 22) (%)	7 (N = 24) (%)
Coarse Thin Orange	16.7	20.0	9.3
Comales	7.7	2.3	2.4
Handled covers	18.1	16.3	6.5
Incised and decorated	27.0	16.6	6.6
Puppet figurines	2.3	10.5	6.7
Foreign wares	2.1	4.9	4.1
Censers	5.6	5.4	8.9
Three-prong burners	3.1	6.0	5.8
Granular Ware	2.7	2.5	1.6
Miniatures	2.0	1.6	1.4
Copas	1.2	0.6	2.9
'Common' *candeleros*	4.9	2.6	14.6
Other *candeleros*	0.9	3.1	9.1
Ollas	5.7	7.5	20.2

whether the hierarchical clustering has done anything but sort sites on the basis of their proportions of regular Thin Orange and San Martín Orange. However, inspection of Table 3 shows that there are several other variables whose means differ enough between clusters, relative to their standard deviations within clusters, to suggest strongly that these variables also really differ between clusters. Indeed, a mechanical application of t-tests shows that many of these differences are 'highly significant'.

There are, however, several good reasons for *not* simply doing a set of t-tests in this situation. First, as is *always* true, multiple t-tests for possible pairwise significant differences should be preceded by a procedure such as analysis of variance which tests for *overall* significance among the groups. Secondly, if our 16 variables were independent, so that we could make 16 independent analyses of variance, the chances would be $1 - (0.95)^{16}$, or 0.56, of getting *at least one* result 'significant at the 5% level' just by chance. With multiple tests, it can be quite hard to ascertain the real significance levels attained. But thirdly, and most importantly, since our variables are percentages, which necessarily add to 100% in each collection, it is a mathematical necessity that the variables in Table 3 *cannot* be independent, but must be complexly interrelated (Chayes 1971). For example, the means for almost every category except regular Thin Orange in cluster 1 are smaller than the corresponding means in cluster 7. This is at least partly because the average percentage of regular Thin Orange in cluster 1 is so high that all other percentages must necessarily be depressed.

To deal with the possibility that regular Thin Orange and San Martín Orange may be constraining percentages of other categories to appear to differ significantly, Cowgill recomputed the means for the other 14 variables so that they, alone,

would add to 100% in each column (Table 4). It is not clear that these are the means that would emerge if it had been feasible to recompute percentages for each site in each cluster, based only on these 14 categories. However, the figures in Table 4 may be good approximations to what would come from such an analysis. Because of our doubts on this score, we interpret Table 4 conservatively. Nevertheless, taken together with Table 3, there is evidence that cluster 7 differs from clusters 1 and 2, not only in having less regular Thin Orange and more San Martín Orange, but also in having more ollas, more *candeleros* of all kinds, and perhaps more *copas*. In addition, cluster 1 differs from both 2 and 7 in having lower proportions of puppet figurines and foreign sherds. Table 4 gives less conclusive hints that cluster 7 may also differ from the others in having lower proportions of coarse Thin Orange and handled covers, while cluster 1 may differ from the others by having a higher proportion of *comales*. Some of these results are reasonable; others are unexpected and difficult to explain.

There is also a marked trend in the average proportion of incised and decorated sherds in Table 4, from high in cluster 1 to intermediate in 2 and quite low in cluster 7. This trend, higher proportions of incised and decorated on the average in higher status sites and more major temples, is just what one might have predicted at the outset. It would be nice if we could stop analyses at this point, seize on this result, and take off into interpretations. Unfortunately, as so often, a bit of further work complicates the matter. In the subsequent analysis summarized in Table 5, the association between status and proportion of decorated sherds fails to appear, even when a compensation similar to Table 4 is made for effects of percentages of regular Thin Orange and San Martín Orange.

One possible interpretation of the present analysis is that three levels of 'state' buildings are being identified. These

Table 5. *Mean percentage of 15 ceramic categories in three groups of sites derived by hierarchical clustering. All sites pertain to three-temple complexes. These three groups are among those shown in Fig. 9. Group 1: mostly main pyramids and sites along the 'Street of the Dead'. Group 2: mostly major temples and platforms of large three-temple complexes. Group 3: many minor platforms of large three-temple complexes and temples and platforms of small three-temple complexes*

Ceramic categories	Clusters		
	1 (N = 18) (%)	2 (N = 25) (%)	3 (N = 12) (%)
Regular Thin Orange	83.1	67.5	53.2
Coarse Thin Orange	4.7	2.2	2.0
Comales	0.1	0.8	0.6
Handled covers	2.6	4.9	5.1
Incised and decorated	2.0	3.3	4.8
Puppet figurines	0.6	0.4	0.6
Foreign wares	0.9	0.1	1.0
Censers	0.8	1.3	0.9
Three-prong burners	1.2	2.2	1.2
Granular Ware	0.5	0.0	0.0
Miniatures	0.2	0.1	0.2
Copas	0.2	0.1	0.9
'Common' *candeleros*	0.4	0.8	1.3
Other *candeleros*	0.0	1.3	1.4
San Martín Orange	2.7	14.9	26.7

would range from those most important, politically and religiously (cluster 1), to a group that is fairly similar but that includes major 'temple' complexes far from the 'Street of the Dead' (cluster 2), to a group of sites that have more in common with neighboring apartment compounds than with other 'state' buildings (cluster 7). It is this last group of sites that we believe should receive close further examination in relation to a *barrio* level of religion and/or political administration.

To explore these issues further, a second analysis was designed (also by Altschul), using 72 sites that are parts of three-temple complexes. Nine sites from the Ciudadela were also included, because of the important role this complex (probably the residence of the head or heads of the state) is believed to have played in the administration of the state and the city. Of these 81 sites, only 16 had been included in the analysis just discussed.

This sequence of cluster and discriminant analyses was planned to examine in greater depth the relations between the main temples of the city and other major 'temple' complexes. We were particularly anxious to determine, through an expanded analysis using only 'temples', whether the major components of three-temple complexes would again be distinguished from the main pyramids of Teotihuacán. We also hoped to clarify the nature of intrasite differentiation within individual three-temple complexes. In our research on the problem of *barrios* we found that different parts of those 'temple' complexes which were located in primarily residential districts often joined different clusters. In many of these

clusters parts of 'temple' complexes were grouped with apartment compounds dispersed throughout the area being analysed. These results suggested to Altschul that different parts of 'temple' complexes may have been associated with different functions, and that some of these functions may have been neighborhood-based. He reasoned that those parts of a 'temple' complex closely associated with the central authority should join with sites along the 'Street of the Dead', while those components of 'temple' complexes that might be centers of neighborhood-based activities would cluster together and would be distinguished by assemblages not associated with very high status.

The final matter addressed by this 81 site analysis concerned the diverse nature of three-temple complexes. They all follow a broadly similar architectural plan, but a number of them, such as Plaza One (Fig. 1, number 14, N5W2) and the Plaza of the Columns (facing the 'Street of the Dead', Fig. 1, inset, number 37, N4W1) are much more imposing than are some of the smaller ones scattered in non-central districts of the city. Earlier analyses had left the position of these smaller complexes in doubt. Some clustered with the larger structures, while others were associated with 'temples' at the neighborhood level.

Thus with this second set of analyses we were trying to tap three levels of variability – between major three-temple complexes and the main temples of the city, between major and minor three-temple complexes, and between the different parts of single complexes.

Figure 8 maps the sites used in this analysis. Figure 9, divided into eight areas, shows the six clusters derived from an average linkage hierarchical clustering, choosing 150 as the similarity level for defining clusters. Table 5, analogous to Table 3, shows mean values of the variables for the three largest clusters. The categories were the same as in the previous analysis, except that ollas were omitted. Variables were again obtained by computing the percentage of each category relative to the total of all 15 categories. Clusters 1 and 2, comprising nearly half the sites in the analysis, are fairly similar to each other (joining at a similarity of about 148) and relatively dissimilar to anything else (they do not cluster with any of the remaining groups at any level about 127). These clusters correspond quite nicely to the two major high status groups of the previous analysis (Table 3).

As hypothesized, cluster 1 contains most of the city's main structures included in our sample, while cluster 2 is composed of the major temples and platforms of the larger three-temple complexes. The only exceptions are major portions of the 5' group (Fig. 1, inset, number 30, N5W1; in part 4 of Fig. 9), some platforms in the Plaza of the Columns, the northern platforms of Plaza One, and one temple from a small complex in N6W1. All these sites joined cluster 1, rather than the expected cluster 2. It is not clear whether these two clusters are capturing a difference based on status, function, or some other dimension. However, it is interesting to note that the temples on the platforms surrounding the Ciudadela are divided about evenly between the two clusters.

Of the eight 'temples' which were in neither cluster 1 nor 2, seven joined cluster 3. As can be seen from Tables 3 and 5, the artifact composition for this cluster is fairly similar to that of cluster 7 (the 'neighborhood temple' cluster) of the previous analysis, even though only two sites are common to both data sets. Also included in cluster 3 are some minor platforms pertaining to the major 'temple' complexes. Although these investigations are still exploratory, they do strengthen the hypothesis that the small outlying 'temples' and 'temple' complexes functioned as links between the central authority and the outlying *barrios*. They also provide evidence for differentiation of activities within single large three-temple complexes.

The remaining three clusters obtained in this analysis were all small, yet highly distinctive. Cluster 4 consisted of several platforms belonging to both large and small complexes, and also the northern palace of the Ciudadela. These sites were all characterized by a high proportion of handled covers. Cluster 5 is composed of four relatively minor platforms pertaining to smaller complexes. In cluster 5, San Martín Orange averaged over 50% of the 15 categories used in this analysis. These sites should be investigated for evidence of possible San Martín Orange manufacture or evidence of storage (as would be indicated if our restudy of the ceramics shows a high proportion of amphoras in these sites). Cluster 6 is a particularly tight cluster, including six parts of the northernmost of the two large three-temple complexes in N6W3 (Fig. 9, part 1), plus one other site.

To investigate cluster 6, yet another cluster analysis was carried out, using 160 sites in N6W3, N6W2, N7W3, and N7W2. Results are mapped in Fig. 10. The six sites just mentioned clustered together with 24 widely dispersed sites that included low, intermediate, and high status residences, workshops, and one possible cemetery. Other sections of the same three-temple complex (12: N6W3) joined together in a highly distinctive cluster (not similar to anything else above a similarity level of 137) that included two apartment compounds bordering the complexes and another two in outlying areas of this district. Of these four apartment compounds, one is believed to be a residential workshop. The differences thus detected within single three-temple complexes may possibly be because some parts may have remained in use later than other parts. But it seems more likely that the differences arise because of distinctive sets of activities: one set is associated with 'state' operations and the other set reflecting community-based functions.

As we hope the results of this and preceding sections amply illustrate, we have found the coupled use of hierarchical clustering and discriminant analysis highly useful as an exploratory technique. Patterns have been identified that had gone unnoticed in the field and that probably would not have been recognized at all without the aid of computers and multivariate statistics. We have also been able to use some hypotheses about Teotihuacán society as guides in designing our studies, and have been able to move some distance toward really good tests of some of these hypotheses. However, we feel that the techniques we have described are most profitably used to identify areas of sufficiently great potential for the understanding of Teotihuacán society to warrant further statistical analyses. Problem-oriented excavations are also called for, and we very much hope that they will be possible, on a fairly large scale, in the future. Further statistical work should move toward formulation of more detailed models and their more rigorous testing, rather than simply identifying patterned variation in the data.

Summary

Even in a discussion of this length, we have had to be highly selective, and we have only touched on a small part of our work. Of more than a hundred maps for publication, we have chosen four examples: density of regular Thin Orange, and proportions of regular Thin Orange, San Martín Orange, and handled covers. In all three examples of ratio maps, the observed spatial distributions differ considerably from our expectations (see Figs. 3–6). It is important to put these kinds of data on record, and also important to try to understand the reasons for the observed spatial patterns. We have also sketched some of our ongoing work on specific questions about Teotihuacán society. Much remains to be done, but we have also learned much. For example, small room groups are distinct from larger apartment compounds in their characteristic artifact assemblages, and this difference is not simply a consequence of different regional tendencies. Some archi-

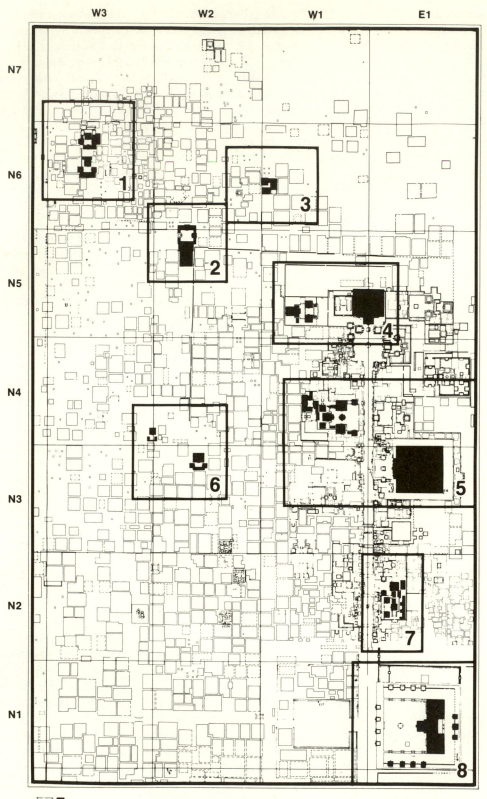

Sites included in the analysis.

Fig. 8. Sites used in study of three-temple complexes.

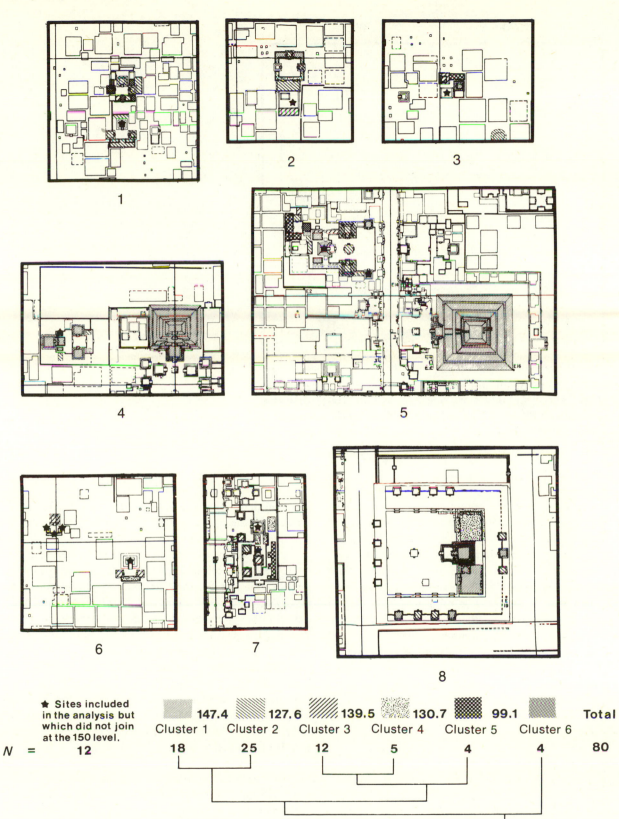

Fig. 9. Clusters obtained in study of three-temple complexes, using average linkage.

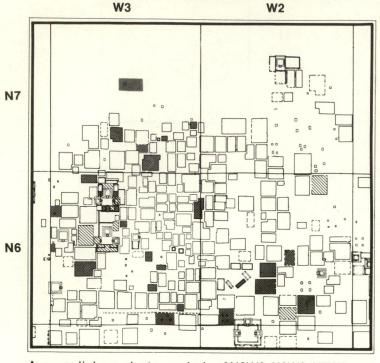

Average linkage cluster analysis of N6W3, N6W2, N7W3, and N7W2 showing only sites associated with parts of three-temple complexes 11:N6W3 or 12:N6W3. Minimum level of cluster similarity = 150.

■ Cluster 1   ▨ Cluster 2

Fig. 10. Cluster analysis in far northwest.

tecturally substantial apartment compounds have been found to have artifact assemblages similar to those from insubstantial structures that we believe were low status dwellings. Other insubstantial structures, near apartment compounds, seem to have been places where special activities were carried out, since their assemblages are unlike either those of nearby apartment compounds or sites we think were low status dwellings. Our investigations of *barrios* have identified not only a number of spatial clusters of sites sharing quite similar artifact assemblages but also many cases where statistical clustering of sites in terms of their assemblages does not lead to tight spatial clusters, and it is more clear than before that many neighborhoods were far from homogeneous. Our techniques have identified sites that are close to one another but have quite different assemblages, and other sites which, in spite of being far from one another, have quite similar assemblages. Most notably, certain sites far from the 'Street of the Dead' have assemblages quite like those from some of the major pyramids and very high status residences close to the Street. These sites are often impressive three-temple complexes. Architecturally more modest pyramids and platforms far from the 'Street of the Dead' are more apt to resemble other sites in their own neighborhoods. Does an assemblage highly similar to that from major pyramids and high status residences reflect local activity of the central authority, or does it reflect a local group so

powerful that it could closely emulate the trappings and activities of the central authority? This is one of many questions that remain unanswered.

In all our investigations, a series of factors have contributed to a richness of possibilities, but also to the complexities we face. One factor is the extraordinary size and intrinsic complexity of the society whose members built and inhabited the city. Another is the wealth of data recovered by the Teotihuacán Mapping Project, unprecedented in the care and detail of coverage of such a large area. Although this was the collective achievement of many people, the essential ingredients were the vision, the dedication, and frequently the charisma, of René Millon. He conceived the project, inspired everyone else, and was far more concerned with what needed to be done than with whether it had ever been done before, or whether it seemed 'feasible' to anyone else. The rise of computer technology has also had a major impact on what we have done and tried to do. As seems to be universal experience in efforts to apply computers to new fields, there have been periods of sheer drudgery, exasperating malfunctions, and some awful messes; times when we felt it might be better to say our work was 'computer-hampered' rather than computer-aided. Nevertheless, a number of things *have* worked out, and we are reaping rewards from years of struggle.

In addition to our efforts to apply new techniques to

exceptional data, we have tried to set high standards in our conceptualization of Teotihuacán society; both in general models and in specific hypotheses. We feel that what we have achieved does not compare too badly with what other archaeologists are doing. We know that we will not be led to all the right answers simply by inspection and analysis of our archaeological data, even though such 'data analytic' approaches have immense heuristic value. It is essential to take account of additional knowledge, much of it derived from study of other societies, in formulating our models to be tested. We are also convinced that 'cultural materialist' paradigms are an insufficient framework within which to cast our models. Beyond this, we are much less satisfied. In archaeology, as in all social and humanistic studies, an enormous amount of work in developing good theory remains to be done.

Besides our dissatisfaction with theory, we are also troubled by gaps between theory and archaeological data, and by what seems to us the quite specious ease by which archaeological reasoning too often leaps these gaps. Although he words the matter differently and might be incensed by our belief that inductive and deductive approaches should be used jointly, we think that Lewis Binford has a somewhat similar concern with linking data and theory, in his discussion of 'middle-range' theory (Binford 1977, pp. 6–7). We ourselves have not bridged as many of these gaps as we would have wished, but at least we have made ourselves aware of their existence, and have taken account of them in offering interpretations of our results.

We have stressed the need to work concomitantly in two directions; from data toward new hypotheses about Teotihuacán and improved sociocultural theory, and from hypotheses toward specific new questions to ask of data. Techniques about which we have most often talked are varieties of mapping, discriminant analysis, and hierarchical clustering. Our maps tend to take data as primary and produce spatial patterns which suggest new hypotheses relevant for theory. Discriminant analysis and hierarchical clustering have tended to take hypotheses suggested by theory as their points of departure. However, the distinction is far from absolute. New hypotheses suggest mapping spatial distributions of novel functions of the 'obvious' variables. Equally, multivariate analyses designed to test specific hypotheses, or at least directed to fairly definite questions, often yield unexpected patterns that suggest new ideas and new questions. This, we take it, is the right general prescription for all good research; what we all need to do is to perform brilliantly within these guidelines!

Notes

1. Fieldwork and much of the data analysis was supported by a series of National Science Foundation grants to the University of Rochester, with René Millon as principal investigator. Further analysis and computer work has been supported by NSF grants to Brandeis University (principal investigator, George Cowgill) and by funds from the Wenner-Gren Society for Anthropological Research, the American Council of Learned Societies, the Canada Council (awarded to Bruce Drewitt and Michael Spence), and the Ivey Foundation of Canada (awarded to Michael Spence). Much of the work described here (especially distribution mapping) has been aided by a National Endowment for the Humanities grant to Brandeis University. Both Altschul and Sload are recipients of NSF doctoral dissertation research support grants. Teotihuacán Mapping Project results, of which our work forms a part, are being published in a series of volumes by the University of Texas Press (Millon 1973; Millon *et al.* 1973). We would like to express our appreciation to all these institutions. Robert Hunt, Paula Krotser, Evelyn Rattray, and Michael Spence have either commented on an earlier version of this paper or shared unpublished data with us, or both, for which we are grateful. We are especially grateful to René Millon, partly for very helpful comments on two earlier drafts of this paper, but above all for having made it all possible.

2. These ceramic studies are also supported by the NEH grant to Brandeis University.

3. A similar point is made by Sanders *et al.* (1979, p. 15), who say
    . . . once the distribution of residences for various prehistoric time periods had been described, how were we to infer what these meant in terms of interaction with the natural environment and other human beings. This was the point at which we floundered, and are still, to some extent, floundering . . . . What we failed to do, and what no one has ever done adequately, is to develop a series of models, by means of which the archaeologist can make reasonable sociological inferences from settlement pattern data.
    Later they ask, 'How were we to translate mounds and concentrations of artifact debris into sociological phenomena . . . ?' (Sanders *et al.* 1979, p. 16).

4. Robert Santley is also among those critical of results from small sampling fractions (Sanders *et al.* 1979, Appendix E).

5. Terms such as 'N7W3' refer to the 500 m × 500 m squares of the Mapping Project grid, identified by the numbers and letters on the margins of the archaeological map (Fig. 1). Each square covers 25 hectares. They should not be confused with our spatial aggregation units, each of which is a 6.25 hectare quarter of one of the 500 m × 500 m grid squares on the archaeological map.

6. More exactly, it is impossible for the ratio to exceed unity, since regular Thin Orange is one of the categories in the denominator, as well as in the numerator. However, a proportion of the regular Thin Orange total, certainly small and probably extremely small, dates to the Tzacualli and Patlachique phases.

7. Computations of X_s for Figs. 5 and 6 lead to exactly the values mapped.

8. 'Street of the Dead' is derived from the name used for it by the Aztecs (*miccaotli* in Nahuatl), apparently in the belief that the mounds lining it were the tombs of dead rulers. Archaeological evidence shows that the significance of the Street for the Teotihuacanos was very different, and we will put the term in quotes to remind the reader that the name is inappropriate. See the discussion by R. Millon (1973, p. 33).

9. Gilbert (1980, pp. 124, 136, and 142) illustrates several metal vessels from ancient China (ranging from about the eighth to fourth centuries B.C.) that have lids that can be inverted to stand alone as separate containers. However, except for this feature, they have nothing in common with Teotihuacán handled covers. In particular, there is no indication that the lids of these Chinese examples might have been held in place by tying.

10. Evelyn Rattray (personal communication, October 1981) thinks that handled covers may have been used as censers. This is a distinct possibility that seems consistent with what we know of their spatial distribution. However, it seems to leave unexplained

their distinctive form, which was apparently intended to enable them to be used as tied-on lids as well as receptacles.

11. Millon (1966, p. 16; 1970*b*, p. 11; Adams 1966, p. 131) has postulated the existence of temple workshops associated with the Pyramid of the Moon. Michael Spence (1979, pp. 22, 25; 1981) sees evidence that some obsidian workers spent part of their time in state or temple workshops. We do not know how extensively the Teotihuacán state demanded labor service, and we do not know whether (as, for example, in the Inca state) there was a reciprocal obligation of the state to feed those performing such service. However, it is entirely possible that this was done.

12. William Sanders (personal communication) feels that 'plaster-smoothers' were in fact used for smoothing plaster. However, we are unconvinced of this.

13. The Brainerd–Robinson similarity coefficient is defined as

$$S_{ij} = 200 - \sum_{k=1}^{M} |X_{ik} - X_{jk}|,$$

where the comparison is between assemblages i and j, X_{ik} is the percentage of category k in assemblage i, X_{jk} is the percentage of category k in assemblage j, and the comparison is in terms of M categories. For each category, the absolute value of the difference of its percentages in the two assemblages is computed, and added to the absolute values of the two percentage differences for all other categories. If two assemblages have no categories at all in common, S_{ij} has its lowest possible value, which is 0. The highest possible value of S_{ij}, for two identical assemblages, is 200. Note that S_{ij} is 200 minus a 'city block' distance term.

References

Abascal M., R. (1974). Análisis por activación de neutrones: una aportación para la arqueología moderna. Thesis. Escuela Nacional de Antropología e Historia, México, D.F.

Acosta, J. R. (1964). *El Palacio del Quetzalpapálotl*, Memorias, No. 10. Instituto Nacional de Antropología e Historia: México, D.F.

Adams, R. McC. (1966). *The Evolution of Urban Society: Early Mesopotamia and Prehispanic Mexico*. Aldine: Chicago.

Altschul, J. H. (1981). Spatial and statistical evidence for social groupings at Teotihuacán, Mexico. Ph.D. thesis, Department of Anthropology, Brandeis University. (University Microfilms, Ann Arbor, Michigan.)

Armillas, P. (1944). Exploraciones recientes en Teotihuacán, México. *Cuadernos Americanos* 3(4): 121–36.

Armillas, P. (1950). Teotihuacán, Tula, y los Toltecas. *Runa* 3(1): 37–70.

Armillas, P. (1964). Northern Mesoamerica. In *Prehistoric Man in the New World*, ed. J. D. Jennings and E. Norbeck, pp. 291–329. University of Chicago Press: Chicago, Ill.

Bennyhoff, J. A. (1967). Chronology and periodization: continuity and change in the Teotihuacán ceramic tradition. In *Teotihuacán, XI Mesa Redonda*, pp. 19–29. Sociedad Mexicana de Antropología: México, D.F.

Bernal, I. (1966). Teotihuacán ¿ Capital de Imperio?, *Revista Mexicana de Estudios Antropológicos* 20: 95–110.

Binford, L. R. (ed.) (1977). *For Theory Building in Archaeology*. Academic Press: New York.

Blalock, H. M. (1979). *Social Statistics*, revised second edition. McGraw-Hill: New York.

Blanton, R. E. (1976). Anthropological Studies of Cities. *Annual Review of Anthropology* 5: 249–64.

Blanton, R. E. (1978). *Monte Albán: Settlement Patterns at the Ancient Zapotec Capital*. Academic Press: New York.

Blucher, D. K. (1971). *Late Preclassic Cultures in the Valley of Mexico: Pre-Urban Teotihuacán*. Ph.D. Thesis. Department of Anthropology, Brandeis University. (University Microfilms, Ann Arbor, Michigan.)

Calnek, E. E. (1976). The internal structure of Tenochtitlan. In *The Valley of Mexico*, ed. E. R. Wolf, pp. 287–302. University of New Mexico Press: Albuquerque, New Mexico.

Carter, G. M. and Rolph, J. E. (1974). Empirical Bayes methods applied to estimating Fire Alarm probabilities. *Journal of the American Statistical Association* 69(348): 880–5.

Chayes, F. (1971). *Ratio Correlation: A Manual for Students of Petrology and Geochemistry*. University of Chicago Press: Chicago, Ill.

Cowgill, G. L. (1967). Evaluación preliminar de la aplicación de metodos de máquinas computadoras a los datos del Mapa de Teotihuacán. In *Teotihuacán, XI Mesa Redonda*, pp. 19–112. Sociedad Mexicana de Antropología: México D.F.

Cowgill, G. L. (1968). Archaeological applications of factor, cluster, and proximity analysis. *American Antiquity* 33: 367–75.

Cowgill, G. L. (1974). Quantitative studies of urbanization at Teotihuacán. In *Mesoamerican Archaeology: New Approaches*, ed. N. Hammond, pp. 363–96. Duckworth: London.

Cowgill, G. L. (1977). Processes of growth and decline at Teotihuacán: the city and the state. In *Los Procesos de Cambio en Mesoamérica y Areas Circunvecinas, XV Mesa Redonda*, vol. 1, pp. 183–93. Sociedad Mexicana de Antropología: México, D.F.

Cowgill, G. L. (1979*a*). Teotihuacán, internal militaristic competition, and the fall of the Classic Maya. In *Maya Archaeology and Ethnohistory*, ed. N. Hammond and G. R. Willey, pp. 51–62. University of Texas Press: Austin, Texas.

Cowgill, G. L. (1979*b*). Politico-economic factors in the disintegration of early states. Paper for Annual Meeting, Society for American Archaeology, Vancouver, B.C. Ms., Brandeis University.

Efron, B. (1975). Biased versus unbiased estimation. *Advances in Mathematics* 16(3): 259–77.

Efron, B. and Morris, C. (1973). Stein's estimation rule and its competitors – An empirical Bayes approach. *Journal of the American Statistical Association* 68(342): 117–30.

Efron, B. and Morris, C. (1975). Data analysis using Stein's Estimator and its generalizations. *Journal of the American Statistical Association* 70(350): 311–19.

Efron, B. and Morris, C. (1977). Stein's Paradox in statistics. *Scientific American* 236(5): 119–27.

Freedman, M. S. (1976). *Barrio definition at Teotihuacán: A preliminary examination*. Paper for Annual Meeting, Society for American Archaeology, St Louis, Ms., Brandeis University.

Gilbert, K. S. (ed.) (1980). *Treasures from the Bronze Age of China: An Exhibition from the People's Republic of China* (The Metropolitan Museum of Art). Ballantine: New York.

Gottscho [Sload], R. S. (1977). Toward more precise status categories at Teotihuacán, Mexico. *Newsletter of Computer Archaeology* 13(1): 1–16.

Keyfitz, N. (1977). *Applied Mathematical Demography*. Wiley: New York.

Klecka, W. R. (1975). Discriminant analysis. In *Statistical Package for the Social Sciences*, second edition, ed. N. H. Nie, C. H. Hull, J. G. Jenkins, K. Steinbrenner and D. H. Bent, pp. 434–67. McGraw-Hill: New York.

Krotser, P. H. (1979). Production and distribution of San Martín Orange Ware: An example of prehistoric specialization. Paper for Annual Meeting, Society for American Archaeology, Vancouver, B.C.

Krotser, P. H. and Rattray, E. (1980). Manufactura y distribución de tres grupos cerámicos de Teotihuacan. *Anales de Antropología* 17(1): 91–104.

Kuhn, T. S. (1970). *The Structure of Scientific Revolutions*, second edition. University of Chicago Press: Chicago, Ill.

Linné, S. (1934). *Archaeological Researches at Teotihuacán, Mexico*, Publication 1, n.s. The Ethnographical Museum of Sweden: Stockholm.

Linné, S. (1942). *Mexican Highland Cultures,* Publication 7, n.s. Ethnographical Museum of Sweden: Stockholm.

Linné, S. (1956). Radiocarbon dates in Teotihuacán. *Ethnos* 2(3–4): 180–93.

McClung de Tapia, E. S. (1979). Plants and Subsistence in the Teotihuacán Valley: A.D. 100–750. Ph.D. Thesis. Department of Anthropology, Brandeis University. (University Microfilms, Ann Arbor, Michigan.)

Miller, A. G. (1973). *The Mural Painting of Teotihuacán.* Dumbarton Oaks Research Library and Collection: Washington, D.C.

Millon, R. (1966). Progress report on the Teotihuacán Mapping Project for the Departamento de Monumentos Prehispánicos, No. 6. Instituto Nacional de Antropología e Historia: México, D.F. (Unpublished.)

Millon, R. (1970a). Teotihuacán: completion of map of giant ancient city in the Valley of Mexico. *Science* 170: 1077–82.

Millon, R. (1970b). Progress report on the Teotihuacán Mapping Project for the Departamento de Monumentos Prehispánicos, No. 10. Instituto Nacional de Antropología e Historia: México, D.F. (Unpublished.)

Millon, R. (1973). *The Teotihuacán Map* Part 1, *Text, Urbanization at Teotihuacán, Mexico.* vol. 1, University of Texas Press: Austin, Texas.

Millon, R. (1974). The study of urbanism at Teotihuacán, Mexico. In *Mesoamerican Archaeology: New Approaches,* ed. N. Hammond, pp. 335–62. Duckworth: London.

Millon, R. (1976). Social relations in ancient Teotihuacán. In *The Valley of Mexico,* ed. E. R. Wolf, pp. 205–48. University of New Mexico Press: Albuquerque, New Mexico.

Millon, R. (1981). Teotihuacán: city, state, and civilization. In *Supplement to the Handbook of Middle American Indians,* vol. 1, *Archaeology,* ed. J. A. Sabloff, pp. 198–243. University of Texas Press: Austin, Texas.

Millon, R., Drewitt, R. B. and Cowgill, G. L. (1973). *The Teotihuacán Map,* Part 2, *Maps, Urbanization at Teotihuacán, Mexico,* vol. 1. University of Texas Press: Austin.

Mosteller, F. and Tukey, J. W. (1977). *Data Analysis and Regression: A Second Course in Statistics.* Addison-Wesley: Reading, Mass.

Müller, F. (1978). *La Cerámica del Centro Ceremonial de Teotihuacán.* Instituto Nacional de Antropología e Historia: México, D.F.

Rattray, E. C. (1973). The Teotihuacán Ceramic Chronology: *Early Tzacualli to Early Tlamimilolpa Phases.* Ph.D. Thesis. Department of Anthropology, University of Missouri. (University Microfilms, Ann Arbor, Michigan.)

Rattray, E. C. (1976). Thin Orange: A Teotihuacán trade ware. Paper for Annual Meeting, Society for American Archaeology.

Rattray, E. (1980). Anaranjado delgado: Cerámica de comercio de Teotihuacán. In *Interacción Cultural en Mexico,* ed. E. Rattray, J. Litvak and C. Diaz, pp. 55–80. Universidad Nacional Autónoma de Mexico: Mexico, D.F.

Rattray, E. C. (1981). The Teotihuacán Ceramic Chronology: Early Tzacualli to Metepec Phases. Ms. for *Urbanization at Teotihuacán, Mexico,* vol. IV, *Ceramics and Chronology,* Part 1, ed. R. Millon. University of Texas Press: Austin, Texas (in press).

Sanders, W. T., Parsons, J. R. and Santley, R. S. (1979). *The Basin of Mexico: Ecological Processes in the Evolution of a Civilization.* Academic Press: New York.

Sayre, E. V. and Harbottle, G. (1979). The analysis by neutron activation of archaeological ceramics related to Teotihuacán: Local wares and trade sherds. Ms., Chemistry Department, Brookhaven National Laboratory, Upton, New York.

Séjourné, L. (1959). *Un Palacio en la Ciudad de los Dioses: Exploraciones en Teotihuacán, 1955–58.* Instituto Nacional de Antropología e Historia: México, D.F.

Séjourné, L. (1966a). *Arqueología de Teotihuacán: La Cerámica.* Fondo de Cultura Económica: México and Buenos Aires.

Séjourné, L. (1966b). *Arquitectura y Pintura en Teotihuacán.* Siglo Ventiuno: México, D.F.

Séjourné, L. and Salicrup, G. (1965). Arquitectura y arqueología. *Revista de la Universidad de México* 19(7): 4–8.

Sload, R. S. (1982). A study of status and function in the Xolalpan–Metepec community at Teotihuacán, Mexico. Ph.D. Thesis. Department of Anthropology, Brandeis University, Waltham, Mass. (University Microfilms, Ann Arbor, Michigan.)

Smith, M. E. (1975). Temples, residences, and artifacts at classic Teotihuacán. Senior Honors Thesis, Department of Anthropology, Brandeis University, Waltham, Mass.

Smith, M. E. (1976). A multivariate analysis of temples and residences in classic Teotihuacán, Mexico. Paper for Annual Meeting, Society for American Archaeology.

Sneath, P. H. A. and Sokal, R. R. (1973). *Numerical Taxonomy: The Principles and Practice of Numerical Classification.* Freeman: San Francisco.

Sotomayor, A. and Castillo C., N. (1963). *Estudio Petrográfico de la Cerámica 'Anaranjado Delgado'.* Pub. 12. Departamento de Prehistoria, Instituto Nacional de Antropología e Historia: México, D.F.

Spence, M. W. (1967). The obsidian industry of Teotihuacán. *American Antiquity* 32: 507–14.

Spence, M. W. (1979). Craft production and polity in Early Teotihuacán. Ms., Department of Anthropology, University of Western Ontario, London, Ontario.

Spence, M. W. (1981). Obsidian production and the state in Teotihuacán. *American Antiquity* 46(4): 769–88.

Spence, M. W., Kimberlin, J. and Harbottle, G. (1979). State controlled procurement and the obsidian workshops of Teotihuacán. Ms., Department of Anthropology, University of Western Ontario, London, Ontario.

Tatsuoka, M. (1970). *Discriminant Analysis: The Study of Group Differences.* Institute for Personality and Ability Testing: Champaign, Ill.

Tolstoy, P. (1958). *Surface Survey of the Northern Valley of Mexico: The Classic and Post-Classic Periods,* vol. 48, Part 5, n.s., Transactions of the American Philosophical Society, Philadelphia.

Vaillant, G. C. (1938). A correlation of archaeological and historical sequences in the Valley of Mexico. *American Anthropologist* 40: 535–73.

Wolf, E. R. (ed.) (1976). *The Valley of Mexico: Studies in Pre-Hispanic Ecology and Society.* University of New Mexico Press: Albuquerque, New Mexico.

Yoffee, N. (1979). The decline and rise of Mesopotamian civilization: an ethnoarchaeological perspective on the evolution of social complexity. *American Antiquity* 44(1): 5–35.

Chapter 11

**Identifying spatial disorder:
a case study of a Mongol fort**
Roland Fletcher

The site, called Taşkun Kale, is the remains of a garrison fort built at some time in the thirteenth–fourteenth centuries A.D. as part of the Ilkhanid Mongol domination of Anatolia (Figs. 1 and 2). The fort was probably intended only to control the local region around the river crossing of the Murat near Aşvan (McNicoll 1973, p. 171). Whatever the original purpose of the fort, its military function seems to have declined during the use of the structure. A fire damaged the southern portion of the fort, after which alterations were made to the Main Gate complex. Access to the passages on either side of the gate was obstructed and rooms were built in the courtyard. The fort was then abandoned. Taşkun Kale was excavated under the direction of Tony McNicoll in 1970, 1971 (McNicoll 1973) and 1973 as part of the Aşvan project (French 1973).

The remains of the fort consist of a roughly oval area enclosed by a thick masonry circuit wall. Towers survive on the southern and western sides of the fort. Entry to the fort was from the south through a single large gateway. Within the circuit wall, room walls of masonry and mud brick are arranged around a central courtyard. The fort is about 40 m long and 30 m wide with the towers projecting about 4 to 5 m from the outer face of the circuit wall. Taşkun Kale is now drowned periodically by the waters of the Aşvan dam.

In 1978 Tony McNicoll asked me to carry out a spatial analysis of the fort. The results of the investigation are published in the excavation report (McNicoll 1983). Details of the structure, occupation, use and development of the fort will be found in that report. The purpose of this paper is to discuss the methodology and the more general consequences of the analysis.

The fort was added to and altered during its use and several possible descriptions of its successive spatial characteristics can be obtained. In addition the site has been affected by post-depositional damage and was, of necessity, selectively excavated. The successive forms of the fort are, in consequence, incompletely represented in the recorded plan. The site offers the opportunity to study spatial changes and to indicate ways in which damage and sampling can affect the study of spatial patterns. Analytic procedures can be pushed as far as possible to assess what policies may help or hinder the investigation of space in archaeological sites. The study of Taşkun Kale is a methodological experiment.

My policy has been to use crude procedures both to handle the problems which result from an inevitable partial representation of the original structures and to describe the arrangement of space in the fort. These procedures could be used during fieldwork and later on in preliminary assessments. One purpose of this paper is to show that *an impression* of the dimensional character of a structure can be obtained by simple methods requiring nothing more than some paper, a writing implement and the ability to add and subtract.

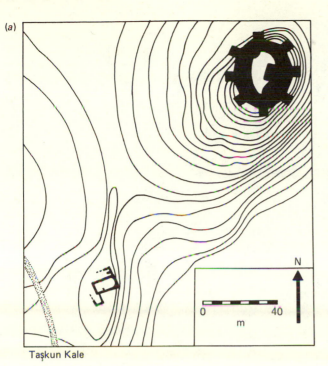

(a)

N

0   40
m

Taşkun Kale

(b)

TK

Anatolia

Fig. 1. (*a*) General site plan and (*b*) regional plan. TK = Taşkun Kale.

The methodology for describing the spatial arrangement is, however, naive and its results suggest several ways in which further rigour and clarification could be introduced.

My overall intention is to assess a proposition that human communities will be liable to generate spatial disorder even if they are trying to produce spatial order. The occurrence of spatial disorder can be understood in terms of a model of the ways in which spatial order is generated. The consequences of spatial disorder can be seen as a corollary of the need for a coherent spatial framework if community life is to remain viable.

The specific role of this chapter is to argue that a simple methodology can identify the absence, as well as the presence, of dimensional order. I then wish to illustrate ways in which a spatial message model can affect our interpretation of the behaviour of human communities, and to indicate how the methodology needs to be made more rigorous and sophisticated.

Basis – the spatial message model

Human beings are habitually able to produce consistent personal spacing behaviour without being fully aware that they are doing so (Hall 1966). Tacit, repetitious ordering of space is an ordinary element of human daily life. People can locate themselves at specific distances relative to other people without being aware that they are doing so, and without using any measuring device other than their eye and brain (Fletcher 1977, p. 49). We can therefore expect that human beings are able to arrange their material spatial context in a similar fashion. Just as personal spacing behaviour is a collection of indicators about how to locate oneself in space, so likewise we can expect that the material form of a settlement should also carry a spatial message of some kind about how space is to be ordered.

Studies of other settlements have indicated that the structures of a settlement act as a communication device transmitting a message about a way in which space can be arranged in the horizontal plane (Fletcher 1980*a*). The message consists of numerous dimensional signals. The width of a door is a signal, a particular dimension. The length of one wall of a room is another signal in the dimensional message of a settlement.

What has appeared from the spatial analyses so far carried out is that, when we obtain central tendency and variation descriptions for the distributions of all the *types* of spacings we can identify in a settlement, those values tend to form a pattern. If the settlement contains many different types of spacings (e.g. door width, room length, room width), then the central tendency values tend to occur in clumps (Fig. 3*a*) (Fletcher 1977, p. 90). Settlement space can apparently carry a dimensional message of considerable redundancy. A given community appears to use very similar spacings to arrange a wide variety of features which may have differing functions and be made of different materials and produced by differing methods of construction. For example, in a settlement, spacings around 3 m might have expression in grave length, room width, length of gaps between timber posts in a platform and so on. In the same settlement spacings around 4 m might occur in room length, courtyard radius, lengths of fencing and the gaps between residence units. What we then find is that these clumps of central tendencies are related to each other in a simple way. The interval or separation between each cluster tends to fall into a regular pattern; for instance each successive interval between the clusters is larger than the preceding interval (Fig. 3*b*). The relationship between these successive intervals can be described by an equation for the regression of the intervals against the central tendencies (see Fig. 4). A shorthand description can then be used by comparing the order of the successive intervals with various standard descriptions of serial patterns e.g. Arithmetic, Geometric and Fibonacci. For example, a *convenient* mnemonic for the pattern in Fig. 5*a* is an Arithmetic series because the successive intervals are approximately constant. An example of an Arithmetic series is 2, 4, 6, 8, 10, 12 . . ., where the constant

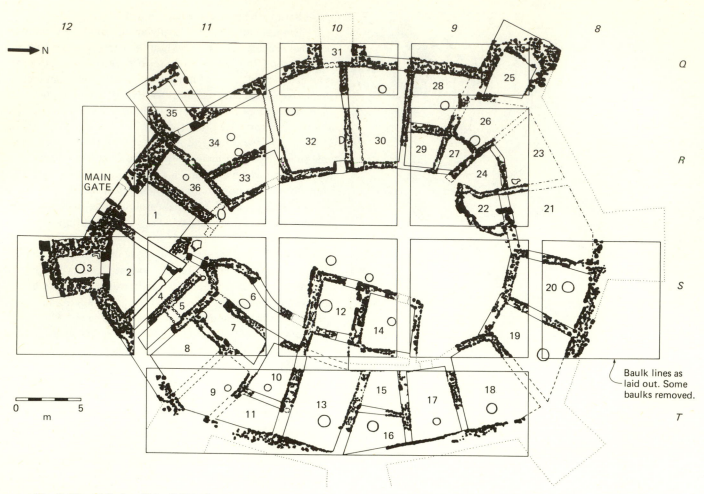

Fig. 2. Plan of Taşkun Kale. Grid indicators are in italic.

interval is 2. By contrast the *convenient* mnemonic for Fig. 5*b* would be a Fibonacci series because the intervals increase with the size of the central tendencies such that each successive central tendency value is the sum of the preceding two central tendencies. An example of a Fibonacci series is 1, 2, 3, 5, 8, 13, 21 . . . .

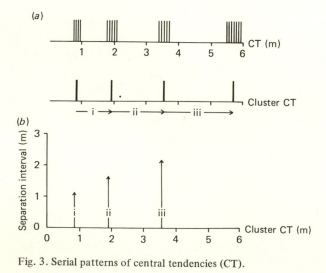

Fig. 3. Serial patterns of central tendencies (CT).

We then have to relate this pattern of central tendencies to the variation values. What we frequently find is that the variation values tend to increase as the central tendencies increase in size (Fig. 4*a*). The nature of the tendency is different for different communities. In terms of a workable message, there is a simple rule relating variation to signals. The clumps of central tendency values linked by the orderly arrangement of intervals are components of a message. Each central tendency clump is different from its neighbours. But the difference depends upon the gap between it and the adjacent clump. The more that gap is narrowed the harder it would be to distinguish between them. What follows is that the variation associated with a central tendency value must be less than the difference between it and its 'nearest' component of the message (Fig. 4*a*) if the differences are to be recognisable to any observer.

This was illustrated in the study of a Ghanaian and an Egyptian settlement (Fletcher 1980*a*) by using the statistical convention of the Mean and Standard Deviation. The result was a trend of variation values less than the major intervals between the successive Means. The important and unexpected result of the studies so far carried out is that situations can arise where some of the intervals in a sequence are less than

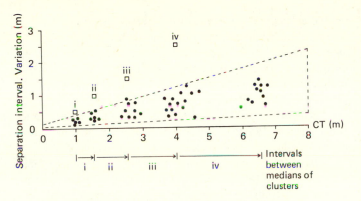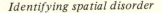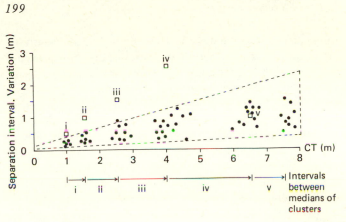

Fig. 4. Variation trends. CT = central tendencies.

the variation values (Fig. 4*b*). What has happened is that the central tendency difference between two adjacent clumps of spacings is less than the variation occurring for those values. In effect, that interval would be unrecognisable to the community because the expected variation is so great that the 'difference' would be insufficiently large to appear as such to them. The dimensional message is coherent up to the central tendencies with which the anomaly occurs. A coherent message can only occur for spacings larger than those involved in the anomaly if the series shifts to much larger intervals, greater than the degree of variation which creates the anomaly (Figs. 4*c*, 5*a*, *b*) (Fletcher 1977, p. 103).

As is plain from these examples there is no inevitability to the relationship between variation and central tendency.

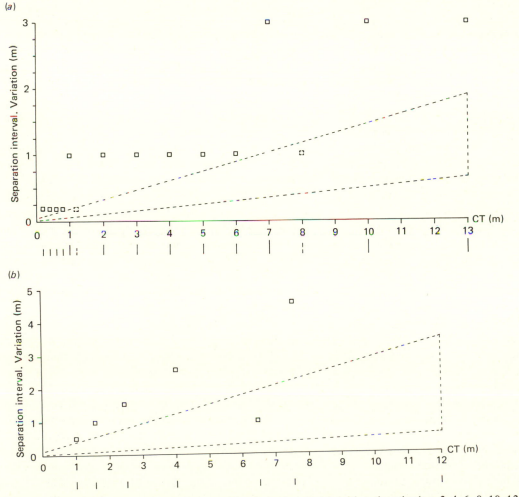

Fig. 5. Relationship between serial patterns and variation trends. (*a*) Arithmetic series (e.g. 2, 4, 6, 8, 10, 12, ...); (*b*) Fibonacci series (e.g. 1, 1, 2, 3, 5, 8, 13, 21, ...). CT = central tendency.

Anomalies of the kind described above can, and apparently do, occur. In the cases described, however, the anomalies do not destroy the overall coherence of the spatial message. But a situation can be envisaged in which the amount of variation associated with the spacing distances in the settlement could be at odds with the intervals of the series of spacing distances. Furthermore, we might also expect loss of serial order. For example, a series 2, 4, 6, 8, 10 could become incoherent with some slight shifts in the spacing distances e.g. 3, 4, 5, 5.5, 8.5, 9. Instead of the interval succession being a constant 2 it has been altered to $1.5 (4.5 - 3)$, $1(5.5 - 4.5)$, $3(8.5 - 5.5)$, $0.5 (9 - 8.5)$. Incoherence can therefore be defined within the terms of this methodology and the description of variation and central tendency which it employs.

(a) If the variation values generally exceed the intervals of the series.

(b) If a variation anomaly occurs with no alteration of series interval size for larger spacings.

(c) If the intervals between clusters of central tendencies cease to be amenable to a simple series description.

At this point it is useful to introduce a version of the concept of 'noise' in communication systems (Cherry 1966, pp. 198–211, 278). This helps to give some idea of the general class of problems caused by incoherence in spatial messages. It also suggests a relationship between energy expenditure and message coherence which offers a general model for the growth and disintegration of the spatial message used by a community.

One difficulty of any message system is signals that are extraneous to the message. A familiar example of 'noise' is the crackling sound coming through a telephone at the same time as the sounds of a conversation. The crackle can become so severe that the conversation is swamped, the words cannot be distinguished from the 'noise'. The 'noise' in a telephone line is a function of various limitations of the way in which the signals of the coherent message are transmitted. If a lot of energy is put into shielding the transmission system from outside interference and into reducing the degeneration of the intended signals then the message will be clear and audible. Message coherence depends upon energy input to control the deleterious effects of transmission.

There is an equivalent situation with spatial messages. In a settlement, the mode of transmission of a spatial message is the construction of structural features. The few initial constructions in a settlement are therefore a weak transmission of the message. The liability is that factors which can affect the form and size of structures will tend to distort or mask any spatial message which the builders might have been tacitly attempting to express. In such a situation the occupants would be living in a spatial context where 'noise' and coherent message could not be unscrambled. However, a spatial message can be made clearer by the addition of further structures, i.e. the expenditure of more energy on message transmission. When some spacing distances are being displayed more frequently than others there will be the basis for a recognisable spatial message. The more features there are carrying the various parts of the message the more redundancy it will possess and the message can be more secure and clear. When a settlement contains many structural features a single oddity created by adverse circumstances or human idiosyncracy will tend to have little effect on the overall message.

The irony of this process of addition and its significance for settlement dynamics is that it need not, in the long run, necessarily lead to further clarification. One of the characteristics of the repeated replication of a message through time is a tendency toward cumulative error, eventually increasing to such a level that the original message is swamped with confusion. Unless large amounts of energy can be put into editing, then the integrity of the message will be lost.

Two possible extreme situations can arise. The first is that order would simply go on cumulating, especially if the community possesses sufficient energy to delete structures, whether old or new, that happen not to fit the prevailing pattern. But more likely is that disorder will in the end increase through time with more and more replication. Some old buildings and features will tend to survive; successive generations of builders will perceive a slightly different spatial context and build in relation to their perception; and editing out structures involves a cost in energy that the community might not be able to sustain *even if* it could consciously recognise an 'out of place' feature.

The implication is that many settlements may never get beyond their early phase of development because the community failed to build up sufficient structures quickly enough to supply a coherent spatial context. Without such a context, the community would lack a predictable milieu for its daily life (Fletcher 1977, p. 107). The theoretical expectation is that the community should cease to function as a viable unit, just as would happen if a basic consensus about other kinds of classifications were lost within a community. If a settlement attains a coherent spatial pattern, we should find later on that it will begin to display loss of spatial order. We might commonly recognise this as the late phase of a settlement shortly before its abandonment. The space in a settlement may therefore go through a cycle from lack of representation of order, to cumulative order and then to cumulative disorder and termination.

Review

It is important to note that there is no implication whatsoever that the community which apparently produced a dimensional message will be aware that it has done so, let alone be aware of the precise mathematical description or the convenient mnemonic which we can use to refer to that message. Material spatial behaviour is such a specific case of the usual characteristic of non-verbal signalling that human beings are rarely aware of its pattern, though they know that such behaviour occurs. Rules of etiquette are the most obvious illustration (Argyle 1975, p. 62). Two characteristics of non-verbal signalling are of particular relevance. The first is that a small number of acts in isolation do not give much clue to regularities in behaviour. Secondly, error is possible. People tend consciously to notice divergence from the expected and they act against it if they have the authority and/or the energy.

Divergence from the expected can always occur. We should not presume that settlements will always produce perfect dimensional order. Individual builders could create structures that might lack a coherent spatial pattern and spatial arrangements could lack pattern when there are so few structures that examples of types of spacings are simply rare. At the other extreme a large number of additions and alterations to a settlement could introduce sufficient errors to obliterate a previously existing pattern. The consequence of persistent loss of spatial message coherence should be the same as the failure of other communication systems. The community should cease to function in the particular settlement that is displaying an incoherent spatial pattern. This does not mean that the human group would necessarily die out. It might, but movement, either individually or as a group, to a different settlement context is an alternative. Ordered spatial messages are not inevitable, they are only to be expected as a corollary of, and necessary basis for, viable community life. If we are to study this interaction we need a methodology which is capable of indicating whether or not a serial pattern and the appropriate associated variation trend occur in a settlement.

PART 1 – ANALYSIS

Research procedure

(i) Analytic procedure

The procedure used is simple and tedious and is an empirical product of work on eight settlements in Ghana. In essence there are two problems in trying to study patterns of signals. First, to find methods of measurement and presentation that will indicate presence or absence of order. Secondly, to assess whether or not any identified regularities describe the thing they are claimed to describe.

Measurement

What to measure is defined by the terms of proxemic analysis (Hall 1968). Proxemics is concerned with spacings between interacting beings and with the relationship between particular spacing distances and particular kinds of social behaviour. The universe of possible measurements is limited to those spacing distances occurring between active, similar linked entities, such as two people in an intimate interaction or the people in a conversation group. The spacing distances are classified in terms of the context in which they occur. Likewise the distances between inert, similar linked entities in settlements are arranged in categories such as door width and room length (Fletcher 1977, pp. 60–7). Diagonals across rooms are not used in this study because they are members of another possible class of space interrelationships.

Presentation

A method of presentation is itself an analytic device, but it is also not the only one possible, nor can any patterns it shows be regarded as the only possible ones. The presentation problem is like the empirical search for the appropriate focal length for a camera lens to produce a sharp picture of the things at which it is pointed. The key feature of this exercise is that as the focal length is altered so different kinds of detail will become visible, ranging down to the microscopic. As you alter the nature of the film you will get a variety of different images of varying clarity not necessarily equivalent with the image that the human eye might pick up from the same object. Only a limited range of camera and film characteristics are any use in producing a clear picture of things at a particular scale, for instance to obtain an overall picture of the features of a landscape.

The same operational characteristics apply to a study of spatial, dimensional phenomena. As you alter the precision of your observation so you will perceive different features and varied relationships between them. For example, as is well known, different class intervals will produce different shapes of distributions from the same sample of values (Fig. 6). What might be regarded as two separate distributions at one class interval could be regarded as one distribution when the same

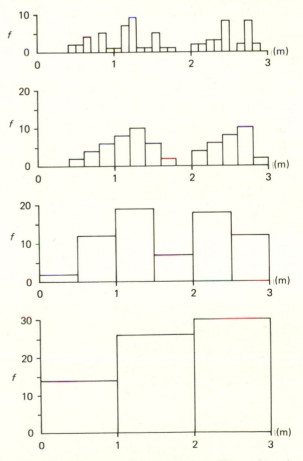

Fig. 6. Class interval and distribution shape. Here and in subsequent similar figures f = frequency.

values are arranged in a larger class interval. Two different descriptions of central tendency and variation could be derived from the two different presentations. Altering the grain of detail produces different kinds of patterns. What is at issue is the grain of detail appropriate to a given enquiry.

A perceiving system like the human eye and brain must inevitably be working on varying criteria of similarity and difference which change according to the precision with which observations are being made. If two objects 10 and 16 cm long are being assessed for similarity or difference in terms of length, then at a grain of detail equivalent to a 5 cm class interval they would be presented as different. Those same objects, when their size is presented at a 10 cm class interval from 10–20 cm are similar. There can be no absolute standard of similarity and difference for a perceiving device, only a statement relative to the grain of detail being used.

Three main points follow from this relativity. One is that there can be many different descriptions of the regularities occurring in a spatial arrangement. If you are close enough to a tapestry to see the warp and weft distinctly, you will not, at the same time, be able to see the entire pattern of the colours of the tapestry. What kind of pattern is recognised, if any, depends upon the grain of observational detail being used. Another consequence is that, when comparing a variety of things of the same type, for example various settlements, you need to be consistent in the grain of observation detail which you use otherwise you will be comparing different levels of detail. The third point is that you must likewise apply a consistent analytic procedure and grain of detail to a site. If you do not, you will be mixing up patterns which relate to different levels of detail within the settlement. The result will probably be very confusing.

The grain of detail used in this study is expressed in a presentation using a 20 cm class interval. This interval has been applied to the other settlements in which serial patterns associated with coherent variation trends have been recognised for spacings of up to 6–8 m. The interval is an empirical product of research on several settlements and I am now using it as a standard comparative procedure. There is no claim that it is the only scale of operational detail which should be used, nor need we presume that dimensional ordering is only expressed at this level of detail.

The procedure used in this study is merely *one way* of perceiving settlement space, a policy which appears to work as a description of the dimensional aspect of spatial behaviour by human groups in settlements. It probably would not work for the description of individual activity and might well be inappropriate if the analysis was to be restricted to any one of the residence units in a settlement. The crude analogy is that you would not expect to obtain a photo-micrograph if you use the lens, focal length, exposure and film that provides you with excellent landscape photographs.

The problem of 'noise'

We have to cope with the distorting effects of post-

depositional damage and selective excavation, and with the 'noise' created by the occupants of the settlement. Some of the former effects can be handled by a reconstruction procedure (see Reconstruction policy, p. 205). But even then the effects of post-depositional damage cannot be either obviated or ignored. Plainly an analysis of minutiae is unlikely to be worthwhile, since the studied sample must be presumed to incorporate idiosyncratic acts by the original occupants, combined with the effects of damage on particular parts of the site.

This is indeed what we find. If distributions with sample sizes of two examples are used to obtain central tendency values, then no dimensional order is evident. Likewise if distributions with fewer than five values are used to obtain variation values then no trend is evident. What appear are low variation values for all central tendencies up to about 10 m. The trend of increasing variation which we might expect at some period in the growth of the fort is swamped. The minimum distribution sample sizes are therefore set at three or more for a central tendency to be obtained, and five or more for a variation value.

Similarly, the specifications for dividing polymodal distributions into their unimodal components cannot be subtle either. Frequency of occurrence in modes, and distance between modes cannot be used in a simple procedure. The use of such attributes would involve the use of statistical descriptions of distribution shape. Rather, the method has to concentrate on the least frequently occurring dimensional values. If we ignore class intervals which contain no dimensional values then no serial or variation patterns are evident among the identifiable distributions. The minimal requirement is that a class interval with no dimensional value in it has to be regarded as a divide between distributions.

Dealing with the 'bridge' values between two modes requires more discussion. Take an ideal situation where the dimensional values are arranged into distinct and discrete modes (Fig. 7a). The pattern of peak occurrences is apparent. But this could be somewhat blurred by the addition of two values in every class interval (Fig. 7b). Plainly, the peaks have not disappeared. But unless some rule is devised to deal with the general but low incidence of values in all the intervals, a description of the entire collection of values can result in only one central tendency description and one variation value, as if the pattern were being described at the grain of detail expressed by a 1 m class interval (Fig. 7c). We need to find out whether or not a simple procedure can be devised to deal with the 'noise' so that the finer detail at the smaller class interval can also be described. A procedure is needed, appropriate to the grain of detail, which will tend to suppress the noise but not obliterate the possible message. Obviously the selectivity with which noise can be handled by a crude procedure will be limited. A crude method is liable to wipe out the message as well! The procedure is the equivalent of adjusting the treble control on a radio to reduce the amount of hiss. If you try to cut out all the 'noise' you also suppress some of the treble

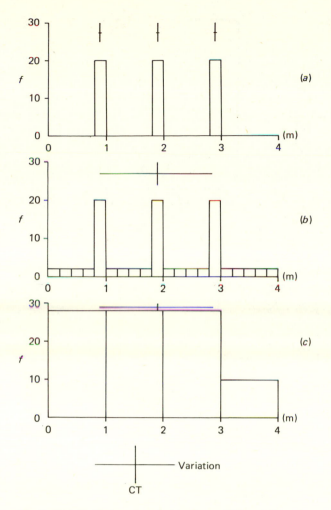

Fig. 7. 'Noise' effects and central tendency (CT) variation descriptions.

sounds of the music thereby missing part of the message which is being transmitted.

The policy must avoid being too gross otherwise the message may also be suppressed. If the restriction on 'noise' is not sufficiently vigorous then 'noise' will prevail. In Taşkun Kale, if a single value occurrence in a class interval is regarded as sufficient to define a divide between distributions, then no serial or variation pattern can be identified. This criterion for suppressing 'noise' would appear to be insufficiently vigorous. The policy chosen therefore specifies that a 'bridge' between two modes is to be identified when *at least* two adjacent class intervals each contain one dimensional value. This 'bridge' is split to create two distributions (Fig. 8).

Many possible ways of coping with 'noise' could be devised, some of them highly sophisticated statistical operations. While I am in no doubt that these will ultimately be necessary, my purpose now is much simpler. All I aim to do is show that a minimum arbitrary ruling, consistently applied, can be used to provide an indication of the presence or absence of dimensional order. It has to be shown that the suppression of 'noise' procedure does not inevitably predefine either the occurrence of order or disorder. Since presence and absence of order are recognisable in the Taşkun Kale data, the latter requirement is satisfied.

A related problem is the issue of the changes in distribution shape which can occur over time. Two initially separate distributions can, by successive additions, be transformed into a single continuous distribution (Fig. 9). But, temporarily, the two merging distributions could be described *either* as one or two distributions. Conversely a single distribution can be split by successive deletions or additions to create two distributions from one. In all such ambiguous cases which occur in Taşkun Kale, both the separate and combined descriptions

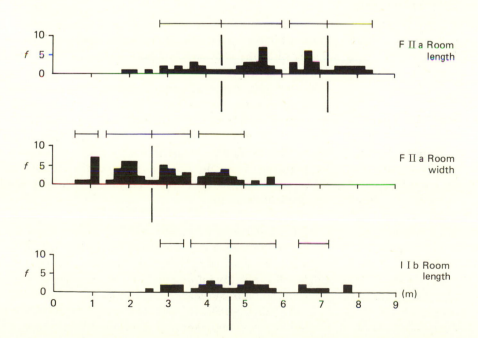

Fig. 8. Splitting polymodal distributions. Examples from Taşkun Kale (see Figs. 12 and 13).

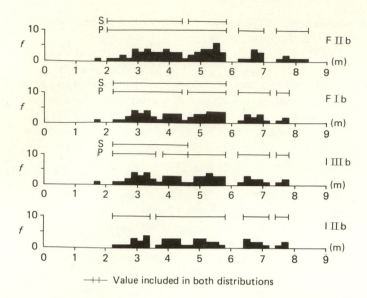

Fig. 9. Merging of distributions. Room width examples from Taşkun Kale (see Figs. 12 and 13). P = primary values; S = secondary values.

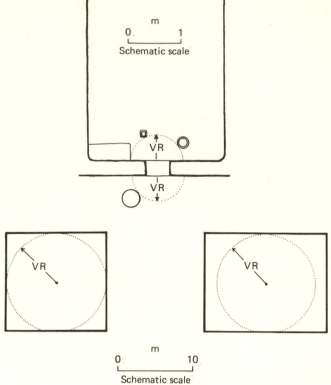

Fig. 10. Visual ranges (VR). The lower two diagrams show how the visual range is controlled by room width.

are given. The alternatives are ranked. When the preceding state shows separate distributions, the separate descriptions are given greater emphasis, and vice versa when the preceding state shows one distribution.

Describing the distributions

The early studies of dimensional order (Fletcher 1980*a*) used a Mean (M) and Standard Deviation (SD) description of central tendency and variation as a convention even though the distributions are not Gaussian Normal. An alternative and simpler description was sought which would give the same trend of variation as the M and SD. It was found that a Median and 40% range description could be substituted (Fletcher 1977, pp. 96–7). Such a description can be produced quickly and easily and requires no mathematical ability beyond subtraction.

Assessing the proposed serial pattern

Identifying dimensional order in a settlement is not a sufficient exercise in itself. What is required is a demonstration that the proposed order tells us something about the pattern of space in the settlement. We have to be able to assess whether or not the implications of a defined series have some correspondence with other descriptions of space in the settlement. In previous studies, a crosscheck has been provided by looking at the location of features in relation to visual commencement points and the visual fields around those points (Fletcher 1977, p. 98, 99; 1980*a*). For example, when you are standing in a doorway you are located at a visual commencement point looking out into some adjacent space which contains the visual field around the door. What we tend to find is that there is a clear area immediately in front of the door. That open area is bounded by the occurrence of features

such as fireplaces and seating platforms. I shall refer to the distance from the door to the nearest features as a visual range. It is this distance which is used as a crosscheck on the dimensional series (Fig. 10).

The argument is that breaks in the dimensional series such as the shift to a new serial sequence (Fig. 5) should be reflected in the areal layout of the features in a settlement. The break in the series suggests that the distance at which the break occurs should be expressed as a boundary of some kind in relation to a visual commencement point. If, for instance, a new series begins for spacings of about 1 m we should find that a marked difference in the arrangement of areal space should occur in an arc about 1 m away from the doorways of the settlement. In other words we would expect to see some expression of visual ranges of about 1 m in the settlement. If such a visual range did not occur then the serial analysis would be called into question.

(ii) Site plan (see Fig. 2)

The study of Taşkun Kale has been carried out entirely from the plan supplied by Tony and Tamara McNicoll (McNicoll 1983). My information about it comes by personal communication from them.

Wherever possible the aim of a spatial analysis should be to use as many kinds of spacings and features as possible. Taşkun Kale poses several problems. The plan is partial, because of post-occupational disturbance (damage) and the necessities of selective excavation. It is also a palimpsest of walls and domestic fittings. Rooms have been added, walls altered and features built on top of each other in the rooms and the courtyard. Fortunately, in Taşkun Kale, though some corners of rooms are missing, the wall alignments are usually available. A procedure can be applied on the plan to renovate the corners. This procedure also serves to provide plans of earlier states of the fort which have been affected by later additions.

Irretrievable damage to walling and the lack of a secure sequence for the domestic fittings such as *tandir* (hearth ovens) have to be accepted as liable distorting factors. The analysis is predicated on an opinion that spatial order should be recognisable even through such distortion. Spatial messages fortunately appear to possess a high degree of redundancy. For example, any one value in a series is usually repeated by dimensions from several types of spacings (Fletcher 1977, p. 90). We might, therefore, expect to recognise spatial patterns even when damage has reduced the available variety of types of spacings and features in a site. Likewise, even though a palimpsest and damage may have blurred the positioning of entities relative to visual commencement points, by the superpositioning of features and the disappearance of doorways, we might expect that enough will survive for the assessment of serial pattern in comparison to visual ranges.

Ironically the logical requirement for identifying spatial disorder is severe. While damage could make the sample so partial that insufficient evidence for pattern would survive, demonstrating the presence of spatial disorder requires positive evidence. The analysis has to show that dimensional and variation values *present in the site* are consistent with spatial disorder. Absence of possible parts of a series would not be acceptable evidence of disorder. Absence merely makes decision impossible. A purpose of this analysis is to show that disorder can be identified and to assess how much damage can be accepted because of the compensatory effect of the redundancy in spatial messages.

Reconstruction policy

Introduction

The fort has suffered varying degrees of damage in different sectors and is also excavated to varying degrees of completeness depending upon the arrangement of the excavation grid. These two factors result in the plan of parts of the site being irretrievably uncertain while other sectors can be reconstructed with little appeal to unknowns. I have therefore chosen a standard reconstruction procedure and have then pointed out the various parts of the site for which reconstruction becomes increasingly uncertain. The magnitude of this uncertainty is described in terms of three degrees of 'repair'. The first degree requires only limited extrapolation of wall alignment. The second degree requires

much longer extrapolations, while in the third degree decisions have to be made about some termini of wall lines.

Procedure

Throughout the plan I have specified as a reconstruction procedure that walls continue on their known track through baulks and across the areas of damage. Straight line projection of the wall direction and parallel correspondence of the opposite sides of walls are used where no other information is available to complete the shapes of some rooms. Straight lines and parallels are used *not* because they are correct, but because they can be applied with consistency. The key corollary of this policy is that walls in Taşkun Kale do *not* run absolutely straight nor are their opposite sides precisely parallel. The restoration procedure does not therefore inevitably guarantee an exact correspondence between the remnant and restored parts of the site. Nor could it be said inevitably to express the same spatial pattern, since no exact correspondence of the restoration and the original walls they represent could be expected. The analytic sacrifice is the price for a consistent procedure which puts the plan into a form usable for a dimensional spatial analysis but does *not* predefine the identification of spatial order.

An additional rule is that no invention can be made of walls entirely concealed by baulks. Such walls could occur in Rooms 6, 13, 28 and 30. Having made the rule, I then have to make one exception! The necessity arose because of the location of the baulk between Rooms 10 and 11 (Fig. 2). In my opinion this baulk must conceal a transverse wall. There is no other case of a transverse wall in Taşkun Kale terminating in this way to produce an L-shaped room. Such a room would be a severe anomaly in the arrangement of rooms around the courtyard (Fig. 11). The position of the wall is delimited by a block which projects from the inner face of the circuit wall and the position of the wall between 33 and 32.

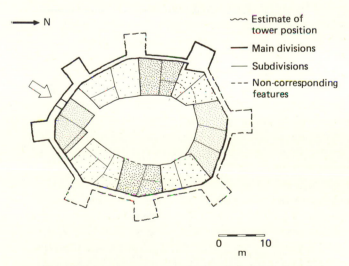

Fig. 11. Room arrangement at Taşkun Kale. Equivalent State sectors are shaded in the same way. The large arrow indicates the Main Gate.

Table 1. *Sequence of probable States of reconstruction at Taşkun Kale (see Fig. 12)*

Abbreviations	States	Notes
End	End State	Site as excavated.
F II	Final II	Rooms added after fire.
F I	Final I	Damaged by fire.
I III	Initial III	See alternative in Start State III.
I II	Initial II	See alternative in Start State II.
I I	Initial I ⎫	Alternative States. Both could not
S III	Start State III ⎭	occur in one actual structural sequence.
S II	Start State II	Rooms 4 and 5 might also be included.
S I	Start State I	Rooms 4 and 5 might also be included.

The product of this first degree of 'repair' is the End State of the Site. Longer, straight-line extrapolation of wall line is required, the second degree of 'repair', to restore the shape of Rooms 8, 9, 11, 18, 19 and 28. It also defines the limits, of 1, 4, 5, 36, 16 and 27 and 24 prior to the room additions in the courtyard in Final II (see sequence in Table I).

The third degree of 'repair' requires a decision about the position of the north-west sector of the circuit wall. The two ends of the inner face of the circuit wall can be derived from the shape of the tower around Room 25 and the fragment of circuit wall in Room 21. This third stage of repair, restores the shape of Rooms 21, 23 and 26. The measurements from this relatively uncertain third stage are identified on the distributions.

The State descriptions from Start State I to Final II are derived from the second and third degree reconstructions.

Sequence (Table 1, Fig. 12)

The interior of the fort has been so disturbed by ploughing that only the broad outline of structural development can be obtained from the vertical stratigraphy. However, the general trend of interior additions can be derived from the layout of the rooms, the various abutments, rearrangements of access and different kinds of wall construction.

To carry out the analysis several procedural restrictions are necessary. First we have to assume as a parsimonious rule, to prevent free invention, that the fort has never contained any major stone or mud brick wall features for which evidence has been completely eradicated. Secondly, the sequence cannot usefully be described in terms of additions of single rooms. Such a policy would require the presentation of a large number of possible room combinations. The effort would be to little gain. A message model does not require that every addition will be consistent with the existing message, only that the persisting occupation of the settlement will require the adjustment of anomalies. Assessment is needed not at the level of each addition as it occurred but rather of various overall States that the fort may have passed through. This will suffice to find out whether or not the methodology can pick up loss of order as an overall characteristic of the site.

The fort appears to have been altered on several occasions. Most obvious is the asymmetrical arrangement of Rooms 6, 12, 14 and 22 (Fig. 2) within the courtyard space. Their late occurrence is evident from the stratigraphy. Several possible development sequences can be suggested for the earlier development of the internal arrangements of Taşkun Kale. These are all based on the premise that the circuit wall and Main Gate were completed first and that additions were then made within that circuit. The sequence proposed depends upon the overall symmetry of the fort around the Main Gate and courtyard. Commencing at the Main Gate, two wings of rooms extend around the periphery of the fort and meet at the far end of the courtyard. Successive additions of rooms can therefore have occurred, starting by the Main Gate and ending with the completion of a continuous zone of rooms. After that, the infilling of the courtyard space would have begun (Fig. 12).

The main problem with the sequence is that several End State rooms can be regarded as subdivisions of larger room spaces, for example 28 and 29 or 15 and 16. There is no way of knowing from the features we have so far recognised in the site or the stratigraphy whether these possible subdivisions occurred early or late or scattered through the development of the fort. To cope with this problem I have chosen to present the distributions from each of the possible States of the fort in two forms, without the subdivisions (Condition 'a') and with them (Condition 'b') (Fig. 13). In Condition 'a', for example, 28 and 29 are treated as one room with two long walls running between the courtyard and the circuit wall, and two short wall sides, one at the courtyard end and the other at the circuit wall end. By contrast, in Condition 'b' this room space 28/29 is regarded as two separate rooms each with two long walls and two short walls. The subdivision values are introduced for the earliest State that could include them. Final II b is the terminal form of both conditions.

Another problem is the alterations made to the Main Gate (1) (Fig. 2). On some unknown occasion a thick wall was built across the internal access to the gate. In Start State I, I have assumed that the access was uninterrupted. In Final II that blocking wall is an inherent part of the alterations to the

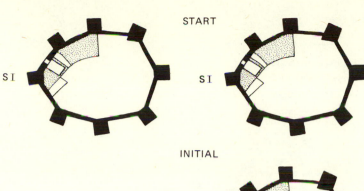

START

S I   S I

INITIAL

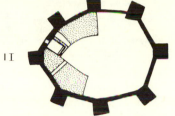

I I

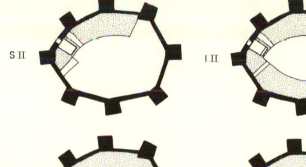

S II   I II

S III   I III

FINAL

F I

N

0   20
m

F II

Tower and circuit wall

Main gate

Roof area

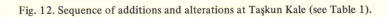

Fig. 12. Sequence of additions and alterations at Taşkun Kale (see Table 1).

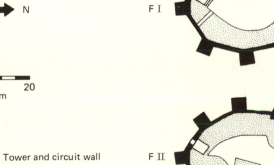

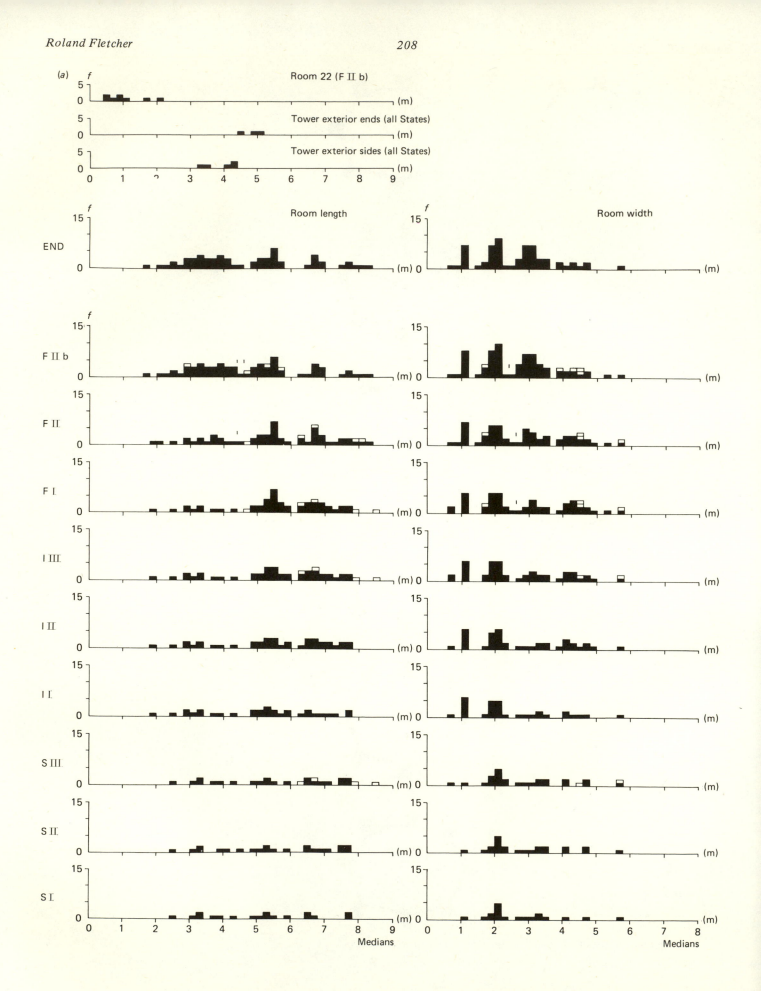

(a)

f   Room 22 (F II b)

Tower exterior ends (all States)

Tower exterior sides (all States)

f   Room length   f   Room width

END

F II b

F II

F I

I III

I II

I I

S III

S II

S I

Medians   Medians

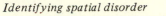

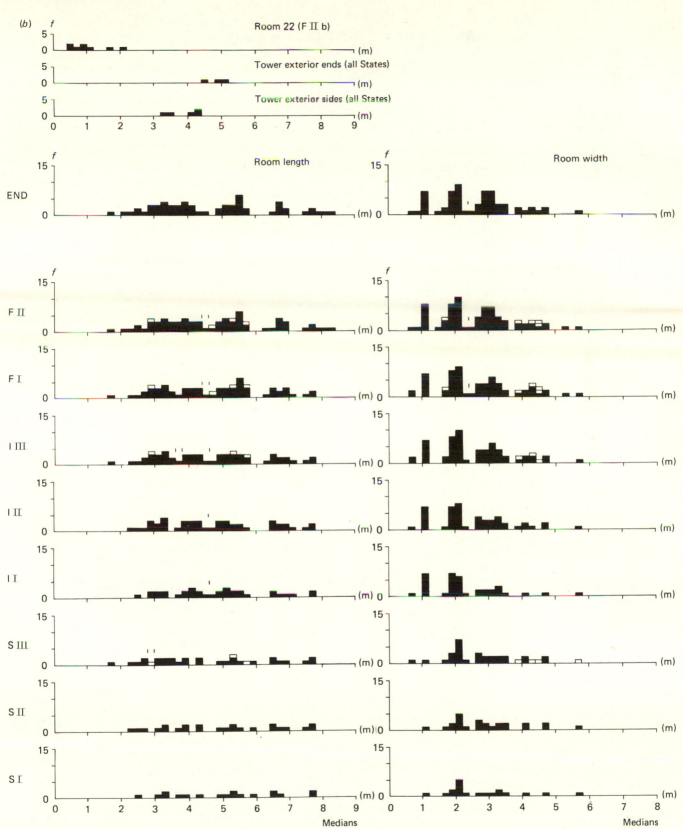

Fig. 13(*a–b*). Sequence of distributions of room widths and lengths at Taşkun Kale.

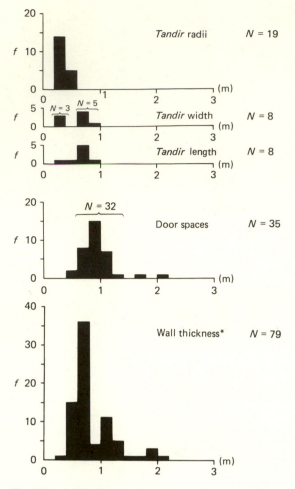

Fig. 14(*a–c*). Distribution for spacings with median values less than 1 m at Taşkun Kale. In (*a*), 'oven' in room 3 (see Fig. 2) is excluded; *tandir* in room 20 (see Fig. 2) is included in radii and width/length. In (*c*), wall thickness is taken at the midpoint of each wall of each room. See Fig. 12 for tower extension sides.

	N	*M* (m)	40% range
Tandir radii	19	0.30	0.12
Tandir width	3	0.35	–
	5	0.66	0.04
Tandir length	8	0.64	0.17
Door space width	32	0.90	0.16

(i) *Tandir* occur in two forms, round and oval. Some of the oval *tandir* also have one straight side or have other features attached to them, e.g. the ribs projecting from the *tandir* by the access to the Main Gate. The dimensions were taken from the external edges of the lip of the *tandir*.
(ii) Door space width refers to the gap which may have contained a door. If the doors had wooden frames then the median would be smaller, possibly about 70 cm.
(iii) For Room 22 in Final II and the End State there is a median of 75 cm and a 40% range value of 30 cm for wall dimensions.

courtyard area. It is therefore included in Final II a and b. For the other States the open access is allocated to the form without subdivision, Condition 'a', and the blocked access to Condition 'b', the form with subdivision.

No claim is being made that the fort actually developed by shifts from one State to the next. The proposed sequence, with its two alternative conditions of 'room amalgamation' (Condition 'a') and 'room subdivision' (Condition 'b') is intended only to provide possible descriptions of a number of forms through which the fort *could* have passed. Assessment of the change in spatial pattern in the fort is made on the basis of the range of possible forms, not from a claim that one particular sequence of additions actually occurred. There is some uncertainty about the layout of the fort which has to be accepted in the description, since there is no apparent way to remedy the problem. To seek more precision would be to demand too much of the battered remains of the fort.

The proposed sequence is therefore a succession of frozen moments in what may have been a continuous and gradual development. Assessment is directed at the broad characteristics of the two alternative Conditions of the successive States. The characteristics of the sequence are reviewed in the light of the dimensional analysis.

Review

The methodology proceeds from a conventionalised reconstruction procedure which is used to bring the fragmentary plan into a usable form. From the layout of the fort and its internal structural characteristics, a broad sequence of development states can be proposed. The states of this sequence have to be presented, of necessity, in two alternative conditions of subdivided and amalgamated room space. No evidence is available on when or even whether particular room subdivisions took place. Measurements of wall dimensions, door width and size of *tandir* (hearth ovens) were obtained from the reconstructed plan. The distributions of these various measurements are presented using a 20 cm class interval and are processed to control for 'noise' whether from the behaviour of the occupants or from post-depositional effects. Central tendency and variation descriptions are given in terms of Median and 40% range. These values are now analysed to find out whether or not serial arrangements of medians and trends of increasing variation with increase in median values occur in the successive states of the fort.

Results

Introduction

One of the main problems with the dimensional analysis of Taşkun Kale is the scarcity of central tendency values compared to those present in other settlements. Since a serial sequence is usually represented by clusters of central tendencies around consecutive modal values the poor representation in any one State can itself be expected to produce small sample ambiguities. To deal with the problem of under-representation, I have presented the data in terms of the occurrence of central tendencies over time (Fig. 15 *a*, *b*). These data have been presented in two ways so that the sequence of central tendencies can be easily seen (Fig. 15*a*)

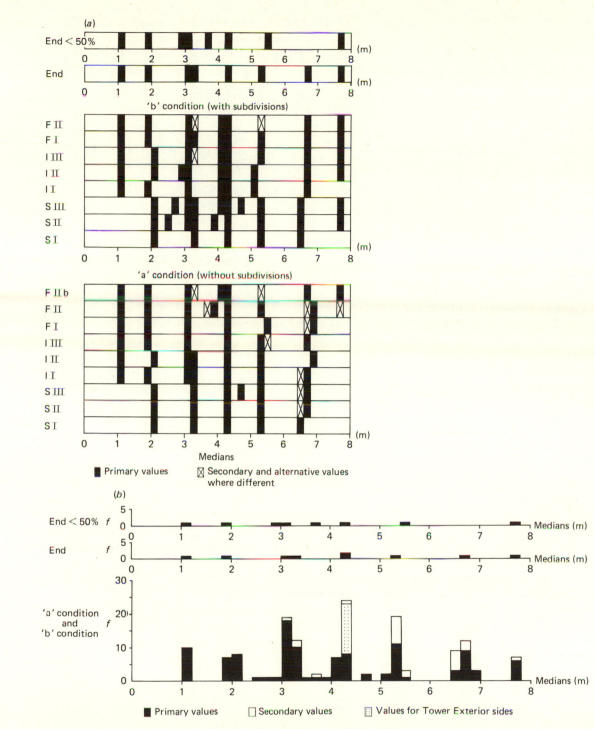

Fig. 15(a–b). Sequence and frequency of medians (1 to 8 m) at Taşkun Kale.

and by frequency of occurrence of the medians so that the most powerful overall signals during the growth of the fort can be recognised (Fig. 15 b). All that can be shown is that some central tendency values are frequently repeated, with a shift toward larger intervals between the larger central tendencies until the 7.70 m values are reached. No definitive description of a series is possible. Nor would the description have much meaning. The recurrent central tendencies can be envisaged as lying in a fuzzy band of values around each com-

ponent of a series. All that can be stated is that the increment of the intervals is small, resembling an Arithmetic series.

(i) Description of the distributions

0 to 1 m central tendencies
In Final II/End State, the medians for door space width, *tandir* dimensions and Room 22 do not produce any readily recognisable pattern (Figs. 13, 14). Wall thickness shows a

marked peak between 60 cm and 80 cm and a lesser peak at 1–1.20 m (Fig. 14). There is insufficient data to claim any series pattern between 0 and 1 m. Though there may be indications of clusters around 30–35 cm and 64–66 cm (if we leave out the 75 cm median for Room 22) there are still not enough values to claim that a particular series can be identified.

1 to 8 m central tendencies (*Fig. 15*a, b)

Throughout the successive States there are medians at approximately 2.00, 3.10, 4.20, 5.30, 6.60 m. There are insufficient dimensions to display a 1 m median in any of the Start States but this median value appears in every other State of the fort. A 7.70 m median is absent from Start State I, Initial I, and Initial II a, III a and Final I a but is present in all the other States and Conditions.

The 'a' condition displays a repetitious pattern of medians except in Start State III, where there is a 4.70 m median, and in Final II, where there is a loss of coherence with the appearance of medians of about 3.70 m which lie between the recurrent median values, 3.20 and 4.30 m. These intervening medians break up the rough series of intervals.

The 'b' condition displays a repetitious pattern of medians except in Start States II and III b. The 3.10 m and 4.20 m values are more strongly represented than in the 'a' condition. The interval is reduced by a 3.30 m value in Final I and Start State III.

40% Range variation (*Fig. 16*)

The variation trend for Start State I contains only three values. And the other Start States do not clearly display the expected trend of variation.

From Initial I onwards a trend from low variation values with small medians to large variation with larger medians occurs throughout the 'a' condition. In the 'b' condition only Initial I and II display the trend of variation. Initial III b, Final I b, and Final II b, all have high variation values for medians around 3 and 4 m, which are inconsonant with the expected trend of variation.

Discussion

Start States I and IIa display serial pattern but the variation trend is poorly represented. However, if only two further rooms, 4 and 5, are added, Start States I and IIa do display a variation trend. Start State III always lacks serial pattern (Fig. 16). From Initial I onwards, the 'a' condition displays both serial pattern and the variation trend, except that in Final II the serial pattern breaks down. By contrast, the 'b' condition displays the serial pattern but involves severe dissonance in the variation trends from Initial III onwards.

The main points of the analysis are:

1. The Final II State, whether in the 'a' or 'b' condition, lacks either serial pattern or a coherent trend of variation. The loss of order is the result of the presence of new features. It is not caused by damage deleting components of the earlier pattern.

2. The subdivision of rooms (Condition 'b') appears to lead to a breakdown of the trend of variation in the later States of the fort. While it is not possible to be specific about particular alterations, the general implication is that the subdivisions did not assist the occurrence of an ordered spatial environment.

3. The construction of the courtyard complex in Final State II, with its alterations to adjacent rooms, contributes to the loss of serial pattern and the break-up of the variation trend.

4. The Start States underrepresent the possible pattern. But the slight addition of Rooms 4 and 5 gives Start States I and IIa a clear variation trend as well as a serial pattern. Both Initial Ia and Start State IIa are equally likely moves in the early development of the fort, if Rooms 4 and 5 were added first. Start State III does not appear to be a probable State of the fort, according to the spatial message model.

(ii) Visual ranges

Introduction

In previously analysed settlements there have been disjunctions in the serial pattern where the intervals of the series have coincided with the rising trend of variation.

There could apparently be many different forms of this relationship between the series interval and the trend of variation. In a near-Arithmetic series there should be abrupt jumps in the series interval size to keep above the rising trend of variation (Fig. 5a).

In Taşkun Kale it is apparent that the overall trend of variation in Final II swamps the separations between the medians of less than 1 m (Fig. 17). The only separation value which lies above the trend is a 29 cm separation between medians for *tandir* width and length. A series with an interval of 29 cm would be swamped by the variation trend near the 1 m median. Though we do not have any direct evidence for the nature of *any* series up to 1 m, we do know that no interval in such a series could have been larger than about 30 cm. The jump to the much larger interval from 1 m onward becomes explicable as the formation of a 'new' series above the trend of variation.

For the earlier States of the fort the same circumstances then arise somewhere beyond the 6.60 m value, possibly for that value but more likely at and beyond the 7.70 m median, where the series interval is again swamped by the rising trend of variation (Fig. 17a). There are then odd dimensional values scattered between 8.80 m and 13.45 m. These values derived from the internal and external façades of the circuit wall. They cannot be ordered into a series by the present methodology. The serial interval allows a median at approximately 8.80 to 9 m. Its only representatives are the façades between towers (35), (31) and (25). The only indication of a further series beyond the 1 to 8 m values is the occurrence of a few widely separated values (Table 2).

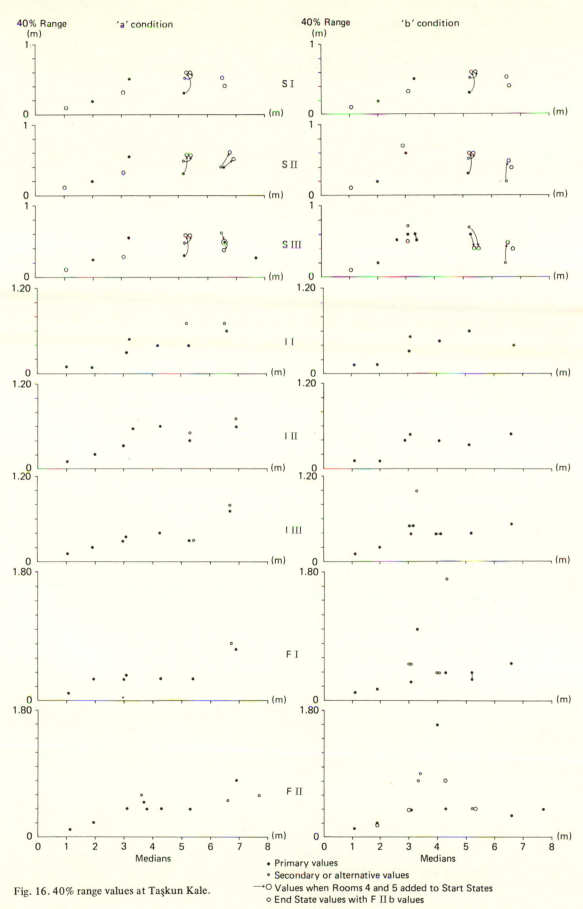

Fig. 16. 40% range values at Taşkun Kale.

- • Primary values
- ◦ Secondary or alternative values
- →O Values when Rooms 4 and 5 added to Start States
- o End State values with F II b values

Table 2. *Visual ranges greater than 8 m in Taşkun Kale*

15 m	Internal courtyard width.
	Distance between centres of towers
24 m	Internal courtyard length
38 m	External fort width
46 m	External fort length

We only have concrete evidence for a serial pattern of some kind from 1 to 8 m, with a break at either end. The 1 m break is more clearly defined than the 7.70 m limit. The 7.70 m limit is swamped by the high variation values of Initial III b and Final II b (Fig. 17*b*).

Visual ranges

The limiting values of the serial pattern should have expression in the settlement, either as a visual range out from a visual commencement point like a doorway or as the distance from the centre to the edge of an open space.

1 m visual range. An indication of a 1 m visual range occurs around the doorways. All the *tandir* inside rooms occur

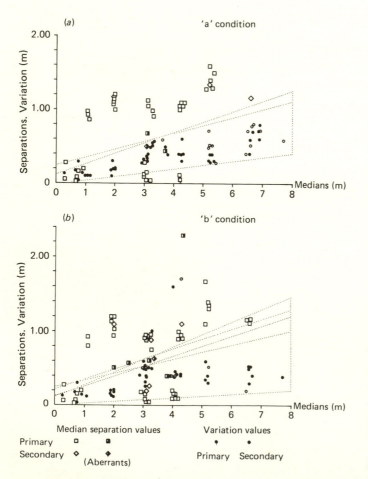

Fig. 17(*a–b*). Medians and 40% range (0 to 8 m) at Taşkun Kale. End and Start III States are excluded.

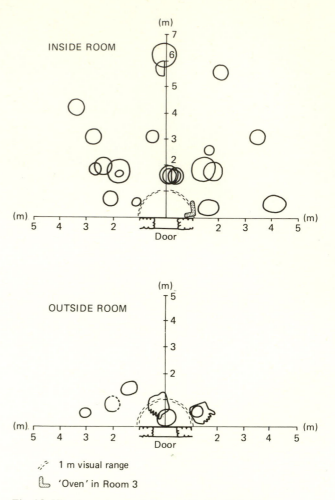

Fig. 18. Visual range around doors at Taşkun Kale. Note that storage jars and pits do not conform to a 1 m visual range. Also, in subdivided room spaces 10/11, 15/16, 26/27 and 28/29, four *tandir* lie close to a wall; access may have been through the roof or through other walls.

at or beyond 1 m from the nearest doorway (Fig. 18*a*). There is one aberrant *tandir*, located in a door space, in the gap leading from room 4 into room 5 and a unique *tandir* in Room 3 which lies across the 1 m visual range.

External *tandir* do not conform to the 1 m zone (Fig. 18*b*). The entries to 4 and 36 are obstructed by *tandir*, though access to and from the Main Gate is clear. These external *tandir* and the *tandir* in the entry to 5 are all late features, structurally associated with alterations made in Final II.

Suggested features. One perplexing feature of Taşkun Kale is that none of the *tandir* is located within 1 m of the inner face of the circuit wall (Fig. 19). If all the *tandir* occurred more than 1 m away from the nearest wall then patterning of space in the rooms would suffice as the explanation. There might, for instance, have been an entirely clear 1 m zone around the edges of the rooms. But several *tandir*, storage jars and pits occur in that zone. Whatever explanation is used, it must therefore involve some specific feature of the relationship between the *tandir* and the circuit wall. The

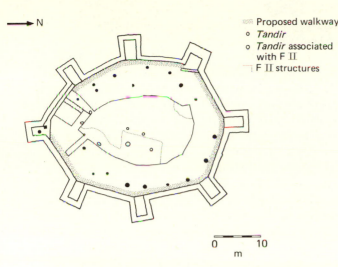

Fig. 19. *Tandir* and the circuit wall as Taşkun Kale. In Figs. 19–24 the towers are schematic.

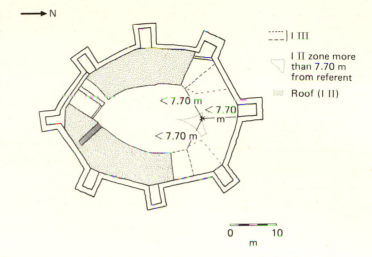

Fig. 21. Visual range in courtyard at Taşkun Kale Initial State III.

implication is that the positions of the *tandir* were also marked at roof level, perhaps by vents for smoke. The vents would have delimited a 1 m wide walk-way behind the parapet. Note that this is not a rationalist argument. Many communities tolerate smoky rooms. The use of roof vents is neither inevitable nor necessarily sensible. Even at 1 m away from the parapet anyone could have tripped over the vents or stepped backwards onto them. Whether or not the vents were present cannot be decided by arguments on what would have been sensible, only by references to the archaeological record. Fragments of such vents should be identifiable.

7.70 m visual range. The most marked correspondence in the spatial pattern of the fort is that the maximum median

distance present in the rooms of the fort is also the limit of visual range on the roof and in the courtyard. The visual commencement points on the roof are the access positions from the towers onto the roof. From those points a visual field extends about 7.70 m to the marked visual limit produced by the edge of the roof (Fig. 20). This effect is produced by the approximate symmetry of the courtyard relative to the circuit wall.

In the Final I courtyard the maximum distance that a person could be from a structural reference point was about 7.70 m (Fig. 20). This applies to Initial III and for either of the possible room additions from Initial II to Initial III (Fig. 21). The 7.70 m visual range disappears when Rooms 9, 12, 14 and 22 are added in the courtyard (Fig. 22).

Suggested features. A problem with the Start States and Initial I and II is whether or not the 7.70 m visual range was

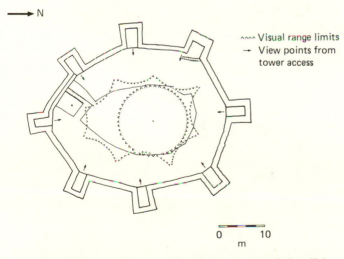

Fig. 20. Visual ranges on roof and in courtyard at Taşkun Kale Final State I. Lengths of the longest rooms do not *determine* visual range on the roof, except from tower 31. It is the symmetry of the courtyard which produces the visual range. As is apparent in Final II, there is no mechanical constraint on the location of small rooms.

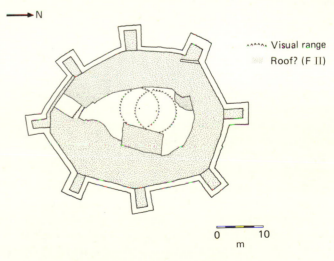

Fig. 22. Visual range in courtyard at Taşkun Kale Final State II.

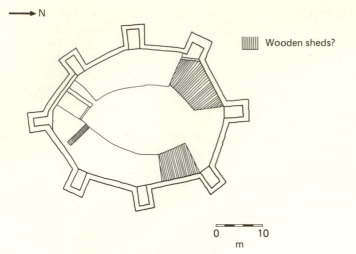

Fig. 23. Proposed arrangement at Taşkun Kale Initial State II.

delimited in the courtyard (Fig. 23). While the Start State could temporarily lack an integrated spatial pattern I would not expect that situation to last for long. Yet it is only with the addition of some of the rooms of Initial III that the 7.70 m visual range is present. One possibility is that the rooms were all added within one building season. But there is an alternative. One suggestion would be that initially there were flimsy wooden sheds built up against the curtain wall. These would have sufficed to delimit the visual field within the fort. The sheds would have been demolished when they could be replaced by rooms build of masonry and mud brick. In Final II, the contraction of the visual range in the courtyard to about 4 m suggests that the behaviour of the occupants no longer involved the larger visual ranges that were present on the roofs. Such would have been the case if the parapets and roofs were decayed and access to the roof no longer went through Rooms 5 and 36. In this State one might also expect to find structures cluttered around the outer face of the circuit wall and towers, as the earlier visual range pattern broke down.

Conclusions

The most important result is that indications of the absence of spatial order can be supplied by the crude methodology. Recognition of spatial order patterns is not therefore an artifact of the methodology. The reconstruction procedure produces dimensional values which aggregate to produce pattern in some cases and absence of pattern in others. Nor is the occurrence of disorder a function of limited sample size, since more and more features are evident up to and including the final disordered state. There were more examples of dimensions of features available from Final II than in Final I and preceding States. The 'noise' control policy does not preclude the occurrence of distributions at odds with either the serial pattern or the expected trend of variation. Furthermore, in Taşkun Kale the absence of dimensional order in both conditions of Final II occurs with other aberrant features of visual range. These are the three 'out of place' *tandir* near the

Main Gate access, and the contraction of the visual range in the courtyard.

In the Start States I and II a serial pattern does occur, but the expected trend of variation is inadequately represented. Later States of the fort display a serial pattern and the expected trend of variation. Taşkun Kale provides sufficient evidence in itself to show that it *can* have possessed spatial order during its development. There are visual ranges in the fort which correspond to that possible spatial order.

In the Final States there is no evidence that the late occupants of Taşkun Kale could be distinguished, by their spatial behaviour, from the fort's earlier occupants. The spatial behaviour of its occupants simply and progressively lost coherence. Room subdivisions and the addition of the rooms in the courtyard appear to be the cause of the loss of spatial message coherence. All that occurs in Final II is a blurring of the distinction between the 3 m and the 4 m values in the series. The blurring is expressed in two ways – in the 'a' condition by a median intermediate to the 3 and 4 m values, and in the 'b' condition by exceptionally high variation values around the 4 m medians. What is being specified is that ambiguity was arising because the dimensional values being added to the message could be members of several distributions rather than only one. The methodology indicates that a situation was arising which had not been present in the preceding States and is in contrast to the expected spatial order.

There are features of the spatial message which suggest that error rather than a different spatial message is involved. First, the overall serial pattern does not change. The crucial central tendency and variation anomalies occur only around the 3 and 4 m medians. Secondly, in Final II b, though the variation values jump for the 3–4 m medians, there is no sign that the serial intervals on either side of that jump were different. The jump in variation cannot therefore be claimed as the start of a new series.

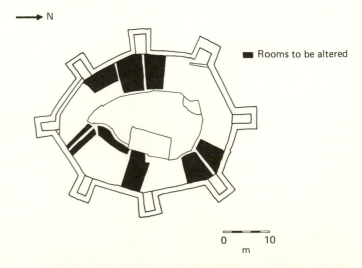

Fig. 24. Taşkun Kale: rooms requiring subdivision if dimensions are greater than 5 m are to be removed from serial arrangement.

In Final II b the high variation values cut off the serial pattern at the 3 m and 4 m medians, producing a paradoxical visual environment. The variation values delimit the serial pattern near the 4 m medians and the visual range in the courtyard had contracted to approximately that distance (Fig. 17*b*). But the structures of the fort were still carrying the earlier serial pattern even though, according to the rising level of variation, the larger dimensions would not have been distinguishable from each other as components of a series. At least nine rooms would have needed subdivisions merely to attain consistent 3 and 4 m medians (Fig. 24). Alterations to the circuit wall and the towers would also have been needed to mask the dimensional values encased in those massive structures. The analytic methodology suggests that Taşkun Kale in its terminal form did not provide a coherent spatial framework for daily life.

PART II – CONSEQUENCES

The study of Taşkun Kale has served its primary purpose by indicating that dimensional order and disorder can be identified in archaeological sites. My concern now is not so much with the specific interpretation of Taşkun Kale as with the methodological and theoretical issues which follow from the analysis.

(i) Methodological

Presentation and analysis

The ambiguities for dimensions less than 1 m and more than 8 m suggest that a rigorous procedure for altering the class interval along the dimensional scale will be necessary. In the study of a Ghanaian settlement (Fletcher 1977, p. 78), progressively larger class intervals were used for larger dimensions. The intervals were set by the level of my measurement error. However, I would prefer to use a shift of class interval based on the mechanical properties of the human eye. Since the variation trend can be related to the nature of the eye as a receptor, it should be possible to devise a standard transformation of class interval based on the way in which visual perception changes with distance of view. Also involved is the problem that different kinds of patterns may be recognisable with differing perception of grain of detail. The dimensions from a settlement should be presented using a range of class intervals to see if particular presentations display marked distribution peaks. What we may find is that dimensional order occurs at many levels of detail. Distinct distributions of small dimensions recognisable in a small class interval should amalgamate in a larger class interval to conform with the arrangement of the other distributions of larger dimensions.

Human beings do not use the same degree of perceptual precision for observing all the parts of their visual universe. The eye allows a continuous change of perceptual detail made up of many small increments of loss of acuity with increased observation distance. But each human group could divide up

that continuum in its own way. The implication of the breaks in serial order, and their relationship to the variation trend, is that the breaks represent visual distances at which a group is making marked jumps in the degree of perceptual acuity on which its behaviour is based. We may find that one class interval will function up to such a break and must then be replaced by another interval size. All that the series break specifies is that the spatial pattern has 'gone out of focus' and that a different grain of perceptual detail is needed to deal with dimensions beyond the break.

The crude methodology also points out other requirements. Statistical methods, such as Fisher's Exact test, are needed to deal with small numbers of examples, specifically with sample populations of less than five. A method is also required to avoid the undue emphasis on single-dimensional values. More work has to be applied to the uncertainties surrounding any one-dimensional value and the relationship of that value to the nearest aggregate of dimensions. In essence the new methodology would involve far more processing. Any one-dimensional value will have to be assessed in a variety of ways, particularly in relation to class intervals. Considerable data storage capacity and rapid analytic procedures will be essential.

An additional aid in the study of spatial patterning may come from communication theory. Once settlements are regarded as dimensional expressions of spatial messages, then the characteristics, requirements and failings of communication systems in general may also apply to the analysis of space in settlements. This would seem a particularly fruitful research programme to pursue. Communication theory and the propositions derived from it can be expressed in mathematical and algebraic form. They should therefore be amenable to applications as a procedure for analysing settlement space.

Dealing with damage

The only estimate which can be obtained from Taşkun Kale for a limit on acceptable damage is that, if about 50% of the structures in a site are destroyed, analysis is probably not worth while. Less than 50% of the original walls of the End State of the fort now survive with both corners intact. Estimates from that sample do not supply positive indications either of the dislocated serial pattern or of the high variation values (Fig. 25). While some information can apparently survive such damage, critical parts may be lost. In addition the loss of all or most of the representatives of one type of spacing can be particularly frustrating. In Taşkun Kale only three of the ten possible outer façade lines of the circuit wall can be measured. It is this lack of data which prevents an assessment of the serial pattern beyond the 8 m values.

The analysis of Taşkun Kale does suggest that damage can be partially rectified by consistent reconstruction. The procedure merely provides more measurable dimensions which partially related to the original form of the site. Some uncertainty has to be accepted in order to obtain the larger sample,

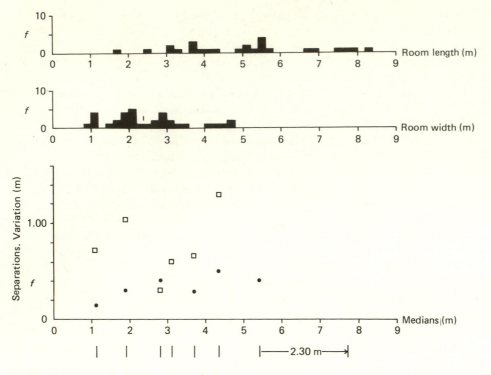

Fig. 25. End State at Taşkun Kale; < 50% survival. Distribution medians and 40% range values produced from walls with extant corners.

but this seems to be tolerable. The reconstruction leads to arrangements of dimensional order or disorder and produces these differing effects even for the same room spaces in their undivided and their segregated forms. The reconstruction procedure does not apparently favour either order or disorder. Surprisingly therefore such a policy is apparently usable. However, closer definition of the reconstruction rules will be needed since there are plainly limits of damage beyond which it would be a futile policy.

For palimpsests of features within a structure, the situation is still unclear. Given that many archaeological sites are terminal occupations, which might not be displaying spatial order, we need some statement of how much ambiguity to expect. In Taşkun Kale two of the normal *tandir* infringe the expected 1 m zone around doorways and one lies within a space linking two rooms. When divided into two classes of internal and external *tandir*, it is the external cases which are markedly 'out of place'. Taking the entire class of *tandir*, an estimate for how much blurring we might expect and tolerate is that if only 10% of the positionings are in the wrong place there may previously have been spatial order in the settlement.

The recognition that loss of order can be present in an archaeological site should be of assistance. When the effects of damage and selective excavation and cultural bias are added, it is not surprising that many archaeologists have failed to perceive either pattern or regularities in archaeological settlement plans. Knowing that loss of order can occur may help to reduce the agony of trying to find spatial patterns where none exists.

Rapid assessments

Large amounts of effort are part of spatial analysis. But the analysis of Taşkun Kale suggests that assessment of spatial behaviour could be carried out by looking at limited classes of data. Room dimensions appear to carry a lot of information. An initial assessment might fruitfully concentrate on them rather than trying to extract data from other poorly preserved spacings. A limited enquiry could attempt to pursue the relationship between the maximum median values for room length and the limits of visual range in the settlement. So far there appears to be a correspondence between these two (Fletcher 1980*a*). But the relationship is unlikely to be simple. We cannot assume that open spaces delimited by walls will be usual. In the Ghanaian settlement there were also identifiable visual ranges *outside* the residence units, defined by platforms, granaries, fires and graves (Fletcher 1980*a*). The positioning of features in the open spaces of a settlement should be part of the overall spatial order. One caution is that the terminal State of a site may have undergone a contraction of visual range, as in Taşkun Kale. Aberrant late additions have to be taken into account.

Products of spatial analysis

In sites which lack secure relative dating for successive additions and alterations, spatial analysis can be used to assess the possible sequence. For example, in Taşkun Kale there is no way to choose, in terms of spatial pattern, between Start State IIa and Initial I. The minimal definition of the sequence is therefore, Start State I, Initial II, Initial III; then Final I

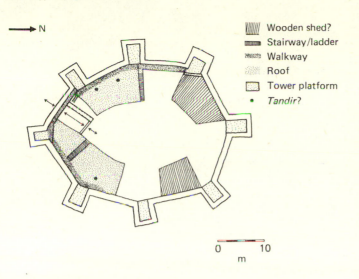

▨	Wooden shed?
▨	Stairway/ladder
▨	Walkway
⣿	Roof
☐	Tower platform
•	*Tandir?*

Fig. 26. Proposed arrangement in Initial State I at Taşkun Kale. Towers are schematic.

followed by Final II. The analysis also specifies that the room subdivisions cannot be ascribed solely to Final II. Their presence early in the development of the fort makes no difference to the nature or the occurrence of spatial order. If, however, in the 'b' condition *all* the States had lacked order, the spatial message model would suggest either that the subdivisions were late or, as is always possible, that something odd was happening. Such odd cases would deserve investigation. There are several possibilities. For example, that the site was only briefly occupied, or that considerable external force was being applied to keep the occupants in an incoherent spatial environment.

The analysis also acts as a spotlight, showing up unexpected aspects of a site or helping to clarify obscure features. For instance, the 1 m visual break draws attention to a possible walkway on the roof behind the parapet. This in turn suggests that the *tandir* may have had roof vents and that the odd feature at the rear of tower 25 (Fig. 2) can be interpreted as a buttress to carry the walkway, before the adjacent rooms were built (Fig. 26). The 7.70 m visual range indicates that the courtyard limits may have been defined by timber sheds during the early States of the fort. Suggestions of this kind, made in the field, might help to guide an excavation and could also offer assistance for pictorial reconstructions.

The 7.70 m range may also offer clues to the height of the circuit wall. If the fort were a coherent visual environment this should be evident outside the fort as well as inside. Though the tower positions are uncertain, a 7.70 m visual range out from the towers is the smallest distance that would have produced a continuous visual field around the fort. This would have ensured that every part of the circuit wall was within the familiar perceptual range of the guards (Fig. 27). In a small fort the same might apply in the vertical plane. Points at the base of the circuit wall ought to have been within the familiar visual range. On that basis, wall height could be estimated (Fig. 28) and checked against other structural evidence.

The most consequential product of the analysis is that the loss of spatial order helps to explain the position of the courtyard rooms. Otherwise it is unclear why Room 22 was added where it was and why Rooms 12 and 14 were 'swung out' from the old courtyard façade. Even though the alterations produced spatial incoherence they can be seen as an attempt to keep the visual range in correspondence with the truncated spatial pattern. Had you asked the occupants they would as likely have remarked that they needed a new sheep pen and cookhouse!

(ii) Theoretical

In more general terms the analysis of Taşkun Kale affects our definition of planning, the identification of human

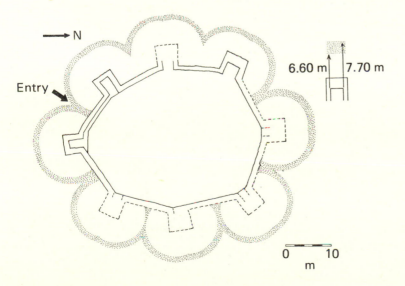

Fig. 27. Visual ranges out from the towers at Taşkun Kale.

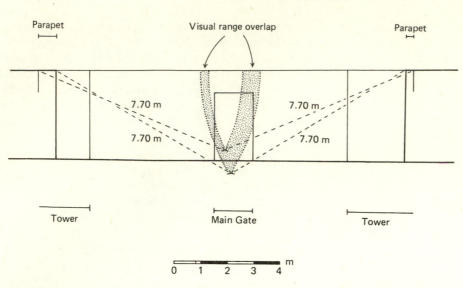

Fig. 28. Visual ranges from the tower parapets to ground level by the Main Gate.

groups in the archaeological record, and the explanation of settlement growth and disintegration.

Planning

A description can be provided of the amount of variation occurring in a structure. That statement refers to the variation which was allowed, or could not be prevented, during construction. The fort of Taşkun Kale does not therefore directly reflect the accuracy of any survey or deliberate measurements on which the layout might have been based. It is a fallacy to suppose that because we can provide a mathematical description of a structure, the mathematics was consciously known by the creators of the building. That confuses the label with the object labelled.

Though the variation in Taşkun Kale was lower than the variation in a user-built Konkomba settlement, the latter had over 60 enclosed spaces compared to the 30–40 of the fort. Since variation tends to increase with an increase in the number of structures the variation for Taşkun Kale is unsurprising (Fig. 30). No appeal to deliberate measurement is required to explain the variability of room size in the fort. Nor is it required for the circuit wall and towers. If the spacings between tower positions on the circuit wall are treated as members of a single distribution, the population of examples does not vary any more than would be expected from the known trends (Fig. 29). A sergeant and some garrison labour would have sufficed to build the rooms. No other professional builders need be suggested for the circuit

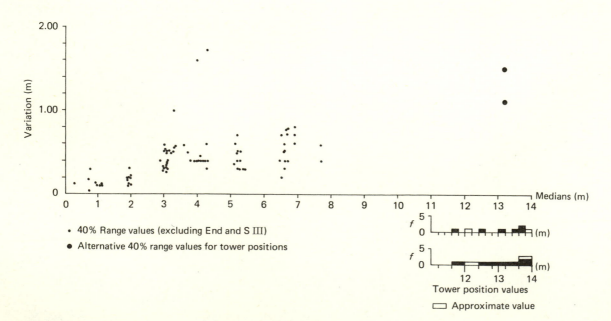

Fig. 29. Variation at Taşkun Kale in all States except End and Start III.

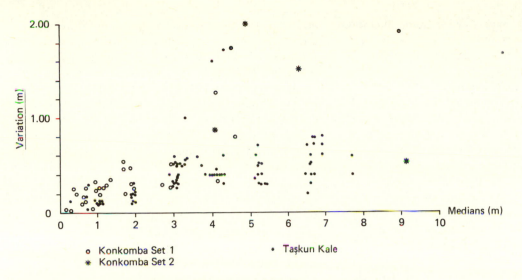

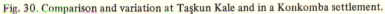

Fig. 30. Comparison and variation at Taşkun Kale and in a Konkomba settlement.

wall and towers. The basic plan of the fort could have been paced out and judged by eye. If it was carefully measured, the construction did not do justice to the plan.

A statement that a structure was planned is therefore severely affected by the recognition that human beings usually produce ordered spatial environments for themselves. To describe a site as planned demands a good deal more than the assumption that someone knew what they were doing and ordered the location of each part of the structure. On such a definition every user-built settlement could be described as planned. The term should be restricted to situations in which *dimensions* were consciously specified and labour was sufficiently controlled to ensure that the dimensions are accurately expressed in the completed structure. What we will then require is a demonstration that some structures express dimensional precision of a kind that cannot be produced by the unaided eye.

Group identification

The alterations made to the fort, after the fire which damaged the rooms around the Main Gate, cannot be ascribed to a different pattern of spatial behaviour. Superficially this seems surprising. It is hard to envisage that a military garrison would continue to use an apparently decrepit fort. But the spatial analysis does not specify that they did, only that whoever did so had a similar pattern of spatial behaviour. Several possibilities may be considered.

The fort may have been built to oversee a potentially unreliable Christian community which had been moved away from the critical ford at Aşvan (McNicoll 1973, p. 171). A non-Christian garrison from a different region may have settled into domestic life, intermarrying with the locals as Ilkhanid authority broke down in the fourteenth century A.D. Or a loyal Christian garrison could have been placed in the fort to control and protect the local community. But we should beware an assumption that the material component of human behaviour merely reflects social and political phenomena. If spatial behaviour was very similar over large regions of Anatolia, a Muslim garrison and a Christian community need not have been distinguishable in spatial terms. Whatever the garrison and the local community said about each other, the characteristics of spatial activity in Taşkun Kale can still be analysed and interpreted in behavioural terms. Conversely, no matter how we try to turn space into statements about social and political entities we will in the end still be describing spatial behaviour. The useful question to ask is how does an analysis of spatial behaviour affect our understanding of settlement growth and change? Space does not have to be translated into other terms to make that assessment possible.

Settlement dynamics

The two critical results of the analysis of Taşkun Kale are that 'Arithmetic' type serial patterns can occur and that settlement space appears to go through a cycle from absence of order, through order, to disintegration of spatial pattern.

As I had suspected (Fletcher 1977, p. 108) human communities are apparently able to produce many different kinds of serial patterns. We should expect that the trend of variation can also differ for settlements of similar size. In a coherent spatial environment the slope and start value of the variation trend is related to the serial pattern. If the series intervals increase very rapidly or the jumps at the series breaks are substantial, then the variation trend can rise steeply.

Given all these possible differences we should find that there has been preferential selection by group behaviour (Fletcher 1980b) and by general circumstances (Fletcher 1977, pp. 137–9) for some, rather than other, spatial patterns. For example, patterns with high variation values might tend to persist longer because they could facilitate shifts to alternative spatial arrangements. A Fibonacci type series could be particularly effective for dividing up space because of the many possible dimensional combinations which it allows. An alternative option is that the marked discontinuous jumps necessary in an Arithmetic type series may be effective in some circumstances because they unambiguously arrange behaviour into discrete spatial sectors.

Dimensional patterns should constrain the stability, rate and nature of change in settlement layout. Low variation would tend to operate against rapid coherent change. But a high level of variation carries the risk that replication will increase so rapidly that spatial order would be lost.

In Taşkun Kale the central tendencies appear to be generally more stable than the variation values. Mechanically, this is to be expected. To get rid of a central tendency demands either the removal or concealment of the existing dimensions. Furthermore, each component of the series will usually be represented by central tendencies from several types of spacings. To shift the median of such a cluster without losing pattern coherence would require alterations to many functionally unrelated entities. By contrast, variation can increase simply by the addition of new features whose dimensions are at the periphery of an existing distribution. We seem to be dealing with a replication system, carrying a considerable amount of redundancy, which tends toward maintaining itself over time but is also liable, because of copying changes, to produce new ordered patterns or else to lose message coherence.

The cycle of spatial arrangement which occurs during the existence of a settlement is the product of a local process of replication error, the growth of undifferentiated chaos, resulting from the cumulative effects of a succession of small events. That replication error can be reversed either by starting a new spatial arrangement elsewhere, or by the input of sufficient energy to remove most of the older spatial format.

In essence, the cycle will occur unless energy is expended to control the changes occurring at any one time. Variation increase can occur because of relatively few new structural additions. But gradual decay and demolition will be affecting primarily the older structures. Dimensions will be deleted regardless of the coherence of the older spatial message. While the adults may remember what the settlement was like, the children will only perceive what is actually there. If the behaviour of children is influenced by their spatial context (Aiello & Aiello 1974), then they would tend to replicate what is there. Spatial disorder would continue to increase. A meticulous editing of old structures might help to retain a tolerable spatial environment. But the editing process is governed by the social–political workings of the community not by any conscious perception of the spatial message involved.

Rather than being a reflection of social/political institutions, the consequences of the development of a settlement would appear to result from dissonance between the daily operations of a community and the nature of its built spatial environment. Plainly, the demands of politics can lead to housing disasters (Newman 1972). We have been confusing two levels of interpretation. Any one structure

may relate to social/political activities. But the cumulative effect of many such events follows from behavioural needs for spatial coherence and tolerable amounts of interaction (Fletcher 1980*b*). If these requirements are absent, sustained community life should become impossible.

According to this thesis, settlements will have a finite existence even without the intervention of outside factors like attack or resource failure. Indeed it may be that some kinds of spatial arrangement so adversely affect group behaviour that the community becomes particularly vulnerable to such dislocations (Fletcher 1980*b*). The specific expression in any one community of the effects of spatial arrangements which are behaviourally disturbing will depend upon the social and political characteristics of the group. That some kind of action will occur leading either to drastic rearrangements or to the abandoning of the settlement follows from the proposed parameters of spatial behaviour.

Loss of spatial order and the ability to identify it in settlements therefore becomes of some consequence. If we can identify loss of spatial order we may then begin to assess how the material behaviour of communities changes in such circumstances. We need to know what a failing community looks like. At present we only know that failure has finally, irretrievably occurred. Studies of short term states in occupied settlements and analyses in the archaeological record of long term occupation will be complementary.

How long can a community tolerate spatial incoherence? If the tolerance can last for decades without improvement of spatial order then plainly that behavioural parameter would be of little consequence. That human beings can be kept in spatially intolerable circumstances should come as no surprise. But two other factors attend. External force needs to be applied and the confined population is usually transient because of death, termination of contract, or release from captivity. The twentieth century A.D. with its concentration camps, military bases, labour camps and detention centres provides a saddening host of examples. The period of tolerance for relatively *unconstrained* communities *should* be short. We need to know what kinds of spatial patterns are likely to throw up sufficient variants for a community to be able to shift to a new coherent pattern within a short time.

Developing a sophisticated methodology to deal with these questions would seem to be worth while. Using the method to describe diverse settlement forms and changes we could begin to explain, within the spatial message model, how and why settlements are altered or abandoned.

Conclusion
The analysis of Taşkun Kale has been used to show that a methodology can be devised which identifies both the presence and the absence of spatial order in settlements. Several consequences follow from the analysis. These suggest that attempts to devise a more sophisticated methodology are necessary and will be productive. We may be able to make use of the theory, mathematical description and procedures

of communication theory to deal with spatial messages. The issues to be pursued involve the effect of structural alterations on community life and the liabilities of rapid spatial change. We need to know more about the many kinds of spatial patterns which can occur, in particular the way in which they affect rates of spatial change. These will be of some relevance for our understanding of the persistence and abandonment of settlements. The spatial message model suggests that settlements will tend to go through a cycle from under-representation of spatial pattern, to the occurrence of spatial order and then eventually to loss of spatial coherence. This cycle should vary in rate and intensity for different kinds of spatial patterns. If the nature of spatial order affects the workings of community life then it is possible that the analysis of spatial messages will help us to gain some further insight into the persistence, mobility and demise of human communities.

References

Aiello, J. R. and Aiello, T. de C. (1974). The development of personal space: proxemic behaviour of children 6 through 16. *Human Ecology* 2: 177–89.

Argyle, M. (1975). *Bodily Communication.* Methuen: London.

Cherry, C. (1966). *On Human Communication.* MIT Press: Cambridge, Mass.

Fletcher, R. (1977). Settlement studies (micro and semi-micro). In *Spatial Archaeology,* ed. D. L. Clarke, pp. 47–162. Academic Press: London.

Fletcher, R. (1980a). Space and community behaviour: spatial order in settlements. In *Universals of Human Thought,* ed. B. Lloyd and J. Gay, pp. 71–110. Cambridge University Press: Cambridge.

Fletcher, R. (1980b). People and space: a case study on material behaviour. In *Pattern of the Past: studies in Honour of David Clarke,* ed. N. Hammond, G. Isaac and I. Hodder, pp. 97–128. Cambridge University Press: Cambridge.

French, D. H. (1973). Aşvan 1968–72. *Anatolian Studies,* vol. XXIII. Special Number.

Hall, E. T. (1966). *The Hidden Dimension.* Doubleday: New York.

Hall, E. T. (1968). Proxemics. *Current Anthropology* 9: 83–108.

McNicoll, A. (1973). Taşkun Kale. *Anatolian Studies,* vol. XXIII: 159–80.

McNicoll, A. (1983). Taşkun Kale. BAR: Oxford.

Newman, O. (1972). *Defensible Space.* Architectural Press: London.

Chapter 12

**Ethnoarchaeology and
intrasite spatial analysis:
a case study from the
Australian Western Desert**
Brian Spurling and
Brian Hayden

ABSTRACT

Using ethnoarchaeologically derived data from two
recently occupied lithic sites in Western Australia, the appropriateness of spatial analysis utilizing crosstabulation procedures on artifact cell counts is evaluated. The cultural item
populations were recovered from two small, open-air campsites
located in the Australian Western Desert. Both sites were
occupied in the 1940s by Pintupi-speaking groups who still
used a lithic technology. Members of these groups assisted in
the site excavations and provided information on the activities
represented at both sites. Fisher's Exact test is employed to
generate item co-associations for each site. The matrices
of exact values are then compared with the known activities
conducted at both sites using the data from questionnaires
as a means of verification and control. Differences between
observed and expected distributions are discussed and the
consequences which this study has for similar attempts at
spatial analyses are explored.

In recent years, the archaeological community has been made
increasingly aware of numerical techniques designed for the
recognition of spatial patterning between and among classes
of archaeological data such as items and features. The application of such techniques can and has been undertaken at all
scales with which the archaeologist must deal – from intrasite
activity areas to regional market systems and from data
recovered by site-specific surface collections to data acquired
in regional, inventory-oriented research.

In this chapter we are interested in associational recognition at the level of the archaeological sites: specifically,
briefly occupied, limited activity loci generically analogous to
Binford's (1980, pp. 9–10) *residential base* type. The stated
rationale for undertaking a programme to discover spatial
patterning in data arrangements (*sensu* Pielou 1969, p. 83)
has been the identification of 'toolkits', activity areas, and site
function. More recently, questions dealing with occupation
intensity and duration as well as processes of post-depositional
disturbance (e.g. Hivernal and Hodder, Chapter 7) have been
addressed using spatial analytical procedures. The ultimate
objective of such studies is, we hope, the better to construct
and interpret cultural units from behavioral perspectives.

Our goal here is the isolation of 'toolkits' or activity
areas which have generally been determined by the dependent
or correlated nature of a pair or more of cultural item classes
over space. Methods currently implemented to discover such
associational patterning include the following: variations on
simple contingency table tests (e.g. Dacey 1973); multivariate,
discrete data ANOVA-like formulations (Hietala and Stevens
1977); and continuous data analyses intended to detect the
scale of patterning. These last procedures are often followed
by seriational, factor, or multi-dimensional scaling methods
(e.g. Whallon 1973*a*; Schiffer 1975; Burley 1976).

Generally, these methods have been applied to data sets recovered from prehistoric sites and the identified patterns have provided an inferential baseline from which prehistoric 'toolkits' or activities have been induced. Whether or not such associations truly represented a functional reality in either a paleoemic or paleoetic sense has not yet been tested to our knowledge. In short, statistically identified data patterns at archaeological sites may only be fortuitous consequences of a researcher's analytical results. Partly because such statistical techniques have not been demonstrated to yield verifiable inferences in archaeological contexts, the claims of intrasite toolkit discovery have occasioned some justifiable scepticism. For example, Doran and Hodson (1975; p. 151) suggest:

> Because spatial patterning may involve irregular shapes, and because it is two-dimensional, it will require very sophisticated numerical procedures indeed before judgement by eye can be bettered. It is valuable to look for such methods but not to imagine that they can be replaced by stereotyped tests of significance and the imposition of grids: these both involve unwarranted assumptions about the data and their structure, and could not in any case detect spatial patterns of varied, irregular shape and size.

Schiffer (1976, p. 11) argues that:

> Between the time artifacts were manufactured and used in the past and the time these same objects are unearthed by the archeologist, they have been subjected to a series of cultural and noncultural processes which have transformed them spatially, quantitatively, formally, and relationally.

Yellen (1977, p. 97), Binford (1978), and others make similar observations. In fact, bearing on the case studies at hand, such activities as 'sweeping' behavior (J. O'Connell, personal communication as cited in South 1979, p. 218, and Rathje 1979, pp. 9–10) may drastically transform the spatial patterning of occupation debris.

In this chapter we undertake a programme which formally tests, in a limited fashion, the proposition that data based associations of artifact classes have a corresponding interpretable set of associated behavioral events responsible for them. The two Australian sites of Ngarulurutja and Walukaritji (herein a.k.a. Ngaru and Walu, respectively), excavated by Hayden, provided data patterns which allow the testing of this proposition. Since both sites had been occupied by still-living, lithic-using groups, Hayden was able to take members of the populations responsible for artifact deposition at the sites back to the site. These individuals were interviewed regarding the activities that had occurred and the location of these activities at each site.

Site information

Both sites were occupied up until the mid 1940s by members of a Pintupi-speaking group, located immediately south of Lake MacDonald (Fig. 1), who did not possess metal tools. Two of the Pintupi men who had inhabited Ngaru and

Walu during this period returned with Hayden to the sites and relocated the hearths that they had used on specific visits. They helped to excavate the areas around these hearths and to identify artifacts recovered.

Before excavation took place, interviews with each of the men were carried out to obtain information concerning the activities which took place at the campsites, co-residents at the campsite, and other aspects of interest for reconstructing events at the sites. During the interviews with individuals involved, it was first ascertained that they had used stone tools when living as traditional hunter–gatherers. This was done by requesting each man to make specific items such as spearthrowers and shields using only stone tools. Invariably, persons who had not used stone tools under traditional circumstances failed in these tasks, while it was clearly evident when individuals had a thorough acquaintance with lithic technology. The results of these technological projects are presented in Hayden (1979). After identifying these individuals, Hayden requested Mr Kenneth Hansen, director of the Summer Institute of Linguistics in Australia and a specialist in the Pintupi dialect, to interview individuals who had proficient knowledge in the use of stone tools and to find out whether they had ever camped at any sites without using metal tools. He then asked if such places could be located exactly, and obtained other ethnographic details in which he was interested. Many of these details were later corroborated by a third member of one of the camping groups who did not travel with him to the site. Informant accounts were further substantiated by the recovery of resharpening debris found within 1 m of where informants said they had resharpened a chopping implement. After excavations were completed, the two Pintupi men were again interviewed with the help of Mr Hansen in order to clarify various observations and reported contexts. The data derived from the resultant excavations are quite unique, since no similar information is available in the literature concerning campsites where only lithic tools were used, i.e. sites where no industrial tools were present or used during occupation.

The total sample of lithic tools (Table 1) may seem small for the implementation of statistical procedures; however, because the manufacturing activities were probably as intensive as was likely to occur in most hunting–gathering societies, and because curation probably did not significantly affect dropping rates, it seems doubtful that many more tools would be discarded per person per week at these types of sites in similar environmental conditions and at similar levels of lithic technology. Related ethnographic studies dealing with rates of stone tool use support such a generalization (Gould 1977, p. 165).

Because some tools were curated at these sites, the previous statement may come as a surprise to many readers. However, the standard assumption that curation (or items generally considered as curated) acts to reduce the numbers of tools deposited may be questionable. Munday (this volume) addresses this question for Middle Paleolithic assemblages in

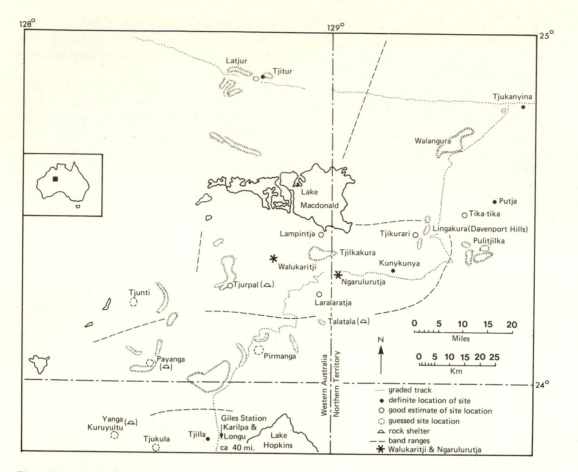

Fig. 1. Map of the Lake MacDonald area of Australia, indicating the two sites analyzed, Walu and Ngaru, located in the center of the range of one band of Pintupi about 1940.

the Near East. Curation studies at this point in time are not conclusive (see also Hayden 1976). In the case of Pintupi speaking groups, however, one extremely curated tool type was present, the chipped stone hafted adze. In this case – the only quantified study of the use of functionally equivalent curated and non-curated tools in the same task – the curated tools actually had higher dropping rates (Hayden 1979). Specifically, a spearthrower was made using only seven core tools (chopping implements), only two of which could be considered exhausted by the end of this task; such core tools are generally considered to be non-curated items. On the other hand a spearthrower made using chipped stone adzes required 16 adzes, all but the last of which were discarded during manufacture. Thus, in terms of number of tools, the curated adzes actually outnumbered the relatively non-curated core tools, when used in functionally identical tasks. The important difference between curated and non-curated tools in this instance was not the relative length of use-life, but the relative portability – the adzes weighing a few grams as opposed to several kilograms for the core tools. Moreover, while Binford (1972*b*, p. 189; 1973, p. 244) characterizes Australian Aboriginal technology as one of the most highly curated in the world, Hayden found during his ethnographic study that

only a very small proportion of the chipped stone used by Aborigines was curated (Hayden 1976, pp. 50–2; 1977, p. 182). There are still other problems with the notion of curation and its effects on assemblages which become apparent when curation is viewed from an ethnoarchaeological perspective (Hayden 1976). Because of all these problematic aspects, curation will not be dealt with further at this point. However, we would like to indicate that there should be a critical reassessment of what archaeological 'living floors', with abundant tools and other cultural items, really represent in terms of the duration and frequency of site occupancy (cf. Yellen 1977, p. 82; Hietala and Stevens 1977, p. 557).

Recovery techniques
Both excavations were of single occupation levels, respectively comprising 4–16 features and representing 7–21 day stays for a group of 4–5 people. For each site, living detritus could be fairly unambiguously related to a specific occupation. The recovery techniques employed by Hayden were conventional. The recovered items were provenienced according to 1 m × 1 m squares of larger 2 m × 2 m excavation units. A 1/16 inch screen was used to dry-sieve the sand deposits. The field crew consisted of the sites' former

Table 1. *Tabular frequency distribution of cultural item classes from Ngaru and Walu with variable definitions for both sites*

Class (+ abbreviation)	Frequency (+ variable No.)	
	Ngarulurutja	Walukaritji
Flakes (fl)	76 (1)	46 (1)
Utilized flakes (uf)	3 (7)	3 (10)
Chopper rejuvenation flakes (cf)	–	1 (8)
Miscellaneous items (mi)	2 (3)	–
Knives (kn)	1 (6)	1 (9)
Scrapers (sc)	3 (9)	–
Adzes (ad)	3 (8)	17 (12)
Notches (no)	3 (4)	3 (5)
Cores (co)	2 (5)	2 (6)
Tjiwa or mortar (tj)	3 (2)	6 (2)
Burins (bu)	–	1 (11)
Rock slabs (rs)	–	1 (4)
Ochre (oc)	–	2 (7)
Hearths[a]	11 (10)	–
Campfire (hc)	–	10 (20)
Cookfire (hk)	–	8 (21)
Large pits (pl)	–	1 (22)
Small pits (ps)	–	2 (19)
Hammerstone for *tjiwa* (hm)	–	6 (3)
Bone – unidentified (bo)	206 (11)	–
Possum elements (po)	–	11 (14)
Wallaby elements (wa)	–	28 (13)
Rabbit elements (ra)	–	28 (17)
Lizard (li)	–	2 (15)
Bandicoot (ba)	–	2 (16)
Rat kangaroo (rk)	–	2 (18)

[a] The number of hearths presented here indicate the number of collection grids in which hearths occurred. In actual fact four hearths (covering 11 1 m × 1 m units) and 9 hearths (covering 18 1 m × 1 m units) were recorded for Ngaru and Walu, respectively.

occupants. These individuals picked out extraordinarily minute material only a few millimetres in length. Only bone fragments larger than 2 cm were used in the bone counts presented in this paper. Additional occupational and contextual details regarding the sites dealt with in this article are presented in the Appendix.

Statistical method – the exact test

The statistical test applied to the quadrat frequencies of the recovered items from Ngaru and Walu is based upon the hypergeometric distribution (Lieberman and Owen 1961). To test for co-associational patterning we use Fisher's Exact test (Siegel 1956; Hietala and Stevens 1977). The test data are constructed according to the mean splitting procedure discussed by Dacey (1973). The data were thus crosstabulated

by the number of quadrats which contain less than or more than the mean cell frequency for each artifact class pair considered. Equality of single quadrat cell counts to mean class frequencies did not occur in any application. Cells containing fewer items than the unrounded class mean are counted as having '0' representatives, those exceeding the unrounded mean are counted as having '1' represented.

Fisher's Exact test was selected because the *p* values are exact, rather than approximate, for the hypothesis of no association and, more importantly, because the TWO-WAY frequencies need not exceed 5. The test is thus useful for sparse data situations such as encountered at Walu and Ngaru. With reference to Tables 1–3 it is clear that the requirement of large samples cannot be met for the majority of variables. And these low sample sizes clearly mitigate against utilization of the recently introduced categorical data procedures based on log linear models (Clark 1976; Hietala and Stevens 1977). However, Fisher's Exact test is applicable to small sample sizes *vis-à-vis* other procedures based on asymptotic (large sample) results. The archaeological sensitivity of this application, with respect to the resulting interpretations, is discussed below.

Methodological considerations

Initially the number of items of each artifact class from each site was separately tabulated This was first performed for the original size of collection grid (1 m × 1 m). This information is presented in Table 2 for Ngaru and Table 3 for Walu. The locations of each grid unit referred to in Tables 2 and 3 are illustrated in Figs. 2 and 3. Only items which were

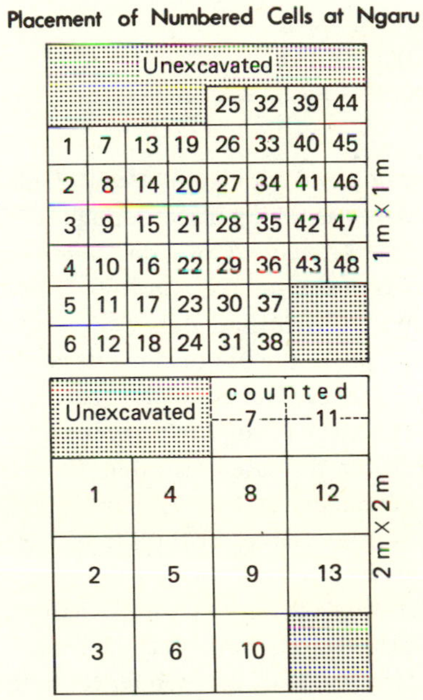

Fig. 2. Schematic representation of numbered quadrats used in this analysis for the Ngaru. Although approximately half of the 2 m × 2 m quadrats numbered 7 and 11 were not excavated, the artifact count was so low in this area of the site that there has probably been no significant effect on the analysis.

Table 2. *Raw data matrix for Ngaru: cell counts by item class*

Index of variables and raw counts ( ) for Ngaru

1. Flakes (76)
2. *Tjiwa* (3)
3. Miscellaneous (2)
4. Notches (3)
5. Cores (3)
6. Knives (1)

7. Utilized flakes (3)
8. Adzes (3)
9. Scrapers (3)
10. Hearths (11)
11. Bone (unidentified) (206)

Cell numbers refer to Fig. 2.

Cell no.	Item class 123456789 10 11	Cell no.	Item class 123456789 10 11	Cell no.	Item class 123456789 10 11
1.	1010000000 0	17.	2000000001 0	33.	0000000000 3
2.	3000000000 2	18.	5000000001 4	34.	0000000000 0
3.	4001101000 0	19.	0000000000 0	35.	3000000000 1
4.	4100000000 0	20.	1000000000 4	36.	1000000100 1
5.	3000000000 3	21.	300001000120	37.	2001000010 1
6.	1000000000 4	22.	200000000158	38.	0010000000 0
7.	0000000000 3	23.	1000001001 0	39.	0000000000 0
8.	1000000000 0	24.	0000000001 0	40.	0100100000 9
9.	2000000000 3	25.	1000000000 0	41.	3000000000 4
10.	2000000000 6	26.	0001000000 0	42.	2000000000 0
11.	2000000000 5	27.	2000000000 2	43.	2000000000 1
12.	800000000017	28.	100000000014	44.	0000000001 0
13.	0000100000 0	29.	000000101017	45.	0000000001 1
14.	0000000001 6	30.	2000000000 0	46.	1000000110 5
15.	1000000001 1	31.	2000000100 0	47.	0000000000 0
16.	5100000001 8	32.	1000000000 0	48.	2000000000 3

recovered during excavation and which could confidently be assigned to depositional events taking place during the last occupation of each site are tabulated (for a discussion of the depositional context of each site see the Appendix). Fisher Exact values were computed from these data.

The following example in the use of this test is provided. The frequencies of the presences and absences (scored 1 for greater than, 0 for less than, the mean) are arrayed in a 2 × 2 contingency table (Fig. 4). In the case illustrated, the number of spatial co-associations of wallaby skeletal elements and the presence of a campfire is investigated for the site of Walu. The size of observational unit (cell or quadrat) is 1 m × 1 m. The computation of this test provides the exact probability of obtaining cell frequencies deviating more extremely from expectation under the hypothesis of independence. In this case the probability of such a 2 × 2 array is $p = 0.0049$ for the one-tailed case, a very unlikely arrangement to have occurred strictly by chance.

The kindest thing that can be said about the computational tasks involved in deriving exact probabilities is that they are tedious. When both column or row totals are less than or equal to 50, tables such as those supplied by Finney *et al.* (1963) or Bennet and Horst (1966) can be consulted. Most large computer facilities should have the IMSL (International Mathematical & Statistical Libraries, Inc.), MIDAS (Michigan Interactive Data Analysis System), or similar packages which have routines performing this test. In the present case the **MIDAS TWOWAY** procedure was utilized. Sokal and Rohlf (1969*a*, 1969*b*) provide a method for computing exact values using factorials of logarithms. Consultation of this source may prove useful if only a very few computations are required or access to statistical packages such as those mentioned above is not readily available. In other cases, the exact test can often be approximated by the ordinary Pearson's Chi-squared test statistic or the log–linear Chi-squared statistic. The user should, however, be appraised of the requisite conditions for valid approximations.

In the first step of the analysis, all recovered classes from both sites were considered. This resulted in 11 classes for Ngaru and twice that number for Walu. Values received

Table 3. *Raw data matrix for Walu: cell counts by item class*

Index of variables and raw counts ( ) for Walu

1. Flakes (46)
2. *Tjiwa* (6)
3. Hammerstone (3)
4. Rock slab (1)
5. Notches (3)
6. Cores (2)
7. Ochre (2)
8. Chopper rejuvenation flakes (1)
9. Knives (1)
10. Utilized flakes (3)
11. Burin (1)

12. Adzes (17)
13. Wallaby (28)
14. Possum (11)
15. Lizard (2)
16. Bandicoot (2)
17. Rabbit (28)
18. Rat kangaroo (2)
19. Small pits (2)
20. Camp fires (10)
21. Cooking fire (8)
22. Large pits (1)

Cell numbers refer to Fig. 3.

Item class

```
            1111111111222
            1234567890123456789012
Cell
no.
  1.   0000000000000000000000
  2.   2000000000000000000000
  3.   2000000000020100100000
  4.   0000000000000000010000
  5.   1000000000002000000100
  6.   2000000000010000000000
  7.   0000000000001000000000
  8.   1100000000000000000000
  9.   0010000000013000000100
 10.   1000000101001100000100
 11.   1000000000001000100100
 12.   1100000000010000000000
 13.   0000000000001000000000
 14.   1000000000001000100000
 15.   1000100010001000000100
 16.   0000011000011100000100
 17.   1000000000000010000100
 18.   2010000000000000000000
 19.   1000000000001000010000
 20.   1000000000001000301000
 21.   1100000000011000100000
 22.   0000000000000200000000
 23.   0010000000001000000101
 24.   0000000000000000000000
 25.   0000000000000000000000
```

Item class

```
            1111111111222
            1234567890123456789012
Cell
no.
 26.   0000000000000000000000
 27.   0000000000000000200000
 28.   0000000000000001000000
 29.   0000000000000000001000
 30.   1000000000001000000000
 31.   1000100000000001400000
 32.   0000000000002100000000
 33.   3000000000000000000000
 34.   0000000000000010000000
 35.   0000000000000000000000
 36.   1000000000000000000010
 37.   1000000000002000000010
 38.   1000000000001000000000
 39.   1110000000000000100010
 40.   0010000000002000100000
 41.   0100000000000000000000
 42.   0000000000010001000000
 43.   0000000000000000000000
 44.   1000000000000000000000
 45.   2000000000000000000000
 46.   1000000000000200000000
 47.   0000000000001000000000
 48.   0000000000010000000000
 49.   0000000000000000000010
 50.   1000100000011000400000
```

Item class

```
            1111111111222
            1234567890123456789012
Cell
no.
 51.   0000010000000000000000
 52.   0000000000000100000000
 53.   1000000000000000000000
 54.   3000000000000000000000
 55.   1000001000010000000000
 56.   0000000000000000100000
 57.   1000000000000100100000
 58.   1000000000000000000000
 59.   0000000000000000000010
 60.   0000000000010100000010
 61.   0000000000000000200000
 62.   0000000000100000000000
 63.   1000000000000000000000
 64.   0100000000010000000100
 65.   0000000001000000100100
 66.   0001000000000000200000
 67.   2000000000010000000000
 68.   0000000000001000000010
 69.   0000000000000000000010
 70.   0000000000000000000000
 71.   1010000000000000000000
 72.   1000000000010000100000
 73.   0000000000010000000000
 74.   0000000000010000000000
 75.   1000000001010000000000
 76.   0000000000000000000000
```

which were less than or equal to $p = 0.15$ (one-tailed) are given in Tables 4 and 5 for Ngaru and Walu, respectively.

In order to determine what effect alterations in cell size would have on the results of the spatial analyses, each site was broken down into 2 m × 2 m grid units – 13 cells for Ngaru and 20 for Walu (see Figs. 2 and 3). In order to utilize all 1 m × 1 m cells for which observations were possible, it was necessary to include 4 m² from each site which has not been excavated but which were surface collected and which were thought to have very low densities of artifacts because

Table 4. *Exact values for item associations at Ngaru*

Exact probabilities of independence between cultural item classes for Ngaru (Quadrat size = 1 m × 1 m: one-tailed)			
	p
Bone and scrapers	0.13
Bone and *tjiwas*	0.13
Exact probabilities of independence between cultural item classes for Ngaru (Quadrat size = 2 m × 2 m: one-tailed)	
	p
Adzes and scrapers	0.00
Tjiwas and cores	0.11

classes and their associations, it is to be expected that a few of the comparisons will individually produce low probabilities by chance. Given spatial independence of all item classes, 5% of the comparisons can be expected to yield significant *p*-values at the alpha = 0.05 level. Therefore, it can be expected that better than 5% non-random patterning will result in testing hypotheses of randomness (c.f. Grieg-Smith 1964). When many comparisons are conducted, random error may account for apparent isolated associations.

Secondly, in a recent article Cowgill (1977) suggests that the widespread acceptance of alpha levels of 5% may be, in some cases, the unquestioning acceptance of 'statistical folkways' which require some reassessment. He argues that, for smaller samples, it may be useful to accept levels of 10% or greater. In the present analyses we have computed exact probabilities for all pairs of recovered items and report all those with a *p*-value less than or equal to 0.30 (in Tables 3 and 4, *p*-value is 0.15 – for the hypothetical one-tailed case). We did so in order to discern what associations occurred when our concern with making a Type 1 Error was relaxed.

Tertiary concerns include the effect of this relaxation of the critical region on the chances of making a Type 2 error (accepting a false null hypothesis) and the impact that empty cells have on the results of contingency table tests. Suffice to say that the former problem represents a known trade-off (see Sokal and Rohlf 1969*a*, pp. 156–66; Cowgill 1977, pp. 356–9) and methods exist, such as combinations of significance tests, to control the possibility of spurious results. The second problem arises when a large number of simultaneously empty cells occur in a TWOWAY analysis. As the number of empty cells increases, as a function of the increasing rarity of the two variables under study, so does the chance of a positive association. Although the number of simultaneously empty cells appears large for the lower frequency artifact classes for the analyses here, only eight cells are always empty for all classes at the 1 m × 1 m unit and no cells are simultaneously empty at the 2 m × 2 m grid size for Walu. At the site of Ngaru, nine cells are empty of artifacts at the 1 m × 1 m grid size but there are no completely empty cells for the 2 m × 2 m analysis. Visual inspection of contingency tables with low frequency input values which produced 'significant' *p* values does not indicate adverse effects resulting from high values for mutual absences.

of peripheral locations and trends in excavated artifact frequencies. Matrices of exact values less than or equal to 0.15 (one-tailed) are also presented in Tables 4 and 5.

Before turning to a discussion of the results of this analysis, some methodological considerations are in order.

First, if we are interested in more than a few artifact

Placement of Numbered Cells at Walu

Unexcavated				25	35	45	54	63	70
				26	36	46	55	64	71
				27	37	47	56	65	72
				28	38	48	57	66	73
1	7	13	19	29	39	49	58	67	74
2	8	14	20	30	40	50	59	68	75
3	9	15	21	31	41	51	60	69	76
4	10	16	22	32	42	52	61		
5	11	17	23	33	43	53	62		
6	12	18	24	34	44				

1 m × 1 m

Unexcavated		7	12	17
		8	13	18
1	4	9	14	19
2	5	10	15	--20-- counted
3	6	11	--16-- counted	

2 m × 2 m

Fig. 3. Schematic representation of numbered quadrats used in this analysis for the site of Walu. Although approximately half of the 2 m × 2 m quadrats numbered 16 and 20 were not excavated, the artifact count was so low in this area of the site that there has probably been no significant effect on the analysis.

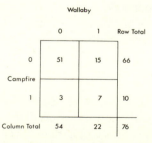

Fig. 4. Example of 2 × 2 table used in analysis for the computation of Fisher's Exact test.

Table 5. *Exact values for item associations at Walu*

Exact probabilities of independence between cultural item classes for Walu (Quadrat size = 1 m × 1 m: one-tailed test)

	p
Adzes and ochre	0.04
Adzes and *tjiwas*	0.10
Notches and flakes	0.10
Notches and knives	0.04
Utilized flakes and chopper rejuvenation flakes	0.04
Cores and ochre	0.05
Possum and chopper rejuvenation flakes	0.12
Campfire and chopper rejuvenation flakes	0.13
Campfire and large pits	0.13
Campfire and knives	0.13
Campfire and utilized flakes	0.04
Rabbit and notches	0.12
Wallaby and campfire	0.00
Bandicoot and notches	0.08
Hammerstone and large pit	0.08

Exact probabilities of independence between cultural item classes for Walu (Quadrat size = 2 m × 2 m: one-tailed)

	p		*p*
Knives and ochre	0.10	Bandicoot and wallaby	0.11
Knives and notches	0.15	Bandicoot and rabbit	0.15
Utilized flakes and chopper rejuvenation flakes	0.15	Rat kangaroo and chopper rejuvenation flakes	0.10
Utilized flakes and adzes	0.11	Hammerstones and campfire	0.06
Cores and knives	0.10	Rat kangaroo and wallaby	0.11
Possum and ochre	0.11		
Possum and adzes	0.03		
Possum and notches	0.03		
Possum and cores	0.11		
Campfire and adzes	0.07		
Wallaby and *tjiwas*	0.08		
Wallaby and small pits	0.11		
Rabbit and flakes	0.05		
Rabbit and small pits	0.15		
Rock slab and utilized flakes	0.15		
Lizards and flakes	0.15		
Lizard and large pits	0.10		

Table 1 gives the overall site artifact class frequencies for the two sites of Ngaru and Walu. Figure 4 presents a particular example displaying co-associational possibilities, with Fisher's Exact test, for the two artifact classes or wallaby skeletal elements and campfires from the site of Ngaru using 1 m × 1 m quadrat units. Figures 5 and 7 display the provenience *in situ* of artifacts found during excavations, while Figs. 6 and 8 display the provenience of artifacts recovered from the screened matrices. General camp features and plans are also illustrated in these figures.

Tables 4 and 5 contain matrices of exact probabilities less than or equal to 0.30 (two-tailed) of the independent arrangement of cultural item classes over both sites gridded into 1 m × 1 m units. The data were re-organized and the values above the mean number of class members per 2 m × 2 m cells were used for a second Exact test series for each site. The results of the two test series differ between cell sizes. The utility of the discovered associations found using the Fisher Exact tests for inferring functional relationships between items is assessed below.

Discussion

The ethnographic data obtained from the informants, as well as that in the literature, portrays activities being carried out in a very unstructured fashion around the central focus of one or more sleeping hearths. Several small fires were

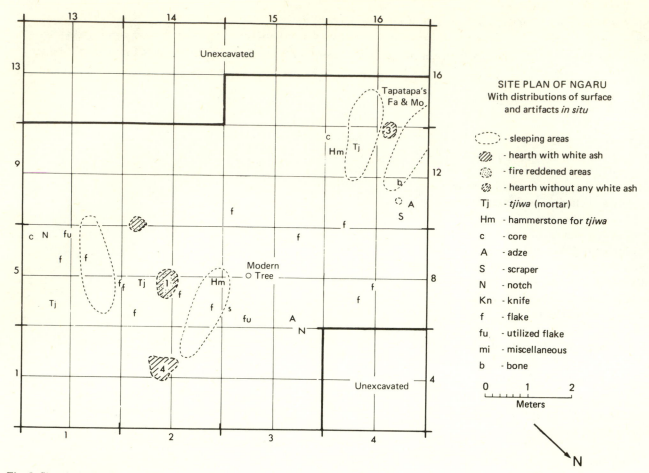

Fig. 5. Site plan of Ngaru, showing the position of artifacts found *in situ*. In Figs. 5–8, numbers along the perimeter refer to the 2 m × 2 m recording units used during excavation.

often lit at night for warmth, although only one was usually used during the day and for cooking. It was around these hearths that one slept, cooked, ate, relaxed during the day, mended hunting or gathering tools before setting out for the day, or carried out other odd jobs. The sleeping areas around the hearths were usually swept clean of irritating vegetation such as thorns, and sometimes were scooped out to form a comfortable lounging area. Some work which might cause an uncomfortable amount of debris, such as cooking and butchering of moderate sized game, straightening spears in the clefts of trees or on angular rocks, or flintknapping, might occur slightly outside of the comfortable prepared area. Items which might make sleeping or walking particularly uncomfortable (such as large bones) were often thrown about 10 m outside the area of immediate occupation.

These observations corroborate those made by Yellen (1977) and, to an extent, those by Binford (1978). Specifically, small bones (rabbit-sized) were usually simply dropped at the site of eating (i.e. around the hearth) or lightly tossed to one side. Lithic debris from work performed near the hearths never seem to have been discarded more than 1 or 2 m from the place of work. One other major factor in determining the position of debris depositions (and work activity)

was the availability of shade. Many individuals utilized the shade of nearby trees for eating, sleeping, and working during the peak of the daily temperatures of the hot season. Yellen's (1977, p. 87) study of the !Kung also indicates that hearths and shaded areas are the 'primary refuse areas' (Schiffer 1976, p. 30). None of the separate shaded activity centers was excavated in the present samples because, where activities were carried out in shaded areas, these were always 15–25 m away from the main campsite and their use was unsuspected during the excavations.

The almost haphazard distribution of specific activities around a central campsite focus has also been noted for the !Kung (Yellen 1977, p. 89) and may be a relatively widespread characteristic of many hunter–gatherers. It may also be that the toolkit patterning which archaeologists pick up at sites containing a substantial number of tools is not activity differentiation within a single occupation but, rather, groups engaging intensively in different activities during different visits to the same campsite (e.g. at one time making spearthrowers, at another butchering meat from an unusually lucky series of kills). Yellen's (1977, p. 82) information again parallels this, i.e.

If a group camps at some place and then departs and

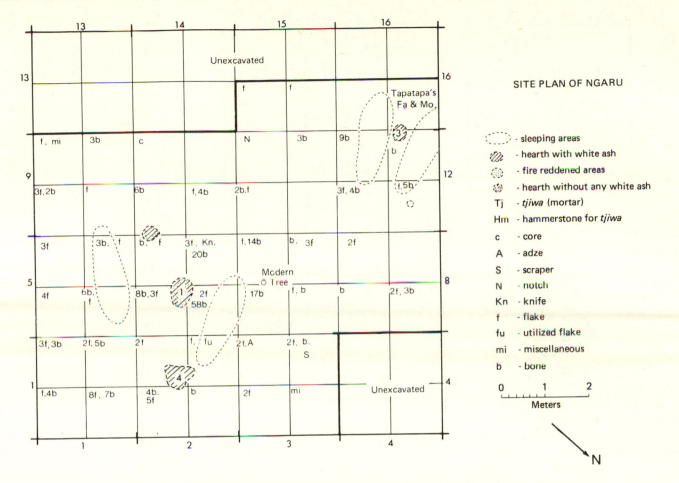

Fig. 6. Site plan of Ngaru, showing the cell unit provenience of artifacts found during screening of deposits.

the same individuals return for the same length of time a year later, it is quite possible that none of the manufacturing activities carried out the first time will be repeated the second.

Thus in general one is not led *a priori* to expect very distinctive toolkits to be manifest in the Australian data. Nor is one led to expect very strong patterning when one takes into account the relatively low number of tools per person per week deposited even in the most ideal circumstances. Nevertheless, distinct activities did occur at both sites which, it was hypothesized, might yield some patterning. We now turn to consider the two sites in sequence.

Ngarulurutja

At Ngaru, two separate camping loci existed in close proximity (Fig. 5). The first (eastern) locus was occupied by two young unmarried men (classificatory brothers), who engaged in the majority of hunting activities and hunting toolkit maintenance (primarily spear sharpening). They also visited a nearby chalcedony quarry and brought back flaked materials for fashioning new chipped stone adzes which they probably continued to work around their sleeping area. The other (western) locus was occupied by one boy's elderly

parents. The father was too elderly to do much more than consume, while the mother gathered vegetable food and may have sharpened her digging stick with some materials.

Each independent economic unit (i.e. Husband–Wife pair, and each unmarried person) had their own small pounding slab which was used to pound lizards and for other similar purposes. Casually selected flakes were habitually used in butchering meat or preparing it for cooking. A summary of activities with associated artifact types which were carried out at Ngaru follows.

1. Flaking for adzes: cores, debitage, flakes, (young men's locus).
2. Replacing used adzes: used (worn out or ineffective) adzes.
3. Eating: primary flakes, knives (for meat), bone, hearths, pounding stones for meat or plant food (no chipped stone tools were used for processing or consuming plant foods), (both loci).
4. Maintenance of wooden implements: utilized flakes, scrapers, adzes, notches, (young men's locus).

Walukaritji

At Walu there were also two camping loci (Fig. 7). Both

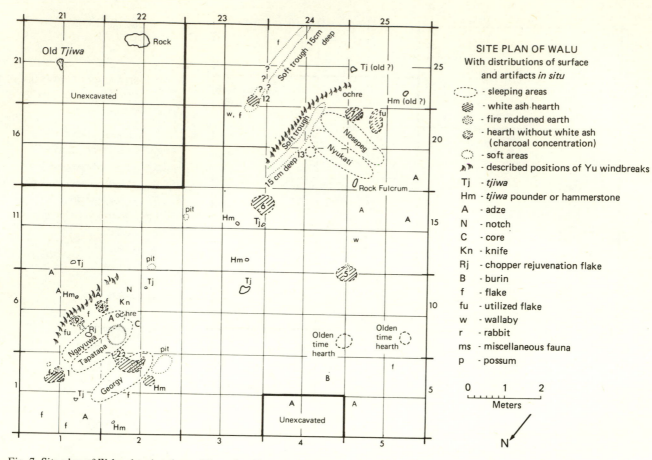

Fig. 7. Site plan of Walu, showing the position of artifacts found *in situ.*

loci at this site were occupied by groups of unmarried men who were classificatory brothers but from different areas. At the first locus (in the northern corner of the excavation) three young men camped; two young men were encamped at the second locus (in the south). All of the men at the first locus engaged in spearthrower manufacturing while only one man at the second locus did; the other member of that locus finished several spears that he had brought with him in an unfinished state. He used the angular rock on the northern edge of the sleeping area for straightening them. All men engaged in hunting activities, and presumably also in spear maintenance activities. Game such as rabbit and wallaby appears to have been cooked in specially prepared hearths (Fig. 7) slightly apart from the main sleeping hearths. One of the younger members of the campsite dug several pits in play activities. While at the site, a serious fight broke out between members of the two loci, resulting in disabling leg wounds to two of them. It is uncertain how these disabilities might have affected activities, movements, and discard patterns in detail, although we do know that the disabled men could not hunt or walk for several days.

The activities and associated artifacts left at Walu were as follows:

1. Chopping-implement resharpening for wood procurement: rejuvenation flake (first locus).

2. Spearthrower manufacture: adzes, possibly utilized flakes.
3. Spear manufacture and maintenance: adzes, scrapers, utilized flakes, notches, and possibly a burin (both loci).
4. Spear straightening: rock slab, plus possibly items in no. 3.
5. Cooking moderate sized game: hearths, wallaby, rabbit, bandicoot, flakes, knives.
6. Eating small game and vegetable food, sleeping area hearths, pounding stones (not included in analysis), bones (possibly flakes and knives).
7. Play activity: pits.
8. Water runoff control: elongated troughs, sleeping areas.
9. Ritual activity (ethnographically unrecorded) ochre.
10. Flint-knapping: cores and debitage (flakes) used to make adzes, utilized flakes, knives in the above activities.

Synthesis

If any separation into toolkits is to be expected from the analysis of the general activity areas at the two sites, we would expect the separation to occur along the activity lines and associated tools indicated above. Several conclusions can be drawn in comparing the possible tool associations based on ethnographic data with the inferred toolkits presented in

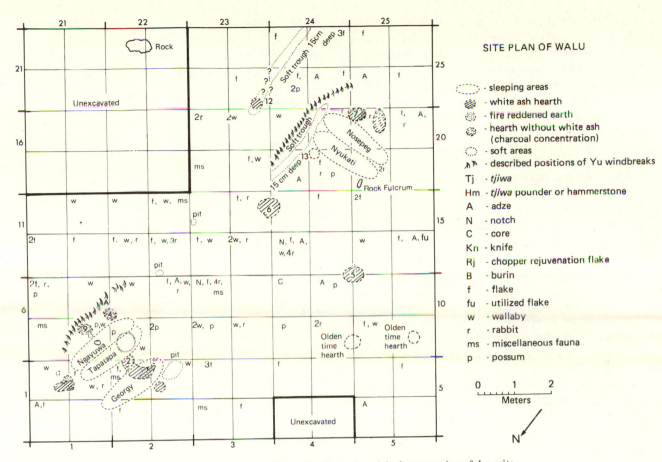

Fig. 8. Site plan of Walu, showing the cell unit provenience of artifacts found during screening of deposits.

Tables 3 and 4 – keeping in mind the relatively generalized nature of the principal activity areas. Given the multifunctional use of the young men's camp at Ngaru, some associations are discovered which are functionally explicable. The isolated woodworking component is apparent at the enlarged quadrat size (2 m × 2 m) where adzes and scrapers are shown not to be independent ($p = 0.00$). At the original collection quadrat size (i.e. 1 m × 1 m) only bone and *tjiwas* appear to be meaningfully associated, although the association is weaker ($p = 0.13 \times 2 = 0.26$). The other associations revealed at the reduced critical region do not belong together on the basis of being discarded in the same task performance. The remaining results for Ngaru are too discordant to be meaningful.

At Walu, a number of strong associations are meaningful in terms of materials used in the same tasks. Using quadrats 1 m on a side, wallaby remains and campfires were strongly related ($p = 0.00$) which is expected as moderate-sized game was cooked in either cooking fires or campfires, but were always consumed around campfires, where meat could be roasted on coals to warm it up if not completely cooked. Knives and campfires ($p = 0.13$) are also related, knives being used in butchering and preparing game for cooking in the hearths.

Using quadrats 2 m on a side, many more sensible associations were produced: rabbits and flakes ($p = 0.05$),

expected since flakes were used for butchering; hammerstones and campfires ($p = 0.06$), expected since hammerstones were used to pound up lizard bone into an edible pulp and lizards were consistently cooked in the campfires; cores may have also been used to produce knives ($p = 0.10$); bandicoot, wallaby, and rabbit bones all tend to occur together ($p = 0.11$) which is expectable because all are of approximately the same size and would have been treated in the same manner in terms of cooking, butchering, consumption and waste discard; utilized flakes and adzes are also associated ($p = 0.11$) which is to be expected because of the functional similarity of these tool classes and the fact that they would be used in different stages of tasks such as spear and spearthrower making. In similar fashion, the rock slab/utilized flake association makes sense ($p = 0.15$) because both were used in making and maintaining spears, while bandicoot and rabbit remains are associated for the same reason previously mentioned ($p = 0.15$). None of the other associations makes any sense in terms of items of facilities used in the context of a single task. However, it is of interest to note that some associations, such as notches and knives, occur at both cell sizes, probably as a result of small sample sizes for both item classes, as they are clearly functionally unassociated.

At both sites some segregational effects occur. That is

some classes of cultural items are arranged so that their spatial occurrences are mutually exclusive. This is true for cookfires versus flakes, campfires and wallaby elements at the Walu site. Segregation also obtains between cores versus flakes, miscellaneous items versus flakes and bone versus notches at Ngaru. These cases of segregation have no appreciable impact on the analyses insofar as the generation of spurious associations is concerned.

Summary and conclusions

For both sites, realistic approximations of some toolkits are provided by Fisher's Exact test at relaxed rejection regions. However, several caveats are in order.

The acceptance of a relaxed critical region, i.e. accepting an increased likelihood of making a type 1 error three out of ten times (alpha = 0.3), will aid in the detection of ethnographically validated tools and faunal associations. This is particularly so when one utilizes weak tests for association. For example, Hietala and Stevens (1977) found that relaxed type 1 error levels were required to detect associations with hypergeometric tests, whereas the associations were found at less relaxed levels with the employment of stronger tests. However, at the same time, this practice promotes the generation of associations which are fortuitous. For the most part these associations occur because of the generalized activities observable at small campsites. And these associations are detected by implementing the Exact test. Without the safeguard available to us, i.e. crosschecking the detected archaeological associations against the real case associations, naive and erroneous tool and faunal correspondences could be advanced for both sites.

While agreeing with Cowgill (1977, p. 359) that accepting increased significance levels is probably warranted in cases where small sample sizes are the norm, we must accept the increased risks which go along with this 'shot-gun' approach (see Grieg-Smith 1964, p. 96). In order to test just what, in the cases under consideration, are the risks incurred by increasing alpha, all Exact probability values less than or equal to 0.30 (for the two-tailed case) or 0.15 (for the one-tailed) were arrayed according to whether or not the associations they describe had some ethnographic validity or whether they represented chance associations attributable to the refuse scatter resulting from general camp activities.

Tables 6 and 7 contain this information for both sites at both quadrat sizes. The right-hand column of these tables contains the percentage of times meaningful associations are detected at alpha levels of 0.05, 0.10, 0.20, and 0.30 (for the two-tailed case). Unfortunately, no trends can be detected.

For the site of Ngaru, at both quadrat sizes, the relaxation of concern with type 1 error to 0.30 provides a 0.5 chance of isolating a true, functional association between items. Importantly, the highest association detected at the 2 m × 2 m cell size is indicative of possibly the pre-eminent activity performed at the site. It should be noted that the associations revealed at the 1 m × 1 m cell size do not corres-

Table 6. *Relationship of size of rejection region to number of ethnographically verifiable associations: Ngaru*

Relationship of rate of success of toolkit identification to increase in chance of making a Type 1 error: Ngaru. (Quadrat size = 2 m × 2 m.)

Significance p	Functionally associated	Activity scatter	Detection of functional relationship
0.00	1 (ad/sc)		1.0
0.01			
0.02			
0.03			
0.04			
0.05			
0.06			
0.07			
0.08			
0.09			
0.10			
0.11		1 (tj/co)	
0.12			
0.13			
0.14			
0.15			

Relationship of rate of success of toolkit identification to increase in chance of making a Type 1 error: Ngaru. (Quadrat size = 1 m × 1 m.)

Significance p	Functionally associated	Activity scatter	Detection of functional relationship
0.00			
0.01			
0.02			
0.03			
0.04			
0.05			
0.06			
0.07			
0.08			
0.09			
0.10			
0.11			
0.12			
0.13	1 (bo/tj)	1 (bo/sc)	
0.14			
0.15			

For abbreviations see Table 1.

Table 7. *Relationship of size of rejection region to number of ethnographically verifiable associations: Walu*

Relationship of rate of success of toolkit identification to increase in chance of making a type 1 error: Walu. (Quadrat size = 1 m × 1 m.)

Significance p	Functionally associated	Activity scatter	Detection of functional relationship
0.00	1 (wa/hc)		1.0
0.01			
0.02			
0.03			
0.04		4 (ad/oc;uf/cf hc/uf;no/kn)	
0.05		1 (oc/co)	0.17
0.06			
0.07			
0.08		2 (ba/no;hm/pl)	
0.09			
0.10		2 (ad/tj;no/fl)	0.10
0.11			
0.12		2 (po/cf;ra/no)	
0.13	1 (hc/kn)	2 (hc/cf;hc/pl)	
0.14			
0.15			0.13

Relationship of rate of success of toolkit identification to increase in chance of making a type 1 error: Walu. (Quadrat size = 2 m × 2 m.)

0.00			
0.01			
0.02			0.0
0.03		2 (po/ad;po/no)	
0.04			
0.05	1 (ra/fl)		0.33
0.06	1 (hm/hc)		
0.07		1 (hc/ad)	
0.08		1 (wa/tj)	
0.10	1 (co/kn)	3 (kn/oc;li/fl rk/cf)	0.30
0.11	3 (uf/ad;ba/wa ra/wa)	3 (po/oc;po/co wa/ps)	
0.12			
0.13			
0.14			
0.15	2 (rs/uf;ba/ra)	5 (no/kn;uf/cf ra/ps;li/fl; rk/fl)	0.35

For abbreviations see Table 1.

pond to those produced by crosstabulation at the 2 m × 2 m cell size. This lack of stability in associations can be easily accounted for but it is difficult to provide a rule of thumb when decisions must be made as to the scale of observations from site to site.

At Walu, 15 co-associations were produced at the 1 m × 1 m cell size and 23 were found at the 2 m × 2 m quadrat size which were $p \leqslant 0.30$. At the smaller cell size a decrease in the percentage of correctly detected associations occurs as the rejection level is relaxed with slight increase in the rate of successful detection (from 0.10 to 0.13) occurring between alpha values of 0.2 and 0.3 (two-tailed). For a quadrat size of 2 m × 2 m we fare somewhat better with a detection rate of 35% at alpha = 0.3. Although it is of interest that the accepted level of risk closely approximates to the percentage of correctly identified associations, as this relationship only appears once out of four cases, we cannot venture that this correspondence has any general interpretability.

Unfortunately no hard and fast rules can be advanced to assist those who wish to select meaningful associations from fortuitous ones at increased significance levels. In the cases considered, the acceptance of all tool and faunal associations at alpha = 0.3 would mean that only between 13 and 50% would be meaningful. It is clear that, had we no foreknowledge of the behavioral correlates of the cultural item associations present, the selection of any of the many different toolkits resulting from our analysis would be arbitrary.

That the specific associations at the two sites were different is not at all surprising given the differences in activities which occurred, the differences in length of occupation, the number and age/sex composition of the occupants, and given the large role which chance apparently plays in determining associations.

Other data comparable to these have yielded similar results. For example, a preliminary examination of one of Yellen's mapped sites (Yellen 1977, pp. 154–8), employing the same research strategy, has been undertaken. Spatial analyses of all 16 of Yellen's mapped campsites is also planned. Camp 2 (No. Tum No. Toa 2) was selected for investigation because, in several respects, key site formation parameters resemble those for Ngaru. The variables of site population, duration of occupation, and size are roughly comparable to Ngaru. Nine item classes were mapped using a Tektronix digitizer, partitioned into two separate cell sizes of 1 m × 1 m and 2 m × 2 m employing a program developed by B. Ball and J. Nance (S.F.U.), and the resultant matrix was crosstabulated using the MIDAS TWOWAY routine. Four associations with $p \leqslant 0.30$ resulted from crosstabulation at the 1 m × 1 m cell size and three resulted from the crosstabulation of 2 m × 2 m cell size.

Two observations which have bearing on the analyses presented here merit comment. First, only two co-associations are common to both cell sizes. These are between (1) the abandoned wooden tray and huts and (2) mongongo nuts and scattered cooking fires from previous occupations. In both

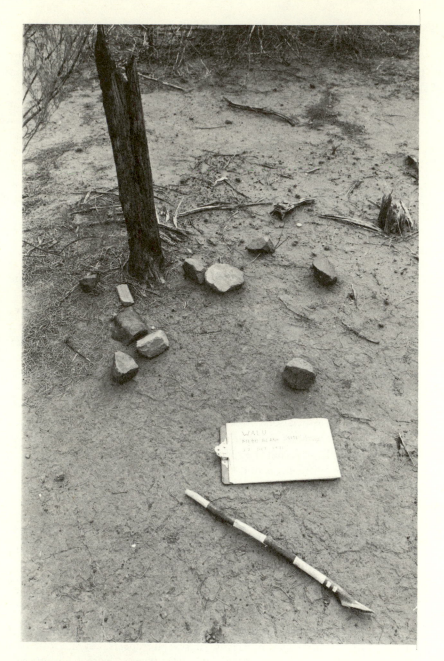

Fig. 9. An unusual concentration of core tools found at Walu at the base of a mulga tree. These tools were spatially isolated from visible remains of campsites and were interpreted by informants as having been used to remove two flitches of wood from the mulga tree stump in the picture. They represent a single functional type and could easily be interpreted as a toolkit and activity area without recourse to statistical analysis. This photograph is reproduced from *Palaeolithic Reflections: Lithic Technology and Ethnographic Excavation among Australian Aborigines,* B. Hayden, published by the Australian Institute of Aboriginal Studies, copies of which are available from the Institute, Canberra.

cases these associations achieved lower *p*-values at the increased cell size. Secondly, the association of mongongo nuts and scattered cooking fires *from previous occupations* would, if interpreted on the basis that lack of statistical independence between items is equivalent to a contemporaneous functional activity, be misleading.

It should be understood that we have discounted the visibility of hut features, wooden trays, and macro-floral remains if sought in a purely archaeological context. The

survivorship of these data might be in the direction of non-detection of the site of No. Tum No. Toa 2 itself.

It is possible that, given exact provenience data for all recovered items, a nearest neighbour analysis (e.g. Whallon 1973*b*; Morlan 1974; Ives 1977) might produce associations with greater ethnographic verisimilitude; however, this procedure is not applicable to the Ngaru and Walu data nor to many other data sets from archaeological excavations or surface collections. In an attempt to improve the results obtained using Fisher's Exact test, mean-splitting procedures were tested including median splits and simple presence/absence in the assignments of the categorical variables used for the Exact tests. Relatively minor differences in co-associated pairs were produced by these options and the mean-split procedure generated the majority of sensible associations in the present data sets.

It is worth repeating that the toolkit patterning which archaeologists sometimes pick up at sites with substantial numbers of tools is not necessarily activity differentiation within a single occupation. It may represent groups engaging intensively in different activities during different visits to the same campsite (e.g. at one time making spearthrowers, at another butchering meat from an unusually lucky series of kills).

Clearly, with regard to the determination of intrasite activity sets, we are not out of the wilderness yet. Much more research based upon experimental arrangements of items (such as undertaken by Greig-Smith 1952), novel techniques such as spectral analysis (e.g. Graham 1980), the fusion of use/wear and refitting studies (Cahen *et al.* 1979), detailed review of the ethnographic literature on discard behavior (such as that recently presented by Murray 1980), and, particularly, the maximum use of the all too few ethnoarchaeological studies must be carried out. The results of the present study should be extended, only with caution, to similar research.

While the use of generalized activity areas is a major factor responsible for masking spatial relationships between tools discarded in the course of a specific task, it must also be emphasized that under special circumstances, activity areas and toolkits can be easily discerned. For example, in prolonged work projects, lasting several hours, hunter–gatherers may, on rare occasions, stay in specific locations and generate highly localized, intensive debris related to a single task. These localized intensive scatters tend to be only $1-2\,\mathrm{m}^2$ in area, are rare, often involve only a single tool type, and, most importantly, are so obvious that no statistical techniques are needed to identify them. One such scatter is depicted in Fig. 9. Activities which take place in areas well separated from camp-fires may also form identifiable activity areas and toolkits. For example, such activities may include cooking moderately sized and large game, procuring wood as in Fig. 9, or skin working. However, it would be unusual for most archaeological excavations to encompass more than one of these areas from a single occupation given the relatively characteristic large distance between loci. Thus, the debris scatters which we have dealt with at Ngaru and Walu are seen to be representative of the types of situations which archaeologists will most often encounter as single occupations, and to which they will attempt to apply statistical analyses.

Whether our assessment of the relative values of the spatial tests discussed above is pertinent only to low density, Australian Western Desert sites of about $60-100\,\mathrm{m}^2$ in area, or whether our assessment is more widely relevent, is a critical desiderata of future research.

Acknowledgements

Foremost, we extend extreme gratitude to Ngayuwa and Tapatapa Tjungala of Papunya Settlement, the two classificatory brothers who returned to their former campsites, helped in excavation and provided so much information with so much patience. We also thank the Australian–American Educational Foundation and the Australian Institute of Aboriginal Studies for making travel to Australia and field work possible. Special thanks are due Dr J. Peter White (Sydney University) and Mr Robert Edwards (AIAS) for their encouragement and help.

Appreciation is extended to Bruce Ball and Jack Nance for supplying their program for partitioning site cell sizes. Moreover, we wish to credit Harold Hietala, Paul Larson, and the anonymous reviewers for their assistance in improving various aspects of this paper. Any remaining errors or omissions are made without complicity.

APPENDIX: EXCAVATIONAL DATA

For both ethnographic sites excavated, Pintupi informants were able, after some searching, to locate the exact places where they had camped on specific occasions some 30 years previously. They located the campfires which they had used, where individuals had slept, where specific activities had taken place (which, in some cases, were remarkably corroborated by subsequent material finds), identified persons who had camped in the immediate vicinity, and related what was generally eaten. For the most part, contamination from previous or subsequent occupations was not significant. Hayden estimated on the basis of stratigraphic position, differential patination, and internal spatial consistency within the assemblage that no more than a few percent of the artifacts might be from other occupations.

The land surfaces on which the encampments were made appeared to be relatively stable, although, since the occupations, small plants had grown up on the site and in some places these plants had captured eolian sediments and accumulated shallow sand deposits. In other areas sheet wash had partially covered hearths and artifacts, or alternatively exposed them. The sites' micro-stratigraphy clearly demonstrated these processes. Thus artifacts from the occupation occurred on the surface, and in some instances under shallow loose sand around plants or embedded in the thin sheet wash deposits. Also, because the site areas were loosened with sticks by the occupants and cleared of annoying vegetation before occupation, many artifacts were also found at depths of up to 3–5 cm from the surface because of trampling and disturbance by the occupants. Because both surface artifacts and materials within 5 cm from the surface were all from the same occupation, it was not useful or meaningful to analyze artifacts according to whether they occurred on the surface or in the matrix. A much more detailed discussion of the stratigraphy of the two sites is given in Hayden (1979) and will not be elaborated upon further here. No floatation, chemical or granulometric analyses of soils were carried out. Unlike some sites observed by Gould (1980, pp. 26–7), no general deflation had taken place and there was no mixing of occupational debris at the specific campsites excavated. Evidence of prior occupation was uncovered in the Walu excavations; however, these artifacts occurred substantially below the occupation level we were dealing with, and artifacts had more pronounced patination.

Because the sites were only 30 years old, no dating program was undertaken, although charcoal samples were collected. The environment and fauna of the Australian Western Desert were essentially the same during the sites' occupations as they are today. The area can be characterized as desert to semi-desert with wide areas of meandering dune fields covered by substantial patches of spinnifex grass or mulga shrub. The meat fare of the Pintupi at the time of occupation consisted primarily of rabbits, wallabies, a number of species of lizards, the bandicoot, an anteater, possum, and, very rarely, kangaroos, emus, feral cats, and dingoes. The male Pintupi informants said they did not collect any vegetable foods or bring any to the campsites, although at Ngaru the women did this, and at Walu women kin sent over vegetable foods to the young men in exchange for meat. Bone preservation at both sites was excellent, with even the most delicate lizard mandibles retaining sharp features. It is unlikely that differential preservation of bone has seriously biased artifact patterning at either of the sites. Again, the complete details of fauna used and subsistence particulars has already been published elsewhere and need not be repeated here (Hayden 1979). The vast majority of bone fragments were unidentifiable probably because of the Western Desert practice of mascerating bones of small animals. In the original analysis at Walu, provenience was recorded for identifiable animal parts in order to determine whether there was any patterning related to meat sharing practices between personnel at the site. Since no patterning was apparent, proveniences were not kept for identifiable bone fragments at Ngaru. Thus, identifiable bone from Walu is analyzed according to provenience, whereas none of the identifiable bone from Ngaru is provenience, i.e. it is all simply recorded as unidentified bone.

Excavation continued at both sites until artifact densities began to drop off to negligible frequencies. At both sites, portions of the site which were least dense in artifacts were left unexcavated because of shortage of water supplies.

References

Bennet, B. M. and Horst, C. (1966). *Supplement to Tables for Testing Significance in a* 2 × 2 *Contingency Table.* Cambridge University Press: Cambridge.

Binford, L. (1972*b*). Model building-paradigms, and the current state of Paleolithic research. *An Archaeological Perspective*, pp. 244–94. Seminar Press: New York.

Binford, L. (1973). Interassemblage variability – the Mousterian and the 'functional argument'. In *The Explanation of Culture Changes: Models in Prehistory*, ed. C. Renfrew, pp, 223–56. University of Pittsburgh Press: Pittsburgh.

Binford, L. (1978). Dimensional analysis of behavior and site structure: learning from an Eskimo hunting stand. *American Antiquity* 43(3): 330–61.

Binford, L. (1980). Willow smoke and dog's tails: hunter–gatherer settlement systems and archaeological site formation. *American Antiquity* 45(1): 4–20.

Burley, D. V. (1976). On the spatial analysis of a plowed site at Bartiboy. *Canadian Archaeological Association Bulletin* No. 8, pp. 82–105.

Cahen, D., Keeley, L. H. and Van Noten, F. L. (1979). Stone tools, toolkits, and human behavior in prehistory. *Current Anthropology* 20(4): 661–83.

Clark, G. A. (1976). More on contingency table analysis, decision making criteria and the use of log linear models. *American Antiquity* 4(3): 259–73.

Cowgill, G. L. (1977). The trouble with significance tests and what we can do about it. *American Antiquity* 42(3): 350–68.

Dacey, M. F. (1973). Statistical tests of spatial association in the locations of tool types. *American Antiquity* 38(3): 320–7.

Doran, J. E. and Hodson, F. R. (1975). *Mathematics and Computers in Archaeology.* Edinburgh University Press: Edinburgh.

Finney, D. J., Latscha, B. M. and Hsu, P. (1963). *Tables for Testing Significance in a* 2 × 2 *Contingency Table.* Cambridge University Press: Cambridge.

Gould, R. (1977). Ethno-archaeology; or, where do models come from? *Stone tools as Cultural Markers,* ed. R. V. S. Wright, pp. 162–8. Australian Institute of Aboriginal Studies: Canberra.

Gould, R. (1980). *Living Archaeology.* Cambridge University Press: Cambridge.

Graham, I. (1980). Spectral analysis and distance methods in the study of archaeological distributions. *Journal of Archaeological Science* 7, 105–29.

Greig-Smith, P. (1952). The use of random and contiguous quadrats in the study of the structure of plant communities. *Annals of Botany* 16: 293–316.

Greig-Smith, P. (1964). *Quantitative Plant Ecology,* second edition. Plenum Press: New York.

Hayden, B. D. (1976). Curation: old and new. In *Primitive Art and Technology,* ed. J. S. Raymond, B. Loveseth, C. Arnold and G. Reardon, pp. 47–59. University of Calgary Archaeological Association: Calgary.

Hayden, B. D. (1977). Stone tool functions in the Western Desert. In *Stone Tools as Cultural Markers,* ed. R. V. S. Wright, pp. 178–88. Australian Institute of Aboriginal Studies: Canberra.

Hayden, B. D. (1979). *Paleolithic Reflections: Lithic Technology of the Western Desert Aborigines.* Australian Institute of Aboriginal Studies: Canberra.

Hietala, H. J. and Stevens, D. S. (1977). Spatial analysis: multiple procedures in pattern recognition. *American Antiquity* 42(4): 539–59.

Hodder, I. and Orton, C. (1976). *Spatial Analysis in Archaeology.* Cambridge University Press: Cambridge.

Ives, J. W. (1977). A spatial analysis of artifact distribution on a boreal forest archaeological site. Master's Thesis, University of Alberta, Edmonton.

Lieberman, G. J. and Owen, D. B. (1961). *Tables of the Hyper-geometric Probability Distribution.* Stanford University Press: Stanford.

Morlan, R. E. (1974). Gladstone: an analysis of horizontal distributions. *Arctic Anthropology* XI, Supplement: 213–37.

Murray, P. (1980). Discard location: the ethnographic data. *American Antiquity* 45(3): 490–502.

Pielou, E. C. (1969). *An Introduction to Mathematical Ecology.* Wiley-Interscience: New York.

Rathje, W. L. (1979). Modern material culture studies. In *Advances in Archaeological Method and Theory*, vol. 2, ed. M. B. Schiffer, pp. 1–38. Academic Press: New York.

Schiffer, M. B. (1975). Factors and 'toolkits': evaluating multivariate analyses in archaeology. *Plains Anthropologist* 20: 61–70.

Schiffer, M. B. (1976). *Behavioral Archaeology.* Academic Press: New York.

Schiffer, M. B. (ed.) (1979). *Advances in Archaeological Method and Theory,* vol. 2. Academic Press: New York.

Siegel, S. (1956). *Nonparametric Statistics for the Behavioral Sciences.* McGraw-Hill: New York.

Sokal, R. R. and Rohlf, P. J. (1969*a*). *Biometry.* W. H. Freeman and Co.: San Francisco.

Sokal, R. R. and Rohlf, P. J. (1969*b*). *Statistical Tables.* W. H. Freeman and Co.: San Francisco.

South, S. (1979). Historic site content, structure and function. *American Antiquity* 44(2): 213–37.

Whallon, R., Jr (1973*a*). Spatial analysis of occupation floors. I. The application of dimensional analysis of variance. *American*

Antiquity 38: 266–78.

Whallon, R. Jr (1973*b*). Spatial analysis of paleolithic occupation areas. In *Models in Prehistory: the Explanation of Culture Change,* ed. C. Renfrew, pp. 115–30. University of Pittsburgh: Pittsburgh, Penn.

Whallon, R. Jr (1974). Spatial analysis of occupation floors. II. The application of nearest neighbor analysis. *American Antiquity* 39(1): 16–34.

Yellen, J. E. (1977). *Archaeological Approaches to the Present: Models for Reconstructing the Past.* Academic Press: New York.

Chapter 13

**Unconstrained clustering for
the analysis of spatial
distributions in archaeology**
Robert Whallon

Introduction

In this chapter I will consider some of the methodological problems in the quantitative analysis of spatial distributions of materials (artifactual and other) over areas of human activity ('occupation' or 'living' floors). I will evaluate and attempt to improve the congruence, or 'fit', between analysis and the models and questions we have in mind when we undertake a study of such spatial distributions. Although there has been a substantial amount of recent interest in this subject and an active development of analytical techniques for spatial analysis, I think it fair to say that there is still a large measure of dissatisfaction with available approaches and their results.

In fact, a substantial proportion of quantitative analyses of archaeological data fails to produce results that are considered 'good' or useful when measured against a large body of acquired experience and knowledge in this field. Understandably, most disappointing or unsuccessful analyses remain unpublished. Of those that are published, it seems the majority are used as negative examples in arguments against the use of certain methods of analysis in situations for which other methods are advocated (e.g. Christenson and Read 1977).

It has been argued that rejection of such results and, consequently, of the quantitative methods which produced them is an unwarranted and conservative reaction. This argument is based on the belief that results generated by rigorous statistical or mathematical methods of analysis must have an objective validity, and that accumulated archaeological experience and knowledge do not provide an equally rigorous or 'objective' basis for rejection of such analytical results and methods.

There is a great deal of resistance to this argument, however, even by avid practitioners and promoters of quantitative analysis in archaeology. Much of this resistance comes from the feeling that traditional archaeological models and accumulated archaeological knowledge cannot be so wrong, or have such large gaps, that they will show little or no relation at all to the results of new, quantitative methods of analysis. Also, no one has yet been able to demonstrate for such results a 'meaning' or interpretation to which the criteria used in judging 'traditional' or 'standard' analytical results are not relevant, or which call upon a model not already well addressed by current archaeological analyses.

It seems to me that the main reason for the failure of so many quantitative analyses is simply that the statistical and mathematical models or principles in terms of which the applied analytical methods operate are not congruent with the questions being asked of the data, are not congruent with the processes by which it is believed that our data base – the archaeological record – was formed, and, consequently, are not congruent with the structure or patterns of variability inherent in archaeological data. There is already some general recognition of these points, and they are bound to be realized more clearly as greater attention is paid to the application of quantitative methods in archaeology.

Such problems of congruence are probably largely the result of the widespread borrowing and often mechanical application of quantitative techniques from other fields of study, on the one hand, and of lack of sufficient care or thought by both archaeologists and statisticians on the other. Archaeologists are particularly ill-trained for, and unused to, the rigorous and logical thought necessary for the informed use of quantitative methods, while the rare statisticians who have tried their hands at archaeology typically have understood the nature of archaeological data, questions, and models only partially, vaguely, or incorrectly, so that their efforts are usually no better than the archaeologists' own.

The solution to this situation is, of course, the development of analytical methods which operate specifically in accord with the problems being investigated, the models believed to represent the processes involved, and the consequent structure of the data which bear on these problems. One approach to laying some foundations for the development of such methods consists of attempts to define explicitly the formal properties of 'traditional' archaeological analyses (e.g. Whallon 1972; Borillo 1974*a*; see also Borillo 1974*b*). One method, developed specifically for archaeological analysis, in which problems of congruence appear largely to have been solved is seriation (see Marquardt 1978).

With respect to spatial analysis, one of the responses to dissatisfaction with currently available methods and results has been a growing interest and activity in ethnoarchaeology. A major focus of ethnoarchaeology has been precisely the investigation of the patterns of behavior and other processes involved in the formation of 'occupation floors', and of the forms of the material distributions which result from these patterns and processes. A major aim of these studies is to aid in the archaeological identification of similar physical results, from which the former existence and operation of similar behavior and processes can be inferred.

The results of such ethnoarchaeological studies minimally have shown the following (see also Spurling and Hayden, Chapter 12):

(*a*) There is a wide range of processes which result in the the deposition and distribution of materials (artifacts and debris) over an occupation area, and there are many variables which affect these processes.

(*b*) Among the technological variables involved, we find:
  (1) different degrees of functional specificity among types of tools – some types being quite restricted in their range of uses, others being used in a wide variety of activities;
  (2) different rates of breakage, wearing out, and discard among types of tools and among different activities as well;
  (3) different rate of curation, repair, or re-use of tools, depending upon tool type, activity, and access to raw materials;

  (4) different space requirements among activities, involving different amounts of space, and shapes of area, as well as different degrees of separation between areas; and
  (5) different patterns of consumption of the various materials being processed.

(*c*) Among the social factors involved are
  (1) the size of the social group occupying or using the site;
  (2) the composition of the group;
  (3) the length of stay at the site;
  (4) the size, shape, and arrangement of structures and other facilities on the site;
  (5) patterns of within-site movement; and
  (6) patterns of rubbish disposal.

(*d*) The time of year (season) may influence activities and the organization of space significantly.

(*e*) Post-depositional disturbance or alteration of materials (e.g. differential preservation, geological sorting and deposition, animal activities, etc.) may influence strongly the form of the archaeological record that remains at an occupation or activity site.

This list is not meant to be exhaustive or systematic, but the points herein imply a series of important consequences for the distribution of materials over archaeological occupation floors. Any approach to the spatial analysis of such distributions must be as congruent as possible with these consequences in order to be applied usefully. Minimally, these consequences are that the scatters or 'clusters' of materials resulting from specific processes or activities – the so-called 'activity areas' of an occupation – can be expected to be

(1) of widely differing size,
(2) of greatly variable and often irregular shapes,
(3) of different densities, and
(4) of variable composition,
(5) with the further implication that the relationships among types of material are likely to vary also from area to area.

Therefore, an appropriate analytical approach to the definition of such scatters or clusters should be able to operate with as much freedom as possible from constraints on the size, shape, density, composition and internal organization or structure of the clusters which are identified. These characteristics – size, shape, density, composition, and internal patterns of covariation or association – should be *variables* in terms of which the defined clusters can be described and differentiated, *not factors* which are held constant in one or another way by the operation of the methods applied in any approach to the spatial analysis of an occupation floor. I will attempt to develop such an approach in this chapter.

A brief consideration of the major and commonly used methods for spatial analysis makes it clear that they all operate with rather severe constraints in one or more of these respects. For example:

(*a*) Dimensional analysis of variance (Whallon 1973) and

other grid-count-dependent tests of non-random cluster-ing (e.g. Dacey 1973) have well-known and severe limitations in terms of the size and shape of the clusters they can define. In addition, they implicitly assume nearly uniform size, shape, and density among clusters.

(*b*) The use of nearest-neighbor analysis to test for non-randomness of distribution, followed by a mapping procedure based on a maximum 'cut-off' distance between points within a cluster (Whallon 1974; Clark 1979) obviously operates on a basic assumption of constant or uniform density among clusters – thus implying a uniform mean and an identical distribution of nearest-neighbor distances among clusters. There are also co-variational restrictions on the application of this method (see Hietala, Chapter 4).

(*c*) The use of principal components or factor analysis of correlation matrices based on grid count data (Vierra and Taylor 1977) assumes the existence of global, linear patterns of covariation among the various kinds of items scattered over the area under analysis. The simpler procedure of defining groups of mutually correlated items from an ordered matrix of such corre-lation coefficients (Whallon 1973) not only assumes that there are global, linear patterns of covariation among items, but, further, strongly tends to result in the definition only of discrete, or, at most, minimally over-lapping groups of spatially correlated items ('toolkits'). Additionally, all these approaches are subject to the previously noted size and shape constraints involved in the use of data collected or organized within grid units over an area.

Considering, therefore, the expected variation in composition and internal organization of scatters or clusters, it can be predicted that the assumptions implicit in the use of correlation, principal components, and factor analysis will seldom correspond to the struc-ture of spatial data. An example will be given below illustrating a severe mismatch between these assumptions and the data from an ethnographically recorded occupation area.

(*d*) Other proposed methods of spatial analysis (e.g. Hietala and Stevens 1977; Johnson 1977; Kintigh and Ammer-man 1982) all similarly make one or more of the above assumptions or work under one or more constraints on cluster size, shape, density, composition, or covariational patterning.

The challenge, then, is to develop an approach to spatial analysis that is in fact free from constraint in all these respects. This approach must define spatial scatters or clusters over an area in such a way that size, shape, density, composition, and patterns of association or covariation are no longer constrain-ing factors, but are variables in terms of which the spatial scatters or clusters may be described. This description would not be conditioned by methods of analysis, therefore, but rather would be informative of structure or patterning

inherent in the data. This structure or patterning, in turn, may be significantly informative of the processes or activities by which the observed spatial distributions were formed.

The approach described below attempts to do just that. It is a general approach or framework for analysis, rather than a sequence of specifically or rigidly prescribed methods. It consists of a series of steps, at each of which a number of options are open to the analyst. In this paper, specific methods are applied and their choice defended. The guiding principles behind the choices of these specific methods are, first, the selection of methods which involve the fewest constraining assumptions, and secondly, the emphasis on local as opposed to global patterning of material distribution over an occupation floor. However, there is ample room for experi-mentation and the testing of other methods within this analytical framework, and it allows for a good deal of 'tailor-ing' of analysis to various specific circumstances, models, or assumptions.

Obviously, this is only a first approximation to an effective approach to spatial analysis. However, analysis within this framework does begin to break away significantly from the many constraints inherent in other approaches, and to provide results from spatial analysis in which these formerly constraining factors become descriptive variables.

Description of the approach

This approach consists, in outline, of the following steps:

(1) The distributional pattern of each type of item is repre-sented by smoothed density contours over the area.

(2) At each data point, then, the densities of each type of item in turn are interpolated from the smoothed den-sities generated in step 1. This creates a vector of den-sities at each point. (The data points are typically the item locations on the floor, but they may also be grid points as discussed below.)

(3) Each of these vectors of densities is converted to a vector of 'relative' or proportional densities by summing the elements of the vector and dividing each of the elements by the sum for that vector.

(4) Cluster analysis is used to combine data points into groups that tend to be homogeneous with respect to these vectors of relative densities.

(5) The data points belonging to each group are plotted on the floor and inspected for spatial integrity or inter-pretable spatial patterning. Spatially distinct sub-groups may be separated if desired.

(6) If step 5 indicates reasonable spatial integrity or inter-pretable spatial patterning of the groups of points defined by the cluster analysis, these groups (and sub-groups if created in step 5) are described in terms of their size, shape, density, composition, and internal patterns of covariation.

(7) The information on these groups generated in step 6 may then be used for interpretation and reconstruction

of the behavior or processes which created the spatial structure or organization of the data.

I will now describe in more detail each of these steps, concentrating, of course, on the first 6, which constitute the methodological framework of this approach.

The approach begins with as unfettered a representation as possible of the distribution of each type of item over an occupation floor (or other area to be analyzed). I take a density contour map for this representation. This involves some degree of generalizing from the data, particularly point location data, but this is necessary. We are interested in distributional pattern, and pattern is a characteristic of the data as a whole rather than of the array of individual item locations. That is, pattern *is* a generalization from the data. The most common constraints on such generalizations are on size and shape, as is particularly evident in the use of grid counts to summarize the distribution of individual point locations of items. A contour map represents the differing densities of items over an area and is quite unrestricted in its representation of the size and shape of regions defined by these different densities.

Technically, however, questions arise immediately. In the first place, how is the density of any type of item measured at any point on the floor? There are several methods from which to choose at this step in the analysis. All involve some procedure of data smoothing, and some are quite complex. In this context, frequencies are smoothed in two dimensions over an occupation floor, but the principles of smoothing are not different from those applied in 'exploratory data analysis' as outlined in detail by Tukey (1977) or Hartwig and Dearing (1979). In the example presented below, I use a simple, two-dimensional running mean (Cole and King 1968, pp. 201–7) or 'floating template' (Tobler 1966) approach, commonly used in geography for the construction of density contour maps from the spatial distributions of point locations.

A second question at this step is what sort of interpolation to use in moving from a series of densities at given points over the floor to the drawing of density isolines, and, as we will see, eventually to the interpolation of densities to data points on the floor for further analysis. Linear interpolation provides greater smoothing of the data. Interpolation using inverse squares of the distances involved allows local fluctuations in density to stand out somewhat more sharply. Again, there are other methods of interpolation which could be used at this step if good arguments for their application, and their typically greater complexity, can be found.

So far, I have been assuming the use of point location data for each item. However, the approach is also applicable to grid count data. In fact, the use of smoothing procedures applied to grid counts to produce a density contour map may produce a clearer picture of areal trends in the data than the raw grid counts alone. Although a large amount of detail and accuracy is always lost with grid counts, analysis is not forestalled, and the approach I describe can be followed in its general outlines.

The methodological problem now becomes one of utilizing the information contained in the several density contour maps in such a way as to reveal clearly the joint patterning of the several kinds of items over the floor. It is true that some of the spatial scatters or clusters revealed by analysis may consist essentially of items of a single type. This is a possible, and not unexpected, result of the approach I describe here, which operates without constraint on the number of kinds of items which must be considered in order to define a spatial scatter or cluster. However, if there are good theoretical or hypothesized reasons to think that it is the distributional patterns of single kinds of items, alone, which are meaningful in terms of the behavior and processes resulting in the formation of the archaeologically (or ethnoarchaeologically) observed occupation floor, then further analysis of the sort I describe is unnecessary. On the contrary, however, considerations largely derived from ethnoarchaeological studies, as discussed above, incline me to believe that it is generally more likely that behaviorally significant patterning will be manifested in the mutual clustering and interrelationships among two or more types of items than in the distributions of single types of items alone.

If attention is, in fact, focused on single kinds of items, then it may be appropriate to consider tests of 'randomness'. In the present approach, however, I propose to forego or bypass any test of the randomness or non-randomness of item distributions over the area under analysis. The focus of this approach to spatial analysis is on the patterns of joint distribution of different materials, not on the quality of randomness or non-randomness of these distributions. Although such tests of non-randomness of distribution might be made outside the present analytical framework, or subsequent to this analysis, it seems to me that the results of presently available tests are so much a function of the scale of observation and measurement of item distributions that it is exceedingly difficult to use them in an informative way. Furthermore, these tests are not well developed (H. J. Hietala, personal communication), and Hietala and Stevens (1977, pp. 553–4) have shown, with grid count data, that such tests can be inappropriate if used as a prior consideration for comparing different items. In general, two items can be individually 'random' while occupying similar or different spaces. All together, therefore, I am inclined to regard such tests as generally uninformative for most spatial analyses of archaeological data.

There are several ways in which density contour maps of two or more variables have been compared in other fields such as geology (e.g. Pelto 1954) and geography (e.g. Robinson 1962), but these all work on the assumption of some global organization to the spatial data. They all assume that some process is operating uniformly over the entire area under analysis. This process may be complex and may be represented by such complex analytical constructs as high-order trend surfaces, but the process is assumed to be uniform over the whole area. Methods of comparison among density distributions in these fields therefore incorporate elements of this assumption. Such an assumption of global processes is not congruent with the postulated variability in associational or covariational patterning within spatial scatters or clusters of archaeological materials. It is this point particularly, whose validity is demonstrated in the example below, that argues forcefully against the use of methods for spatial analysis which assume the existence of global processes or patterns in the data. Hietala and Larson (1979), also, have documented the point that global approaches, such as trend-surface analysis, generally are not congruent with archaeological processes, and that such descriptive tools as SYMAP density contouring are better for defining distributional patterns of materials within archaeological sites.

To implement an approach that emphasizes local variation and patterning in spatial distributions, I focus on local densities at a series of points over the area under analysis. The first and most obvious choice for such points is the actual locations of the items on the floor. However, if the number of items is large enough to create computational problems, a series of grid points across the floor may be substituted for the item points. Detail is lost, of course, if grid points are substituted for actual item points, but, as will be seen below, the result of such a substitution can be reasonably satisfactory. The use of grid points obviously is obligatory if grid count data, only, are available for analysis.

The object is to use these local densities to associate each point with one of a series of scatters or clusters on the floor, each of which can be characterized differently by size, shape, density, content, and internal patterns of covariation among types of items. None of these variables will be held constant by the analysis across scatters or clusters.

Although all these variables must be free to change among clusters, at least one must be held relatively constant *within* clusters to provide clear distinctions among clusters on at least one variable, and a central tendency to that variable for each cluster. This variable, then, should provide the criterion in terms of which points initially are assigned to various scatters or clusters. It is desirable to have only a single criterion in order to place the least possible constraint on the characteristics of the clusters defined by the analysis.

I have chosen internal homogeneity of composition, or content, as the best candidate for this criterion. We cannot use actual local densities for this criterion, however, because this would introduce into the analysis an unwanted effect from absolute density variations. For example, points in high density areas would tend to be grouped together regardless of possibly noticeable variations in proportions of different kinds of items in these areas. The use of relative or proportional density, on the other hand, does not appear to have any unwanted influence on the size, shape, density, range of contents, or internal covariation of the scatters or clusters defined. Composition can vary freely among clusters and is constrained to be as homogeneous as possible only within individual clusters.

Furthermore, this criterion appears to accord well with the models devised from ethnoarchaeological studies, in which particular constellations of items (tools, raw materials, by-products) in various given proportions seem to be characteristic of particular activities. The absolute frequencies, or densities, of these items often are a function of length of occupation, number of persons engaged in the activity, number of times the activity is repeated, etc. (see e.g. Yellen 1977). However, the relative frequencies (local proportions) of various kinds of items, while not fixed as constants, generally appear to be more stable and to reflect the nature of the activities more directly.

Therefore, the next step of our analytical procedure is to calculate the relative (proportional) densities of each type of item at each data point (item point or grid point). These densities are derived from the smoothed density estimates (density contours) which were used to represent the distributional patterns of each type of item in the first step of the analysis. These density contours are free from any assumption or constraint of global patterning and vary freely in response to local density fluctuations. They are smoothed, using moving-averages or a 'floating template', in order to generalize from point distribution plots to local density estimates. It is exactly such local density estimates that we now wish to generate for each data point.

The estimate of local density of any type of item at any specific point on the floor is given, theoretically, by the value of the density isoline (contour) passing through that point. Practically, however, the most direct and accurate density estimate is derived by interpolation from the smoothed densities from which the density contour maps were actually constructed. Therefore, we find, for each data point, the closest surrounding locations at which these initial, smoothed densities were calculated. The local density estimate for the data point is then found by interpolation. In the example below, I use a weighted mean, in which the weights are the inverse squares of the distances from the data points to the four surrounding smoothed densities. The use of inverse squares of these distances maintains an emphasis on local density fluctuations. Simple, linear interpolation is an alternative which would provide a slightly greater smoothing of the pattern of density distributions over the floor.

At each data point in turn, then, densities are estimated for each type of item on the floor. I call these estimates the *absolute densities* of all items at the data points. Later in the analysis these absolute densities become important in the description of density characteristics and variations among spatial scatters or clusters. I do not enter the absolute densities directly into further analysis, however, because to do so would introduce, as mentioned above, a tendency for variation in density itself to play a large role in, or dominate, the analysis. In the next step, the cluster analysis, the use of absolute densities would lead to at least a partial tendency for points in high density areas to be clustered together, points in low density areas to be clustered together, etc., and this tendency would mask or dominate potentially significant variations in the proportions of different types of items within these areas. A major goal of the approach outlined here was to prevent density (i.e. abundance), among other factors, from playing a determining, and largely uncontrolled, role in spatial analysis.

The absolute densities, therefore, are converted to *relative densities* for analysis. These are simply proportions, calculated by summing all the local density estimates at each data point and then dividing each of these densities by their sum. Multiplied by 100, of course, the results can be expressed as the percentages of total density at that point represented by each type of item. These relative densities thus are the smoothed estimates of the local 'assemblage composition' at each point, and are the data to be used in the cluster analysis of these points on the floor. The use of relative densities thus makes the clustering criterion one of internal homogeneity of composition or content.

The next step is to define groups of the data points through the use of cluster analysis. Before proceeding to this step, however, a number of possible approaches to the analysis of the data, as now organized, may well come to mind. Correlations among the different types of items can be calculated from their varying relative densities at points on the floor, and factor or principal components analysis can be used to define major axes of variability in these data. These analyses may appear attractive at first glance, but they are not appropriate to the analytical approach being developed here because they immediately introduce strong assumptions of global or uniform patterning or process over the area under analysis, as discussed above. The linear model, on which all of these analytical techniques are based, assumes a uniform pattern of covariation among types of items across the different scatters and clusters definable on the occupation floor: an assumption which is most unlikely to be valid and which I have taken some pains to avoid so far.

Therefore, the next step of the analysis is simply to group the data points directly, using cluster analysis. The cluster analysis is based upon the array of relative densities of all types of items calculated at each data point. Every pair of points is compared in terms of the vector of relative density (local proportion) estimates at each point, and a measure of the degree of similarity/dissimilarity between the points is calculated. Various different measures, or coefficients, may be used here, but Euclidean distance is the measure which most obviously and immediately comes to mind for this purpose, and it is the measure I use below. A clustering algorithm applied to Euclidean distances clearly follows the criterion adopted above of internal homogeneity of composition of clusters.

There are, of course, many algorithms that could be used for the clustering of the data points. Avoiding the well-known problems of complete linkage and single linkage clustering, there is still a variety of choices among algorithms which produce relatively homogeneous clusters (see Sneath and Sokal 1973, pp. 201–45). My personal preference, at this stage, tends to be either average linkage or minimization of error sums of squares (Ward's method) clustering. However, here, as in many other archaeological applications of cluster analysis, very similar, if not identical, results might be obtained from centroid, k-means, or perhaps other algorithms. Within broad limits, it seems that there is little basis for a definitive choice among these algorithms, all of which make use of group central tendencies for clustering, and, given reasonably well-defined structure in the data, results are closely comparable among them. In any case, unweighted clustering is desirable, since we do not want the size of a cluster necessarily to influence the assignment of points to it. In the example below I use Ward's method (Ward 1963; Veldman 1967, pp. 308–17; Cormack 1971, p. 332).

Note that this approach to the grouping of data points from an 'occupation' floor does not cluster them in terms of their spatial proximity or patterning over the area under analysis, and, clearly, it does not cluster the various types of materials or items from the total assemblage into discrete groups, or 'toolkits'. Rather, the vectors of relative, or proportional, densities calculated at each point represent estimates of the 'assemblage composition' at those locations. A cluster analysis based on such estimates of assemblage composition therefore is searching, in effect, for a partition of this data that best represents the pattern of assemblage similarities and differences among these points.

Spatial relations have not been considered so far in this analysis. Neither have the spatial variables of size, shape, or density of distribution, nor the patterns of covariation among types of items, been used thus far in the analysis. Proportional composition of the assemblages defined at each point has been the sole, critical, defining factor in terms of which grouping of the data points has been accomplished. Obviously, the next step now is to examine the actual spatial and covariational characteristics of the groups of points defined by the cluster analysis.

To reveal, finally, the spatial aspects of the structure or organization of the assemblage of materials distributed over the area under analysis, each point on the original distribution map, with which the analysis began, is identified as to the group to which it was assigned by the cluster analysis. Data points belonging to group 1 from the cluster analysis are identified and plotted on the map. The same is done successively for data points belonging to group 2, group 3, etc. When this is done, areas of homogeneous assemblage composition on the 'floor' naturally will appear as clusters or scatters of points belonging to the same group. Points belonging to the same group may appear, however, in separate spatial clusters or scatters on the ground, or even as a series of isolated points. The former situation simply represents different, separate areas with similar assemblages of items, something that is not at all astonishing, but even to be expected, given our present understanding of the spatial organization of human activities, at least in simple sites, and the material distributional consequences of this organization. A series of isolated points from any given group defined by the cluster analysis simply represents the distribution of isolated items of the same type on the floor.

The first thing to do with such a plot of data points by group on the floor is to examine the distribution of points belonging to each group in turn for spatial integrity and spatial separation from the distributions of points in other groups. At this stage it is possible to subdivide groups whose points fall clearly into two or more spatially discrete locations. The points visually identified with each distinct location may simply be assigned to separate sub-groups. This may be an important step before calculation of the descriptive statistics that will be used to define and characterize the final results of analysis, because such distinct spatial clusters or scatters, while sharing identical assemblages of items, may well exhibit noticeable differences in size, shape, density, covariational patterning, etc. Sometimes, however, these descriptive characteristics may not vary to any great degree between spatially distinct scatters of points belonging to the same group. In such cases, an overall characterization of the spatial clusters of these points can probably best be developed on the basis of the total sample of points, with the exception of the size, shape, and location of the distinct spatial locations in which these points are found.

The most important role of a visual inspection for spatial integrity, however, is the assurance that it gives of interpretable structure, both in the spatial patterning of items and in assemblage variability over the area under analysis. Experimental 'disturbance' of ethnoarchaeologically recorded campsites (to be reported in detail elsewhere) has shown that spatial integrity of the distribution of points by group is maintained in a remarkably stable manner until disturbance and disruption of the original structure reaches a critical stage at which all aspects of original structure or organization are lost extremely rapidly. When this stage is reached, the plot of points by group quickly becomes a jumble in which no spatial coherence is discernible. A check for the spatial integrity of the plots of points by group thus becomes also a test for preservation of significant, interpretable structure over an area and allows the identification of situations in which disturbances, of whatever sort, have irretrievably destroyed such structure.

The scatters or clusters on the ground of the points belonging to each group defined by the cluster analysis can clearly be described in terms of size and shape, impressionistically or by various measurements, subdividing groups from the cluster analysis as necessary when clusters are spatially separated. The composition of each group, and subgroup, can be specified easily by calculating the means of the relative densities of each type of item from the vectors of estimates associated with each point within the group. A group's internal homogeneity of composition can be measured from the standard deviations of these means and inspected from histograms of the relative densities within the group.

Similarly, since no constraints are placed by this

approach upon the patterns of covariation among items, as the proportional density of each varies, from point to point, around its group central tendency, we can also expect groups to differ significantly in this respect. These patterns of covariation among the various kinds of items within any group may be examined by the calculation of correlation coefficients and inspection of the scatter plots of the paired values on which these correlations are calculated, using as data only the relative densities estimated for points included within the group. Finally, the absolute densities of material within the spatial extent of any group can be calculated directly, by taking the original measures of total artifact densities at the data points (the summed density estimates which were used to calculate the relative densities upon which the subsequent analysis was based) and calculating the mean and standard deviation of these measured densities.

When all the above has been carried out for each of the groups, and subgroups, defined in the analysis, it comprises a rather exhaustive description of the spatial organization of material distribution over the area analyzed. The description thus developed covers how many different scatters or clusters of items can be defined over this area, the varying sizes, shapes, and absolute densities of these scatters or clusters, the patterns of covariation among different kinds of items within these clusters, and the composition or content of these clusters in terms both of the types of items present in those areas of the floor and of the relative or proportional densities of these items. None of these descriptions is constrained in its variability by the analysis, and none is held constant, or within predefined limits over all clusters. All are *variables* which describe the nature of the spatial units identified by the analysis. This is the goal for which this approach to analysis was designed.

An example: analysis of the Mask site

To illustrate this approach, we will apply it to the Mask site (Binford 1978), a small Eskimo campsite, some 9 m × 12 m in size, containing several hearths, and over which five kinds of material remains are distributed: tools, projectile components (cartridge cases), scraps of wood, large bones, and bone scrap. As a test case for the approach to spatial analysis outlined here, however, I will provisionally treat this camp as if it were simply an archaeological site. I will analyze and interpret it as such, and later will compare the results to the ethnographically known activities and patterns of behavior that created this site.

As the first step in analysis, density contours for each kind of material are constructed over the site, using the moving-average or floating-template method mentioned above, in this case with densities being measured within a 1 m radius around each grid point. Inspection of these density contours, superimposed on the original item scatters, shows that they provide a satisfactory and accurate representation of the distributional pattern of each kind of material on the site (Figs. 1–5).

From the density contours for each kind of material, then, measures of absolute density at each item point on the site map are obtained by interpolation, and these measures are transformed into proportional or relative densities at each point.

As discussed above, interesting analyses might already be made from spatial data in this form. A matrix of correlations among items, calculated on the basis of their relative densities at each point shows one high and significant positive and several high and significant negative correlations, along with several instances of null or random correlation (Table 1). A principal components analysis of this matrix reveals a series of significant components of the strong variability and patterning of this data (Table 2). On component 1, projectiles and wood scrap load highly and together, while bone scrap loads highly in the opposite direction. Here we have a classic picture of two highly associated variables, both of which are negatively

correlated with a third variable. In terms of their proportional densities over this site, projectiles and wood scrap are clearly correlated with each other. Both tend to be relatively common in areas where bone scrap is present in lower densities, and vice versa. Component 2 exhibits the same kind of patterning, with both tools and large bones loading together and bone scrap loading in the opposite direction. Component 3 shows large bones loading highly in one direction versus tools loading highly in the other. These three components account for 91% of the total variation in the local densities.

It is possible to draw some conclusions and to create a picture of the spatial structure of the materials scattered on the site from these analyses. We see correlations which suggest various craft or maintenance activities, primary processing activities, secondary processing or consumption activities, and discard or disposal activities. Further, it is obvious from the

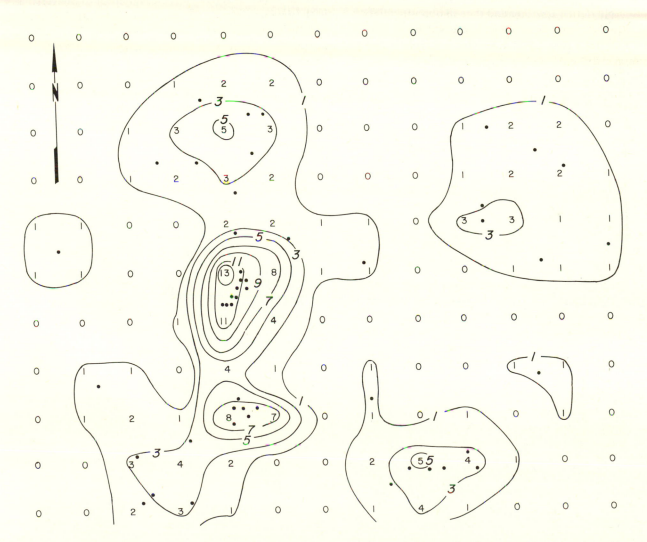

Figs. 1–5. Point locations of individual items on the Mask site, counts of items within 1 m of each corner of the 1 m × 1 m grid over the site (roman numbers), and density contours (italic numbers) of these counts. (Item locations were measured from the maps by Binford (1978). Points are omitted here when, at this scale, they would conflict with one of the grid corner counts.)
Fig. 1. The distribution of tools.

Table 1. *Correlation matrix using relative densities at item points*

Variable:	Tools	Projectiles	Wood scrap	Large bones	Bone scrap
Tools	1.0000				
Projectiles	−0.2976	1.0000			
Wood scrap	−0.3318	0.5026	1.0000		
Large bones	0.0346	−0.0662	−0.2910	1.0000	
Bone scrap	−0.1196	−0.8280	−0.6546	−0.0064	1.0000

$N = 490$ $DF = 488$ r @ $0.05 = 0.0886$ r @ $0.01 = 0.1163$, where N = number of items; DF = degrees of freedom; r = Pearson correlation.

results of the principal components analysis that the patterning or structure of spatial distributions of materials on this site is not simple. Item types are not sorted out into discrete groups that load together on distinct components. The same pairs of items load first together and then in opposite directions on different components. The picture which emerges could not have been revealed by the simple ordering of the correlation matrix, and principal components analysis was necessary to reveal the structure in the data that was obscured in the correlation matrix alone.

Nevertheless, even principal components analysis may obscure as well as reveal patterns and much of the variability in the data may remain to be discovered by other approaches to analysis. In this case, as in so many others, it is useful and instructive to begin with simple descriptive and display techniques.

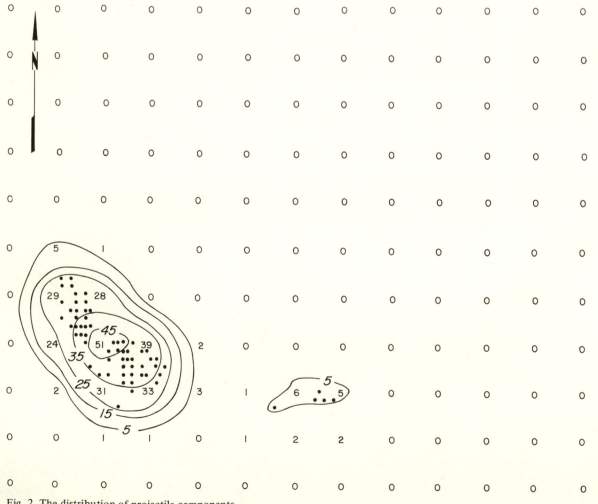

Fig. 2. The distribution of projectile components.

Table 2. *Principal components analysis using relative densities at item points*

Component	(1)	(2)	(3)	(4)	(5)
Eigenvalue	2.4168	1.1440	0.9977	0.4414	0.0000
% Variance	48.34	71.22	91.17	100.0	100.0
Tools	0.20227	0.68247	− 0.60478	0.08709	0.34638
Projectiles	− 0.57165	0.13436	0.16522	− 0.60642	0.51001
Wood scraps	− 0.54052	− 0.20413	− 0.10564	0.72979	0.34989
Large bones	0.14008	0.53398	0.76632	0.30268	0.12798
Bone scrap	0.56614	− 0.43517	0.09242	− 0.02157	0.69361

Inspection of the histograms of item frequencies (Fig. 6) and of the scatter plots of the relative local densities of various pairs of items (Figs. 7–13) makes it obvious that linear correlation and orthogonal axes are, in many cases, poor representations of the structure of the data, i.e. of the many different patterns of relationships among the relative densities of these items on this site. Most histograms demonstrate extremely strong skewed distributions, while one (bone scrap) exhibits a strong and dramatic bimodal distribution. The complexity of the data, however, is clearest in the scatter plots. Some suggest multiple lines of positively correlated points, defined by different parameters – slope and intercept (e.g. Fig. 7). Others indicate a similar pattern, but of multiple negative lines (e.g. Fig. 8). More common is a mixture of scatters

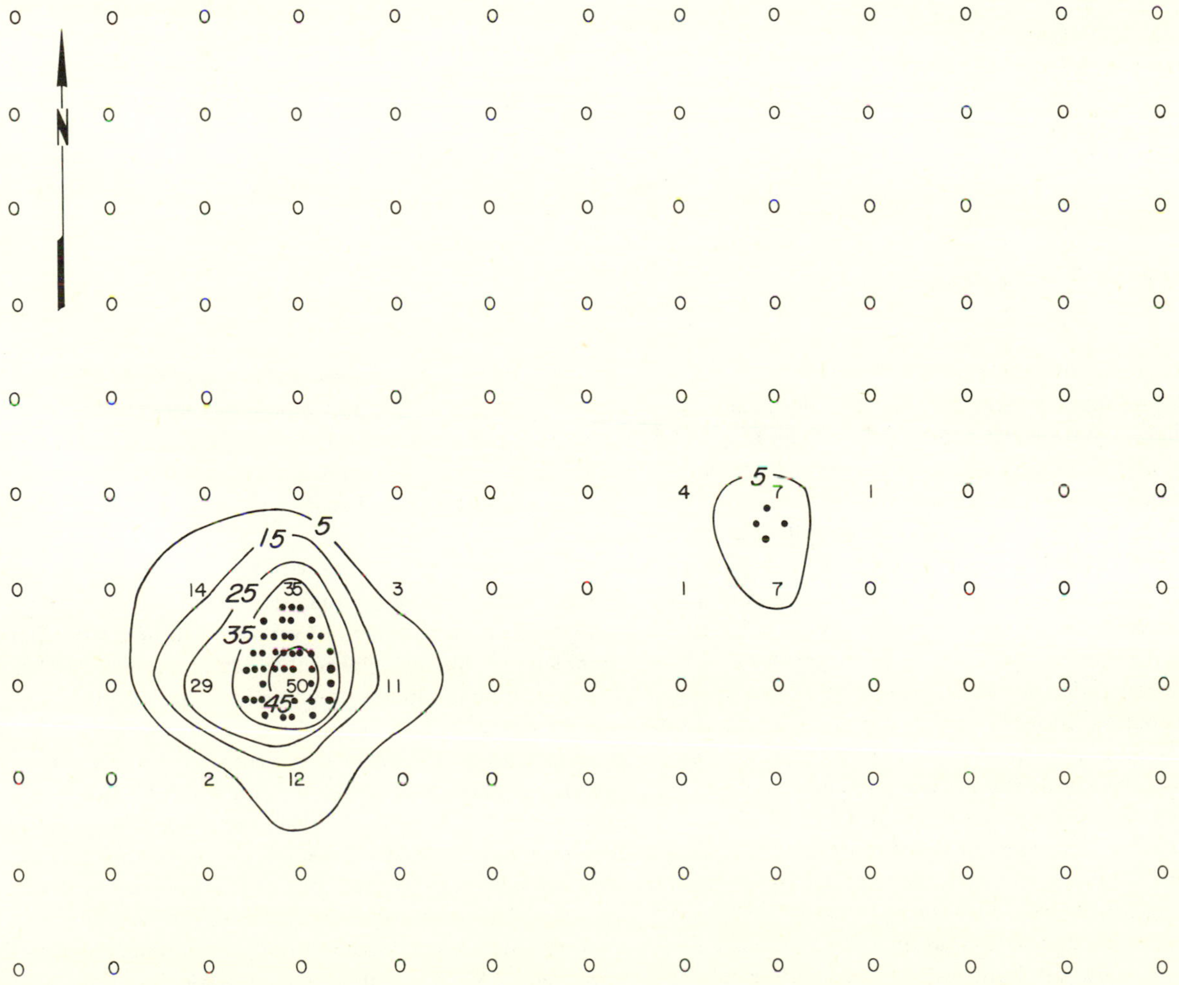

Fig. 3. The distribution of wood scrap.

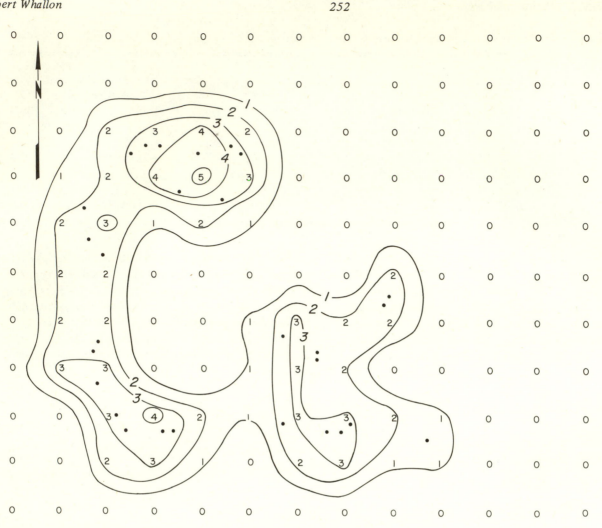

Fig. 4. The distribution of large bones.

indicative of both positive and negative correlations among the points. This sometimes takes the form of a dominant negative correlation and several minor positive ones (e.g. Figs. 9, 10), but can also be seen in examples with equally important positive and negative correlations criss-crossing each other (e.g. Figs. 11, 12). Finally, from some scatter plots it is clear that the form of relationship is not one of linear correlation but of absolute presence/absence disassociation (e.g. Fig. 13).

This complexity is not unanticipated, given the propositions and understanding, with which we began this study, concerning the generation of spatial patterning of materials on human occupation floors. From the beginning it was taken as to be expected *a priori* that there might be significant and definitive variability among the scatters and clusters of material items across an occupation area in terms of the associations or correlations among items as well as in terms of the other variables of size, shape, density, and content. Clearly, it would be inappropriate and misleading to use routinely any specific or uniform model of covariation among variables – linearity of correlation, orthogonality of axes, etc – as a basis for the analysis of such spatial distributions. Fortunately, our

approach makes no such assumptions and, as we will see below, most if not all of the complexity and confusion in these histograms and scatter plots is cleared up and reduced to simple patterns of distribution and covariation by the analysis and definition of spatial groups of the items on this floor.

The analysis continues with the grouping of the data (item) points. The cluster analysis applied in this example uses a criterion of minimization of variance within clusters (an 'error sum of squares' criterion) to group items hierarchically. The procedure is commonly known as Ward's method and was chosen because of its quality of producing tight, homogeneous clusters. Euclidean distances among points were calculated on the basis of the unstandardized relative densities of item types at each point. Again, there are obvious alternative approaches at this stage of the analysis. Other methods of cluster analysis can be used, but I think that the results of average linkage clustering, for example, another immediately reasonable approach, would not differ significantly from those produced by Ward's method. One possible direction to investigate in this respect might be that of methods with fewer

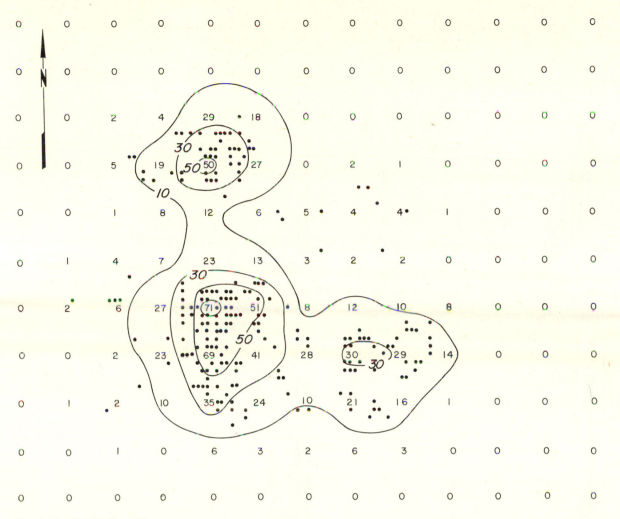

Fig. 5. The distribution of bone scrap.

inherent constraints on the form or structure of the clusters they define – i.e. some variant of single linkage analysis. I think in any case, however, that weighted clustering, in which the sizes of the clusters being formed play a role in the subsequent grouping, is clearly an undesirable alternative which violates the principle of 'no constraints' in spatial analysis with which we began. The use of Euclidean distances seems reasonable, but they could be squared and the relative densities on which they are calculated could be standardized. I think plausible arguments can be made both for and against standardization. I elected not to standardize in this case.

Grouping of the item points on the floor of this site proceeds smoothly by Ward's method until a series of marked jumps in the error sum of squares are produced by the fusion of relatively dissimilar groups (Fig. 14). These sudden jumps in the clustering criterion indicate significant increases in the heterogeneity of the groups being defined. This is classic 'good' clustering and in this case indicates clear cut-off points at either 13 or 7 groups, depending upon the degree with which we want to work and how we interpret more detailed or more general groupings.

Plotting the members of each of the 13 groups defined

by this cluster analysis on the occupation floor shows remarkably clear and unambiguous spatial integrity of these groups (Fig. 15), this although no constraints of spatial proximity were built into the analysis in any way. Also, the spatial distributions thus found are obviously free from constraints of size, shape, or density: some are small, compact, and dense, forming tight spatial clusters; others are large, spread out, occasionally even in irregular patches, and sparse, defining broader areas of the occupation surface which are characterized by artifact scatters of particular composition. This, in fact, is the only constraint to which the groups formed by the analysis are held – a well-defined homogeneity of composition in terms of the relative or proportional densities of the different kinds of items found in the areas of the points forming these clusters or scatters.

It is possible to subdivide several of these 13 groups on the basis of separate spatial clusterings on the floor. This would be the next step in analysis and was carried out here. However, the results of this subdivision showed that the only significant differences among these subgroups were in their size, shape, and absolute density on the occupation floor, i.e. the characteristics in terms of which they were separated as

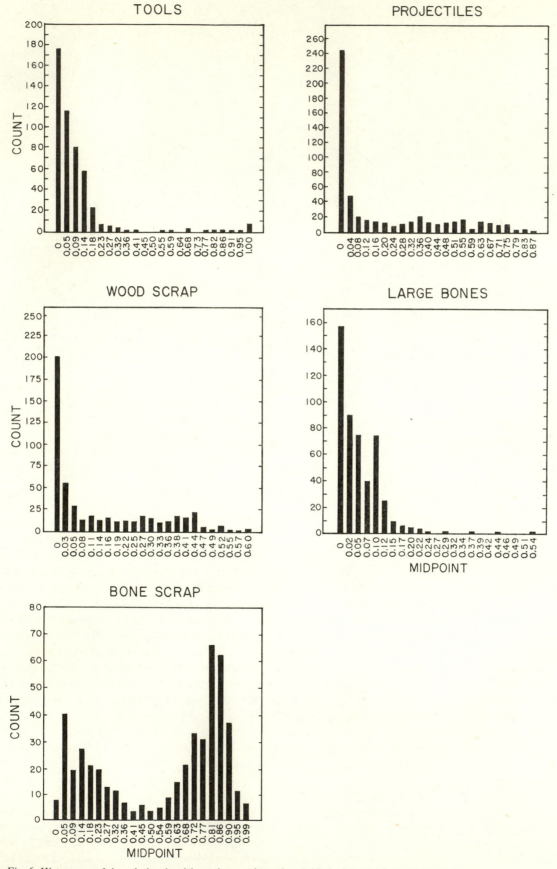

Fig. 6. Histograms of the relative densities at item points of each kind of material on the Mask site.

Table 3. *Means and standard deviations of relative densities by group for 13 groups*

Group	Materials				
	Tools	Projectiles	Wood scrap	Large bones	Bone scrap
1	0.90 ± 0.11	0.01 ± 0.02	0.00 ± 0.00	0.05 ± 0.08	0.04 ± 0.06
2	0.01 ± 0.02	0.33 ± 0.07	0.39 ± 0.08	0.01 ± 0.02	0.25 ± 0.06
3	0.01 ± 0.00	0.51 ± 0.05	0.33 ± 0.05	0.03 ± 0.01	0.12 ± 0.04
4	0.02 ± 0.04	0.02 ± 0.04	0.50 ± 0.07	0.09 ± 0.07	0.36 ± 0.09
5	0.02 ± 0.02	0.70 ± 0.07	0.17 ± 0.08	0.06 ± 0.01	0.57 ± 0.02
6	0.17 ± 0.13	0.20 ± 0.13	0.01 ± 0.01	0.38 ± 0.12	0.24 ± 0.14
7	0.51 ± 0.12	0.02 ± 0.04	0.00 ± 0.00	0.14 ± 0.02	0.33 ± 0.10
8	0.04 ± 0.02	0.18 ± 0.05	0.00 ± 0.00	0.11 ± 0.02	0.67 ± 0.06
9	0.07 ± 0.02	0.08 ± 0.07	0.21 ± 0.07	0.01 ± 0.01	0.64 ± 0.08
10	0.19 ± 0.05	0.03 ± 0.03	0.01 ± 0.02	0.03 ± 0.03	0.74 ± 0.04
11	0.10 ± 0.04	0.01 ± 0.01	0.07 ± 0.04	0.01 ± 0.01	0.83 ± 0.02
12	0.08 ± 0.03	0.00 ± 0.01	0.00 ± 0.00	0.11 ± 0.04	0.81 ± 0.06
13	0.03 ± 0.03	0.01 ± 0.01	0.01 ± 0.01	0.05 ± 0.03	0.91 ± 0.04

subgroups. Characteristics of composition and relations of association or covariation among item types were virtually uniform over subgroups. Therefore, we will present the characteristics of the 13 groups, mentioning the significant spatial subdivisions of each in turn, rather than redefining each of these subdivisions as a separate group.

The primary descriptive characteristics of these groups are the relative densities of all item types at the points which make up each group. Of course, it would be possible to tally by type the points in each group and to calculate proportions or percentages directly from these counts. However, it was computationally easier for us to calculate the mean relative densities for each type over all the points in a group. This approach gave us the additional advantage of being able to use the range, standard deviation, and the histogram of the relative densities of each type over all the points included within a group as measures or indicators of the homogeneity of the group.

Table 3 gives the means and standard deviations of the relative densities of all item types in all 13 groups. The range

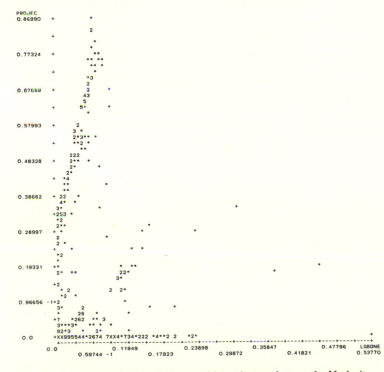

Figs. 7–13. Scatter plots of relative densities at item points on the Mask site.
Fig. 7. Projectile elements (PROJEC) versus large bones (LGBONE).

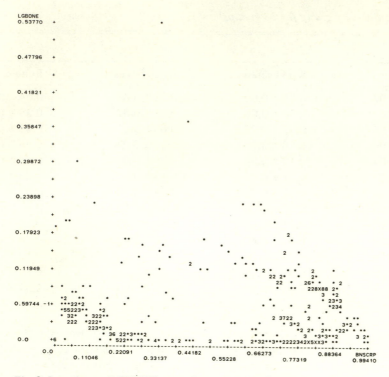

Fig. 8. Large bones (LGBONE) versus bone scrap (BNSCRP).

of characteristic composition is considerable. Some groups are dominated by a single kind of item; others are characterized by a mixture of artifact types in widely varying proportions. However, an examination of the ranges and standard deviations of the relative densities within groups and an inspection of the histograms of these densities indicate clearly that

the obvious lack of overall homogeneity evident when examining densities over the entire floor now disappears. This result should be predictable from the analysis.

Not necessarily so predictable, however, and striking in terms of the significance of the groups defined and the spatial structure or organization of the occupation floor area, are the

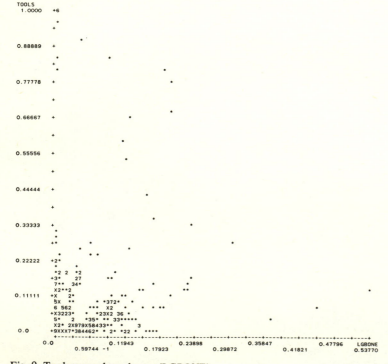

Fig. 9. Tools versus large bones (LGBONE).

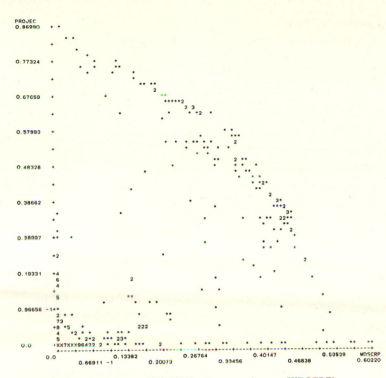

Fig. 10. Projectile elements (PROJEC) versus wood scrap (WDSCRP).

changes in the patterns of association or covariation among types of items within the spatial groups. An inspection of the scatter plots between paired item types within clusters reveals a general homogeneity within groups that, as expected, usually breaks the multiple patterning pointed out on scatter plots of relative densities from the entire site down into its separate components (e.g. Figs. 16–22). This means, of course, that not only are the patterns of covariation among different types of items relatively uniform within groups, but also that they are frequently strikingly different between groups. This can be seen on the scatter plots, but Table 4 gives the correlation coefficients between all pairs of items within all

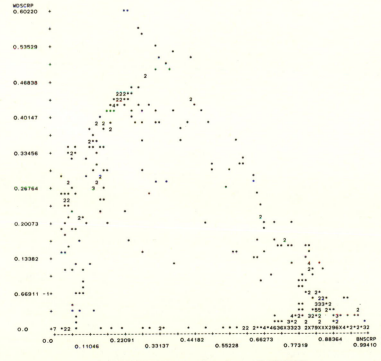

Fig. 11. Wood scrap (WDSCRP) versus large bones (LGBONE).

Table 4. *Correlations between all pairs of item types by group for 13 groups*

Group	(n)	Correlation between variables: 1&2	1&3	1&4	1&5	2&3	2&4	2&5	3&4	3&5	4&5
1	(14)	−0.63	0.00	−0.82	−0.46	0.00	0.54	0.02	0.00	0.00	−0.10
2	(53)	0.11	−0.86	0.72	0.47	−0.40	0.43	−0.71	−0.87	−0.34	0.14
3	(45)	0.50	−0.59	0.61	−0.19	−0.70	0.75	−0.68	−0.98	−0.04	−0.06
4	(15)	−0.04	0.13	−0.48	−0.11	−0.10	−0.75	0.20	0.19	−0.95	−0.38
5	(44)	−0.22	−0.12	0.63	0.05	−0.89	0.49	0.17	−0.77	−0.48	0.38
6	(5)	0.60	0.68	−0.71	−0.92	0.36	−0.88	−0.75	−0.69	−0.46	0.66
7	(5)	−0.41	0.00	−0.84	−0.93	0.00	0.40	0.06	0.00	0.00	0.68
8	(22)	−0.45	0.00	−0.41	0.17	0.00	0.85	−0.95	0.00	0.00	−0.87
9	(33)	−0.42	−0.20	0.26	0.21	−0.30	0.67	−0.54	−0.54	−0.57	−0.27
10	(50)	−0.57	−0.30	−0.04	−0.58	−0.03	0.16	−0.12	−0.42	0.20	−0.53
11	(65)	−0.45	−0.83	−0.71	0.17	0.41	−0.11	−0.23	0.54	−0.67	−0.13
12	(72)	−0.04	0.00	0.68	−0.87	0.00	−0.15	−0.09	0.00	0.00	−0.92
13	(67)	0.01	−0.14	−0.32	−0.43	−0.23	0.29	−0.51	−0.24	0.00	−0.61

Variable 1 = tools; 2 = projectiles; 3 = wood scrap; 4 = large bones; 5 = bone scrap.

groups and illustrates these differences more dramatically. An important point to note from this table is that there is no tendency for an item to exhibit only negative correlation with all or most other items, a tendency which is often observed in using relative or proportional measures. Also, there is no tendency for correlations to be related to sample sizes, either of items or of groups. Thus, the picture of significantly varying correlation from group to group of any pair of items is a real indication of variable relationships among items across the floor of this site. Such correlations can be plotted on the floor, of course, graphically illustrating this point (e.g. Fig. 23). Such spatial patterning in this aspect of material item distribution was a possibility to be expected which we advanced at the beginning of our analysis. Clearly it is a real, significant, and potentially important aspect of spatial distributions that would not be detected by, and even runs counter to, any methods of analysis which are based on the use of correlations calculated across entire occupation areas.

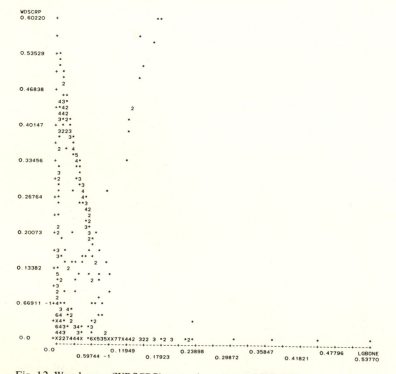

Fig. 12. Wood scrap (WDSCRP) versus bone scrap (BNSCRP).

Table 5. *Absolute densities (items per square meter) by group for 13 groups*

Group	Average density	Standard deviation
1	0.82	0.41
2	28.24	6.29
3	24.79	3.87
4	8.70	8.42
5	14.37	3.22
6	1.78	0.70
7	2.32	0.33
8	7.72	1.24
9	23.82	4.19
10	12.31	5.13
11	21.35	6.54
12	11.55	3.92
13	10.08	3.99

It is of interest now to investigate the characteristics of the individual groups of items and to see to what interpretive conclusions this brings us concerning the distribution of materials over the area of this site.

Group 1 forms a broad and sparse scatter over the far eastern portion of the site, with a small, separate cluster of three points on the southwestern edge of the site area. The absolute density of material in these areas is low, averaging less than one item per square meter (Table 5) and not varying significantly between the two locations. The composition of this group consists overwhelmingly only of 'tools'.

It makes sense next to take groups 5, 3, 2, 4, and 9 in that order. All form relatively small, compact, slightly elongate or ovoid clusters on the southwestern side of the site, except group 4 which follows this pattern in part but also exhibits a second spatial cluster just to the east of the site center. The spatial separation of group 4 perhaps warrants the definition of a subgroup in this case, since the histogram of absolute item densities for that group (Fig. 24) makes it clear that the average local density is very high (ca 22.1) in the area to the southwest and, to the contrary, quite low in the cluster just east of the site center (ca 3.8). The average densities within the other groups being considered are very high, as in group 4 in their vicinity. It seems that we can speak of a real spatial cluster or concentration in this part of the site (Table 5).

Compositionally, all of these groups are characterized by various combinations and proportions of projectiles, wood scrap, and bone scrap (Table 3). More specifically, there is a clear gradient of change in composition among these closely juxtaposed groups. Beginning with group 5 on the southwest, there is a clear preponderance of projectiles, with an important secondary component of scrap bone and a smaller but noticeable proportion of scrap wood. Next to the northeast, group 3 is characterized by a high proportion of projectiles, a high proportion of wood scrap, and some scrap bone. Adjacent to this, group 2 exhibits almost equal proportions of wood scrap and projectiles, with wood, however, gaining a slight advantage over projectiles, followed by a relatively high and significant amount of bone scrap. With the small concentration of group

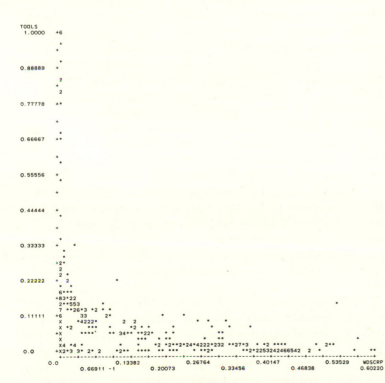

Fig. 13. Tools versus wood scrap (WDSCRP).

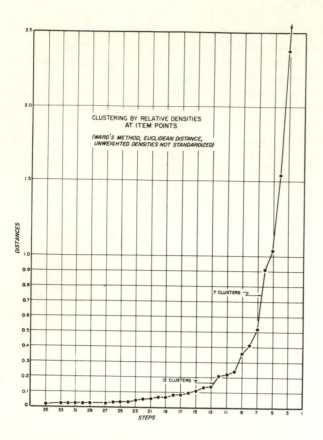

Fig. 14. Graph of the increase in clustering coefficient (error sum of squares) over the last several steps in the cluster analysis of item points at the Mask site.

3, 2, and 4. The scatter of group 4 items just east of the center of the site marks a similar area in which a concentration of scrap wood is found on the periphery of the major area of bone scrap distribution. Finally, group 9 is essentially the beginning of the major, central area of distribution of bone scrap and only incidentally touches on the concentration of wood scrap, marked primarily by groups 4 and 2.

Now, this discussion points out the one major and truly troubling problem with the analytical approach which I have described and applied here. It defines groups discretely. Points are discretely assigned to clusters on the basis of the local composition of the material scattered on the occupation floor. Consequently, using this approach, it is difficult to identify and deal with overlapping distributions. Often they will be evident from sharply defined gradients of change among adjacent clusters. This may be quite adequate and satisfactory in many cases. However, I perceive this difficulty to be a real weakness of the approach, and would hope that this can be an area of future improvements.

The several clusters covering the central area of the site are defined by groups 10, 11, 12, and 13 and are all characterized by predominant proportions of scrap bone. Of these, group 13 consists virtually entirely of scrap bone and covers a relatively large area in the south-central portion of the site. The others are differentiated by small variations in the proportions of minor components. Group 10 contains a significant quantity of tools. Group 11 contains a noticeable but much smaller quantity of tools. Both form a series of discontinuous patches scattered about in the middle of the occupation. Group 12, while following roughly the same spatial pattern, contains essentially no tools but a small quantity of large bone fragments. Most of these groups are of moderate absolute density (Table 5). Groups 10, 11 and 13 show some local variation from patch to patch. Only group 11 shows a high degree of concentration adjacent to the area of high density of material in the southwestern corner of the site.

Group 8 seems to continue the same patterns as groups 10–13, only in a scatter of much lower density on the southern margin of the occupation. In addition to a large proportion of bone scrap, there is a significant amount of projectiles and also some large bone in this area.

Finally, both groups 6 and 7 are small, on the periphery of the site, and show very low absolute densities. Group 7 contains tools, large bones, and bone scrap. Group 6 seems to contain a little of everything except wood scrap.

If we were to try now to interpret the results of this analysis, to what conclusions would we come concerning the meaning of the above patterns of material distribution over this site in terms of the activities or processes which might have produced them? A more or less common or standard approach would see the distributions of tools as indicative of working (activity) areas of various sorts; the presence of projectiles would normally indicate the special maintenance activities of re-armament, while debris such as wood scrap would be considered to be the result of manufacturing

4, projectiles become insignificant, while wood scrap is clearly the major component in this area, followed by an ever-growing proportion of bone scrap. The concentration of group 9 marks the culmination of this trend in an area highly dominated by scrap bone, followed by a much smaller, though noticeable quantity of wood scrap. The increasing dominance of bone scrap in this direction can be followed over the central portion of the site in group 10, which will be discussed below.

I think the meaning of this pattern is clear. We have an area of relatively dense concentration of materials in which three separate components or trends can be discerned. First, there appears to be a general dominance of scrap bone over the central to the northern portions of the site in groups 9 through 13, which will be discussed below. This distribution of scrap bone decreases in proportional importance across the area of clusters 9, 4, 2, 3, and 5, forming an underlying and declining component in the composition of these areas. Then, within this general concentration of materials, it appears clear that there are two overlapping components whose degree of overlap is 'measured' by the analysis as a sequential series of groups which vary in their constituent proportions of these two components. One is an area characterized by a concentration of projectiles, identifiable in the analysis as covering roughly the areas of groups 5, 3, and 2. The second is a concentration of wood scrap, identifiable with the areas of groups

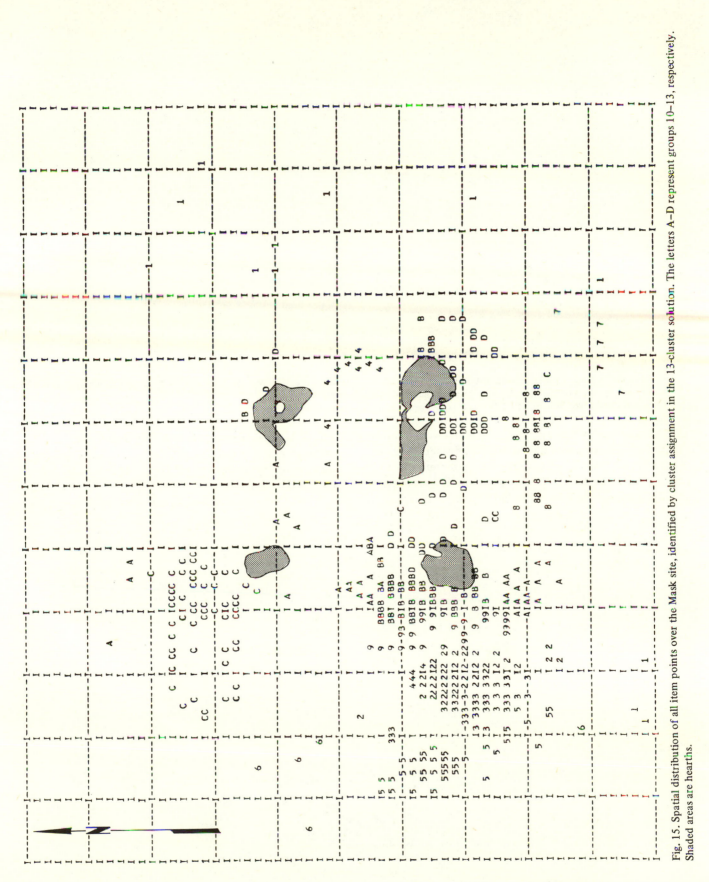

Fig. 15. Spatial distribution of all item points over the Mask site, identified by cluster assignment in the 13-cluster solution. The letters A–D represent groups 10–13, respectively. Shaded areas are hearths.

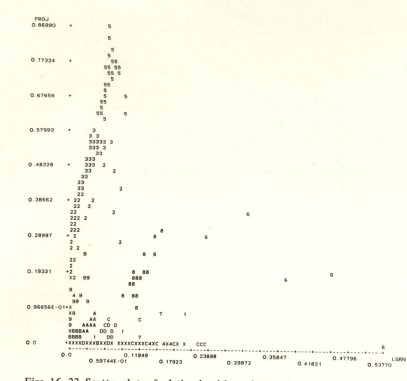

Figs. 16–22. Scatter plots of relative densities at item points on the Mask site, with each point identified by cluster assignment as in Fig. 15 (X indicates the superpositioning of points belonging to different clusters).
Fig. 16. Projectile elements (PROJ) versus large bones (LGBN).

(maintenance) activities. Larger, whole bones would normally indicate to archaeologists the locations of dismemberment or butchering, while scrap bones or bone splinters are usually interpreted as the debris of final processing or consumption. Putting these general interpretations together with considera-

tion of the spatial associations among these categories of material remnants and the size, shape, concentration and location of spatial clusters relative to other cultural features on this site, we come to the following general interpretation.

The most obvious and striking features of the spatial

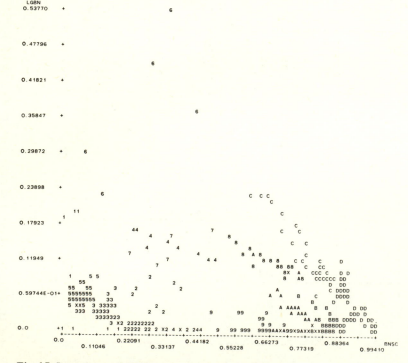

Fig. 17. Large bones (LGBN) versus bone scrap (BNSC).

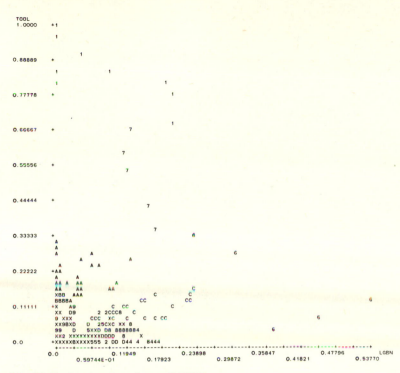

Fig. 18. Tools versus large bones (LGBN).

organization of the material on this site, as revealed by the above analysis, are the series of concentrations or 'patches' of moderate density over the central portion of the site, which are characterized primarily by high proportions of scrap bone. Their composition and central location, dispersed around the several hearths, leads immediately and readily to a primary interpretation of these groups – nos. 8 to 13 –

as representative or indicative of the activities of final processing and consumption of meat around the campfires of this site. However, a finer and more specific interpretation is possible for these groups individually. Cluster 9 overlaps slightly an area of maintenance activities involving woodworking. If we discount the resultant proportion of scrap wood in this area, it is very similar to the adjacent group 11.

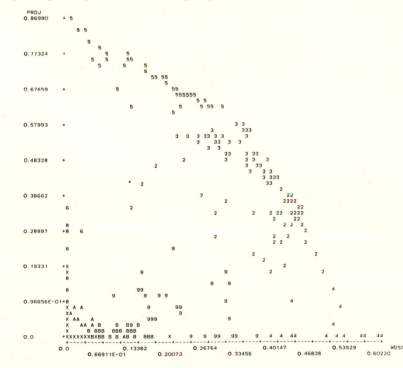

Fig. 19. Projectile elements (PROJ) versus wood scrap (WDSC).

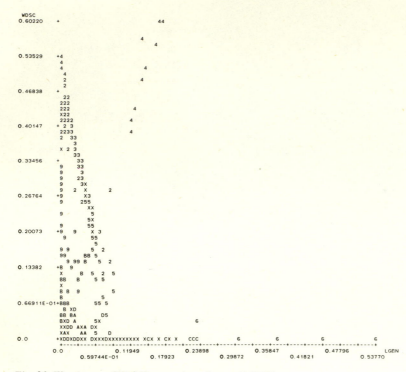

Fig. 20. Wood scrap (WDSC) versus large bones (LGBN).

Both groups, then, demonstrate a small component of tool-using activity, minor and probably associated with the final processing and consumption activities in their areas. The higher proportion of tools in group 10 may indicate something more than this, some craft or maintenance activity in addition to final processing and consumption. The area

of group 8 may have been the locus of some butchering, some final processing and consumption, and some special armament or maintenance activity. Group 12 seems to mark an area both of butchering and of final processing and consumption, while group 13 seems to represent only the final debris of consumed food.

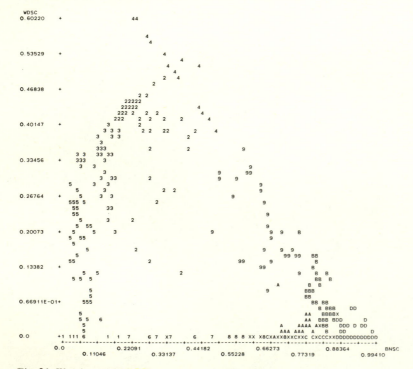

Fig. 21. Wood scrap (WDSC) versus bone scrap (BNSC).

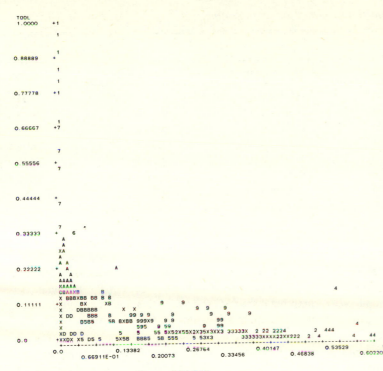

Fig. 22. Tools versus wood scrap (WDSC).

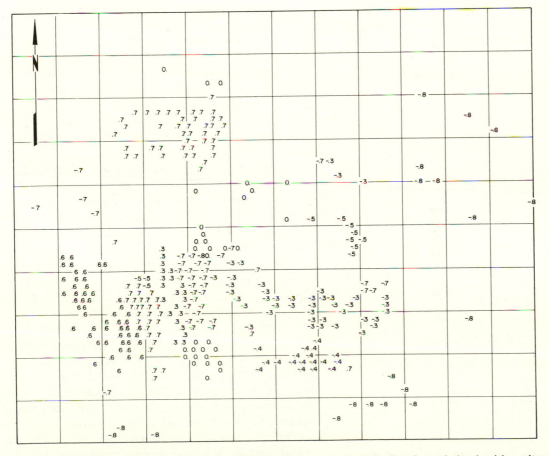

Fig. 23. Correlation coefficients between tools and large bones at the Mask site, based on relative densities at item points, but calculated separately for each of the 13 clusters and plotted by cluster as in Fig. 15.

Table 6. *Means and standard deviations of relative densities by group for seven groups*

Group	Material				
	Tools	Projectiles	Wood scrap	Large bones	Bone scrap
1	0.90 ± 0.11	0.01 ± 0.02	0.00 ± 0.00	0.05 ± 0.08	0.04 ± 0.06
2	0.01 ± 0.01	0.41 ± 0.11	0.36 ± 0.08	0.02 ± 0.02	0.19 ± 0.08
3	0.02 ± 0.04	0.02 ± 0.04	0.50 ± 0.07	0.09 ± 0.07	0.36 ± 0.09
4	0.02 ± 0.02	0.70 ± 0.67	0.17 ± 0.08	0.06 ± 0.01	0.06 ± 0.02
5	0.34 ± 0.22	0.11 ± 0.13	0.00 ± 0.01	0.26 ± 0.15	0.29 ± 0.12
6	0.06 ± 0.03	0.12 ± 0.08	0.13 ± 0.12	0.05 ± 0.06	0.65 ± 0.07
7	0.09 ± 0.06	0.01 ± 0.02	0.02 ± 0.04	0.05 ± 0.05	0.83 ± 0.07

The other major and obvious activity areas are, first, those two areas of maintenance activities associated with woodworking and, secondly, the special armament or maintenance area adjacent to and overlapping one of the woodworking areas. The maintenance activities involving woodworking are marked primarily by the areas of group 4, with strong overlap in the area of group 2 and minor overlap further with group 3. Maintenance activities primarily involving projectiles and armament can be identified with the area of groups 5 and 3, slightly overlapping that of group 2.

Group 1 is difficult to interpret. The presence of tools alone would indicate a widely dispersed activity, but the lack of other, associated remains and the lack of clear typological characterization of these tools makes interpretation of this

hypothetical activity difficult. The area of group 7, however, would most reasonably be interpreted as a butchering/consumption area on the basis of the local association of tools, large bones, and bone scrap. Finally, the small, peripheral area of group 6, with some of everything except wood scrap, might be interpreted best as a minor amount of randomly discarded material.

Generalizing now, we can identify a large, central area of this site within which the primary activity was the final processing and consumption of meat around a series of small hearths, combined here and there with various minor craft or maintenance activities. At two places on the edge of this central zone there were special activity areas devoted to specific craft and maintenance activities, two involving woodworking and one related to armament or working with projectiles. Finally, peripheral to both the central zone and the special craft or activity areas is a possible butchery area, a small refuse scatter of random artifacts, and a broad zone of sparsely scattered tools which may represent the area of some unidentifiable activity or, alternatively, a light scatter of discarded or 'tossed' refuse.

Just such a general picture may be obtained by abandoning the details provided by the 13-group results of the cluster analysis and taking the next major jump in the fusion values of the clustering to define only seven groups (Fig. 14). These groups may be defined in the same manner as the 13 groups just described, but a glance only at the relative proportions of items in each group and at their spatial distribution over the site will suffice to show that, indeed, they provide exactly the same picture which we have created by generalizing from a study of the 13-group solution (Fig. 25; Table 6).

With only seven groups, spatial patterning on the site floor is still clear and strong. Groups 7 and 6 both contain predominant proportions of bone scrap and only a minor proportion of tools. Broadly, they cover the central zone of the site in a series of patches of generally moderate density and clearly represent the general area of final processing and consumption of meat in this area around the hearths, occasionally coupled with minor craft or maintenance activities. Group 6 overlaps slightly the area of special woodworking activity. The special craft areas probably associated with maintenance

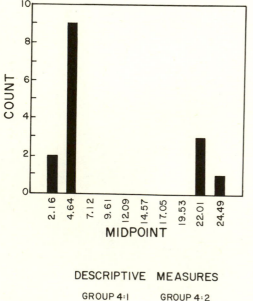

DESCRIPTIVE MEASURES

	GROUP 4:1	GROUP 4:2
N	11	4
MINIMUM	2.16	21.08
MAXIMUM	4.84	24.49
MEAN	3.83	22.09
ST. DEVIATION	0.81	1.61

Fig. 24. Histogram of absolute densities of all material around each item point in group 4 of the 13-cluster solution in the spatial analysis of the Mask site.

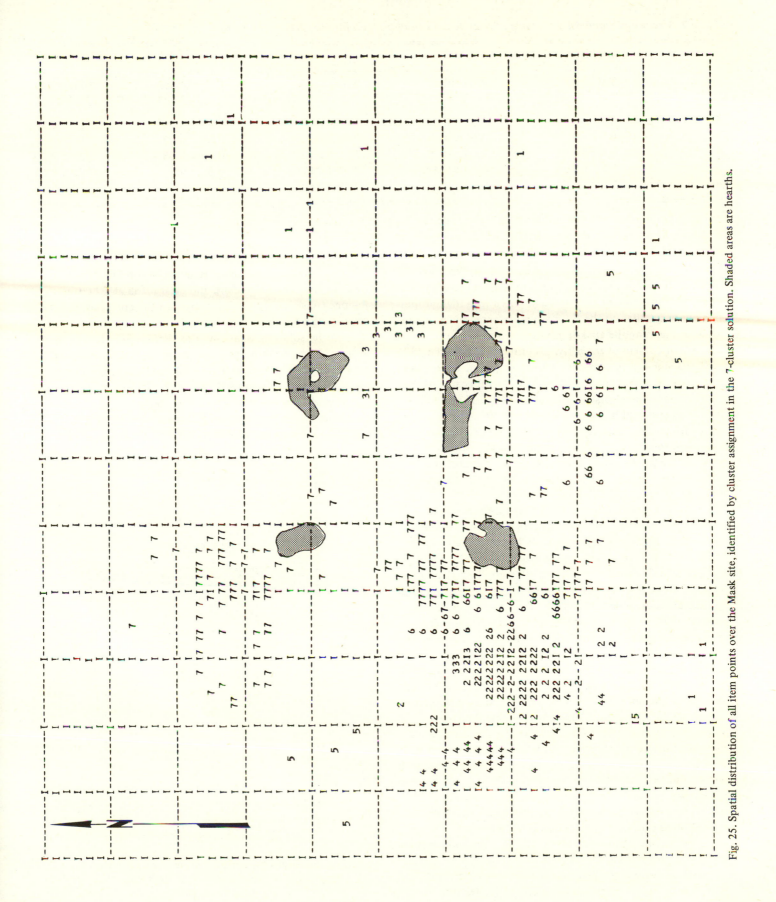

Fig. 25. Spatial distribution of all item points over the Mask site, identified by cluster assignment in the 7-cluster solution. Shaded areas are hearths.

Table 7. *Means and standard deviations of relative densities by group for 6(5) grid point groups*

Group	Material Tools	Projectiles	Wood scrap	Large bones	Bone scrap
1[a]					
2	0.34 ± 0.23	0.03 ± 0.06	0.00 ± 0.00	0.42 ± 0.30	0.21 ± 0.16
3	0.05 ± 0.08	0.62 ± 0.18	0.14 ± 0.17	0.06 ± 0.07	0.11 ± 0.08
4	0.03 ± 0.06	0.00 ± 0.00	0.62 ± 0.23	0.06 ± 0.08	0.28 ± 0.20
5	0.08 ± 0.10	0.03 ± 0.07	0.01 ± 0.02	0.08 ± 0.09	0.79 ± 0.16
6	0.99 ± 0.04	0.00 ± 0.00	0.00 ± 0.00	0.01 ± 0.04	0.00 ± 0.00

[a] Group 1 consists of those grid points falling outside the limits of the site.
There are no artifacts in the surrounding grid squares.

activities are represented by groups 3, 2, and 4. Woodworking is primarily represented by group 3, overlapping into the area of group 2. Armament activities associated with high proportions of projectiles on the floor are represented by group 4, again overlapping the area of group 2. In short, group 2 marks the area of overlap of the activities principally represented by groups 3 and 4 in the southwest area of the site. There is also a separate area of group 3 materials on the other side of the central zone characterized by groups 6 and 7. The combination of items important in group 5 would traditionally be associated with butchering activities, although we previously identified some of these points as peripherally dispersed refuse. Finally, the broad scatter of tools in group 1 is identical with group 1 as discussed above for the 13-group analysis.

A final variation in the analytical approach can be presented, which also produces a more generalized picture, and which may be not only adequate but inescapable in some cases. Instead of using the actual item points or locations in analysis, it is equally possible to calculate the relative densities of the various kinds of materials on an occupation floor at each point on an arbitrary grid placed over the area. The analysis then proceeds as in the case of actual item points. This approach may be necessary or desirable in cases where the number of item points is large and the volume of computation, particularly at the step of cluster analysis, becomes prohibitively cumbersome or expensive. Of course, it becomes the only approach by which data collected as counts per grid square can be analyzed by the approach described here. Depending upon the size of the grid on the site area, the picture of spatial organization of materials over the area will be more or less generalized, compared to the detail obtainable when using the individual item points. If the individual points are known, but are simply overwhelmingly abundant, a relatively small-scale grid may provide as much detail or resolution as can be interpreted meaningfully.

In the case of the Mask site, the use of grid points from a 1 m grid provides virtually as much resolution, and certainly the same picture, as the 7-group solution using individual item points. Figure 26 shows the graph of cluster fusions using

140 grid points as data rather than the 490 actual item points over the site. There is a sharp and clear break at a 9 (effectively 8 – one consists only of empty areas of the grid) cluster solution and a second major jump in the level of fusion at a 6(5)-cluster solution. Spatially, the distribution of grid points grouped in the 6-cluster solution show much more cohesiveness or integrity and clear patterning than the larger number of groups. Figure 27 presents the site grid with the points labelled according to the group to which they belong.

Evaluating these groups with respect to their composition (Table 7) and spatial patterning, we find a picture

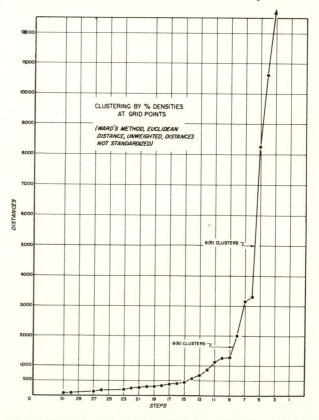

Fig. 26. Graph of the increase in clustering coefficient (error sum of squares) over the last several steps in the cluster analysis of grid points at the Mask site.

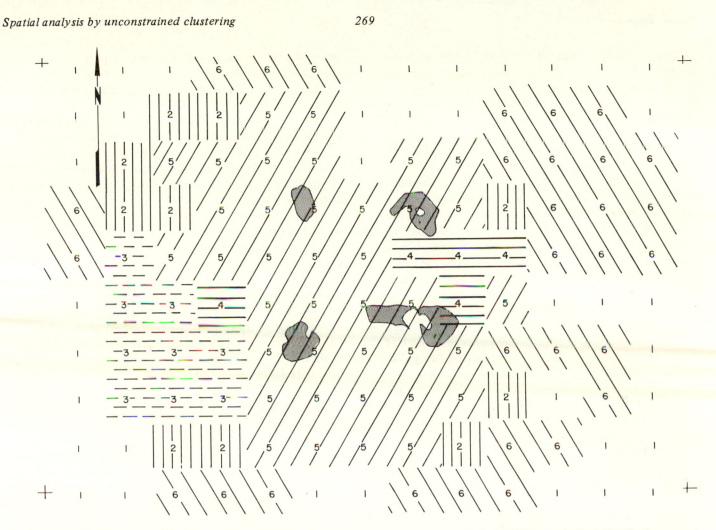

Fig. 27. Distribution of grid points by cluster assignment in the 6(5)-cluster solution at the Mask site. Different shadings identify the square around each point by cluster (cluster 1 consists of squares containing no material at all). Shaded areas are hearths.

essentially the same as that derived above from the seven groups of item points. Group 5 covers the central area of the site and is characterized by a preponderance of scrap bone, with only a minor proportion of tools and, in this case, also of large bone fragments – essentially the same picture of an area of final processing and consumption activities, with minor additional activities of crafts and maintenance, as obtained from interpretation of the groups defined from item points in this same part of the site. Group 4 clearly indicates areas of maintenance woodworking activities. Group 3 similarly represents the special activity area involving work with projectiles, but also encompasses the zone of overlap both with woodworking activities and with adjacent final processing and consumption areas. Group 2 contains significant amounts of tools, large bone, and bone scrap and occurs in small patches or strips just adjacent to the central zones of consumption and special maintenance activities on the site. The first interpretation to come to mind is, of course, localized episodes of butchering or processing in these areas. Finally, group 6 is composed essentially only of tools and is broadly dispersed over the peripheral areas of the site.

This picture is basically the same as we have seen before from the analysis of item points. It appears clear that analysis by grid points is a viable and usable alternative approach which can be relied upon in cases either where item points are too numerous or where only counts per grid square are available for analysis. In addition to characterization by content or composition and by spatial location, the groups identified by an analysis of grid points can be defined in terms of varying absolute density of materials, variable size, and varying relationships of covariation or association among item types, just as the groups defined from item points. The spatial shape of grid point groups is somewhat less flexibly defined, depending on the scale of the grid, but is not too restricted to provide a general picture of the spatial organization of an occupation floor, and potentially can be quite detailed with a fine-grained grid. In short, analysis of grid point data offers basically all the features of analysis of item point data at a slightly more general level. It thus forms a reliable and valuable alternative method of analysis within the general approach which I have outlined.

Evaluation of the Mask site analysis

Now, this is not an archaeological site for which the above interpretations must remain inferences, but, as I have

said, an ethnoarchaeologically recorded Eskimo camp, the
Mask site (Binford 1978), for which the patterns of activity
on the site and the processes generating the observed scatters
and clusters of materials are known. Therefore, we can test
the accuracy and usefulness of our analyses and interpretations
against the real situation in this case.

We will examine the results of the 13-group analysis
first. Groups 8–13 were interpreted as indicative of the
locations of final processing and consumption of food (meat).
Differences among these groups were interpreted as indications of overlap with adjacent, special activity areas, the
combined location of craft and consumption activities, and the
presence of butchering activities as well as consumption in
some areas. Superimposing Binford's representation of
locations of eating and talking and of craft activities on the
maps of these distributions allows us to assess these interpretations. We find that cluster 8 coincides with a card-
playing area, but more importantly it is directly adjacent to
areas of eating around the hearths, although at the back of
the men at these locations (Fig. 28). In this case we know
that this is a discard zone for rubbish and not an area of
butchering as well as consumption. Groups 9 and 11 contained
a minor amount of tools in addition to bone scrap, and it was
inferred that this was simply incidental to the final processing
and consumption activities at these locations. We do find, in
fact, that eating activities were prominent at these spots
(Fig. 28), but more striking is the direct association of these
spatial clusters with the location of individuals engaged in
crafts (Fig. 29). We underestimated the significance of a minor
component of tools in the assemblages here. However, we had
proposed the existence of craft activities alongside consumption at locations characterized by group 10. Eating was,
indeed, characteristic of most of these locations (Fig. 28) and
these locations are immediately adjacent to or in front of the
locations of various craft activities as well (Fig. 29). Group 12
is apparently not an area of butchering, but coincides most
closely with the location of a craftsman (Fig. 29). In this case
the spatial associations among items are partly fortuitous. The
bone scrap results from adjacent eating; the tools are apparently related to craft activity; the large bones are debris tossed
out from the adjacent eating area. Finally, the areas of group
13 seem to correspond well to eating areas on the site
(Fig. 28).

The inferred special activity areas on the site are rather
nicely associated with the known locations of special activities.
The points of groups 5 and 3, and partially those of groups 2
lie directly in front of the stations taken up by marksmen
practicing at target shooting and dropping the 'projectiles'
(shell casings) in front of them (Fig. 28). Woodworking
activities are clearly localized in relation to craftsmen at
work on the site and are well marked by the locations of
group 4 and to a lesser and partial extent by groups 2 and
3 (Fig. 29).

The areas of groups 1, 7, and 6 were given different
interpretations, but all turn out to be peripheral areas of
refuse disposal – tossed out over a broad zone in the area of
the various tools of group 1 and concentrated peripherally
to areas of activity in the cases of the more diverse groups
7 and 6 (Fig. 28).

The correspondence between the groups defined in the
more general 7-group solution and the actual locations of
various activities on the site as recorded by Binford are
naturally generally similar to those just described for 13
groups (Figs. 30 and 31). Groups 7 and 6 were interpreted
as representing a broad area of final processing and consumption activities, occasionally combined with a minor component
of craft or maintenance activities. In fact they do coincide
remarkably well with the major zone of eating and occasional
craft activities as observed by Binford around the various
hearths. Special craft areas were indicated by groups 3, 2, and
4. Groups 3 and 4 here are identical to groups 4 and 5 of the
13-group solution and thus coincide precisely with woodworking and target shooting activities as observed on the site.
Group 2 simply combines the former groups 2 and 3 into one
larger area of overlap between the two activities of woodworking and target practice. Both group 5 and group 1 are peripheral to the other distributions of materials. Group 5 is close to
other clusters and appears to represent peripheral dumping or
scattering of refuse, although the traditional or common interpretation of this combination of items in this location would
probably be that it represents the locus of some butchering
activity on the site. Finally, group 1 here is identical with
group 1 discussed above in the 13-group solution and corresponds to a zone of widely scattered, 'tossed' refuse.

Given the above correspondences and the general congruence of results from analyzing item points and grid points,
it is not surprising that there is also a good correspondence
between the spatial organization of the site as defined by the
analysis of relative densities at grid points and the areas of
activity as observed and recorded by Binford (Figs. 32 and
33). The area of group 5, interpreted as a zone of final
processing, consumption and some maintenance activities,
indeed covers the areas of eating and minor craft activities
around the hearths at this site. The two clusters of group 4
points clearly locate the observed woodworking activities.
The area of group 3 not only covers the zone of overlap
between woodworking and target shooting activities but
also clearly represents the location of the latter activity
on the site. Group 2 very nicely represents patches and
strips of refuse discarded adjacent to the main locations of
other activities, although the common interpretation might
have missed the mark for this group, unless, perhaps, the
specific types of tools associated with this group could have
been taken into account. And, finally, the broad scatter of
discarded tools peripheral to the main site area is clearly indicated by the distribution of the points of group 2.

Conclusion

In summary, a practical application of the method I have
here described, on a site for which the activities and processes

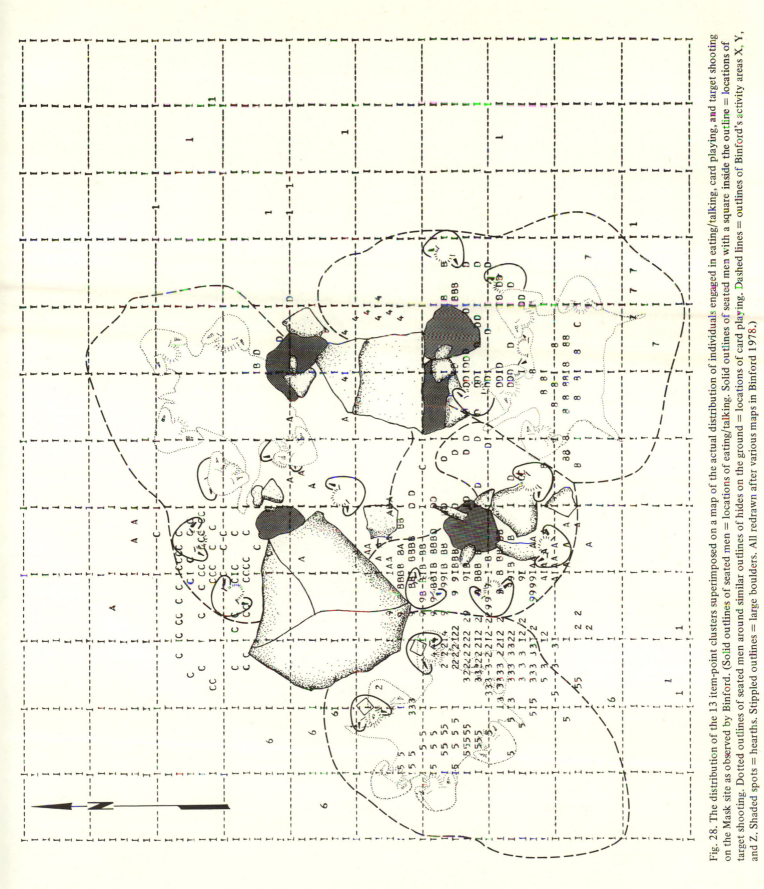

Fig. 28. The distribution of the 13 item-point clusters superimposed on a map of the actual distribution of individuals engaged in eating/talking, card playing, and target shooting on the Mask site as observed by Binford. (Solid outlines of seated men = locations of eating/talking. Solid outlines of seated men with a square inside the outline = locations of target shooting. Dotted outlines of seated men around similar outlines of hides on the ground = locations of card playing. Dashed lines = outlines of Binford's activity areas X, Y, and Z. Shaded spots = hearths. Stippled outlines = large boulders. All redrawn after various maps in Binford 1978.)

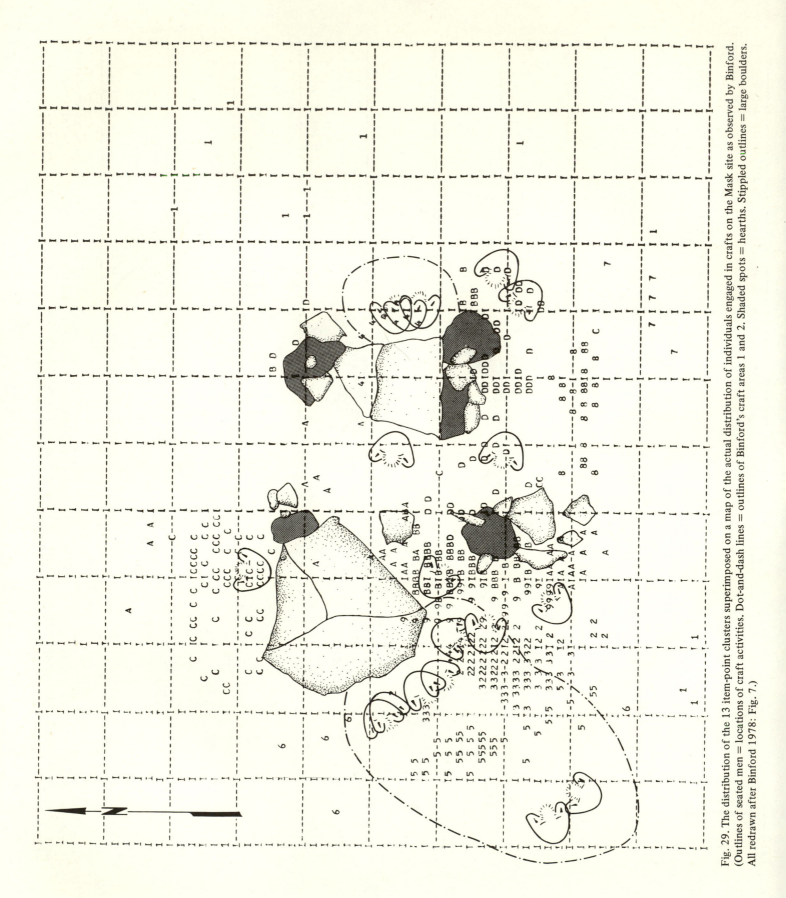

Fig. 29. The distribution of the 13 item-point clusters superimposed on a map of the actual distribution of individuals engaged in crafts on the Mask site as observed by Binford. (Outlines of seated men = locations of craft activities. Dot-and-dash lines = outlines of Binford's craft areas 1 and 2. Shaded spots = hearths. Stippled outlines = large boulders. All redrawn after Binford 1978: Fig. 7.)

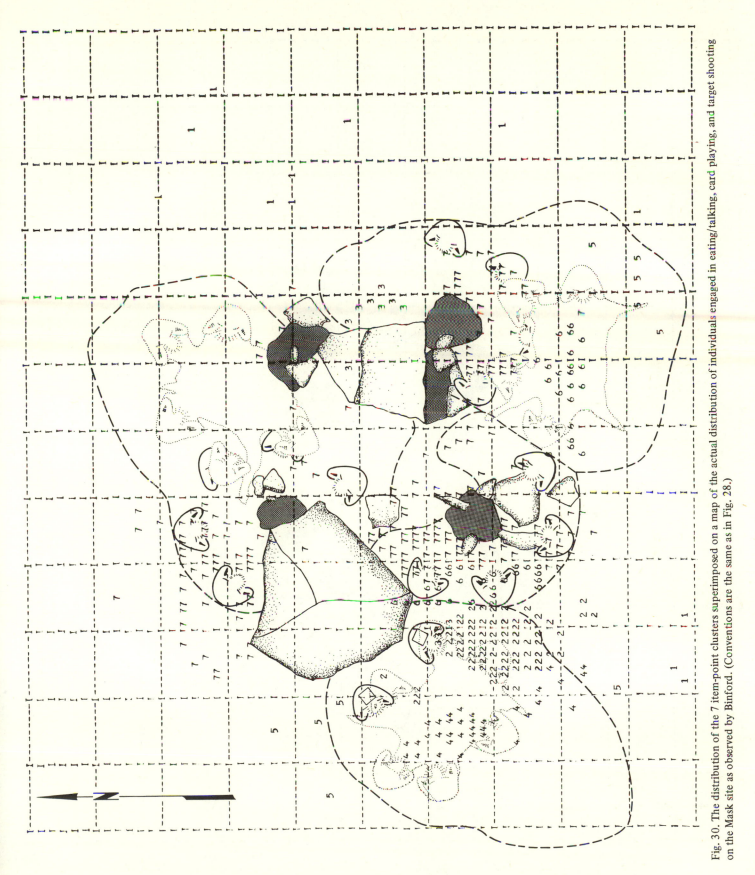

Fig. 30. The distribution of the 7 item-point clusters superimposed on a map of the actual distribution of individuals engaged in eating/talking, card playing, and target shooting on the Mask site as observed by Binford. (Conventions are the same as in Fig. 28.)

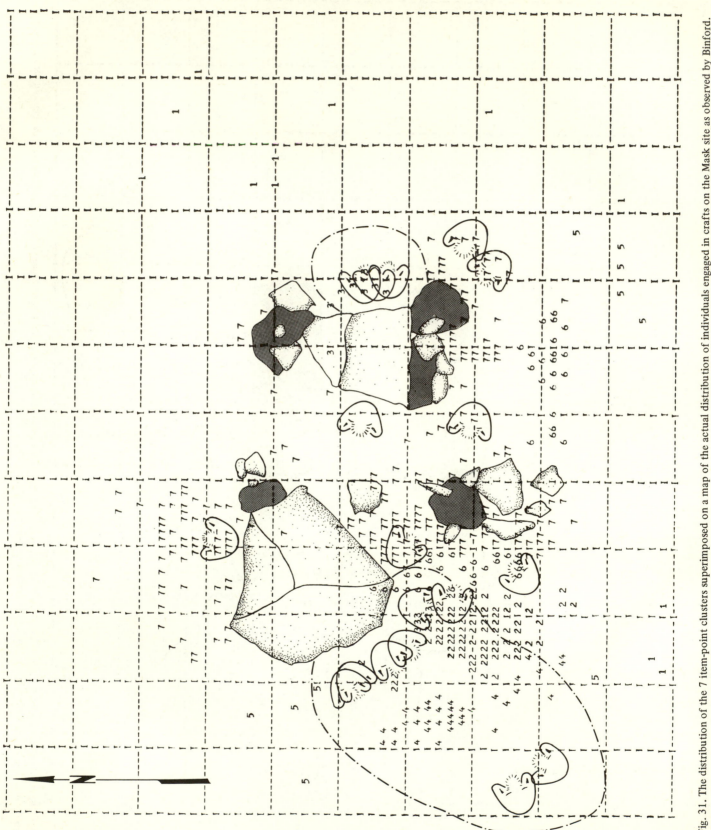

Fig. 31. The distribution of the 7 item-point clusters superimposed on a map of the actual distribution of individuals engaged in crafts on the Mask site as observed by Binford. (Conventions = the same as in Fig. 29.)

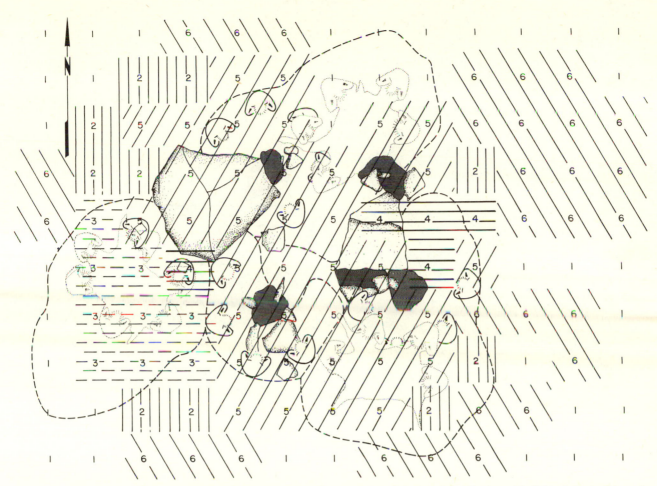

Fig. 32. The distribution of the 6(5) grid-point clusters superimposed on a map of the actual distribution of individuals engaged in eating-talking, card playing, and target shooting on the Mask site as observed by Binford. (Conventions = the same as in Fig. 28.)

involved in the formation of clusters and scatters of material items were known and could serve as a check on the accuracy and usefulness of the approach, has rather convincingly illustrated that it can be practicable and does largely produce the kind of results desired. Obviously, this is not yet the final word on the spatial analysis of occupation floors, but I would like to stress two significant and salient advantages it possesses over other approaches. In the first place it is simple. The most complicated step is the cluster analysis of item or grid points into a series of groups. Even this step, however many calculations may be involved, especially with a large set of points, is mathematically and statistically simple. In effect, our whole method is hardly more than an elaborate approach to a descriptive summary or display of the data, or a series of such summaries and displays. Thus, interpretation of the results is also relatively easy and straightforward, although it can go far beyond what a simple inspection of the raw data would enable us to make.

The second, and I think really important, advantage of this method is that it is largely free of the many and various constraints that are inbuilt in virtually all other approaches to spatial analysis. These constraints patently conflict with the models and information we now have, both on the

processes by which distributions of material items on occupation areas (sites, floors) are formed, and on the variables in terms of which these distributions may vary as a consequence of these processes. These models and the knowledge of formation processes, provide us with keys or clues to the interpretation of spatial patterns in the archaeological record and are derived both from theory and from empirical, ethno-archaeological studies. They form a framework to which our analytical methods must conform or be congruent if they are to be relied upon to produce results which make sense and are interpretable within our current models and understanding of what we are studying.

Thus, factors which are used as constraints or criteria in other methods of spatial analysis (size of cluster, shape of cluster, density of cluster, discrete sets or combinations of items within clusters, and patterns of association or correlation among items) are now all treated as variables. They are not predetermined in any way by the analysis. Instead, they now form a set of descriptors in terms of which the clusters or scatters defined may be characterized and which may be at least partially indicative of the activities or processes which generated the clusters or scatters.

The most serious problem with the method described

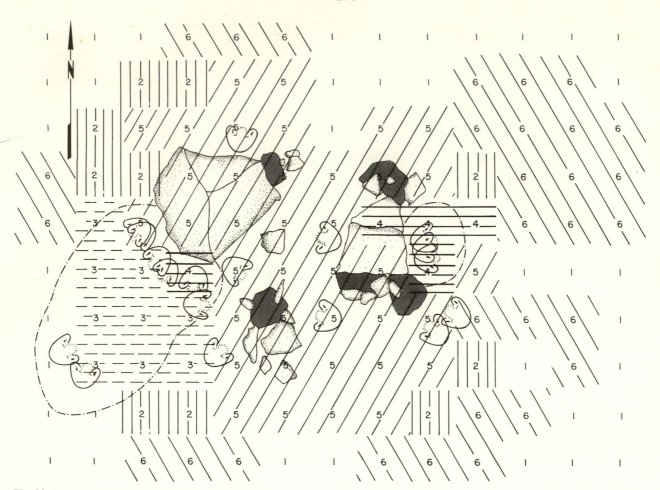

Fig. 33. The distribution of the 6(5) grid-point clusters superimposed on a map of the actual distribution of individuals engaged in crafts on the Mask site as observed by Binford. (Conventions = the same as in Fig. 29.)

has already been seen above, and this is its inability to define overlapping distributions. Points on the area being analyzed are grouped into discrete clusters according to the composition of the material assemblage at each location. Thus, if a point falls in a zone of overlap or mixture, the likelihood is that it will be assigned to a group reflecting the mixed character of the assemblage at that spot. Two overlapping clusters or scatters are separated into a series of groups of points representing the changing composition of materials on the floor across the zone of overlap, as in the case of groups 5, 3, 2, and 4 from the 13-group solution above. Such overlapping can often be defined and identified as above, but the manner in which it is revealed by this method is not directly obvious nor particularly satisfactory. More work is certainly needed on this aspect of the approach.

Another possible point of weakness in this approach is the fact that there is nothing inherent in the procedure which guarantees that the groups of points formed by the cluster analysis will indeed be contiguous and form spatially coherent clusters or scatters. In fact, in the example presented, they largely do this, although the points in a single group may form more than one spatial unit. However, there is nothing in the method itself that guarantees such an outcome.

If this is seen as a serious deficiency or as an undesirable feature of the method, it is easy enough to introduce a feature into the cluster analysis that will force the creation of groups that are spatially coherent. Such a spatially restricted grouping procedure could be introduced by limiting the possibilities for fusion in the clustering process to only proximate points or clusters on the floor. One could simply take the matrix of distances (or similarities) among points, calculated on the basis of relative densities of the various kinds of materials on the floor, for example, and retain only those distances between spatially adjacent pairs of points, say the first six or so nearest neighbors of each point. All other distances would be set to some arbitrarily large value, like 10^{12}.

On the other hand, there are advantages to letting the method run freely, without such a spatial restriction on the clustering process. In the first place, it is informative to see the extent to which any group, defined by composition alone, forms a single spatial cluster or scatter, occurs as two or more cohesive clusters or scatters, or forms a 'patchy' or discontinuous spatial distribution. Keeping in mind that the points in these different patterns of distribution represent areas of similar assemblage composition, the patterns of distribution themselves may be informative about the meaning of these areas on the site or the processes responsible for the formation of such spatial patterning. For example, in the grouping of grid points over the Mask site, it was found that the points of group 2 were distributed in a series of separate spots and bands peripheral to the main concentration of consumption and maintenance activity areas. In retrospect it is now clear that this pattern is the result of the disposition of refuse irregularly around the centers of activity on the site, largely by the 'tossing' out of debris from these centers. It is now possible to see the spatial pattern of this group as indicative of such activity rather than of butchering activities which might be expected to be more clearly localized in a limited number of larger and certainly less linear areas.

Secondly, although the groups of points defined in the above example generally appeared on the ground as spatially coherent and identifiable clusters and scatters, it is easy to imagine a situation in which this would not occur and in which the points belonging to the different groups would be scattered widely and would be highly interspersed among each other. Such situations have been generated by simulated 'disturbance' of ethnoarchaeological sites, as mentioned above. A useful conclusion therefore might be that such a situation may be taken as a sign of random dispersal and mixture of materials over a site, with no archaeologically meaningful clusters, scatters, or 'activity areas', as opposed to a situation, as in the example above, in which they can be successfully defined and interpreted.

Acknowledgement

I would like to thank Harold Hietala for many valuable, informative, and useful comments on this chapter. He has helped considerably to improve its clarity and accuracy.

References

Binford, L. R. (1978). Dimensional analysis of behavior and site structure: learning from an Eskimo hunting stand. *American Antiquity* 43: 330–61.

Borillo, M. (1974*a*). Construction of a deductive model by simulation of a traditional archaeological study. *American Antiquity* 39: 243–52.

Borillo, M. (1974*b*). A few remarks on Whallon's 'A new approach to pottery typology'. *American Antiquity* 39: 371–3.

Christenson, A. L. and Read, D. W. (1977). Numerical taxonomy, *r*-mode factor analysis, and archaeological classification. *American Antiquity* 42: 163–79.

Clark, G. A. (1979). Spatial association at Liencres, an early Holocene open site on the Santander coast, north-central Spain. In *Computer Graphics in Archaeology*, ed. S. Upham, pp. 121–43. Tempe, Arizona State University, Anthropological Research Paper 15.

Cole, J. P. and King, C. A. M. (1968). *Quantitative Geography. Techniques and Theories in Geography*. John Wiley and Sons: London.

Cormack, R. M. (1971). A review of classification. *Journal of the Royal Statistical Society* (*A*) 134: 321–67.

Dacey, M. F. (1973). Statistical tests of spatial association in the locations of tool types. *American Antiquity* 38: 320–8.

Hartwig, F. and Dearing, B. E. (1979). *Exploratory Data Analysis*. Quantitative applications in the social sciences 16. Sage: Beverly Hills.

Hietala, H. J. and Larson, P. A. Jr (1979). SYMAP analyses in archaeology: intrasite assumptions and a comparison with TREND analysis, *Norwegian Archaeological Review* 12: 57–64.

Hietala, H. J. and Stevens, D. S. (1977). Spatial analysis: multiple procedures in pattern recognition studies. *American Antiquity* 42: 539–59.

Johnson, I. (1977). Local density analysis: a new method for quantitative spatial analysis. In *Computer Applications in Archaeology 1977*. Proceedings of the annual conference at the Computer Centre, University of Birmingham, pp. 90–2. University of Birmingham: Birmingham.

Kintigh, K. W. and Ammerman, A. J. (1982). Heuristic approaches to spatial analysis in archaeology. *American Antiquity* 47: 31–63.

Marquardt, W. H. (1978). Advances in archaeological seriation. In *Advances in Archaeological Method and Theory*, vol. 1, ed. M. B. Schiffer, pp. 257–314. Academic Press: New York.

Pelto, C. R. (1954). Mapping of multicomponent systems. *Journal of Geology* 62: 501–11.

Robinson, A. H. (1962). Mapping the correspondence of isarithmic maps. *Annuals of the Association of American Geographers* 52: 414–25. [Reprinted (1968) in *Spatial Analysis. A Reader in Statistical Geography*, ed. B. J. L. Berry and D. F. Marble, pp. 301–12.] Prentice-Hall: Englewood Cliffs, New Jersey.

Sneath, P. H. A. and Sokal, R. R. (1973). *Numerical Taxonomy. The Principles and Practice of Numerical classification*. W. H. Freeman: San Francisco.

Tobler, W. R. (1966). *Numerical Map Generalization*. Michigan Inter-university Community of Mathematical Geographers, Discussion Paper 8. University of Michigan Department of Geography: Ann Arbor, Mich.

Tukey, J. W. (1977). *Exploratory Data Analysis*: Addison-Wesley: Reading, Mass.

Veldman, D. J. (1967). *Fortran Programming for the Behavioral Sciences*. Holt, Rinehart and Winston: New York.

Vierra, R. K. and Taylor, R. L. (1977). Dummy data distributions and quantitative methods: an example applied to overlapping spatial distributions. In *For Theory Building in Archaeology. Essays on Faunal Remains, Aquatic Resources, Spatial Analysis, and Systemic Modeling*, ed. L. R. Binford, pp. 317–24. Academic Press: New York.

Ward, J. H. Jr (1963). Hierarchical grouping to optimize an objective function. *Journal of the American Statistical Association* 58: 236–44.

Whallon, R. Jr (1972). A new approach to pottery typology. *American Antiquity* 37: 13–33.

Whallon, R. Jr (1973). Spatial analysis of occupation floors. I. Application of dimensional analysis of variance. *American Antiquity* 38: 266–78.

Whallon, R. Jr (1974). Spatial analysis of occupation floors. II. The application of nearest neighbor analysis. *American Antiquity* 39: 16–34.

Yellen, J. E. (1977). *Archaeological Approaches to the Present. Models for Reconstructing the Past*. Academic Press: New York.

Chapter 14

**Intrasite spatial analysis:
future directions**
Harold J. Hietala

The understanding of activity patterns and human behavior in space can be realized with the proper combination of archaeological and statistical methods. For example, the pioneering efforts of Cahen *et al.* (1979) utilized wear pattern studies in combination with artifact refitting efforts to determine certain aspects of behavior at the Late Upper Paleolithic site of Meer in Belgium. Their observations typify the notion that local analyses must prevail if we are adequately to understand spatial patterning in Paleolithic sites:

> Our examples offer the warning that the spatial clustering of artifacts, particularly tools, does not necessarily reflect their actual association in use. Also, correspondence between morphological types and functions cannot be assumed, but must be the subject of detailed investigation. Moreover, the typological characterization of whole lithic assemblages, while supremely important as a method of summarizing data and a means of communication among prehistorians, provides a poor and confusing unit of analysis. Our goal should be to make comparisons not from assemblage to assemblage but from tool to tool, activity to activity, and even 'hut' to 'hut'. (Cahen *et al.* 1979, p. 672)

In contrast, Whallon (Chapter 13) used a statistical approach (local) which gave reasonably satisfactory results in interpreting the known behavior at the Mask site. Interestingly, Spurling and Hayden (Chapter 12) found that a global approach was not satisfactory.

All in all, the weight of general evidence leads me to conclude, most decidedly, that statistical procedures to analyze spatial data should not generally be global in nature. This does not mean that global approaches should never be used. Prior to application, however, one should test the appropriateness of the global assumptions. For example, an assumption of a linear correlation is definitely testable. On the other hand, if we can develop procedures which do not make global assumptions and which are only slightly less efficient than competing global procedures, then why use global procedures at all. In fact, potentially there are many directions to explore here. For example, there are many non-parametric methods in statistics which compete very well with classical parametric methods. In addition, for large data sets one can always use multivariate discrete methods (Hietala, Chapter 4) which have the capability of simultaneous local and global analysis. Since statistical considerations are of importance, it is useful to consider possibilities different from currently accepted methods.

Statistical alternatives
The alternatives to currently accepted methods, considered in this section, are based on the principle that local methods are preferable to global methods. This principle should not be attributed to all other authors in this volume, since they might not all agree with the statement. Nevertheless, I will give consideration to local and global space by con-

sidering the conceptual areas of descriptive statistics, associational statistics, multivariate statistics, nearest-neighbor statistics, spatial autocorrelation statistics and spatial series. These areas are not disjoint and, thus, comments in one area might apply to another area.

Descriptive statistics

Although Whallon (Chapter 13) uses smoothed averages to estimate the probability density (in space) for each artifact class, there are other non-parametric alternatives with better statistical properties. The procedure used by Whallon, however, is probably better than some series estimators (Tapia and Thompson 1978, p. 50) but is certainly not as good as other non-parametric density estimators. The different non-parametric estimators fall into four classes called series estimators, spline function estimators, kernal estimators and penalized maximum likelihood estimators (Tapia and Thompson 1978). I favor the last approach, because most archaeologists are familiar with the method of maximum likelihood estimation and this approach seems to work as well as the others. Applications of the penalized maximum likelihood estimator in two-dimensional space are given by Tapia and Thompson (1978, p. 141–3). Other procedures are referenced by Whallon (Chapter 13).

Associational statistics

If the associational statistic is based on chi-squared tables, then there does not exist a real problem since the multidimensional categorical statistic can be partitioned into local and global components (Hietala, Chapter 4). For linear association measures (Pearson's, the non-parametric measure due to Spearman or the monotonic measure due to Kendall) there exists the obvious problem of spurious or uninformative global associations generated through the principle of abundance. For example, if two artifact classes are randomly distributed in local space, then low and high density clusters (with proportional contents) will yield a positive spatial correlation between the classes. One obvious approach is to consider the impact of local variability by testing for the equality of locally based coefficients across areas of the site. It is presumed that the local coefficients would be statistically indistinguishable from the global coefficient. The important point, here, is that a global measure of linear association not only assumes linearity but assumes the existence of a common linear association for all subregions or areas of the site.

Other associational measures or tests suffer from the same problematic considerations. For example, the permutation statistic (MRPP), considered by Berry, Mielke and Kvamme (Chapter 5), and the 'A' statistic, utilized by Hivernel and Hodder (Chapter 7), may be extended, in principle, to statistics which consider both local and global variability. At the least, statistical procedures need to be developed to test the hypothesis that the global association is uniform in space (i.e. the local associations do not radically differ from one area to another). The local density approach (Johnson, Chapter 6) may also be extended, in principle, to within-area and between-area considerations although an understanding of the distribution of the local density statistic, under a null hypothesis of no association, needs to be derived first.

Multivariate statistics

Hietala (Chapter 4) and Whallon (Chapter 13) give approaches which are local and non-parametric in concept. My methodological suggestions have obvious sample size constraints while Whallon's method of 'unconstrained clustering' could be improved by clustering on subgroups of the variables (pairs) so that overlapping areas are definable. Other multivariate and non-parametric approaches have been considered in the statistical literature, independent of spatial analysis applications.

Although I am aware of the non-parametric volume published by Puri and Sen (1970), I would be less than sanguine if I thought that their results would lead to reasonable expectations. This is a judgement based on the fact that although their volume was published in 1970, to date, software packages are still not available. The obvious alternative is to consider local versus global space. If local patterns are unimportant, then we should, at least, find intermediate results that are comparable to global findings. In addition, one can always retrieve the original data to give further verification of the conclusions. For example, if two or more artifact classes are considered to represent a specific activity when found together, then one can statistically test this hypothesis through the application of multiple-dimensional contingency table theory. For large samples one can use the approach given in Chapter 4. For small samples, one can test the proposition by using the hypothesis of quasi-independence, defined by Fienberg (1977), where the statistical cell consisting of mutual absences is a structural zero. The only case that cannot be handled, when considering structural zeros, is the (2×2) table. In many cases, however, the two-way table can be extended by letting one (or both) of the variables be categorically defined as frequencies more than one, equal to one, and equal to zero. A hypothesis of quasi-independence is still possible in this case.

Nearest-neighbor statistics

These statistics may be extended in at least two directions. First, a local and global partitioning of nearest-neighbor variability may be accomplished through the technique suggested in Chapter 4. Secondly, one should be able, at least in principle, to compare local results through testing an hypothesis of area-wise homogeneous statistics.

Spatial autocorrelation statistics

Moran's and Geary's statistics are well defined by Cliff and Ord (1981). Local and global adjustments are considered by C. Tiedemann, B. Gladfetter and B. Hole. Although they delivered a paper on this topic in 1981, they issued an explicit instruction that the paper was not to be cited. We anxiously look forward to their publication (Tiedemann *et al.* 1984).

Spatial series

The application of trend surface results are of questionable value since they are based on global assumptions (Hietala and Larson 1979). Fourier series and spectral analysis applications, on the other hand, also employ global assumptions. Haggett *et al.* (1977, p. 399) state that '... estimation of the power spectrum is based upon the assumption that the data are stationary in ... space'. Stationarity is, in essence, an assumption that the association between two variables is invariant relative to spatial locations. Since stationarity is a global assumption, one wonders about its potential usefulness. On the other hand, the assumption is potentially testable prior to its application.

Other than the above considerations, it would be useful for the reader to contemplate approaches in the books by Bartlett (1975), Davis and McCullagh (1975), Hodder and Orton (1976), Clarke (1977), Bennett (1979) and Ripley (1981).

For the final point of discussion, I would like to make a personal plea. Outside of the effort given at the archaeological site of Meer (Cahen *et al.* 1979) there exists a wonderful possibility for unraveling relationships between social behavior, activities and depositional data at the site of Boker Tachtit (Marks 1983). At this Middle to Upper Paleolithic transitional site there exist three major occupational floors spanning the end of the Middle Paleolithic and the beginning of the Upper Paleolithic. Among the transitional floors, there are approximately 6700 complete pieces of debitage of which over 70 % were conjoined (refitted). Over 60 % of the cores had associated refits and there were more than 400 tools for which 40 % were refitted onto reconstructed cores. Since the artifact locations are known (Hietala 1983*a*, 1983*b*) and since we have completed the spatial analyses, it is of interest if our interpretive model is correct and would be more interesting if it were false. Someone needs to do a micro-wear study on the tools, and perhaps a sample of the debitage, to determine the nature of the activities taking place within Boker Tachtit. This would be of exceptional use for interpretations of behavioral change between the Middle and Upper Paleolithic at Boker Tachtit, and for the applicability of statistical techniques for recognizing change. The tools for Boker Tachtit are currently stored at the Israeli Department of Antiquities while the spatial information is available through Southern Methodist University. The completion of a micro-wear study for Boker Tachtit materials should be of outstanding use in intrasite spatial studies.

References

Bartlett, M. S. (1975). *The Statistical Analysis of Spatial Pattern.* Chapman & Hall: London.

Bennett, R. J. (1979). *Spatial Time Series.* Pion: London.

Cahen, D., Keeley, L. H. and Van Noten, F. L. (1979). Stone tools, tool kits, and human behavior. *Current Anthropology* 20: 661–83.

Clarke, D. L. (1977). *Spatial Archaeology.* Academic Press: London.

Cliff, A. D. and Ord, J. K. (1981). *Spatial Processes: Models and Applications.* Pion: London.

Davis, J. C. and McCullagh, M. (1975). *Display and Analysis of Spatial Data.* John Wiley & Sons: New York.

Fienberg, S. E. (1977). *The Analysis of Cross-Classified Categorical Data.* MIT Press: Cambridge, Mass.

Haggett, P., Cliff, A. D. and Frey, A. (1977). *Locational Models,* second edition. Halstead Press, John Wiley & Sons: New York.

Hietala, H. J. (1983*a*). Boker Tachtit: spatial distributions. In *Prehistory and Paleoenvironments in the Central Negev, Israel,* vol. III, *The Avdat/Aqev Area,* Part 3, ed. A. E. Marks, pp. 191–216. Department of Anthropology, Southern Methodist University: Dallas, Texas.

Hietala, H. J. (1983*b*). Boker Tachtit: intralevel and interlevel spatial analyses. In *Prehistory and Paleoenvironments in the Central Negev, Israel,* vol. III, *The Avdat/Aqev Area,* Part 3, ed. A. E. Marks, pp. 217–81. Department of Anthropology, Southern Methodist University: Dallas, Texas.

Hietala, H. J. and Larson, P. (1979). SYMAP analyses in archaeology: intrasite assumptions and a comparison with TREND analysis. *Norwegian Archaeological Review* 12: 57–64.

Hodder, I. and Orton, C. (1976). *Spatial Analysis in Archaeology,* Cambridge University Press: Cambridge.

Marks, A. E. (1983). The sites of Boker Tachtit and Boker: a brief introduction. In *Prehistory and Paleoenvironments in the Central Negev, Israel,* vol. III, *The Avdat/Aqev Area,* Part 3, ed. A. E. Marks, pp. 15–37. Department of Anthropology, Southern Methodist University: Dallas, Texas.

Puri, M. L. and Sen, P. K. (1970). *Nonparametric Methods in Multivariate Analysis.* John Wiley & Sons: New York.

Ripley, B. D. (1981). *Spatial Statistics.* John Wiley & Sons: New York.

Tapia, R. A. and Thompson, J. R. (1978). *Nonparametric Probability Density Estimation.* Johns Hopkins University Press: Baltimore, Maryland.

Tiedemann, C., Gladfetter, B. and Hole, B. (1984). The Contiguity–Anomaly method: a nonstandard approach to spatial autocorrelation. In *Statistical Analysis of Archaeological Data Structures,* ed. C. Carr. Academic Press: New York. (In press.)

Index